济南统计年鉴

JINAN STATISTICAL YEARBOOK

2024

（总第 42 期　NO.42）

济 南 市 统 计 局
国家统计局济南调查队 编

Jinan Municipal Bureau of Statistics
NBS Survey Office in Jinan

中国统计出版社
China Statistics Press

图书在版编目（CIP）数据

济南统计年鉴. 2024 = Jinan Statistical Yearbook 2024 : 汉英对照 / 济南市统计局，国家统计局济南调查队编. -- 北京 : 中国统计出版社，2024. 11. -- ISBN 978-7-5230-0575-0

Ⅰ. C832.521-54

中国国家版本馆 CIP 数据核字第 202462WU41 号

济南统计年鉴 2024

作　　者 / 济南市统计局 国家统计局济南调查队
责任编辑 / 周小睿
执行编辑 / 刘　琛
装帧设计 / 山东麦德森文化传媒有限公司
出版发行 / 中国统计出版社有限公司
通信地址 / 北京市丰台区西三环南路甲6号　邮政编码/100073
发行电话 / 邮购（010）63376909　书店（010）68783171
网　　址 / http://www.zgtjcbs.com/
印　　刷 / 山东麦德森文化传媒有限公司
经　　销 / 新华书店
开　　本 / 890mm×1240mm　1/16
字　　数 / 1500千字
印　　张 / 24 彩页1.25
版　　别 / 2024年11月第1版
版　　次 / 2024年11月第1次印刷
定　　价 / 396.00元　Price：396.00 yuan (RMB)

编辑委员会及编辑工作人员

编辑委员会

编辑工作人员

Editorial Board and Editorial Staff

编辑说明

一、《济南统计年鉴2024》是一部全面反映济南市国民经济和社会发展情况的资料性统计年刊。本书收录了济南市及所辖县、区2023年经济和社会发展各方面大量的统计数据，以及历史重要年份的主要统计数据，是认识和研究济南市情、经济和社会发展，制定宏观政策、指导工作的重要工具书。

二、本年鉴以丰富、翔实的统计资料为主，辅以直观的统计图、特载，全面反映了济南市国民经济和社会发展状况。全书统计资料共分为二十二个部分，即：1. 行政区划；2. 人口；3. 综合；4. 国民经济核算；5. 劳动就业；6. 固定资产投资；7. 城市公用事业和环境保护；8. 财政、金融和保险；9. 物价；10. 人民生活；11. 农业；12. 工业；13. 建筑业；14. 运输与邮电；15. 国内贸易；16. 对外贸易与国际旅游；17. 科技；18. 教育与文化；19. 体育与卫生；20. 民政、司法和其他；特载和附录。各篇末附有《主要统计指标解释》，对主要统计指标的含义、统计范围、统计方法以及历史变动情况作了简要说明。

三、本年鉴中使用的度量衡均采用国际统一标准计量单位，统计口径除特别注明外，均包括济南市区、平阴县、商河县。资料取自济南市统计局、国家统计局济南调查队及有关部门的统计报表。

四、本年鉴中部分数据合计数或相对数由于计量单位取舍不同而产生的计算误差，均未做机械调整。

五、本年鉴表中的符号使用说明：

“空格”表示该项统计指标数据不足本表最小单位数、数据不详或无该项数据；

“-”表示无此项事实；

“#”表示其中的主要项；

“*”或“①”表示本表下有注解。

《济南统计年鉴》自出版以来，受到了社会各界的关心和支持，对此我们深表感谢。同时，欢迎使用《济南统计年鉴2024》，敬请广大读者提出宝贵意见。帮助我们进一步提高统计年鉴编辑工作，更好地为社会各界服务，谢谢！（网址：http://jntj.jinan.gov.cn/）

编　者

2024年10月

EDITOR'S NOTES

I. *Jinan Statistical Yearbook 2024* is a statistical reference book published yearly that comprehensively reflects the development of Jinan's national economy and society. With a vast amount of statistical data on various aspects of economic and social development in Jinan and the counties and districts under its jurisdiction in 2023, as well as the main statistical data of important historical years, the yearbook is an important reference book for people to understand and study Jinan and its economic and social development, for government to formulate macro policies and guidance work.

II. The yearbook is centered on rich and detailed statistical data with intuitive statistical charts and special articles added, comprehensively reflecting Jinan's economic and social development. Statistical data of the yearbook contains 22 parts, namely:1. Division of Administrative Areas;2. Population;3. General Survey;4. National Accounts;5. Labor and Employment;6. Investment in Fixed Assets;7. Urban Public Utilities and Environmental Protection;8. Government Finance、Financial and Insurance;9. Price;10. People's Livelihood;11.Agriculture;12. Industry;13. Construction;14. Transportation, Post and Telecommunications;15. Domestic Trade;16. Foreign Trade and International Tourism;17. Science and Technology;18. Education and Culture;19. Sports and Public Health;20. Social Welfare Civil Administration and Justice; Special Report and Appendix. We edit *Exploratory Notes on Main Statistical Indicators* at the end of every article, briefly explaining the meaning, statistical scope, methods and historical changes of the main statistical indicators.

III. The units of measurement used in this yearbook are internationally unified and standard measurement units. The statistical caliber includes Jinan City, Pingyin County and Shanghe County unless otherwise noted. The data in this yearbook are from the statistical reports of Jinan Municipal Bureau of Statistics, Jinan Investigation Team of National Bureau of Statistics and relevant departments.

IV. The statistical discrepancies caused by the unit of measurement in the total or relative numbers of some data in this yearbook are not adjusted.

V. Notations used in this yearbook:

"Blank Space" indicates that the statistical index data is not large enough to be measured with the smallest unit in this table, or data are unknown or not available;

"-" means that there is no such fact;

"#" indicates the main item;

"*" or "①" means there are annotations in this table.

Since its publication, *Jinan Statistical Yearbook* has received the concern and support of all sectors of society, for which we are deeply grateful. At the same time, welcome to use *Jinan Statistical Yearbook 2024* and offer valuable suggestions, so as to help us further improve the editing of statistical yearbooks and better serve all sectors of society, thank you! (Website: http://jntj.jinan.gov.cn/)

Editor

October 2024

目　录

特载　Special Report

一　行政区划　Divisions of Administrative Areas

二　人　口　Population

三　综　合　General Survey

四 国民经济核算 National Accounts

五 劳动就业 Labor and Employment

六　固定资产投资　Investment in Fixed Assets

七　城市公用事业和环境保护 Urban Public Utilities and Environmental Protection

八　财政、金融和保险　Government Finance、Financial and Insurance

九 物 价 Price

十 人民生活 People's Livelihood

十一 农 业 Agriculture

十二　工　业　Industry

十三　建筑业　Construction

十四 运输与邮电 Transportation, Post and Telecommunications

十五 国内贸易 Domestic Trade

十六 对外贸易与国际旅游 Foreign Trade and International Tourism

十七 科 技 Science and Technology

十八　教育与文化　Education and Culture

十九　体育与卫生　Sports and Public Health

二十 民政、司法和其他
Social Welfare Civil Administration and Justice

附录 Appendix

特载

SPECIAL REPORT

济南概况

济南是中国东部沿海经济文化大省—山东省的省会，全国文明城市，黄河流域中心城市，是中国的特大城市和副省级城市之一，是全省的政治、经济、科创、金融、贸易、文化、教育和交通中心，是山东半岛城市群和省会经济圈核心城市。与德州、滨州、淄博、泰安、聊城等市相邻，辖历下、市中、槐荫、天桥、历城、长清、章丘、济阳、莱芜、钢城十区和平阴、商河二县。2023年末常住人口943.7万，现有汉、回、蒙古、满、苗、壮、朝鲜等55个民族。

济南位于山东省中部，地理位置介于北纬 36° 02′ 至 37° 54′ 、东经 116° 21′ 至 117° 93′ 之间，面积10244平方千米。南依泰山，北跨黄河，地处鲁中南低山丘陵与鲁西北冲积平原的交接带上，地势南高北低。境内矿产资源丰富，主要有煤、石油、天然气、铁、地热和建筑材料等。

自然景色秀丽，名胜古迹众多，是中国历史文化名城之一。尤以泉水遍布、清冽甘美而闻名于世，有“济南泉水甲天下”和“泉城”之美誉。主要风景名胜有趵突泉、黑虎泉、珍珠泉、五龙潭、百脉泉五大泉群，大明湖、千佛山、灵岩寺等文化遗址。

文化底蕴厚重，是中华文明的重要发祥地之一，是齐鲁文化和儒家文化传承弘扬的重要承载地。龙山文化、泉水文化、诗词文化等特色文化融汇交织，拥有城子崖遗址、齐长城遗址等全国重点文物保护单位，是中国非物质文化遗产博览会永久落户地。

综合实力雄厚。2023 年，全市地区生产总值达到12757.4亿元，比上年增长 6.1%。其中，第一产业增加值429.5亿元，增长4.1%；第二产业增加值4312.0亿元，增长 7.8%； 第三产业增加值8015.9亿元，增长5.2%，三次产业构成比为3.4∶33.8∶62.8。一般公共预算收入1060.8亿元。年末金融机构本外币各项存款余额27952.7亿元，比上年增长7.8%；金融机构本外币各项贷款余额28756.6亿元，增长10.1%。全年社会消费品零售总额 5199.0 亿元，比上年增长6.6%。市场主体总量达到154.8万户，“四上”企业数量达到15143家。

区位优势突出。济南北接京津冀、南连长三角、东承环渤海经济圈、西通中原经济区，具有承东启西、衔南接北的区位优势。2023 年年末，公路通车里程18356.5公里。其中，高速公路里程828.4公里，增长4.2%。公路货运量2.5亿吨，增长3.1%；货运周转量615.5亿吨公里，增长1.1%。公共交通旅客运输量5.3亿人次。济南机场全年累计完成航班起降13.7万架次，旅客吞吐量1756.1万人次，货邮吞吐量14.4万吨。全年货物进出口总额2161.0亿元，比上年增长0.3%。

创新资源富集。2023 年，济南拥有山东大学等驻济高校52所，全日制在校大学生69.1万人。新获批全国重点实验室6家，新认定国家级企业技术中心3家，新备案省级院士工作站11家。

产业活力较强。2023年，“四新”经济增加值达到5160.5亿元，占GDP比重提高到40.5%。现代高效农业增加值79.7亿元，比上年增长5.5%，占农林牧渔业增加值比重17.6%。全市规模以上高技术制造业实现增加值增长6.1%，拉动规模以上工业增长1.3个百分点。现代服务业实现增加值4809.1亿元，增长4.4%，占服务业增加值比重60.0%。

民生福祉增强。全年居民人均可支配收入 51757元，比上年增长 6.0%。其中，城镇居民人均可支配收入62506元，增长5.1%；农村居民人均可支配收入25587元，增长7.3%。年末拥有卫生机构8136个。城市居民最低生活保障标准每月1045元；农村居民最低生活保障标准每月814元。

Special Report–1

Overview of Jinan

Jinan is the capital of Shandong Province, a major coastal economic and cultural province in eastern China, and listed as a national civilized city, a central city in the Yellow River Basin and is one of China's megalopolises and deputy provincial cities.It is the political, economic, technological innovation, financial, trade, cultural, educational and transportation center of the whole province, and the core city of urban agglomeration in Shandong Peninsula and provincial economic circle. It has borders with Dezhou, Binzhou, Zibo, Taian and Liaocheng, it has jurisdiction over 10 districts including Lixia, Shizhong, Huaiyin, Tianqiao, Licheng, Changqing, Zhangqiu, Jiyang, Laiwu and Gangcheng, and two counties of Pingyin and Shanghe. By the end of 2023, the city had a permanent resident population of about 9.437 million, with 55 ethnic groups including Han, Hui, Mongolia, Manchu, Miao, Zhuang and Chinese Korean, among others.

Jinan sits in the central part of Shandong province.Located between 36°02'-37°54' northern latitude and 116°21'-117°93' east of Greenwich, covering an area of 10,244 square kilometers. with Mount Tai to the south and the Yellow River to the north, Jinan is located at the junction of low hills in central and southern Shandong and alluvial plain in northwestern Shandong, and the terrain is high in the south and low in the north. Jinan is rich in mineral resources, Mainly coal, oil, natural gas, iron, geothermal and building materials, etc.

With beautiful natural scenery and numerous scenic spots and historical sites, it is one of the famous historical and cultural cities in China. Especially, it is famous all over the world for its pervading, clear and sweet springs, and has the reputation of "Jinan Spring is the finest over the world" and "Spring City". The main scenic spots are Baotu Spring, Black Tiger Spring, Pearl Spring, Five Dragons Pond and Baimai Spring, and cultural sites such as Daming Lake, Qianfo Mountain and Lingyan Temple.

Rich in cultural deposits, it is one of the important birthplaces of Chinese civilization, and an important bearing place for the inheritance and promotion of Qilu culture and Confucian culture. Longshan culture, spring culture, poetry culture and other characteristic cultures are intertwined. It has national key cultural relics protection units such as Chengziya Site and Great Wall of Qi remains, and is the permanent settlement of China Intangible Cultural Heritage Expo.

Great comprehensive strength. In 2023, the GDP of the whole city reached 1,275.74 billion yuan, up by 6.1 percent over the previous year. Of this total, the value added of the primary industry was 42.95 billion yuan, up by 4.1 percent; that of the secondary industry was 431.2 billion yuan, up by 7.8 percent; that of the tertiary industry was 801.59 billion yuan, up by 5.2 percent. The composition ratio of the three industries in Jinan was 3.4 :33.8 :62.8. The general public budget revenue amounted to 106.08 billion yuan. At the end of the year, the balance of the deposits of financial institutions in local currency and foreign currency amounted to 2,795.27 billion yuan, up by 7.8 percent over the previous year; the balance of various deposits of financial institutions in local currency and foreign currency amounted to 2,875.66 billion yuan, up by 10.1 percent. The gross amount of retail sales of consumer goods in the whole year was 519.9 billion yuan, up by 6.6 percent over the previous year. There were totally 1.548 million market entities, and the number of "four-upper" enterprises reached 15,143.

Outstanding location advantages. Jinan is bordered by Beijing-Tianjin-Hebei Region in the north, the Yangtze River Delta in the south, the Bohai Economic Circle in the east and the Central Plains Economic Zone in the west. It has the geographical advantages of connecting the east with the west and linking the south with the north. By the end of 2023, the mileage of highways was 18,356.5 kilometers, of which the mileage of expressways was 828.4 kilometers, up by 4.2 percent. The freight volume of highways was 250 million tons, up by 3.1percent; the freight turnover was 61.55 billion ton-kilometers, up by 1.1percent. The number of public transport passengers was 530 million. Jinan Airport completed a total of 137,000 takeoffs and landings; the passenger throughput was 17.561 million; the postal throughput was 144,000 tons. The gross export-import volume of goods in 2023 was 216.1 billion yuan, up by 0.3 percent over the previous year.

Extensive and concentrated innovative resources. In 2023, there were 52 universities in Jinan, including Shandong University, with 691,000 full-time college students. There were 6 national key laboratories newly approved, three national level enterprise technology centers had been newly recognized, 11 provincial academician workstations newly filed.

Strong industry vitality. In 2023, the added value of the "four new" economy was up to 516.05 billion yuan, accounting for 40.5 percent of GDP. The added value of modern efficient agriculture was 7.97 billion yuan, up by 5.5 percent over the previous year, accounting for 17.6 percent of the added value of agriculture, forestry, animal husbandry and fishery. The added value of high-tech manufacturing industries above designated size in the whole city increased by 6.1 percent, driving the growth of industries above designated size by 1.3 percent. The added value of modern service industry was up to 480.91 billion yuan, up by 4.4 percent, accounting for 60.0 percent of the service industry's value added.

People's livelihood and well-being have been enhanced. The per capita disposable income of households across the whole city was 51757 yuan, up by 6.0 percent over the previous year. Of this total, the per capita disposable income of urban residents was 62,506 yuan, up by 5.1 percent; the per capita disposable income of rural residents is 25,587 yuan, up by 7.3 percent. At the end of the year, there were 8,136 health institutions. The minimum living security standard for urban residents was 1,045 yuan per month; the minimum living security standard for rural residents was 814 yuan per month.

特载-2

2023 年济南市
国民经济和社会发展统计公报[1]

济 南 市 统 计 局

国家统计局济南调查队

2023 年，全市上下坚持以习近平新时代中国特色社会主义思想为指导，深入学习贯彻党的二十大和二十届二中全会精神，坚决落实习近平总书记对山东、对济南工作的重要指示要求，锚定“走在前、开新局”，聚焦聚力“项目突破年”，坚持稳中求进工作总基调，完整、准确、全面贯彻新发展理念，主动服务和融入新发展格局，更好统筹发展和安全，全面深化改革开放，抢抓重大战略机遇，推动绿色低碳高质量发展，新旧动能转换加快推进，群众生活水平稳步提高，全市经济社会发展持续向好、量质齐升，“强新优富美高”新时代社会主义现代化强省会建设取得新成绩。

一、综合

经济总量稳步提升。根据市级生产总值统一核算结果，2023 年全市地区生产总值[2]12757.4 亿元，按不变价格计算，比上年增长[3]6.1%，其中，第一产业增加值 429.5 亿元，增长 4.1%；第二产业增加值 4312.0 亿元，增长 7.8%；第三产业增加值 8015.9 亿元，增长 5.2%。三次产业构成比 3.4∶33.8∶62.8。

图1 2019—2023年地区生产总值及增速

人口规模持续增长。年末常住人口 943.7 万人，比上年增长 0.2%，其中，城镇常住人口 710.4 万人，占总人口比重（常住人口城镇化率）75.3%，提高 1.0 个百分点。户籍人口 825.3 万人，增长 0.7%。全年申报出生率 7.6‰，申报死亡率 5.7‰，人口自然增长率 1.8‰。全年人才流入 27.5 万人，净流入 14.6 万人。

就业形势总体稳定。市场主体增至 154.8 万户，比上年增长 3.3%。全年新增城镇就业 17.8 万人，增长 2.3%。建强创业孵化基地，全市共有市级创业孵化基地 86 家，孵化总面积 366 万平方米，在孵企业 1.2 万个，发放创业担保贷款 7.8 亿元，落实各类创业补贴 4600 万元，累计带动就业 10 万人以上。成功举办首届“海右人才节”，第六届中国（济南）新动能创新创业大赛引进院士团队 12 个，全市新增国家级、省级重点人才 126 人，人才资源总量达到 278.2 万人，连续两年获评“中国最佳引才城市”。

居民消费价格温和上涨。全年居民消费价格指数（CPI）上涨 0.6%，涨幅较上年回落 0.8 个百分点，保供稳价成效明显。从居民消费的八大类商品及服务项目价格构成看，呈“六涨一落一持平”态势。新建商品住宅销售价格同比保持增长，环比指数前高后低。

表 1 2023 年居民消费价格比上年涨跌幅度

指标	比上年增长（%）
居民消费价格指数	0.6
其中：食品烟酒	1.0
衣着	1.4
居住	0.0
生活用品及服务	0.3
交通和通信	-1.8
教育文化和娱乐	2.3
医疗保健	0.8
其他用品和服务	3.9

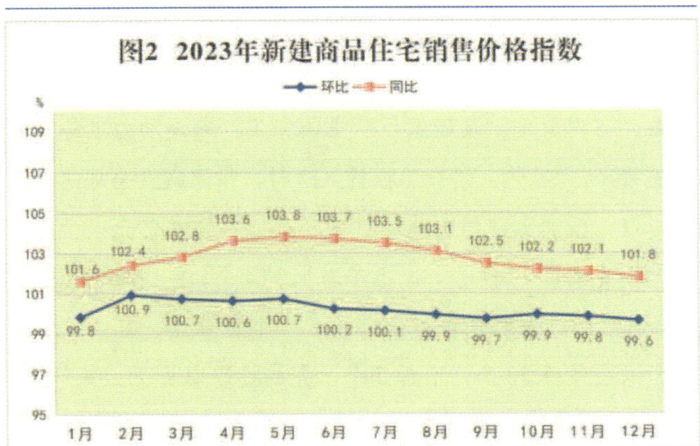

图2 2023年新建商品住宅销售价格指数

抓住用好重大战略机遇。深入实施黄河流域生态保护和高质量发展战略，白云湖湿地保护、鹊山水库除险加固、东部城区四库连通等重点工程基本完成，黄河安澜保障水平明显提升，节水型社会建设实现区县全覆盖。济南新旧动能转换起步区建设加力提速，济南黄河国际会展中心启用，中科新经济科创园等产业载体集聚效应明显增强，示范区电视塔、市博物馆新馆等一批地标建筑启动建设，新引进高端优质项目26个、计划总投资946亿元。科创金融改革试验区建设成效显著，在全国率先组织开展科技金融机构评价，认定科技支行10家、科技金融事业部（专营部门）3家、科技金融特色机构9家，科创板上市公司6家，上市数量居全省首位，成功发行全省首笔REITs（不动产投资信托基金）产品，完成全国首单供应链财司票签发+贴现业务，获批国家资本市场金融科技创新试点，数字人民币总交易额突破63亿元。数字济南建设取得突破性进展，入选全国首批中小企业数字化转型试点城市，连续6年获评中国领军智慧城市，全市算力规模居全省首位，成功跻身数字生态总指数全国十强。深度参与共建“一带一路”，全年中欧班列开行1006列，比上年增长25.6%，首次突破千列大关。

新旧动能转换加快推进。“四新”经济增加值达到5160.5亿元，占GDP比重40.5%，比上年提高1.6个百分点。“四新”经济投资比上年增长27.4%，增速高于全市平均25.3个百分点，占全市投资比重50.6%，提高10.5个百分点。高技术产业投资增长16.6%，占全市投资比重9.1%，拉动全市投资增长1.3个百分点。工业技改投资增长12.4%。规模以上高技术制造业实现增加值增长6.1%，拉动规模以上工业[4]增长1.3个百分点。规模以上高技术服务业企业实现营业收入1425.1亿元，增长5.9%，占规模以上服务业[5]企业营业收入比重33.4%。现代服务业[6]实现增加值4809.1亿元，增长4.4%，占服务业增加值比重60.0%。

“项目突破年”成果丰硕。绿色低碳高质量发展重大项目达到2413个，产业项目提速强劲。招商引资成效明显，成功举办承办第三届儒商大会、中国企业论坛、民营企业500强峰会、中日产业创新发展交流大会、中德（欧）中小企业合作交流大会等重大活动，新设德国、日本国际投资促进联络站。省内首个“零碳工厂”主体完工，弗迪动力电池二期建成投产，“石热入济”工程投入运行，邦德激光全球总部开工建设，爱旭太阳能电池项目成功落地。全市亿元以上固定资产投资项目1767个，比上年增加114个，完成投资比上年增长15.1%，拉动全市投资增长8.7个百分点，其中，五十亿元以上项目50个，增加7个，完成投资增长71.8%。全市“四上”[7]单位总数首次突破15000家，达到15143家，增长16.0%。

二、农业、农村

农林牧渔业总产值稳步增长。全年农林牧渔业总产值800.6亿元，按不变价格计算，比上年增长4.9%，其中，农业总产值543.9亿元，增长4.4%；畜牧业总产值164.0亿元，增长5.6%。农林牧渔业增加值453.0亿元，增长4.4%。

表2 2023年农林牧渔业总产值

指标	产值（亿元）	比上年增长（%）
农林牧渔业总产值	800.6	4.9
农业	543.9	4.4
林业	32.1	3.8
畜牧业	164.0	5.6
渔业	8.9	4.4
农林牧渔服务业	51.7	9.6

农业生产再获丰收。全年粮食播种面积728.7万亩，比上年增长0.3%；粮食总产量302.9万吨，增长2.3%。全年油料总产量6.7万吨，增长1.0%。

林业生产再添新绿。全年完成造林面积826.7公顷，森林抚育面积5893.3公顷，林业有害生物防治作业面积328.6万亩，打造市绿化示范村100个。持续推进林业产业升级，改造低产低效园674公顷。新建山体公园2座，总数达到89座。森林覆盖率23.7%。

畜牧业生产稳定发展。全年生猪出栏203.7万头，比上年下降2.8%；牛出栏10.7万头，下降3.2%；羊出栏130.0万只，下降4.5%；禽出栏6171.8万只，增长8.6%。全年猪牛羊禽肉总产量29.5万吨，增长1.4%，其中，猪肉产量16.7万吨，下降0.9%；牛肉产量2.3万吨，下降4.2%；羊肉产量1.9万吨，下降3.8%；禽肉产量8.6万吨，增长9.3%。全年禽蛋产量29.2万吨，增长8.2%；牛奶产量45.4万吨，增长4.5%。全年水产品产量1.5万吨，增长4.1%。

表3 2023年主要农产品种植面积和产量

指标	单位	面积/产量	比上年增长（%）
粮食总播种面积	万亩	728.7	0.3
棉花种植面积	万亩	4.5	1.3
油料种植面积	万亩	26.5	0.5
粮食总产量	万吨	302.9	2.3
棉花产量	万吨	0.4	2.5
油料产量	万吨	6.7	1.0
生猪出栏	万头	203.7	-2.8
牛出栏	万头	10.7	-3.2

指标	单位	面积/产量	比上年增长(%)
羊出栏	万只	130.0	-4.5
禽出栏	万只	6171.8	8.6
猪肉产量	万吨	16.7	-0.9
牛肉产量	万吨	2.3	-4.2
羊肉产量	万吨	1.9	-3.8
禽肉产量	万吨	8.6	9.3
禽蛋产量	万吨	29.2	8.2
牛奶产量	万吨	45.4	4.5
水产品产量	万吨	1.5	4.1

现代高效农业增势良好。全年现代高效农业增加值79.7亿元，比上年增长5.5%，占农林牧渔业增加值比重17.6%，比上年提高0.5个百分点。全年新建“菜篮子”保供园区22个。生猪规模化养殖场达到357家，国家级畜禽养殖标准化示范场达到33个。省级以上农业知名品牌达到61个，全市“三品一标”农产品有效用标总量513个。

乡村振兴成绩显著。全面完成40个省级和美乡村示范村创建任务，创建完成3个省级乡村振兴齐鲁样板示范区。新认定市级以上示范性新型农业经营主体118家。市级以上农业龙头企业发展到525家，家庭农场、农民合作社分别达到8803家、11320家。持续巩固脱贫攻坚成果，将4.4万脱贫群众纳入全市农村低保和农村特困人员供养范围。

三、工业和建筑业

工业强市势头强劲。全年全部工业增加值2886.1亿元，比上年增长7.9%。规模以上工业增加值增长12.4%。工业大类行业中，24个行业实现增加值增长，增长面58.5%，其中，11个行业增速超过全市平均水平。重点行业中，汽车制造业增加值增长133.3%，计算机通信和其他电子设备制造业增长21.2%，通用设备制造业增长19.1%，石油煤炭及其他燃料加工业增长6.7%，医药制造业增长3.1%，黑色金属冶炼和压延加工业下降4.8%。

盈利状况明显改善。全年规模以上工业企业实现营业收入9208.1亿元，比上年增长10.0%，利润总额419.7亿元，增长26.8%。营业收入利润率、成本费用利润率分别比上年提高0.6、0.7个百分点，亏损企业家数减少26家，亏损总额下降36.7%。大中型企业稳健发展，实现营业收入6559.3亿元，增长11.2%，利润总额达到320.3亿元，增长30.2%，分别领先全市平均1.2、3.4个百分点。

表4　2023年规模以上工业重点行业营业收入增长速度

行业名称	比上年增长（%）
黑色金属冶炼和压延加工业	0.6
汽车制造业	91.2
计算机、通信和其他电子设备制造业	4.6
电气机械和器材制造业	27.4
通用设备制造业	21.8
非金属矿物制品业	-13.6
石油、煤炭及其他燃料加工业	-4.4
医药制造业	2.1
化学原料和化学制品制造业	2.4
金属制品业	1.6
专用设备制造业	-6.6
电力、热力生产和供应业	-1.5
农副食品加工业	5.9
食品制造业	-1.4
黑色金属矿采选业	-19.0
燃气生产和供应业	4.9

工业产品供应稳定。全年规模以上工业产品销售率96.7%。全市生产的207种工业大类产品中，有104种产品产量实现增长，增长面50.2%，其中，增幅超过20%的大类产品有45种，占比21.7%。装备制造产品中，载货汽车产量比上年增长48.9%，发电机组（发电设备）、金属切削机床分别增长27.8%、26.1%。原材料产品中，石墨及碳素制品产量增长9.6%。

表5　2023年规模以上工业企业主要产品产量及增长速度

产品名称	单位	产量	比上年增长（%）
鲜、冷藏肉	万吨	19.4	17.5
乳制品	万吨	48.7	-3.6
饮料酒	万千升	26.0	-1.2
合成氨（无水氨）	万吨	77.7	275.6
初级形态塑料	万吨	91.6	17.4
中成药	吨	9305.3	17.7
石墨及碳素制品	万吨	208.6	9.6
钢材	万吨	1943.6	-4.1
锻件	万吨	127.5	1.1
粉末冶金零件	万吨	1.5	17.6
发动机	万千瓦	2826.4	59.6
数控金属切削机床	台	4983	17.8
气动元件	万件	1915.4	131.2
工业机器人	套	3414	-16.0
载货汽车	万辆	23.9	48.9
变压器	万千伏安	15918.5	0.3
太阳能电池（光伏电池）	万千瓦	25.5	529.8
电子计算机整机	万台	68.4	-11.8
服务器	万台	67.9	-11.9
工业控制计算机及系统	万台	2.8	74.3
传感器	万只	1524.0	42.4

建筑业实现平稳增长。全市具有总承包和专业承包资质的有工作量的建筑业企业 1492 家，比上年增加 121 家。全年签订合同额 14885.9 亿元，比上年增长 12.6%，其中，新签合同额 7177.3 亿元，增长 10.4%。实现建筑业总产值 4772.9 亿元，增长 7.0%，其中，国有及国有控股企业产值 3897.8 亿元，增长 13.6%。房屋施工面积 20516.6 万平方米，增长 2.7%。

四、服务业

服务业发展提质增效。全年服务业增加值 8015.9 亿元，比上年增长 5.2%。规模以上服务业企业实现营业收入 4264.0 亿元，增长 14.4%。重点行业加力提速，规模以上交通运输、仓储和邮政业，租赁和商务服务业，信息传输、软件和信息技术服务业企业营业收入分别增长 25.3%、12.1%、6.6%。

表 6　2023 年规模以上服务业分门类营业收入

门类	营业收入（亿元）	比上年增长（%）
合　计	4264.0	14.4
交通运输、仓储和邮政业	1851.5	25.3
信息传输、软件和信息技术服务业	864.6	6.6
房地产业（不包含房地产开发经营）	206.3	8.1
租赁和商务服务业	547.8	12.1
科学研究和技术服务业	546.7	6.1
水利、环境和公共设施管理业	32.6	-39.9
居民服务、修理和其他服务业	25.7	9.1
教育	32.1	21.9
卫生和社会工作	67.4	12.0
文化、体育和娱乐业	89.2	12.0

交通运输稳健运行。全市年末公路通车里程 18356.5 公里，比上年增长 0.3%，其中，境内高速公路里程 828.4 公里，增长 4.2%。公路客运量 2137.0 万人，增长 48.6%，旅客周转量 46.2 亿人公里，增长 56.2%。公路货运量 2.5 亿吨，增长 3.1%；货运周转量 615.5 亿吨公里，增长 1.1%。年末拥有民用机动车 389.8 万辆，其中，民用汽车 338.7 万辆，增长 5.7%。全市新能源汽车保有量 17.1 万辆，获批全国首批公共领域车辆全面电动化先行区试点城市。公交线路 779 条，比上年增加 23 条，线路总长度 15671.8 公里，增加 48.5 公里，旅客运输量 5.3 亿人次，增加 1.4 亿人次。轨道交通运营线路 3 条，长度 84.1 公里，年客运量 9621.0 万人次，增长 76.4%。全年累计完成航班起降 13.7 万架次，增长 73.6%，旅客吞吐量 1756.1 万人次，增长 113.1%，货邮吞吐量 14.4 万吨，增长 4.6%。

邮政业、电信业健康发展。全年邮政行业业务收入（不包括邮政储蓄银行直接营业收入）121.0 亿元，比上年增长 14.9%；邮政行业寄递业务量 10.8 亿件，增长 8.0%。快递业务收入 92.3 亿元，增长 12.5%；业务量（不包含邮政公司包裹业务）8.5 亿件，增长 10.0%。年末移动电话用户 1287.9 万户，增长 1.7%，其中，5G 移动电话用户 922.2 万户，增长 34.6%。固定互联网宽带接入用户 522.6 万户，增长 4.2%。

旅游业、会展业持续升温。全年接待国内游客 10631.1 万人次，比上年增长 61.9%。实现国内旅游收入 1132.9 亿元，增长 65.5%。A 级旅游景区 89 家，其中，5A 级旅游景区 1 家，4A 级旅游景区 19 家。省级旅游度假区 2 家。全市星级酒店新增 12 家，总数达到 52 家，其中，五星级酒店新增 2 家，总数达到 7 家。明水古城开业试运营，“二安”文化旅游节、“济南城市美丽季”系列活动、“涌动泉城”济南游泉打卡系列活动、书博会、文旅博览会、韩美林艺术展等重大文旅活动成功举办，超然楼、起凤桥、老商埠等景点成为网红打卡地，印象济南 · 泉世界获评国家级旅游休闲街区，济南荣获“2023 年度活力城市”。全年举办展会活动 125 场，增长 64.5%，展览面积 230 万平方米，增长 64.3%，获评“中国会展品牌城市”。

五、固定资产投资

固定资产投资保持增长。全年固定资产投资比上年增长 2.1%。第一产业投资下降 16.5%，第二产业投资增长 25.3%，第三产业投资下降 2.2%。基础设施投资增长 49.1%。高技术服务业投资增长 23.5%。工业投资增长 25.4%，其中，制造业投资增长 7.2%。

房地产市场低位运行。全年房地产开发完成投资 1399.7 亿元，比上年下降 19.7%，其中，住宅完成投资 994.8 亿元，下降 18.4%。房屋施工面积 8143.6 万平方米，下降 5.4%，其中，住宅施工面积 4985.6 万平方米，下降 6.6%。房屋竣工面积 970.9 万平方米，增长 35.8%，其中，住宅竣工面积 679.0 万平方米，增长 39.1%。商品房销售面积 1170.2 万平方米，下降 5.8%，其中，住宅销售面积 825.5 万平方米，下降 9.0%。商品房销售额 1553.2 亿元，增长 2.6%，其中，住宅销售额 1218.0 亿元，下降 0.3%。

六、国内贸易

消费品市场稳步恢复。全市社会消费品零售总额 5199.0 亿元，比上年增长 6.6%。按经营单位所在地分，全市城镇消费品零售额4561.6亿元，增长6.5%；全市乡村消费品零售额637.4亿元，增长7.5%。按消费类型分，全市商品零售4436.7亿元，增长5.8%；餐饮收入762.3亿元，增长11.5%。

线上消费增长较快。全市限额以上[8]批发和零售业单位通过公共网络实现的零售额429.2亿元，比上年增长24.3%，占全市限额以上单位零售额比重22.1%，比上年提高4.0个百分点。

出行类商品销售增势良好。全市限额以上单位汽车类、石油及制品类商品零售额分别比上年增长10.5%、18.8%，分别拉动全市限额以上单位零售额增长3.4、1.9个百分点。新能源汽车表现亮眼，新能源汽车零售额增长83.3%，占全市限额以上单位零售额比重10.9%，比上年提高4.9个百分点。

生活类消费保持稳定。全市限额以上单位吃类、穿类商品零售额分别比上年增长4.9%、10.8%，分别拉动全市限额以上单位零售额增长0.7、0.6个百分点。限额以上单位金银珠宝类、通讯器材类商品零售额分别增长12.8%、11.6%。

表7　2023年限额以上批发和零售业单位主要商品零售额及增长速度

商品类别	零售额（亿元）	比上年增长（%）
粮油、食品类	194.1	3.6
饮料类	19.9	4.3
烟酒类	49.6	10.5
服装、鞋帽、针纺织品类	113.6	10.8
化妆品类	56.8	-16.0
金银珠宝类	48.7	12.8
日用品类	35.7	1.4
书报杂志类	96.3	-0.9
家用电器和音像器材类	107.3	-14.6
中西药品类	84.3	11.9
通讯器材类	67.0	11.6
石油及制品类	208.4	18.8
汽车类	662.4	10.5
其中：新能源汽车	211.4	83.3

七、对外经济

进出口保持平稳增长。全年货物进出口总额2161.0亿元人民币，比上年增长0.3%。其中，出口1373.4亿元，下降1.1%；进口787.6亿元，增长2.8%。一般贸易进出口1927.6亿元，增长2.9%，占比提高2.3个百分点。对欧盟和非洲进出口分别增长10.3%、12.3%；对中亚五国进出口增长63.4%。出口商品中，机电产品出口834.9亿元，增长2.4%；锂电池、新能源汽车分别增长16.6%、15.3%。进口商品中，成品油进口29.5亿元，增长792.7%；煤及褐煤进口27.4亿元，增长122.5%；原油进口11.4亿元，增长75.5%。

利用外资结构实现优化。全市实际使用外资24.8亿美元，其中，高技术产业实际使用外资6.4亿美元，占比25.7%，比上年提高13.1个百分点；第三产业使用外资17.3亿美元，占比达到69.8%。全年实现合同外资58.7亿美元。新设外商投资企业家数267家。总投资过亿美元项目17个，总投资过亿美元项目合同外资16.6亿美元。

对外合作纵深推进。全年对外承包工程新签合同额38.0亿美元，完成营业额42.9亿美元，比上年增长4.7%。备案设立境外企业（机构）78家，增长73.3%；实际完成投资22.3亿美元，增长27.6%。派出各类劳务人员7302人，增长62.7%。

八、财政和金融

财政保障坚实有力。全市地域税收收入1506.6亿元，比上年增长11.5%。一般公共预算收入1060.8亿元，增长6.0%，其中，税收收入797.9亿元，增长15.1%，税收比重75.2%，比上年提高6.0个百分点。一般公共预算支出1365.3亿元，增长11.4%，其中，科学技术支出46.5亿元，增长64.8%；农林水支出77.0亿元，增长12.7%；社会保障和就业支出223.5亿元，增长13.7%，重点事务保障有力。

表8　2023年一般公共预算收入和支出情况

指标	总量（亿元）	增速（%）
一般公共预算收入	1060.8	6.0
其中：税收收入	797.9	15.1
增值税	274.9	38.3
企业所得税	115.2	-0.2
一般公共预算支出	1365.3	11.4
其中：科学技术支出	46.5	64.8
农林水支出	77.0	12.7
社会保障和就业支出	223.5	13.7

存、贷款余额稳定增长。年末金融机构本外币各项存款余额27952.7亿元，比上年增长7.8%；金融机构本外币各项贷款余额28756.6亿元，增长10.1%。

科创金融发展向好。全市科创企业贷款余额1747.1亿元，比上年增长40.6%；科创企业有贷户数3608家，增长26.0%；贷款加权平均利率3.5%，下降37个基点。“济南市创新科创金融服务体系”入选“中国改革2023年度地方全面深化改革典型案例”。

保险业保持健康发展。全市保险业实现保费收入694.8亿元，比上年增长9.9%，较上年同期提高3.7个百分点，其中，财产险保费收入129亿元，增长1.4%；人身险保费收入565.8亿元，增长12.0%。

信贷质量持续改善。全市银行业金融机构不良贷款余额192.4亿元，较年初减少41.8亿元；不良贷款率0.7%，较年初下降0.2个百分点。

资本市场更加活跃。全市新增直接融资规模4108.0亿元，比上年增长31.2%，其中，股权融资61.9亿元，增长2.0%；债券融资4046.1亿元，增长31.7%。全市新增首发上市企业5家，上市公司总数达到60家、股票62只。

九、科技、教育、文化、卫生和体育事业

研发投入不断加大。全年研究与试验发展（R&D）经费投入[9]346.8亿元，比上年增长13.1%，其中，基础研究29.9亿元，增长11.9%；应用研究44.4亿元，增长14.9%；试验发展272.5亿元，增长12.9%。R&D经费投入占GDP比重2.9%，比上年提高0.2个百分点。规模以上工业企业研发人员51599人，增长19.9%；规模以上工业企业设立研发机构841个，增长66.2%。新认定国家级企业技术中心3家，总数达到32家。新认定省级企业技术中心15家，总数达到249家。

创新能力提质升级。全年万人有效发明专利拥有量61.9件，比上年增长26.5%。发明专利授权量13693件，增长15.5%。技术合同实现交易额806.5亿元，增长31.4%。获得省级科技进步一等奖18项，二等奖66项；获得省级自然科学一等奖2项，二等奖25项。新获批全国重点实验室6家，总数达到11家；新增省级工程研究中心48家，总数达到237家；新备案省级院士工作站11家，总数达到73家。国家科技型中小企业达到8323家，增长9.3%。

教育事业成绩斐然。全市普惠性幼儿园覆盖率达到94%，公办幼儿园在园幼儿占比超过60%。开工新建、改扩建中小学校、幼儿园60所，新增学位4万余个。全国职业院校技能大赛获奖总数44项，其中一等奖16项。立项市校融合发展战略工程项目125个。

表9　2023年教育事业基本情况

学校类别	学校数量（所）	在校生（万人）	专任教师（万人）
驻济高等学校	52	69.1	4.0
中等职业学校（不含技工学校）	32	6.1	0.4
技工学校	31	9.0	0.4
普通中学	332	43.7	3.6
小学	574	70.6	4.1
特殊教育学校	13	0.2	0.1
幼儿园	2117	30.9	2.6

文化事业繁荣稳定。年末拥有国有艺术表演团体11个，文化馆（站）174个，公共图书馆13个，公共博物馆13个，档案馆13个。市级以上文物保护单位437处，其中，国家级30处。城市可统计票房数字影院73家，观众1107.6万人次，票房收入4.8亿元。电视人口混合覆盖率100%，广播人口混合覆盖率99.7%。建成泉城书房52处，基层综合性文化服务中心覆盖率100%。规模以上文化及相关产业企业营业收入比上年增长15.3%，其中，文化制造业增长28.5%，文化批发和零售业增长13.2%，文化服务业增长14.8%。

医疗卫生服务水平持续提升。年末共有医疗卫生机构8136个，其中医院320个，在医院中有公立医院98个，民营医院222个；基层医疗卫生机构7704个，其中，卫生院48个，社区卫生服务中心（站）423个，门诊部214个，诊所（卫生所、医务室）3528个，村卫生室3491个；专业公共卫生机构55个，其中，疾病预防控制中心16个，卫生监督所（中心）12个。年末卫生技术人员12.2万人，其中，执业医师和执业助理医师4.7万人，注册护士5.6万人。医疗卫生机构床位8.2万张，其中，医院7.1万张，镇卫生院0.4万张。全年总诊疗人次9091.2万人次，出院人数293.2万人。建成社区医院13家，人口育儿托位数4.3万个。入选建设国家儿童友好城市名单，“泉心托”成为全国首个托育城市品牌。广安门医院济南医院、宣武医院济南医院获批国家区域医疗中心。

群众体育事业蓬勃发展。全年新成立体育社会组织7个，培训社会体育指导员4089人。组织各类全民健身活动（赛事）3431次，参与人数500万人次（含线上活动）。获省级及以上金牌286枚，银牌191枚，铜牌218枚。

十、能源、环境、城市建设和安全生产

绿色低碳转型成效显著。能源消费结构不断优化，煤炭消费控制在合理区间，天然气保障能力增强。规模以上工业煤炭消费2800.3万吨，比上年下降1.7%；焦炭消费774.5万吨，下降4.7%；天然气消费10.6亿立方米，增长5.3%。新能源发电稳步提升，规模以上企业风力发电量25.0亿千瓦时，增长7.9%；太阳能发电量3.5亿千瓦时，增长15.7%；垃圾焚烧发电量10.3亿千瓦时，增长6.9%；生物质发电量7.4亿千瓦时，增长11.5%。

表10　2023年规模以上工业能源消费情况

指标	累计	比上年增长（%）
煤炭（万吨）	2800.3	-1.7
天然气消费量（亿立方米）	10.6	5.3
焦炭（万吨）	774.5	-4.7
汽油（万吨）	0.4	15.0
柴油（万吨）	4.7	30.2

表 11 2023 年规模以上企业能源生产情况

指标	累计	比上年增长（%）
原煤（万吨）	59.0	20.6
发电量（亿千瓦时）	323.0	1.0
火力发电量（亿千瓦时）	294.4	0.3
垃圾焚烧发电量（亿千瓦时）	10.3	6.9
生物质发电量（亿千瓦时）	7.4	11.5
风力发电量（亿千瓦时）	25.0	7.9
太阳能发电量（亿千瓦时）	3.5	15.7

全社会用电量稳步增长。全社会用电量 540.9 亿千瓦时，比上年增长 8.2%，其中，居民生活用电量 104.3 亿千瓦时，增长 6.8%。分产业看，第一产业用电量 4.1 亿千瓦时，增长 15.2%；第二产业用电量 291.6 亿千瓦时，增长 6.5%；第三产业用电量 140.9 亿千瓦时，增长 13.0%。工业用电量 280.7 亿千瓦时，占全社会用电量比重 51.9%，增长 6.7%。

表 12 2023 年全市用电量情况

指标	累计（亿千瓦时）	比上年增长（%）
全社会用电	540.9	8.2
城乡居民生活用电	104.3	6.8
第一产业	4.1	15.2
第二产业	291.6	6.5
工 业	280.7	6.7
第三产业	140.9	13.0

生态环境质量加力改善。空气质量综合指数 4.59，市区空气质量良好以上天数 204 天，优良天数比率 62.6%。细颗粒物（PM2.5）浓度 38 微克/立方米，可吸入颗粒物（PM10）年均浓度 73 微克/立方米，二氧化硫 9 微克/立方米，二氧化氮 33 微克/立方米。国控断面好Ⅲ类水体比例达到 100%，小清河出境断面辛丰庄化学需氧量和氨氮浓度分别为 13.8 毫克/升、0.37 毫克/升，指标浓度达到地表水环境质量标准（GB3838-2002）Ⅱ类水体。区域环境噪声昼间平均等效声级 53.8 分贝，市区道路交通噪声昼间平均等效声级 67.2 分贝。

城市建设水平全面提升。年末城市建成区面积 860.0 平方公里，比上年增加 6.1 平方公里。新建各类公园 100 处、绿道 111 公里、森林步道 100 公里。建成区绿地率 40.2%，人均公园绿地面积 14.4 平方米。全年天然气供气量 18.7 亿立方米。液化石油气供气量 4.6 万吨，比上年增长 19.1%。集中供热面积 3.6 亿平方米，增长 8.8%。自来水供水量 5.5 亿吨，增长 8.5%。持续推动市民泉水直饮工程，累计建设 118 处市民泉水直饮工程，覆盖人口达到 38 万人。生活垃圾无害化处理率 100%。充电基础设施保有量 7.9 万个，其中，公共充换电站共 735 座，车桩比达到 2.14: 1，建成区内公共充换电站平均服务半径 0.6 公里。公共充电设施日均充电量 82.2 万度，日均充电次数 2.7 万次，全年公共充电设施电力消费量 3.1 亿度。

社会治安保持良好。全年共破获刑事案件 25418 起，命案现案破案率保持 100%，连续 13 年实现命案全破，获评首批全国社会治安防控体系建设示范城市。八类严重暴力案件破现案率 100%，“两盗”案件现案破案率 58.5%，抓获各类逃犯 3075 人；打掉恶势力犯罪集团 11 个、恶势力团伙 8 个。

安全生产形势稳定。全市发生各类生产安全事故 104 起，比上年下降 25.2%，死亡 87 人，下降 20.9%。未发生重大及以上生产安全事故。

十一、居民生活和社会保障

城乡居民收入差距进一步缩小。全市居民人均可支配收入 51757 元，比上年增长 6.0%。分城乡看，城镇居民人均可支配收入 62506 元，增长 5.1%；农村居民人均可支配收入 25587 元，增长 7.3%。城乡居民收入比由上年同期的 2.49: 1 下降至 2.44: 1。城镇居民恩格尔系数[10]23.6%，农村居民恩格尔系数 30.3%。

表 13 2023 年居民人均可支配收入及增长速度

指标	全体居民		城镇居民		农村居民	
	2023 年（元）	比上年增长（%）	2023 年（元）	比上年增长（%）	2023 年（元）	比上年增长（%）
可支配收入	51757	6.0	62506	5.1	25587	7.3
工资性收入	29676	5.0	36150	4.2	13913	5.9
经营净收入	5453	11.5	3810	17.2	9455	8.1
财产净收入	7629	5.7	10523	4.4	584	15.6
转移净收入	8999	6.4	12023	5.1	1635	12.4

表 14 2023 年末每百户居民家庭主要耐用消费品拥有量[11]

指标	单位	城镇居民	农村居民
家用汽车	辆	67	49
电冰箱(柜)	台	102	99
洗衣机	台	99	95
热水器	台	100	91
空调	台	179	97
彩色电视机	台	100	101
计算机	台	77	38
移动电话	部	243	240

社会保障体系更加健全。年末城镇职工基本养老保险参保人数 456.6 万人；职工医疗保险参保人数 367.3 万人，比

上年增加 14.4 万人；失业保险参保人数 239.7 万人，增加 4.3 万人；工伤保险参保人数 310.6 万人，增加 3.2 万人；生育保险参保人数 254.0 万人，增加 8.4 万人。居民养老保险和医疗保险参保人数分别达到 312.1 万人和 499.8 万人。

最低生活保障不断提高。城市居民最低生活保障标准 1045 元/月，保障城镇居民 7951 户、10548 人，发放保障金及各类补贴 1.2 亿元；农村居民最低生活保障标准 814 元/月，保障农村居民 60342 户、85340 人，发放保障金及各类补贴 6.6 亿元。城市特困人员基本生活标准 1492 元/月，农村特困人员基本生活标准 1356 元/月。照料护理标准按照自理、半自理和完全不能自理分别为 281 元/月、466 元/月、932 元/月，城市特困保障 910 人，农村特困保障 14422 人，共发放特困供养救助金及补贴 3.4 亿元。

救助帮扶更有温度。全市共有社会救助综合服务机构 14 处，其中，救助管理站 1 处，未成年人救助保护中心 16 处。培训残疾人 4711 人次，安置残疾人员就业 2788 人，帮扶救助残疾人投入资金 3.3 亿元。

民生福祉显著改善。全市建成各类养老服务设施 4142 处，社区养老服务设施配建达标率 100%，长者食堂等各类助餐场所达到 2590 处、累计服务 3000 万人次，城乡居民基础养老金月标准提高至 178 元。居民医保财政补助标准提高至 730 元，职工门诊统筹年度支付限额由 3000 元提高到 4500 元。发放育儿补贴 1.1 亿元，惠及家庭 2.5 万个。

注释：

[1] 2023 年统计数据为统计快报数或初步核算数，正式数据以出版的《济南统计年鉴 2024》为准。部分数据因四舍五入影响，存在总计与分项合计不等情况。

[2] 全市地区生产总值、各产业增加值绝对数按现价计算，增长速度按不变价格计算，当年数据为初步核算数。根据年度核算，对国内生产总值、各产业增加值等相关指标的历史数据进行了修订。

[3] 本公报中的增长，如无特殊表述，均为本期数据较上年同期数据的增长率。

[4] 规模以上工业企业指年主营业务收入 2000 万元及以上的工业法人单位。

[5] 规模以上服务业包括：交通运输、仓储和邮政业，信息传输、软件和信息技术服务业，房地产业（不包含房地产开发经营），租赁和商务服务业，科学研究和技术服务业，水利、环境和公共设施管理业，居民服务、修理和其他服务业，教育，卫生和社会工作，文化、体育和娱乐业。

[6] 现代服务业包括：信息传输、软件和信息技术服务业，金融业，房地产业，租赁和商务服务业，科学研究和技术服务业，水利、环境和公共设施管理业，居民服务、修理和其他服务业，教育，卫生和社会工作，文化、体育和娱乐业。

[7] “四上”单位指规模以上工业、有资质的建筑业、限额以上批发和零售业、限额以上住宿和餐饮业、房地产开发经营业、规模以上服务业。

[8] 限额以上单位是指年主营业务收入 2000 万元及以上的批发业单位、500 万元及以上的零售业单位、200 万元及以上的住宿和餐饮业单位。单位包括法人企业、产业活动单位和个体户。

[9] 研究与试验发展（R&D）经费投入相关指标错年使用 2022 年数据。

[10] 恩格尔系数是指食品支出在消费支出中的比重。

[11] 数据来自住户收支与生活状况调查。

资料来源：本公报中黄河流域生态保护和高质量发展战略、企业技术中心、充电基础设施数据来自发展改革部门；教育数据来自教育部门；科技数据来自科技部门；电信相关数据来自工业和信息化部门；户籍、社会治安、民用机动车数据来自公安部门；城乡最低生活保障、特困人员救助供养、养老服务设施相关数据来自民政部门；地域税收数据来自税务部门；财政数据来自财政部门；城镇新增就业、城镇职工保险参保、技工学校数据来自人力资源和社会保障部门；环境保护相关数据来自生态环境部门；城市建设相关数据来自住房和城乡建设部门；垃圾处理数据来自城市管理部门；交通运输数据来自交通运输部门；民航数据来自济南国际机场；泉水直饮工程建设数据来自城乡水务部门；水产品产量、农业数据来自农业农村部门；林业数据来自园林和林业部门；进出口、展会、新设境外企业、外派劳务人员数据来自商务部门；旅游、文化数据来自文化和旅游部门；档案数据来自市档案馆；卫生、育儿补贴数据来自卫生健康部门；生产安全数据来自应急管理部门；知识产权数据来自市场监管部门；体育数据来自体育部门；医疗保险类数据来自医疗保障部门；金融数据来自地方金融监督管理部门；招商引资、外资数据来自投资促进部门；市场主体数据来自行政审批服务部门；物流数据来自口岸物流部门；残疾人保障数据来自残联；邮政、快递数据来自邮政管理部门；居民收入与支出数据、恩格尔系数、价格指数、粮食畜牧数据、城乡家庭主要耐用消费品拥有量来自国家统计局济南调查队；济南新旧动能转换起步区数据来自济南新旧动能转换起步区管委会；其他数据均来自市统计局。

Special Report–2

STATISTICAL COMMUNIQUÉ OF THE JINAN MUNICIPAL ON THE 2023 NATIONAL ECONOMIC AND SOCIAL DEVELOPMENT [1]

Jinan Municipal Bureau of Statistics
NBS Survey Office in Jinan

In 2023, the whole city adhered to the guidance of Xi Jinping Thought on Socialism with Chinese Characteristics for a New Era, deeply studied and implemented the spirit of the 20th National Congress of the Communist Party of China and the second Plenary Session of the 20th Central Committee of the Communist Party of China, resolutely implemented the important instructions and requirements of General Secretary Xi Jinping on the governance work of the governments of Shandong Province and Jinan City, anchored "leading the way and embedding on a new stage all around", focused and concentrated on "the year of major project breakthrough". The municipal economy witnessed the momentum of recovery with adherence to the general tone of seeking progress while maintaining stability, by fully and accurately implementing the new development concept, actively serving and integrating into the new development pattern, following the general principle of pursuing progress while ensuring stability, and comprehensively deepening reform and opening up, seized the major strategic opportunities, promoted high-quality development of the green, low-carbon and circular economy development concept, deepen the transition from old to new kinetic energy, and improve the living standards of the masses, both quantitative and qualitative progress across the whole city's economic and social development had been achieved, with all citizens witnessing new great progress in building a powerful socialist modern provincial capital with the advantages of "strong, new, excellent, rich, beautiful, and high-level" in the new era.

I. General Outlook

The economic aggregate was steadily increasing. According to the unified accounting results of the municipal gross domestic product (GDP), the city's regional GDP in 2023 was [2]1275.74 billion yuan, up by [3]6.1 percent over 2022 at constant prices. Of this total, the added value of the primary industry was 42.95 billion yuan, up by 4.1 percent, and that of the secondary industry was 431.2 billion yuan, up by 7.8 percent ,and that of the tertiary industry was 801.59 billion yuan, up by 5.2 percent. The composition ratio of the three industries in Jinan was 3.4:33.8:62.8.

Figure 1 Gross Domestic Product Between 2019 to 2023

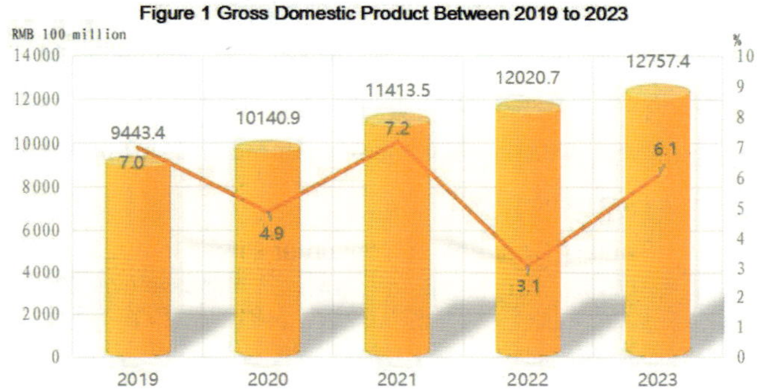

The population size was consistently increasing. By the end of 2023, the permanent population of Jinan reached 9.437 million, up by 0.2 percent over that of the previous year. Of this total, the urban permanent population amounted to 7.104 million, accounting for 75.3 percent of the total population (urbanization rate of the permanent population), up by 1.0 percent. The registered population amounted to 8.253 million, up by 0.7 percent. The declared birth rate for the whole year was 7.6 per thousand, the declared death rate was 5.7 per thousand, and the natural population growth rate was 1.8 per thousand. The annual inflow of talent amounted to 0.275 million, with a net inflow of 0.146 million.

The overall employment situation was generally stable. The number of market entities reached 1.548 million, up by 3.3 percent over that of the previous year. Throughout 2023, the newly added employed population amounted to 0.178 million, up by 2.3 percent. For the establishment of entrepreneurship incubation bases, there were 86 municipal level entrepreneurship incubation bases across the whole city, with a total incubation area of 3.66 million square meters and 12000 incubating enterprises. The city granted entrepreneurship guarantee loans of 780 million yuan, carried out various entrepreneurship subsidies of 46 million yuan, and created more than 0.1 million job opportunities cumulatively. The city successfully held the 1st "Haiyou Talent Festival" and the sixth China (Jinan) New Energy Innovation and Entrepreneurship Competition, which imported 12 academician teams. There were newly added 126 national and provincial key talents across the whole city, making the total talent size of 2.782 million, and Jinan was well deserved for the "China's Best Talent Introduction City" for two consecutive years.

The consumer prices increased moderately. The annual consumer price index (CPI) went up by 0.6 percent, down by 0.8 percent than that of the previous year, indicating a significant effect in ensuring market supply and stable prices. From the price composition of the eight major categories of goods and services consumed by residents, it showed a trend of "six increases, one decrease, and one balanced". The selling prices of newly-built residential properties continuously grew year-on-year, with the month-on-month index fluctuating from growth to reduction.

Table 1 Changes of Consumer Prices in 2023

Item	Increase over 2022 (%)
Consumer Price Index	0.6
Of which:Food,Tobacco and Liquor	1.0
Clothing	1.4
Residence	0.0
Household facilities, articles and services	0.3
Transportation and telecommunication	-1.8
Education, culture and recreation	2.3
Health care and medical services	0.8
Miscellaneous goods and services	3.9

FIGURE 2 SALES PRICE INDEX OF NEWLY-BUILT COMERCIAL HOUSING IN 2023

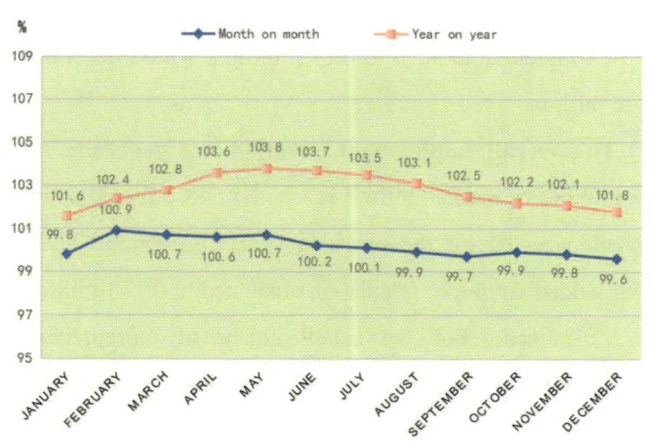

Seized and made good use of major strategic opportunities. In depth implementation of the ecological protection and high-quality development strategy in the Yellow River Basin, key projects such as the protection of Baiyun Lake wetland, the reinforcement of Queshan Reservoir, and the connection of the four reservoirs in the eastern urban area were completed basically. The level of security for the Yellow River had been significantly improved, and the construction of a water-saving society had reached full coverage of districts and counties. The construction of the starting area for the transformation of old and new kinetic energy in Jinan was accelerated, the Jinan Yellow River International Convention and Exhibition Center had been put into use, and the agglomeration effect of industrial carriers such as the Zhongke New Economy Science and Technology Innovation Park enhanced significantly. The construction of landmark buildings such as the TV tower in the demonstration zone and the new museum across the whole city was initiated, and 26 high-end and high-quality projects had been newly introduced with a planned total investment of 94.6 billion yuan. The construction of the Sci Tech Innovation Financial Reform Pilot Zone had reached remarkable results. It had taken the lead in organizing evaluations of science and technology financial institutions nationwide, recognizing 10 science and technology branches, 3 science and technology finance business units (specialized departments), 9 science and technology finance characteristic institutions, and 6 companies listed on the Sci Tech Innovation Board, ranking first in the province in terms of the number of listings. It had successfully issued the first REITs (Real Estate Investment Trust Funds) product in the province, completed the first supply chain finance company ticket issuance and discounting business in the country, and was approved as a pilot for financial technology innovation in the national capital market. The total transaction volume of digital RMB had exceeded 6.3 billion yuan. Breakthroughs had been made in the construction of Digital Jinan, making the city selected as one of the first pilot cities for digital transformation of small and medium-sized enterprises in China. It had been awarded the title of China's leading smart city for six consecutive years, and its computing power scale ranks first in the province. It had successfully entered the top ten of the national digital ecosystem index. Deeply participated in the joint construction of the "the Belt and Road", and 1006 China EU trains were launched throughout 2023, up by 25.6 percent over that of the previous year, breaking the 1000 train mark for the first time.

Accelerated the transition from old to new kinetic

energy. The value added of the "Four New" economy reached 516.05 billion yuan, accounting for 40.5 percent of the whole city's GDP, up by 1.6 percent over that of the previous year. The investment in the "Four New" economy went up by 27.4 percent compared with that of the previous year, up by 25.3 percent higher than the average investment growth rates across the city, accounting for 50.6 percent of the city's total investment amount, up by 10.5 percent. The investment amount in high-tech industries went up by 16.6 percent, accounting for 9.1 percent of the city's total investment amount, and advancing the city's investment growth by 1.3 percent. Industrial technological transformation investment went up by 12.4 percent. The value added of high-tech manufacturing industry above designated size went up by 6.1 percent, driving the growth of industries[4] above designated size by 1.3 percent. High tech service industry enterprises above designated size reached a revenue of 142.51 billion yuan, up by 5.9 percent, accounting for 33.4 percent of the revenue of service industry[5] enterprises above designated size. The modern service industry [6]reached an added value of 480.91 billion yuan, up by 4.4 percent, accounting for 60.0 percent of the service industry's added value.

The "year of major project breakthrough" had yielded fruitful progress. The number of major projects for green, low-carbon, and high-quality development had reached 2413, and industrial projects were with a strong growth momentum. The investment promotion attained outstanding progress, successfully hosting major events such as the 3rd Confucian Business Conference, China Enterprise Forum, Top 500 Private Enterprises Summit, China Japan Industrial Innovation and Development Exchange Conference, and China Germany (Europe) Small and Medium sized Enterprise Cooperation and Exchange Conference. New international investment promotion liaison stations had been established in Germany and Japan. The first "Zero-Carbon Factory" in the province had been completed, the second phase of the FinDreams Battery Project was completed and put into operation, the "Transporting electrical energy from Tai'an Shiheng Power Plant to Jinan" project had been put into operation, the Bodor Laser global headquarters had started construction, and the AIKO solar cell project had been successfully landed. There were 1767 fixed assets investment projects worth more than 100 million yuan across the whole city, up by 114 over that of the previous year, and the completed investment went up by 15.1 percent over that of the previous year, driving the city's investment growth by 8.7 percent. Of this total, there were 50 projects worth more than 5 billion yuan, up by 7, and the completed investment went up by 71.8 percent. The total number of [7]"enterprises in four industries with operating income above designated size" across the city had exceeded 15000 for the first time, reaching 15143, up by 16.0 percent.

II. Agriculture and Rural Area

The Gross Output Value of agriculture, forestry, animal husbandry, and fishery increased steadily. The Gross Output Value of agriculture, forestry, animal husbandry and fishery in 2023 amounted to 80.06 billion yuan, up by 4.9 percent over that of the previous year at constant prices. Of this total, the Gross Output Value of agriculture reached 54.39 billion yuan, up by 4.4 percent, and that of animal husbandry reached 16.4 billion yuan, up by 5.6 percent. The value added of agriculture, forestry, animal husbandry, and fishery amounted to 45.3 billion yuan, up by 4.4 percent.

Table 2 Gross Output Value of Agriculture, Forestry, Animal Husbandry and Fishery In 2023

Item	Output value (100 million yuan)	Increase over 2022 (%)
Gross output value of agriculture, forestry, animal husbandry and fishery	800.6	4.9
Agriculture	543.9	4.4
Forestry	32.1	3.8
Animal husbandry	164.0	5.6
Fishery	8.9	4.4
Agriculture,forestry, animal husbandry and fishery services	51.7	9.6

Agricultural production secured another bumper harvest. The annual grain sowing area amounted to 7.287 million mu, up by 0.3 percent over that of the previous year, and the total annual grain output reached 3.029 million tons, up by 2.3 percent. The total annual oil production reached 67000 tons, up by 1.0 percent.

New achievements in forestry production were created. Throughout 2023, the completed afforestation area across the city amounted to 826.7 hectares, forest tending area amounted to 5893.3 hectares, forestry pest control operation area amounted to 3.286 million mu, and with 100 demonstration villages for urban greening. The city continuously improved the forestry industry and transformed 674 hectares of greening trees with low yield and efficiency. The city finished construction of 2 mountain parks with a total number of 89, making the forest coverage rate reach 23.7 percent.

The animal husbandry output developed steadily. The annual output of live pigs amounted to 2.037 million, up by 2.8 percent over that of the previous year, and that of cattle amounted to 0.107 million, down by 3.2 percent, and that of sheep amounted to 1.30 million, down by 4.5 percent, and that of poultry amounted to 61.718 million, up by 8.6 percent. The total output of pork, beef, mutton, and poultry meat for 2023 reached 0.295 million tons, up by 1.4 percent. Of this total, pork output was 0.167 million tons, down by 0.9 percent, and beef output was 0.023 million tons, down by 4.2 percent, and mutton output was 0.019 million tons, down by 3.8 percent, and poultry meat output was 0.086 million tons, up by 9.3 percent. The annual Poultry-egg output amounted to 0.292 million tons, up by 8.2 percent, and milk output was 0.454 million tons, up by 4.5 percent, and the annual output of Aquatic products reached 0.015 million tons, up by 4.1 percent.

Table 3 Main Agricultural Product Planting Area and Output In 2023

Item	Unit	Area/ output	Increase over 2022 (%)
Total sown area of grain	10,000 mu	728.7	0.3
Cotton planting area	10,000 mu	4.5	1.3
Oil planting area	10,000 mu	26.5	0.5
Total grain output	10,000 tons	302.9	2.3
Cotton yield	10,000 tons	0.4	2.5
Oil yield	10,000 tons	6.7	1.0
Slaughtered Pigs	10 000 heads	203.7	-2.8
Slaughtered Cattle	10 000 heads	10.7	-3.2
Slaughtered Sheep	10 000 heads	130.0	-4.5
Slaughtered Poultry	10 000 heads	6171.8	8.6
Output of Pork	10,000 tons	16.7	-0.9
Output of Beef	10,000 tons	2.3	-4.2
Output of Mutton	10,000 tons	1.9	-3.8
Output of Poultry Meat	10,000 tons	8.6	9.3
Output of Poultry & Eggs	10,000 tons	29.2	8.2
Output of Cow Milk	10,000 tons	45.4	4.5
Output of Aquatic Products	10,000 tons	1.5	4.1

The scale of modern and efficient agricultural production maintained good growth momentum. The value added of modern and efficient agriculture for the whole year amounted to 7.97 billion yuan, up by 5.5 percent over that of the previous year, accounting for 17.6 percent of the value added of agriculture, forestry, animal husbandry and fishery industries, up by 0.5 percent over that of the previous year. The city created 22 annual new parks(vegetable basket project) for vegetables supply and guarantee, 357 large-scale live pig breeding farms and 33 state-level standardized demonstration farms for livestock and poultry breeding. 61 well-known agricultural brands reached or beyond the provincial level, and the green, organic, geographical indication and compliant agricultural products (Three Certificates Plus One Registration) amounted to 513 across the whole city.

Great achievements had been made in rural revitalization cause. The city successfully accomplished the task of creating 40 provincial-level and beautiful rural demonstration villages, and created 3 provincial-level model demonstration zones for rural revitalization in Shandong Province. The city newly affirmed 118 demonstration new agricultural business entities at or beyond the city level. The number of leading agricultural enterprises at or above the city level amounted to 525, with 8803 family farms and 11320 farmer cooperatives respectively. The city continuously expanded the scope of poverty alleviation, incorporated 44000 getting rid of poverty residents into the scope of rural subsistence allowances and support for rural extremely poor people across the whole city.

III. Industry and Construction

The industrial production scale expanded stronger. The annual total industrial value added amounted to 288.61 billion yuan, up by 7.9 percent over that of the previous year. The added value of industrial companies above designated size went up by 12.4 percent. Among the major industrial sectors, 24 industries reached value-added growth, up by 58.5 percent. Of this total, 11 industries had growth rates exceeding the city's average level. Among the key industries, the value added of automobile manufacturing went up by 133.3 percent, computer communication and other electronic equipment manufacturing went up by 21.2 percent, general equipment manufacturing went up by 19.1 percent, petroleum, coal and other fuel processing industry went up by 6.7 percent, pharmaceutical manufacturing industry went up by 3.1 percent, and smelting and pressing of ferrous metals industry down by 4.8 percent.

The profitability improved significantly. The annual

industrial enterprises above designated size reached a revenue of 920.81 billion yuan, up by 10.0 percent over that of the previous year, with a total profit of 41.97 billion yuan, up by 26.8 percent. The operating income profit margin and cost profit margin went up by 0.6 and 0.7 percent respectively over that of the previous year, while the number of loss making entrepreneurs down by 26 and the total loss amount down by 36.7 percent. Large and medium-sized enterprises developed steadily in achieving a revenue of 655.93 billion yuan, up by 11.2 percent, with a total profit of 32.03 billion yuan, up by 30.2 percent, higher than the city average by 1.2 and 3.4 percent respectively.

Table 4 Growth Rate of Operating Revenue of Key Industries Above Designated Size In 2023

Industry	Increase over 2022 (%)
Smelting and Pressing of Ferrous Metals	0.6
Manufacture of Automobiles	91.2
Manufacture of Computers, Communication and Other Electronic Equipment	4.6
Manufacture of Electrical Machinery and Apparatus	27.4
Manufacture of General Purpose Machinery	21.8
Manufacture of Non-metallic Mineral Products	-13.6
Processing of Petroleum, Coal and Other Fuels	-4.4
Manufacture of Medicines	2.1
Manufacture of Raw Chemical Materials and Chemical Products	2.4
Manufacture of Metal Products	1.6
Manufacture of Special Purpose Machinery	-6.6
Production and Supply of Electric Power and Heat Power	-1.5
Processing of Food from Agricultural Products	5.9
Manufacture of Foods	-1.4
Mining and Processing of Ferrous Metal Ores	-19.0
Production and Supply of Gas	4.9

The supply of industrial products was stable. The sales rate of industrial products above designated size for the whole year was 96.7 percent. Among the 207 industrial products produced by the whole city, the output of 104 types of products increased with a growth rate of 50.2 percent. Of this total, 45 products were with an increase rate of over 20 percent accounted for 21.7 percent. For equipment manufacturing products, the output of trucks went up by 48.9 percent over that of the previous year, while the output of generator sets (power generation equipment) and metal cutting machine tools went up by 27.8 percent and 26.1 percent respectively. For raw material products, the production of graphite and carbon products went up by 9.6 percent.

Table 5 Output and Growth Rate of Main Products of Industrial Enterprises Above Designated Size In 2023

Product Designation	Unit	Output	Increase over 2022 (%)
Frozen,Fresh Meat	10,000 tons	19.4	17.5
Milk Products	10,000 tons	48.7	-3.6
Liquor	10,000 kiloliter	26.0	-1.2
Synthetic Ammonia	10,000 tons	77.7	275.6
Primary Plastic	10,000 tons	91.6	17.4
Traditional Chemical Medicine	ton	9305.3	17.7
Graphite and Carbon Products	10,000 tons	208.6	9.6
Rolled Steel	10,000 tons	1943.6	-4.1
Forge Piece	10,000 tons	127.5	1.1
Sintered Metal Products	10,000 tons	1.5	17.6
Engine	10,000 kW	2826.4	59.6
CNC Metal Cutting Machine Tools	Unit	4983	17.8
Pneumatic Components	10,000 unit	1915.4	131.2
Industrial Robot	Unit	3414	-16.0
Trucks	10,000 units	23.9	48.9
Transformers	10,000 KVA	15918.5	0.3
Solar Cells (Photovoltaic Cells)	10,000 kW	25.5	529.8
Computers	10,000 units	68.4	-11.8
Servers	10,000 units	67.9	-11.9
Industrial control computer and system	10,000 units	2.8	74.3
Transducer	10,000 units	1524.0	42.4

The construction industry grew steadily. There were 1492 construction enterprises across the whole city with general contracting and professional contracting qualifications and workload, up by 121 over that of the previous year. The total amount of signed contracts for 2023 was 1.48859 trillion yuan, up by 12.6 percent over that of the previous year. Of this total, the amount of newly signed contracts was 717.73 billion yuan, up by 10.4 percent. The total output value of the construction industry reached 477.29 billion yuan, up by 7.0 percent. Of this total, the output value of state-owned and state-controlled enterprises was 389.78 billion yuan, up by 13.6 percent. The construction area of the house was 205.166 million square meters, up by 2.7 percent.

IV. Service Sector

The service industry had seen improvements in both quality and efficiency. The added value of the service industry for the whole year was 801.59 billion yuan, up by 5.2 percent over that of the previous year. Service industry enterprises above designated size reached a revenue of 426.4 billion yuan, up by 14.4 percent. Key industries are accelerating their efforts, with the operating income of large-scale transportation, warehousing, and postal services, leasing and business services, and information transmission, software, and information technology services went up by 25.3 percent, 12.1 percent, and 6.6 percent respectively.

Table 6 Operating Revenue of Service Enterprises Above Designated Size by Sector In 2023

Sector	Operating Revenue (100 Million yuan)	Increase over 2022 (%)
Total	4264.0	14.4
Transport, Storage and Post	1851.5	25.3
Information Transmission, Software and Information Technology	864.6	6.6
Real Estate (Excluding Real Estate Development and Operation)	206.3	8.1
Leasing and Business Services	547.8	12.1
Scientific Research,Technical Services	546.7	6.1
Management of Water Conservancy, Environment and Public Facilities	32.6	-39.9
Services to Households, Repair and Other Services	25.7	9.1
Education	32.1	21.9
Health and Social Work	67.4	12.0
Culture, Sports and Recreation	89.2	12.0

The transportation developed steadily. The annual total traffic mileage of highways across the whole city reached 18356.5 kilometers, up by 0.3 percent over that of the previous year. Of this total, the traffic mileage of domestic expressways was 828.4 kilometers, up by 4.2 percent, and the highway passenger transportation volume was 21.37 million, up by 48.6 percent, and the passenger turnover was 4.62 billion person-kilometers, up by 56.2 percent. The road freight volume was 250 million tons, up by 3.1 percent; The freight turnover was 61.55 billion ton-kilometers, up by 1.1 percent. Annual civilian vehicles amounted to 3.898 million , of which 3.387 million were civilian cars, up by 5.7 percent. The total number of new energy vehicles across the whole city reached 0.171 million, and the city had been approved as one of the first batch of pilot cities for comprehensive electrification of public sector vehicles in China. The number of bus routes amounted to 779, up by 23 over that of the previous year, with a total traffic mileage of 15671.8 kilometers, up by 48.5 kilometers. The passenger transportation volume was 530 million, up by 140 million. There were 3 operating rail transit lines with a traffic mileage of 84.1 kilometers and an annual passenger transportation volume of 96.21 million, up by 76.4 percent. Annually, a total of 0.137 million flights taking off and landing, up by 73.6 percent. The passenger throughput was 17.561 million, up by 113.1 percent, and the cargo and mail transportation handling volume was 0.144 million tons, up by 4.6 percent.

The postal and telecommunications industries developed healthily. The annual business revenue of the postal industry (excluding direct operating revenue of Postal Savings Bank of China Co., Ltd.) reached 12.1 billion yuan, up by 14.9 percent over that of the previous year; The delivery volume in postal industry reached 1.08 billion items, up by 8.0 percent. The revenue of express delivery business reached 9.23 billion yuan, up by 12.5 percent; The business volume (excluding postal company parcel business) reached 850 million, up by 10.0 percent. At the end of 2023, there were 12.879 million mobile phone users in total, up by 1.7 percent, of which 9.222 million were 5G mobile phone users, up by 34.6 percent, and the volume of fixed Internet broadband users reached 5.226 million, up 4.2 percent.

The tourism and exhibition industries developed flourishing. The tourism and exhibition industries market serviced 106.311 million domestic tourists annually, up by 61.9 percent over that of the previous year. Domestic tourism revenue amounted to 113.29 billion yuan, up by 65.5 percent. There were eighty-nine of A-level tourist attractions, including one of 5A-level tourist attraction and nineteen of 4A-level tourist attractions, and two of provincial-level tourist resorts. 12 new star rated hotels had been added to the city, bringing the total to 52. Of this total, two of new 5-star hotels had been added, with the total of 7. Mingshui Ancient City Shuangquan Resort opened for trial operation, and major cultural and tourism events such as the Double An Cultural Tourism Festival, the "Jinan City Beautiful Season", the "Rushes on Spring City" Jinan Spring Tour, the Book Expo, the Cultural and Tourism Expo, and the Han Meilin Art Exhibition were successfully held. Scenic spots such as Chaoran Tower, Qifeng Bridge, and the former trading port became popular check-in attractions, and the Impression Jinan Spring World was awarded the state-level tourism and leisure street, Jinan was also awarded the title of "Most Dynamic City 2023". Annually, 125 exhibition events were held, up by 64.5 percent, with an exhibition area of 2.3 million square meters, up by 64.3 percent, and Jinan also be involved into the list of "China Exhibition Brand City".

V. Investment in Fixed Assets

Fixed assets investment size grew steadily. Fixed assets investment went up by 2.1 percent over that of the previous year. The investment in the primary industry down by 16.5 percent, and that in the secondary industry went up by 25.3 percent, and that in the tertiary industry down by 2.2 percent. Infrastructure investment went up by 49.1 percent, and the investment in high-tech service industry went up by 23.5 percent. Industrial investment went up by 25.4 percent, with manufacturing investment went up by 7.2 percent.

The development of the real estate market was still in a stagnant state. The total investment in real estate development for 2023 reached 139.97 billion yuan, down by 19.7 percent over that of the previous year. Of this total, the investment in residential development was 99.48 billion yuan, down by 18.4 percent. The construction area of houses was 81.436 million square meters, down by 5.4 percent. Of this total, the construction area of residential buildings was 49.856 million square meters, down by 6.6 percent. The completed area of houses was 9.709 million square meters, up by 35.8 percent. Of this total, the completed area of residential buildings was 6.79 million square meters, up by 39.1 percent. The sales area of commercial housing amounted to 11.702 million square meters, down by 5.8 percent, of which the sales area of residential housing was 8.255 million square meters, down by 9.0 percent. The sales revenue of commercial housing was 155.32 billion yuan, up by 2.6 percent, of which the sales revenue of residential housing was 121.8 billion yuan, down by 0.3 percent.

VI. Domestic Trade

The consumer goods market was steadily recovering. The total retail sales of consumer goods across the whole city reached 519.9 billion yuan, up by 6.6 percent over that of the previous year. According to the location of the operating units, the retail sales of consumer goods in urban areas of the city reached 456.16 billion yuan, up by 6.5 percent; The retail sales of consumer goods in rural areas of the city reached 63.74 billion yuan, up by 7.5 percent. By consumption type, the whole city's retail sales of goods reached 443.67 billion yuan, up by 5.8 percent, and the catering revenue reached 76.23 billion yuan, up by 11.5 percent.

Online consumption grew rapidly. The retail sales of wholesale and retail units [8]above designated size across the whole city through public networks reached 42.92 billion yuan, up by 24.3 percent over that of the previous year, accounting for 22.1 percent of the total retail sales of units above designated size across the whole city, up by 4.0 percent over that of the previous year.

The sales of travel related products had good growth. The retail sales of automobiles, petroleum and products by units above designated size across the whole city went up by 10.5 percent and 18.8 percent respectively over that of the previous year, advancing the retail sales of enterprises above designated size across the whole city to go up by 3.4 and 1.9 percent, respectively. The performance of new energy vehicles is impressive, with retail sales of new energy vehicles went up by 83.3 percent, accounting for 10.9 percent of the total retail sales of units above designated size across the whole city, up by 4.9 percent over that of the previous year.

Life related consumption size remained stable. The retail sales of food and clothing products by enterprise above designated size across the whole city went up by 4.9 percent and 10.8 percent respectively over that of the previous year, advancing the retail sales of units above designated size across the whole city went up by 0.7 and 0.6 percent, respectively. The retail sales of gold, silver and jewelry, and communication equipment by enterprises above designated size went up by 12.8 percent and 11.6 percent respectively.

Table 7 Retail Sales Amount and Growth Rate of Main commodities of wholesale and retail units In 2023

Commodity Category	Retail sales (100 million yuan)	Increase over 2022 (%)
Grain and Oil, Food	194.1	3.6
Beverages	19.9	4.3
Tobacco and Liquor	49.6	10.5
Clothing, Shoes, Hats and Textiles	113.6	10.8
Cosmetics	56.8	-16.0
Gold, Silver and Jewellery	48.7	12.8
Articles for Daily Use	35.7	1.4
Newspapers and Magazines	96.3	-0.9
Household Appliances and Audio-Visual Equipment	107.3	-14.6
Traditional Chinese and Western Medicine	84.3	11.9
Communication Appliances	67.0	11.6
Petroleum and Related Products	208.4	18.8
Motor Vehicles	662.4	10.5
Of which: New energy vehicles	211.4	83.3

VII. Foreign Economic Relations

Imports and exports maintained steady growth. The total import and export volume of goods for 2023 amounted to 216.1 billion yuan, up by 0.3 percent over that of the previous year. Of this total, exports amounted to 137.34 billion yuan, down by 1.1 percent; Imports amounted to 78.76 billion yuan, up by 2.8 percent. The imports and exports of general trade amounted to 192.76 billion yuan, up by 2.9 percent, representing went up by 2.3 percent in proportion. Imports and exports to the European Union and Africa markets went up by 10.3 percent and 12.3 percent respectively, and that to the Central Asia region (CA) market went up by 63.4 percent. Among the exported goods, the export of mechanical and electrical products reached 83.49 billion yuan, up by 2.4 percent, and lithium-ion batteries and new energy vehicles went up by 16.6 percent and 15.3 percent respectively. For imported goods, refined oil imports amounted to 2.95 billion yuan, up by 792.7 percent, and coal and lignite imports amounted to 2.74 billion yuan, up by 122.5 percent, and crude oil imports amounted to 1.14 billion yuan, up by 75.5 percent.

Utilized foreign investment structure optimizated. The actual use of foreign investment across the whole city amounted to 2.48 billion US dollars, of which the actual use of foreign investment in high-tech industries was 640 million US dollars, accounting for 25.7 percent, up by 13.1 percents over that of the previous year; The tertiary industry's utilized foreign investment amounted to 1.73 billion US dollars, accounting for 69.8 percent. The total contracted foreign investment for 2023 reached 5.87 billion US dollars. 267 foreign-invested entrepreneurs newly established. There were 17 projects with a total investment of over 100 million US dollars, and the contracted foreign investment for these projects amounted to 1.66 billion US dollars.

External cooperation deepened. The newly signed contracts for foreign contracted projects for the whole year amounted to 3.8 billion US dollars, with the completed revenue of 4.29 billion US dollars, up by 4.7 percent over that of the previous year. 78 overseas enterprises (institutions) were registered and established, up by 73.3 percent; The actual completed investment amounted to 2.23 billion US dollars, up by 27.6 percent, and there were 7302 laborers in various types went global, up by 62.7 percent.

VIII. Finance and Financial Intermediation

The financial guarantee was solid and powerful. The whole city's regional tax revenue amounted to 150.66 billion yuan, up by 11.5 percent over that of the previous year. The general public budget revenue was 106.08 billion yuan, up by 6.0 percent, of which the tax revenue was 79.79 billion yuan, up by 15.1 percent, and the tax proportion was 75.2 percent, up by 6.0 percent over that of the previous year. The general public budget expenditure was 136.53 billion yuan, up by 11.4 percent, of which science and technology expenditure was 4.65 billion yuan, up by 64.8 percent, and that on agriculture, forestry, and water conservancy was 7.70 billion yuan, up by 12.7 percent, and social security and employment expenditures amounted to 22.35 billion yuan, up by 13.7 percent, with strong support for key affairs.

Table 8 General Public Budget Revenue and Expenditure In 2023

Item	Number (100 Million yuan)	Increase over 2022(%)
General Public Budget Revenue	1060.8	6.0
Of which: Tax Revenue	797.9	15.1
Value-added Tax	274.9	38.3
Enterprise Income Tax	115.2	-0.2
General Public Budget Expenditure	1365.3	11.4
Of which: Science and Technology	46.5	64.8
Farming、Forestry and Irrigation Affairs	77.0	12.7
Social Security and Employment	223.5	13.7

The balance of deposits and loans increased steadily. By the end of 2023, the balance of deposits in domestic and foreign currencies for financial institutions amounted to 2795.27 billion yuan, up by 7.8 percent over that of the previous year; The balance of loans in domestic and foreign currencies for financial institutions amounted to 2875.66 billion yuan, up by 10.1 percent.

The development of science and technology innovation finance sector improved flourishing. The balance of loans for science and technology innovation enterprises across the whole city was 174.71 billion yuan, up by 40.6 percent over that of the previous year; There were 3608 loan accounts for science and technology innovation enterprises, up by 26.0 percent; The weighted average interest rate for loans was 3.5 percent, down by 37 basis points. The "Jinan Innovative Science and Technology Innovation Financial Service System" has been selected as a "Typical Case of Local Comprehensive Deepening Reform in China 2023 ".

The insurance industry developed healthy. The insurance industry across the whole city reached premium income of 69.48 billion yuan, up by 9.9 percent over that of the previous year and 3.7 percent higher than the same period last year. Of this total, property insurance premium income was 12.9 billion yuan, up by 1.4 percent; The premium income of personal insurance was 56.58 billion yuan, up by 12.0 percent.

Credit quality continues to improve. The balance of non-performing loans of banking and financial institutions across the whole city amounted to 19.24 billion yuan, down by 4.18 billion yuan from the beginning of 2023; The non-performing loan ratio was 0.7 percent, down by 0.2 percent from the beginning of 2023.

The capital market was more active. The city's newly added direct financing scale was 410.8 billion yuan, up by 31.2 percent over that of the previous year, of which 6.19 billion yuan was equity financing, up by 2.0 percent; Bond financing reached 404.61 billion yuan, up by 31.7 percent. There were 5 newly listed companies across the whole city, with a total of 60 listed companies and 62 stocks.

IX. Technology, education, culture, public health, and sports enterprises

R&D investment continues to increase. The annual research and experimental development (R&D) expenditure was [9]34.68 billion yuan, up by 13.1 percent over that of the previous year, of which 2.99 billion yuan was for basic research, up by 11.9 percent; Applied research amounted to 4.44 billion yuan, up by 14.9 percent; The experimental development amounted to 27.25 billion yuan, up by 12.9 percent. R&D expenditure accounted for 2.9 percent of GDP, up by 0.2 percent over that of the previous year. R&D personnel in industrial enterprises above designated size reached 51599, up by 19.9 percent; Industrial enterprises above designated size established 841 R&D institutions, up by 66.2 percent. Three national level enterprise technology centers had been newly recognized, bringing the total number to 32. The provincial-level enterprise technology centers that had been newly recognized reached 15, with the total number of 249.

The quality of innovation capability upgraded. The total number of valid invention patents held by 10000 people throughout 2023 was 61.9, up by 26.5 percent over that of the previous year. The number of authorized invention patents was 13693, up by 15.5 percent. The technology contract reached a transaction volume of 80.65 billion yuan, up by 31.4 percent. Received 18 first prizes and 66 second prizes for provincial-level scientific and technological progress; Received 2 first prizes and 25 second prizes in provincial natural sciences. 6 new national key laboratories had been approved, bringing the total number to 11; 48 provincial-level engineering research centers had been added, bringing the total to 237; There were 11 newly registered provincial-level academician workstations, bringing the total number to 73. The number of national technology-based small and medium-sized enterprises reached 8323, up by 9.3 percent.

The education industry reached remarkable results. The coverage rate of universal kindergartens across the whole city had reached 94 percent, and the proportion of children in public kindergartens exceeds 60 percent. We have started construction, renovation, and expansion of 60 primary and secondary schools, kindergartens, and more than 40000 new school places. The total number of awards in the National Vocational College Skills Competition was 44, including 16 first prizes. 125 strategic engineering projects for the integration of city and school had been approved.

Table 9 Basic Situation of Education In 2023

School Categories	Number Of Schools (place)	Students At School (10 000 persons)	Full-time teacher (10 000 persons)
Colleges and Universities Stationed in Ji'nan	52	69.1	4.0
Secondary Vocational Schools (excluding technical schools)	32	6.1	0.4
Vestibule School	31	9.0	0.4
Ordinary Middle School	332	43.7	3.6
Elementary School	574	70.6	4.1
Special Education School	13	0.2	0.1
Kindergartens	2117	30.9	2.6

The cultural industry was prosperous and stable. At the end of 2023, there were 11 state-owned art performance groups, 174 cultural centers (stations), 13 public libraries, 13 public museums, and 13 archives. There were 437 cultural relics protection units at or above the city level, including 30 at the national level. There were 73 digital cinemas across the whole city with a total of 11.076 million viewers and a box office revenue of 480 million yuan. The TV population mixed coverage rate was 100 percent, and the broadcasting population mixed coverage rate was 99.7 percent. 52 study rooms had been built in Quancheng, and the coverage rate of grassroots comprehensive cultural service centers was 100 percent. The operating income of cultural and related industry enterprises above designated size went up by 15.3 percent over that of the previous year, of which the cultural manufacturing industry went up by 28.5 percent, the cultural wholesale and retail industry went up by 13.2 percent, and the cultural service industry went up by 14.8 percent.

The level of medical and health services continues to improve. At the end of 2023, there were 8136 medical and health institutions, including 320 hospitals, of which 98 were public hospitals and 222 were private hospitals; There were 7704 primary healthcare institutions, including 48 health centers, 423 community health service centers (stations), 214 outpatient departments, 3528 clinics (health centers, medical rooms), and 3491 village clinics; There were 55 professional public health institutions, including 16 disease prevention and control centers and 12 health supervision centers. At the end of 2023, there were 0.122 million health technicians, including 47000 practicing doctors and assistant practicing doctors, and 56000 registered nurses. There were 82000 beds in medical and health institutions, including 71000 in hospitals and 4000 in town health centers. The total number of diagnosed and treated patients throughout 2023 was 90.912 million, and the number of discharged patients was 2.932 million. Thirteen community hospitals were built, with 43000 childcare centers for the population. Selected for the list of national child friendly cities, "Quanxintuo" has become the first childcare city brand in China. Guang'anmen Hospital Jinan Hospital and Xuanwu Hospital Jinan Hospital had been approved as national regional medical centers.

The mass sports industry developed flourishing. Seven new sports social organizations were established throughout 2023, and 4089 social sports instructors were trained. Organize 3431 national fitness activities (competitions) with 5 million participants (including online activities). Obtained 286 provincial and above gold medals, 191 silver medals, and 218 bronze medals.

X. Energy, Environment, Urban Construction, and Safety Production

The green and low-carbon transformation had reached significant results. The energy consumption structure was continuously optimized, coal consumption was controlled within a reasonable range, and the ability to guarantee natural gas was enhanced. Industrial coal consumption above designated size was 28.003 million tons, down by 1.7 percent over that of the previous year; The consumption of coke was 7.745 million tons, down by 4.7 percent; Natural gas consumption reached 1.06 billion cubic meters, up by 5.3 percent. New energy power generation had steadily increased, with wind power generation of 2.5 billion kilowatt hours by enterprises above designated size, up by 7.9 percent; Solar power generation reached 350 million kilowatt hours, up by 15.7 percent; The power generation from garbage incineration reached 1.03 billion kilowatt hours, up by 6.9 percent; The biomass power generation reached 740 million kilowatt hours, up by 11.5 percent.

Table 10 Energy Consumption of Industrial Enterprises Above Designated Size In 2023

Item	Consumption	Increase over 2022 (%)
Coal (10,000tons)	2800.3	-1.7
Natural Gas (100 million cu.m)	10.6	5.3
Coke (10,000 tons)	774.5	-4.7
Gasoline (10,000 tons)	0.4	15.0
Diesel Oil (10,000 tons)	4.7	30.2

Table 11 Energy Production of Enterprises Above Designated Size In 2023

Item	Production	Increase over 2022 (%)
Coal（10,000 tons）	59.0	20.6
Electricity Generation（100 million kWh）	323.0	1.0
Thermal Power（100 million kWh）	294.4	0.3
Garbage Incineration（100 million kWh）	10.3	6.9
Biomass（100 million kWh）	7.4	11.5
Wind Power（100 million kWh）	25.0	7.9
Solar Power（100 million kWh）	3.5	15.7

The electricity consumption of the whole society increased steadily. The total electricity consumption of the whole society was 54.09 billion kilowatt hours, up by 8.2 percent over that of the previous year, of which the residential electricity consumption was 10.43 billion kilowatt hours, up by 6.8 percent. From the perspective of different industries, the electricity consumption of the primary industry was 410 million kilowatt hours, up by 15.2 percent; The electricity consumption of the secondary industry reached 29.16 billion kilowatt hours, up by 6.5 percent; The electricity consumption of the tertiary industry reached 14.09 billion kilowatt hours, up by 13.0 percent. The industrial electricity consumption was 28.07 billion kilowatt hours, accounting for 51.9 percent of the total electricity consumption in society, up by 6.7 percent.

Table 12 Electricity Consumption of the Whole City In 2023

Item	Electricity Consumption (100 million kWh)	Increase over 2022 (%)
Total Electricity Consumption	540.9	8.2
Household Electricity Consumption	104.3	6.8
Primary industry	4.1	15.2
Secondary industry	291.6	6.5
Industrial Electricity Consumption	280.7	6.7
Tertiary industry	140.9	13.0

Strive to improve the quality of the ecological environment. The comprehensive air quality index was 4.59, with 204 days of good or above air quality in the urban area, and a 62.6 percent rate of excellent days. The concentration of fine particulate matter ($PM_{2.5}$) was 38 micrograms per cubic meter, the annual average concentration of inhalable particulate matter (PM_{10}) was 73 micrograms per cubic meter, sulfur dioxide was 9 micrograms per cubic meter, and nitrogen dioxide was 33 micrograms per cubic meter. The proportion of Class III water bodies in the national control section reached 100 percent. The chemical oxygen demand and ammonia nitrogen concentration in Xinfengzhuang, the exit section of Xiaoqing River, were 13.8 mg/L and 0.37 mg/L respectively, and the indicator concentration meets the Class II water body environmental quality standard (GB3838-2002) for surface water. The average equivalent sound level of regional environmental noise during the day was 53.8 decibels, and the average equivalent sound level of urban road traffic noise during the day was 67.2 decibels.

The level of urban construction comprehensively improved. At the end of 2023, the built-up area of the city was 860.0 square kilometers, up by 6.1 square kilometers over that of the previous year. Construct 100 new parks, 111 kilometers of greenways, and 100 kilometers of forest trails. The green space ratio of the built-up area was 40.2 percent, and the per capita park green area was 14.4 square meters. The annual natural gas supply was 1.87 billion cubic meters. The supply of liquefied petroleum gas was 46000 tons, up by 19.1 percent over that of the previous year. The area of centralized heating was 360 million square meters, up by 8.8 percent. The tap water supply reached 550 million tons, up by 8.5 percent. Continuously promote the construction of direct drinking spring water projects for citizens, with a total of 118 projects built, covering a population of 0.38 million people. The harmless treatment rate of household waste was 100 percent. The number of charging infrastructure is 79000, including 735 public charging and swapping stations, with a vehicle to pile ratio of 2.14:1. The average service radius of public charging and swapping stations within the built-up area was 0.6 kilometers. The daily average charging capacity of public charging facilities was 0.822 million kWh, with a daily charging frequency of 27000 times. The annual electricity consumption of public charging facilities was 310 million kWh.

Good social security situation. A total of 25418 criminal cases were solved throughout 2023, with a 100 percent success rate in solving homicide cases. For 13 consecutive years, all homicide cases had been solved, and it was awarded as one of the first demonstration cities for the construction of the national social security prevention and control system. The rate of solving eight types of serious violent cases was 100 percent, the rate of solving "Two-Thefts" cases was 58.5 percent, and 3075 fugitives of various types arrested, and 11 criminal groups and 8 evil gangs were dismantled.

A stable safety production situation. There were 104 production safety accidents of various types across the whole city, down by 25.2 percent over that of the previous year, with 87 deaths, down by 20.9 percent. No major or above production safety accidents have occurred.

XI. Households' Livelihood and Social Security

The income gap between urban and rural households had further narrowed. The per capita disposable income of households across the whole city was 51757 yuan, up by 6.0 percent over that of the previous year. Looking at urban and rural areas, the per capita disposable income of urban households was 62506 yuan, up by 5.1 percent; The per capita disposable income of rural households was 25587 yuan, up by 7.3 percent. The income ratio of urban and rural households decreased from 2.49:1 in the same period last year to 2.44:1. The Engel coefficient for urban households was [10]23.6 percent, while for rural households it was 30.3 percent.

Table 13 Per Capita Disposable Income and Growth Rates of Urban and Rural Households In 2023

Item	All Households		Urban Households		Rural Households	
	2023 (yuan)	Increase over 2022 (%)	2023 (yuan)	Increase over 2022 (%)	2023 (yuan)	Increase over 2022 (%)
Disposable Income	51757	6.0	62506	5.1	25587	7.3
Income of Wages and Salaries	29676	5.0	36150	4.2	13913	5.9
Net Business Income	5453	11.5	3810	17.2	9455	8.1
Net Income from Property	7629	5.7	10523	4.4	584	15.6
Net Income from Transfer	8999	6.4	12023	5.1	1635	12.4

Table 14 At the End of 2023, Number of Major Durable Consumer Goods Owned Per 100 Households [11]

Item	Unit	Urban Residents	Rural Residents
Automobile	Unit	67	49
Refrigerator (cabinet)	Set	102	99
Washing Machine	Set	99	95
Water Heater	Set	100	91
Air Conditioner	Set	179	97
Colour Television Set	Set	100	101
Computer	Set	77	38
Mobile Phone	Set	243	240

The social security system was more sound. At the end of 2023, 4.566 million people participated in the basic old-age insurance for urban employees; The number of employees participating in medical insurance was 3.673 million, up by 144000 over that of the previous year; The number of people participating in unemployment insurance was 2.397 million, up by 43000; The number of people participating in work-related injury insurance was 3.106 million, up by 32000; The number of people participating in maternity insurance was 2.54 million, up by 84000. The number of people participating in households' pension insurance and medical insurance reached 3.121 million and 4.998 million respectively.

The minimum living allowance continues to increase. The minimum living guarantee standard for urban households was 1045 yuan/month, which guarantees 7951 households and 10548 urban households, and distributes 120 million yuan in security funds and various subsidies; The minimum living guarantee standard for rural households was 814 yuan/month, which guarantees 60342 households and 85340 people in rural areas, and distributes 660 million yuan in security funds and various subsidies. The basic living standard for urban extremely poor people was 1492 yuan/month, and for rural extremely poor people it was 1356 yuan/month. The nursing standards for self-care, semi self-care, and complete inability to self-care are 281 yuan/month, 466 yuan/month, and 932 yuan/month, respectively. 910 people in urban areas and 14422 people in rural areas are covered by the special hardship allowance, with a total of 340 million yuan in special hardship support and subsidies.

Rescue and assistance were more warm. There were a

total of 14 comprehensive social assistance service institutions across the whole city, including 1 assistance management station and 16 juvenile assistance and protection centers. Trained 4711 disabled people, provided employment for 2788 disabled people, and invested 330 million yuan in assisting and aiding disabled people.

The well-being of the people significantly improved. 4142 various types of elderly care service facilities had been built across the whole city, and the compliance rate of community elderly care service facilities was 100 percent. There are 2590 elderly canteens and other types of meal assistance places, serving a total of 30 million people. The monthly standard for basic pension for urban and rural households had been raised to 178 yuan. The financial subsidy standard for resident medical insurance had been raised to 730 yuan, and the annual payment limit for employee outpatient pooling had been increased from 3000 yuan to 4500 yuan. A childcare subsidy of 110 million yuan was distributed, benefiting 25000 families.

Notes:

[1] The statistical data for 2023 is based on statistical reports or preliminary calculations, and the official data is subject to the published *Jinan Statistical Yearbook 2024*. Due to rounding, some data may have discrepancies between the total and sub total.

[2] The absolute figures of the city's gross domestic product and the added value of various industries are calculated at current prices, and the Growth Rates is calculated at constant prices. The data for that year is a preliminary calculation. Based on annual accounting, the historical data of relevant indicators such as GDP and added value of various industries had been revised.

[3] The growth mentioned in this bulletin, unless otherwise stated, refers to the Growth Rates of this period's data compared to the same period last year.

[4] Industrial enterprises above designated size refer to industrial legal entities with an annual main business income of 20 million yuan or more.

[5] The service industries above designated size include: transportation, warehousing, and postal services, information transmission, software, and information technology services, real estate (excluding real estate development and operation), leasing and business services, scientific research and technology services, water conservancy, environmental, and public facility management, resident services, repairs, and other services, education, health, and social work, culture, sports, and entertainment.

[6] Modern service industries include: information transmission, software and information technology services, finance, real estate, leasing and business services, scientific research and technology services, water conservancy, environmental and public facility management, resident services, repairs and other services, education, health and social work, culture, sports and entertainment.

[7] The "four above" units refer to industries above designated size, qualified construction industry, wholesale and retail industry above designated size, accommodation and catering industry above designated size, real estate development and operation, and service industry above designated size.

[8] Units above designated size refer to wholesale enterprises with an annual main business income of 20 million yuan or more, retail enterprises with an annual main business income of 5 million yuan or more, and accommodation and catering enterprises with an annual main business income of 2 million yuan or more. Units include legal entities, industrial activity units, and individual businesses.

[9] The indicators related to research and experimental development (R&D) funding investment uses the data of 2022.

[10] The Engel coefficient refers to the proportion of food expenditure in consumer expenditure.

[11] The data comes from a survey on household income, expenditure, and living conditions.

Data source: The ecological protection and high-quality development strategy, enterprise technology center, and charging infrastructure data in the Yellow River Basin in this bulletin are from the development and reform department; Education data comes from the education department; Technology data comes from the technology department; Telecommunications related data comes from the industrial and information technology departments; The data of registered residence, social security and civil motor vehicles are from the public security department; The data related to the minimum living guarantee for urban and rural areas, assistance and support for extremely poor people, and elderly care service facilities comes from the civil affairs department; Regional tax data comes from the tax department; Financial data comes from the finance department; The data on new urban employment, urban employee insurance participation, and technical schools comes from the human resources and social security departments; Environmental protection related data comes from the ecological environment department; The data related to urban construction comes from the housing and urban-rural development departments; The garbage disposal data comes from the urban management department; Transportation data comes from the transportation department; The civil aviation data comes from Jinan International Airport; The construction data for the Spring Water Direct Drinking Project comes from the urban and rural water department; The production of Aquatic product and agricultural data come from the agricultural and rural sectors; Forestry data comes from the landscaping and forestry departments; Import and export, exhibitions, newly established overseas enterprises, and dispatched labor personnel data come from the commerce department; Tourism and cultural data come from the cultural and tourism sector; The archival data comes from the Municipal Archives; The data on health and childcare subsidies comes from the health department; Production safety data comes from the emergency management department; Intellectual property data comes from market regulatory authorities; Sports data comes from the sports department; Medical insurance data comes from the medical security department; Financial data comes from local financial supervision and management departments; The data on investment attraction and foreign investment comes from the investment promotion department; Market entity data comes from administrative approval service departments; The logistics data comes from the port logistics department; Data on disability protection comes from the Disabled Persons' Federation; Postal and express data come from the postal management department; The data on households' income and expenditure, Engel coefficient, price index, grain and livestock data, and the ownership of major durable consumer goods by urban and rural households are from the Jinan survey team of the National Bureau of Statistics; The data for the Jinan New and Old Kinetic Energy Conversion Starting Zone comes from the Jinan New and Old Kinetic Energy Conversion Starting Zone Management Committee; All other data comes from the Municipal Bureau of Statistics.

2023年的济南
Jinan in 2023

12757.4
地区生产总值（亿元）
Gross Domestic Product
(100 million yuan)

62.8
第三产业比重(%)
Proportion of Tertiary
Industry(%)

943.7
常住人口（万人）
Permanent Population
(10 000 persons)

1060.8
一般公共预算收入（亿元）
General Public Budget
Revenue(100 million yuan)

2.1
全社会固定资产投资增长幅度(%)
Growth Rate Total Investment in
Fixed Assets(%)

307.4
海关进出口总额（亿美元）
International Trade in Goods of
Customs(100 million USD)

135347
人均地区生产总值（元）
Per Capita Gross Domestic
Product(yuan)

5199.0
社会消费品零售总额（亿元）
Total Retail Sale of Consumer
Goods(100 million yuan)

62506
城镇居民人均可支配收入（元）
Per Capita Disposable Income of
Urban Households(yuan)

25587
农村居民人均可支配收入（元）
Per Capita Disposable Income of
Rural Households(yuan)

100.6
居民消费价格指数
Consumer Price Index

济南一日

A Day in Jinan

每日创造

Daily Production

29063.6
一般公共预算收入
（万元 / 天）
General Public Budget Revenue
(10 000 yuan/day)

37405.3
一般公共预算支出
（万元 / 天）
General Public Budget Expenditure
(10 000 yuan/day)

8422.2
海关进出口总额
（万美元 / 天）
International Trade in Goods of Customs
(10 000 USD/day)

58548
公路客运量
（人 / 天）
Highways Passenger Traffic
(person/day)

11767.9
第一产业（万元 / 天）
Primary Industry(10 000 yuan/day)

349518.4
地区生产总值（万元 / 天）
Gross Domestic Product (10 000 yuan/day)

48112
民航客运量
（人 / 天）
Civil Aviation Passenger Traffic
(person/day)

118137.3
第二产业（万元 / 天）
Secondary Industry(10 000 yuan/day)

654
生产汽车
（辆 / 天）
Automobile Manufacturing
(unit/day)

219613.2
第三产业（万元 / 天）
Tertiary Industry(10 000 yuan/day)

8848
发电量
（万千瓦时 / 天）
Electricity Generation
(10 000 kWh/day)

19901
蔬菜产量
（吨 / 天）
Output of Vegetables
(ton/day)

8298
粮食产量
（吨 / 天）
Output of Grain Crops
(ton/day)

1860
生产服务器
（台 / 天）
Server Manufacturing
(unit/day)

每日生活
Daily Life

171
出生人口
（人 / 天）
Population of Birth
(person/day)

129
死亡人口
（人 / 天）
Population of Death
(person/day)

2857.3
城乡居民生活用电量
（万千瓦时 / 天）
Household Electricity Consumption of Urban and Rural Residents
(10 000 kWh/day)

156
登记结婚
（对 / 天）
Registered Marriages
(couple/day)

365
城镇非私营单位在岗职工平均工资
（元 / 天）
Average Wages of Staff and Workers in Urban Non Private Units(yuan/day)

71
离婚
（对 / 天）
Divorces
(couple/day)

171
城镇居民人均可支配收入
（元 / 天）
Per Capita Disposable Income of Urban Households(yuan/day)

150.5
自来水供水量
（万吨 / 天）
Volume of Water Supply
(10 000 tons/day)

121459.4
批发零售业零售额
（万元 / 天）
Total Retail Sale of Wholesale and Retail Trades (10 000 yuan/day)

920.2
住宿业零售额（万元 / 天）
Total Retail Sale of Accommodation
(10 000 yuan/day)

20059.5
餐饮业零售额（万元 / 天）
Total Retail Sale of Catering Industry
(10 000 yuan/day)

142439.1
社会消费品零售总额（万元/天）
Total Retail Sale of Consumer Goods
(10 000 yuan/day)

513.1
天然气供气量
（万立方米 / 天）
Total Natural Gas Supply
(10 000 cu.m/day)

8159
生活垃圾清运量
（吨 / 天）
Volume of Domestic Garbage Collected and Transported(ton/day)

45
农村居民人均消费支出
（元 / 天）
Per Capita Consumer Expenditure of Rural Households(yuan/day)

104
城镇居民人均消费支出
（元 / 天）
Per Capita Consumer Expenditure of Urban Households(yuan/day)

70
农村居民人均可支配收入
（元 / 天）
Per Capita Disposable Income of Rural Households(yuan/day)

综 合
General

地区生产总值（亿元）
Gross Domestic Product (100 million yuan)

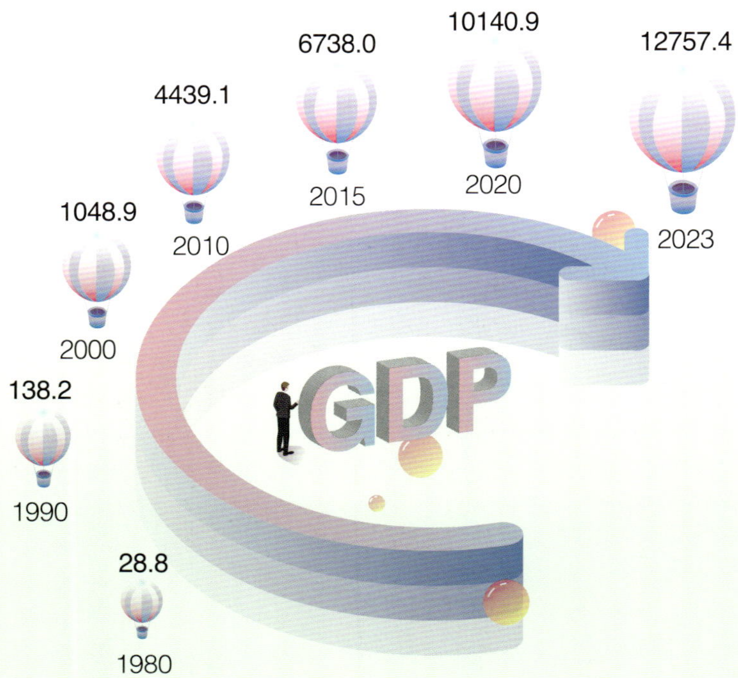

人均地区生产总值（元）
Per Capita Gross Domestic Product (yuan)

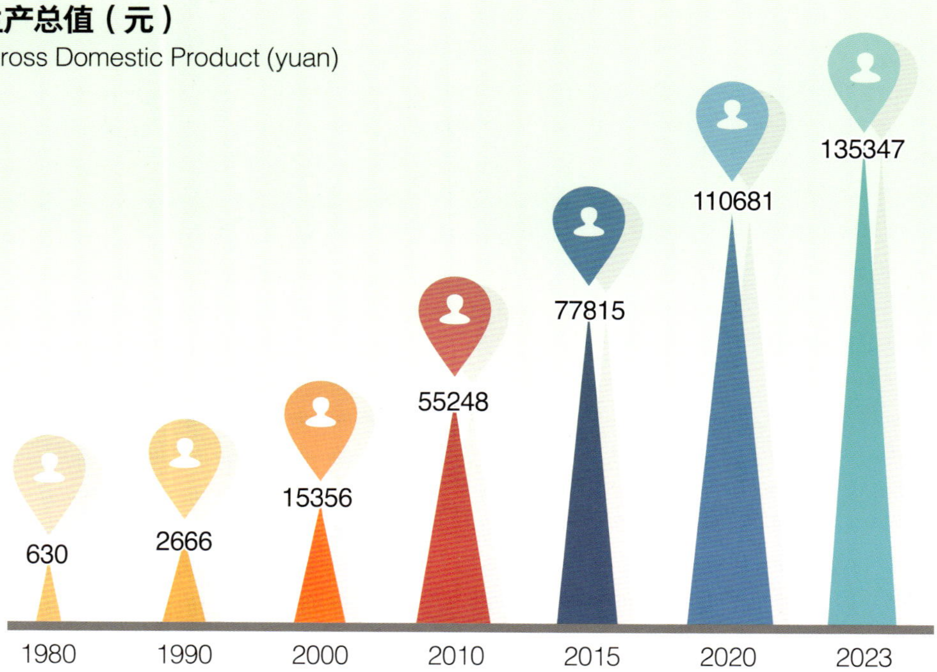

人口
Population

年末户籍总人口（万人）
Registered Population Year-end (10 000 persons)

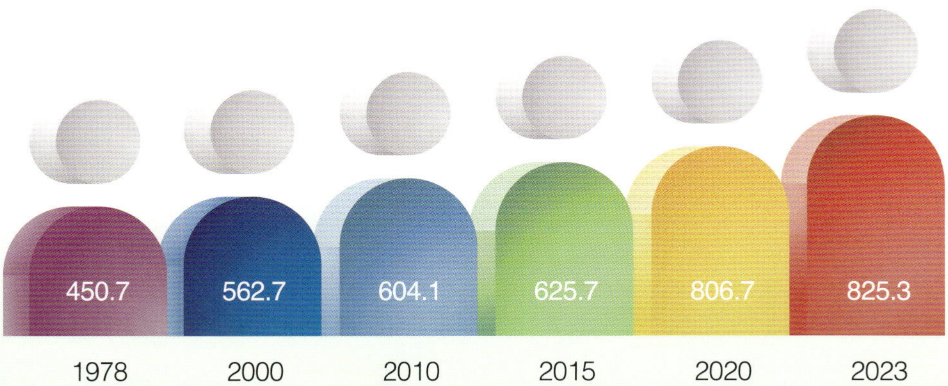

人口自然变动情况（‰）
Natural Changes of Population (‰)

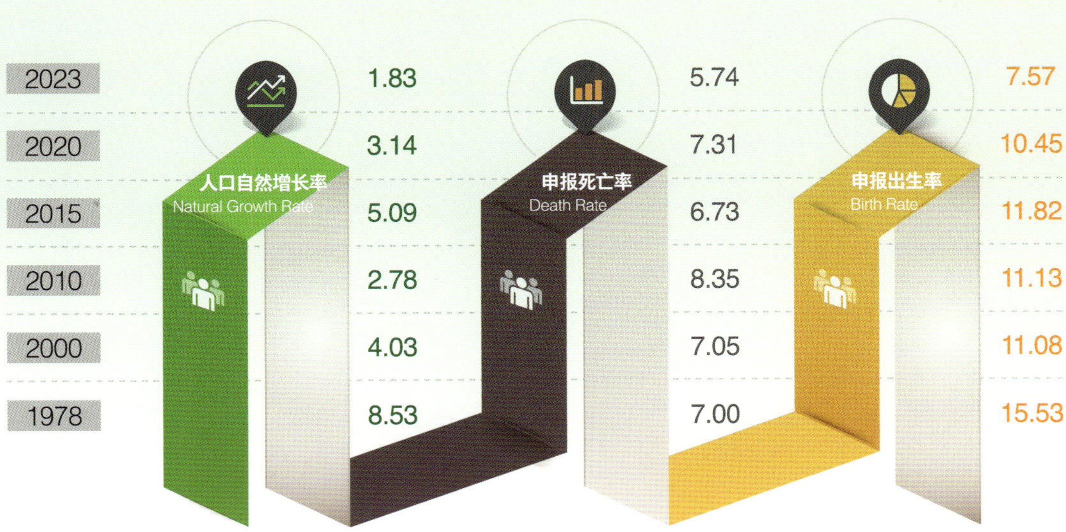

就 业
Employment

全社会从业人员（万人）
Total Employed Persons (10 000 persons)

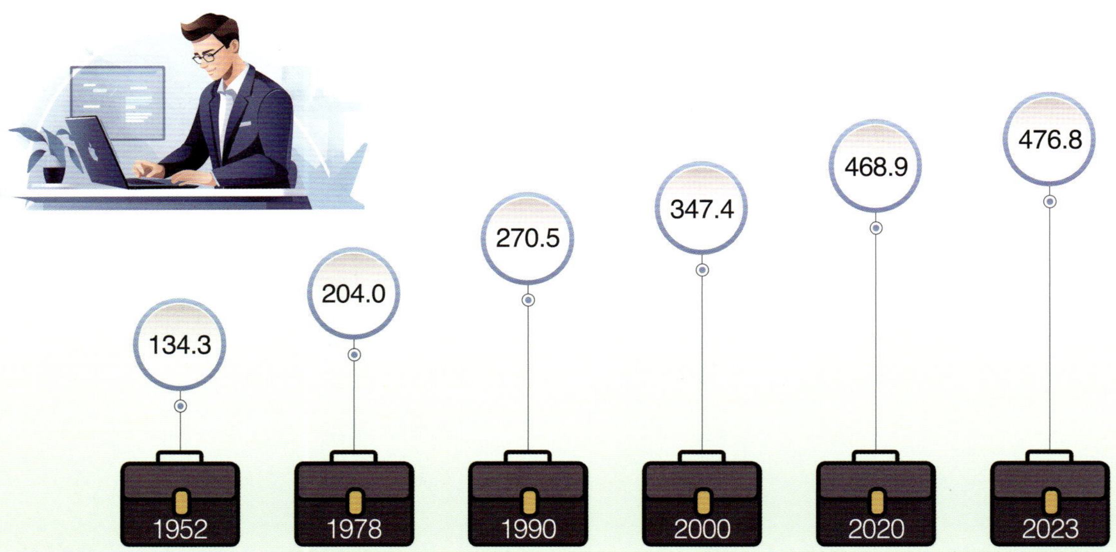

在岗职工平均工资（元）
Average Wage of Staff and Workers (yuan)

注：1．2006 年以后为法人单位在岗职工口径；2．2019 年以后为城镇非私营单位在岗职工口径。

Notes: 1.The data after 2006 are based on the caliber of Staff and Workers of legal entities.
2.The data after 2019 are based on the caliber of Staff and Workers in Urban Non Private Units.

财政 金融
Government Finance Financial

一般公共预算收入支出（亿元）
General Public Budget Revenue and Expenditure (100 million yuan)

一般公共预算收入
General Public Budget Revenue

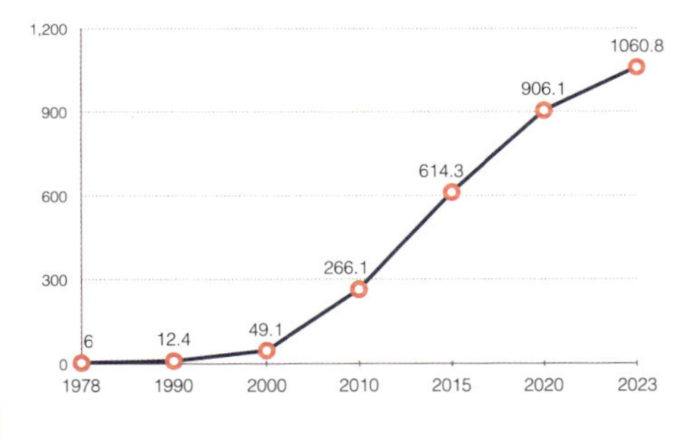

一般公共预算支出
General Public Budget Expenditure

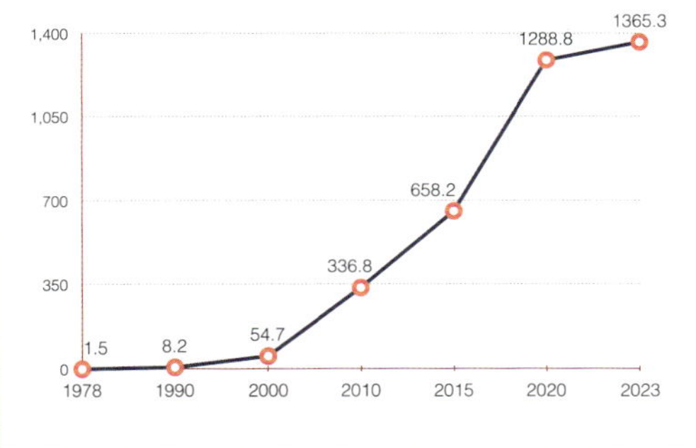

金融机构人民币存、贷款余额（亿元）
The Ending Balance of all Deposits and Loans in RMB of Financial Institutions (100 million yuan)

存
Deposits

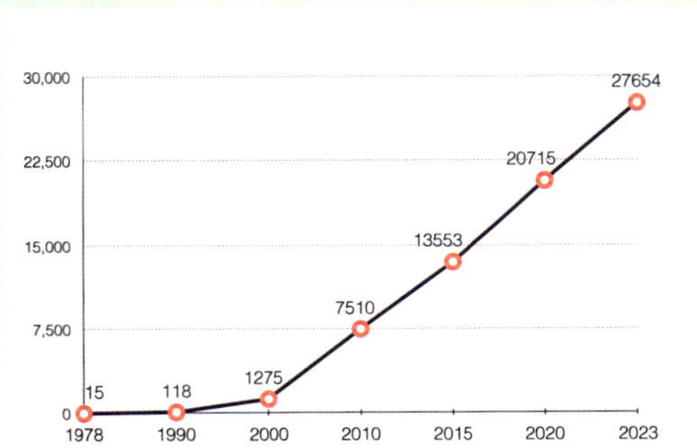

贷
Loans

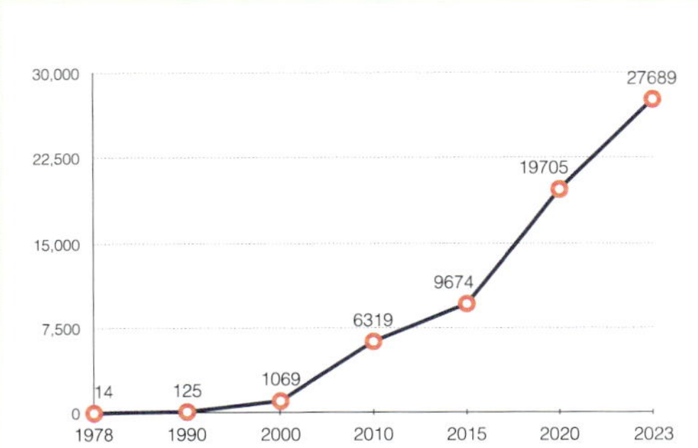

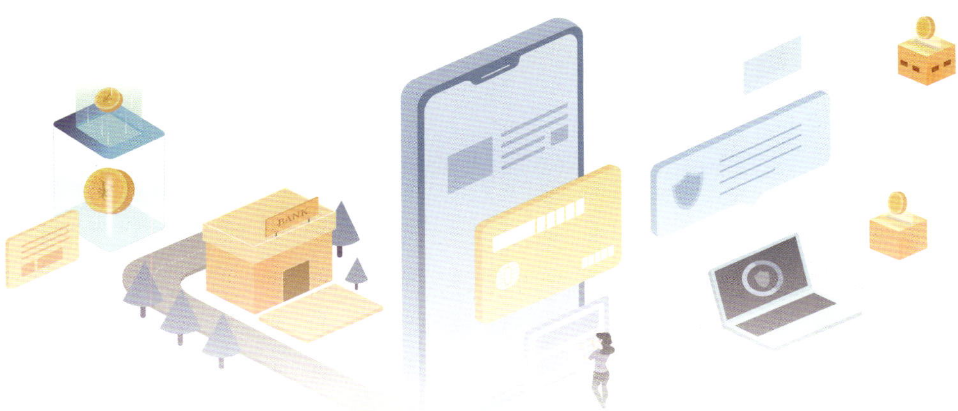

人民生活
People's Livelihood

城乡居民人均可支配收入（元）
Per Capita Disposable Income of Urban and Rural Households（yuan）

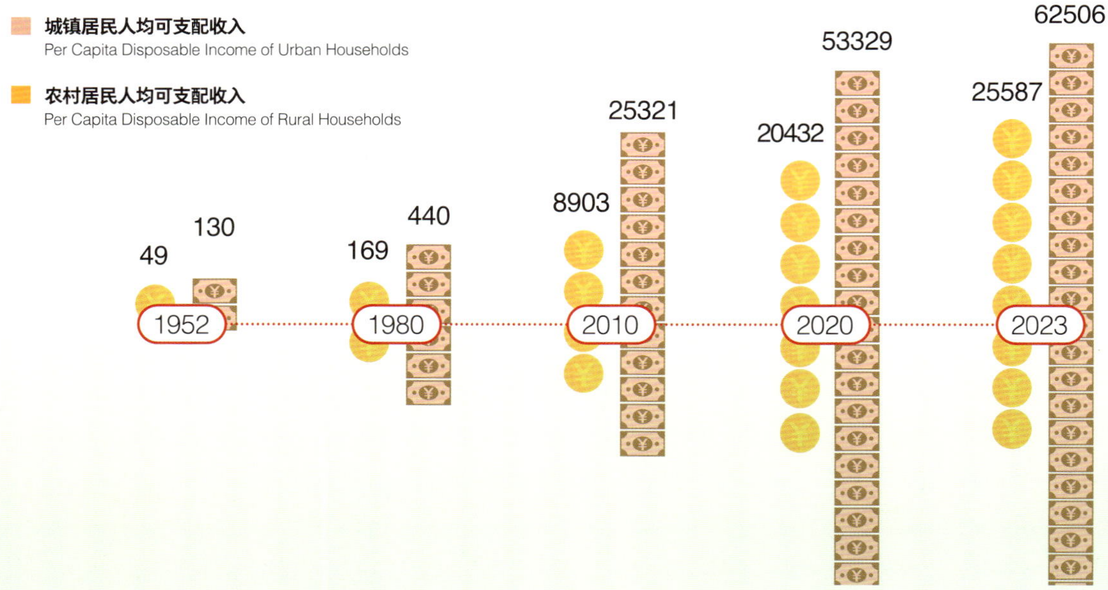

注：城乡一体化改革，2015年起为城镇居民人均可支配收入和农村居民人均可支配收入口径；之前年份为城市居民人均可支配收入和农民人均纯收入口径。
Note: The urban-rural integration reform has been based on the caliber of per capita disposable income of urban and rural households since 2015; the urban-rural integration reform in previous years was based on the caliber of per capita disposable income of urban households and the per capita net income of farmers.

城乡居民人均消费支出（元）
Per Capita Consumption Expenditure of Urban and Rural Households（yuan）

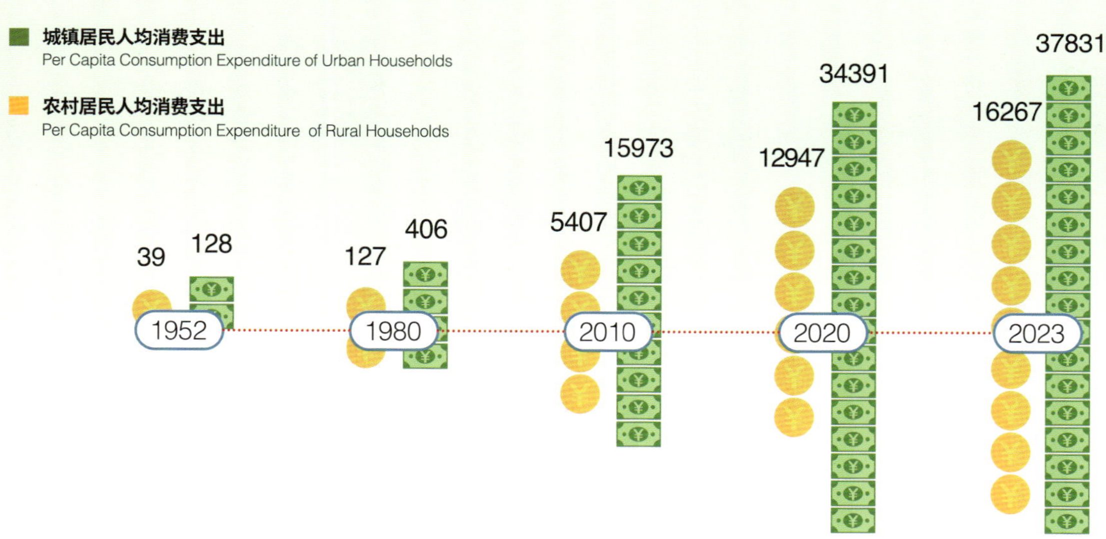

注：从2015年开始，本市居民收支调查指标采用新口径。“农村居民人均消费支出”2014年以前为农民人均生活费支出口径。
Note: Starting from 2015, the city's residents' income and expenditure survey indicators adopt a new caliber. "Per capita consumption expenditure of rural households" was the “per capita living expenses of farmers” before 2014.

城乡居民恩格尔系数（%）
Engel's Coefficient of Urban and Rural Households (%)

城镇居民恩格尔系数
Engel's Coefficient of Urban Households

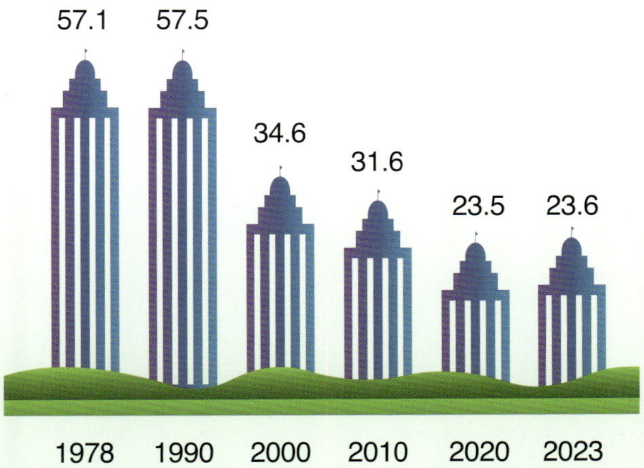

农村居民恩格尔系数
Engel's Coefficient of Rural Households

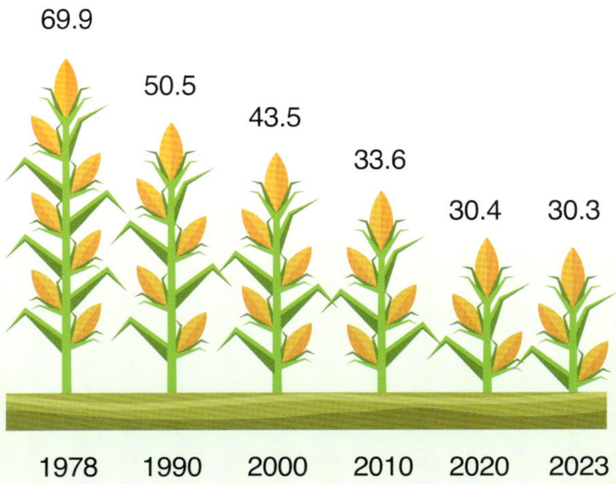

人民币住户存款余额（亿元）
The Balance RMB Household Deposits（100 million yuan）

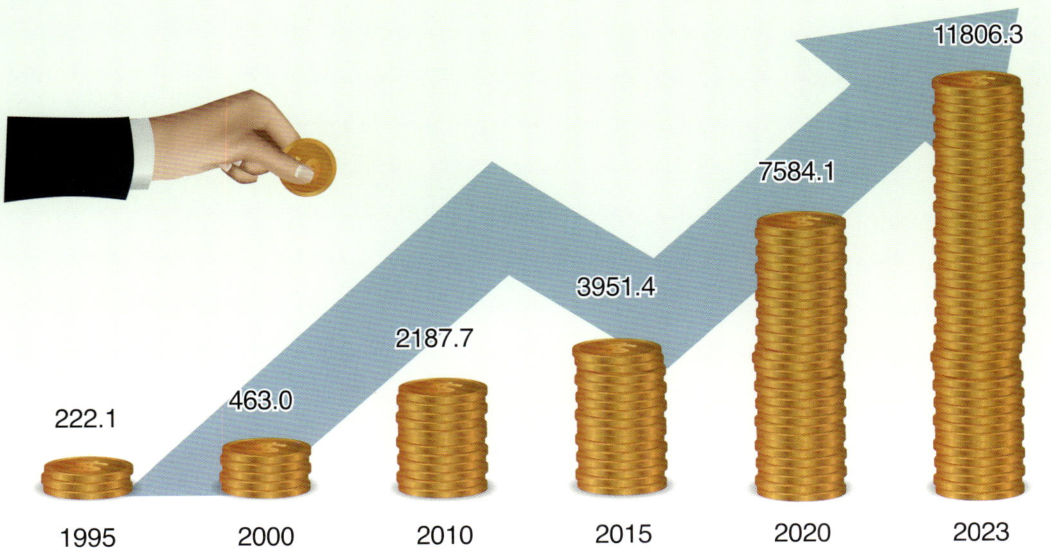

注：2015 年之前为城乡居民人民币储蓄存款余额口径，2015 年调整为住户存款余额口径。
Note: Before 2015, the caliber was the balance of saving deposit (RMB) of urban and rural Households, and has been adjusted to balance held on deposit of households since 2015.

物 价
Price

居民消费价格指数（以上年为 100）
Consumer Price Index (Preceding Last Year=100)

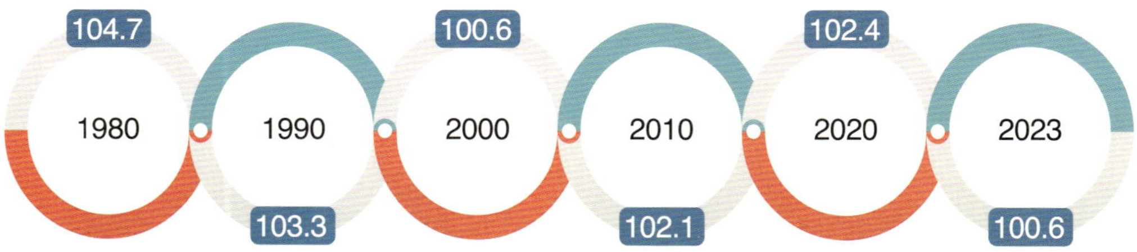

工业生产者出厂价格指数与工业生产者购进价格指数（以上年为 100）
Producer Price Index and Purchasing Price Index for Industrial Products (Preceding Last Year=100)

工业生产者出厂价格指数
Producer Price Index for Industrial Products

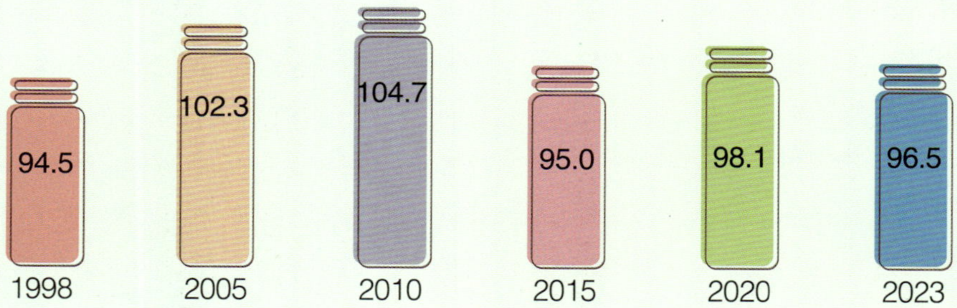

工业生产者购进价格指数
Purchasing Price Index for Industrial Products

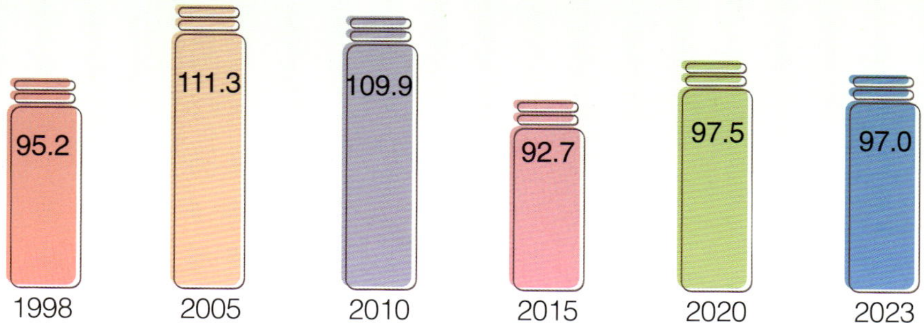

注：2020 年起，“工业生产者出厂价格指数”与“工业生产者购进价格指数”指标为全省数据。
Note: Starting in 2020,the“Producer Price Indices for Industrial Products”and“ Purchasing Price Index for Industrial Producer ”are province-wide data.

农业
Agriculture

农林牧渔业总产值（亿元）
Gross Output Value of Farming, Forestry, Animal Husbandry and Fishery(100 million yuan)

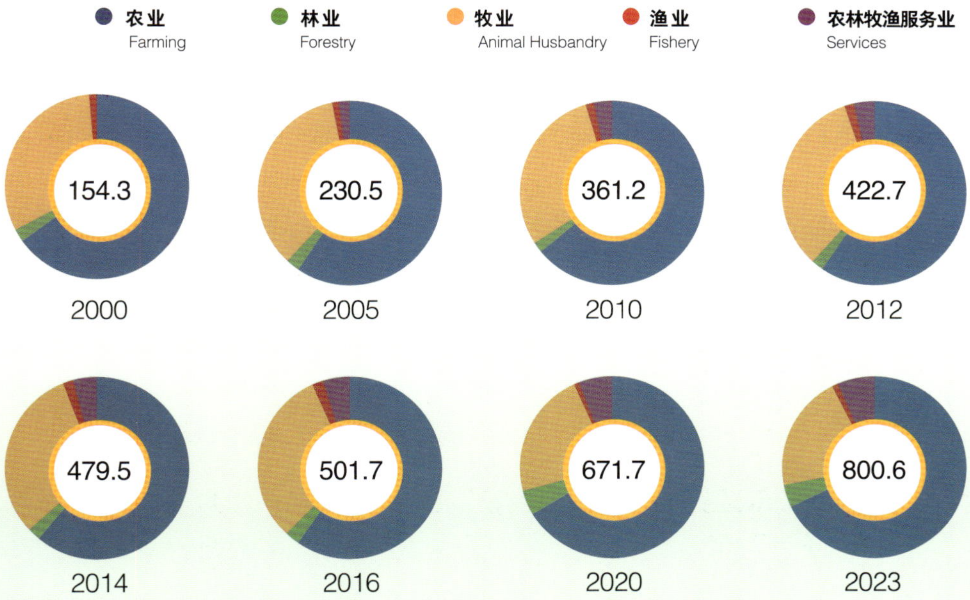

主要农产品产量（万吨）
Output of Main Agricultural Products (10 000 tons)

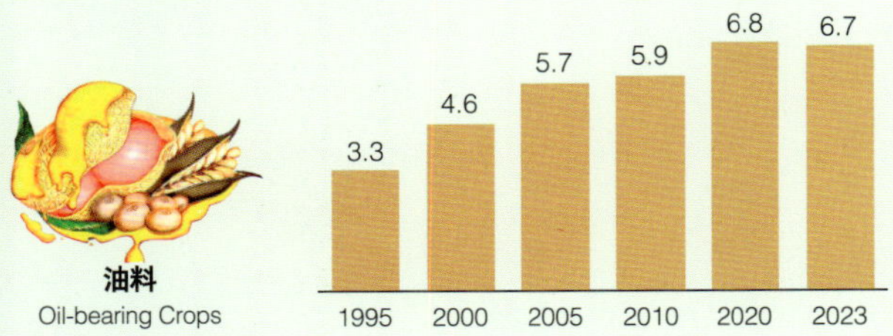

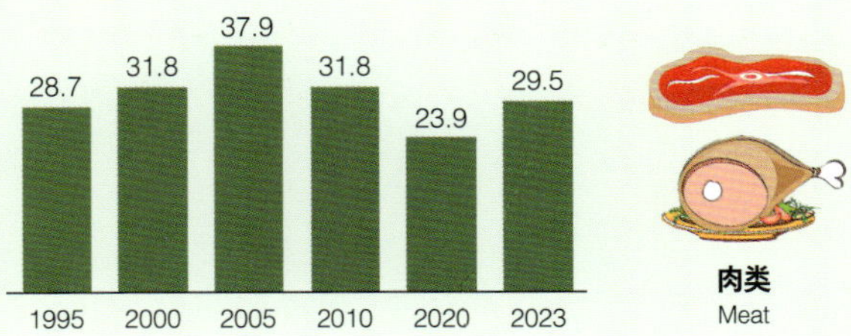

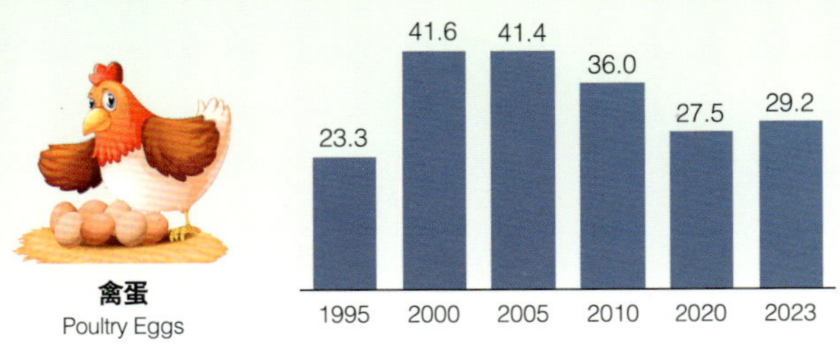

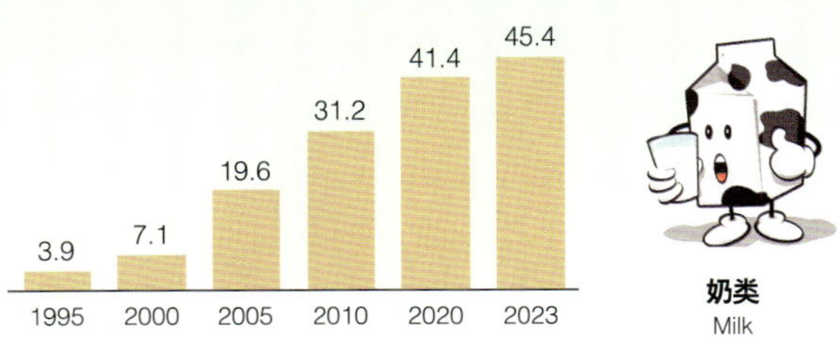

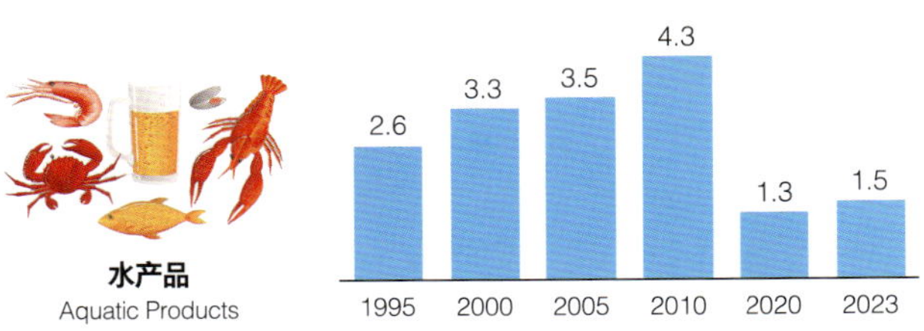

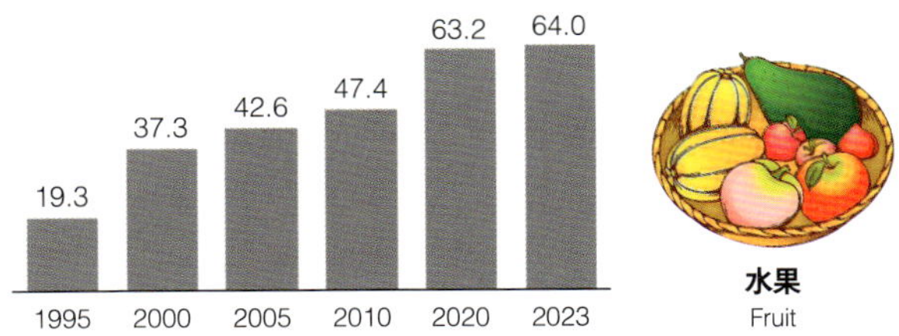

工 业
Industry

规模以上工业营业收入（亿元）
Business Revenue of Industrial Enterprises Above Designated Size (100 million yuan)

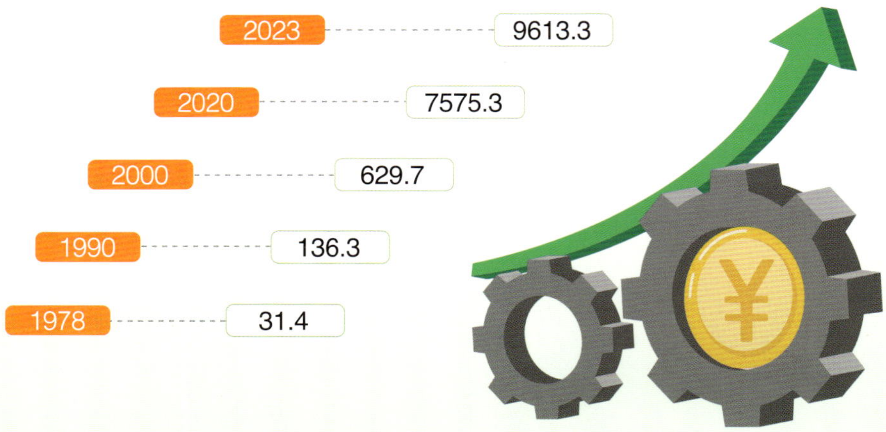

注：2018 年以前为主营业务收入口径。
Note: Before 2018, the main business income caliber.

规模以上工业利税总额（亿元）
Total Profits and Taxes of Industrial Enterprises Above Designated Size (100 million yuan)

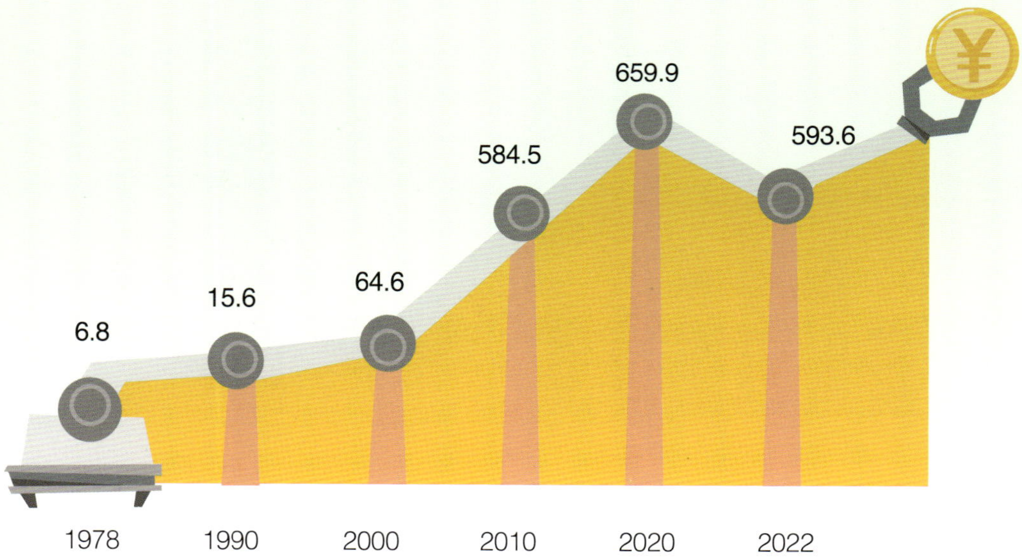

注：自 2023 年起，山东省统计局不再反馈“利税总额”相关数据。
Note:Since 2023,Shandong Provincial Bureau of Statistics no longer provide relevant data of “total profits and taxes”.

规模以上工业利润总额（亿元）
Total Profits of Industrial Enterprises Above Designated Size (100 million yuan)

Year	Total Profits
2023	448.1
2020	423.3
2010	339.8
2000	21.7
1990	3.2
1978	3.9

主要工业产品产量
Output of Major Industrial Products

发电量（亿千瓦时）
Electricity Generation (100 million kWh)

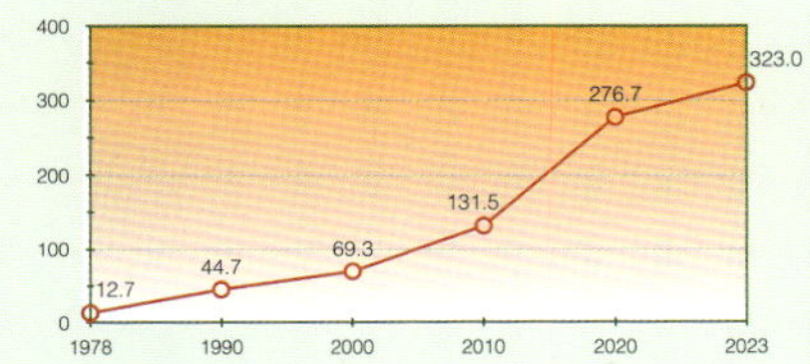

服务器（万台）
Servers (10 000 unit)

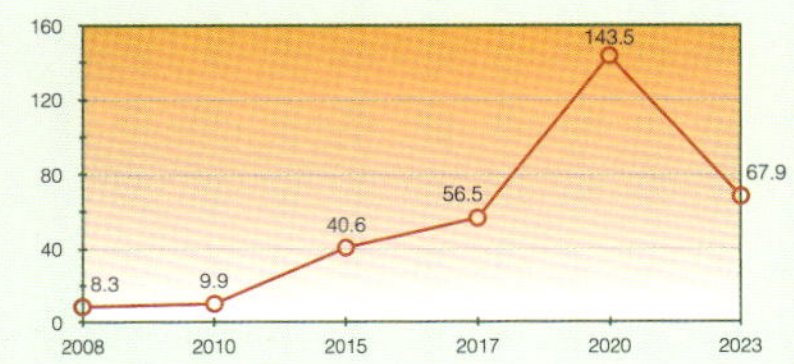

原油加工量（万吨）
Crude Processing Volume (10 000 tons)

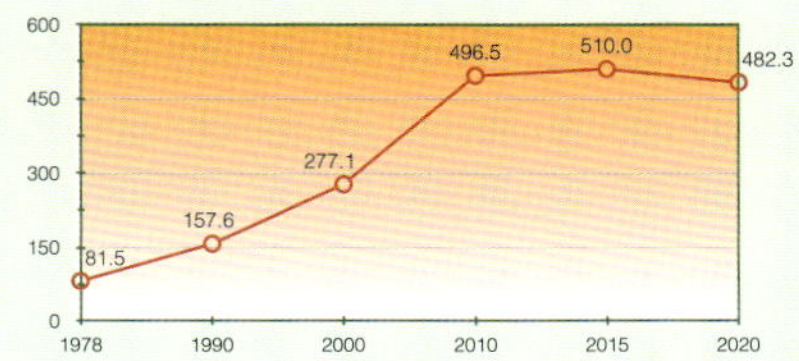

化肥（万吨）
Chemical Fertilizer (10 000 tons)

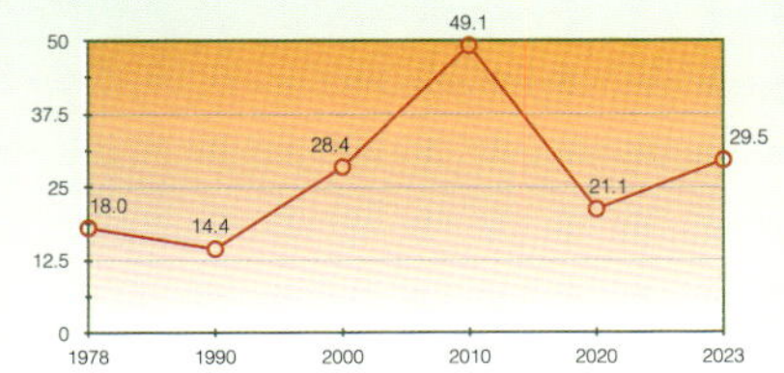

水泥（万吨）
Cement (10 000 tons)

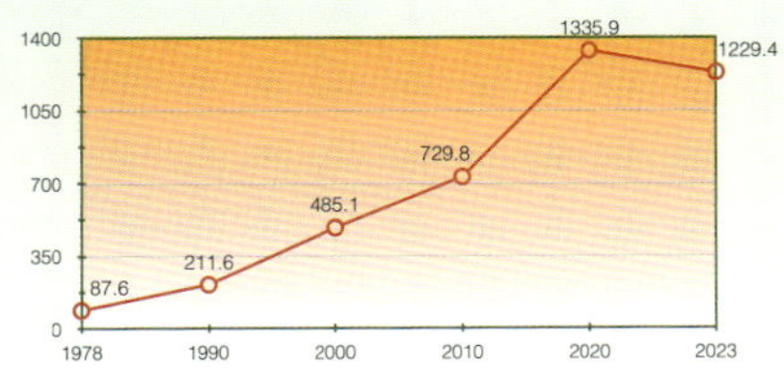

啤酒（万千升）
Beer (10 000 kiloliter)

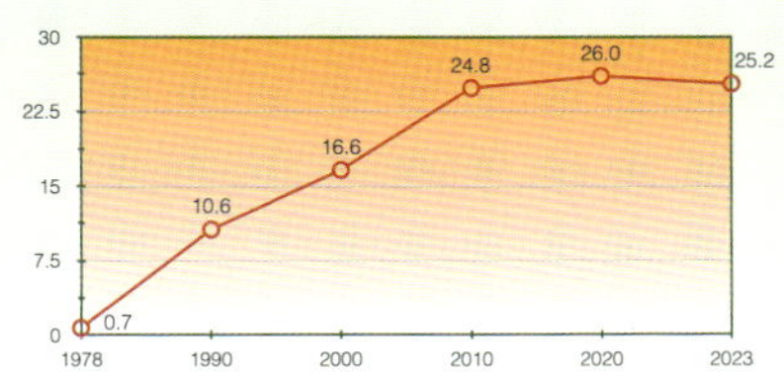

汽车（辆）
Motor Vehicles (unit)

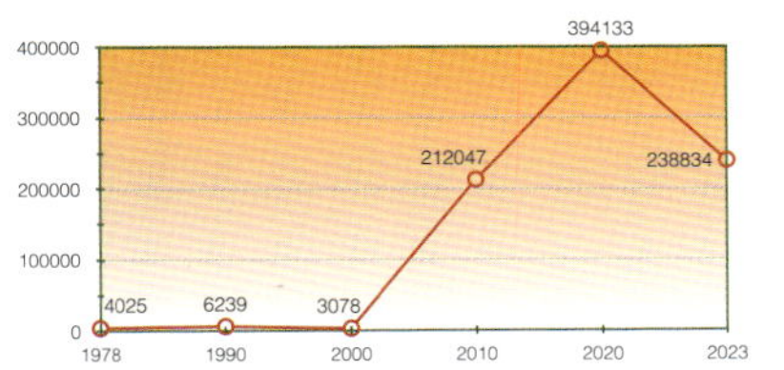

钢（万吨）
Steel (10 000 tons)

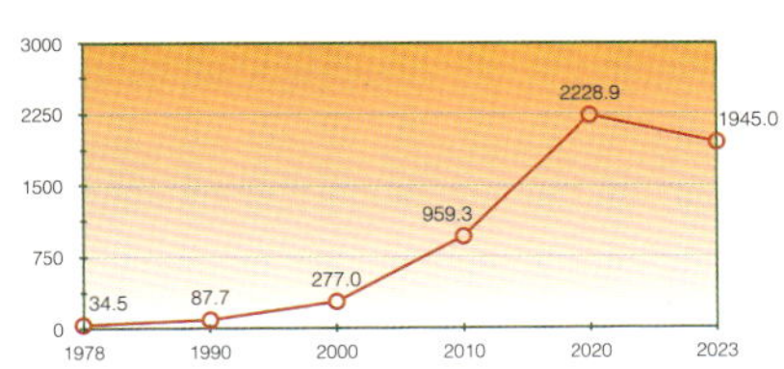

初级形态塑料（万吨）
Primary Plastic (10 000 tons)

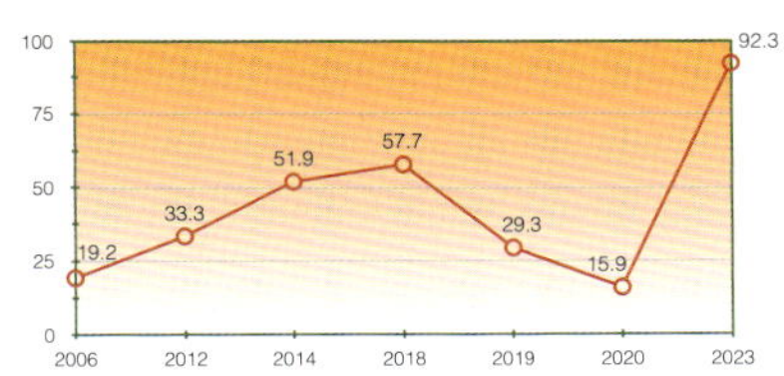

投资
Investment

固定资产投资增长幅度 (%)
Growth Rate of Investment in Fixed Assets(%)

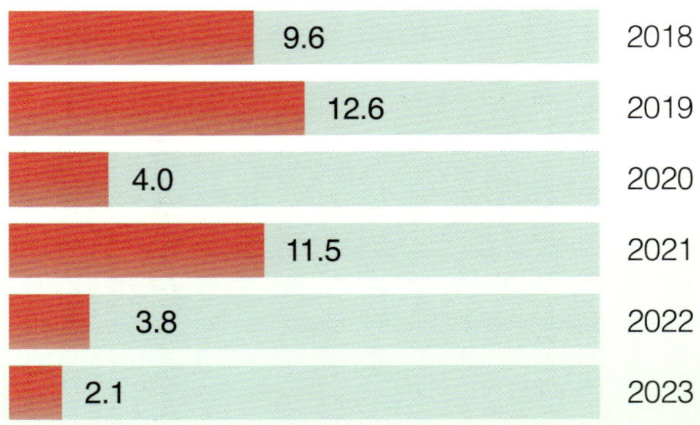

房地产开发投资总额（亿元）
Estate Development Investment(100 million yuan)

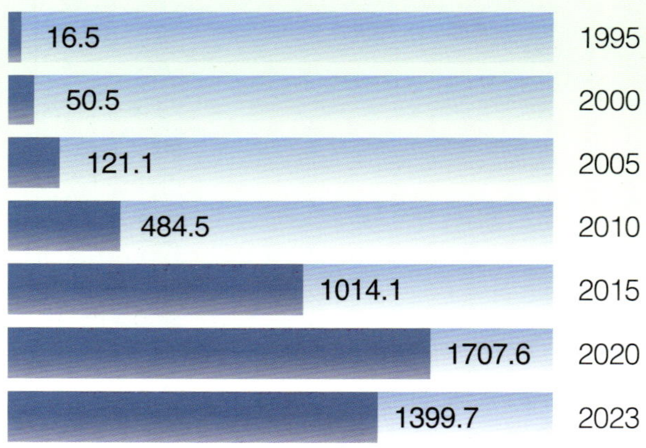

贸易外经
Domestic and Foreign Trade

社会消费品零售总额（亿元）
Total Retail Sales of Consumer Goods (100 million yuan)

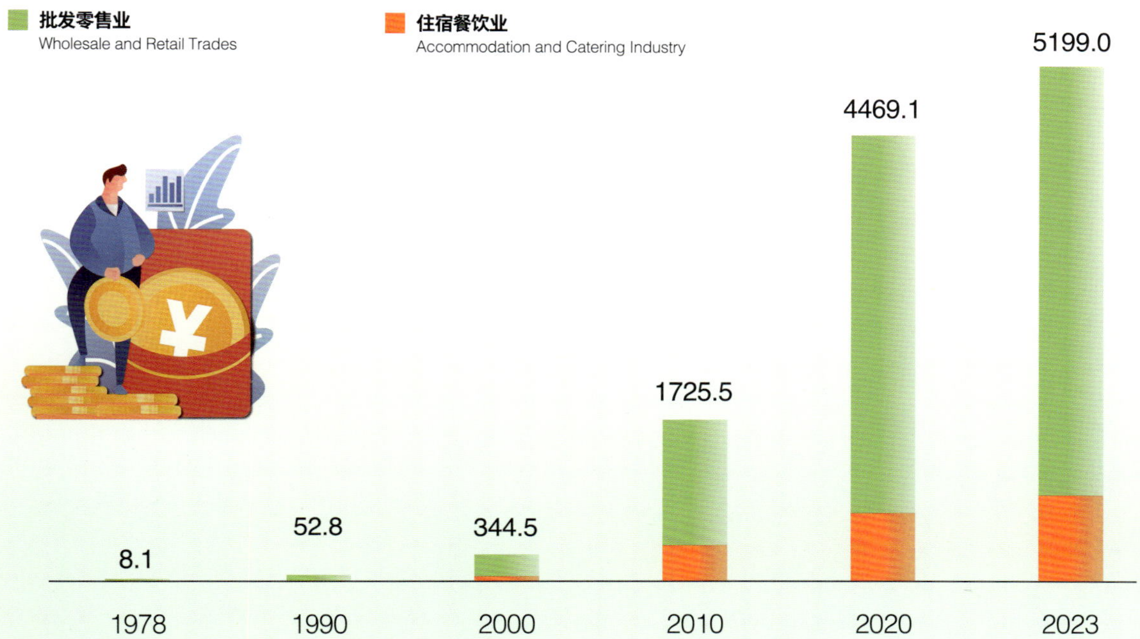

实际使用外资金额（万美元）
Actual Use of Foreign Capital (10 000 USD)

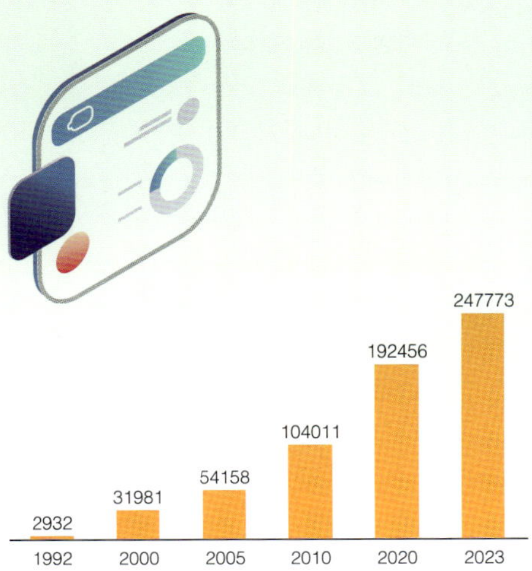

海关进出口总额（万美元）
International Trade in Goods of Customs (10 000 USD)

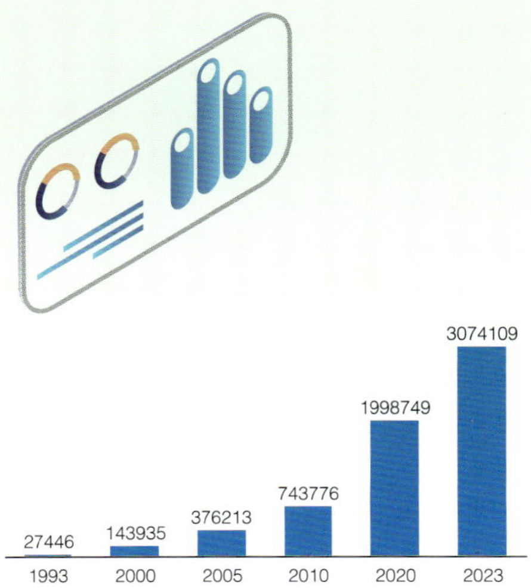

城市建设
Urban Public

全社会用电量（亿千瓦时）
Electricity Consumption (100 million kWh)

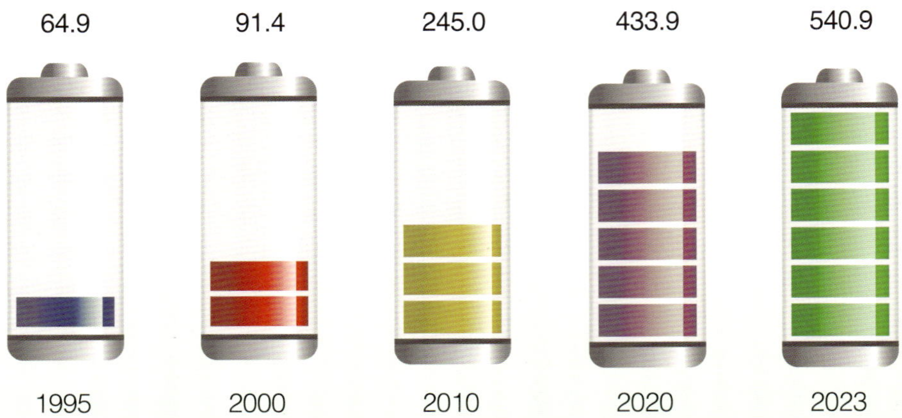

全社会供气量
Total Social Gas Supply

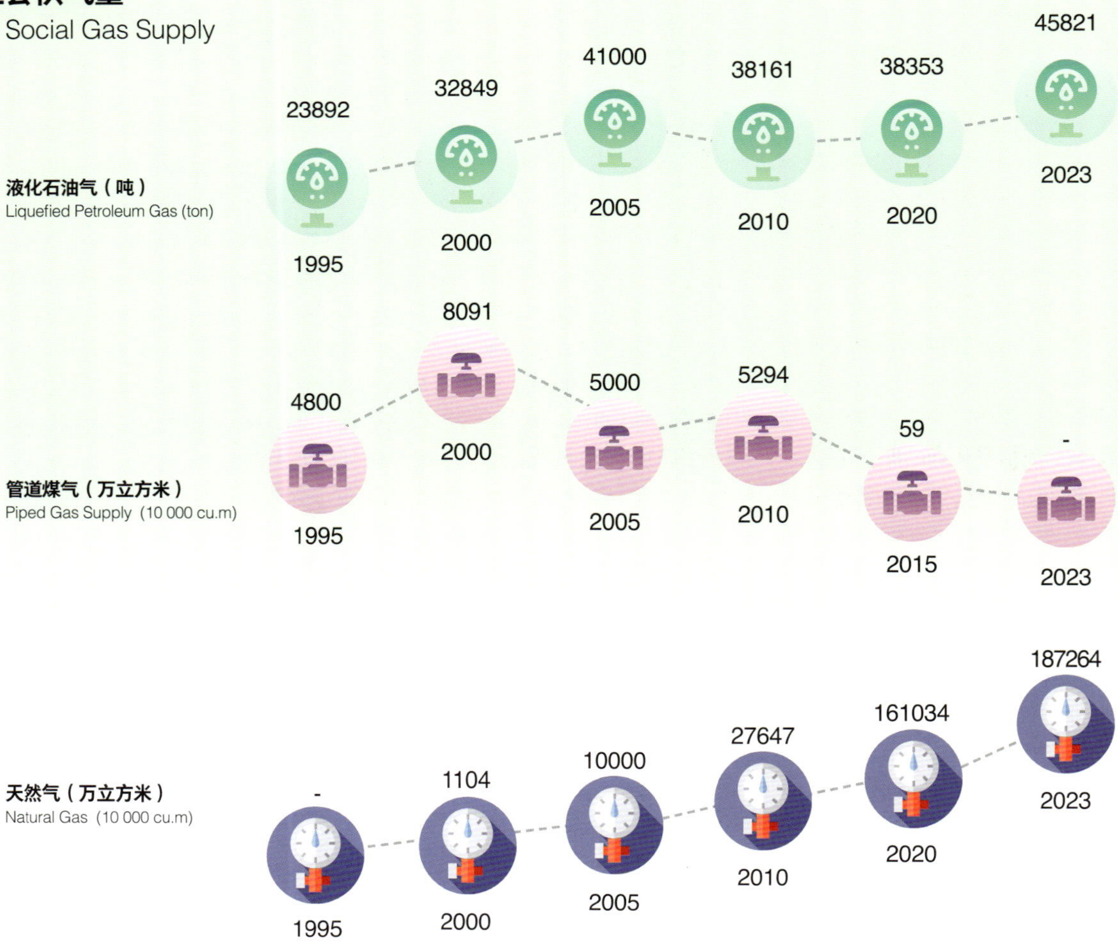

供热面积（万平方米）
Area of Central Heating (10 000 sq.m)

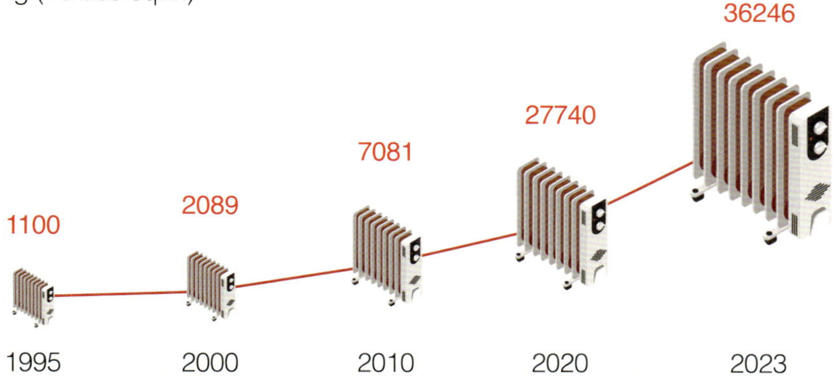

公共交通客运量（万人次）
Public Transportation of Passenger Traffic (10 000 person-times)

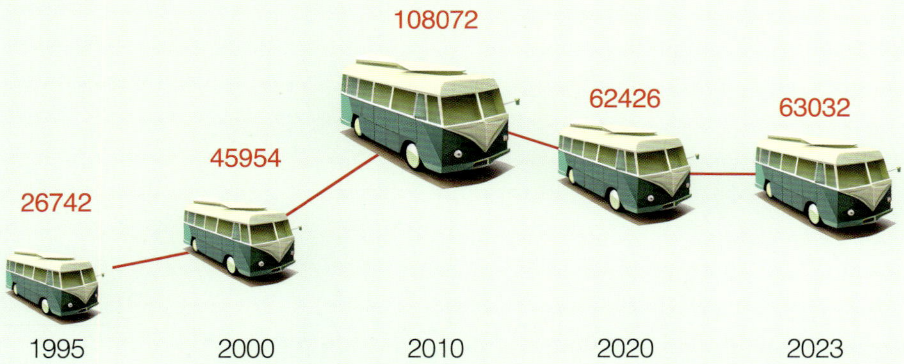

人均公园绿地面积（平方米/人）
Per Capita Public Green Area (sq.m/person)

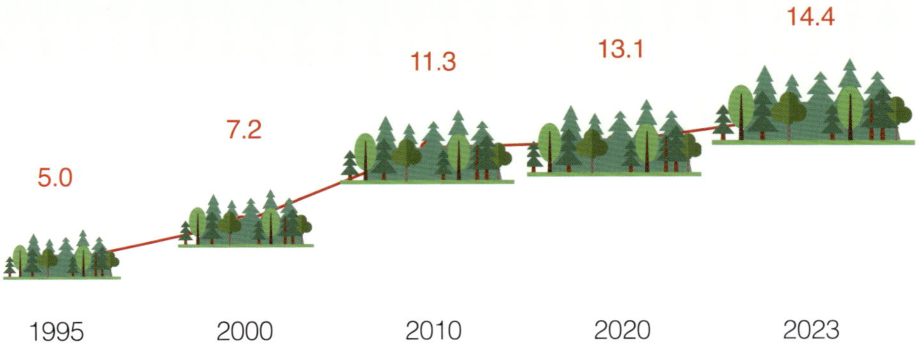

交通 邮电
Transportation Post and Telecommunication

公路通车里程(公里)
Length of Highways in Operation(km)

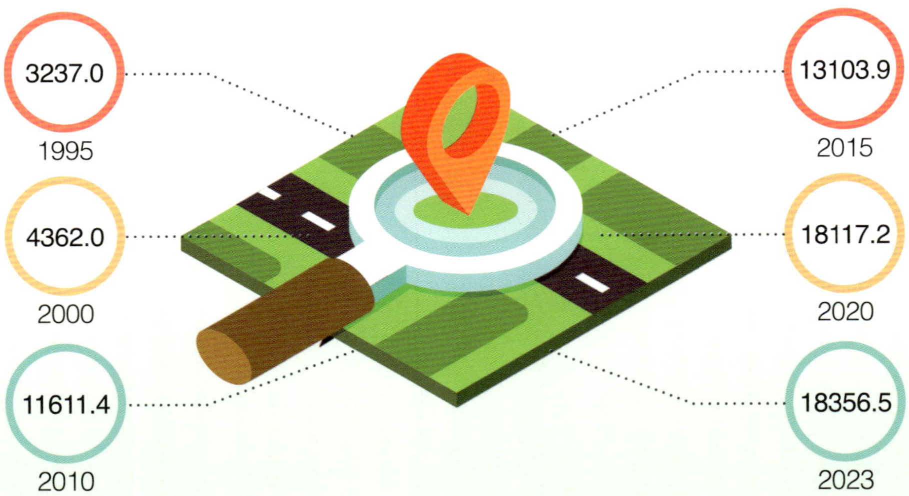

高速公路(公里)
Expressway(km)

移动电话用户、 宽带互联网接入用户数（万户）
Number of Mobile Telephone Subscribers, Subscribers of Broad Band Internet(10 000 subscribers)

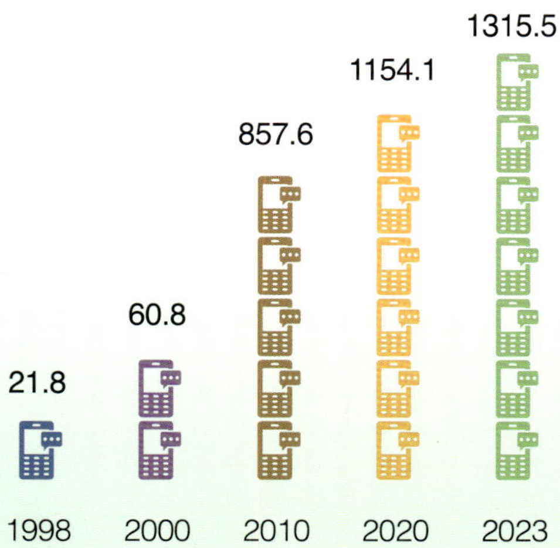

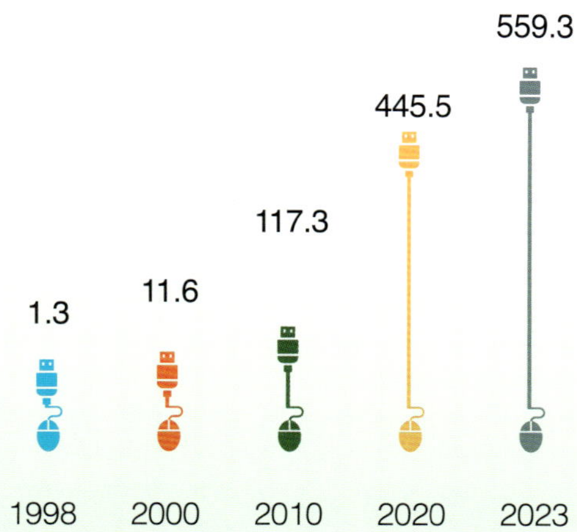

客运量（万人）
Passenger Traffic(10 000 persons)

货运量（万吨）
Freight Traffic(10 000 tons)

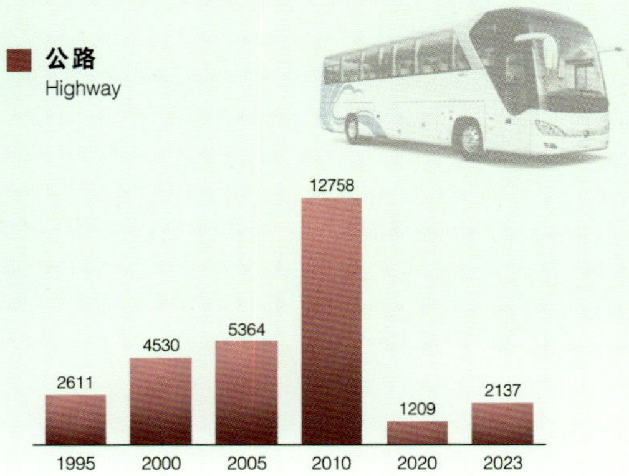

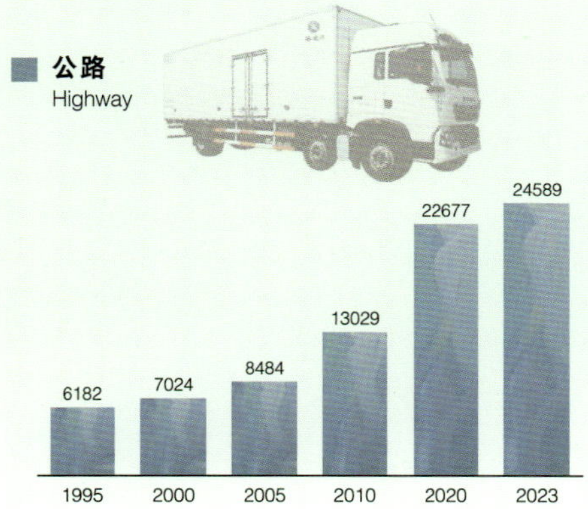

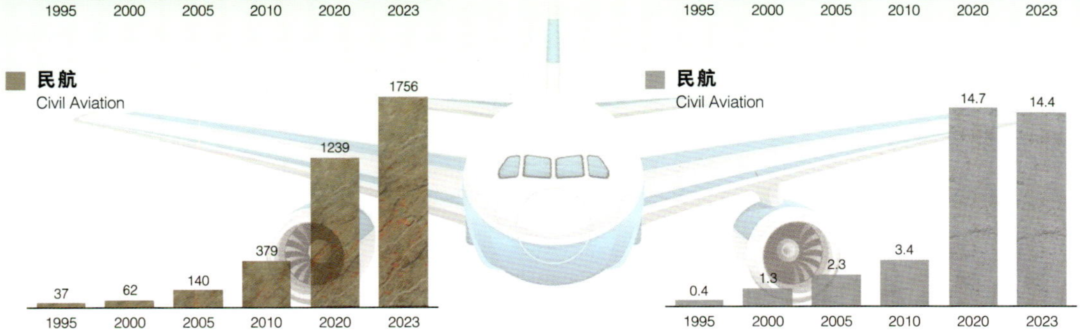

科技 教育 卫生
Science and Technology Education Health

发明专利授权量（件）
The number of invention patents granted(pieces)

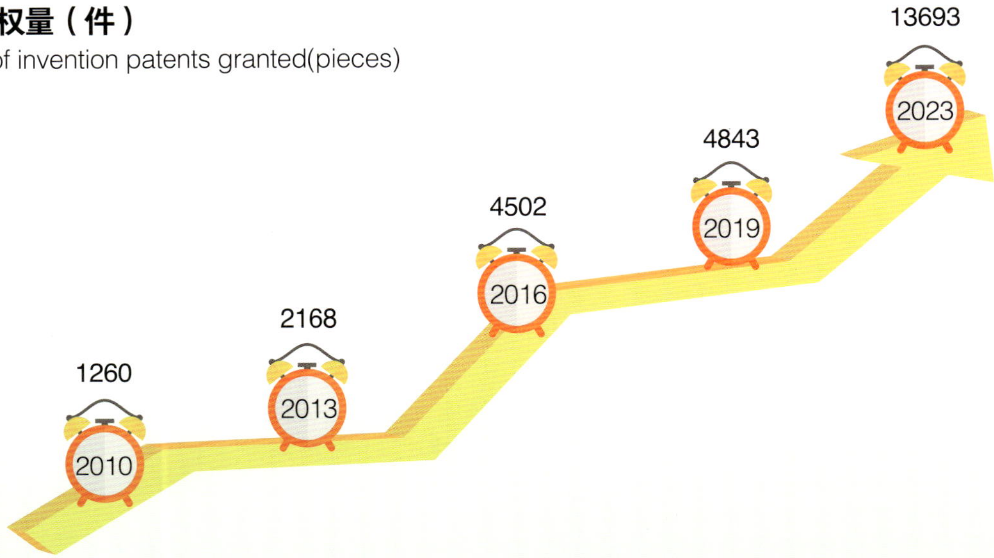

各类学校专任教师（万人）
Full-time Teachers (10 000 persons)

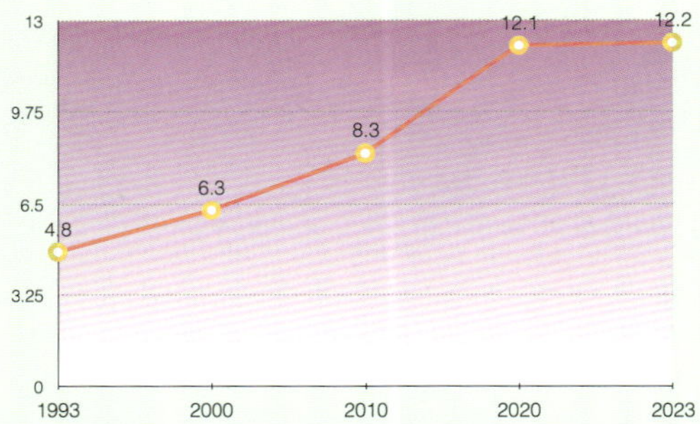

各类学校在校学生（万人）
Total Enrollment (10 000 persons)

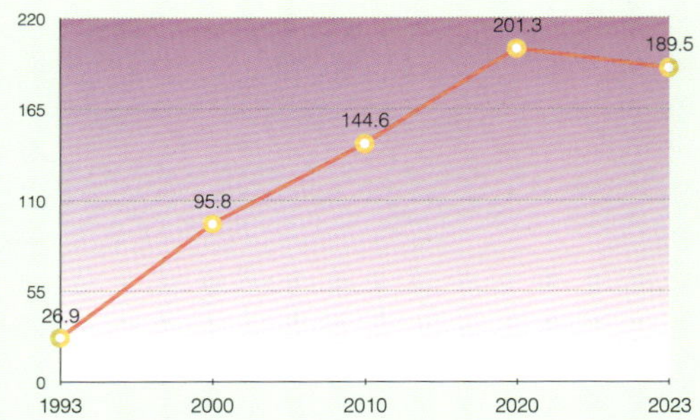

每万人拥有医院床位数（张）
Number of Hospitals Beds per 10000 Population (set)

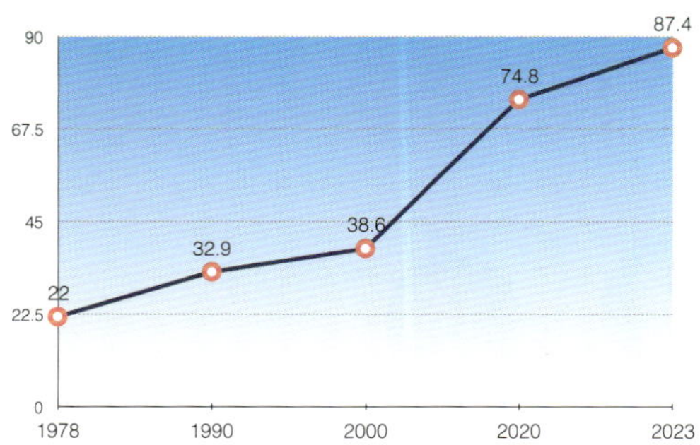

每万人拥有医生数（人）
Number of Doctors per 10000 Population (person)

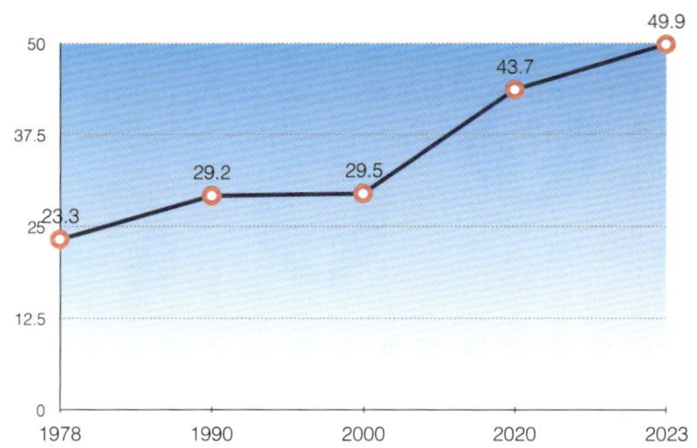

1

行 政 区 划

DIVISIONS OF ADMINISTRATIVE AREAS

1-1 行政区划
Divisions of Administrative Areas

单位：个 (unit)

年份地区	Year and Region	乡 Townships	镇 Towns	街道 Street Communities	村 Village	居委会 Neighborhood committee	土地面积(平方公里) Land Area (sq.km)
全市主要年份							
1989		57	54	53	4710	702	8227
1990		57	54	48	4752	669	8227
1991		57	54	48	4752	670	8227
1992		57	54	48	4759	670	8227
1993		56	55	48	4756	670	8227
1994		55	56	48	4759	670	8227
1995		48	63	49	4723	721	8227
1996		42	68	49	4704	685	8154
1997		42	68	50	4696	616	8154
1998		42	69	50	4711	505	8154
1999		42	69	50	4714	468	8154
2000		42	69	50	4702	416	8154
2001		28	64	54	4677	417	8177
2002		27	65	54	4657	487	8177
2003		27	61	58	4657	487	8177
2004		27	61	58	4657	487	8177
2005		12	53	64	4628	400	8177
2006		11	53	64	4604	487	8177
2007		11	50	73	4563	500	8177
2008		11	50	73	4551	521	8177
2009		11	50	75	4553	522	8177
2010		6	49	86	4552	532	8177
2011		4	51	86	4538	556	8177
2012		4	51	86	4532	586	8177
2013		2	51	90	4548	597	7998
2014		2	51	90	4547	627	7998
2015		2	46	95	4546	641	7998
2016			39	104	4547	669	7998
2017			29	112	4548	711	7998
2018			29	112	4546	740	7998
2019			40	121	5551	847	10244
2020			29	132	5530	861	10244
2021			29	132	4699	992	10244
2022			29	132	4698	1000	10244
2023			29	132	4691	1057	10244
2023年分地区							
历下区	Li xia			14		138	101
市中区	Shi zhong			17	77	141	281
槐荫区	Huai yin			16	93	112	152
天桥区	Tian qiao			15	48	152	259
历城区	Li cheng			21	266	110	1301
长清区	Chang qing		2	8	585	51	1209
章丘区	Zhang qiu		1	17	525	67	1719
济阳区	Ji yang		2	8	566	52	1099
莱芜区	Lai wu		7	8	792	69	1740
钢城区	Gang cheng			5	211	41	506
济南高新区	Jinan Gao xin				147	63	
济南起步区(直管)	Jinan Start-up Area (Directly under)				303	5	
南部山区	Nan shan				254	1	
平阴县	Ping yin		6	2	308	30	715
商河县	Shang he		11	1	516	25	1162

注：1.指标“土地面积”2013年起为第二次全市土地调查数据。
2.本表内数据由相关主管部门提供。

Notes:1. Indicator "land area" is the city land survey data for the second time as of 2013.
2.The data in this table are provided by the relevant authority departments.

1–2 县区所辖镇、街道办事处(2023年末)
Town and Street Communities Under the Jurisdiction(End of 2023)

县区	Region	镇、街道办事处数量(个) Number of Towns and Street Communities (unit)	镇、街道办事处名称 Name of Towns and Street Communities
历下区	Li xia	14	解放路街道办事处 千佛山街道办事处 趵突泉街道办事处 泉城路街道办事处 大明湖街道办事处 东关街道办事处 文化东路街道办事处 建筑新村街道办事处 甸柳新村街道办事处 燕山街道办事处 姚家街道办事处 智远街道办事处 龙洞街道办事处 舜华路街道办事处
市中区	Shi zhong	17	大观园街道办事处 杆石桥街道办事处 四里村街道办事处 魏家庄街道办事处 二七新村街道办事处 七里山街道办事处 六里山街道办事处 舜玉路街道办事处 泺源街道办事处 王官庄街道办事处 舜耕街道办事处 白马山街道办事处 七贤街道办事处 十六里河街道办事处 兴隆街道办事处 党家街道办事处 陡沟街道办事处
槐荫区	Huai yin	16	振兴街街道办事处 中大槐树街道办事处 道德街街道办事处 西市场街道办事处 五里沟街道办事处 营市街街道办事处 青年公园街道办事处 南辛庄街道办事处 段店北路街道办事处 张庄路街道办事处 匡山街道办事处 美里湖街道办事处 兴福街道办事处 玉清湖街道办事处 腊山街道办事处 吴家堡街道办事处
天桥区	Tian qiao	15	无影山街道办事处 工人新村北村街道办事处 工人新村南村街道办事处 天桥东街街道办事处 堤口路街道办事处 北坦街道办事处 制锦市街道办事处 官扎营街道办事处 宝华街街道办事处 纬北路街道办事处 药山街道办事处 北园街道办事处 泺口街道办事处 桑梓店街道办事处 大桥街道办事处
历城区	Li cheng	21	山大路街道办事处 洪家楼街道办事处 东风街道办事处 全福街道办事处 荷花路街道办事处 鲍山街道办事处 唐冶街道办事处 华山街道办事处 王舍人街道办事处 郭店街道办事处 港沟街道办事处 彩石街道办事处 董家街道办事处 唐王街道办事处 孙村街道办事处 巨野河街道办事处 遥墙街道办事处 临港街道办事处 仲宫街道办事处 柳埠街道办事处 西营街道办事处
长清区	Chang qing	10	文昌街道办事处 崮云湖街道办事处 平安街道办事处 五峰山街道办事处 归德街道办事处 张夏街道办事处 万德街道办事处 孝里街道办事处 马山镇 双泉镇
章丘区	Zhang qiu	18	明水街道办事处 双山街道办事处 枣园街道办事处 龙山街道办事处 埠村街道办事处 圣井街道办事处 普集街道办事处 绣惠街道办事处 相公庄街道办事处 文祖街道办事处 官庄街道办事处 曹范街道办事处 宁家埠街道办事处 高官寨街道办事处 白云湖街道办事处 刁镇街道办事处 黄河街道办事处 垛庄镇
济阳区	Ji yang	10	济阳街道办事处 济北街道办事处 回河街道办事处 垛石街道办事处 曲堤街道办事处 崔寨街道办事处 太平街道办事处 孙耿街道办事处 仁风镇 新市镇
莱芜区	Lai wu	15	凤城街道办事处 张家洼街道办事处 高庄街道办事处 鹏泉街道办事处 口镇街道办事处 羊里街道办事处 方下街道办事处 雪野街道办事处 牛泉镇 苗山镇 大王庄镇 寨里镇 杨庄镇 茶业口镇 和庄镇
钢城区	Gang cheng	5	艾山街道办事处 里辛街道办事处 汶源街道办事处 颜庄街道办事处 辛庄街道办事处
平阴县	Ping yin	8	榆山街道办事处 锦水街道办事处 东阿镇 孝直镇 孔村镇 洪范池镇 玫瑰镇 安城镇
商河县	Shang he	12	许商街道办事处 殷巷镇 怀仁镇 玉皇庙镇 龙桑寺镇 郑路镇 贾庄镇 白桥镇 孙集镇 韩庙镇 沙河镇 张坊镇

2

人口

POPULATION

2-1 主要年份总户数、总人口(户籍人口)

Total Household and Population in Major Years(registered population)

年份 year	年末总户数 (万户) Total year-end Households (10 000 households)	年末总人口 (万人) Total year-end Population (10 000 persons)	按性别分(万人) Grouped by Sex (10 000 persons)		性别比 (女=100) Sex Ratio (Female= 100)	年平均人口 (万人) Annual Average Population (10 000 persons)	比上年增长 (‰) Growth Rate (‰)	人口密度 (人/平方公里) Density of Population (person/sq.km)
			男性 Male	女性 Female				
1952	70.19	318.66	157.68	160.98	97.95	315.94	3.30	387
1957	76.44	346.38	170.30	176.09	96.71	343.25	17.40	421
1962	81.45	351.44	174.55	176.89	98.68	350.18	-4.60	427
1965	83.01	373.22	186.08	187.14	99.43	370.24	19.50	454
1970	89.48	407.50	203.16	204.34	99.42	404.17	16.60	495
1975	96.54	437.73	217.82	219.91	99.05	435.15	9.90	532
1976	98.63	442.09	220.89	221.20	99.86	439.91	10.90	537
1977	100.60	445.05	222.46	222.59	99.94	443.57	8.30	541
1978	102.93	450.67	226.31	224.36	100.87	447.86	9.70	548
1979	105.34	456.37	228.57	227.80	100.34	453.52	12.60	555
1980	106.83	458.61	230.47	228.15	101.02	457.49	8.80	557
1981	110.52	467.93	235.35	232.58	101.19	463.27	12.60	569
1982	112.51	474.23	238.99	235.26	101.59	471.08	16.80	576
1983	114.92	479.38	242.02	237.36	101.54	476.81	12.20	583
1984	116.92	483.85	244.32	239.53	102.00	481.62	10.10	588
1985	120.19	488.39	246.86	241.53	102.21	486.12	9.30	594
1986	122.67	494.06	250.09	243.97	102.51	491.23	10.50	601
1987	125.43	501.03	253.95	247.08	102.78	497.55	12.90	609
1988	130.32	507.18	257.22	249.86	102.95	504.11	13.20	616
1989	134.77	513.39	260.79	252.61	103.24	510.29	12.30	624
1990	140.36	523.60	265.91	257.69	103.19	518.50	16.10	636
1991	143.42	527.43	267.78	259.65	103.13	525.52	13.50	641
1992	147.50	530.70	269.46	261.25	103.14	529.07	6.70	645
1993	149.42	533.53	270.77	262.76	103.05	532.12	5.80	649
1994	153.60	537.31	272.76	264.54	103.11	535.42	6.20	653
1995	156.45	542.12	274.98	267.14	102.93	539.72	8.00	656
1996	156.42	543.45	275.59	267.86	102.89	542.79	5.70	666

2-1 续表 continued

年份 year	年末总户数 (万户) Total year-end Households (10 000 households)	年末总人口 (万人) Total year-end Population (10 000 persons)	按性别分(万人) Grouped by Sex (10 000 persons)		性别比 (女=100) Sex Ratio (Female= 100)	年平均人口 (万人) Annual Average Population (10 000 persons)	比上年增长 (‰) Growth Rate (‰)	人口密度 (人/平方公里) Density of Population (person/sq.km)
			男性 Male	女性 Female				
1997	157.66	549.20	278.30	270.90	102.73	546.33	6.50	674
1998	160.93	553.54	279.91	273.63	102.30	551.37	9.20	679
1999	163.52	557.63	281.71	275.93	102.09	555.59	7.70	684
2000	166.63	562.65	284.19	278.46	102.06	560.14	8.20	690
2001	168.46	569.00	287.39	281.61	102.06	565.83	10.20	696
2002	170.10	575.01	290.58	284.43	102.16	572.00	10.90	703
2003	172.18	582.56	294.04	288.52	101.91	578.78	11.90	712
2004	173.24	590.08	297.25	292.82	101.51	586.32	13.03	722
2005	177.69	597.44	300.42	297.02	101.15	593.76	12.69	731
2006	179.48	603.35	302.72	300.63	100.70	600.39	11.17	738
2007	181.88	604.85	302.87	301.98	100.29	604.10	6.17	740
2008	184.63	603.99	302.00	301.99	100.00	604.42	0.53	739
2009	187.70	603.27	301.26	302.01	99.75	603.63	-1.30	738
2010	190.65	604.08	301.28	302.80	99.50	603.68	0.08	739
2011	193.61	606.64	302.19	304.44	99.26	605.36	2.78	742
2012	195.79	609.21	303.30	305.91	99.15	607.92	4.23	745
2013	199.67	613.25	304.93	308.32	98.90	611.23	5.44	767
2014	201.93	621.61	309.09	312.52	98.90	617.43	15.64	777
2015	203.59	625.73	310.92	314.80	98.77	623.67	10.11	782
2016	205.45	632.83	314.28	318.55	98.66	629.28	9.00	791
2017	208.08	643.62	319.21	324.41	98.40	638.22	14.21	805
2018	216.64	655.90	324.74	331.15	98.06	649.76	19.08	820
2019	270.26	796.74	395.30	401.44	98.47	726.32	21.47	778
2020	276.35	806.72	399.61	407.11	98.16	801.73	12.45	788
2021	283.04	816.61	404.03	412.57	97.93	811.67	12.40	797
2022	286.64	819.95	405.11	414.84	97.65	818.28	8.14	800
2023	290.46	825.30	407.23	418.07	97.41	822.63	5.32	806

2-2 主要年份市区总户数、总人口(户籍人口)
Total Household and Population of Urban in Major Years(registered population)

年份 year	年末总户数 (万户) Total year-end Households (10 000 households)	年末总人口 (万人) Total year-end Population (10 000 persons)	按性别分(万人) Grouped by Sex (10 000 persons)		年平均人口 (万人) Annual Average Population (10 000 persons)
			男性 Male	女性 Female	
1952	26.46	124.96	63.95	61.01	123.83
1957	29.13	143.17	72.05	71.13	140.11
1962	32.25	153.35	78.52	74.83	154.18
1965	34.03	162.82	83.20	79.62	161.90
1970	37.21	167.82	85.61	82.21	168.51
1975	40.67	178.78	90.83	87.95	177.74
1976	41.59	180.99	91.83	89.16	179.88
1977	42.34	181.49	91.92	89.57	181.24
1978	43.79	186.43	94.70	91.73	183.96
1979	45.33	189.26	96.22	93.04	187.84
1980	46.12	190.01	97.22	92.79	189.63
1981	48.64	194.05	99.37	94.69	192.03
1982	50.60	201.31	101.44	99.87	197.68
1983	52.32	205.48	103.42	102.07	203.39
1984	54.30	209.55	105.57	103.99	207.52
1985	56.88	213.28	107.96	105.33	211.42
1986	58.65	216.98	111.54	105.43	215.13
1987	60.54	221.49	113.79	107.70	219.23
1988	63.03	225.00	115.51	109.39	223.25
1989	65.29	228.88	117.49	111.39	226.94
1990	81.22	283.66	145.29	138.36	
1991	83.30	286.20	146.55	139.65	284.93
1992	85.87	288.52	145.19	143.33	287.36
1993	88.02	291.24	149.07	142.17	289.88
1994	90.10	294.60	150.75	143.85	292.92
1995	92.04	299.20	152.97	146.23	296.90
1996	93.12	302.78	154.58	148.20	300.99
1997	93.90	306.98	156.54	150.44	304.88
1998	96.65	309.90	157.58	152.32	308.44

2-2 续表 continued

年份 year	年末总户数 (万户) Total year-end Households (10 000 households)	年末总人口 (万人) Total year-end Population (10 000 persons)	按性别分(万人) Grouped by Sex (10 000 persons)		年平均人口 (万人) Annual Average Population (10 000 persons)
			男性 Male	女性 Female	
1999	97.74	313.18	159.19	153.99	311.54
2000	99.25	317.20	161.03	156.17	315.19
2001	100.53	322.45	163.73	158.72	319.83
2002	101.62	327.55	166.43	161.12	325.00
2003	102.71	334.80	169.84	164.96	331.18
2004	102.68	341.73	172.91	168.82	338.27
2005	104.87	347.87	175.41	172.45	344.80
2006	106.19	352.29	177.10	175.19	350.08
2007	107.55	352.71	176.70	176.01	352.50
2008	109.26	350.23	175.08	175.15	351.47
2009	111.07	348.24	173.71	174.53	349.24
2010	112.91	348.02	173.19	174.83	348.13
2011	114.75	349.44	173.51	175.93	348.73
2012	116.49	352.17	174.55	177.62	350.81
2013	118.50	355.38	175.86	179.52	353.78
2014	120.33	360.99	178.55	182.44	358.19
2015	121.96	364.54	180.12	184.42	362.77
2016	154.64	473.33	233.74	239.59	418.94
2017	157.42	483.75	238.48	245.27	478.54
2018	182.76	554.13	273.31	280.82	518.94
2019	236.31	695.09	343.90	351.19	689.31
2020	242.04	705.33	348.36	356.97	700.21
2021	248.66	715.55	352.90	362.66	710.44
2022	252.43	719.84	354.40	365.45	717.70
2023	256.23	725.42	356.60	368.82	722.63

注：1990年以前的数据中不包括长清区。2016年起数据包括章丘区。2018年起数据包括济阳区。 2019年起数据包括莱芜区、钢城区。

Note: The data before 1990 excludes Changqing. The data as of 2016 includes Zhangqiu. The data as of 2018 includes Jiyang. Data after the year of 2019 involves Laiwu and Gangcheng.

2-3 主要年份人口自然变动情况
Natural Change of Population in Major Years

年份 Year	申报出生人口 (人) Population of Birth (person)	申报出生率 (‰) Birth Rate (‰)	申报死亡人口 (人) Population of Death (person)	申报死亡率 (‰) Death Rate (‰)	人口自然增长 (人) Population of Natural Growth (person)	人口自然增长率 (‰) Natural Growth Rate(‰)
1952	72861	23.06	29949	9.48	42912	13.58
1957	108432	31.59	38082	11.09	70350	20.50
1962	108029	30.85	44464	12.70	63565	18.15
1965	121364	32.78	39355	10.63	82009	22.15
1970	111861	27.68	29965	7.41	81896	20.27
1975	82939	19.06	33837	7.78	49102	11.28
1976	70065	15.93	34693	7.89	35372	8.04
1977	67413	15.20	33723	7.60	33690	7.60
1978	69541	15.53	31343	7.00	38198	8.53
1979	72596	16.01	30205	6.66	42391	9.35
1980	60336	13.19	32004	7.00	28332	6.19
1981	70327	15.18	31671	6.84	38656	8.34
1982	74147	15.74	28679	6.09	45468	9.65
1983	56454	11.84	30080	6.31	26374	5.53
1984	61156	12.70	32277	6.70	28879	6.00
1985	55386	11.39	31678	6.52	23708	4.87
1986	69901	14.23	30790	6.27	39111	7.96
1987	86752	17.44	30007	6.03	56745	11.41
1988	78922	15.66	32850	6.52	46072	9.14
1989	76380	14.97	30721	6.02	45659	8.95
1990	66806	12.88	33916	6.54	32890	6.34
1991	59374	11.30	32675	6.20	26699	5.10
1992	52825	9.98	34969	6.61	17856	3.37
1993	46007	8.65	35317	6.64	10690	2.01
1994	49940	9.30	35308	6.60	14632	2.70
1995	54132	10.03	34107	6.32	20025	3.71
1996	58254	10.73	36452	6.71	21802	4.02

2-3 续表 continued

年份 Year	申报出生人口 (人) Population of Birth (person)	申报出生率 (‰) Birth Rate (‰)	申报死亡人口 (人) Population of Death (person)	申报死亡率 (‰) Death Rate (‰)	人口自然增长 (人) Population of Natural Growth (person)	人口自然增长率 (‰) Natural Growth Rate(‰)
1997	62245	11.39	35768	6.55	26477	4.84
1998	62490	11.33	36497	6.64	25893	4.69
1999	55931	10.07	34956	6.29	20975	3.78
2000	62059	11.08	39499	7.05	22560	4.03
2001	55536	9.82	33816	5.98	21720	3.84
2002	57317	10.02	36234	6.33	21083	3.69
2003	54599	9.43	42539	7.35	12060	2.08
2004	60670	10.35	38158	6.51	22512	3.84
2005	60240	10.15	37782	6.36	22458	3.78
2006	57706	9.61	39040	6.50	18666	3.11
2007	58367	9.66	39752	6.58	18615	3.08
2008	59600	9.86	39887	6.60	19713	3.26
2009	56694	9.39	40911	6.78	15783	2.61
2010	67162	11.13	50380	8.35	16782	2.78
2011	66563	11.00	40310	6.66	26253	4.34
2012	71449	11.75	49148	8.08	22301	3.67
2013	69351	11.35	41713	6.82	27638	4.53
2014	110503	17.90	41887	6.78	68616	11.11
2015	73688	11.82	41999	6.73	31689	5.09
2016	91941	14.61	39460	6.27	52481	8.34
2017	113766	17.83	62958	9.86	50808	7.96
2018	94694	14.57	45374	6.98	49320	7.59
2019	101723	12.86	52396	6.62	49327	6.24
2020	83782	10.45	58568	7.31	25214	3.14
2021	66666	8.21	44228	5.45	22438	2.76
2022	64267	7.85	79727	9.74	-15460	-1.89
2023	62271	7.57	47248	5.74	15023	1.83

2-4 分地区户数、人口数(2023年)(户籍人口)
Household and Population by Region(2023)(registered population)

地区	Region	户数(万户) Households (10 000 households)	人口数(万人) Population (10 000 persons)	按性别分(万人) Grouped by Sex (10 000 persons)	
				男性 Male	女性 Female
全市	**Total**	**290.46**	**825.30**	**407.23**	**418.07**
市区	Districts	256.23	725.42	356.60	368.82
历下区	Li xia	27.46	78.70	38.07	40.63
市中区	Shi zhong	26.64	70.62	34.18	36.44
槐荫区	Huai yin	18.63	49.71	23.72	25.99
天桥区	Tian qiao	20.36	54.88	26.42	28.46
历城区	Li cheng	43.53	122.24	59.80	62.44
长清区	Chang qing	18.91	56.65	28.20	28.45
章丘区	Zhang qiu	32.26	104.46	51.62	52.84
济阳区	Ji yang	18.08	59.99	30.16	29.83
莱芜区	Lai wu	38.79	98.82	49.45	49.37
钢城区	Gang cheng	11.57	29.35	14.99	14.36
平阴县	Ping yin	13.58	36.52	18.32	18.20
商河县	Shang he	20.65	63.36	32.31	31.05

2-5 分地区人口机械变动情况(2023年)
Mechanical Changes of Population by Region (2023)

地区	Region	迁入人口 (人) Move Into the Population (person)	迁入率 (‰) Move In Rate (‰)	迁出人口 (人) Move Out the population (person)	迁出率 (‰) Move Out Rate (‰)	人口机械增长 (人) Mechanical Growth of Population (person)	人口机械增长率 (‰) Mechanical Growth Rate of Population (‰)
全市	**Total**	**74354**	**9.04**	**35891**	**4.36**	**38463**	**4.68**
市区	Districts	68388	9.46	25904	3.58	42484	5.88
历下区	Li xia	11497	14.71	5307	6.79	6190	7.92
市中区	Shi zhong	8465	12.04	3580	5.09	4885	6.95
槐荫区	Huai yin	9667	19.58	2642	5.35	7025	14.23
天桥区	Tian qiao	8287	15.14	2213	4.04	6074	11.10
历城区	Li cheng	21929	18.20	5059	4.20	16870	14.00
长清区	Chang qing	1820	3.21	1366	2.41	454	0.80
章丘区	Zhang qiu	2142	2.05	2020	1.93	122	0.12
济阳区	Ji yang	2208	3.69	1077	1.80	1131	1.89
莱芜区	Lai wu	1861	1.88	2001	2.02	-140	-0.14
钢城区	Gang cheng	512	1.74	639	2.17	-127	-0.43
平阴县	Ping yin	1899	5.19	3537	9.67	-1638	-4.48
商河县	Shang he	4067	6.41	6450	10.17	-2383	-3.76

2-6 分地区人口自然变动情况(2023年)
Natural Changes of Population by Region (2023)

地区	Region	申报出生人口 (人) Population of Birth (person)	申报出生率 (‰) Birth Rate (‰)	申报死亡人口 (人) Population of Death (person)	申报死亡率 (‰) Death Rate (‰)	人口自然增长 (人) Population of Natural Growth (person)	人口自然增长率 (‰) Natural Growth Rate (‰)
全市	**Total**	**62271**	**7.57**	**47248**	**5.74**	**15023**	**1.83**
市区	Districts	56202	7.78	42945	5.94	13257	1.84
历下区	Li xia	6551	8.38	2658	3.40	3893	4.98
市中区	Shi zhong	5351	7.61	3727	5.30	1624	2.31
槐荫区	Huai yin	4501	9.12	2243	4.54	2258	4.57
天桥区	Tian qiao	4041	7.38	3092	5.65	949	1.73
历城区	Li cheng	13903	11.54	6276	5.21	7627	6.33
长清区	Chang qing	3773	6.65	4702	8.28	-929	-1.64
章丘区	Zhang qiu	6302	6.02	9049	8.64	-2747	-2.62
济阳区	Ji yang	4604	7.69	3096	5.17	1508	2.52
莱芜区	Lai wu	5626	5.69	6674	6.75	-1048	-1.06
钢城区	Gang cheng	1550	5.26	1428	4.85	122	0.41
平阴县	Ping yin	1972	5.39	1579	4.32	393	1.07
商河县	Shang he	4097	6.46	2724	4.30	1373	2.17

2-7 结婚情况
Number of Marriages

单位：对 (couple)

地区	Region	2019年	2020年	2021年	2022年	2023年
总计	**Total**	**52300**	**50521**	**49380**	**48079**	**56948**
历下区	Li xia	5456	5634	6196	6382	8002
市中区	Shi zhong	5092	5074	4927	4948	6113
槐荫区	Huai yin	3452	3434	3802	3977	4575
天桥区	Tian qiao	4287	3869	3445	3219	3823
历城区	Li cheng	6809	6094	5591	5742	6407
长清区	Chang qing	3930	3547	3273	3049	3144
章丘区	Zhang qiu	6000	6016	5315	5055	6087
济阳区	Ji yang	3629	3154	2146	2041	2478
莱芜区	Lai wu	4514	4054	3970	3581	4043
钢城区	Gang cheng	1183	1117	1060	995	1086
济南高新区	Jinan Gao xin	2533	2783	2982	3055	4148
济南起步区(直管)	Jinan Start-up Area(Directly under)		560	1312	1181	1417
南部山区	Nan shan			816	991	1112
平阴县	Ping yin	1974	1881	1632	1408	1509
商河县	Shang he	3441	3304	2913	2455	3004

2-8 离婚情况
Number of Divorces

单位：对 (couple)

地区	Region	2019年	2020年	2021年	2022年	2023年
总计	**Total**	**36224**	**36515**	**24563**	**23544**	**25849**
法院离婚结案数	**Divorce Case Handled**	**7326**	**6887**	**7057**	**6479**	**8019**
民政数	**Divorces Handled through Civil**	**28898**	**29628**	**17506**	**17065**	**17830**
历下区	Li xia	3644	3889	2331	2277	2017
市中区	Shi zhong	3441	3785	2254	2268	2270
槐荫区	Huai yin	2416	2530	1701	1704	1630
天桥区	Tian qiao	3031	2936	1665	1656	1661
历城区	Li cheng	4195	4398	2261	2082	2181
长清区	Chang qing	1864	1953	1092	982	1003
章丘区	Zhang qiu	2793	2763	1633	1572	1663
济阳区	Ji yang	1745	1587	652	586	737
莱芜区	Lai wu	1418	1220	817	877	1025
钢城区	Gang cheng	502	432	240	292	333
济南高新区	Jinan Gaoxin	1322	1495	1005	911	1050
济南起步区(直管)	Jinan Start-up Area(Directly under)		269	373	358	379
南部山区	Nan shan			319	418	612
平阴县	Ping yin	968	938	490	480	529
商河县	Shang he	1559	1433	673	602	740

注：“法院离婚结案数”根据部门数据进行修订。
Note: "Divorce Cases Handled through Court Trial" Revision should be based on departmental data.

主要统计指标解释

人口数 指一定时点、一定地区范围内的有生命的个人的总和。年度统计的年末人口数指每年12月31日24时的人口数。

出生率（又称粗出生率） 指在一定时期内(通常为一年)一定地区的出生人数与同期内平均人数(或期中人数)之比，用千分率表示。本资料中的出生率指年出生率，其计算公式为：

出生率＝年出生人数／年平均人数×1000‰

式中：出生人数指活产婴儿，即胎儿脱离母体时(不管怀孕月数)，有过呼吸或其他生命现象。年平均人数指年初、年底人口数的平均数，也可用年中人口数代替。

死亡率（又称粗死亡率） 指在一定时期内(通常为一年)一定地区的死亡人数与同期内平均人数(或期中人数)之比，用千分率表示。本资料中的死亡率指年死亡率，其计算公式为：

死亡率＝年死亡人数／年平均人数×1000‰

人口自然增长率 指在一定时期内(通常为一年)人口自然增加数(出生人数减死亡人数)与该时期内平均人数(或期中人数)之比，用千分率表示。计算公式为：

人口自然增长率＝（本年出生人数－本年死亡人数）／年平均人数×1000‰

人口自然增长率＝人口出生率－人口死亡率

人口机械增长率 是反映迁移变动的一个相对指标。它表明一个地区在一定时间内迁入人口数与迁出人口数相抵后的差额与总人口数的比率，用千分率表示。计算公式为：

人口机械增长率=一定时期的迁入迁出人口差额/该时期的平均人口×100%

人口密度 指一定时点，一定地区的人口数与该时点、该地区的面积之比，即一定时点的单位土地面积上的人口数，通常以每平方公里的居民人数来表示：

人口密度＝该地区人口数／该地区土地面积×100%

性别比 反映两性人口间比例的指标，指在总人口中或各年龄组人口中，男性人数与女性人数之比。通常以每100个女性人口相对应的男性人口数。计算公式：

性别比＝男性人口／女性人口×100%

Explanatory Notes on Main Statistical Indicators

Total Population refers to the total number of people alive at a certain point of time within a given area.The annual statistics on total population is taken at midnight, the 31st of December.

Birth Rate (or Crude Birth Rate) refers to the ratio of the number of births to the average population (or mid-year population) during a certain period of time (usually a year), expressed in ‰. Birth rate in the chapter refers to annual birth rate. The following formula is used:

Birth rate = number of births/annual average population *1000‰

Number of births in the formula refers to live births, i.e. when a baby has breathed or showed any vital phenomena regardless of the length of pregnancy.Annual average population is the average of the number of population at the beginning of the year and that at the end of the year. Sometimes it is substituted by the mid-year population.

Death Rate (or Crude Death Rate) refers to the ratio of the number of deaths to the average population (or mid-year population) during a certain period of time (usually a year), expressed in ‰. Death rate in the chapter refers to annual death rate. The following formula is used:

Death rate = number of deaths/annual average population *1000‰

Natural Growth Rate of Population refers to the ratio of natural increase in population (number of births minus number of deaths) in a certain period of time (usually a year) to the average population (or mid-year population) of the same period, expressed in ‰. The following formula is applied:

Natural Growth Rate of Population=(number of births - number of deaths)/ annual average population * 1000‰

Natural Growth Rate of Population=Birth Rate-Death Rate

Mechanical Growth Rate of Population is a relative indicator that reflects changes in the population migration. It shows the ratio of the balance (between the people count moving in and out of a given area) to total population during a certain period of time, expressed in ‰. The following formula is used:

Mechanical growth rate = the balance between people count moving in and out of a given area during a certain period of time/average population * 1000‰

Population Density refers to the ratio of total population in a given area at a certain point of time to the area at this point of time, namely total population per area of land at a certain point of time, expressed in number of residents per square kilometers:

Population density= Total population in the region/Land area in the region*100%

Sex ratio refers to the ratio of male to female population in total population or age groups, male population to per 100 female populations. The following formula is used:

Sex ratio= Male population/Female population*100%

3

综 合

GENERAL SURVEY

3-1 国民经济和社会发展总量指标
Principal Aggregate Indicators on National Economic and Social Development

指标	Item	单位 Unit	1978年
面积	**Area**		
土地面积	Land Area	平方公里(sq.km)	
#建成区面积	Area of Built Districts	平方公里(sq.km)	85
人口	**Population**		
年末总户数(户籍人口)	Total year-end Households(Household Population)	万户(10 000 households)	102.93
年末总人口(户籍人口)	Total year-end Population(Household Population)	万人(10 000 persons)	450.67
#市区	Population	万人(10 000 persons)	186.43
#男性	Male	万人(10 000 persons)	226.31
年末常住总人口	Total Resident Population at the Year-end	万人(10 000 persons)	
就业	**Employment**		
全社会从业人员	Employed Persons	万人(10 000 persons)	204.04
第一产业	Primary Industry	万人(10 000 persons)	136.30
第二产业	Secondary Industry	万人(10 000 persons)	46.06
第三产业	Tertiary Industry	万人(10 000 persons)	21.68
职工平均工资	Average Wage of Staff and Workers	元(yuan)	578
城镇非私营单位就业人员平均工资	Average Wage of Employed Persons in Urban Non Private Units	元(yuan)	
城镇非私营单位在岗职工平均工资	Average Wage of Staff and Workers in Urban Non Private Units	元(yuan)	
城镇私营单位就业人员平均工资	Average Wage of Employed Persons in Urban Private Units	元(yuan)	
城镇登记失业人员数	Registered Urban Unemployed Persons	万人(10 000 persons)	
城镇登记失业率	Registered Urban Unemployment Rate	%	
国民经济核算	**National Accounting**		
地区生产总值	Gross Domestic Product	亿元(100 million yuan)	23.60
#非公有制经济	Non-public Economy	亿元(100 million yuan)	
第一产业	Primary Industry	亿元(100 million yuan)	4.16
第二产业	Secondary Industry	亿元(100 million yuan)	13.32
第三产业	Tertiary Industry	亿元(100 million yuan)	6.12
人均地区生产总值	Per Capita GDP	元(yuan)	527
固定资产投资	**Investment in Fixed Assets**		
固定资产投资	Investment in Fixed Assets	亿元(100 million yuan)	3.19
第一产业	Primary Industry	亿元(100 million yuan)	0.55
第二产业	Secondary Industry	亿元(100 million yuan)	1.15
#工业	Industry	亿元(100 million yuan)	0.75
第三产业	Tertiary Industry	亿元(100 million yuan)	1.29
#房地产投资	Real Estate Investment	亿元(100 million yuan)	
财政税收	**Fiscal Tax Revenue**		
一般公共预算收入	General Public Budget Revenue	亿元(100 million yuan)	5.90
一般公共预算支出	General Public Budget Expenditure	亿元(100 million yuan)	1.50
地域税收收入	Regional Tax Revenue	亿元(100 million yuan)	

1990年	1995年	2000年	2005年	2010年	2015年	2020年	2021年	2022年	2023年
8227	8227	8154	8177	8177	7998	10244	10244	10244	10244
103	114	120	295	347	497	840	841	854	860
140.36	156.45	166.63	177.69	190.65	203.59	276.35	283.04	286.64	290.46
523.60	542.12	562.65	597.44	604.08	625.73	806.72	816.61	819.95	825.30
232.30	247.57	317.20	347.87	348.02	458.16	705.33	715.55	719.84	725.42
265.91	274.98	284.19	300.42	301.28	310.92	399.61	404.03	405.11	407.23
				681.80	713.20	924.16	933.61	941.47	943.67
270.54	324.22	347.37	360.00	373.70	388.70	468.90	470.78	469.00	476.80
125.73	116.13	109.98	99.10	76.66	71.80				
87.75	106.68	110.81	114.20	120.20	124.70				
57.06	101.41	126.58	146.70	176.84	192.20				
2211	5851	10422	20866	31096	58578				
						104990	114596	123902	129222
						108391	119245	128703	133232
						60348	60914	61538	64500
	2.45	3.90	5.75	5.97	3.20				
	2.30	3.70	3.86	3.84	2.04	2.03			
138.24	473.52	1048.85	2086.44	4439.05	6738.01	10140.91	11413.51	12020.73	12757.42
		238.32	768.50	1664.43	2599.60				
23.93	67.64	109.27	150.50	238.19	326.09	361.66	408.77	420.54	429.53
67.36	220.37	468.23	1005.54	1918.55	2516.99	3542.73	3946.10	4095.20	4312.01
46.95	185.51	471.35	930.40	2282.31	3894.93	6236.52	7058.64	7504.99	8015.88
2666	8773	15356	27338	55248	77815	110681	122873	128216	135347
30.60	112.76	305.95	857.00	1987.44	3498.42				
0.52	3.24	13.57	38.28	68.08	102.52				
14.62	46.26	73.14	362.05	677.28	1217.39				
2.05	45.35	67.72	352.27	667.35	1147.87				
13.94	63.27	219.24	456.67	1242.08	2178.51				
2.18	16.46	50.53	121.09	484.50	1014.14	1707.63	1928.00	1830.80	1399.72
12.40	16.99	49.05	106.15	266.13	614.32	906.08	1007.61	1001.14	1060.82
8.20	19.63	54.72	120.66	336.80	658.20	1288.80	1293.08	1225.57	1365.29
	53.49	112.35	231.34	527.70	959.33	1369.16	1555.89	1351.69	1506.58

3-1 续表 1 continued 1

指标	Item	单位 Unit	1978年
国税税收收入	National Tax Revenue	亿元(100 million yuan)	
地税税收收入	Land Tax Revenue	亿元(100 million yuan)	
金融保险	**Finance and Insurance**		
金融机构人民币存款余额	RMB Deposits Balance of Financial Institutions	亿元(100 million yuan)	15.43
#住户存款	Deposits of Households	亿元(100 million yuan)	1.14
金融机构人民币贷款余额	RMB Loans Balance of Financial Institutions	亿元(100 million yuan)	14.08
#短期贷款	Short-term Loans	亿元(100 million yuan)	-
保险金额	Insured Amount	亿元(100 million yuan)	
保费收入	Premium Income	万元(10 000 yuan)	
赔付支出	Claim Payment	万元(10 000 yuan)	
农业	**Agriculture**		
农林牧渔业总产值	Gross Output Value of Farming, Forestry, Animal Husbandry and Fishery	亿元(100 million yuan)	6.57
农用机械总动力	Total power of agricultural machinery	万千瓦(10 000kW)	69.70
年末实有耕地面积	Actual cultivated Area at Year-end	千公顷(1000 ha)	373.19
粮食总产量	Total Output of Grain	万吨(10 000 tons)	115.38
蔬菜总产量	Total Output of Vegetable	万吨(10 000 tons)	49.19
肉类总产量	Total Output of meat	万吨(10 000 tons)	2.50
奶类总产量	Total Output of Milk	万吨(10 000 tons)	0.40
棉花总产量	Total Output of Cotton	万吨(10 000 tons)	0.51
规模以上工业	**Industry Enterprises above Designated Size**		
单位数	Number of Enterprises	个(unit)	1319
工业总产值	Gross Industrial Output Value	亿元(100 million yuan)	37.67
营业收入	Revenue from Principal Business	亿元(100 million yuan)	31.39
利税总额	Total Profits and Taxes	亿元(100 million yuan)	6.80
利润总额	Total Profits	亿元(100 million yuan)	3.88
资产总计	Total Assets	亿元(100 million yuan)	25.68
所有者权益	Owner's Equities	亿元(100 million yuan)	7.47
建筑业	**Construction**		
资质以上企业个数	Number of Qualification Enterprises	个(unit)	10
建筑业总产值	Gross Output Value of Construction Enterprises	亿元(100 million yuan)	0.68
施工面积	Floor Space under Construction	万平方米(10 000 sq.m)	
竣工面积	Floor Space of Completed	万平方米(10 000 sq.m)	49
其中：住宅	Residential	万平方米(10 000 sq.m)	
交通运输	**Transport**		
货运量	Freight Traffic		
铁路	Railways	万吨(10 000 tons)	2191
公路	Highways	万吨(10 000 tons)	1670
航空	Airways	万吨(10 000 tons)	

1990年	1995年	2000年	2005年	2010年	2015年	2020年	2021年	2022年	2023年
	39.55	72.54	144.20	309.87	494.43	-	-	-	-
	13.94	39.80	87.14	217.82	464.90	-	-	-	-
117.95	438.01	1274.96	3483.34	7510.44	13552.99	20714.97	23029.20	25589.51	27653.74
51.08	222.06	463.04	1024.42	2187.68	3951.42	7584.12	8558.43	10226.27	11806.31
124.76	337.26	1069.31	3259.86	6319.09	9674.22	19704.88	22349.91	25077.98	27689.22
98.50	239.31	527.31	1240.49	1898.61	2692.81	3829.14	4329.33	4809.27	5296.33
						927748	659267	615535	3595569
						6280398	5984712	6324536	6948217
						1603108	2124574	1915636	2160735
36.92	114.07	154.30	230.46	361.24	493.04	671.66	758.41	784.24	800.56
183.40	241.20	349.47	426.76	509.68	584.98	543.48	570.10	594.94	618.43
347.56	339.30	333.72	366.99	362.30	358.57	342.29	342.56	342.88	347.12
181.47	252.48	240.27	260.11	289.43	264.55	290.81	293.07	296.19	302.89
126.09	253.54	405.95	529.37	572.05	626.23	673.73	691.76	712.61	726.39
11.38	28.68	31.82	37.93	31.79	34.18	23.92	27.36	29.10	29.50
1.87	3.48	7.09	19.61	31.20	23.27	41.43	42.10	43.43	45.38
5.00	2.91	2.73	3.55	2.94	0.74	0.42	0.38	0.35	0.36
2008	2648	1038	1670	2021	2021	2215	2543	2665	2811
174.89	526.48	680.04	2237.51	4485.61	5339.97	6765.08	7591.25	7246.05	8272.05
136.29	432.17	629.72	2142.84	4497.17	5417.16	7575.34	8492.55	8370.30	9613.31
15.57	53.59	64.62	244.61	584.53	685.71	659.87	645.49	593.57	
3.23	16.30	21.69	131.30	339.76	396.13	423.31	408.38	344.86	448.14
125.25	578.55	958.10	1868.06	3904.42	4987.76	7724.85	8494.19	9637.65	11412.84
36.82	180.86	363.37	630.06	1481.75	2159.78	2967.31	3380.30	3779.62	4350.58
46	141	569	737	739	463	1033	1182	1371	1519
12.56	58.78	141.92	462.65	894.30	1663.83	3748.12	4126.03	4460.75	4777.09
269	1030	1611	3298	4655	10189	17090	19410	19971	20690
170	306	701	1400	1306	2039	3323	3730	3128	3735
77	141	396	884	773	1178	1916	2247	1808	1921
3416	3877	5168	7211	9913	15794	23189	22895	24717	25349
3970	6182	7024	8484	13029	20419	22677	24669	23843	24589
	0.4	1.3	2.0	3.4	4.2	14.7	16.8	13.8	14.4

3-1 续表 2 continued 2

指标	Item	单位 Unit	1978年
客运量	Passenger Traffic		
铁路	Railways	万人(10 000 persons)	1302
公路	Highways	万人(10 000 persons)	505
航空	Airways	万人(10 000 persons)	
民用汽车拥有量	Possession of Private Vehicles	辆(unit)	1684
#载客	Passenger Vehicles	辆(unit)	1353
#载货	Trucks	辆(unit)	224
邮电通信	**Post and Telecommunication Services**		
固定电话	Fixed Telephone	万户(10 000 households)	2.68
#城市	Districts	万户(10 000 households)	2.27
移动电话	Mobile Telephone	万户(10 000 households)	
互联网用户	Internet Broad Band	万户(10 000 households)	
国内贸易	**Domestic Trade**		
社会消费品零售总额	Total Retail Sales of Consumer Goods	亿元(100 million yuan)	8.13
#批发零售业	Wholesale and Retail Trade	亿元(100 million yuan)	7.07
#餐饮业	Catering Services	亿元(100 million yuan)	0.29
对外经济和国际旅游	**Foreign Economy and Trade,Tourism**		
全年货物进出口总额(海关)	Total Value of Imports and Exports(Customs)	万美元(10 000 USD)	
进口	Imports	万美元(10 000 USD)	
出口	Exports	万美元(10 000 USD)	
全年货物进出口总额	Total Value of Imports and Exports	亿元(100 million yuan)	
进口	Imports	亿元(100 million yuan)	
出口	Exports	亿元(100 million yuan)	
全年实际使用外资	Total Amount of Foreign Capital Actually Utilized	万美元(10 000 USD)	
全年实现合同外资	Total Amount of Contracted Foreign Capital	万美元(10 000 USD)	
入境游客人数	International Tourists	人(person)	
外国人	Foreigners	人(person)	
港澳台同胞	Chinese Compatriots from Hong Kong Macao and Taiwan Province	人(person)	
国际旅游(外汇)收入	Earnings from International Tourism	亿美元(100 million USD)	
教育	**Education**		
普通高等学校在校生	Total Enrollment of Regular Institutions of Higher Education	万人(10 000 persons)	1.09
普通高等学校专任教师	Full-time Teachers of Regular Institutions of Higher Education	人(person)	2947
中等专业学校在校生	Total Enrollment of Secondary Professional Schools	万人(10 000 persons)	0.68
中等专业学校专任教师	Full-time Teachers of Secondary Professional Schools	人(person)	1020
普通中学在校生	Total Enrollment of Regular Senior Secondary Schools	万人(10 000 persons)	30.61
普通中学专任教师	Full-time Teachers of Regular Senior Secondary Schools	人(person)	19275
小学在校生	Total Enrollment of Regular Primary Schools	万人(10 000 persons)	60.91
小学专任教师	Full-time Teachers of Regular Primary Schools	人(person)	24926

1990年	1995年	2000年	2005年	2010年	2015年	2020年	2021年	2022年	2023年
1438	1519	1693	1924	3327	10681	9797	12164	7322	18265
1801	2611	4530	5364	12758	3663	1209	2024	1438	2137
2.6	37.0	62.0	140.0	379.2	533.1	1238.5	1361.6	824.2	1756.1
39748	86766	129204	347687	807378	1541045	2794278	3025326	3203381	3386516
26032	33968	68625	196415	627849	1400588	2556622	2759683	2925704	3092893
12141	47790	56627	71588	117994	123801	224713	250200	261017	275868
9.87	39.18	106.34	258.90	213.30	165.30	144.78	145.31	147.66	163.20
9.12	36.48	83.08	206.30	177.40	141.00	127.65			
	2.3	60.8	239.0	857.6	1090.4	1154.1	1216.3	1266.0	1315.5
		11.57	74.34	117.30	231.66	445.48	463.04	501.40	559.30
52.82	183.76	344.45	772.65	1725.46	3141.04	4469.13	5126.10	4878.11	5199.03
38.20	134.53	228.75	657.55	1402.27	2648.44	3857.01	4388.16	4192.16	4433.27
2.56	13.35	37.76	108.44	308.11	473.23	586.62	707.78	658.79	732.17
	66587	143935	376213	743776	911424	1998749	3003034	3270583	3074109
	29812	143935	198370	338888	311763	909323	1184182	1157632	1122634
	36775	143935	177843	404888	599661	1089426	1818852	2112951	1951475
						1382.7	1944.2	2208.9	2161.0
						627.6	770.1	777.1	787.6
						755.0	1174.1	1431.8	1373.4
	25294	31981	54158	104011	157851	192456	265840	313738	247773
	47449	44074	112072	120903	303100	585244	968530	784185	587039
20583	54468	103990	120164	230985	332942	108524			
12705	30011	40990	69762	153327	205477	90926			
7878	24457	63000	50402	77658	127465	17700			
0.15	0.19	0.32	0.42	1.14	1.84	0.33			
3.73	5.66	9.30	38.04	50.53	53.62	89.85	69.40	67.07	69.11
7245	7500	8267	18434	26870	30873	42202	41894	41936	40098
2.51	4.79	5.75	4.79	2.12	1.57	6.28	6.40	6.49	6.05
2890	2890	2916	1578	1334	763	3642	4040	4273	4315
22.45	27.15	33.82	30.91	30.18	30.16	39.84	40.70	42.10	43.73
16065	17621	20585	21915	21943	23643	34796	35587	36165	36440
47.57	49.23	41.40	37.88	38.40	41.44	57.01	61.00	64.42	70.64
26922	27417	27417	25201	24801	25795	37219	38467	39874	41373

3-1 续表 3 continued 3

指标	Item	单位 Unit	1978年
文化	**Culture**		
图书馆藏书量	Number of Books in Library	万册(10 000 copies)	341.0
图书出版种数	Number of Publication	种(kind)	389
图书量	Books	万册(10 000 copies)	20166
报纸量	Newspapers	万册(10 000 copies)	25055
杂志量	Magazines	万份(10 000 copies)	2209
卫生	**Public Health**		
卫生机构数	Number of Health Institutions	个(unit)	1017
#医院及卫生院	Hospitals and Township Hospitals	个(unit)	148
卫生机构床位数	Number of Beds	张(bed)	11496
#医院及卫生院	Hospitals and Township Hospitals	张(bed)	9856
卫生工作人员	Medical Personnel	人(person)	24949
#卫生技术人员	Medical Technical Personnel	人(person)	19198
人民生活	**People's Livelihood**		
城镇居民人均可支配收入	Per Capita Disposable Income of Urban Households	元(yuan)	337.8
城镇居民人均消费支出	Per Capita Consumption Expenditure of Urban Households	元(yuan)	317.9
#食品	Food	元(yuan)	181.6
农村居民人均可支配收入	Per Capita Disposable Income of Rural Households	元(yuan)	110.5
农村居民人均消费支出	Per Capita Consumption Expenditure of Rural Households	元(yuan)	83.2
#食品	Food	元(yuan)	58.2
农民人均住宅居住面积	Rural Residential Area Per Capita	平方米(sq.m)	9.6
社会治安	**Public security**		
交通事故起数	Number of Traffic Accidents	起(case)	
交通事故死伤人数	Deaths and Injuries from Traffic Accidents	人(person)	
交通事故损失折款	Property Losses from Traffic Accidents	万元(10 000 yuan)	
火灾事故起数	Number of Fire Accidents	起(case)	
火灾事故死伤人数	Deaths and Injuries from Fire Accidents	人(person)	
火灾事故损失折款	Property Losses from Fire Accidents	万元(10 000 yuan)	

注：1.“职工平均工资”2006年以前为在岗职工口径，2006年及以后为法人单位在岗职工口径。
2.“建成区面积”为全市口径。
3.工业统计指标1997年及以前统计口径为乡及乡以上工业企业，1998年及以后为全部国有及年销售收入500万元以上工业企业，2011年及以后为年主营业务收入2000万元及以上工业法人单位。
4.货运量、客运量中的“铁路”指标，2013年3月铁路系统改革，铁路系统统计数据按新口径执行；“公路指标”自2014年起交通部门执行新的公路运输量统计方案，调查范围较老口径有所缩小，2014年及2013年数据均为新口径下交通运输部反馈数据。
5.从2015年起，全市居民收支调查指标采用新口径。“农村居民人均可支配收入”2014年以前为农民人均纯收入口径；“农村居民人均生活消费支出”2014年以前为农民人均生活费支出口径。
6.规模以上工业“营业收入”，2018年以前为“主营业务收入”口径。

1990年	1995年	2000年	2005年	2010年	2015年	2020年	2021年	2022年	2023年
476.0	524.6	591.7	725.1	941.2	1195.0				
2001	2603	3851	5389	6586	10234				
31685	39025	38471	27919	26603	43860				
46930	54460	109199	113751	184706	136480				
3321	4579	11177	7195	6995	8572				
1300	1185	1414	2138	5086	5947	7514	7515	7665	8136
178	216	231	246	277	269	343	336	329	368
18214	20747	21698	24695	31947	49311	68831	72832	76367	82473
17216	19534	20830	23524	29844	45195	62072	66258	69642	74310
41444	43648	45166	41499	54711	89117	126681	131269	137111	147040
31130	32848	35669	34129	39366	71778	102172	108401	113536	122229
1619.5	4720.6	8471.3	13578.5	25321.1	39888.7	53328.6	57449	59459	62506
1360.1	3830.4	6891.8	9226.6	15973.3	26318.7	34390.8	36866	35788	37831
781.6	1823.6	2387.1	3046.9	5051.2	6415.0	8071.9	8654	8520	8942
731.1	1812.7	3046.8	4812.3	8903.3	14231.8	20432.1	22580	23844	25587
569.8	1373.6	1976.8	2902.8	5406.6	8597.2	12946.9	14591	14883	16267
287.7	770.8	860.0	1134.8	1818.3	2775.5	3931.3	4446	4538	4935
22.5	24.7	28.6	33.8	40.2	52.6	50.3	49.8	47.5	49.2
509	1231	1306	911	774	2946	3313	3317	3257	2937
518	1345	1364	1186	1121	3885	3747	3631	3771	2827
64	369	357	316	189	840	1006	1207	857	704
309	110	1281	1071	791	2609	4319	5907	5892	6535
67	87	26	3	9	12	16	35	13	14
166	925	471	76	462	1571	2153	6232	3817	5494

Notes: 1. The average salary of employees is the caliber data of employees in the post before 2006, and the caliber data of employees in the legal entity in 2006 and later.

2.The "area of built districts" refers to the entire city.

3. Industrial statistical indicators In 1997 and before, the statistical caliber was industrial enterprises at or above the township level. In 1998 and after, they were all state-owned and with an annual sales income of more than 5 million yuan. In 2011 and beyond, the annual main business income was 20 million yuan and above industrial enterprises legal entities.

4. The "railway" indicator in freight volume and passenger volume, the railway system reform in March 2013, the railway system statistics are implemented according to the new caliber; the "road indicators" since 2014, the transportation department has implemented a new road traffic statistics program. The scope of the survey has been narrower than that of the old one. The data for 2014 and 2013 are the feedback data of the Ministry of Communications under the new caliber.

5. Starting from 2015, the city's residents' income and expenditure survey indicators adopt a new caliber. "per capita disposable income of Rural Residents" was the "per capita net income of Rural Residents" before 2014; "Per capita consumption expenditure of Rural Residents"was the "per capita living expenses of farmers" before 2014.

6."Main operating revenue" of industrial enterprises above designated size adopts the statistical scale of "main operating revenue" before 2018.

3–2 国民经济和社会发展比例和效益指标
Indicators on Proportions and Efficiency in National Economic and Social Development

指标	Item	单位 Unit	1978年	1985年
人口	**Population**			
申报出生率	Birth Rate	‰	15.53	11.39
申报死亡率	Death Rate	‰	7.00	6.52
自然增长率	Natural Growth Rate	‰	8.53	4.87
就业	**Employment**			
就业者负担人口	Dependency of Employed Population	人(person)	2.21	1.99
三次产业从业者比例	Composition of Employed Population			
第一产业	Primary Industry	%	66.8	47.5
第二产业	Secondary Industry	%	22.6	31.0
第三产业	Tertiary Industry	%	10.6	21.5
城镇登记失业率	Registered Unemployment Rate in Urban Areas	%		
国民经济核算	**National Accounting**			
三次产业增加值比例	Composition of Gross Domestic Product			
第一产业	Primary Industry	%		21.1
第二产业	Secondary Industry	%		51.8
第三产业	Tertiary Industry	%		27.1
人均生产总值	Per Capita GDP	元(yuan)		1263
资本形成率(投资率)	Capital Formation Rate	%		
最终消费率(消费率)	Final Consumption Rate	%		
固定资产投资	**Investment in Fixed Assets**			
固定资产投资占生产总值比重	Proportion of Fixed Assets Investment in GDP	%		23.7
财政	**Finance**			
一般公共预算收入占生产总值比重	Proportion of General Public Budget Revenue in GDP	%	25.2	14.5
一般公共预算支出占生产总值比重	Proportion of General Public Budget Expenditure in GDP	%	6.3	5.6
农业	**Agriculture**			
人均耕地面积	Per Cultivated Area	亩(mu)	1.24	1.10
每公顷耕地化肥施用量(折纯)	Consumption of Chemical Fertilizers per Hectare	千克(kg)		225
每公顷播种面积粮食产量	Grain Yield Per Hectare of Sown Area	千克(kg)	2475	3864
机耕率	Machine-cultivated Rate	%		
规模以上工业	**Industry Enterprises above Designated Size**			
产品销售率	Product Sales Rate	%		

1990年	1995年	2000年	2010年	2015年	2019年	2020年	2021年	2022年	2023年
12.88	10.03	11.08	11.13	11.82	12.77	10.45	8.21	7.85	7.57
6.54	6.32	7.05	8.35	6.73	6.58	7.31	5.45	9.74	5.74
6.34	3.71	4.03	2.78	5.09	6.19	3.14	2.76	-1.89	1.83
1.94	1.67	1.62	1.62	1.61	1.5	1.3	1.4	1.4	1.3
46.5	35.8	31.7	20.5	18.5	15.7				
32.4	32.9	31.9	32.2	32.1	31.3				
21.1	31.3	36.4	47.3	49.4	52.9				
	2.45	3.70	3.84	2.04	2.01	2.03			
17.3	14.3	10.0	5.5	5.0	3.6	3.6	3.6	3.5	3.4
48.7	46.5	43.9	41.9	37.8	34.6	34.8	34.7	34.8	33.8
34.0	39.2	46.1	52.6	57.2	61.8	61.6	61.7	61.7	62.8
2666	8773	15356	55248	77815	104180	110681	122873	128287	135347
39.1	39.5	40.2	52.6	63.0					
37.8	41.9	56.9	46.9	52.3					
22.1	23.8	32.1	50.8	57.3					
9.0	3.6	5.2	15.2	10.1	9.3	8.9	8.8	8.3	8.3
5.9	4.1	5.8	16.9	10.8	12.7	12.7	11.3	10.2	10.7
1.00	0.94	0.88	0.90	0.87	0.64	0.71	0.63	0.63	0.63
330	569	641	646	626	623	599	584	567	546
4273	5512	5354	6192	6117	5956	6053	6060	6112	6235
					92.0	94.1	96.5	96.6	97.5
	97.12	98.24	98.71	98.23	96.80				

3-2 续表 continued

指标	Item	单位 Unit	1978年	1985年
总资产贡献率	Total Asset Contribution Rate	%		
流动资产周转次数	Turnover of Current Asset	次(times)		
邮电通讯业	**Post and Telecommunication Services**			
每百人拥有电话用户数	Number of Phones Per 100 Population	户(subscriber)	0.60	1.26
每百人拥有移动电话用户数	Number of Mobile Phone Per 100 Population	户(subscriber)		
国内商业	**Domestic Commerce**			
人均消费品零售总额	Total Sales of Consumption Good Per Capita	元(yuan)	182	500
教育	**Education**			
学龄儿童入学率	School-age Children Enrollment Rate	%		99.44
学校教师负担人数	Teacher-student Ratio	人(person)	21.28	16.75
高等教育	Higher Education	人(person)	2.47	6.55
中等教育	Secondary Education	人(person)	16.65	14.46
小学	Primary Schools	人(person)	34.99	20.33
卫生	**Public Health**			
每万人拥有医院卫生院数	Number of Health Institutes per 10000 Population	个(unit)	0.33	0.34
每万人拥有医生数	Number of Doctors per 10000 Population	人(person)	23.3	26.3
每万人拥有医院床位数	Number of Hospitals Beds per 10000 Population	张(bed)	22.0	28.2
市政建设	**City Construction**			
城市人口用水普及率	Coverage Rate of Water Supply	%	99.0	100.0
城市用气普及率	Coverage Rate of Natural Gas Supply	%	17.8	26.3
建成区绿化覆盖率	Coverage Rate of Urban Green Areas	%	12.0	23.0
生活	**Life**			
城镇居民恩格尔系数	Engel's Coefficient of Urban Households	%	57.1	56.5
农村居民恩格尔系数	Engel's Coefficient of Rural Households	%	69.9	51.8

注：1.“一般公共预算收入占生产总值比重”2012年(含)以前为“地方财政收入”口径；“一般公共预算支出占生产总值比重”2012年(含)以前为“地方财政支出”口径。
2.人均生产总值，2000年及以后数据根据全国第四次经济普查修订。

1990年	1995年	2000年	2010年	2015年	2019年	2020年	2021年	2022年	2023年
	12.25	8.45	15.98	13.37	8.90	9.11	8.07	6.69	6.77
	1.69	1.52	2.11	1.82	1.65	1.61	1.63	1.46	1.41
1.89	7.23	18.98	35.31	26.48	18.81	18.06	17.90	18.05	19.84
	0.43	10.81	141.97	174.26	140.93	143.06	148.95	154.40	159.40
1009	3389	6149	27343	50369	55882	55744	63155	59614	63200
99.03	99.40	99.93	100.00	100.00	100.00	100.00	100.00	100.00	100.00
14.20	15.60	15.24	17.40	17.37	15.44	16.58	14.89	14.73	15.51
5.15	7.55	11.25	21.76	22.53	18.76	21.29	16.57	15.99	17.24
12.99	15.30	16.78	14.72	13.33	12.71	11.00	12.37	12.02	12.21
17.67	18.20	15.10	15.48	16.07	15.01	15.32	15.87	16.16	17.07
0.34	0.40	0.41	0.46	0.43	0.44	0.43	0.41	0.40	0.45
29.2	27.9	29.5	29.1	46.0	43.0	43.7	45.5	46.7	49.9
32.9	36.0	38.6	52.9	69.1	74.8	73.3	77.5	80.8	85.8
100.0	100.0	100.0	100.0	99.0	100.0	100.0	100.0	100.0	100.0
45.7	72.2	90.7	95.5	97.7	100.0	100.0	100.0	100.0	100.0
30.0	30.5	36.1	36.9	39.9	41.2	40.7	41.7	41.9	44.5
57.5	47.6	34.6	31.6	24.4	23.8	23.5	23.5	23.8	23.6
50.5	56.1	43.5	33.6	32.3	30.1	30.4	30.5	30.5	30.3

Notes: 1."The proportion of general public budget revenue in total output value" was the caliber of "local financial revenue" before 2012 (inclusive); "The proportion of general public budget expenditure in total output value" was the caliber of "local financial expenditure".

2.Per Capita GDP，The data of 2000 and later are revised data after the Fourth National Economic Census.

3-3 平均每天主要社会经济活动
Selected Indicators on Average Daily Social and Economic Activities

指标	Item	单位 Unit	1978年
每天创造的财富			
地区生产总值(当年价)	Gross Domestic Product	万元(10 000 yuan)	646
第一产业	Primary Industry	万元(10 000 yuan)	114
第二产业	Secondary Industry	万元(10 000 yuan)	365
第三产业	Tertiary Industry	万元(10 000 yuan)	167
一般公共预算收入	General Public Budget Revenue	万元(10 000 yuan)	163
一般公共预算支出	General Public Budget Expenditure	万元(10 000 yuan)	41
固定资产投资	Investment in Fixed Assets	万元(10 000 yuan)	
每天生产主要工、农业产品	**Production of Major Industrial Product and Agricultural Products on Average Daily**		
粮食	Grain	吨(ton)	3161
棉花	Cotton	吨(ton)	14
蔬菜	Vegetable	吨(ton)	1348
猪肉	Pork	吨(ton)	67
奶类	Milk	吨(ton)	11
钢材	Steel	吨(ton)	689
发电量	Electric Energy Capacity	万千瓦时(10 000 kWh)	347
水泥	Cement	吨(ton)	2399
化肥	Chemical Fertilizer	吨(ton)	494
金切机床	Metal-cutting Machine Tools	台(unit)	10
汽车	Motor Vehicles	辆(unit)	12
服务器	Server	台(unit)	-
布	Cloth	万米(10 000 m)	38
每天其他经济活动	**Other Economic Activity on Average Daily**		
最终消费量	Final Consumption	万元(10 000 yuan)	
居民消费	Households Expense	万元(10 000 yuan)	
农业居民	Rural Households	万元(10 000 yuan)	
城镇居民	Urban Households	万元(10 000 yuan)	
政府消费	Government Expense	万元(10 000 yuan)	
社会消费品零售总额	Total Sales of Consumption Good Per Capita	万元(10 000 yuan)	261
公路货运量	Highways Freight Traffic	万吨(10 000 tons)	3.2
公路客运量	Highways Passenger Traffic	万人(10 000 persons)	1.4
自来水供水量	Water Supply	万吨(10 000 tons)	36.9
用电量	Electricity Consumption	万千瓦时(10 000 kWh)	754
市内公共车辆乘客人数	Number of City Bus Passengers	万人次(10 000 person-times)	34.0
实际使用外资额	Total Amount of Foreign Capital Actually Utilized	万美元(10 000 USD)	
港澳台及外国来济旅游人数	Compatriots from Hong Kong Macao and Taiwan and Foreigners	人(person)	
每天人口变动和婚姻	**Daily Population Changes and Marriages**		
出生	Birth	人(person)	191
死亡	Death	人(person)	86
结婚	Marriages	对(couple)	
离婚	Divorces	对(couple)	

注：1.“一般公共预算收入”指标1978年到1995年为“地方财政收入”口径，“一般公共预算支出”指标1978年到1995年为“地方财政支出”口径。
2.按照国家统计局经济普查年度数据使用规定，部分涉及国民经济核算的指标数据空缺。

1985年	1990年	1995年	2000年	2010年	2015年	2020年	2021年	2022年	2023年
1682	3787	12973	28657	121618	184603	277074	312699	329335	349518
354	656	1853	2986	6526	8934	9881	11199	11522	11768
872	1845	6038	12793	52563	68959	96796	108112	112197	118137
456	1286	5082	12878	62529	106710	170397	193387	205616	219613
244	339	465	1344	7291	16831	24757	27605	27429	29064
94	224	537	1499	9227	18032	35213	35427	33577	37405
399	838	3089	8382	54450	95847				
4479	4972	6917	6583	7930	7248	7946	8030	8115	8298
136.2	137	79.7	74.7	81	20.2	12	10	10	10
2304	3455	6946	14733	16478	17157	18408	18953	19524	19901
138	215	390	478	597	508	350	422	463	458
23	51	95	194	855	638	1132	1153	1190	1243
1197	1576	2856	6507	26857	19852	63839	57690	55381	53287
724	1225	1884	1898	3601	4818	7560	8633	8717	8848
3699	5796	11644	13291	19994	21411	36290	42770	37304	33683
313	396	384	778	1345	644	577	458	116	807
18	14	11	8	6	10	29	38	34	53
31	17	16	8	581	263	1077	878	450	654
				271	1112	3921	3115	2112	1860
50	55	41	45	22	44	3	3	2	5
780	1580	5524	14833	50253	87412				
638	1274	4567	11098	39460	55221				
367	624	1938	3596	5142	7120				
271	650	2629	7502	34317	48101				
142	306	957	3735	10794	32192				
640	1447	5151	9718	49382	93433	122107	140441	133647	142439
6.9	10.9	16.9	19.2	35.7	55.9	76.5	67.6	65.3	67.4
3.1	4.9	7.2	12.4	35.0	10.0	3.3	5.5	3.9	5.9
40	45.3	57.5	76.7	64.5	87.2	123.0	136.2	138.7	150.5
747	1255	1779	2505	6713.3	7238.5	11855.2	13020.9	13690.8	14817.9
62.2	73.3	73.3	125.9	296.1	256.5	170.6	200.2	134.2	172.7
	8.5	69.3	87.6	285.0	432.5	524.6	728.3	859.6	678.8
27	56	149	285	633	912.2	298.0			
152	183	148	170	184	202	230	183	176	171
87	93	94	108	138	115	160	121	218	129
	103	137	120	153	138	138	135	132	156
		17	20	50	70	100	67	65	71

Notes: 1. The indicator-"general public budget revenue" was the caliber of "local financial revenue" from 1978 to 1995 and the indicator-"general public budget expenditure" was the caliber of "local fiscal expenditure" from 1978 to 1995.

2. Part of index data regarding national economic accounting is missing according to economic census year data use provisions of National Bureau of Statistics.

3-4 国民经济人均指标
Per Indicators of National Economic

指标	Item	单位 Unit	1978年
地区生产总值	**Gross Domestic Product**	**元(yuan)**	**527**
主要农产品产量	**Output of Major Agricultural Products**		
粮食	Grain	千克(kg)	258
棉花	Cotton	千克(kg)	1.14
猪肉	Pork	千克(kg)	5.44
水果	Fruits	千克(kg)	12.65
禽蛋	Eggs	千克(kg)	
蔬菜	Vegetable	千克(kg)	109.84
牛奶	Milk	千克(kg)	0.88
水产品	Aquatic Products	千克(kg)	0.29
主要工业产品产量	**Output of Major Industrial Products**		
钢材	Steel	千克(kg)	48.1
发电量	Electric Energy Capacity	千瓦小时(kWh)	282.5
水泥	Cement	千克(kg)	195.5
化肥	Chemical Fertilizer	千克(kg)	29.5
服务器	Server	台(unit)	-
布	Cloth	米(m)	30.8
其他经济活动	**Other Economic Activity**		
社会消费品零售总额	Total Sales of Consumption Good Per Capita	元(yuan)	182
一般公共预算收入	General Public Budget Revenue	元(yuan)	133
一般公共预算支出	General Public Budget Expenditure	元(yuan)	33
城乡居民人民币储蓄存款余额	RMB Deposits Balance of Urban and Rural Households	元(yuan)	33
城镇居民人均可支配收入	Per Capita Disposable Income of Urban Households	元(yuan)	338
城镇居民人均消费支出	Per Capita Life Consumption Expenditure of Urban Households	元(yuan)	318
农村居民人均可支配收入	Per Capita Disposable Income of Rural Households	元(yuan)	111
农村居民人均消费支出	Per Capita Life Consumption Expenditure of Rural Households	元(yuan)	83

注：1.“一般公共预算收入”指标1978年到1995年为“地方财政收入”口径。“一般公共预算支出”指标1978年到1995年为“地方财政支出”口径。
2.从2015年起，全市发布城乡住户调查一体化改革新口径数据，居民收支调查指标与2014年前分别实施的城镇和农村住户调查的调查范围、方法、指标口径、名称有所不同。
3.根据年末反馈人口数据，修订2020年相关数据。

1985年	1990年	1995年	2000年	2010年	2015年	2019年	2020年	2021年	2022年	2023年
1263	**2666**	**8773**	**15356**	**55248**	**77815**	**104180**	**110681**	**122873**	**128216**	**135347**
336	350	468	429	479	424	322	320	316	316	321
10.22	9.64	5.38	4.87	4.87	2.36	0.61	0.47	0.41	0.37	0.38
10.33	15.13	26.33	31.15	36.10	36.46	19.22	14.11	16.60	18.02	17.75
14.70	12.88	35.81	66.56	78.58	61.89	70.93	69.64	66.64	66.12	67.89
	18.27	41.29	74.29	59.68	56.86	41.22	30.27	32.83	28.79	30.98
173.02	243.10	469.77	960.06	996.29	1041.79	756.41	742.39	744.72	760.09	770.65
1.76	3.46	6.44	12.65	51.68	46.75	36.21	45.65	45.32	46.32	48.15
0.41	1.80	4.72	5.87	7.06	7.63	1.82	1.46	1.51	1.58	1.63
69.6	169.1	195.7	424.0	1623.8	1161.8	2541.7	2574.6	2266.9	2156.1	2063.5
543.9	862.3	1237.0	1231.5	2177.5	2819.9	3326.0	3049.0	3392.2	3393.6	3426.3
277.9	408.0	728.4	866.1	1208.9	1253.1	1451.2	1463.6	1680.6	1452.3	1304.3
18.7	23.6	23.0	46.5	80.3	37.7	19.1	23.3	18.0	4.5	31.3
-	-	-	-	0.016	0.065	0.1	0.2	0.1	0.1	0.1
37.2	38.9	19.9	29.5	13.6	25.7	4.6	1.2	1.2	0.9	1.9
500	1009	3468	6332	25577	44243	49812	49245	55185	52031	55158
183	239	315	876	4409	9850	9851	9984	10847	10678	11255
70	158	363	977	5579	10553	13492	14201	13921	13072	14485
236	985	4115	8266	36239	63358	72550	83570	92136	109076	125257
732	1620	4721	8471	25321	39889	51913	53329	57449	59459	62506
704	1369	3830	6892	15973	26319	33439	34391	36866	35788	37831
439	731	1813	3047	8903	14232	19454	20432	22580	23844	25587
330	570	1374	1977	5407	8597	12300	12947	14591	14883	16267

Notes: 1. The indicator-"general public budget revenue" was the caliber of "local financial revenue" from 1978 to 1995 and the indicator-"general public budget expenditure" was the caliber of "local fiscal expenditure" from 1978 to 1995.

2. From 2015, new caliber data about urban and rural household survey integration reform was published by the city and the survey index of residents' income and expenditure was different from survey scope, method, indicator caliber and name of urban and rural residents implemented before 2014.

3.Relevant data in 2020 was revised according to population data at the end of the year.

3-5 国民经济主要指标及占全国、全省比重(2023年)

Main Indicators of National Economy and Their Proportion in China and Shandong Province(2023)

指标	Item	单位 Unit	全国 Country
区划面积	Area	万平方公里(10 000 sq.km)	960
年末总人口	Total year-end Population	万人(10 000 persons)	140967
生产总值(当年价)	Gross Domestic Product	亿元(100 million yuan)	1260582.0
第一产业	Primary Industry	亿元(100 million yuan)	89755.0
第二产业	Secondary Industry	亿元(100 million yuan)	482589.0
第三产业	Tertiary Industry	亿元(100 million yuan)	688238.0
规模以上工业营业收入	Revenue from Business of Industrial Enterprises above Designated Size	亿元(100 million yuan)	1334390.8
规模以上工业利润总额	Total Profits of Industrial Enterprises above Designated Size	亿元(100 million yuan)	76858.3
粮食总产量	Total Output of Grain	万吨(10 000 tons)	69541.0
棉花总产量	Total Output of Cotton	万吨(10 000 tons)	562.0
固定资产投资额	Investment in Fixed Assets	亿元(100 million yuan)	503036.0
公路货物周转量	Highways Freight Turnover	亿吨公里(100 million ton-km)	73950.20
社会消费品零售总额	Total Sales of Consumption Good Per Capita	亿元(100 million yuan)	471495.0
实际使用外资	Total Amount of Foreign Capital Actually Utilized	亿美元(100 million USD)	1633.0
一般公共预算收入	General Public Budget Revenue	亿元(100 million yuan)	216784.0
一般公共预算支出	General Public Budget Expenditure	亿元(100 million yuan)	274574.0
普通本专科在校学生	Enrollment of Regular Institutions of Higher Education	万人(10 000 persons)	3775.0
中等职业教育在校学生	Enrollment of Secondary Professional Schools	万人(10 000 persons)	1737.9
卫生机构数	Number of Health Institutions	个(unit)	1070785
卫生技术人员	Medical Technical Personnel	万人(10 000 persons)	1248.8
#执业(助理)医师	Licensed Doctors	万人(10 000 persons)	478.2
城镇居民人均可支配收入	Per Capita Disposable Income of Urban Households	元(yuan)	51821
农村居民人均可支配收入	Per Capita Disposable Income of Rural Households	元(yuan)	21691

全省 Province	济南 Jinan	济南占全国比重 (%) Jinan Account for Proportion of Country (%)	济南占全省比重 (%) Jinan Account for Proportion of Province (%)
15.8	1.0244	0.11	6.48
10123.0	943.7	0.67	9.32
92068.7	12757.4	1.01	13.86
6506.2	429.5	0.48	6.60
35987.9	4312.0	0.89	11.98
49574.6	8015.9	1.16	16.17
113496.2	9613.3	0.72	8.47
5586.1	448.1	0.58	8.02
5655.3	302.89	0.44	5.36
12.6	0.4	0.06	2.86
7999.40	615.50	0.83	7.69
36141.8	5199.0	1.10	14.39
175.3	24.8	1.52	14.15
7464.7	1060.8	0.49	14.21
12582.7	1365.3	0.50	10.85
267.3	69.1	1.83	25.85
133.1	15.1	0.87	11.34
88240	8136	0.76	9.22
93.4	12.2	0.98	13.06
37.20	4.7	0.98	12.63
51571	62506		
23776	25587		

主要统计指标解释

国民经济行业分类 自2017年年报和2018年定期报表开始使用新的《国民经济行业分类》（GB/T4754-2017）。该分类是由国家统计局组织修订，原国家质量监督检验检疫总局和中国国家标准化管理委员会于2017年6月30日发布。这次修订是在2011年分类标准的基础上，结合我国经济活动特点，参照联合国《全部经济活动的国际标准产业分类》（ISIC/Rev.4）进行的。修订后的《国民经济行业分类》（GB/T4754-2017）共有门类20个，大类97个，中类473个，小类1382个。

Explanatory Notes on Main Statistical Indicators

Industrial Classification of the National Economy The new Industrial Classification of the National Economy (GB/T 4754-2017) is introduced starting from the compilation of 2017 annual statistics and 2018 monthly or quarterly statistics. The revision, based on the 2011 classification, was organized by the National Bureau of Statistics taking into consideration of the characteristics of economic activities in China and the International Standards of the Industrial Classification of All Economic Activities (ISIC/Rev.4) of the United Nations. The new Classification was promulgated by the former National Administration of Quality Supervision, Inspection and Quarantine and the Standardization Administration of the People's Republic of China on June 30, 2017. The revised version of the Industrial Classification of the National Economy (GB/T 4754-2017) is composed of 20 sections, 97 divisions, 473 groups and 1382 classes.

4

国民经济核算

NATIONAL ACCOUNTS

4-1 各时期生产总值(按当年价格计算)
Gross Domestic Product in Each Period(Calculated at Current Prices)

年份 Year	地区生产总值 (亿元) Gross Domestic Product (100 million yuan)	其中 of which 第一产业 Primary Industry	第二产业 Secondary Industry	第三产业 Tertiary Industry	#工业 Industry	人均生产总值 (元) Per Capita GDP (yuan)
1952	3.83	1.45	1.13	1.25	1.09	121
1957	6.66	1.93	2.24	2.50	2.18	194
1962	6.21	1.03	2.43	2.74	2.36	177
1965	9.68	1.88	4.44	3.36	4.34	262
1970	13.61	2.16	7.69	3.76	7.56	337
1975	16.24	2.90	8.65	4.69	8.46	373
"五五"时期						
1976	18.18	3.34	9.98	4.85	9.72	413
1977	19.98	3.58	11.23	5.16	10.98	450
1978	23.60	4.16	13.32	6.12	12.89	527
1979	26.56	5.01	14.77	6.78	14.10	586
1980	28.80	5.96	15.86	6.98	14.24	630
"六五"时期						
1981	31.56	6.56	17.65	7.35	15.11	681
1982	36.06	8.80	18.55	8.70	15.79	765
1983	42.01	11.62	20.48	9.92	17.96	881
1984	47.99	10.35	25.47	12.18	20.10	997
1985	61.37	12.92	31.82	16.63	27.54	1263
"七五"时期						
1986	71.28	14.82	34.48	21.99	28.69	1451
1987	84.54	17.52	40.29	26.74	32.88	1699
1988	114.22	22.23	57.07	34.92	47.49	2266
1989	125.83	23.77	61.52	40.54	54.66	2466
1990	138.24	23.93	67.36	46.95	60.43	2666
"八五"时期						
1991	163.39	25.38	76.56	61.45	67.73	3109
1992	207.84	27.74	98.36	81.73	86.85	3928
1993	270.76	32.66	133.15	104.96	115.36	5088
1994	371.88	49.44	176.82	145.61	154.49	6946
1995	473.52	67.64	220.37	185.51	194.16	8773
"九五"时期						
1996	580.84	74.24	274.93	231.67	238.31	10701
1997	709.95	82.52	327.97	299.46	278.87	12995

4–1 续表 continued

年份 Year	地区生产总值 (亿元) Gross Domestic Product (100 million yuan)	其中 of which 第一产业 Primary Industry	第二产业 Secondary Industry	第三产业 Tertiary Industry	#工业 Industry	人均生产总值 (元) Per Capita GDP (yuan)
1998	802.16	90.20	366.43	345.53	298.41	14549
1999	881.32	92.52	399.80	389.00	318.80	15863
2000	1048.85	109.27	468.23	471.35	379.07	15356
“十五”时期						
2001	1175.98	112.59	499.58	563.81	405.00	17062
2002	1323.06	114.79	572.55	635.72	465.89	19032
2003	1529.34	118.47	687.31	723.56	570.04	21765
2004	1827.84	135.60	858.25	833.99	725.46	25729
2005	2086.44	150.50	1005.54	930.40	859.24	27338
“十一五”时期						
2006	2417.78	161.70	1134.84	1121.24	961.73	31390
2007	2811.23	169.67	1292.43	1349.13	1091.74	36071
2008	3378.97	194.87	1514.48	1669.62	1280.66	42931
2009	3705.96	206.20	1603.76	1896.00	1313.89	46735
2010	4439.05	238.19	1918.55	2282.31	1572.50	55248
“十二五”时期						
2011	4931.10	259.32	2058.29	2613.49	1661.94	60207
2012	5328.00	272.85	2132.64	2922.51	1711.76	63988
2013	5765.76	302.08	2276.14	3187.54	1764.60	68343
2014	6330.51	315.73	2424.33	3590.45	1861.37	74028
2015	6738.01	326.09	2516.99	3894.93	1924.96	77815
“十三五”时期						
2016	7274.94	328.42	2601.27	4345.25	1966.07	82820
2017	7933.87	323.08	2800.42	4810.37	2062.26	89285
2018	8678.64	332.73	2997.08	5348.83	2100.16	96682
2019	9443.37	343.06	3265.22	5835.09	2167.87	104180
2020	10140.91	361.66	3542.73	6236.52	2382.27	110681
“十四五”时期						
2021	11413.51	408.77	3946.10	7058.64	2706.06	122873
2022	12020.73	420.54	4095.20	7504.99	2777.20	128216
2023	12757.42	429.53	4312.01	8015.88	2886.07	135347

注：1.2000年及以后数据根据全国第四次经济普查修订。
2.经济普查年度，2023 年地区生产总值相关指标为快报数据。(以下相关各表同)
Note: 1.The data of 2000 and later are revised data after the Fourth National Economic Census.
2.In the economic census year, Gross Domestic Product related indicator in 2023 is the express data.(the same below)

4-2 各时期生产总值环比指数(以上年为100)
Circle Indices of Gross Domestic Product in Each Period(preceding year=100)

年份 Year	地区生产总值 Gross Domestic Product	其中 of which				人均生产总值 Per Capita GDP
		第一产业 Primary Industry	第二产业 Secondary Industry	第三产业 Tertiary Industry	#工业 Industry	
1957	97.5	91.7	89.0	112.7	92.3	95.7
1962	105.6	116.7	82.7	121.9	81.3	105.9
1965	120.8	120.4	138.8	105.3	132.9	120.7
1970	113.7	95.9	131.9	100.5	130.8	108.7
1975	139.0	121.5	160.4	117.6	167.8	133.9
“五五”时期						
1976	104.9	93.2	114.6	104.5	113.1	104.6
1977	106.8	95.0	112.3	106.3	113.9	104.7
1978	113.0	99.3	114.2	119.0	111.9	109.1
1979	112.1	120.0	110.5	110.4	109.0	110.8
1980	113.6	124.5	112.5	107.9	105.7	112.6
“六五”时期						
1981	109.5	110.1	111.2	105.1	106.1	108.0
1982	116.0	136.2	106.7	120.2	106.1	114.1
1983	117.0	132.5	110.8	114.5	114.2	115.6
1984	118.4	92.3	128.9	127.3	116.0	117.3
1985	105.4	102.9	103.0	112.6	112.9	104.4
“七五”时期						
1986	110.8	109.4	103.4	126.1	99.4	109.6
1987	112.2	111.9	110.5	115.0	108.4	110.8
1988	119.0	111.8	124.8	115.0	127.2	117.5
1989	103.2	100.1	101.0	108.8	107.8	101.9
1990	108.3	99.2	107.9	114.2	109.0	106.6
“八五”时期						
1991	112.8	101.2	108.5	124.9	107.0	111.3
1992	122.8	105.5	124.0	128.4	123.8	122.0
1993	121.4	109.7	126.1	119.7	123.8	120.7
1994	118.9	131.0	115.0	120.1	115.9	118.2
1995	113.3	121.7	110.9	112.3	111.8	112.4
“九五”时期						
1996	114.9	102.8	116.9	117.0	115.0	114.3

4-2 续表 continued

年份 Year	地区生产总值 Gross Domestic Product	其中 of which 第一产业 Primary Industry	第二产业 Secondary Industry	第三产业 Tertiary Industry	#工业 Industry	人均生产总值 Per Capita GDP
1997	119.6	108.8	116.7	126.3	114.5	118.8
1998	113.8	110.1	112.6	116.3	107.8	112.8
1999	113.1	109.5	111.8	115.4	110.6	112.2
2000	112.1	106.1	110.8	114.9	112.2	111.2
“十五”时期						
2001	111.9	104.3	110.3	115.2	111.7	110.9
2002	113.2	102.7	114.8	113.9	115.2	112.2
2003	115.6	102.2	117.8	116.0	120.5	114.4
2004	115.8	108.8	118.9	113.9	122.2	114.5
2005	113.9	106.7	119.0	109.9	119.9	106.0
“十一五”时期						
2006	115.6	105.6	116.5	116.2	118.0	114.5
2007	115.7	100.4	114.9	118.7	115.3	114.3
2008	112.9	104.4	109.5	117.5	109.8	111.8
2009	112.1	104.9	111.2	113.8	109.2	111.3
2010	112.5	104.6	110.1	115.5	109.5	111.0
“十二五”时期						
2011	110.3	104.0	110.8	110.5	110.9	108.2
2012	109.5	104.7	108.9	110.5	108.9	107.7
2013	109.4	103.6	110.9	108.7	108.7	108.0
2014	108.6	103.9	108.0	109.5	107.4	107.1
2015	107.9	103.9	107.1	108.8	106.4	106.5
“十三五”时期						
2016	107.6	104.1	105.9	108.9	105.6	106.0
2017	107.9	103.4	106.8	109.1	106.7	106.7
2018	107.3	102.7	106.1	108.5	104.5	106.3
2019	107.0	101.3	107.8	107.0	104.1	106.0
2020	104.9	102.2	107.0	103.7	108.2	103.7
“十四五”时期						
2021	107.2	107.1	103.2	109.4	104.4	105.7
2022	103.1	103.0	102.2	103.5	101.4	102.1
2023	106.1	104.1	107.8	105.2	107.9	105.5

4-3 分地区生产总值(2023年)
Value of Gross Domestic Product by Region(2023)

单位：亿元 (100 million yuan)

指标	Item	济南市 Total City	历下区 Li xia	市中区 Shi zhong	槐荫区 Huai yin	天桥区 Tian qiao	历城区 Li cheng	长清区 Chang qing	章丘区 Zhang qiu
地区生产总值	**Gross Domestic Product**	**12757.4**	**2446.9**	**1350.4**	**801.8**	**765.6**	**1327.8**	**400.4**	**1165.1**
第一产业	Primary Industry	429.5		1.8	2.5	1.6	25.3	41.4	99.7
第二产业	Secondary Industry	4312.0	526.0	351.6	227.8	259.1	354.8	167.5	565.5
第三产业	Tertiary Industry	8015.9	1920.9	996.9	571.5	504.9	947.7	191.5	500.0

4-3 续表 continued

单位：亿元 (100 million yuan)

指标	Item	济阳区 Ji yang	莱芜区 Lai wu	钢城区 Gang cheng	济南高新区 Jinan Gao xin	济南起步区(直管) Jinan Start-up Area (Directly under)	南部山区 Nan shan	平阴县 Ping yin	商河县 Shang he
地区生产总值	**Gross Domestic Product**	**268.5**	**1030.2**	**350.1**	**1767.3**	**113.2**	**72.7**	**281.2**	**246.1**
第一产业	Primary Industry	41.0	74.8	12.9	3.5	12.6	10.6	42.2	59.8
第二产业	Secondary Industry	125.4	414.7	226.5	772.2	68.4	18.5	153.7	80.2
第三产业	Tertiary Industry	102.1	540.7	110.7	991.6	32.3	43.7	85.3	106.1

4–4 生产总值(2023年)(分行业，按当年价格计算)
Value of Gross Domestic Product(2023)(Sub Industry, Calculated at Current Prices)

单位：亿元 (100 million yuan)

指标	Item	2023年
地区生产总值	**Gross Domestic Product**	**12757.42**
农、林、牧、渔业	**Agriculture, Forestry, Animal Husbandry and Fishery**	**453.02**
农、林、牧、渔服务业	Services of Agriculture,Forestry,Animal Husbandry and Fishing	23.49
工业	**Industry**	**2886.07**
#开采辅助活动	Mining Support Activities	0.02
#金属制品、机械和设备修理业	Metal Products, Machinery and Equipment Repair Industry	12.36
建筑业	**Construction**	**1438.32**
批发和零售业	**Wholesale and Retail Trade**	**1760.25**
批发业	Wholesale	984.84
零售业	Retail Trade	775.41
交通运输、仓储和邮政业	**Transport, Storage and Post**	**757.34**
住宿和餐饮业	**Hotels and Catering Services**	**173.37**
住宿业	Hotels	16.51
餐饮业	Catering Services	156.86
金融业	**Financial Intermediation**	**1081.71**
房地产业	**Real Estate**	**824.82**
房地产业(K门类)	Real estate industry(K category)	556.80
自有房地产经营活动	Own Real Estate Operating Activities	268.02
其他服务业	**Other Services**	**3382.52**
营利性服务业	Profit service industry	2045.18
非营利性服务业	Non-Profit service industry	1337.34
第一产业	**Primary Industry**	**429.53**
第二产业	**Secondary Industry**	**4312.01**
第三产业	**Tertiary Industry**	**8015.88**

主要统计指标解释

国内生产总值（GDP） 指一个国家所有常住单位在一定时期内生产活动的最终成果。国内生产总值有三种表现形态，即价值形态、收入形态和产品形态。从价值形态看，它是所有常住单位在一定时期内生产的全部货物和服务价值与同期投入的全部非固定资产货物和服务价值的差额，即所有常住单位的增加值之和；从收入形态看，它是所有常住单位在一定时期内创造的各项收入之和，包括劳动者报酬、生产税净额、固定资产折旧和营业盈余；从产品形态看，它是所有常住单位在一定时期内最终使用的货物和服务价值与货物和服务净出口价值之和。在实际核算中，国内生产总值有三种计算方法，即生产法、收入法和支出法。三种方法分别从不同的方面反映国内生产总值及其构成。对于一个地区来说，称为地区生产总值或地区 GDP。

三次产业 三次产业的划分是世界上较为常用的产业结构分类，但各国的划分不尽一致。根据《国民经济行业分类》（GB/T 4754—2017）和《三次产业划分规定》，我国的三次产业划分是：

第一产业是指农、林、牧、渔业（不含农、林、牧、渔专业及辅助性活动）。

第二产业是指采矿业（不含开采专业及辅助性活动），制造业（不含金属制品、机械和设备修理业），电力、热力、燃气及水生产和供应业，建筑业。

第三产业即服务业，是指除第一产业、第二产业以外的其他行业。

Explanatory Notes on Main Statistical Indicators

Gross Domestic Product (GDP) refers to the final products produced by all resident units in a country during a certain period of time. Gross domestic product is expressed in three different perspectives, namely value, income, and products respectively. GDP in its value perspective refers to the balance of total value of all goods and services produced by all resident units during a certain period of time, minus the total value of input of goods and services of the nature of non-fixed assets; in other words, it is the sum of the value-added of all resident units. GDP from the perspective of income refers to the sum of all kinds of revenue, including compensation of employees, net taxes on production, depreciation of fixed assets, and operating surplus. GDP from the perspective of products refers to the value of all goods and services for final demand by all resident units plus the net exports of goods and services during a given period of time. In the practice of national accounting, gross domestic product is calculated by three approaches, namely production approach, income approach and expenditure approach, which reflect gross domestic product and its composition from different angles.

For a region, it is called as gross regional product(GRP) or regional GDP.

Three Strata of Industry Classification of economic activities into three strata of industries is a common practice in the world, although the grouping varies to some extent from country to country. In China, according to Industrial Classification for National Economic Activities (GB/T 4754—2017) and Rules on Division of Three Strata of Industries, economic activities are categorized into the following three strata of industries:

Primary industry refers to agriculture, forestry, animal husbandry and fishery industries (not including services in support of agriculture, forestry, animal husbandry and fishery industries).

Secondary industry refers to mining and quarrying (not including support activities for mining), manufacturing (not including repair service of metal products, machinery and equipment), production and supply of electricity, heat, gas and water, and construction.

Tertiary industry refers to all other economic activities not included in the primary or secondary industries.

5

劳动就业

LABOR AND EMPLOYMENT

5-1 按三次产业分就业人员及构成
Number of Employed Persons and Structure by Type of Industry

年份 Year	就业人员 (万人) Total Employed Persons (10 000 persons)				构成 (合计=100) Composition in Percentage (Total=100)		
	合计 Total	第一产业 Primary Industry	第二产业 Secondary Industry	第三产业 Tertiary Industry	第一产业 Primary Industry	第二产业 Secondary Industry	第三产业 Tertiary Industry
1952	134.26	109.87	5.86	18.53	81.8	4.4	13.8
1957	144.29	118.65	13.12	12.52	82.2	9.1	8.7
1962	137.58	106.50	16.45	14.63	77.4	12.0	10.6
1965	143.67	107.68	20.96	15.03	74.9	14.6	10.5
1970	161.18	118.15	30.32	12.71	73.3	18.8	7.9
1975	192.59	135.95	41.56	15.08	70.6	21.6	7.8
1978	204.04	136.30	46.06	21.68	66.8	22.6	10.6
1980	214.21	135.16	51.30	27.75	63.1	23.9	13.0
1985	245.32	116.59	76.08	52.65	47.5	31.0	21.5
1990	270.54	125.73	87.75	57.06	46.5	32.4	21.1
1991	276.18	130.36	87.99	57.83	47.2	31.9	20.9
1992	280.19	127.09	85.59	67.51	45.4	30.5	24.1
1993	285.69	124.25	89.91	71.53	43.5	31.5	25.0
1994	303.46	122.62	91.64	89.20	40.4	30.2	29.4
1995	324.22	116.13	106.68	101.41	35.8	32.9	31.3
1996	332.33	107.70	113.91	110.72	32.4	34.3	33.3
1997	337.43	108.17	113.93	115.33	32.0	33.8	34.2
1998	341.63	109.32	113.38	118.93	31.9	33.2	34.9
1999	344.48	109.56	112.98	121.94	31.8	32.8	35.4
2000	347.37	109.98	110.81	126.58	31.7	31.9	36.4
2001	350.10	109.99	109.24	130.87	31.4	31.2	37.4
2002	352.70	108.01	109.14	135.55	30.6	30.9	38.5
2003	355.30	104.90	110.60	139.80	29.5	31.1	39.4

5-1 续表 continued

年份 Year	就业人员(万人) Total Employed Persons (10 000 persons)				构成(合计=100) Composition in Percentage (Total=100)		
	合计 Total	第一产业 Primary Industry	第二产业 Secondary Industry	第三产业 Tertiary Industry	第一产业 Primary Industry	第二产业 Secondary Industry	第三产业 Tertiary Industry
2004	358.50	99.30	113.30	145.90	27.7	31.6	40.7
2005	360.00	99.10	114.20	146.70	27.5	31.7	40.8
2006	361.80	99.00	115.20	147.60	27.4	31.8	40.8
2007	364.30	98.80	116.30	149.20	27.1	31.9	41.0
2008	367.36	98.01	116.95	152.40	26.7	31.8	41.5
2009	372.25	97.80	119.15	155.30	26.3	32.0	41.7
2010	373.70	76.66	120.20	176.84	20.5	32.2	47.3
2011	375.50	74.95	120.70	179.85	20.0	32.1	47.9
2012	379.30	74.30	123.10	181.90	19.6	32.5	47.9
2013	382.30	73.40	122.19	186.71	19.20	32.00	48.80
2014	385.70	72.50	123.30	189.90	18.80	31.97	49.24
2015	388.70	71.80	124.70	192.20	18.47	32.08	49.45
2016	394.93	70.90	126.90	197.13	17.95	32.13	49.92
2017	405.38	69.50	129.35	206.53	17.14	31.91	50.95
2018	419.27	68.80	132.17	218.30	16.41	31.52	52.07
2019	492.36	77.42	154.27	260.67	15.72	31.33	52.94
2020	468.90						
2021	470.78						
2022	469.00						
2023	476.80						

注：2020年起，山东省统计局不再反馈“就业人员”分产业相关数据。

Note:Since 2020, Shandong Provincial Bureau of Statistics will no longer provide relevant data of practitioners by industry.

5-2 主要年份职工工资
Wage of Staff and Workers in Major Years

年份 Year	职工工资总额 (万元) Total Wages of Staff and Workers (10 000 yuan)				职工平均工资 (元) Average Wage of Staff and Workers (yuan)			
	合计 Total	国有经济 State-owned Units	城镇集体经济 Urban Collective-owned Units	其他经济 Others	合计 Total	国有经济 State-owned Units	城镇集体经济 Urban Collective-owned Units	其他经济 Others
1952	4881	4587	294	-	442	453	324	-
1957	14553	11654	2899	-	586	621	480	-
1962	19412	16409	3003	-	577	607	451	-
1965	20367	16821	3546	-	617	664	461	-
1970	21226	17314	3912	-	549	578	449	-
1975	29239	22662	6577	-	557	615	420	-
1978	37840	28733	9107	-	578	626	465	-
1980	55900	41809	14091	-	776	821	668	-
1985	92092	67756	24330	6	1104	1169	954	894
1986	111934	84269	27643	22	1298	1384	1092	882
1987	126263	96322	29673	268	1422	1515	1185	1603
1988	166206	130287	35515	404	1806	1946	1427	2304
1989	190106	150899	38654	553	2037	2199	1577	2614
1990	210618	166250	43003	1365	2211	2370	1751	2460
1991	229540	181185	46091	2264	2368	2535	1872	2658
1992	267295	214311	49565	3419	2710	2938	2020	2919
1993	327226	264252	54442	8532	3323	3547	2524	3553
1994	465966	371403	67351	27212	4736	5209	2975	4922
1995	581432	465311	79932	36189	5851	6561	3623	5663
1996	700636	562645	89126	48865	7031	7839	4290	6875
1997	792368	636694	67999	57675	7896	8761	4954	7303
1998	717927	578788	68455	70684	8326	9022	5459	7410
1999	756696	608052	67273	81371	9083	9929	5766	7818
2000	857337	639312	59468	158557	10422	11761	6211	8651
2001	950851	713222	60818	176811	11980	13462	7061	9945
2002	1120837	846978	74672	199187	14395	16362	8188	11729
2003	1256160	930392	69554	256214	16027	18197	9331	12942

5-2 续表 continued

年份 Year	职工工资总额 (万元) Total Wages of Staff and Workers (10 000 yuan)				职工平均工资 (元) Average Wage of Staff and Workers (yuan)			
	合计 Total	国有经济 State-owned Units	城镇集体经济 Urban Collective-owned Units	其他经济 Others	合计 Total	国有经济 State-owned Units	城镇集体经济 Urban Collective-owned Units	其他经济 Others
2004	1420491	1049033	73150	298308	18029	20759	10587	13974
2005	1966782	1126918	77722	762142	20866	24626	11890	18164
2006	2459044	1326412	140974	991658	21808	26550	12332	19305
2007	3086928	1680494	166960	1239474	26085	31910	15763	22500
2008	3735956	2049453	202995	1483509	30798	37191	19296	26645
2009	4241838	2227992	177020	1836825	34544	41239	21365	30368
2010	4695402	2462874	179365	2053164	36833	43339	22593	32740
2011	5569118	2647111	169476	2752531	41959	49342	26646	37851
2012	6458632	2811390	161513	3485729	45924	52845	32180	42294
2013	7927677	2766005	170176	4991497	53650	58842	37264	51891
2014	8464904	2912941	148424	5403539	59534	66810	40170	56945
2015	8885256	3282169	143078	5460009	67112	78733	47013	62283
2016	10068893	3715397	162695	6190800	74834	88887	51370	69107
2017	10694345	3776127	124702	6793516	82192	98770	54790	75814
2018	11496722	3869498	98327	7528898	89168	109052	62941	81935
2019	14170697	4846897	87776	9236024	97482	123249	66047	88204
2020	16196772				104990			
2021	18110031				114596			
2022	19250769				123902			
2023	20384867				129222			

注：1.本表中1998年及以后年份数据均为在岗职工口径，国有、集体、其他分组按1998年新标准。2006年及以后年份数据为非私营单位从业人员口径。
2.2020年起，国家统计局修订劳动工资统计报表制度，山东省统计局未反馈国有经济、城镇集体经济、其他经济相关分类数据。

Notes:1.In this table, the data for 1998 and subsequent years are the caliber of on-the-job workers, and the data of state-owned, collective and other groups base the new standard in 1998. Data for 2006 and subsequent years are the caliber of employees in non-private units.
2.Since 2020, the National Bureau of Statistics has revised the statistical system of labor wages and salaries, and the Provincial Bureau of Statistics has not given classified data of state-owned economy, urban collective economy and other economies.

5-3 城镇非私营单位就业人员人数(2023年)
Number of Employed Persons in Urban Non-Private Units(2023)

单位：人 (person)

指标	Item	就业人员 Employed Persons	#在岗职工 Staff and Workers
合计	**Total**	**1565449**	**1459220**
按国民经济行业分组	**Grouped by Sector**		
农、林、牧、渔业	Agriculture,Forestry,Animal Husbandry and Fishing	778	749
采矿业	Mining	11246	11008
制造业	Manufacturing	250380	245177
电力、热力、燃气及水生产和供应业	Production and Distribution of Electricity, Heating Power, Gas and Water	18293	17947
建筑业	Construction	236668	190880
批发和零售业	Wholesale and Retail Trade	102524	99941
交通运输、仓储和邮政业	Traffic,Transport,Storage and Post	69032	68065
住宿和餐饮业	Hotels and Catering Services	29603	28140
信息传输、软件和信息技术服务业	Information Transfer, Software and Information Technology Services	80964	80920
金融业	Financial Intermediation	80823	62294
房地产业	Real Estate	73551	72349
租赁和商务服务业	Leasing and Business Services	92551	79081
科学研究和技术服务业	Scientific Research and Development,Technical Services	76682	75155
水利、环境和公共设施管理业	Management of Water Conservancy, Environment and Public Facilities	18419	16567
居民服务、修理和其他服务业	Services to Households, Repair and Other Services	7156	6244
教育	Education	155236	150698
卫生和社会工作	Health and Social Work	107379	100736
文化、体育和娱乐业	Culture,Sports and Entertainment	21763	20976
公共管理、社会保障和社会组织	Public Administration, Social Security and Social Organizations	132402	132293

5-4 城镇非私营单位就业人员工资总额(2023年)
Total Wage Bill of Employed Persons in Urban Non-Private Units(2023)

单位：万元 (10 000 yuan)

指标	Item	就业人员工资总额 Total Wage Bill of Employed Persons	#在岗职工工资总额 Total Wage Bill of Staff and Workers
合计	**Total**	**20384867**	**19585751**
按国民经济行业分组	**Grouped by Sector**		
农、林、牧、渔业	Agriculture,Forestry,Animal Husbandry and Fishing	7322	7286
采矿业	Mining	130578	129217
制造业	Manufacturing	2874057	2852406
电力、热力、燃气及水生产和供应业	Production and Distribution of Electricity, Heating Power, Gas and Water	233286	231524
建筑业	Construction	2649392	2303168
批发和零售业	Wholesale and Retail Trade	1030116	1016718
交通运输、仓储和邮政业	Traffic,Transport,Storage and Post	832267	828245
住宿和餐饮业	Hotels and Catering Services	175071	171301
信息传输、软件和信息技术服务业	Information Transfer, Software and Information Technology Services	1304556	1302075
金融业	Financial Intermediation	1507635	1335695
房地产业	Real Estate	551805	548453
租赁和商务服务业	Leasing and Business Services	941570	837946
科学研究和技术服务业	Scientific Research and Development,Technical Services	1096379	1078805
水利、环境和公共设施管理业	Management of Water Conservancy, Environment and Public Facilities	167713	162885
居民服务、修理和其他服务业	Services to Households, Repair and Other Services	44905	43386
教育	Education	2377836	2356591
卫生和社会工作	Health and Social Work	1933041	1884282
文化、体育和娱乐业	Culture,Sports and Entertainment	305649	277444
公共管理、社会保障和社会组织	Public Administration, Social Security and Social Organizations	2221687	2218320

5-5 城镇非私营单位就业人员平均工资(2023年)
Average Wage of Employed Persons in Urban Non-Private Units(2023)

单位：元 (yuan)

指标	Item	就业人员平均工资 Average Wage of Employed Persons	#在岗职工平均工资 Average Wage of Staff and Workers
合计	**Total**	**129222**	**133232**
按国民经济行业分组	**Grouped by Sector**		
农、林、牧、渔业	Agriculture,Forestry,Animal Husbandry and Fishing	94455	97246
采矿业	Mining	115502	116781
制造业	Manufacturing	113977	115524
电力、热力、燃气及水生产和供应业	Production and Distribution of Electricity, Heating Power, Gas and Water	128259	128783
建筑业	Construction	108985	116897
批发和零售业	Wholesale and Retail Trade	100330	101666
交通运输、仓储和邮政业	Traffic,Transport,Storage and Post	120166	121342
住宿和餐饮业	Hotels and Catering Services	58903	60247
信息传输、软件和信息技术服务业	Information Transfer, Software and Information Technology Services	158503	158442
金融业	Financial Intermediation	179760	210096
房地产业	Real Estate	75122	75916
租赁和商务服务业	Leasing and Business Services	102499	106032
科学研究和技术服务业	Scientific Research and Development,Technical Services	142634	143124
水利、环境和公共设施管理业	Management of Water Conservancy, Environment and Public Facilities	80239	86229
居民服务、修理和其他服务业	Services to Households, Repair and Other Services	59742	66056
教育	Education	154279	157115
卫生和社会工作	Health and Social Work	182915	190382
文化、体育和娱乐业	Culture,Sports and Entertainment	140621	132902
公共管理、社会保障和社会组织	Public Administration, Social Security and Social Organizations	168291	168152

5-6 社会保障基本情况
Basic Conditions of Social Security

单位：万人 (10 000 persons)

指标	Item	2019年	2020年	2021年	2022年	2023年
职工基本养老保险参保人数	Urban Basic Pension Insurance	408.33	437.30	472.68	488.62	456.57
#企业	Enterprise	378.63	345.26	441.90	457.23	424.53
事业机关	Institution and Government Agency	29.70	18.99	30.78	31.39	32.04
职工基本医疗保险参保人数	Medical Care Insurance	288.04	313.52	336.20	352.82	367.26
参加失业保险人数	Unemployment Insurance	189.70	213.60	226.91	235.43	239.72
工伤保险参保人数	Work Injury Insurance	262.56	278.60	293.47	307.37	310.59
生育保险参保人数	Maternity Insurance	201.24	213.10	235.77	245.62	254.01

注："职工基本养老保险参保人数""企业"及"事业机关"包含离退休人员。
Note: The caliber "number of employees with basic endowment insurance", " enterprise" and "business organ" contains the retired after.

主要统计指标解释

单位就业人员 指报告期末最后一日在本单位工作，并取得工资或其他形式劳动报酬的人员数。该指标为时点指标，不包括最后一日当天及以前已经与单位解除劳动合同关系的人员，是在岗职工、劳务派遣人员及其他就业人员之和。就业人员不包括：

(1)离开本单位仍保留劳动关系，并定期领取生活费的人员；

(2)在本单位实习的各类在校学生；

(3)本单位以劳务外包形式使用的人员，如：建筑业整建制使用的人员。

在岗职工 指在本单位工作且与本单位签订劳动合同，并由单位支付各项工资和社会保险、住房公积金的人员，以及上述人员中由于学习、病伤、产假等原因暂未工作仍由单位支付工资的人员。在岗职工还包括：

(1)应订立劳动合同而未订立劳动合同人员(如使用的农村户籍人员)；

(2)处于试用期人员；

(3)编制外招用的人员，如临时人员；

(4)派往外单位工作，但工资仍由本单位发放的人员(如挂职锻炼、外派工作等情况)。

工资总额 指根据《关于工资总额组成的规定》(1990年1月1日国家统计局发布的一号令)进行修订，本单位在报告期内(季度或年度)直接支付给本单位全部就业人员的劳动报酬总额。包括计时工资、计件工资、奖金、津贴和补贴、加班加点工资、特殊情况下支付的工资，是在岗职工工资总额、劳务派遣人员工资总额和其他就业人员工资总额之和。

工资总额是税前工资，包括单位从个人工资中直接为其代扣或代缴的房费、水费、电费、住房公积金和社会保险基金个人缴纳部分等。

工资总额不论是计入成本的还是不计入成本的，不论是以货币形式支付的还是以实物形式支付的，均应列入工资总额的计算范围。

平均工资 指单位就业人员在一定时期内平均每人所得的工资额。它表明一定时期工资收入的高低程度，是反映就业人员工资水平的主要指标。计算公式为：

平均工资=报告期就业人员工资总额/报告期就业人员平均人数

Explanatory Notes on Main Statistical Indicators

Persons Employed in Various Units refer to the total number of employees who work at his unit on the last day and obtain wages or other forms of payment at the end of the reporting period. This indicator is a kind of time point index and it equals to the sum of the number of employed staff and workers, labor dispatch personnel and other employed persons, excluding those who have terminated labor contracts with working unit on or before the last day of the reporting period. Employed persons do not include:

1)persons who have left their working units while keeping their labour contract (employment relation) unchanged and receiving regular alimony;

2)all kinds of enrolled students who do internship in various units;

3)persons employed due to labor outsourcing, for example, persons employed in the organizational system of construction industry.

Employed Staff and Workers refer to persons who signed labor contracts with working units and working units would pay wages, social insurance and housing funds for them. Persons who have their work posts but are temporarily absent from work for reasons of study or on sick, injury or maternal leave and still receive wages from their working units are also included. Employed staff and workers also include:

1)Persons who should have signed the labor contracts but not (like people with rural household registration);

2)Employees on probation;

3)Employees beyond the staffing quota, for example, temporary employees;

4)Employees who are sent to other working units but still obtain wages from their original units (situations like on-the-job placement, expatriated assignment, etc.)

Total Wage Bill It is revised according to the "Provision of Composition of Total Wages" (Order No.1 by National Bureau of Statistics on January, 1st, 1990), total wage bill refers to the total remuneration payment to all employed persons in various units during the reporting period (by quarter or by year), including hourly-paid wages, piece-rate wages, bonuses, allowance and subsidies, overtime wages and wages paid under special circumstances. It equals to the sum of total wages of employed staff and workers, dispatch labors and other employed persons.

Total wage bill is pre-tax wages, including the room charges, utility bills, housing funds and social insurance paid or withheld by employee's units.

Total wage bill, whether or not included in cost, whether or not paid in money or in kind, shall be included in the calculation of total wage.

Average Wage refers to the average per capita wage during a certain period of time for employed persons. It shows the general level of wage income during a certain period of time and it's one major indicator to reflect the wage level. It is calculated as follows:

Average Wage=Total wage bill of employed persons at reference time/Average number of employed persons at reference time

6

固定资产投资

INVESTMENT IN FIXED ASSETS

6-1 固定资产投资
Total Investment in Fixed Assets

单位：万元 (10 000 yuan)

指标	Item	2011年	2012年	2013年	2014年	2015年	2016年	2017年
固定资产投资	**Investment in Fixed Assets**	**19343389**	**21860756**	**26383337**	**30634425**	**34984158**	**39743278**	**43635821**
按管理渠道分	**By Management Channels**							
城镇集体以上投资	Above Urban Collective Investment	13059328	14005706	18189147	20297503	23817574	27091510	30334660
房地产开发投资	Real Estate Development Investment	5271575	6633153	7211744	9173706	10141433	11639381	12325712
农村投资	Rural Investment	1012486	1221898	982446	1163216	1025151	1012387	975449
按经济类型分	**Registration Status**							
国有经济	State-owned	7334983	6595774	8770551	6421555	8236033	7175934	8700130
集体经济	Collective-owned	1802483	1920132	2165782	2309282	1809902	1298005	1458316
联营经济	Joint Ownership Units		195897	100213	17820	30882	1808	
股份制经济	Share-holding	5682038	1234405	1448535	5814573	7403146	10826143	12722943
外商投资经济	Fund from Overseas	408736	466383	336618	384940	284944	771449	410019
港澳台投资经济	Fund from Hong Kong,Macao and Taiwan	586347	634574	546675	177167	270022	961601	1129955
个体经济	Self-employed	2956158	3318099	30342	4423319	4447149	6788160	39804
其他经济	Others	572644	1169661	2044857	1912063	2360647	1683680	1002734
按投资用途分	**By Investment Purpose**							
第一产业	Primary Industry	486482	624114	982446	1163216	1025151	1012387	975449
第二产业	Secondary Industry	6073178	7337047	9078831	10985386	12173905	13019930	14418169
#工业	Industry	5767374	7018465	8060463	10410562	11478708	12373806	13176351
第三产业	Tertiary Industry	12783729	13899596	16322060	18485823	21785102	25710961	28242203
投资资金来源	**Fund of Different Sources**							
国家资金	State Appropriations	1317777	1693582	1302138	1240862	691574	1360695	1353707
国内贷款	Domestic Loans	1579846	517431	2173131	341374	73212	3656032	3343213
债券	Bond							40902
利用外资	Overseas Funds	68300	226374	262823	32757	44835	327727	250555
自筹资金	Self-raised Fund	14843051	16405182	19166006	19058000	23594834	28216931	28042143
其他资金	Others	3469710	4139026	5741361	454265	342083	10839004	10267805

注：自2011年起固定资产投资统计口径由50万元调整为500万元。
Note: Statistical caliber of fixed-asset investment as of 2011 was adjusted to RMB 5 million from 0.5 million.

6-2 固定资产投资分类(2023年)
Classification of Investment in Fixed Assets(2023)

指标	Item	固定资产投资额比上年增长(%) Growth rate of Investment in Fixed Assets (%)
本年完成投资	**Investment Completed This Year**	**2.1**
按构成分	**Investment by Structure**	
建筑安装工程	Construction and Installation	5.4
设备工器具购置	Purchase of Equipment and Instruments	17.8
#购置旧设备	Purchase of Second-hand Equipment	-36.6
其他费用	Others	-6.5
按产业分	**Grouped by Three Strata of Industry**	
第一产业	Primary Industry	-16.5
第二产业	Secondary Industry	25.3
第三产业	Tertiary Industry	-2.2
按登记注册类型分	**By Status of Registration**	
内资企业	Domestic Invested Enterprises	**7.1**
港澳台投资企业	Enterprises with Investment from Hong Kong,Macao and Taiwan	**-18.8**
外商投资企业	Foreign Invested Enterprises	**4.1**
个体工商户	Individual Industrial and Commercial Households	**-11.0**
按建设性质分	**Investment by Type of Construction**	
新建	New Construction	13.2
扩建	Expansion	17.3
改建和技术改造	Reconstruction and Technical Transformation	19.9
其他	Others	-17.5

6-2 续表 continued

指标	Item	固定资产投资额比上年增长(%) Growth rate of Investment in Fixed Assets (%)
按国民经济行业分	**by Sector**	
农、林、牧、渔业	Farming, Forestry, Animal Husbandry and Fishery	-13.6
采矿业	Mining	-38.0
制造业	Manufacturing	7.2
电力、热力、燃气及水生产和供应业	Production and Supply of Electricity, Heat, Gas and Water	109.1
建筑业	Construction	-32.4
批发和零售业	Wholesale and Retail Trade	23.1
交通运输、仓储和邮政业	Transport, Storage and Post	47.0
住宿和餐饮业	Hotels and Catering Services	37.6
信息传输、软件和信息技术服务业	Information Transmission, Software and Information Technology	-18.9
金融业	Financial Intermediation	-16.3
房地产业	Real Estate	-10.1
租赁和商务服务业	Leasing and Business Services	-10.6
科学研究和技术服务业	Scientific Research and Technical Services	18.4
水利、环境和公共设施管理业	Management of Water Conservancy,Environment and Public Facilities	25.0
居民服务、修理和其他服务业	Service to Households, Repair and Other Service	136.2
教育	Education	-5.8
卫生和社会工作	Health and Social Service	-26.6
文化、体育和娱乐业	Culture, Sports and Entertainment	-0.4
公共管理、社会保障和社会组织	Public Management,Social Security and Social Organizations	-26.5
新增固定资产(万元)	**Newly Increased Fixed Assets(10 000 yuan)**	**11024306**
施工项目个数(个)	**Number of Project under Construction(unit)**	**4363**
#新开工	Started This Year	1463
竣工项目个数(个)	**Number of Buildings Completed(unit)**	**1106**
房屋施工面积(万平方米)	**Floor Space of Buildings under Construction(10 000 sq.m)**	**8137.75**
#住宅	Residential Buildings	4987.75
房屋竣工面积(万平方米)	**Floor Space of Buildings Completed(10 000 sq.m)**	**985.50**
#住宅	Residential Buildings	692.47

6-3 房地产开发投资分类(2023年)
Classification of Estate Development Investment(2023)

单位：万元　　(10 000 yuan)

指标	Item	房地产开发投资 Estate Development Investment
本年完成投资额	**Investment Completed This Year**	**14892441**
按构成分	**Investment by Structure**	
建筑工程	Construction	7834311
安装工程	Installation	488094
设备、工器具购置	Purchase of Equipment and Instruments	14918
其他费用	Others	6555118
按登记注册类型分	**By Status of Registration**	
内资企业	Domestic Invested Enterprises	14370066
港澳台投资企业	Enterprises with Investment from Hong Kong,Macao and Taiwan	378018
外商投资企业	Foreign Invested Enterprises	144357
新增固定资产	**Newly Increased Fixed Assets**	**5376105**
施工项目个数(个)	**Number of Project under Construction(unit)**	**833**
#新开工	Started This Year	93
竣工项目个数(个)	**Number of Buildings Completed(unit)**	**125**
房屋施工面积(万平方米)	**Floor Space of Buildings under Construction(10 000 sq.m)**	**8137.75**
#住宅	Residential Buildings	4987.75
房屋竣工面积(万平方米)	**Floor Space of Buildings Completed(10 000 sq.m)**	**985.50**
#住宅	Residential Buildings	692.47

6–4 固定资产投资资金来源(2023年)
Investment by Source of Funds (2023)

指标	Item	固定资产投资额比上年增长(%) Growth rate of Investment in Fixed Assets(%)	房地产开发投资(万元) Estate Development Investment (10 000 yuan)
本年资金来源合计	**Total Funds of All Sources**	**-1.7**	**24812442**
上年末结余资金	**Fund Left from Last Year**	**-13.9**	**8640597**
本年资金来源小计	**Fund of All Sources in Current Year**	**1.6**	**16171845**
国家预算资金	State Budget	-3.8	
国内贷款	Domestic Loans	27.7	2145524
债券	Bond	481.3	
利用外资	Foreign Investment	27.4	
其中：外商直接投资	Foreign Direct Investment		
自筹资金	Self-Raising Funds	-1.5	4549564
其中：企、事业单位自有资金	Enterprise and Institutions Own Funds		
其他资金来源	Other Funds	-3.4	9476757

6–5 新增主要生产能力和效益(2023年)
Newly Increased Production Capacity and Administrative(2023)

项目 Item	单位 Unit	新增生产能力 Newly Increased This Year
年产5万辆新能源商用车项目	辆/年(unit/year)	2197
汽车发动机部件生产线技术改造项目	辆/年(unit/year)	2000
山东豪驰智能汽车有限公司AC072并线改造项目	辆/年(unit/year)	1152
年产15万吨机械配件改扩建技术改造项目	万吨/年(10 000 tons/year)	15
年产12万吨分条线改扩建技术改造项目	万吨/年(10 000 tons/year)	12
先行区崔寨污水处理厂一期工程	万吨/日(10 000 tons/day)	4
济南市钢城区城市供水能力提升项目	万吨/日(10 000 tons/day)	3
钢城区里辛街道乡村振兴项目	万吨/日(10 000 tons/day)	1.1
在水一方商务休闲服务中心项目	万吨/日(10 000 tons/day)	1.1
高钙新材料项目	万吨/日(10 000 tons/day)	1.1

6-6 房地产开发建设情况
Basic Situations of Real Estate Development

单位：万元 (10 000 yuan)

指标	Item	2019年	2020年	2021年	2022年	2023年
计划总投资	**Intended Investment**	**111989855**	**120132064**	**122030897**	**114367104**	**115376567**
本年完成投资	**Investment Completed in Current Year**	**15769302**	**17076304**	**19280018**	**18308037**	**14892441**
按构成分	**Grouped by Use of Funds**					
建筑工程	Construction	9183871	10195398	9012796	8861731	7834311
安装工程	Installation	1606223	1172528	828597	384031	488094
设备、工器具购置	Purchase of Equipment and Instruments	406018	265076	44903	24731	14918
其他费用	Others	4573190	5443302	9393722	9037544	6555118
#旧建筑物购置费	Purchase of Used Building	9701	6041	2211	15800	6368
土地购置	Value of Land Purchased	4231601	5040479	8497926	8471035	5877508
按工程用途分	**Grouped by Use of Buildings**					
住宅	Residential Buildings	11356997	12043120	13513858	12476265	10842945
办公楼	Office Buildings	1312853	1693130	1433323	2098742	1382748
商业营业用房	Buildings for Business Use	1662057	1693638	1734079	1216401	1118608
其他	Others	1437395	1646416	2598758	2516629	1548140
本年新增固定资产	**Newly Increased Fixed Assets**	**3988646**	**5297407**	**7149999**	**4160000**	**5376105**
待开发土地面积(万平方米)	Area of Land Pending for Development (10 000 sq.m)	455.30	278.98	349.94	272.00	309.30
本年土地购置面积(万平方米)	Area of Land Purchased in the Year(10 000 sq.m)	280.40	106.04	189.99	46.89	
房屋施工面积(万平方米)	Floor Space of Buildings under Construction(10 000 sq.m)	9979.96	10353.04	10156.54	8604.93	8137.75
房屋竣工面积(万平方米)	Floor Space of Buildings Completed(10 000 sq.m)	1070.03	1272.97	1115.66	714.99	985.50
竣工房屋价值	Value of Buildings Completed	2844724	3321996	3335553	2038727	3928428
竣工住宅(套)	Residential Buildings Completed(unit)	60422	77790	64928	40794	55617

注：2023年起，指标“本年土地购置面积”不再进行统计。
Note:Starting from 2023, the item "Area of Land Purchased in the Year" shall not be calculated for statistics.

6–7 房地产开发公司经营情况
Real Estate Development and Management

单位：万元 (10 000 yuan)

指标	Item	2019年	2020年	2021年	2022年	2023年
开发公司个数(个)	**Number of Real Estate Enterprises(unit)**	**710**	**704**	**655**	**674**	**658**
企业资本金	**Enterprises Funds**	**14920358**	**15884470**	**16394299**	**17588114**	**18388529**
资产与负债	**Assets and Liabilities**					
资产总计	Total Assets	128868654	136819137	142473813	144643628	139821803
负债总计	Total Liabilities	106654306	113236782	117808688	118769495	112246943
所有者权益	Owners' Equity	22214348	23582355	16394299	25874133	27574860
损益情况	**Net Income or Loss**					
营业收入	Business Revenue	14411472	14853884	18351536	16591169	18599842
土地转让收入	Revenues from Land Transfer	150739	344311	339936	228303	127
商品房销售收入	Revenues from Commercial Housing Sold	11656310	11934688	15836088	14185254	17312216
房屋出租收入	Revenue from House Leasing	99996	109568	170083	133884	122106
其他收入	Others	134461	472363	877906	572082	787138
营业成本	Business Cost	10131040	11087743	14419864	14049279	15116085
税金及附加	Taxes and Other Charges	1036931	977022	989222	772482	882317
利润总额	Total Profits	2287980	1719277	1715428	470150	1285032
房屋销售与出租	**House for Sales and Rent**					
本年实际销售房屋面积(平方米)	Floor Space of Commercial Buildings Sold(sq.m)	12464708	13357486	15481974	12419469	11702186
#住宅(平方米)	Residential Buildings(sq.m)	10206808	11452394	13001987	9070928	8255244
本年房屋实际销售额	Total Sale of Commercial Buildings	13807789	15719460	19569740	15145712	15534755
#住宅	Residential Buildings	11738543	14065259	17216533	12217238	12182917
待售房屋面积(平方米)	Floor Space of Waiting For Sold(sq.m)	1064915	1474183	2100169	2481683	4523484
#住宅(平方米)	Residential Buildings(sq.m)	635088	906322	1203741	1382209	2270791
出租房屋面积(平方米)	Floor Space of House Leasing(sq.m)	39132	2385	1165	76236	76298

6-8 房地产开发公司经营情况(2023年)
Real Estate Development and Management(2023)

单位：万元 (10 000 yuan)

指标	Item	合计 Total	内资企业 Domestic Invested Enterprises 小计 Total	#国有 State-owned	港澳台投资企业 Enterprises with Investment from Hong Kong, Macao and Taiwan	外商投资企业 Foreign Invested Enterprises
开发公司个数(个)	**Number of Real Estate Enterprises(unit)**	**658**	**629**	**183**	**24**	**5**
按资质分	**by Qualification Criteria**					
#一级资质	First Grade	29	28	18	1	
二级资质	Second Grade	224	218	76	6	
三级资质	Third Grade	45	44	9		1
四级资质	Forth Grade	6	5	2	1	
企业资本金	**Enterprises Funds**	**18388529**	**16319640**	**7476224**	**1942720**	**126168**
资产与负债	**Assets and Liabilities**					
资产总计	Total Assets	139821803	134903235	77275401	4379136	539431
负债总计	Total Liabilities	112246943	109491344	60995411	2361076	394523
所有者权益	Owners' Equity	27574860	25411891	16279990	2018060	144909
损益情况	**Net Income or Loss**					
营业收入	Business Revenue	18599842	17597483	7611696	899266	103094
土地转让收入	Revenues from Land Transfer	127	127	127		
商品房销售收入	Revenues from Commercial Housing Sold	17312216	16399483	6738557	809716	103017
房屋出租收入	Revenue from House Leasing	122106	79938	58212	42091	77
其他收入	Others	787138	774729	594071	12409	
营业成本	Business Cost	15116085	14339174	6074779	674788	102124
税金及附加	Taxes and Other Charges	882317	827750	472195	53976	591
利润总额	Total Profits	1285032	1209554	732418	127496	-52018

主要统计指标解释

固定资产投资 指以货币形式表现的在一定时期内建造和购置固定资产的工作量以及与此有关的费用的总称。

房地产开发投资 指房地产开发企业本年完成的全部用于房屋建设工程、土地开发工程的投资额以及公益性建筑和土地购置费等的投资。

国家预算内资金 国家预算包括一般预算、政府性基金预算、国有资本经营预算和社保基金预算。各类预算中用于固定资产投资的资金全部作为国家预算资金填报，其中一般预算中用于固定资产投资的部分包括基建投资、车购税、灾后恢复重建基金和其他财政投资。各级政府债券也应归入国家预算资金。

国内贷款 指报告期固定资产投资项目单位向银行及非银行金融机构借入用于固定资产投资的各种国内借款，包括银行利用自有资金及吸收存款发放的贷款、上级拨入的国内贷款、国家专项贷款（包括煤代油贷款、劳改煤矿专项贷款等），地方财政专项资金安排的贷款、国内储备贷款、周转贷款等。

债券 指企业或金融机构为筹集用于固定资产投资的资金向投资者出具的承诺按一定发行条件还本付息的债务凭证，包括金融债券和企业债券。

利用外资 指报告期收到的境外（包括外国及港澳台地区）资金(包括设备、材料、技术在内)。包括对外借款(外国政府贷款、国际金融组织贷款、出口信贷、外国银行商业贷款、对外发行债券和股票)、外商直接投资、外商其他投资(包括补偿贸易、加工装配由外商提供的设备价款、国际租赁、外商投资收益的再投资资金)。不包括我国自有外汇资金(国家外汇、地方外汇、留成外汇、调剂外汇和国内银行自有资金发放的外汇贷款等)。各类外资按报告期的外汇牌价（中间价）折成人民币计算。

自筹资金 指在报告期内筹集的用于项目建设和购置的资金。包括自有资金、股东投入资金和借入资金，但不包括各类财政性资金、从各类金融机构借入资金和国外资金。

其他资金来源 指在报告期收到的除以上各种资金之外的用于固定资产投资的资金。包括社会集资、个人资金、无偿捐赠的资金及其他单位拨入的资金等。

固定资产投资按国民经济行业分 指根据其从事的社会经济活动性质对各类单位进行的分类。应根据建设项目建成投产后的主要产品种类或主要用途及社会经济活动种类来划分，不能根据项目单位本身的行业类别来划分。如果项目投产后有几种产品，应根据主要产品来确定行业类别。一般情况下，一个建设项目只能属于一种国民经济行业。

固定资产投资按建设性质分 按整个建设项目情况来确定。建设项目的性质一般分为新建、扩建、改建和技术改造、单纯建造生活设施、迁建、恢复、单纯购置。农户投资不划分建设性质。

（1）新建 指从无到有“平地起家”开始建设的项目。现有企业、事业、行政单位投资的项目一般不属于新建。但如有的单位原有基础很小，经过建设后新增的固定资产价值超过该企业、事业、行政单位原有固定资产价值（原值）三倍以上的，也应作为新建。

（2）扩建 指在厂内或其他地点，为扩大原有产品的生产能力（或效益）或增加新的产品生产能力，而增建的生产车间（或主要工程）、分厂、独立的生产线等项目。行政、事业单位在原单位增建业务性用房（如学校增建教学用房、医院增建门诊部、病房等）也作为扩建。

现有企、事业单位为扩大原有主要产品生产能力或增加新的产品生产能力，增建一个或几个主要生产车间（或主要工程）、分厂，同时进行一些更新改造工程的，也应作为扩建。

（3）改建和技术改造 指现有企业、事业单位对原有设施进行技术改造或更新（包括相应配套的辅助性生产、生活福利设施）的建设项目。改建项目包括企业、事业单位为适应市场变化的需要，而改变企业的主要产品种类（如军工企业转民用产品等）的建设项目；原有产品生产作业线由于各工序（车间）之间能力不平衡，为填平补齐充分发挥原有生产能力而增建但不增加主要产品生产能力的建设项目。技术改造是指企业、事业单位在现有基础上用先进的技术代替落后的技术，用先进的工艺和装备代替落后的工艺和装备，以改变企业落后的技术经济面貌，实现以内涵为主的扩大再生产，达到提高产品质量、促进产品更新换代、节约能源、降低消耗、扩大生产规模、全面提高社会经效益的目的。技术改造具体包括以下内容：机器设备和工具的更新改造；生产工艺改革、节约能源和原材料的改造；厂房建筑和公共设施的改造；保护环境进行的“三废”治理改造；劳动条件和生产环境的改造等。

固定资产投资按构成分

（1）建筑工程 指各种房屋、建筑物的建造工程。这部分投资额必须兴工动料，通过施工活动才能实现，是固定资产投资额的重要组成部分。

（2）安装工程 指各种设备、装置的安装工程。

在安装工程中，不包括被安装设备本身价值。

（3）设备工器具购置 指报告期内购置或自制的，达到固定资产标准的设备、工具、器具的价值。新建单位及扩建单位的新建车间，按照设计或计划要求购置或自制的全部设备、工具、器具，不论是否达到固定资产标准均计入“设备工器具购置”中。

（4）其他费用 指在固定资产建造和购置过程中发生的，除建筑安装工程和设备、工器具购置投资完成额以外的应当分摊计入固定资产投资的费用，不指经营中财务上的其他费用。

新增生产能力(或工程效益)名称 指建成投产项目或工程新增生产能力(或工程效益)的名称。

待开发土地面积 指房地产开发企业经有关部门批准，通过各种方式获得土地使用权，但尚未开工建设的土地面积。

本年土地购置面积 指房地产开发企业本年通过各种方式获得土地使用权的土地面积。房屋施工面积 指报告期内施工的全部房屋建筑面积。

房屋施工面积 指房地产开发企业本年施工的全部房屋建筑面积。包括本年新开工的房屋建筑面积、上年跨入本年继续施工的房屋建筑面积、上年停缓建在本年恢复施工的房屋建筑面积、本年竣工的房屋建筑面积以及本年施工后又停缓建的房屋建筑面积。多层建筑应填各层建筑面积之和。

房屋竣工面积 指房地产开发企业本年按照设计要求已全部完工，达到住人和使用条件，经验收鉴定合格或达到竣工验收标准，可正式移交使用的各栋房屋建筑面积的总和。

商品房销售面积 指房地产开发企业本年出售商品房屋的合同总面积(即双方签署的正式买卖合同中所确定的建筑面积)。

商品房销售额 指房地产开发企业本年出售商品房屋的合同总价款(即双方签署的正式买卖合同中所确定的合同总价)。该指标与商品房销售面积同口径。

Explanatory Notes on Main Statistical Indicators

Total Investment in Fixed Assets refers to the volume of activities in construction and purchases of fixed assets and related fees during a certain period of time, expressed in monetary terms.

Investment in Real Estate Development refers to the investment made by real estate development enterprises in the construction of buildings, development of land, nonprofit buildings and value of land purchased.

Fund from the State Budget State budget consists of general budget, government fund budget, operation budget of state-owned assets and social security fund budget. Funds for investment in fixed assets from various budgets are reported as fund from the state budget, of which, the general budget utilized on fixed assets investment includes investment on infrastructure construction, vehicle purchase tax, post-disaster restoration and reconstruction funds and other financial investment. Government bonds at all levels should also be included.

Domestic Loans refer to loans of various forms borrowed by investing units from banks and non-bank financial institutions during the reference period for the purpose of investment in fixed assets, including loans issued by banks from their self-owned funds and deposit, loans appropriated by higher responsible authorities, special loans by government (including loan for substituting petroleum with coal, special loans for reform-through-labour coal mines), loans arranged by local government from special funds, domestic reserve loan, and revolving loan, etc.

Bond refer to the certificate of indebtedness issued by the enterprise or the financial institution to the investor for raising the capital of fixed-asset investment with capital and interest promised to be repaid as per certain issue terms, including financial bond and enterprise bond.

Foreign Investment refers to overseas (including foreign countries, Hongkong, Macao and Taiwan) funds received during the reference period (covering equipment, materials and technology), including foreign borrowings (loans from foreign governments and international financial institutions, export credit, commercial loans from foreign banks, issue of bonds and stocks overseas), foreign direct investment and other foreign investments (including funds from foreign direct investment income that are reinvested in fixed assets domestically). Excluded from this category is capital in foreign exchanges owned by China (foreign exchanges owned by the central and local governments, foreign exchanges retained by enterprises, foreign exchanges by enterprises through the regulating mechanism, loans in foreign exchanges issued by the Bank of China with its own fund, etc.). In calculating the utilization of foreign capital, foreign currencies are converted into Chinese Renminbi applying the exchange rate (central parity rate) at the end of the reference period.

Self-raised Funds refer to funds for investment in fixed assets received during the reference period by investing units, including investment in fixed assets using own funds of various enterprises and institutions or funds raised from other units other than financial funds, funds borrowed from financial institutions and overseas funds.

Other Funds refer to funds for investment in fixed assets received from sources other than those listed above, including funds raised from individuals and through donations, and funds transferred from other units.

Investment in Fixed Assets by Sector refers to the classification of investment by the nature of social economic activities the investing units are engaged in. The classification of construction projects by sector is determined by the major products or the purpose of the projects when they are put into production or use, and by the nature of their social economic activities, instead of being determined by industrial classification of the project enterprises. The project will be classified according to major product if there are several kinds of products yielded. In general, one project can only be classified into one sector.

Investment in Fixed Assets by Type of Construction Construction projects in general can be classified, by the type of construction, into new construction, expansion, reconstruction and technical transformation, purely construction of living facilities, moving, restoration and purely purchasing. However, investment by type of construction is not applied to investment by real-estate development units and investment by rural households.

(1) New construction in general refers to construction projects, which start from scratch. The existing projects invested by enterprises, institutions and administrative agencies cannot be classified as new construction. In case the size of the existing unit is quite small, and the value of newly added fixed assets is more than three times of the original value, the expansion will be considered as new construction.

(2) Expansion refers to projects of construction of new production workshop, branch factory or independent production line within a factory or in other locations, for the purpose of increasing the production capacity (or improving efficiency) or adding new production capacity. Newly constructed accommodation for the operation of institutions and administrative organizations (such as newly constructed buildings for teaching in schools, buildings for clinics or wards in hospitals, etc.) are also classified as expansion.

Also included in expansion are investments by existing enterprises or institutions in building major production line(s) or branch factory (ies) along with some work on innovation, for the purpose of expanding the production capacity of original products or producing new products.

(3) Reconstruction and technical transformation refers to construction projects by existing enterprises or institutions in innovation

or technical transformation of the old facilities (including auxiliary production equipment and welfare facilities). Also considered as reconstruction is the construction of new workshops by the existing enterprises or institutions to change the variety of products to meet the market demand (such as the production of civil products by defence industries), or to bring the designed production capacity into full play through a more balanced production process on production lines. Technical transformation refers to replacement of old technology or equipment by new technology or equipment, in order to expand the reproduction through improvement of technology contents in production, to improve product quality, to promote new products, to save energy, to reduce consumption, to expand the production scale and to improve overall social-economic efficiency. Contents of technical transformation include: updating of machinery, equipment and tools; reforming production process by using energy or materials saving technology; construction of factory workshops and transformation of public facilities; treatment transformation of "three wastes" (waste gas, waste water and industrial residue) aiming at environmental protection; improvement of working conditions and environment, etc.

Investment in Fixed Assets by Structure

(1) Construction refers to the construction of houses and buildings, also known as work volume of construction. This part of investment can only be achieved through construction activities, it is the major component of the total investment in fixed assets.

(2) Installation refers to the installation of various kinds of equipment and instruments, also known as work volume of installation.

The value of equipment installed itself is not included in the value of installation projects.

(3) Purchase of equipment and instruments refers to the total value of equipment, tools, and instruments purchased or self-produced which come up to the cut-off point for fixed assets during the reference period. Equipment, tools and instruments purchased or self-produced for new workshops by newly established or expanded units are categorized as "purchase of equipment and instruments" no matter whether they come up to the cut-off point for fixed assets.

(4) Other expenses refer to expenses arising during the construction or purchase of fixed assets other than those expenses on construction, installation and purchase of equipment and instruments. Other financial expenses arising in operation are not included.

Newly Increased Production Capacity (or Project Efficiency) refers to the name of new production capacity (or project benefit) of the project or the engineering completed and put into operation.

Area of Land Pending for Development refers to the area of land with its use rights already approved by authorities and obtained by real estate development enterprises but the land development not yet started.

Area of Land Purchased in the Year refers to the area of land with its use rights already obtained in the year by real estate development enterprises.

Floor Space of Buildings under Construction refers to the total space area of the buildings under construction in the year by real estate development enterprises. It includes buildings started in the year, continued from the previous year, suspended in earlier years but restarted in the year, completed in the year, and buildings under construction but suspended in the year. The floor space of a multi-storied building should be the sum of floor space of all the stories.

Floor Space of Buildings Completed refers to the total floor space area of each building completed in the year by real estate development enterprises, which meet the requirements as designed, up to the standard for being resided in and put into use, has been checked and accepted by departments concerned as qualified or up to the standard of buildings completed and can be handed over for putting into use.

Floor Space of Commercial Buildings Sold refers to total contracted area of commercial buildings (i.e. area of floor space as designated in the formal contracts signed by both sides) sold by real estate development enterprises in the year.

Sales of Commercial Buildings refers to the total contracted value (i.e. value of sales/purchase for selling/ purchase of commercial buildings as designated in the contract signed by both sides) received from the sales of the buildings by real estate development enterprises in the year. This indicator has the same statistical coverage as the area of commercial buildings sold.

7

城市公用事业和环境保护

URBAN PUBLIC UTILITIES AND ENVIRONMENTAL PROTECTION

7-1 城市道路与公共交通
Basic Statistics on Municipal Engineering and Public Transportation

指标	Item	2019年	2020年	2021年	2022年	2023年
城市道路	**City Roads**					
道路长度(公里)	Length of Roads (km)	6987	7301	7847	8064	8211
道路面积(万平方米)	Area of Roads (10 000 sq.m)	12653	13138	14212	14776	15166
城市桥梁(座)	Number of City Bridges (unit)	1136	978	1004	1044	1084
#立交桥(座)	Interchange (unit)	95	79	79	79	79
路灯(盏)	Number of Streetlights (unit)	213259	185188	204404	231892	260611
人均拥有道路面积(平方米)	Per Capita Road Arae (sq.m)	20.30	20.66	20.88	21.50	21.75
公共交通	**Public Transportation**					
年末营运车辆(辆)	Number of Operating Vehicles (unit)	19676	18915	19219	18134	18335
公共汽车	Buses	8383	8188	8833	7630	7624
#无轨电车	Trolley Buses	109	126	126	278	431
出租汽车	Number of Taxis	11293	10727	10386	10504	10711
客运总量(万人次)	Total Passenger Traffic (10 000 person-times)	99389.9	62425.9	73058.0	48974.7	63031.8
轨道交通	**Rail Traffic**					
配属车辆数(辆)	Number of Vehicles (unit)	204	204	408	408	408
运营里程(公里)	Length in Operation (km)	47.7	47.7	84.1	84.1	84.1
客运总量(万人次)	Total Passenger Traffic (10 000 person-times)	573.5	867.6	5602.9	5455.4	9620.9

注：2020年起，“城市桥梁”使用新统计口径。
Note:Since 2020, “Urban Bridge” will be subject to new statistic specifications.

7-2 水、电、气、热供应情况
Basic Statistics on Water, Electricity, Gas and Heating in Cities

指标	Item	单位 Unit	2019年	2020年	2021年	2022年	2023年
自来水	**Water**						
年末水厂生产能力	Production Capacity of Water Supply	万吨/日(10 000 tons/day)	241.00	243.00	288.90	288.90	288.90
年末管线长度	Length of Water Supply Pipelines	公里(km)	5703.60	6033.59	7077.25	7531.00	8134.10
全年供水量	Volume of Water Supply	万吨(10 000 tons)	44452.30	45182.90	49712.36	50636.04	54939.20
人均日生活用水	Per Capita Daily Water Consumption	升(litre)	134.79	131.58	141.07	143.93	153.93
供水普及率	Coverage Rate of Urban Population with Access to Tap Water	%	100.00	100.00	100.00	100.00	100.00
用电量	**Electricity Consumption**						
全社会用电量	Total Electricity Consumption	万千瓦时(10 000 kWh)	4143022	4338712	4752639	4997126	5408519
工业用电量	Industrial Electricity Consumption	万千瓦时(10 000 kWh)	2215281	2395876	2565881	2630417	2807205
城乡居民生活用电量	Household Electricity Consumption	万千瓦时(10 000 kWh)	776162	796871	865304	976315	1042900
液化石油气和天然气	**Liquefied Petroleum Gas and Gas**						
液化石油气全年供气量	Total Liquefied Petroleum Gas Supply	吨(ton)	45518.0	38353.0	25160.0	38471.0	45820.6
生活用	Residential Use	吨(ton)	25935	22119	12981	14134	9787
居民用气人口	Population Uses Gas	万人(10 000 persons)	59.90	52.59	40.70	41.08	11.08
天然气供气量	Total Natural Gas Supply	万立方米(10 000 cu.m)	143576.00	161034.00	179895.21	197735.00	187264.10
生产用	Production Use	万立方米(10 000 cu.m)	96706.80	113916.82	100508.71	116850.46	123583.20
生活用	Residential Use	万立方米(10 000 cu.m)	46869.20	47117.18	79386.50	80884.54	63680.90
居民用气人口	Population Uses Gas	万人(10 000 persons)	560.90	614.20	639.78	646.09	686.29
供气普及率	Coverage Rate of Urban Population with Access to Gas	%	99.97	100.00	100.00	100.00	100.00
集中供热	**Central Heating**						
管道长度	Length of Heating Pipelines	公里(km)	8893	10426	12836	14381	14835
供热面积	Heating Area	万平方米(10 000 sq.m)	26073	27740	30465	33305	36246

7-3 环境状况及污染治理情况
Basic Statistics on Environment and Treatment of Pollution

指标	Item	单位 Unit	2019年	2020年	2021年	2022年	2023年
环境质量状况	**Environment Condition**						
环境空气细颗粒物($PM_{2.5}$)浓度年均值	Annual Average Concentration of $PM_{2.5}$	mg / m^3	0.053	0.047	0.040	0.037	0.038
环境空气二氧化硫浓度年均值	Annual Average Concentration of SO_2	mg / m^3	0.015	0.012	0.011	0.011	0.009
环境空气二氧化氮浓度年均值	Annual Average Concentration of NO_2	mg / m^3	0.041	0.035	0.033	0.031	0.033
环境空气可吸入颗粒物(PM_{10})浓度年均值	Annual Average Concentration of PM_{10}	mg / m^3	0.103	0.086	0.078	0.071	0.073
集中式饮用水源地水质达标率	Standard rate of concentrate Water Source Area	%	100.00	100.00	100.00	100.00	100.00
区域环境噪声昼间平均等效声级	Area Whole-day Average Noise Value	分贝(db)	54.9	54.4	53.8	55.0	53.8
道路交通噪声平均等效声级	Traffic Average Noise Value	分贝(db)	69.6	69.1	68.8	66.5	67.2
污染物排放情况	**Discharge of Major Pollutants**						
废水排放总量	Volume of Waste Water Discharged	万吨 (10 000 tons)	29261	46493	49649	44595	
#工业废水排放量	Volume of Industrial Waste Water Discharged	万吨 (10 000 tons)	5120	5886	6084	5667	
化学需氧量排放量	Volume of COD Emission	吨(ton)	19131	49922	44799	39166	
#工业化学需氧量排放量	Volume of Industrial COD Emission	吨(ton)	1425	1744	1557	1384	
氨氮排放量	Volume of Ammonia Nitrogen	吨(ton)	1447	3016	2568	2335	
#工业氨氮排放量	Volume of Industrial Ammonia Nitrogen	吨(ton)	78	54	52	45	
二氧化硫排放量	Volume of Sulphur Dioxide Discharged	吨(ton)	17124	15920	13601	12650	
#工业二氧化硫排放量	Volume of Industrial Sulphur Dioxide Discharged	吨(ton)	13353	11356	9458	8838	
氮氧化物排放量	Volume of Nitrogen Oxides Discharged	吨(ton)	41533	52729	55787	48584	
#工业氮氧化物排放量	Volume of Industrial Nitrogen Oxides Discharged	吨(ton)	38022	25382	22763	20539	
机动车氮氧化物排放量	Volume of Vehicle Nitrogen Oxides	吨(ton)		24814	30628	25553	
烟(粉)尘排放量	Volume of Soot and Dust Discharged	吨(ton)	31258	25871	22580	19952	
#工业烟(粉)尘排放量	Volume of Industrial Soot and Dust Discharged	吨(ton)	22404	13414	11047	9426	

注：1.生态环境部以第二次污染源普查成果为基准，依法组织对2016–2019年污染源统计初步数据进行更新，2019年数据为更新后的数据。根据统计规则，2020年之前未对机动车氮氧化物排放量进行统计。
2.根据生态环境部统一工作安排，2020年开始统计农村生活污水污染物产排量；目前2023年环境统计工作只完成了工业源统计部分，生活源、机动车统计正在开展中，尚未定库。

Notes:1.Based on the results of the Second Pollution Sources Census of China, the Ministry of Ecology and Environment organized to update preliminary statistic data of pollution sources from 2016 to 2019 under laws, and data in 2019 are the updated data. According to the statistic rules, the emission of nitrogen oxides from motor vehicles was not counted before 2020.
2.According to the unified work arrangement of the Ministry of Ecology and Environment, the output and discharge of pollutants in rural domestic sewage have been counted since 2020; At present, the environmental statistics work in 2023 has only completed for the statistics of industrial sources, while the statistics of living sources and motor vehicles are undergoing,and the database has not yet been fixed.

7-4 城市园林绿化、环境卫生及其他
Basic Statistics on Parks Green Areas and Urban Sanitation in Cities

指标	Item	单位 Unit	2019年	2020年	2021年	2022年	2023年
园林绿化	**Parks Gardens and Green Areas**						
年末园林绿地面积	Area of Green Space at Year-end	公顷 (ha)	28199.3	31087.8	31761.9	32405.1	35313.9
#公园面积	Area of Parks	万平方米(10 000 sq.m)	3688	3754	4339	4421	4546
人均公园绿地面积	Per Capita Area of Green Space	平方米/人(sq.m/person)	13.2	13.1	13.0	13.1	14.4
建成区绿化覆盖率	Coverage of Green Area	%	41.18	40.69	41.69	41.94	44.51
城市卫生	**Urban Health**						
污水集中处理率	Centralized Sewage Treatment Rate	%	97.73	98.17	98.20	98.23	98.38
清运垃圾	Garbage Clearance	万吨(10 000 tons)	278.75	278.03	296.96	277.77	297.80
公共厕所	Public Lavatory	座 (unit)	1122	1203	1267	1298	1286

主要统计指标解释

年末自来水生产能力 指年底城建部门管理的自来水厂和自备水源的社会单位取水、净化、送水、出厂输水干管等环节的实际生产能力。

供水管道长度 指从送水泵至各类用户引入管之间所有市政管道的长度。不包括新安装尚未使用、水厂内以及用户建筑物内的管道。

供水总量 指公用自来水厂和自备水源的社会单位全年的供水总量，包括有效供水量及损失水量。

生活用水 包括公共服务用水和居民家庭用水。公共服务用水指为城区社会公共生活服务的用水。包括行政事业单位、部队营区和公共设施服务、批发零售业、住宿餐饮业以及社会服务业等单位的用水。居民家庭用水指城市范围内所有居民家庭的日常生活用水。包括城市居民、农民家庭、公共供水站用水。

供水普及率 指报告期末城区用水人口数与城市人口总数的比率。计算公式：

供水普及率=城区用水人口（含暂住人口）/（城区人口+城区暂住人口）*100%

燃气普及率 指报告期末城区使用燃气的城市人口数与城市人口总数的比率。其中燃气包括人工煤气、天然气、液化石油气三种。计算公式为：

燃气普及率=城区用气人口（含暂住人口）/（城区人口+城区暂住人口）*100%

供热管道长度 指从各类热源到热用户建筑物接入口之间的全部蒸汽和热水的管道长度。不包括各类热源厂内部的管道长度。

城市桥梁 指为跨越天然或人工障碍物而修建的构筑物。包括跨河桥、立交桥、人行天桥以及人行地下通道等。

绿地面积 指报告期末用作园林和绿化的各种绿地面积。包括公园绿地、防护绿地、广场用地、附属绿地和位于建成区范围内的区域绿地面积。

公园绿地 向公众开放，以游憩为主要功能，兼具生态、景观、文教和应急避险等功能，有一定游憩和服务设施的绿地。

工业废水排放量 指报告期内经过企业厂区所有排放口排到企业外部的工业废水量。包括生产废水、外排的直接冷却水、废气治理设施废水、超标排放的矿井地下水和与工业废水混排的厂区生活污水，不包括独立外排的间接冷却水(清浊不分流的间接冷却水应计算在内)。

化学需氧量 (COD) 测量有机和无机物质化学分解所消耗氧的质量浓度的水污染指数。废气排放总量 指燃料燃烧和生产工艺过程中排放的各种废气总量，以标准状态下每年万标立方米表示。

二氧化硫排放量 指报告期内企业在燃料燃烧和生产工艺过程中排入大气的二氧化硫总质量。工业中二氧化硫主要来源于化石燃料(煤、石油等)的燃烧，还包括含硫矿石的冶炼或含硫酸、磷肥等生产的工业废气排放。

氮氧化物排放量 指报告期内企业在燃料燃烧和生产工艺过程中排入大气的氮氧化物总质量。

烟(粉)尘排放量 指报告期内企业在燃料燃烧和生产工艺过程中排入大气的烟尘及工业粉尘的总质量之和。烟尘或工业粉尘排放量可以通过除尘系统的排风量和除尘设备出口烟尘浓度相乘求得。

工业粉尘排放量 指企业在生产工艺过程中排放的颗粒物重量。如钢铁企业的耐火材料粉尘、焦化企业的筛焦系统粉尘、烧结机的粉尘、石灰窑的粉尘、建材企业的水泥粉尘等。不包括电厂排放大气的烟尘。

Explanatory Notes on Main Statistical Indicators

Year-end Tap Water Production Capacity refers to actual capacity of such links as water intaking, purification, water carriage and leaving factory water main pipe of the waterworks managed by urban construction department and social unit water source prepared at the end of the year.

Length of Water Supply Pipelines refers to the total length of all municipal pipelines between the water pumps and the user service pipes, excluding pipelines newly installed but not in use yet, pipelines in the water factories, and pipelines in the users' buildings.

Total Volume of Water Supply refers to the total volume of water supplied by water-works (units) during the reference period, including both the effective water supply and loss during the water supply.

Consumption of Water for Daily Use includes consumption of water for public service use and consumption of water for household use. Consumption of water for public service use refers to water consumption for public service in the urban areas, including water consumption of administrative institutions, military barracks, public facilities, wholesale and retail, accommodation and catering industries and social service industry, etc. Consumption of water for household use refers to consumption of water for daily life of all households in cities, including households of urban residents and farmers, and public water supply stations.

Coverage Rate of Urban Population with Access to Tap Water refers to the ratio of the urban population with access to tap water to the total urban population at the end of reference period. The formula is:

Coverage rate of urban population with access to tap water=Urban population with access to tap water/Urban population*100%

Coverage Rate of Urban Population with Access to Gas refers to the ratio of the urban population with access to gas to the total urban population at the end of the reference period. Gas here includes gaswork gas, natural gas and liquefied petroleum gas. The formula is:

Coverage Rate of Urban Population with Access to Gas= Urban population with access to gas/ Urban population*100%

Length of Urban Heating Pipelines refers to the total length of steam or hot water pipelines for sources of heat to the leading pipelines of the buildings of the users, excluding internal pipelines in heat generating enterprises.

Urban Bridges refer to bridges built to cross over natural or man-made barriers, including bridges over rivers, overpasses for traffic and for pedestrians, underpasses for pedestrians, etc.

Area of Green Space refers to the total area occupied for green projects at the end of the reference period, including public recreational green space, protection green land, land for squares, green land attached to institutions, and other green areas.

Public Recreational Green Space refers to green areas open to the public for amusement and rest with the facilities of amusement, rest and services. Its function also includes improving ecology, beautifying landscape, education and preventing and reducing disaster.

Industrial Waste Water Discharged refers to the volume of industrial waste water discharged through all of the drainage system to the outside of factory complex by enterprises during the report period. It includes discharged waste water from production, direct cooling water, waste gas treatment facilities, mine groundwater beyond the standard and domestic sewage mixed with industrial waste water, does not include independently discharged indirect cooling water (voicing split-less indirect cooling water should be taken into account).

Chemical Oxygen Demand (COD) refers to index of water pollution measuring the mass concentration of oxygen consumed by the chemical breakdown of organic and inorganic matter. Total exhaust emission refers to total quantity of various exhaust gases discharged in the process of fuel burning and production which is expressed with 10,000 standard cubic meters each year under the standard state.

SO2 Emission refers to total volume of SO2 discharged into air during the process of fuel combustion and industrial production in enterprises in a given time, and is mainly caused by the combustion of fossil fuel, ore smelting and the discharge of industrial waste gas during the production of sulfuric acid and phosphate fertilizers.

Nitrogen Oxides Emission refers to total volume of nitrogen oxides discharged into air during the process of fuel combustion and industrial production.

Industrial Soot and Dust Emission refers to volume of soot and dust in smoke emitted in process of fuel burning and industrial production in premises of enterprises in the report period. It is calculated by multiplying exhaust volume of dust removal system by dust concentration.

Emission Load of Industrial Dust refers to the weight of particulate matters discharged in the process of production (such as fireproofing dust of the iron and steel enterprise, coke screening system dust of the coke making enterprise, dust of the sintering machine, dust of the lime kiln and cement dust of the building material industry), excluding smoke discharged by the power plant in to the atmosphere.

8

财政、金融和保险

GOVERNMENT FINANCE、FINANCIAL AND INSURANCE

8-1 各时期地方财政收支及指数
Local Government Revenue, Expenditures and Indices in Each Period

年份 Year	一般公共预算收入 (万元) General Public Budget Revenue (10 000 yuan)	一般公共预算支出 (万元) General Public Budget Expenditure (10 000 yuan)	指数(以上年为100) (Preceding Year=100)	
			一般公共预算收入 General Public Budget Revenue	一般公共预算支出 General Public Budget Expenditure
1999	460690	497667	119.9	110.8
2000	490485	547210	110.5	110.4
“十五”时期				
2001	596061	703720	121.5	128.6
2002	662511	775046	115.4	110.2
2003	761064	884597	119.6	114.3
2004	890364	1016953	120.9	115.0
2005	1061547	1206643	120.7	118.7
“十一五”时期				
2006	1284388	1469762	121.0	121.8
2007	1570192	1799787	122.3	122.5
2008	1860155	2213190	118.5	123.1
2009	2101923	2599178	113.0	117.4
2010	2661314	3368037	126.6	129.6
“十二五”时期				
2011	3249315	3968831	122.1	117.8
2012	3808218	4656731	117.0	117.3
2013	4820722	5193190	113.9	111.5
2014	5431278	5714138	112.7	110.0
2015	6143172	6581813	113.1	115.2
“十三五”时期				
2016	6412167	7412641	104.4	112.6
2017	6772100	8340600	105.6	112.5
2018	7528162	10183179	111.2	122.1
2019	8741898	11973158	107.2	107.0
2020	9060751	12887953	103.6	107.6
“十四五”时期				
2021	10076073	12930814	111.2	108.4
2022	10011421	12255733	99.4	94.8
2023	10608223	13652948	106.0	111.4

注：1.2013年财政部门对一般公共预算收入口径进行调整，2013年一般公共预算收入指数为可比口径。2018年以前为区划调整前数据。
2. “一般公共预算收入”与“一般公共预算支出”为预算数据，以下各表同。

Notes:1. In 2013, the financial department adjusted the caliber of general public budget revenue. In 2013, the index of general public budget income index was comparable caliber.Data before the year of 2018 are the data of administrative division before the adjustment.
2."General public budget revenue" and "general public budget expenditure" are estimates, the same for the following tables.

8-2 地方财政收入(2023年)
Local Financial Revenue(2023)

单位：万元 (10 000 yuan)

指标	Item	合计 Total	市本级 Cities 小计 Total	市直 Departments Directly Under the Municipal Government	济南起步区(直管) Jinan Start-up Area (Directly under)	南部山区 Nan shan	县区级 Counties
一般公共预算收入	**General Public Budget Revenue**	**10608223**	**1205155**	**1085436**	**105297**	**14422**	**9403068**
增值税	Value-added Tax	2749481	28190		20841	7349	2721291
企业所得税	Enterprise Income Tax	1151762	16602		15794	808	1135160
个人所得税	Personal Income Tax	484132	2730		2179	551	481402
资源税	Resource Tax	62979	239		111	128	62740
城市维护建设税	Tax on City Maintenance and Construction	453729	12274	7138	3803	1333	441455
房产税	Tax on Real Estates	355397	7653		7349	304	347744
印花税	Stamp Tax	213793	4315		4159	156	209478
城镇土地使用税	Holding tax on urban and county land	263146	5164		4896	268	257982
土地增值税	Land Value Added Tax	1370008	3313		2933	380	1366695
车船税	Tax on vehicles and Their Registration	140246	3		2	1	140243
耕地占用税	Farmland Occupation Tax	70451	11039		11039		59412
契税	Contract tax	652208	20556		20305	251	631652
环境保护税	Environmental Protection Tax	10475	56		53	3	10419
专项收入	Specific Revenue	833960	513136	508636	3522	978	320824
行政事业性收费收入	Income from Administrative Fees	360554	165381	159116	5857	408	195173
罚没收入	Penalty and Confiscatory Income	193161	81209	80810	264	135	111952
国有资本经营收入	Profits of State-owned Enterprises	8801	400	400			8401
国有资源(资产)有偿使用收入	Revenue of Compensable Use of State-owned Resources (Assets)	978477	108995	105436	2190	1369	869482
捐赠收入	Donation Income	2555	212	212			2343
政府住房基金收入	Government Housing Fund Income	238577	223674	223674			14903
其他收入	Others	12875	14	14			12861
政府性基金收入	**Government Funds Income**	**4772689**	**4147702**	**3685096**	**462388**	**218**	**624987**
#城市基础设施配套收入	Urban Infrastructure Supporting Income	544052	333010	282984	49876	150	211042

8-3 各区财政收入(2023年)
Financial Revenue by District(2023)

单位：万元

指标	Item	合计 Total	历下区 Li xia	市中区 Shi zhong
一般公共预算收入	**General Public Budget Revenue**	**8852204**	**1883905**	**982156**
增值税	Value-added Tax	2596462	537476	260388
企业所得税	Enterprise Income Tax	1096249	302183	128869
个人所得税	Personal Income Tax	470392	133659	65019
资源税	Resource Tax	54034	1008	8942
城市维护建设税	Tax on City Maintenance and Construction	429069	91098	35324
房产税	Tax on Real Estates	335419	89410	38228
印花税	Stamp Tax	204067	53153	23640
城镇土地使用税	Holding tax on urban and county land	237993	12144	11715
土地增值税	Land Value Added Tax	1353019	322405	192963
车船税	Tax on vehicles and Their Registration	79038	25091	11696
耕地占用税	Farmland Occupation Tax	53293	16944	2339
契税	Contract tax	611276	131936	76908
环境保护税	Environmental Protection Tax	9483	291	223
专项收入	Specific Revenue	303787	60381	21192
行政事业性收费收入	Income from Administrative Fees	181404	13996	9751
罚没收入	Penalty and Confiscatory Income	96534	3829	3854
国有资本经营收入	Profits of State-owned Enterprises	7948		
国有资源(资产)有偿使用收入	Revenue of Compensable Use of State-owned Resources (Assets)	704548	87262	91080
捐赠收入	Donation Income	1669		17
政府住房基金收入	Government Housing Fund Income	14855	1154	
其他收入	Others	10209	1	2
政府性基金收入	**Government Funds Income**	**383343**		
#城市基础设施配套收入	Urban Infrastructure Supporting Income	171514		

(10 000 yuan)

槐荫区 Huai yin	天桥区 Tian qiao	历城区 Li cheng	长清区 Chang qing	章丘区 Zhang qiu	济阳区 Ji yang	莱芜区 Lai wu	钢城区 Gang cheng	济南高新区 Jinan Gao xin
567393	**410867**	**1401229**	**302407**	**604581**	**300788**	**469408**	**222911**	**1706559**
202543	142989	280523	84206	209530	93997	154188	74164	556458
54078	43625	96944	23120	43558	31196	31355	23896	317425
31742	22319	53226	8329	25229	4782	13845	3993	108249
326	456	2369	3251	10176	971	14190	5781	6564
25565	18290	48204	11164	28481	12392	20422	8429	129700
21890	18089	29622	9656	22124	6736	19863	9147	70654
10471	9376	21010	3493	11275	3515	14062	7551	46521
13368	11670	31342	14169	52217	14284	33429	16387	27268
72019	72655	430013	27880	19946	11022	17370	208	186538
1025	3064	7585	4086	6027	9964	8190	2042	268
614	1085	7772	4906	2505	5349	3403	1310	7066
62851	32859	143634	21028	31550	16489	24360	3578	66083
99	149	772	102	958	318	3383	3031	157
15293	10740	30097	13058	27479	11774	24312	7696	81765
17966	7648	34847	28266	14028	6723	27617	8284	12278
5576	1844	22555	8101	31615	2811	9969	2616	3764
322			7225	101			300	
30348	13983	160146	20905	67462	67955	40010	44172	81225
16	9	531	600	18	466	12		
			8852	275				4574
1096	1	1	1	6	36	9003	60	2
	2504		**16375**	**49115**	**23433**	**177103**	**49463**	**65350**
	2504		13706	45405	21489	23034	1913	63463

8–4 各县财政收入(2023年) Financial Revenue by County(2023)

单位：万元 (10 000 yuan)

指标	Item	合计 Total	平阴县 Ping yin	商河县 Shang he
一般公共预算收入	**General Public Budget Revenue**	**550864**	**324596**	**226268**
增值税	Value-added Tax	124829	66191	58638
企业所得税	Enterprise Income Tax	38911	25702	13209
个人所得税	Personal Income Tax	11010	6269	4741
资源税	Resource Tax	8706	8063	643
城市维护建设税	Tax on City Maintenance and Construction	12386	6853	5533
房产税	Tax on Real Estates	12325	6813	5512
印花税	Stamp Tax	5411	3219	2192
城镇土地使用税	Holding tax on urban and county land	19989	8269	11720
土地增值税	Land Value Added Tax	13676	2577	11099
车船税	Tax on vehicles and Their Registration	61205	27071	34134
耕地占用税	Farmland Occupation Tax	6119	2535	3584
契税	Contract tax	20376	7595	12781
环境保护税	Environmental Protection Tax	936	824	112
专项收入	Specific Revenue	17037	9942	7095
行政事业性收费收入	Income from Administrative Fees	13769	6632	7137
罚没收入	Penalty and Confiscatory Income	15418	7994	7424
国有资本经营收入	Profits of State-owned Enterprises	453	453	
国有资源(资产)有偿使用收入	Revenue of Compensable Use of State-owned Resources (Assets)	164934	126886	38048
捐赠收入	Donation Income	674	660	14
政府住房基金收入	Government Housing Fund Income	48	48	
其他收入	Others	2652		2652
政府性基金收入	**Government Funds Income**	**241644**	**92837**	**148807**
#城市基础设施配套收入	Urban Infrastructure Supporting Income	39528	13913	25615

8-5 地方财政支出(2023年)
Local Financial Expenditures (2023)

单位：万元 (10 000 yuan)

指标	Item	合计 Total	市本级 Cities 小计 Total	市直 Departments Directly Under the Municipal Government	济南起步区(直管) Jinan Start-up Area (Directly under)	南部山区 Nan shan	县区级 Counties
一般公共预算支出	**General Public Budget Expenditure**	**13652948**	**5507488**	**4485326**	**827714**	**194448**	**8145460**
一般公共服务支出	General Public Service	1366066	382457	327136	38808	16513	983609
国防支出	Defence Expenditure	21491	15069	15019		50	6422
公共安全支出	Public Security	733462	542405	536073	4965	1367	191057
教育支出	Education	2452843	593888	529669	17626	46593	1858955
科学技术	Science and Technology	465282	119183	105449	13734		346099
文化体育与传媒支出	Culture、Sports and Media	143004	92799	91477	421	901	50205
社会保障和就业支出	Social Security and Employment	2234847	723499	646462	36942	40095	1511348
医疗卫生与计划生育支出	Health and Family Planning	1360294	637715	593212	20094	24409	722579
节能环保支出	Energy-saving and Environment Protection	250451	125795	113495	8980	3320	124656
城乡社区支出	Urban and Rural Community Affairs	2577440	1451774	791277	651210	9287	1125666
农林水支出	Farming、Forestry and Irrigation Affairs	770101	301203	233493	25427	42283	468898
交通运输支出	Transport	385723	262577	259474	174	2929	123146
资源勘探信息等支出	Exploration and Information Affairs	192970	25395	25178	97	120	167575
商业服务业等支出	Commerce and Services Affairs	57439	12387	11883	197	307	45052
金融支出	Financial Supervision Affairs	16444	4248	3848	400		12196
援助其他地区支出	Aid to Other Area	35974	15443	15443			20531
自然资源海洋气象等支出	Natural Resources Marine Meteorological	110709	51587	49704	108	1775	59122
住房保障支出	Housing Security Affairs	282650	53888	41834	8507	3547	228762
粮油物资储备支出	Grain and Oil Reserves	17794	9660	9660			8134
债务付息支出	Pay Principle and Interest for Public Debt	79815	28981	28981			50834
其他支出	Other Expenditure	8776	3131	3131			5645
政府性基金支出	**Government Funds Expenditure**	**9526921**	**5693371**	**4438510**	**1248945**	**5916**	**3833550**

8-6 各区地方财政支出(2023年)
Local Financial Expenditures by District(2023)

单位：万元

指标	Item	合计 Total	历下区 Li xia	市中区 Shi zhong
一般公共预算支出	**General Public Budget Expenditure**	**7246806**	**970466**	**615078**
一般公共服务支出	General Public Service	891144	161333	86223
国防支出	Defence Expenditure	4578	1369	544
公共安全支出	Public Security	158695	24704	13324
教育支出	Education	1661054	250384	209407
科学技术	Science and Technology	345431	5797	3780
文化体育与传媒支出	Culture、Sports and Media	45179	8754	2445
社会保障和就业支出	Social Security and Employment	1356083	164235	126037
医疗卫生与计划生育支出	Health and Family Planning	647616	80047	61056
节能环保支出	Energy-saving and Environment Protection	115371	1637	7840
城乡社区支出	Urban and Rural Community Affairs	997109	192776	67265
农林水支出	Farming、Forestry and Irrigation Affairs	347667	5347	11271
交通运输支出	Transport	111710	290	419
资源勘探信息等支出	Exploration and Information Affairs	153750	6812	3357
商业服务业等支出	Commerce and Services Affairs	43493	3262	276
金融支出	Financial Supervision Affairs	11550	4606	80
援助其他地区支出	Aid to Other Area	20168	3010	2407
国土海洋气象等支出	Land and Weather Affairs	52194	19641	11385
住房保障支出	Housing Security Affairs	196250	26804	5931
粮油物资储备支出	Grain and Oil Reserves	6943	297	
国债还本付息支出	Pay Principle and Interest for Public Debt	43124	24	941
其他支出	Other Expenditure	5645		
政府性基金支出	**Government Funds Expenditure**	**3442998**	**588457**	**214502**

(10 000 yuan)

槐荫区 Huai yin	天桥区 Tian qiao	历城区 Li cheng	长清区 Chang qing	章丘区 Zhang qiu	济阳区 Ji yang	莱芜区 Lai wu	钢城区 Gang cheng	济南高新区 Jinan Gao xin
495693	**323537**	**982526**	**426889**	**848263**	**437163**	**760992**	**269756**	**1116443**
79360	53313	137533	55994	81247	45474	79056	27274	84337
823	507	168	46	417	46	171	287	200
16233	10953	23429	11998	13095	8544	13755	6363	16297
120340	96784	184436	97282	255068	73380	185883	47159	140931
2015	3193	120768	160	917	1195	4538	699	202369
2372	1629	4526	3641	5675	2884	11876	777	600
127949	72494	148480	130391	183251	101548	181718	47143	72837
62333	44461	74721	46891	77887	37904	93612	32332	36372
2896	2056	5845	3515	16910	9156	11531	6689	47296
36705	17234	162971	10259	36605	80986	21403	54432	316473
13383	9938	32640	41083	69270	45172	78779	17031	23753
62	6	32793	2453	14453	5787	26219	2229	26999
6015	936	2342	2197	40753	2906	10418	1971	76043
1335	79	3299	321	827	363	2006	403	31322
217		219	184	198	6	891	17	5132
737	649	2213		5151	267	2199	1918	1617
2032	907	3435	1772	2957	3016	4977	1733	339
17080	4170	36315	15007	34282	13340	11595	10209	21517
100		1926	1665	2163	780		12	
1829	2676	455	806	5321	3479	16322	7896	3375
		1704	215			909		2817
137556	**176240**	**427264**	**264005**	**216083**	**300352**	**469519**	**206589**	**442431**

8–7 各县地方财政支出 (2023年)
Local Financial Expenditures by County(2023)

单位：万元 (10 000 yuan)

指标	Item	合计 Total	平阴县 Ping yin	商河县 Shang he
一般公共预算支出	**General Public Budget Expenditure**	**898654**	**407074**	**491580**
一般公共服务支出	General Public Service	92465	43102	49363
国防支出	Defence Expenditure	1844	1463	381
公共安全支出	Public Security	32362	18505	13857
教育支出	Education	197901	98729	99172
科学技术	Science and Technology	668	280	388
文化体育与传媒支出	Culture、Sports and Media	5026	3480	1546
社会保障和就业支出	Social Security and Employment	155265	53545	101720
医疗卫生与计划生育支出	Health and Family Planning	74963	28977	45986
节能环保支出	Energy-saving and Environment Protection	9285	5475	3810
城乡社区支出	Urban and Rural Community Affairs	128557	63724	64833
农林水支出	Farming、Forestry and Irrigation Affairs	121231	46703	74528
交通运输支出	Transport	11436	5866	5570
资源勘探信息等支出	Exploration and Information Affairs	13825	13096	729
商业服务业等支出	Commerce and Services Affairs	1559	542	1017
金融支出	Financial Supervision Affairs	646	5	641
援助其他地区支出	Aid to Other Area	363	231	132
自然资源海洋气象等支出	Natural Resources Marine Meteorological	6928	5266	1662
住房保障支出	Housing Security Affairs	32512	10841	21671
粮油物资储备支出	Grain and Oil Reserves	1191	881	310
国债还本付息支出	Pay Principle and Interest for Public Debt	7710	4760	2950
其他支出	Other Expenditure			
政府性基金支出	**Government Funds Expenditure**	**390552**	**170304**	**220248**

8–8 金融机构本外币各项存、贷款期末余额

The Ending Balance of all Deposits and Loans in RMB and Foreign Currencies of Financial Institutions

单位：万元　　(10 000 yuan)

指标	Item	2019年	2020年	2021年	2022年	2023年
金融机构本外币各项存款余额	**The Balance of RMB and Foreign Currencies Deposits in Financial Institutions**	**186460860**	**210649849**	**234369588**	**259410006**	**279527032**
#住户存款	Household Deposits	64970029	76475384	86204521	102917118	118706505
非金融企业存款	Non-financial Corporate Deposits	77067935	87238924	93393082	93495869	97759614
广义政府存款	General Government Deposits	35087861	36351481	41171421	43285939	45113044
非银行业金融机构存款	Non-bank Financial Intermediary Deposits	7629436	9239886	11598655	18448374	16686464
金融机构本外币各项贷款余额	**The Balance of RMB and Foreign Currencies Loans in Financial Institutions**	**187687420**	**207202433**	**233132266**	**261122538**	**287565811**
#住户贷款	Household Loans	47041192	54682406	61126528	65261003	69702659
非金融企业及机关团体贷款	Non-financial Corporate and Institution Loans	129406853	142485017	162082669	185229003	207503499
短期贷款	Short-term Loans	34665784	38736145	43586160	48464423	53684308
中长期贷款	Medium and Long-term Loans	82655910	91489364	102739117	117226259	138122458
票据融资	Bill Financing	8682607	8566014	11195931	14017627	10215946
融资租赁	Finance Lease	3240815	3592611	3971136	4718117	5416722
各项垫款	Bill Financing	161737	100884	590324	802577	64065
非银行业金融机构贷款	Non-bank Financial Intermediary Loans	200000			40000	30000

8-9 金融机构人民币各项存、贷款期末余额
The Ending Balance of all Deposits and Loans in RMB of Financial Institutions

单位：万元 (10 000 yuan)

指标	Item	2019年	2020年	2021年	2022年	2023年
金融机构人民币各项存款余额	**The Balance of RMB Deposits in Financial Institutions**	**183032033**	**207149738**	**230292028**	**255895137**	**276537387**
#住户存款	Household Deposits	64380943	75841225	85584289	102262713	118063148
非金融企业存款	Non-financial Corporate Deposits	75805636	85613093	91691729	72925888	96493361
广义政府存款	General Government Deposits	34923450	36297466	41156864	43276614	45104588
非银行业金融机构存款	Non-bank Financial Intermediary Deposits	7571079	9193889	11550960	18425891	16663424
金融机构人民币各项贷款余额	**The Balance of RMB Loans in Financial Institutions**	**176242063**	**197048849**	**223499074**	**250779821**	**276892189**
#住户贷款	Household Loans	47038338	54680859	61124765	65258011	69698891
非金融企业及机关团体贷款	Non-financial Corporate and Institution Loans	128277535	141659442	161539618	184738842	206405122
短期贷款	Short-term Loans	34002100	38291441	43293345	48092662	52963294
中长期贷款	Medium and Long-term Loans	82190276	91128303	102488882	117107858	137745095
票据融资	Bill Financing	8682607	8566014	11195931	14017627	10215946
融资租赁	Finance Lease	3240815	3592611	3971136	4718117	5416722
各项垫款	Bill Financing	161737	81074	590324	802577	64065
非银行业金融机构贷款	Non-bank Financial Intermediary Loans	200000			40000	30000

8-10 保险业务情况
Insurance Business

指标	Item	2019年	2020年	2021年	2022年	2023年
保险金额(亿元)	**Insurance Amount(100 million yuan)**	**438422**	**927748**	**659267**	**615535**	**3595569**
保费收入(万元)	**Premium Income(10 000 yuan)**	**5322643**	**6280398**	**5984712**	**6324536**	**6948217**
财产险	Property Insurance	1174143	1255657	1091694	1523355	1289784
人身险	Life Insurance	4148500	5024741	4893017	4801181	5658434
赔付支出(万元)	**Claim Payment(10 000 yuan)**	**1219250**	**1603108**	**2124574**	**1915636**	**2160735**
财产险	Property Insurance	562261	683340	778634	905599	963898
人身险	Life Insurance	656989	919768	1345940	1010037	1196837

注：数据由地方金融监管部门提供。
Note: Data are provided by the Data are provided by the Financial Regulatory Authority.

8-11 证券机构及证券交易情况
Institution and Trading Summary for Stocks

单位：亿元 (100 million yuan)

指标	Item	2019年	2020年	2021年	2022年	2023年
注册地在济南证券公司数(个)	**Stocks Institutions in Jinan(unit)**	**1**	**1**	**1**	**1**	**1**
证券营业部(个)	**Securities Business Department(unit)**	**92**	**91**	**120**	**92**	**87**
证券交易额	**Trading Volume of Securities Business Department**	**36453**	**47753**	**55847**	**57576**	**55947**
股票	Stock	18621	28606	35660	34147	30757
基金	Fund	2197	3528	2872	3119	2416
债券	Bond	15536	15444	17045	19714	22501
其他	Others	99	174	271	593	272

注：数据由地方金融监管部门提供。
Note: Data are provided by the Data are provided by the Financial Regulatory Authority.

主要统计指标解释

一般公共预算收入 指国家财政参与社会产品分配所取得的收入，是实现国家职能的财力保证。主要包括：（1）各项税收：包括国内增值税、国内消费税、进口货物增值税、进口消费品消费税、出口货物退增值税、出口消费品退消费税、企业所得税、个人所得税、资源税、城市维护建设税、房产税、印花税、城镇土地使用税、土地增值税、车船税、船舶吨税、车辆购置税、关税、耕地占用税、契税、烟叶税、环境保护税等。（2）非税收入：包括专项收入、行政事业性收费收入、罚没收入、国有资本经营收入、国有资源（资产）有偿使用收入和其他收入。财政收入按现行分税制财政体制划分为中央本级收入和地方本级收入。

一般公共预算支出 指国家财政将筹集起来的资金进行分配使用，以满足经济建设和各项事业的需要。主要包括：一般公共服务、外交、国防、公共安全、教育、科学技术、文化旅游体育与传媒、社会保障和就业、卫生健康、节能环保、城乡社区、农林水、交通运输、资源勘探工业信息等、商业服务业等、金融、援助其他地区、自然资源海洋气象等、住房保障、粮油物资储备、灾害防治及应急管理、债务付息、债务发行费用等方面的支出。财政支出根据政府在经济和社会活动中的不同职权，划分为中央财政支出和地方财政支出。

各项存款 金融机构资金来源的主要项目，包括住户存款、非金融企业存款、机关团体存款、财政性存款、非银行业金融机构存款和境外存款。

各项贷款 金融机构资金运用的主要项目，包括住户贷款、非金融企业及机关团体贷款、非银行业金融机构贷款和境外贷款。

保险金额 指保险人承担赔偿或者给付保险金责任的最高限额。

Explanatory Notes on Main Statistical Indicators

General Public Budget Revenue refers to income for the government finance through participating in the distribution of social products. It is the financial guarantee to ensure government functioning. The government revenue includes the following main items: (1) Various tax revenues including domestic value added tax (VAT), domestic consumption tax, VAT from imports, consumption tax from imports, VAT rebate for exports, consumption tax rebate for exports, corporate income tax, individual income tax, resource tax, city maintenance and construction tax, house property tax, stamp tax, urban land use tax, land appreciation tax, tax on vehicles and boat operation, ship tonnage tax, vehicle purchase tax, tariffs, farm land occupation tax, deed tax, and tobacco tax, environment protection tax, etc. (2) Non-tax revenue, including special program receipts, charge income of administrative and institutional units, penalty receipts, operating income from government capital, income from use of state-owned resources (assets) and others non-tax receipts.

General Public Budget Expenditure refers to the distribution and use of the funds which the government finance has raised, so as to meet the needs of economic construction and various undertakings. It includes the following main items: expenditure for general public services, expenditure for foreign affairs, expenditure for national defence expenditure for public security, expenditure for education, expenditure for science and technology, expenditure for culture, tourism, sport and media, expenditure for social safety net and employment effort, expenditure for health care, expenditure for energy conservation and environment protection, expenditure for urban and rural community affairs, expenditure for agriculture, forestry and water conservancy, expenditure for transportation, expenditure for resource exploration and industrial information, expenditure for affairs of commerce and services, expenditure for finance, aid to other regions, expenditure for nature resources, ocean and weather, expenditure for housing security, expenditure for grain & oil reserves, expenditure for prevention of disasters and emergency management, interest payment for public debts, expenditure for issuing debts. General public budget expenditure is divided into general public budget expenditure of central government and general public budget expenditure of local government according to the different functions of the governments played in economic and social activities.

Total Deposits are the main items of financial sources of financial institutions, which include deposits of households, deposits of non-financial enterprises, deposits of government departments & organizations, fiscal deposits, deposits of non-banking financial institutions and overseas deposits.

Total Loans are the main items of financial uses of financial institutions, which include loans to households, loans to non-financial enterprises and government departments & organizations, loans to non-banking financial institutions and overseas loans.

Amount Insured refers to the maximum that the insurant will get for the claim of the case insured.

9

物价

PRICE

9-1 主要年份物价指数(以上年为100)
Price Indices in Major Years(Preceding Year=100)

年份 Year	居民消费价格指数 Consumer Price Index	#食品 Food	#服务项目 Services	零售物价指数 Retail Price Index
1951	108.5	105.3	98.7	109.8
1952	101.5	103.9	101.0	101.2
1955	101.6	101.3	103.4	101.4
1956	100.5	100.7	100.6	100.5
1965	107.3	111.5	97.5	108.0
1970	98.4	99.0	100.0	98.3
1971	100.0	100.5	100.0	100.0
1972	100.1	100.3	100.0	100.1
1973	99.5	99.6	97.9	99.7
1974	99.4	99.1	99.9	99.5
1975	100.2	100.0	100.0	100.2
1976	100.4	100.0	100.0	100.4
1977	99.2	99.9	91.2	100.0
1978	100.3	100.3	100.0	100.3
1979	101.1	101.7	100.5	101.1
1980	104.7	107.9	100.0	105.0
1981	101.9	102.2	100.1	102.0
1982	101.1	101.6	100.3	101.2
1983	100.1	100.3	100.9	100.1
1984	101.9	101.1	109.8	101.3
1985	108.7	112.2	103.3	109.1
1986	106.2	107.6	104.9	106.3
1987	109.5	111.9	104.9	109.8
1988	122.4	128.0	108.8	123.4
1989	116.2	111.2	113.5	116.4
1990	103.3	102.6	108.0	103.0
1991	106.7	107.6	106.9	106.7
1992	110.4	108.7	122.2	109.3
1993	114.7	109.8	138.0	112.1

9-1 续表 continued

年份 Year	居民消费价格指数 Consumer Price Index	#食品 Food	#服务项目 Services	零售物价指数 Retail Price Index
1994	124.8	133.9	114.5	122.7
1995	117.3	123.0	115.1	113.2
1996	109.1	109.7	116.2	106.3
1997	102.9	101.8	107.8	101.5
1998	100.9	99.4	119.0	98.9
1999	99.1	97.3	127.6	96.9
2000	100.6	97.9	129.0	98.0
2001	100.3	100.8	106.1	98.8
2002	98.8	100.2	101.3	97.8
2003	99.9	103.6	100.3	98.0
2004	102.5	107.4	101.2	100.6
2005	101.1	102.7	101.2	100.4
2006	100.9	102.4	100.9	100.3
2007	103.9	111.6	101.8	102.2
2008	105.7	115.5	101.8	104.5
2009	100.3	102.7	102.4	98.7
2010	102.1	107.3	100.6	101.3
2011	105.4	111.3	104.4	104.6
2012	102.4	103.6	102.2	101.8
2013	102.8	104.9	102.7	101.3
2014	102.2	103.2	102.9	101.2
2015	101.9	101.4	101.6	100.3
2016	102.7	103.9	103.5	100.8
2017	102.0	98.5	104.2	101.0
2018	102.6	102.8	102.1	102.6
2019	103.3	112.0	101.4	102.5
2020	102.4	112.3	99.0	101.9
2021	101.5	100.5	101.4	101.3
2022	101.4	103.3	100.1	102.2
2023	100.6	99.7	101.0	

9-2 主要年份物价指数(以1950年为100)

Price Indices in Major Years(Preceding 1950=100)

年份 Year	居民消费价格指数 Consumer Price Index	#食品 Food	#服务项目 Services	零售物价指数 Retail Price Index
1951	108.5	105.3	98.7	109.8
1952	110.1	109.4	103.7	111.1
1955	117.2	123.7	108.2	118.4
1956	117.8	124.6	108.8	119.0
1965	127.7	141.5	116.9	130.7
1970	123.0	141.6	110.1	126.0
1971	123.0	142.3	110.1	126.0
1972	123.1	142.7	110.1	126.1
1973	122.5	142.1	107.8	125.8
1974	121.8	140.9	107.7	125.1
1975	122.0	140.9	107.7	125.4
1976	122.5	140.9	107.7	125.9
1977	121.5	140.7	98.2	125.9
1978	121.9	141.1	98.2	126.3
1979	123.2	143.5	98.6	127.6
1980	129.0	154.9	98.6	134.0
1981	131.5	158.3	98.7	136.7
1982	132.9	160.8	99.0	138.3
1983	133.0	161.3	99.9	138.5
1984	135.6	163.1	109.7	140.3
1985	147.4	183.0	113.3	153.0
1986	156.5	195.8	118.9	162.7
1987	171.4	219.1	124.7	178.6
1988	209.8	280.4	135.7	220.4
1989	234.8	311.8	154.0	256.5
1990	251.8	319.9	166.3	264.2
1991	268.7	344.2	177.8	281.9
1992	296.6	376.2	217.3	308.1
1993	340.2	413.1	299.8	345.4

9-2 续表 continued

年份 Year	居民消费价格指数 Consumer Price Index	#食品 Food	#服务项目 Services	零售物价指数 Retail Price Index
1994	424.6	570.4	343.3	423.8
1995	498.1	709.7	395.1	479.7
1996	543.4	797.7	459.1	509.9
1997	559.2	782.5	494.9	551.6
1998	564.2	777.8	588.9	545.5
1999	559.1	756.8	751.4	528.6
2000	562.4	740.9	969.3	518.0
2001	564.1	746.8	1028.4	511.8
2002	557.3	748.3	1041.8	500.5
2003	556.7	775.2	1044.9	490.5
2004	570.6	832.6	1057.4	493.4
2005	576.9	855.1	1070.1	495.4
2006	582.1	875.6	1079.7	496.9
2007	604.8	977.2	1099.1	507.8
2008	639.3	1128.7	1118.9	530.7
2009	641.2	1159.2	1145.8	523.8
2010	654.7	1243.8	1152.7	530.6
2011	690.2	1384.7	1203.1	555.1
2012	706.8	1434.5	1229.5	565.1
2013	726.6	1504.8	1262.7	572.4
2014	742.6	1553.0	1299.3	579.3
2015	756.7	1574.7	1320.1	581.0
2016	777.1	1636.1	1366.3	585.6
2017	792.6	1611.6	1423.7	591.5
2018	813.3	1656.7	1453.6	606.8
2019	840.1	1855.5	1473.9	622.0
2020	860.3	2083.7	1459.2	633.8
2021	873.2	2094.1	1479.6	642.1
2022	885.4	2163.2	1481.1	656.2
2023	890.7	2156.7	1495.9	

9-3 分月居民消费价格指数(2023年，以上年为100)
Consumer Price Indices by Month(2023，Preceding Year=100)

指标	Item	全年 Annual	一月 January	二月 February
居民消费价格总指数	**Consumer Price Index**	**100.6**	**102.1**	**101.5**
非食品烟酒价格指数	**Non-food,tobacco and alcohol Price Index**	**100.5**	**101.3**	**100.9**
服务价格指数	**Services Price Index**	**101.0**	**101.2**	**101.0**
工业品价格指数	**Industrial Products Price Index**	**99.7**	**101.3**	**100.7**
消费品价格指数	**Consumer Goods Price Index**	**100.3**	**102.7**	**101.8**
扣除食品和能源价格指数	**Excluding Food and Energy Price Index**	**101.1**	**101.1**	**101.0**
一、食品烟酒	**Food,Tobacco and Liquor**	**101.0**	**104.6**	**103.3**
1.食品	Food	99.7	106.2	104.3
(1)粮食	Grain	101.9	105.1	104.7
(2)薯类	Tuber	102.9	120.5	118.2
(3)豆类	Beans	102.1	104.0	103.3
(4)食用油	Edible Oil	98.7	104.2	106.4
食用植物油	Edible Vegetable Oil	98.7	104.2	106.4
(5)菜及食用菌	Vegetable and Edible Fungi	97.7	98.9	96.4
鲜菜	Fresh Vegetable	97.8	98.8	96.2
(6)畜肉类	Meat of Livestock	95.3	112.0	106.7
猪肉	Pork	88.1	122.1	110.6
(7)禽肉类	Meat of Poultry	100.2	105.8	101.9
(8)水产品	Aquatic Products	99.9	104.6	101.9
(9)蛋类	Poultry & Eggs	102.7	113.4	112.3
鸡蛋	Eggs	101.4	115.0	113.3
(10)奶类	Milk	103.8	104.4	110.7
(11)干鲜瓜果类	Fruits and Nuts	100.5	112.3	107.6
鲜果	Fresh Fruits	100.0	114.4	108.6
(12)糖果糕点类	Candy and Cake	104.8	100.7	101.7
(13)调味品	Flavoring	98.5	97.2	97.3
(14)其他食品类	Other Foods	99.7	102.4	103.5
2.茶及饮料	Tea and Beverages	101.1	102.0	102.0
3.烟酒	Tobacco and Alcohol	103.2	102.6	101.1

三月 March	四月 April	五月 May	六月 June	七月 July	八月 August	九月 September	十月 October	十一月 November	十二月 December
100.9	**100.5**	**100.5**	**100.6**	**100.3**	**100.6**	**100.4**	**100.0**	**99.7**	**99.8**
100.4	**100.3**	**100.2**	**99.7**	**100.4**	**100.7**	**100.7**	**100.6**	**100.1**	**100.3**
101.0	**101.5**	**101.2**	**101.2**	**101.6**	**101.5**	**101.1**	**100.7**	**100.3**	**100.4**
99.6	**98.9**	**98.9**	**98.0**	**98.9**	**99.8**	**100.2**	**100.4**	**99.9**	**100.2**
100.8	**99.9**	**100.0**	**100.2**	**99.3**	**100.1**	**100.0**	**99.6**	**99.3**	**99.5**
100.9	**101.1**	**101.0**	**101.1**	**101.6**	**101.4**	**101.3**	**101.0**	**100.8**	**100.9**
102.3	**101.3**	**101.4**	**103.1**	**99.9**	**100.4**	**99.7**	**98.6**	**98.5**	**98.5**
102.7	100.7	100.8	102.8	97.7	98.4	97.1	95.5	95.2	95.3
102.8	100.2	102.2	101.3	101.1	102.7	99.8	100.8	101.6	100.6
110.2	103.4	98.3	111.5	112.2	102.8	101.3	94.0	85.8	80.0
102.6	103.7	103.1	102.9	102.1	100.7	100.1	100.8	100.7	101.3
103.9	100.7	99.2	96.8	96.4	97.9	95.2	97.3	95.4	92.2
103.9	100.7	99.2	96.8	96.4	97.9	95.2	97.3	95.4	92.2
83.8	86.2	98.8	126.3	99.1	100.1	95.2	93.3	100.2	105.8
82.8	84.8	98.4	130.8	99.5	100.7	96.3	93.5	99.8	106.5
109.0	105.9	102.0	99.5	86.3	90.7	90.9	84.1	82.2	85.6
119.3	107.6	99.6	96.0	72.9	82.7	81.5	69.2	65.7	72.0
101.7	101.0	101.6	101.9	98.4	97.5	99.2	99.4	98.4	96.4
105.9	103.1	100.3	102.8	103.2	101.6	97.9	95.3	91.1	90.3
112.5	105.6	102.9	101.4	99.0	104.2	103.4	95.1	93.5	93.9
114.2	105.0	101.1	99.7	96.7	104.1	102.6	92.0	89.7	90.3
107.4	104.9	102.4	101.6	103.9	101.3	101.3	102.7	103.4	102.3
109.7	102.3	99.2	95.7	96.3	95.2	96.2	99.5	99.6	94.3
111.1	102.0	98.4	94.7	94.9	94.2	95.2	98.7	98.6	92.5
103.9	105.8	106.4	106.2	105.4	105.4	105.9	104.2	105.2	106.2
97.2	99.1	97.2	98.2	98.9	100.0	99.2	100.6	98.9	99.0
101.4	100.6	98.6	97.2	99.7	99.8	98.1	100.0	99.1	96.3
100.6	101.2	100.3	101.5	101.7	100.7	99.4	102.0	100.5	101.3
100.9	101.4	103.3	103.2	103.3	104.4	103.9	103.4	105.6	105.3

9-3 续表 1 continued 1

指标	Item	全年 Annual	一月 January	二月 February
(1)卷烟	Cigarette	101.8	101.9	101.9
(2)酒类	Alcohol	104.5	103.2	100.4
4.在外餐饮	Dining Out	103.8	100.9	101.4
二、衣着	**Clothing**	**101.4**	**102.1**	**102.2**
1.服装	Garments	101.7	102.1	102.3
(1)男式服装	Men's Clothing	101.9	102.4	102.9
(2)女式服装	Women's Clothing	101.8	102.0	102.0
(3)儿童服装	Children's Clothing	102.1	103.4	103.4
(4)衣着材料及配件	Clothing and Accessories	98.9	99.9	99.4
(5)衣着服务费	Clothing service fee	100.0	100.0	100.0
2.鞋类	Footwear	100.3	102.1	101.8
(1)鞋	Shoes	100.4	102.2	101.8
(2)鞋类服务	Footwear Services	100.0	100.0	100.0
三、居住	**Residence**	**100.0**	**100.3**	**100.4**
1.租赁房房租	Rent of Rental Housing	100.6	100.8	101.0
2.住房保养维修及管理	Housing Maintenance and Management	99.9	100.0	100.0
(1)住房装潢材料	Housing Decoration Materials	99.9	99.9	99.9
(2)住房维修管理费用	Housing Maintenance Management Fee	100.0	100.0	100.0
3.水电燃料	Water, Electricity and Fuels	100.3	100.2	100.4
(1)水	Water	100.0	100.0	100.0
(2)电	Electricity	100.0	100.0	100.0
(3)燃气	Gas	102.5	102.0	103.0
(4)其他水电燃料类	Other Fuel	100.0	100.0	100.0
4.自有住房	Self-owned House	99.9	100.3	100.5
四、生活用品及服务	**Articles for Daily Use and Services**	**100.3**	**102.1**	**101.5**
1.家具及室内装饰品	Furniture and Interior Decorations	101.1	100.9	101.0
(1)家具	Furniture	100.4	99.9	99.9
(2)室内装饰品	Interior Decorations	105.5	107.2	107.7
2.家用器具	Home Appliances	98.3	100.4	98.3
(1)大型家用器具	Large Home Appliances	98.6	100.5	98.1
(2)小家电	Small Home Appliances	96.9	100.0	99.9

三月 March	四月 April	五月 May	六月 June	七月 July	八月 August	九月 September	十月 October	十一月 November	十二月 December
101.9	101.9	101.9	101.9	101.9	101.9	101.9	101.9	100.9	100.9
100.1	100.9	104.5	104.4	104.6	106.6	105.6	104.7	109.6	109.0
101.9	102.9	102.5	104.1	104.9	104.8	105.7	105.4	105.5	105.2
102.1	**102.1**	**102.0**	**101.7**	**101.6**	**101.2**	**101.0**	**100.3**	**100.3**	**100.5**
102.4	102.3	102.4	102.2	102.1	101.5	101.1	100.5	100.5	100.6
102.8	102.6	102.7	102.5	102.5	101.8	101.1	100.8	100.5	100.5
102.4	102.3	102.3	101.9	102.0	101.8	101.5	100.9	101.0	101.2
103.4	103.4	104.2	103.9	103.5	101.6	100.7	99.4	99.1	99.0
98.8	98.8	98.9	99.0	98.7	97.8	98.6	98.6	99.1	99.5
100.0	100.0	100.0	100.0	100.0	100.0	100.0	100.0	100.0	100.0
101.1	101.2	100.2	99.5	99.2	99.5	100.4	99.4	99.6	100.2
101.1	101.2	100.2	99.5	99.2	99.5	100.4	99.3	99.6	100.2
100.0	100.0	100.0	100.0	100.0	100.0	100.0	100.0	100.0	100.0
100.3	**100.3**	**100.3**	**100.2**	**100.2**	**100.0**	**99.8**	**99.3**	**99.6**	**99.7**
101.0	101.1	101.1	101.2	101.3	101.0	100.4	99.4	99.5	99.8
100.0	100.0	100.0	99.9	99.9	99.9	99.9	99.9	99.9	99.9
99.9	99.9	99.9	99.9	99.9	99.9	99.8	99.8	99.8	99.8
100.0	100.0	100.0	100.0	100.0	100.0	100.0	100.0	100.0	100.0
100.1	100.1	100.1	100.1	100.1	100.1	100.6	100.6	100.6	100.6
100.0	100.0	100.0	100.0	100.0	100.0	100.0	100.0	100.0	100.0
100.0	100.0	100.0	100.0	100.0	100.0	100.0	100.0	100.0	100.0
101.0	101.0	101.0	101.0	101.0	101.0	104.8	104.8	104.7	104.7
100.0	100.0	100.0	100.0	100.0	100.0	100.0	100.0	100.0	100.0
100.4	100.3	100.3	100.2	100.2	99.8	99.4	98.9	99.2	99.4
101.1	**99.9**	**99.5**	**99.1**	**100.0**	**100.0**	**100.0**	**100.0**	**100.1**	**100.5**
100.7	100.6	100.3	100.2	101.2	101.4	101.6	101.4	101.8	101.5
99.9	99.9	100.0	99.5	100.8	100.8	100.8	100.8	100.8	100.8
105.2	104.9	102.3	104.1	103.7	105.1	106.9	104.7	108.4	105.8
99.2	98.0	97.2	97.1	97.3	97.2	97.4	99.2	99.7	99.2
99.3	97.9	97.2	97.3	97.7	97.6	97.9	100.0	100.1	99.5
98.5	98.2	97.1	95.8	94.8	95.0	94.4	94.5	97.3	97.1

9-3 续表 2 continued 2

指标	Item	全年 Annual	一月 January	二月 February
3.家用纺织品	Home Textiles	100.2	101.1	101.2
(1)床上用品	Bedding Article	100.0	100.0	100.0
(2)窗帘门帘	Curtain	100.0	100.0	100.0
(3)其他家用纺织品	Other Home Textiles	101.9	111.3	112.5
4.家庭日用杂品	Daily Use Household Articles	99.4	103.1	102.6
(1)洗涤卫生用品	Washing Sanitary Articles	99.1	104.8	104.5
(2)厨具餐具茶具	Kitchenware, Tableware, Tea Set	100.7	103.4	100.6
(3)其他家庭日用杂品	Other Daily Use Household Articles	99.1	100.1	100.6
5.个人护理用品	Personal-care Supplies	102.3	108.7	107.0
(1)化妆品	Cosmetics	102.3	110.4	108.1
(2)其他护理用品类	Other Personal-care Supplies	102.1	106.1	105.3
6.家庭服务	Household Services	102.7	97.6	99.8
五、交通通信	**Transport and Communications**	**98.2**	**101.6**	**100.3**
1.交通	Transport	97.9	102.3	100.6
(1)交通工具	Transport Facility	97.8	97.3	98.2
(2)交通工具用燃料	Fuels for Transport Facility	94.2	105.3	100.1
(3)交通工具使用和维修	Use and Maintenance of Transport Facility	100.6	101.2	101.2
(4)交通费	Traffic Fee	104.9	112.9	109.4
2.通信	Communications	99.6	99.0	99.2
(1)通信工具	Communication Tools	98.7	97.5	98.0
(2)通信服务	Communication Services	100.0	100.0	100.0
(3)邮递服务	Mailing Services	101.2	100.0	100.0
六、教育文化娱乐	**Education Culture and Recreation**	**102.3**	**102.4**	**101.5**
1.教育	Education	100.3	100.2	100.2
(1)教育用品	Education Articles	99.5	100.1	100.0
(2)教育服务	Education Services	100.3	100.2	100.2
2.文化娱乐	Culture and Recreation	105.9	106.1	103.7
(1)文娱耐用消费品	Durable Consumer Goods for Culture and Recreation	97.8	100.1	100.3

三月 March	四月 April	五月 May	六月 June	七月 July	八月 August	九月 September	十月 October	十一月 November	十二月 December
100.5	100.0	100.0	100.0	100.0	100.0	99.6	100.0	100.0	100.0
100.0	100.0	100.0	100.0	100.0	100.0	100.0	100.0	100.0	100.0
100.0	100.0	100.0	100.0	100.0	100.0	100.0	100.0	100.0	100.0
104.9	100.1	100.1	100.1	100.1	100.1	95.8	100.1	100.1	100.1
102.2	98.5	98.7	97.4	98.6	98.3	98.6	97.1	98.5	100.1
102.0	98.1	98.1	96.5	97.7	98.0	98.2	94.9	96.3	100.8
103.8	99.4	98.7	96.8	99.6	100.4	102.2	101.7	103.3	99.1
101.4	98.6	99.6	99.2	99.3	97.2	96.9	97.8	99.1	99.5
103.4	103.2	102.6	101.2	103.0	101.9	100.6	100.0	97.8	98.7
103.5	104.2	102.6	101.2	103.2	102.2	100.6	99.9	96.0	97.5
103.1	101.5	102.6	101.3	102.6	101.4	100.7	100.1	100.6	100.7
101.3	101.6	101.0	101.9	102.8	104.9	105.4	105.4	105.4	105.4
98.2	**97.0**	**96.4**	**94.8**	**96.3**	**98.8**	**99.1**	**99.7**	**98.2**	**98.7**
97.9	96.4	95.6	93.4	95.3	98.6	99.0	99.9	97.8	98.3
97.4	96.8	96.9	98.2	97.9	98.0	98.0	98.2	98.4	98.3
93.2	89.2	88.5	81.9	86.3	95.1	98.5	101.5	96.8	98.2
101.0	101.0	101.0	100.3	100.3	100.3	100.4	100.4	100.4	100.4
109.4	109.9	105.0	104.2	106.6	107.5	101.9	100.6	96.2	96.6
99.1	99.4	99.5	100.5	100.1	99.6	99.5	99.2	99.7	100.2
97.6	98.2	98.5	101.1	99.9	98.7	98.4	97.7	98.9	100.3
100.0	100.0	100.0	100.0	100.0	100.0	100.0	100.0	100.0	100.0
101.5	101.5	101.5	101.5	101.5	101.5	101.5	101.5	101.5	101.5
101.6	**102.7**	**102.1**	**102.4**	**103.5**	**103.2**	**103.0**	**102.6**	**101.4**	**101.5**
100.2	100.2	100.2	100.2	100.1	100.2	100.4	100.4	100.4	100.4
99.9	99.8	99.8	99.3	99.3	99.3	99.2	99.1	99.2	99.3
100.2	100.2	100.2	100.2	100.2	100.2	100.5	100.5	100.5	100.5
103.9	107.1	105.5	106.2	109.3	108.4	107.4	106.3	103.1	103.3
99.9	98.8	98.7	98.3	96.5	95.8	95.8	96.4	96.8	96.4

9–3 续表 3 continued 3

指标	Item	全年 Annual	一月 January	二月 February
(2)其他文娱用品	Other Articles	100.2	102.0	101.4
(3)文化娱乐服务	Services for Culture and Recreation	100.8	101.8	96.5
(4)旅游	Touring	118.7	116.8	115.4
七、医疗保健	**Health Care**	**100.8**	**100.3**	**100.4**
1.药品及医疗器具	Medicine and Medical Instruments	102.0	100.2	100.5
(1)中药	Traditional Chinese Medicines	110.3	100.3	101.1
(2)西药	Western Medicines	99.5	99.9	100.0
(3)滋补保健品	Health Products	98.7	102.8	102.5
(4)医疗卫生器具	Medical and Health Equipment	100.9	94.3	95.8
(5)保健器具	Healthcare Apparatus	100.2	99.6	99.8
2.医疗服务	Medical Services	100.3	100.4	100.4
(1)综合医疗类	Comprehensive Health Care	100.1	100.3	100.3
(2)诊断类	Diagnostic	100.0	100.1	100.1
(3)治疗类	Therapeutic	100.0	100.0	100.0
(4)康复类	Rehabilitation	108.0	108.8	108.8
(5)中医医疗服务类	Chinese Medicine Services	100.0	100.0	100.0
(6)其他医疗保健服务	Other Medical Services	100.0	100.0	100.0
八、其他用品及服务	**Other Articles and Services**	**103.9**	**102.2**	**102.0**
1.其他用品	Other Articles	105.6	105.3	103.4
(1)首饰手表	Jewelry Watches	109.3	106.6	103.3
(2)母婴用品	Maternal and Infant Supplies	101.8	109.0	109.5
(3)其他杂项用品	Other Miscellaneous Supplies	99.3	100.5	100.4
2.其他服务	Other Services	102.2	99.3	100.6
(1)在外住宿	Hotel Accommodation	113.7	90.9	99.1
(2)美容美发洗浴	Hairdressing Bath	100.4	98.2	99.6
(3)养老服务	Pension Services	100.3	101.7	101.7
(4)金融及保险服务	Finance and Insurance Services	101.4	101.2	101.2
(5)中介法律及其他服务	Legal Intermediary and Other Service	99.9	99.7	99.7

三月 March	四月 April	五月 May	六月 June	七月 July	八月 August	九月 September	十月 October	十一月 November	十二月 December
101.3	100.6	100.3	99.7	99.8	100.1	100.2	98.9	98.8	98.8
96.7	98.7	97.4	104.6	104.8	104.7	105.2	100.0	100.6	99.3
116.2	125.2	121.8	115.8	125.6	122.7	119.4	121.5	111.1	112.9
100.2	**100.1**	**100.9**	**100.7**	**101.1**	**101.3**	**101.2**	**101.2**	**101.2**	**101.1**
99.6	99.7	102.3	101.6	102.9	103.5	103.3	103.3	103.2	103.5
101.3	101.3	111.3	114.5	115.1	115.6	115.5	116.2	115.8	116.1
100.0	100.0	100.0	99.2	99.2	99.2	99.2	99.2	99.2	99.2
98.1	98.1	97.7	94.7	98.3	98.3	98.3	98.3	98.3	99.1
98.6	98.6	104.4	101.5	104.8	104.8	104.8	101.9	100.9	101.7
96.9	98.4	96.5	94.2	96.6	105.9	103.8	103.8	103.7	103.8
100.4	100.3	100.3	100.3	100.3	100.3	100.3	100.3	100.3	100.0
100.3	100.0	100.0	100.0	100.0	100.0	100.0	100.0	100.0	100.0
100.1	100.0	100.0	100.0	100.0	100.0	100.0	100.0	100.0	100.0
100.0	100.0	100.0	100.0	100.0	100.0	100.0	100.0	100.0	100.0
108.8	108.8	108.8	108.8	108.8	108.8	108.8	108.8	108.8	100.0
100.0	100.0	100.0	100.0	100.0	100.0	100.0	100.0	100.0	100.0
100.0	100.0	100.0	100.0	100.0	100.0	100.0	100.0	100.0	100.0
101.7	**103.5**	**104.2**	**103.3**	**105.2**	**104.6**	**105.7**	**105.5**	**104.4**	**104.3**
103.0	104.4	104.4	104.0	107.7	106.7	108.3	107.1	106.5	106.4
103.2	106.7	108.3	108.6	113.2	111.7	114.7	112.9	111.1	111.4
108.5	102.8	99.0	95.8	101.1	100.0	100.7	98.9	99.1	99.5
99.4	99.9	98.6	98.4	99.1	99.0	98.3	98.8	100.0	98.7
100.5	102.6	103.9	102.7	102.9	102.7	103.2	104.0	102.3	102.3
102.3	119.5	130.4	117.9	118.7	116.5	120.0	127.9	111.9	111.4
99.8	99.8	100.7	100.9	100.9	100.9	100.9	100.9	100.9	100.9
100.0	100.0	100.0	100.0	100.0	100.0	100.0	100.0	100.0	100.0
100.6	101.2	101.2	101.2	101.2	101.2	101.7	101.7	101.7	101.7
99.7	99.7	99.7	100.0	100.0	100.0	100.0	100.0	100.0	100.0

9-4 主要年份零售商品和服务项目年平均价格
Per Retail and Services Price of Major Years

商品名称	Name	规格等级牌号 Grade	单位 Unit	1978年	1980年	1985年
面粉	Flour	特一	元/千克(yuan/kg)	0.50	0.50	0.50
粳米	Japonica	标一	元/千克(yuan/kg)	0.34	0.34	0.40
小米	Millet	一等	元/千克(yuan/kg)	0.27	0.27	0.44
土豆	Potato		元/千克(yuan/kg)	0.19	0.22	0.30
豆腐	Tofu	水豆腐	元/千克(yuan/kg)	0.16	0.18	0.26
猪肉	Pork	净肉	元/千克(yuan/kg)	1.72	1.95	2.65
牛肉	Beef	净肉	元/千克(yuan/kg)	1.26	1.76	2.91
羊肉	Mutton	净肉	元/千克(yuan/kg)	1.38	1.88	2.80
鸡蛋	Hen's Egg	新鲜完整	元/千克(yuan/kg)	1.58	2.20	2.60
海带	Kelp	盐干一级	元/千克(yuan/kg)	1.18	1.26	1.32
大白菜	Chinese Cabbage	一等	元/千克(yuan/kg)	0.11	0.07	0.09
菠菜	Spinage	一等	元/千克(yuan/kg)	0.08	0.09	0.28
油菜	Oilseed rape	一等	元/千克(yuan/kg)	0.05	0.07	0.26
芹菜	Celery	一等	元/千克(yuan/kg)	1.13	0.11	0.39
韭菜	Chinese Chives	一等	元/千克(yuan/kg)	0.15	0.16	0.54
黄瓜	Cucumber	一等	元/千克(yuan/kg)	0.19	0.18	0.47
西红柿	Tomato	一等	元/千克(yuan/kg)	0.15	0.18	0.53
茄子	Eggplant	一等	元/千克(yuan/kg)	0.14	0.11	0.27
青椒	Green Pepper	一等	元/千克(yuan/kg)	0.23	0.20	0.47
大葱	Allium Fistulosum	一等	元/千克(yuan/kg)	0.11	0.12	0.28
黑木耳	Black Fungus	甲级	元/千克(yuan/kg)	30.00	32.00	34.86
精盐	Salt	再制盐	元/500克(yuan/500g)	0.16	0.16	0.14
酱油	Soy Sauce	二级	元/千克(yuan/kg)	0.22	0.22	0.34
味精	Aginomoto	含麸酸钠80%以上	元/千克(yuan/kg)	10.80	9.68	12.60
绵白糖	Soft Sugar	国产机制一级	元/千克(yuan/kg)	1.60	1.70	1.70
红糖	Brown Sugar	一级	元/千克(yuan/kg)	1.30	1.30	1.30
啤酒	Beer	熟12度瓶装	元/瓶(yuan/unit)	0.58	0.58	0.73
苹果	Apple	一级	元/千克(yuan/kg)	0.82	0.90	1.19
桔子	Orange	一级	元/千克(yuan/kg)	1.30	1.52	2.35
西瓜	watermelon	一级	元/千克(yuan/kg)	0.24	0.28	0.32
香蕉	Banana	一级	元/千克(yuan/kg)	1.46	1.65	1.82
自来水	Tap Water	生活用水	元/吨(yuan/tons)	0.08	0.08	0.09
照明用电	Lighting Electricity	民用220V	元/度(yuan/kWh)	0.18	0.18	0.18
平信	Ordinary Mail	外埠	元/封(yuan/unit)	0.08	0.08	0.08
注射费	Injection Fees	肌肉注射	元/次(yuan/unit)	0.10	0.10	0.10
住院费	Hospitalization Fees	普通床位	元/天(yuan/day)			
学杂费	Tuition and Fees	高中学生	元/学期(yuan/semester)	2.50	2.50	2.50
公园门票	Park Tickets	大明湖	元/张(yuan/unit)	0.03	0.03	0.03
理发	Haircut	男理一级全活	元/次(yuan/unit)	0.30	0.30	0.45
洗澡	Bath		元/次(yuan/unit)	0.24	0.24	0.30
课本	Textbook	高中语文一年级	元/本(yuan/unit)			
银花	Silver	一等	元/千克(yuan/kg)	6.65	8.00	18.00

注：1.大明湖景区2017年开始免费入园。
2.由于居民消费价格是指数比较，所以理发和洗澡所选的规格品与上年不一致，绝对价格无可比性。
3.因消费升级，商品和服务规格变化较大，零售商品和服务项目年平均价格自2019年起停止更新。

1990年	1995年	2000年	2005年	2010年	2013年	2014年	2015年	2016年	2017年	2018年
0.50	2.24	1.78	2.86	4.14	5.07	5.41	5.43	5.46	5.64	8.54
1.04	3.33	2.03	3.08	4.76	5.91	5.91	6.04	6.05	6.00	6.06
1.32	2.66	2.07	3.26	6.99	8.58	14.10	14.63	10.51	11.49	10.87
0.36	1.48	1.48	1.92	4.53	3.61	3.72	3.80	3.84	3.53	3.84
0.70	1.43	1.55	2.14	4.31	5.21	5.99	6.24	5.97	5.88	6.11
5.52	12.91	12.87	14.90	25.18	33.04	30.57	32.37	35.78	35.49	32.88
5.43	12.06	10.99	16.34	36.47	64.52	65.00	66.58	69.02	69.46	69.25
5.91	15.49	15.04	22.07	44.80	75.33	79.23	76.29	76.85	69.67	79.86
4.96	5.99	3.99	5.72	7.48	8.52	10.87	9.25	8.41	8.18	9.75
3.60	5.35	5.36	8.76	19.29	30.35	33.43	32.50	28.87	27.15	25.51
0.13	0.72	0.91	1.64	3.23	2.77	2.29	2.84	2.80	2.41	2.93
0.50	0.90	1.57	2.21	6.69	7.61	6.53	7.91	8.53	7.41	8.81
0.63	1.11	1.26	1.83	5.05	5.84	5.17	6.43	7.14	6.08	7.46
0.60	1.22	1.25	2.28	4.99	5.46	4.07	5.62	5.06	5.13	5.68
1.01	1.80	1.98	2.99	6.55	7.05	6.47	7.42	5.33	4.97	5.59
0.99	2.45	2.53	3.16	5.67	6.26	5.36	5.96	6.03	5.67	7.53
1.02	2.66	2.07	2.90	6.01	6.60	6.37	7.02	6.97	7.24	7.69
0.89	2.67	2.51	3.07	6.05	6.34	5.60	6.14	6.66	6.14	7.48
1.34	4.13	3.15	4.10	6.45	7.48	6.38	8.07	7.61	7.00	9.03
0.54	1.46	1.31	2.51	6.16	6.95	5.94	6.56	9.59	6.44	6.19
48.95	59.16	68.57	65.13	86.80	121.45	128.14	122.59	118.11	122.67	128.34
0.31	0.70	1.10	2.02	1.50	3.83	3.84	4.28	5.17	5.97	6.18
0.68	1.83	2.40	4.53	6.74	7.04	6.75	6.61	7.14	7.05	8.69
16.50	22.81	14.26	15.67	19.33	21.02	21.34	22.19	21.94	22.56	22.92
2.60	6.89	6.12	5.43	9.75	15.15	15.89	16.08	14.38	14.25	15.39
2.21	6.32	5.90	5.54	9.80	15.62	15.54	14.70	15.68	18.29	21.07
1.41	2.13	2.30	2.42	2.61	2.68	2.77	2.76	2.72	2.49	2.62
2.48	3.86	2.72	3.19	8.93	12.04	14.96	15.11	10.86	11.86	11.85
2.27	3.37	2.35	3.30	7.45	10.29	11.97	9.06	10.72	13.86	11.96
0.58	3.20	2.70	3.06	4.72	5.56	5.88	5.57	5.16	5.60	5.26
2.93	4.78	4.05	4.02	6.39	7.28	9.70	7.01	7.04	6.63	8.24
0.19	0.51	1.60	2.78	3.15	3.15	3.15	4.00	4.21	4.21	4.21
0.18	0.29	0.43	0.53	0.55	0.55	0.56	0.56	0.56	0.56	0.56
0.13	0.20	0.80	0.80	1.20	1.20	1.20	1.20	1.20	1.20	1.20
0.20	0.25	1.67	2.00	2.00	2.00	2.00	2.00	2.00	2.00	2.00
2.50	4.00	7.67	15.00	26.67	26.67	23.33	23.33	33.89	36.67	36.67
12.00	49.00	600.00	800.00	800.00	800.00	800.00	800.00	800.00	800.00	800.00
0.30	4.33	13.48	15.63	30.00	30.00	30.00	30.00	30.00		
1.30	5.63	10.00	17.50	20.50	25.00	25.21	25.21	32.38	25.10	27.70
0.58	5.00	8.00	12.00	30.00	38.00	53.00	58.00	58.00	68.00	68.00
2.00	2.55	6.41	4.60	6.47	6.47	6.47	6.47	6.47	6.44	6.39
28.00	70.00	93.00	87.22	325.00	314.10	361.17	352.71	325.00	324.39	403.83

Notes: 1.Daming Lake Scenic spot has been free since 2017.

2.Because the consumer price of residents is an index comparison, the standard products selected for haircut and bath are inconsistent with the previous year, and the absolute price is incomparable.

3.Because of consumption upgrading and large exchanges in commodity and service specifications, the annual average price of retail commodity and service items has not been updated since 2019.

9-5 住宅销售价格指数(2023年，以上月为100)
Sales Price Indices of Residential Buildings(2023,Preceding month=100)

指标	Item	一月 January	二月 February	三月 March	四月 April	五月 May	六月 June
新建住宅	**New Residential Buildings**	**99.8**	**100.9**	**100.7**	**100.6**	**100.7**	**100.2**
新建商品住宅	New Commercial Residential Buildings	99.8	100.9	100.7	100.6	100.7	100.2
90平方米及以下	Buildings below 90sq.m	99.9	100.5	101.1	100.6	101.0	100.1
90-144平方米	Buildings 90-144 sq.m	99.9	101.0	100.6	100.6	100.6	100.3
144平方米以上	Buildings above 144sq.m	99.4	100.6	100.6	100.4	100.7	100.0
二手住宅	**Second-hand House**	**99.7**	**100.2**	**100.4**	**100.2**	**99.8**	**99.7**
90平方米及以下	Buildings below 90sq.m	99.4	100.0	100.1	100.3	99.8	100.0
90-144平方米	Buildings 90-144 sq.m	99.9	100.4	100.6	100.1	99.7	99.6
144平方米以上	Buildings above 144sq.m	99.6	100.2	100.4	100.2	100.4	99.8

9-5 续表 continued

指标	Item	七月 July	八月 August	九月 September	十月 October	十一月 November	十二月 December
新建住宅	**New Residential Buildings**	**100.1**	**99.9**	**99.7**	**99.9**	**99.8**	**99.6**
新建商品住宅	New Commercial Residential Buildings	100.1	99.9	99.7	99.9	99.8	99.6
90平方米及以下	Buildings below 90sq.m	100.1	100.1	99.8	100.1	99.3	98.6
90-144平方米	Buildings 90-144 sq.m	100.0	99.7	99.6	99.7	99.9	99.8
144平方米以上	Buildings above 144sq.m	100.3	100.4	99.8	100.4	99.8	99.8
二手住宅	**Second-hand House**	**99.9**	**99.5**	**98.9**	**99.7**	**99.4**	**99.6**
90平方米及以下	Buildings below 90sq.m	100.2	99.6	99.0	99.5	98.6	99.0
90-144平方米	Buildings 90-144 sq.m	99.9	99.3	99.0	99.9	99.7	99.8
144平方米以上	Buildings above 144sq.m	99.4	99.7	98.4	99.7	99.8	99.9

9-6 住宅销售价格指数(2023年，以上年为100)

Sales Price Indices of Residential Buildings(2023,Preceding year=100)

指标	Item	一月 January	二月 February	三月 March	四月 April	五月 May	六月 June
新建住宅	**New Residential Buildings**	**101.6**	**102.4**	**102.8**	**103.6**	**103.8**	**103.7**
新建商品住宅	New Commercial Residential Buildings	101.6	102.4	102.8	103.6	103.8	103.7
90平方米及以下	Buildings below 90sq.m	102.3	102.3	102.9	104.2	103.7	103.9
90–144平方米	Buildings 90-144 sq.m	101.2	102.1	102.5	103.2	103.6	103.7
144平方米以上	Buildings above 144sq.m	102.6	103.3	103.8	104.5	104.7	104.0
二手住宅	**Second-hand House**	**96.5**	**96.8**	**97.4**	**98.3**	**98.6**	**98.4**
90平方米及以下	Buildings below 90sq.m	96.6	96.8	96.9	97.7	97.9	98.3
90–144平方米	Buildings 90-144 sq.m	96.4	97.1	97.6	98.8	98.5	98.0
144平方米以上	Buildings above 144sq.m	96.4	96.4	97.4	98.2	99.7	99.7

9-6 续表 continued

指标	Item	七月 July	八月 August	九月 September	十月 October	十一月 November	十二月 December
新建住宅	**New Residential Buildings**	**103.5**	**103.1**	**102.5**	**102.2**	**102.1**	**101.8**
新建商品住宅	New Commercial Residential Buildings	103.5	103.1	102.5	102.2	102.1	101.8
90平方米及以下	Buildings below 90sq.m	104.0	103.6	103.3	102.8	102.4	101.3
90–144平方米	Buildings 90-144 sq.m	103.4	103.0	102.3	101.8	101.8	101.7
144平方米以上	Buildings above 144sq.m	103.3	103.1	102.6	103.0	102.7	102.3
二手住宅	**Second-hand House**	**98.5**	**98.3**	**97.3**	**97.3**	**97.2**	**97.1**
90平方米及以下	Buildings below 90sq.m	98.4	98.1	97.5	97.1	96.3	95.5
90–144平方米	Buildings 90-144 sq.m	98.0	97.9	97.0	97.1	97.5	97.8
144平方米以上	Buildings above 144sq.m	99.8	99.8	97.5	98.2	98.0	97.6

9-7 主要年份工业生产者出厂、购进价格指数(以上年为100)

Producer Price Indices for Industrial Products and Purchasing Price Indices for Industrial Producers in Main Years(Preceding year=100)

年份 Year	工业生产者出厂价格指数 Producer Price Indices for Industrial Products	工业生产者购进价格指数 Purchasing Price Indices for Industrial Producer
1998	94.5	95.2
1999	98.9	97.6
2000	104.8	114.5
2001	99.8	101.4
2002	97.9	100.4
2003	103.2	111.2
2004	106.7	116.4
2005	102.3	111.3
2006	100.2	105.6
2007	103.9	105.0
2008	109.2	116.9
2009	96.2	94.3
2010	104.7	109.9
2011	105.3	108.2
2012	98.4	99.4
2013	98.8	97.8
2014	99.0	98.0
2015	95.0	92.7
2016	99.8	99.0
2017	105.7	113.9
2018	104.8	108.3
2019	100.3	98.6
2020	98.1	97.5
2021	110.3	109.5
2022	105.1	105.8
2023	96.5	97.0

注：2020年起，“工业生产者出厂价格指数”与“工业生产者购进价格指数”指标为全省数据。
Note:Starting in 2020,the"Producer Price Indices for Industrial Products"and" Purchasing Price Index for Industrial Producer "are province-wide data.

主要统计指标解释

居民消费价格指数 是反映一定时期内城乡居民所购买的生活消费品和服务项目价格变动趋势和程度的相对数。

商品零售价格指数 是反映一定时期内城乡商品零售价格变动趋势和程度的相对数。

工业生产者出厂价格指数 是反映一定时期内全部工业产品第一次出售时的出厂价格总水平的变动趋势和变动幅度的相对数。

工业生产者购进价格指数 是反映作为中间投入的原材料、燃料、动力购进价格总水平的变动趋势和变动幅度的相对数。

Explanatory Notes on Main Statistical Indicators

Consumer Price Indices are relative figures reflecting the trend and degree of changes in prices of consumer goods and services purchased by urban and rural households during a given period.

Retail Price Indices are relative figures reflecting the trend and degree of changes in retail prices of commodities during a given period.

Producer Price Indices for Industrial Products are relative figures reflecting the trend and degree of changes in general ex-factory prices of all manufactured goods for first sale during a given period.

Purchasing Price Indices for Industrial Producers are relative figures reflecting changes in the level and degree of purchasing prices such as intermediate input such as raw materials, fuels and power.

10

人民生活

PEOPLE'S LIVELIHOOD

10-1 人民物质文化生活提高情况
Improvement in People's Material and Cultural Life

指标	Item	单位 unit	1978年
就业	**Employment**		
每一农村劳动力负担人数	Average Dependents Per Labor Force	人(person)	1.70
每一城镇就业者负担人数	Dependents Per Urban Employee	人(person)	1.89
城镇登记失业率	Registered Urban Unemployment Rate	%	
收入与支出	**Income and Expenditure**		
农村居民人均可支配收入	Per Capita Disposable Income of Rural Households	元(yuan)	111
农村居民人均消费支出	Per Capita Consumer Expenditure of Rural Households	元(yuan)	83
农村居民恩格尔系数	Engel's Coefficient of Rural Households	%	69.9
城镇居民人均可支配收入	Per Capita Disposable Income of Urban Households	元(yuan)	338
城镇居民人均消费支出	Per Capita Consumer Expenditure of Urban Households	元(yuan)	318
城镇居民恩格尔系数	Engel's Coefficient of Urban Households	%	57.1
居民储蓄	**Household Savings**		
城乡居民年末储蓄存款余额	Deposits of Urban and Rural Households	亿元(100 million yuan)	1.3
人均储蓄存款余额	Per Capita Savings Balance	元(yuan)	28.5
住房面积	**Area of Building**		
农村人均住房建筑面积	Rural Per Capita Living Space	平方米(sq.m)	9.6
城镇人均住房建筑面积	Urban Per Capita Living Space	平方米(sq.m)	4.1
交通通讯	**Traffic and Communication**		
农村每百户拥有摩托车	Number of Motorcycles Owned by Per 100 Rural Households	辆(unit)	
城镇每百户拥有摩托车	Number of Motorcycles Owned by Per 100 Urban Households	辆(unit)	
城市公用事业	**Urban Utilities**		
供水普及率	Coverage Rate of Urban Population with Access to Tap Water	%	99
每万人拥有公园绿地面积	Green Area of Park Per 10 000 Population	公顷(ha)	1.6
文化生活	**Culture Life**		
农村每百户拥有彩色电视机	Number of Color TV Sets Owned by Per 100 Rural Households	台(set)	-
城镇每百户拥有彩色电视机	Number of Color TV Sets Owned by Per 100 Urban Households	台(set)	-
教育卫生	**Education and Public Health**		
每万人口中在校大学生数	Number of College Students Per 10 000 Population	人(person)	22
每万人拥有卫生技术人员	Number of Health Technical Personnel Per 10 000 Population	人(person)	10.98
每万人拥有医院病床	Number of Beds of Hospitals and Health Centers Per 10 000 Population	张(set)	22.01

注：1. "城镇居民人均消费支出"1990年以前为"生活费支出"。
2. "人均住宅建筑面积"，2009年以前(不含)为"使用面积"口径，2002年以前(不含)为"居住面积"口径。
3.从2015年起，全市发布城乡住户调查一体化改革新口径数据，居民收支调查指标与2014年前分别实施的城镇和农村住户调查的调查范围、方法、指标口径、名称有所不同。(以下相关表同)
4. "农村居民人均可支配收入"2014年以前为"农民人均纯收入"口径。

1990年	2000年	2010年	2020年	2021年	2022年	2023年
1.61	1.40	1.35	1.4	1.3	1.4	1.4
1.72	1.71	1.67	1.3	1.4	1.4	1.3
	3.70	3.84	2.03			
731	3047	8903	20432	22580	23844	25587
570	1977	5407	12947	14591	14883	16267
50.5	43.5	33.6	30.4	30.5	30.5	30.3
1620	8471	25321	53329	57449	59459	62506
1360	6892	15973	34391	36866	35788	37831
57.5	34.6	31.6	23.5	23.5	23.8	23.6
51.1	463.0	2187.7	7584.1	8558.4	10226.3	11806.3
975.5	8229.6	36239.0	94596.7	105441.9	124972.7	143519.1
22.5	28.6	40.2	50.3	49.8	47.5	49.2
7.5	10.5	29.7	39.3	39.4	39.7	41.2
4.0	61.0	84.9	57.7	51.7	50.7	43.0
7.7	34.3	13.3	13.1	11.1	10.4	11.1
100	100	100	100.00	100.00	100.00	100.00
4	7.2	11.3	13.06	12.95	13.14	14.35
70.0	125.0	122.2	110.0	104.3	101.8	100.7
61.3	132.3	115.5	105.9	104.8	102.5	100.0
71	165	1064	1121	743	820	840
59.45	63.40	65.20	127.44	133.55	138.75	148.58
32.88	38.57	52.9	73.3	77.5	80.8	85.8

Notes: 1. "Per capita living expenditure of urban residents" was "cost of living expenses" before 1990.

2. "Per capita housing area" was the caliber of "usable area" before 2009 (excluding) and was the caliber of "living area" before 2002.

3. Since 2015, the city has released new caliber data for the integrated reform of urban and rural household surveys. The survey indicator of residents' income and expenditure was different from the survey scope, method, index caliber and name of urban and rural households carried out before 2014. (The same below)

4. "Per capita disposable income of rural residents" was the caliber of "rural per capita net income" before 2014.

10-2 各时期城镇居民生活情况
Basic Conditions of Urban Households in Each Period

年 份 Year	人均可支配收入 (元) Per Capita Disposable Income (yuan)	人均消费支出(元) Per Capita Consumer Expenditure(yuan) 小 计 Total	#人均食品支出 Per Capita Food Expenditure	就业者负担人数 (人) Average Dependents Per Employee (person)	人均住宅建筑面积 (平方米) Per Capita Floor Space (sq.m)
1949	64.53	61.30	37.39		4.09
1952	130.00	127.84	77.98		4.11
1957	206.50	194.15	117.69		3.64
1962	201.74	209.84	131.42		3.48
1965	219.51	212.82	131.59		3.31
1970					3.51
1975					3.66
1978	337.80	317.88	181.56	1.89	4.06
1980	440.09	405.53	230.11	1.67	4.22
"六五"时期					
1981	487.19	452.77	256.67	1.73	4.40
1982	502.97	468.03	275.30	1.70	4.57
1983	552.37	484.87	293.32	1.66	4.93
1984	671.89	537.27	326.97	1.69	5.10
1985	783.00	703.82	397.33	1.68	5.21
"七五"时期					
1986	946.46	836.50	474.62	1.70	7.40
1987	1057.48	943.58	534.12	1.73	7.30
1988	1272.83	1150.44	635.11	1.70	7.50
1989	1487.91	1355.64	745.32	1.71	7.50
1990	1619.50	1360.08	781.58	1.72	7.50
"八五"时期					
1991	1854.33	1569.26	896.62	1.71	7.60
1992	2148.49	1781.21	979.03	1.73	7.65
1993	2873.94	2394.03	1146.02	1.74	7.80
1994	3951.94	3224.73	1566.59	1.72	7.90
1995	4720.55	3830.38	1823.64	1.80	8.00
"九五"时期					
1996	5681.49	4422.91	2161.00	1.71	8.00
1997	6261.21	5210.40	2185.11	1.62	8.10
1998	6757.12	5440.10	2179.99	1.61	9.89
1999	7162.48	6415.39	2204.76	1.66	10.00
2000	8471.32	6891.75	2387.06	1.71	10.50

10–2 续表 continued

年 份 Year	人均可支配收入(元) Per Capita Disposable Income (yuan)	人均消费支出(元) Per Capita Consumer Expenditure(yuan)		就业者负担人数(人) Average Dependents Per Employee (person)	人均住宅建筑面积(平方米) Per Capita Floor Space (sq.m)
		小 计 Total	#人均食品支出 Per Capita Food Expenditure		
“十五”时期					
2001	9564.99	7465.04	2386.84	1.74	10.70
2002	10094.13	7818.33	2575.21	1.72	17.83
2003	11012.86	8395.36	2610.75	1.68	18.85
2004	12005.06	8580.54	2784.87	1.65	19.50
2005	13578.46	9226.61	3046.93	1.73	19.55
“十一五”时期					
2006	15340.17	10713.13	3335.31	1.74	20.1
2007	18005.10	12389.69	3900.91	1.72	21.0
2008	20802.17	13904.59	4466.18	1.87	21.5
2009	22721.65	14764.28	4836.78	1.86	29.4
2010	25321.06	15973.32	5051.18	1.67	29.7
“十二五”时期					
2011	28891.97	18045.58	5722.65	1.71	30.3
2012	32569.75	20031.67	6162.16	1.72	
2013	35647.59	21666.94	6624.32		
2014	38762.77	22980.67	6814.14	2.04	
2015	39888.71	26318.72	6415.00	1.80	44.9
“十三五”时期					
2016	43052.16	28536.93	6908.01	1.87	45.5
2017	46642.40	30728.60	7229.30	1.35	47.8
2018	50146	32977	7758	1.4	46.5
2019	51913	33439	7956	1.4	39.0
2020	53329	34391	8072	1.3	39.3
“十四五”时期					
2021	57449	36866	8654	1.4	39.4
2022	59459	35788	8520	1.4	39.7
2023	62506	37831	8942	1.3	41.2

注：1.可支配收入1983年以前为生活费收入,消费支出1992年以前为生活费支出。
2.“人均住宅建筑面积”，2009年以前(不含)为“使用面积”口径，2002年以前(不含)为“居住面积”口径。

Notes: 1. The disposable income was living expenditure income before 1983, and the consumption expenditure was previously the cost-of-living expenditure before 1992.
2. "Per capita housing area", was the caliber of "usable area" before 2009 (excluding) and was the caliber of "living area" before 2002.

10-3 各时期农村居民生活情况
Basic Conditions of Rural Households in Each Period

年份 Year	人均可支配收入(元) Per Capita Disposable Income (yuan)	人均消费支出(元) Per Capita Consumer Expenditure (yuan)		每一劳动力负担人数(人) Average Dependents Per Labor Force (person)	人均住宅建筑面积(平方米) Per Capita Floor Space (sq.m)
		小计 Total	#人均食品支出 Per Capita Food Expenditure		
1952	49.4	39.2	29.2	1.8	7.5
1957	63.6	57.9	34.8	1.8	7.8
1962	67.7	59.9	36.3	1.8	8.0
1965	92.6	69.7	46.1	1.8	8.2
1970	82.7	67.2	42.2	1.7	8.5
1975	79.1	59.5	40.8	1.7	9.0
1978	110.5	83.2	58.2	1.7	9.6
1980	168.9	127.1	85.8	1.6	10.5
1985	439.2	330.5	171.1	1.6	16.9
1990	731.1	569.8	287.7	1.6	22.5
1991	810.1	610.6	303.7	1.6	23.7
1992	865.3	660.5	335.1	1.6	21.1
1993	1031.4	724.8	371.4	1.6	22.9
1994	1401.0	942.5	511.0	1.6	24.1
1995	1812.7	1373.6	770.8	1.4	24.7
1996	2328.1	1728.1	926.2	1.4	26.9
1997	2600.0	1799.7	922.0	1.4	27.1
1998	2826.4	1872.5	935.9	1.4	27.4
1999	2943.7	1841.2	876.7	1.4	28.3
2000	3046.8	1976.8	860.0	1.4	28.6
2001	3215.7	2057.8	852.5	1.5	29.9
2002	3355.8	2133.9	849.5	1.4	30.6
2003	3619.3	2316.2	900.7	1.4	32.5
2004	4198.7	2543.1	1040.4	1.4	32.9
2005	4812.3	2902.8	1134.8	1.4	33.8
2006	5480.0	3415.3	1199.8	1.4	35.3
2007	6300.1	3789.8	1423.0	1.4	37.3
2008	7180.2	4385.4	1628.2	1.4	38.7
2009	7804.8	4733.1	1686.3	1.4	39.4
2010	8903.3	5406.6	1818.3	1.4	40.2
2011	10411.8	5905.1	2147.3	1.4	41.2
2012	11786.2	6932.2	2465.4	1.4	42.9
2013	13247.6	7798.7	2640.8	1.4	43.9
2014	14726.0	8581.4	2831.4	1.4	
2015	14231.8	8597.2	2775.5	1.4	52.6
2016	15345.6	9396.3	3028.0	1.4	53.8
2017	16593.8	10327.3	3253.2	1.3	55.2
2018	17924	11172	3409	1.4	54.3
2019	19454	12300	3703	1.4	51.1
2020	20432	12947	3931	1.4	50.3
2021	22580	14591	4446	1.3	49.8
2022	23844	14883	4538	1.4	47.5
2023	25587	16267	4935	1.4	49.2

注：1. "人均可支配收入" 2014年以前为"农民人均纯收入"口径。
2. "人均住宅建筑面积"，2009年以前(不含)为"使用面积"口径，2002年以前(不含)为"居住面积"口径。

Notes: 1. "Per capita disposable income" was the caliber of "rural per capita net income" before 2014.
2. "Per capita housing area" was the caliber of "usable area" before 2009 (excluding) and was the caliber of "living area" before 2002 (excluding).

10–4 城镇每百户居民家庭主要耐用消费品拥有量
Main Durable Goods Owned Per 100 Urban Households

单位：台　　(set)

商品名称	Item	1995年	2000年	2005年	2010年	2015年	2020年	2022年	2023年
家用汽车(辆)	Automobile(unit)			5.4	22.7	47.6	58.5	66.1	66.8
摩托车(辆)	Motorcycle(unit)	13.0	34.3	30.1	13.3	15.1	13.1	10.4	11.1
洗衣机	Washing Machine	91.5	100.0	97.0	93.2	98.5	98.4	98.6	98.8
电冰箱	Refrigerator	92.0	99.3	97.0	96.7	101.8	104.0	100.5	101.5
彩色电视机	Color Television Set	95.0	132.3	126.8	115.5	110.5	105.9	102.5	100.0
空调器	Air Conditioner	16.0	65.0	104.4	121.5	146.3	166.4	175.3	179.3
热水器	Water Heaters	36.5	81.3	79.3	82.0	100.3	100.6	99.8	99.9
照相机	Camera	40.5	76.0	59.2	54.0	56.1	33.8	26.7	25.0
住宅电话(部)	Fixed-line Phones(unit)	38.0	86.7	88.6	46.3	54.7	19.2	10.1	8.9
移动电话(部)	Mobile Phones(unit)		28.7	145.2	179.7	213.5	225.7	239.5	243.0
计算机	Computer		20.0	54.2	81.0	90.8	83.2	79.5	77.0

10-5 农村每百户居民家庭主要耐用消费品拥有量
Main Durable Goods Owned Per 100 Rural Households

单位：台 (set)

商品名称	Item	2011年	2012年	2013年	2015年	2019年	2020年	2022年	2023年
家用汽车(辆)	Automobile(unit)					39	37	46	49
摩托车(辆)	Motorcycle(unit)	71	62	65	79	58	58	51	43
洗衣机	Washing Machine	82	86	88	86	93	91	93	95
电冰箱	Refrigerator	88	91	92	91	99	98	97	99
彩色电视机	Color Television Set	116	118	119	114	113	110	102	101
空调器	Air Conditioner	36	39	46	56	93	90	97	97
热水器	Water Heaters	64	69	69	74	82	86	90	90
照相机	Camera	15	14	16	8	6	3	6	5
住宅电话(部)	Fixed-line Phones(unit)	60	58	55	47	21	20	9	6
移动电话(部)	Mobile Phones(unit)	175	186	195	214	232	229	236	240
计算机	Computer	36	39	43	40	39	43	42	38

10-6 居民人均可支配收入和消费支出(2023年)
Per Capita Disposable Income and Consumer Expenditure(2023)

单位：元 (yuan)

指标名称	Item	全体居民 All Households	城镇居民 Urban households	农村居民 Rural households
可支配收入	**Disposable Income**	**51757**	**62506**	**25587**
工资性收入	Income of Wages and Salaries	29676	36150	13913
经营净收入	Net Business Income	5453	3810	9455
财产净收入	Net Income from Properties	7629	10523	584
转移净收入	Net Income from Transfers	8999	12023	1635
消费支出	**Consumption Expenditure**	**31553**	**37831**	**16267**
食品烟酒	Food,Tobacco and liquor	7775	8942	4935
衣着	Clothing and Footwear	1747	2135	801
居住	Housing	9126	11461	3439
生活用品及服务	Household Equipments, Furnishings and Services	2236	2728	1038
交通通信	Transport and Communications	4216	4909	2528
教育文化娱乐	Education, Culture and Recreation	3321	3998	1674
医疗保健	Health care and Medical Services	2459	2819	1583
其他用品和服务	Miscellaneous Goods and Services	673	839	269

主要统计指标解释

居民可支配收入 指居民可用于最终消费支出和储蓄的总和，即居民可用于自由支配的收入。既包括现金收入，也包括实物收入。按照收入的来源，可支配收入包含四项，分别为：工资性收入、经营净收入、财产净收入和转移净收入。

工资性收入 指就业人员通过各种途径得到的全部劳动报酬和各种福利，包括受雇于单位或个人、从事各种自由职业、兼职和零星劳动得到的全部劳动报酬和福利。

经营净收入 指住户或住户成员从事生产经营活动所获得的净收入，是全部经营收入中扣除经营费用、生产性固定资产折旧和生产税之后得到的净收入。计算公式为：

经营净收入=经营收入-经营费用-生产性固定资产折旧-生产税

财产净收入 指住户或住户成员将其所拥有的金融资产、住房等非金融资产和自然资源交由其他机构单位、住户或个人支配而获得的回报并扣除相关的费用之后得到的净收入。财产净收入包括利息净收入、红利收入、储蓄性保险净收益、转让承包土地经营权租金净收入、出租房屋净收入、出租其他资产净收入和自有住房折算净租金等。财产净收入不包括转让资产所有权的溢价所得。

转移净收入 计算公式为：转移净收入=转移性收入-转移性支出

转移性收入 指国家、单位、社会团体对住户的各种经常性转移支付和住户之间的经常性收入转移。包括养老金或退休金、社会救济和补助、政策性生产补贴、政策性生活补贴、经常性捐赠和赔偿、报销医疗费、住户之间的赡养收入，本住户非常住成员寄回带回的收入等。转移性收入不包括住户之间的实物馈赠。

转移性支出 指调查户对国家、单位、住户或个人的经常性或义务性转移支付。包括缴纳的税款、各项社会保障支出、赡养支出、经常性捐赠和赔偿支出以及其他经常转移支出等。

根据住户收支与生活状况调查，分城镇和农村的居民人均可支配收入等数据的覆盖人群主要变化：一是计算城镇居民人均可支配收入时分母包括了在城镇地区常住的农民工，计算农村居民人均可支配收入时分母不包括在城镇地区常住的农民工；二是由本户供养的在外大学生视为常住人口。

居民消费支出 指居民用于满足家庭日常生活消费需要的全部支出，既包括现金消费支出，也包括实物消费支出。消费支出可划分为食品烟酒、衣着、居住、生活用品及服务、交通通信、教育文化娱乐、医疗保健以及其他用品及服务八大类。

食品烟酒 指用于各种食品和烟草、酒类的支出。

衣着 指与居民穿着有关的支出，包括服装、服装材料、鞋类、其他衣类及配件、衣着相关加工服务的支出。

居住 指与居住有关的支出，包括房租、水、电、燃料、物业管理等方面的支出，也包括自有住房折算租金。

生活用品及服务 指家庭及个人的各类生活品及家庭服务。包括家具及室内装饰品、家用器具、家用纺织品、家庭日用杂品、个人用品和家庭服务。

交通通信 指用于交通和通信工具及相关的各种服务费、维修费和车辆保险等支出。

教育文化娱乐 指用于教育、文化和娱乐方面的支出。

医疗保健 指用于医疗和保健的药品、用品和服务的总费用。包括医疗器具及药品，以及医疗服务。

其他用品及服务 指无法直接归入上述各类支出的其他用品与服务支出。

服务性消费 指住户用于各种生活服务的消费支出，包括餐饮服务、衣着鞋类加工服务、居住服务、家庭服务、交通通信服务、教育文化娱乐服务、医疗服务和其他服务等。

Explanatory Notes on Main Statistical Indicators

Disposable Income of Residents refers to the income of residents for purpose of final expenditure and savings. It includes income both in cash and in kind. By sources of income, disposable income includes four categories: income from wages and salaries, net business income, net income from properties and net income from transfer.

Income from Wages and Salaries refers to remuneration and benefits of all kinds of employed persons, including those employed by other units or individuals, freelance workers, part-time jobs, and sporadic workers.

Net Business Income refers to net income earned by households and their members engaged in production and business activities. It refers to the net income of operating revenue minus operating costs, depreciation of productive fixed assets, and production tax. The formula is:

Net business income = operating revenue-operating costs -depreciation of productive fixed assets-production tax

Net Income from Properties refers to the net income received as returns by households or members through lending of their financial assets, non-financial assets such as housing, to other institutions, households or individuals, minus relevant costs. Net income from properties includes net income of interest, bonus income, net income of saving insurance, net income from transferring management right of contract land, income from lending of housing, income from lending other assets, net converted rents of self-owned housing. Net income from properties do not include premium of transferring ownership of assets.

Net Income from Transfer The formula is:

Net income from transfer = income from transfer - expenditure from transfer

Income from Transfer refers to the regular transfer received from governments, institutions, social organizations to households and between households. It includes old-age and retirement pension, regular donation and compensation, reimbursement of medical fees, supporting income between households, income from non-resident members of households, etc. Income from transfer do not include gifts in kinds between households.

Expenditure from Transfer refers to regular or obligatory transfer paid to government, institutions, households or individuals. It includes tax payment, expenditure on all kinds of social security, supporting expenditure, regular donation, compensation payment and other regular transfer expenditure.

According to Household Survey on Income and Expenditure and Living Conditions, main changes of population coverage of per capita disposable income of urban and rural residents includes: migrant workers residing in urban areas are included in the denominator when calculating per capita disposable income of urban residents, and not included in denominator when calculating per capita disposable income of rural residents; students studying in universities or colleges in other places who are supported by the households are regarded as permanent residents of the households.

Consumption Expenditure of Residents refers to all expenditure of residents for living expenditure to satisfy family daily living. It includes expenditure in cash and in kind. It includes eight categories: food, tobacco and liquor; clothing and footwear; housing; household equipments, furnishings and services; transport and communications; education, culture and recreation; health care and medical services, and miscellaneous goods and services.

Food, Tobacco and Liquor refers to expenditure for food, tobacco and liquor of all kinds.

Clothing and Footwear refers to expenditure related to clothing, including clothes, clothing materials, footwear, other clothing and accessories, processing services related to clothing.

Housing refers to expenditure related to housing, including rents, water, electricity, fuel, property management, as well as imputed rent on owner-occupied dwellings.

Household Equipments, Furnishings and Services refers to expenditure of households and individuals on equipments, furnishings and articles for living purpose and on household services. It includes furniture and interior decoration, home appliances, home textiles, household miscellaneous daily articles, personal articles, and household services.

Transport and Communications refers to expenditure on transport and communication and related services, maintenance and repairs, and vehicle insurance.

Education, Culture and Recreation refers to expenditure on educational, cultural and recreational activities.

Health Care and Medical Services refers to expenditure on drugs, supplies and services of medical and health care. It includes medical appliances and drugs, and medical services.

Miscellaneous Goods and Services refers to expenditure on all other articles and services that can not classified into the above categories.

Service Consumption refers to consumption expenditure of households for various living services, including catering services, clothing and footwear processing services, housing services, household services, transportation and communication services, education, culture and entertainment services, medical services and other services.

11

农 业

AGRICULTURE

11-1 各时期农业主要经济指标
Major Economic Indicators of Agriculture in Each Period

年份 Year	农村劳动力 (万人) Rural Labor (10 000 persons)	农林牧渔业总产值(亿元) Gross Output Value of Farming, Forestry,Animal Husbandry and Fishery (100 million yuan)	农业机械总动力 (万千瓦) Total Agricultural Machinery Power (10 000 kW)	年末实有耕地面积 (千公顷) Actual Cultivated Area (1000 ha)	粮食总产量 (万吨) Output of Grain (10 000 tons)	蔬菜总产量 (万吨) Output of Vegetables (10 000 tons)	肉类总产量 (万吨) Output of Meat (10 000 tons)	粮食单产 (千克/公顷) Output Per Hectare of Grain (kg/ha)
1949	106.51	1.50	-	469.85	51.63	10.72	0.24	825
1952	112.35	1.91	-	481.17	62.75	8.61	0.40	960
1957	121.09	2.79	0.32	479.58	67.92	15.86	0.66	1065
1962	108.44	1.33	2.98	412.34	39.74	27.67	0.72	765
1965	111.74	2.61	4.84	410.02	73.80	29.12	1.12	1350
1970	123.91	2.75	14.32	396.49	75.47	31.81	1.21	1470
1975	141.00	4.07	48.04	382.05	100.46	42.00	2.07	2025
1978	140.05	6.57	69.70	373.19	115.38	49.19	2.50	2475
1979	141.60	7.48	80.63	372.45	122.56	49.42	2.92	2610
1980	143.19	7.79	88.45	370.87	116.54	58.13	3.69	2565
“六五”时期								
1981	146.52	11.73	94.47	369.80	121.27	49.85	3.99	2865
1982	149.07	14.47	106.60	369.22	121.13	63.45	4.31	3060
1983	152.39	18.07	112.19	368.45	147.41	65.66	4.66	3570
1984	158.23	19.00	123.92	367.35	160.60	86.91	5.03	3915
1985	162.51	18.36	130.41	357.41	163.50	84.11	5.43	3915
“七五”时期								
1986	165.86	20.91	147.36	353.96	168.16	118.86	6.44	3855
1987	168.56	24.65	156.23	352.18	167.25	101.52	7.13	3945
1988	171.44	34.24	172.89	350.56	167.95	122.83	8.68	4080
1989	173.38	35.14	182.40	349.59	162.45	117.99	9.70	3945
1990	176.83	36.92	183.40	347.56	181.47	126.09	11.38	4273
“八五”时期								
1991	180.09	40.13	191.00	344.76	207.55	146.87	13.50	4779
1992	182.51	45.14	191.50	343.29	198.29	170.61	15.36	4655
1993	183.78	57.81	194.40	341.54	232.21	205.62	19.12	4963
1994	183.42	85.37	207.40	339.97	237.66	226.39	26.14	5237
1995	183.55	114.07	241.20	339.30	252.48	253.54	28.68	5512
“九五”时期								
1996	184.68	117.65	247.07	337.25	267.08	350.36	30.43	5602
1997	186.68	131.69	258.50	335.90	240.34	328.64	24.75	5064
1998	186.54	141.45	273.30	334.83	273.10	344.67	27.38	5634
1999	188.27	148.61	297.55	333.72	279.01	366.78	29.89	5752
2000	189.15	154.30	349.47	333.72	240.27	405.95	31.82	5354

注：1.自2005年始年末实有耕地面积有国土资源局提供，暂无2009年数据。
2.依据2006年农业普查数据，对1997年至2007年蔬菜面积、产量做了相应调整。
3.粮食作物产量、播种面积自2012年开始由国家统计局山东调查总队反馈。
4.按照国务院农普办要求，由国家统计局山东调查总队根据第三次农业普查数据，对2016-2017年市.县(区)粮食播种面积.单产和总产量等数据进行了修订。
5.依据2016年农业普查数据，对2007年至2017年农林牧渔业总产值做了相应调整。
6.依据2016年农业普查数据，对2008年至2017年蔬菜总产量、肉类总产量做了相应调整。
7.2019年农业数据为区划调整后的数据，以下各表同。
8.由于市农业农村局未提供农业机械类指标数据，2020年延用 2019 年数据。以下相关各表同。
9.根据国家统计局最新报表制度，“农村劳动力”指标2022年起不再进行统计。

11-1 续表 continued

年份 Year	农村劳动力(万人) Rural Labor (10 000 persons)	农林牧渔业总产值(亿元) Gross Output Value of Farming, Forestry,Animal Husbandry and Fishery (100 million yuan)	农业机械总动力(万千瓦) Total Agricultural Machinery Power (10 000 kW)	年末实有耕地面积(千公顷) Actual Cultivated Area (1000 ha)	粮食总产量(万吨) Output of Grain (10 000 tons)	蔬菜总产量(万吨) Output of Vegetables (10 000 tons)	肉类总产量(万吨) Output of Meat (10 000 tons)	粮食单产(千克/公顷) Output Per Hectare of Grain (kg/ha)
"十五"时期								
2001	189.87	162.27	409.07	331.75	239.08	435.20	33.23	5480
2002	190.98	167.99	410.17	329.35	189.86	478.34	31.87	4440
2003	192.71	180.30	417.43	325.18	220.56	504.81	33.29	5448
2004	191.31	204.39	418.54	324.89	242.74	515.26	35.35	5807
2005	190.21	230.46	426.76	366.99	260.11	529.37	37.93	5932
"十一五"时期								
2006	190.80	247.70	429.62	361.74	267.91	536.28	38.74	6042
2007	191.16	262.51	446.60	358.80	268.01	522.24	31.85	6064
2008	190.45	302.00	466.00	361.33	281.50	520.25	30.22	6230
2009	195.56	318.06	486.00		289.47	560.83	31.39	6246
2010	196.85	361.24	509.68	362.30	289.43	572.05	31.79	6192
"十二五"时期								
2011	197.38	399.90	527.39	361.25	295.84	590.02	32.43	6315
2012	198.74	422.75	538.66	360.28	286.03	606.11	33.22	6285
2013	199.80	470.55	552.06	361.01	266.60	629.54	33.59	5997
2014	199.73	479.50	567.02	360.24	271.19	638.22	34.10	6109
2015	200.45	493.04	584.98	358.57	264.55	626.23	34.18	6117
"十三五"时期								
2016	200.46	501.72	447.83	357.60	275.43	611.25	31.72	5778
2017	198.91	505.08	442.90	355.66	255.57	591.63	32.50	5660
2018	189.10	514.90	454.62	353.65	251.42	527.22	29.82	5659
2019	239.03	637.30	543.48	344.82	285.46	671.24	35.86	5956
2020	222.13	671.66	543.48	342.29	290.81	673.73	23.92	6053
"十四五"时期								
2021	212.69	758.41	570.10	342.56	293.07	691.76	27.36	6060
2022		784.24	594.94	342.88	296.19	712.61	29.10	6112
2023		800.56	618.43	347.12	302.89	726.39	29.50	6235

Notes: 1. Since 2005, the actual cultivated area has been provided by Land Resources Bureau. No data for 2009.

2. According to the data of the agricultural census in 2006, the area and yield of the vegetables from 1997 to 2007 were adjusted accordingly.

3. Grain crop yield and sown area have been reported by Survey Office of the National Bureau of Statistics in Shandong since 2012.

4. According to the requirements of Agricultural Census Office of the State Council, Survey Office of the National Bureau of Statistics in Shandong revised the grain sown area, yield per unit and total yield of each city and country (district) from 2016-2017 based on the data from the third agricultural census.

5. According to the data of the agricultural census in 2016, the gross output value of farming, forestry, animal husbandry and fishery in the period from 2007 to 2017 was adjusted accordingly.

6. According to the data of the agricultural census in 2016, the total output value of vegetable and meat in the period from 2008 to 2017 was adjusted accordingly.

7.The data of agriculture in 2019 is the adjusted data by the administrative division (the same below).

8.Due to the municipal bureau of agriculture and rural affairs didn't provide data on agricultural machines index, thus the data of 2019 is adopted. The same for the following tables.

9.The index of "rural labor" will not be counted from 2022 in light of the latest report system of National Bureau of Statistics.

11-2 农村基层组织和农业基本情况
Basic Conditions of Rural Grassroots Units and Agriculture

指标	Item	单位 Unit	2019年	2020年	2021年	2022年	2023年
乡镇数量	Number of Towns	个(Unit)	40	29	29	29	29
#镇	Towns	个(Unit)	40	29	29	29	29
村民委员会	Village Committee	个(Unit)	5551	5530	4699	4698	4691
耕地	Cultivated Land	公顷(ha)	344821	342289	342562	342881	347124
其中：水浇地	Irrigated Land	公顷(ha)	269859	268186	270893	271483	275370
园地	Garden Land	公顷(ha)	101941	102052	101351	99552	98496
林地	Forest Land	公顷(ha)	248283	247879	244444	242315	236867
草地	Pasture Land	公顷(ha)	27048	27300	26994	28903	28790
城镇村及工矿用地	Land for Urban Village, Mining and Manufacturing	公顷(ha)	187602	189766	191113	191650	192355
交通运输用地	Land for Transport Facilities	公顷(ha)	19176	19391	20837	22006	23164
水域及水利设施用地	Land for Water Conservancy Facilities	公顷(ha)	58953	58956	60144	59975	59866
农业机械总动力	Total Agricultural Machinery Power	万千瓦(10 000 kW)	543.48	543.48	570.10	594.94	618.43
农用大中型拖拉机	Large and Medium-sized Tractors	台(set)	23553	23553	25498	27040	28727
农用小型拖拉机	Small Tractors	台(set)	49911	49911	48261	47705	47211
谷物联合收割机	Combine Harvester	台(set)	15746	15746	16838	9364	9749
脱粒机	Thresher	台(set)	27007	27007	25932	25821	26388
农用化肥使用量	Consumption of Chemical Fertilizer	吨(折纯) (ton) (convert to pure volume)	214814	205007	199919	194361	189641
农药使用量	Pesticides Consumption	吨(ton)	3477.5	3231.4	2960.8	2846.5	2722.0
农作物总播种面积	Total Sown Area of Farm Crops	千公顷(1000 ha)	615.6	614.3	614.8	617.7	620.7

11-3 分地区农村基层组织和农业基本情况(2023年)
Basic Conditions of Rural Grassroots Units and Agriculture by Region(2023)

指标	Item	单位 Unit	济南市 Jinan	历下区 Li xia
乡镇数量	Number of Towns	个(Unit)	29	
#镇	Towns	个(Unit)	29	
村民委员会	Village Committee	个(Unit)	4691	
耕地	Cultivated Land	公顷(ha)	347124	63
其中：水浇地	Irrigated Land	公顷(ha)	275370	8
园地	Garden Land	公顷(ha)	98496	74
林地	Forest Land	公顷(ha)	236867	2562
草地	Pasture Land	公顷(ha)	28790	94
城镇村及工矿用地	Land for Urban Village, Mining and Manufacturing	公顷(ha)	192355	7142
交通运输用地	Land for Transport Facilities	公顷(ha)	23164	89
水域及水利设施用地	Land for Water Conservancy Facilities	公顷(ha)	59866	37
农业机械总动力	Total Agricultural Machinery Power	万千瓦(10 000 kW)	618.4	2.7
农用大中型拖拉机	Large and Medium-sized Tractors	台(set)	28727	45
农用小型拖拉机	Small Tractors	台(set)	47211	461
谷物联合收割机	Combine Harvester	台(set)	9749	13
脱粒机	Thresher	台(set)	26388	16
农用化肥使用量	Consumption of Chemical Fertilizer	吨(折纯) (ton) (convert to pure volume)	189641	
农药使用量	Pesticides Consumption	吨(ton)	2722.0	
农作物总播种面积	Total Sown Area of Farm Crops	千公顷(1000 ha)	620.7	

市中区 Shi zhong	槐荫区 Huai yin	天桥区 Tian qiao	历城区 Li cheng	长清区 Chang qing	章丘区 Zhang qiu	济阳区 Ji yang	莱芜区 Lai wu	钢城区 Gang cheng	平阴县 Ping yin	商河县 Shang he
				2	1	2	7		6	11
				2	1	2	7		6	11
77	93	48	266	585	525	566	792	211	308	516
3039	1546	8119	13283	31619	62729	64729	46450	11280	27682	76585
785	641	7967	9656	18262	47701	64018	26218	2087	21449	76578
2795	313	516	29285	17938	13808	1330	19308	5223	7417	491
9134	1846	2936	42157	39836	36343	9129	52632	15657	16793	7842
957	301	539	3316	4095	7963	537	7163	1941	1415	470
10312	7648	8713	29857	15819	31849	16950	26940	10344	10199	16584
825	1049	1027	4697	1926	3330	2283	3724	979	1275	1959
379	2278	3655	4818	4397	8997	12357	8463	2078	2743	9664
13.0	3.7	20.6	54.2	55.4	110.9	110.7	74.0	20.5	51.8	100.9
403	257	831	1848	3212	4155	5596	2565	524	2081	7210
412	288	1254	5383	3489	2243	4136	15580	4525	5005	4435
65	110	304	738	859	2366	1487	547	118	525	2617
121	2276	1031	1227	888	2193	6483	6967	1302	705	3179
500	185	2737	9963	11629	41296	28227	23125	3218	13564	55199
18.6	3.9	25.5	226.6	306.4	364.5	568.0	527.3	196.7	124.7	359.8
4.2	2.3	12.8	25.8	56.9	141.0	116.6	60.2	11.5	49.8	139.7

11-4 各时期农林牧渔业总产值(按当年价格计算)

Gross Output Value of Farming, Forestry, Animal Husbandry and Fishery in Each Period(Calculated at Current Prices)

单位：亿元 (100 million yuan)

年份 Year	合计 Total	其中 of which 农业 Farming	林业 Forestry	牧业 Animal Husbandry	渔业 Fishery	农林牧渔服务业 Services of Farming, Forestry,Animal Husbandry and Fishing
1952	1.91	1.67	0.04	0.18	0.02	-
1957	2.79	2.41	0.09	0.28	0.01	-
1962	1.33	1.18	0.03	0.12		-
1965	2.61	2.25	0.07	0.28	0.01	-
1970	2.75	2.32	0.10	0.32	0.01	-
1975	4.07	3.48	0.13	0.44	0.02	-
1978	6.57	5.63	0.20	0.72	0.02	-
1980	7.78	6.66	0.18	0.93	0.01	-
1985	18.36	14.63	0.75	2.93	0.05	-
“七五”时期						
1986	20.91	16.81	0.79	3.23	0.08	-
1987	24.65	19.50	0.99	4.05	0.11	-
1988	34.24	24.83	1.42	7.67	0.32	-
1989	35.14	25.04	1.24	8.47	0.39	-
1990	36.92	24.70	1.41	10.36	0.45	-
“八五”时期						
1991	40.13	26.44	1.47	11.64	0.58	-
1992	45.14	29.01	1.70	13.71	0.72	-
1993	57.81	36.00	1.98	18.86	0.97	-
1994	85.37	52.36	2.80	29.38	0.83	-
1995	114.07	71.48	2.71	38.69	1.19	-
“九五”时期						
1996	117.65	77.16	3.35	35.25	1.89	-
1997	131.69	87.91	3.86	38.04	1.88	-
1998	141.45	93.56	3.55	42.17	2.17	-
1999	148.61	96.81	3.12	46.27	2.41	-
2000	154.30	100.18	3.64	48.34	2.14	-
“十五”时期						
2001	162.27	105.54	3.27	51.16	2.30	-
2002	167.99	106.27	3.51	55.84	2.37	-
2003	180.30	109.41	4.11	60.90	2.05	3.83
2004	204.39	121.28	4.49	71.87	2.50	4.25
2005	230.46	137.01	5.56	80.56	2.69	4.64
“十一五”时期						
2006	247.72	147.98	6.44	84.86	2.89	5.55
2007	262.51	154.32	7.28	91.33	3.18	6.41
2008	302.00	173.32	10.63	104.53	4.54	8.97

11-4 续表 continued

单位：亿元 (100 million yuan)

年份 Year	合计 Total	其中 of which 农业 Farming	林业 Forestry	牧业 Animal Husbandry	渔业 Fishery	农林牧渔服务业 Services of Farming, Forestry,Animal Husbandry and Fishing
2009	318.06	192.96	11.16	98.96	4.79	10.18
2010	361.24	231.08	6.87	106.40	5.31	11.58
“十二五”时期						
2011	399.90	240.80	7.98	131.55	6.05	13.51
2012	422.75	251.57	9.00	139.90	6.88	15.39
2013	470.55	284.66	10.34	149.46	8.01	18.07
2014	479.50	291.94	11.19	147.57	8.76	20.03
2015	493.04	296.93	12.15	153.12	9.32	21.52
“十三五”时期						
2016	501.72	298.63	13.20	156.28	9.88	23.74
2017	505.08	296.75	15.25	159.23	7.80	26.06
2018	514.90	318.55	17.72	141.48	7.28	29.88
2019	637.30	424.04	24.99	144.53	6.79	36.96
2020	671.66	447.15	29.82	149.14	6.10	39.46
“十四五”时期						
2021	758.41	501.98	34.41	170.99	8.20	42.83
2022	784.24	526.03	32.02	170.22	8.48	47.48
2023	800.56	543.88	32.06	164.02	8.89	51.72
2023年分地区Region						
历下区 Li xia						
市中区 Shi zhong	3.39	1.22	0.04	1.91		0.22
槐荫区 Huai yin	4.50	2.75	0.56	0.39	0.62	0.17
天桥区 Tian qiao	2.80	1.29	0.05	1.27	0.10	0.08
历城区 Li cheng	75.06	52.09	7.49	6.44	1.65	7.38
长清区 Chang qing	75.96	50.65	4.67	15.98	1.49	3.17
章丘区 Zhang qiu	187.92	130.35	5.33	37.22	1.35	13.67
济阳区 Ji yang	97.17	74.95	2.65	13.70	1.46	4.41
莱芜区 Lai wu	134.44	98.86	1.78	28.43	1.12	4.24
钢城区 Gang cheng	23.71	10.34	2.11	10.00	0.14	1.13
平阴县 Ping yin	81.06	49.51	3.80	19.57	0.45	7.74
商河县 Shang he	114.55	71.86	3.57	29.10	0.51	9.50

注：1.依据2016年农业普查数据，对2007年至2017年农林牧渔业总产值做了相应调整。
2.天桥区农林牧渔业总产值仅包含桑梓店街道农林牧渔业产值。

Notes: 1.According to the data of the agricultural census in 2016, the total output value of farming, forestry, animal husbandry and fishery in the period from 2007 to 2017 was adjusted accordingly.
2.The gross output value of farming, forestry, animal husbandry and fishery in Tianqiao District only includes the output value of farming, forestry, animal husbandry and fishery in Sangzidian Sub-District.

11-5 各时期农林牧渔业总产值指数(以1952年为100)

Gross Output Value Indices of Farming, Forestry, Animal Husbandry and Fishery in Each Period(1952=100)

年份 Year	合计 Total	其中 of which			
		农业 Farming	林业 Forestry	牧业 Animal Husbandry	渔业 Fishery
1952	100.00	100.00	100.00	100.00	100.00
1957	116.18	114.55	170.35	119.90	109.96
1962	73.32	74.42	69.10	69.25	20.68
1965	123.31	121.76	147.34	141.38	28.95
1970	151.35	146.28	254.82	184.02	58.65
1975	201.09	196.80	317.61	226.74	78.38
"五五"时期					
1976	198.67	185.64	340.19	269.52	118.70
1977	197.95	190.19	373.20	218.87	56.26
1978	208.10	203.90	304.32	239.93	57.89
1979	233.93	224.05	316.47	293.89	53.70
1980	264.53	259.07	286.30	330.80	43.98
"六五"时期					
1981	279.36	279.29	281.28	377.56	55.36
1982	312.68	308.75	346.83	460.13	51.95
1983	402.03	369.18	434.91	460.59	57.98
1984	493.28	436.59	572.67	651.29	69.52
1985	505.48	460.68	992.56	841.94	161.47
"七五"时期					
1986	531.29	488.47	964.62	857.25	229.32
1987	560.14	506.85	1075.00	960.76	291.92
1988	585.14	510.86	992.11	1191.92	383.08
1989	571.95	483.32	886.96	1320.55	495.30
1990	607.77	449.63	1126.99	1931.15	695.49
"八五"时期					
1991	670.19	488.17	1189.04	2204.93	830.45
1992	712.62	491.78	1298.34	2574.55	1007.33
1993	844.31	566.55	1420.51	3221.58	1209.21
1994	945.74	603.90	1671.10	2864.71	1064.29
1995	1093.57	657.49	1508.72	4905.57	1945.11
"九五"时期					
1996	1197.20	727.03	1818.36	5258.95	2224.25

11-5 续表 continued

年 份 Year	合计 Total	其中 of which			
		农业 Farming	林业 Forestry	牧业 Animal Husbandry	渔业 Fishery
1997	1273.56	820.27	2002.99	5116.96	2202.07
1998	1426.28	914.05	1858.14	5907.41	2516.54
1999	1486.09	934.64	2110.21	6277.65	2639.47
2000	1569.90	991.58	2255.81	6620.62	2441.73
“十五”时期					
2001	1599.32	1005.16	1700.16	6905.18	2646.43
2002	1638.09	997.16	1826.57	7349.57	2712.97
2003	1711.88	1072.24	1977.78	7726.93	2324.25
2004	1804.32	1132.29	1979.76	8121.00	2803.05
2005	1930.62	1188.90	2237.13	8770.68	2802.30
“十一五”时期					
2006	2046.15	1249.31	2454.25	9245.35	3003.10
2007	2046.15	1334.26	2610.83	9006.43	3540.65
2008	2148.45	1422.32	2783.14	9231.59	3204.85
2009	2260.17	1524.73	2964.04	9342.35	3323.43
2010	2367.76	1584.02	1815.08	10311.68	3416.48
“十二五”时期					
2011	2471.94	1658.47	2016.56	10600.40	3508.72
2012	2588.12	1724.80	2216.20	11151.62	3768.36
2013	2689.05	1762.74	2491.01	11809.56	3877.64
2014	2801.99	1845.58	2724.66	12116.60	3916.41
2015	2919.67	1924.93	2986.23	12540.68	4033.90
“十三五”时期					
2016	3045.21	2007.70	3317.70	12967.06	4187.19
2017	3157.88	2126.15	3689.28	13278.26	4203.93
2018	3095.96	2215.44	4105.56	12733.85	4330.04
2019	3123.82	2290.76	5037.52	11587.80	3814.77
2020	3205.04	2361.77	5979.54	11460.33	3715.59
“十四五”时期					
2021	3474.26	2456.24	6942.25	14142.05	5164.67
2022	3630.61	2571.68	6970.01	14523.88	5474.55
2023	3808.50	2684.84	7234.88	15337.22	5715.43

11-6 主要农作物播种面积及产量
Sown Areas and Output of Major Farm Crops

指标	Item	2019年	2020年	2021年	2022年	2023年
农作物总播种面积(万公顷)	**Total Sown Area of Crops(10 000 ha)**	**61.56**	**61.43**	**61.48**	**61.77**	**62.07**
粮食作物	Grain Crops	47.93	48.04	48.36	48.46	48.58
谷物	Cereals	46.33	46.38	46.74	46.71	46.89
小麦	Wheat	21.89	21.73	21.95	21.96	21.96
稻谷	Rice	0.14	0.06	0.08	0.09	0.07
玉米	Corn	23.18	23.53	23.64	23.60	23.85
谷子	Millet	1.09	1.03	1.04	1.05	1.00
高粱	Jowar	0.01	0.01	0.01	0.01	0.01
其他	Others	0.01	0.01	0.01	0.01	
豆类	Beans	0.77	0.77	0.75	0.86	0.92
薯类	Tubers	0.83	0.90	0.88	0.89	0.77
油料作物	Oil-bearing Crops	1.92	1.81	1.75	1.76	1.77
#花生	Peanuts	1.81	1.67	1.62	1.63	1.63
棉花	Cotton	0.38	0.35	0.33	0.30	0.30
蔬菜	Vegetable	10.03	9.86	9.74	9.93	10.08
果用瓜	Melon	0.98	0.96	1.00	1.01	1.03
其他作物	Other Farm Crops	0.32	0.40	0.30	0.31	0.32
果园种植面积(万公顷)	**Orchard Area(10 000 ha)**	**3.89**	**3.95**	**3.83**	**3.82**	**3.84**
#苹果	Apple	1.24	1.20	1.20	1.19	1.18
梨	Pear	0.18	0.19	0.21	0.20	0.19
葡萄	Grape	0.11	0.11	0.11	0.12	0.12
桃	Peach	1.00	1.03	0.97	0.95	0.95
农作物总产量(万吨)	**Total Output of Farm Crops(10 000 tons)**					
粮食作物	Grain Crops	285.46	290.81	293.07	296.19	302.89
谷物	Cereals	276.48	280.74	283.22	286.13	294.12
小麦	Wheat	135.31	137.37	139.25	139.69	141.36
稻谷	Rice	1.21	0.52	0.63	0.66	0.56
玉米	Corn	136.11	139.16	139.56	142.11	148.69
谷子	Millet	3.80	3.64	3.73	3.64	3.49
高粱	Chinese Sorghum	0.03	0.02	0.03	0.02	0.02
其他	Other Cereals	0.03	0.03	0.03	0.02	
豆类	Beans	2.12	2.13	2.05	2.25	2.35
薯类	Tubers	6.86	7.93	7.80	7.80	6.42
油料作物	Oil-bearing Crops	6.57	6.82	6.60	6.62	6.68
#花生	Peanuts	6.31	6.48	6.29	6.34	6.39

11-6 续表 continued

指标	Item	2019年	2020年	2021年	2022年	2023年
棉花	Cotton	0.54	0.42	0.38	0.35	0.36
蔬菜	Vegetable	671.24	673.73	691.76	712.61	726.39
果用瓜	Melon	48.02	49.49	50.54	52.28	53.42
水果总产量(万吨)	**Output of Fruits(10 000 tons)**	**62.95**	**63.20**	**61.90**	**61.99**	**63.99**
#苹果	Apple	20.22	18.92	19.26	19.13	19.80
梨	Pear	4.19	3.80	4.16	4.01	3.80
葡萄	Grape	3.13	3.21	3.33	3.49	3.47
桃	Peach	21.40	21.87	20.12	19.56	20.57
杏	Apricot	4.11	4.01	3.47	3.54	3.55
枣(鲜)	Jujube	1.21	1.01	0.97	1.00	0.80
柿子(鲜)	Persimmon	2.29	2.51	2.63	2.69	2.65
山楂	Hawthorn	2.19	2.80	3.15	3.32	3.26
樱桃	Cherry	2.78	3.82	3.60	3.93	4.55
其他	Others	1.19	0.98	0.90	11.70	0.99
农作物单位面积产量(公斤/公顷)	**Output per Hectare of Farm Crops(kg/ha)**					
粮食作物	Grain Crops	5956	6053	6060	6112	6235
谷物	Cereals	5968	6053	6060	6126	6273
小麦	Wheat	6181	6321	6344	6362	6437
稻谷	Rice	8334	8250	7771	7327	7749
玉米	Corn	5872	5914	5903	6022	6236
谷子	Millet	3490	3522	3586	3477	3478
高粱	Chinese Sorghum	1941	1958	2324	2115	1976
其他	Others	2750	2813	2838	2737	
豆类	Beans	2747	2784	2738	2630	2548
薯类	Tubers	8248	8835	8886	8766	8347
油料作物	Oil-bearing Crops	3418	3761	3761	3762	3778
#花生	Peanuts	3495	3878	3883	3881	3928
棉花	Cotton	1410	1193	1170	1180	1194
蔬菜	Vegetable	66895	68337	71058	71748	72090
果用瓜	Melon	48797	51472	50569	51520	52126

注：粮食作物产量、播种面积由国家统计局山东调查总队反馈。
Note: Grain crop yield and sown area have been reported by Survey Office of the National Bureau of Statistics in Shandong.

11-7 林、牧、渔业生产情况
Basic Statistics on Forestry, Animal Husbandry and Fishery

指标	Item	单位 Unit	2019年	2020年	2021年	2022年	2023年
林业生产	**Production of Forestry**						
造林面积	Forested Area	公顷(ha)	10758	10939	5333	774	828
四旁植树	Surrounding Tree Planting	万株(10000 trees)	1576	1527	845	1714	1510
育苗面积	Area of Nursery Garden	公顷(ha)	11579	10750	7781	5229	3897
果品产量	Output of Fruits	吨(ton)	686868	653290	643282	568611	612947
木材采伐量	Timber Cut	立方米(cu.m)	355596	298532	223579	189631	299224
牧业生产	**Production of Animal Husbandry**						
大牲畜存栏	Stocked Large Livestock	万头(10 000 heads)	24.42	15.26	17.18	16.89	15.97
#牛	Cattle	万头(10 000 heads)	24.27	15.20	17.16	16.86	15.95
猪存栏	Stocked Pigs	万头(10 000 heads)	129.26	122.86	131.95	121.21	90.62
羊存栏	Stocked Sheep	万只(10 000 heads)	100.13	66.01	73.56	77.73	71.18
家禽存栏	Stocked Poultry	万只(10 000 heads)	3440.94	2523.33	2763.07	2488.34	3060.81
猪出栏数	Slaughtered Pigs	万头(10 000 heads)	217.66	157.03	192.00	209.60	203.67
羊出栏数	Slaughtered Sheep	万只(10 000 heads)	164.26	86.91	126.84	136.20	130.04
肉类总产量	Output of Meat	吨(ton)	358655	239186	273577	291021	294989

11-7 续表 continued

指标	Item	单位 Unit	2019年	2020年	2021年	2022年	2023年
#猪牛羊肉	Meat	吨(ton)	236601	164537	201638	212521	209163
猪肉	Pork	吨(ton)	170584	128052	154189	168901	167302
牛肉	Beef	吨(ton)	40698	21020	28807	24306	23289
羊肉	Mutton	吨(ton)	25319	15465	18642	19314	18571
禽肉	Poultry Meat	吨(ton)	120194	73887	71686	78492	85826
奶类	Milk	吨(ton)	321323	414297	420987	434263	453831
#牛奶	Cow Milk	吨(ton)	321321	414297	420987	434263	453831
禽蛋	Poultry & Eggs	吨(ton)	365810	274673	304983	269925	292042
#鸡蛋	Eggs	吨(ton)	343650				
渔业生产	**Aquatic Products**						
水产品产量	Total Aquatic Products	吨(ton)	16167	13294	14068	14778	15380
捕捞	Fishing	吨(ton)	3513	3291	1187	729	805
养殖	Cultured	吨(ton)	12654	10003	12881	14049	14575
养殖面积	Breeding Area of Aquatic Products	公顷(ha)	4380	4304	4336	4341	4350
养殖单产	Aquaculture Yield	公斤/公顷(kg/ha)	2889	2324	2971	3236	3351

11-8 分地区主要农作物播种面积及产量(2023年)
Sown Areas and Output of Main Farm Crops by Region(2023)

指标	Item	济南市 Jinan	历下区 Li xia	市中区 Shi zhong
农作物播种总面积(公顷)	**Total Sown Area of Crops(ha)**			
粮食	Grain	485819		4097
谷物	Cereals	468896		4060
小麦	Wheat	219595		1437
稻谷	Rice	723		
玉米	Corn	238451		2500
谷子	Millet	10041		124
高粱	Jowar	87		
其他	Others			
豆类	Beans	9226		34
薯类	Tubers	7697		3
油料作物	Oil-bearing Crops	17691		3
#花生	Peanuts	16273		3
棉花	Cotton	3004		6
蔬菜	Vegetable	100761		89
果用瓜	Melon	10249		15
其他作物	Other Farm Crops	3206		
果园种植面积(公顷)	**Orchard Area(ha)**	**38372**		**292**
#苹果	Apple	11798		47
梨	Pear	1860		8
葡萄	Grape	1197		17
桃	Peach	9474		111
农作物产量(吨)	**Total Output of Farm Crops(ton)**			
粮食作物	Grain Crops	3028926		20461
谷物	Cereals	2941173		20369
小麦	Wheat	1413575		8639
稻谷	Rice	5600		
玉米	Corn	1486906		11448
谷子	Millet	34920		282
高粱	Jowar	172		
其他	Other Cereals			
豆类	Beans	23506		70
薯类	Tubers	64247		23
油料作物	Oil-bearing Crops	66829		8
#花生	Peanuts	63923		8

槐荫区 Huai yin	天桥区 Tian qiao	历城区 Li cheng	长清区 Chang qing	章丘区 Zhang qiu	济阳区 Ji yang	莱芜区 Lai wu	钢城区 Gang cheng	平阴县 Ping yin	商河县 Shang he
2155	12442	19999	44493	107731	101094	31693	4334	35593	122189
2050	12394	19481	41814	102680	99819	29749	3484	31658	121708
825	5693	5809	16740	52118	53777	6079	514	17038	59566
447		107		15	100			53	
779	6701	12272	21572	47974	45942	22662	2729	13179	62142
		1293	3500	2489		1007	241	1388	
			3	84					
101	48	321	1346	3061	1248	325	40	2302	401
4		198	1333	1990	27	1619	809	1633	80
	23	181	3765	1777	313	5223	4094	2300	11
	23	174	3276	1637	297	5206	4094	1554	9
	22	18	97	647	164	427	235	1085	303
148	256	3521	8227	25683	13638	22702	2713	9149	14637
5	10	2044	115	5195	1344	105	87	1028	303
		26	180	4	33	4		693	2266
11	**272**	**10251**	**3442**	**6132**	**735**	**5667**	**3245**	**7775**	**549**
0	32	2929	116	2501	95	711	345	4927	95
1	100	772	40	276	103	254	121	92	92
0	8	100	19	361	37	244	20	296	95
7	118	3850	715	828	393	1026	2051	236	138
13670	71742	107256	269256	642698	636189	197913	25812	203044	840884
13400	71662	104764	253657	617945	632749	182386	18930	185674	839638
5153	34706	35161	99598	332864	348350	38950	3094	98187	408872
3491		821		114	766			409	
4756	36956	64360	139093	277295	283633	141069	15010	82520	430766
		4422	14961	7504		2367	826	4558	
			5	167					
245	80	912	3510	8124	3214	783	106	5651	812
25		1580	12090	16629	226	14745	6776	11719	434
	101	867	18079	5593	1387	20070	11094	9588	41
	101	853	17186	5375	1385	20033	11094	7853	35

11-8 续表 continued

指标	Item	济南市 Jinan	历下区 Li xia	市中区 Shi zhong
棉花	Cotton	3587		10
蔬菜	Vegetable	7263908		4435
果用瓜	Melon	534245		882
水果总产量(吨)	**Output of Fruits(ton)**	**639893**		**3608**
#苹果	Apple	197986		1508
梨	Pear	37980		108
葡萄	Grape	34687		620
桃	Peach	205659		1045
杏	Apricot	35455		74
枣(鲜)	Jujube	8000		120
柿子(鲜)	Persimmon	26468		0.1
山楂	Hawthorn	32601		
樱桃	Cherry	45548		90
其他	Others	9858		27
农作物单位面积产量(公斤/公顷)	**Output per Hectare of Farm Crops(kg/ha)**			
粮食作物	Grain Crops	6235		4994
谷物	Cereals	6273		5017
小麦	Wheat	6437		6012
稻谷	Rice	7746		
玉米	Corn	6236		4579
谷子	Millet	3478		2274
高粱	Jowar	1977		
其他	Others			
豆类	Beans	2548		2059
薯类	Tubers	8347		7667
油料作物	Oil-bearing Crops	3778		2895
#花生	Peanuts	3928		2895
棉花	Cotton	1194		1475
蔬菜	Vegetable	72090		49980
果用瓜	Melon	52126		59580

注：粮食作物产量、播种面积由国家统计局山东调查总队反馈。
Note: Grain crop yield and sown area have been reported by Survey Office of the National Bureau of Statistics in Shandong.

槐荫区 Huai yin	天桥区 Tian qiao	历城区 Li cheng	长清区 Chang qing	章丘区 Zhang qiu	济阳区 Ji yang	莱芜区 Lai wu	钢城区 Gang cheng	平阴县 Ping yin	商河县 Shang he
	31	26	126	700	198	527	339	1251	379
11778	11057	181120	572011	1932073	1273709	1318229	209401	686760	1063335
223	279	99774	4949	264357	72986	4582	3502	67941	14770
284	**7885**	**113992**	**65620**	**75678**	**21492**	**123716**	**104492**	**106363**	**16763**
8	993	25952	3401	40326	3443	21791	17939	80294	2330
35	2931	12195	1616	3354	2715	6615	1977	2576	3858
9	215	2709	439	10730	1125	5645	529	7704	4961
188	3536	52889	13891	11966	11050	28649	73184	5367	3892
	88	3333	15299	599	421	11505	747	2550	838
	107	476	448	3259	831	1783	244	399	334
		1814	5688	141	790	15602	1992	417	22
		11031	148	662	158	15935	3970	686	12
23		2547	24049	3265	2	11163	2233	1886	290
20	14	796	85	294	928	1780	1272	4417	226
6343	5766	5363	6052	5966	6293	6245	5956	5705	6882
6537	5782	5378	6066	6018	6339	6131	5433	5865	6899
6246	6096	6053	5950	6387	6478	6407	6019	5763	6864
7810		7673		7600	7660			7717	
6105	5515	5244	6448	5780	6174	6225	5500	6261	6932
		3420	4275	3015		2351	3427	3284	
			1667	1988					
2426	1667	2841	2608	2654	2575	2409	2650	2455	2025
6250		7980	9070	8356	8370	9107	8376	7176	5425
	4365	4785	4800	3147	4425	3840	2710	4169	3826
	4365	4905	5250	3285	4665	3847	2710	5052	3826
	1391	1425	1305	1083	1207	1235	1443	1152	1253
79695	43245	51445	69525	75225	93390	58065	77170	75060	72645
44520	28845	48810	43065	50895	54315	43800	40440	66075	48795

11-9 分地区林、牧、渔业生产情况(2023年)
Basic Statistics on Forestry, Animal Husbandry and Fishery by Region(2023)

指标	Item	单位 Unit	济南市 Jinan	历下区 Li xia	市中区 Shi zhong
林业生产	**Production of Forestry**				
造林面积	Forested Area	公顷(ha)	828		67
四旁植树	Surrounding Tree Planting	万株(10000 trees)	1510	107	120
育苗面积	Area of Nursery Garden	公顷(ha)	3897		10
果品产量	Output of Fruits	吨(ton)	612947		7520
木材采伐量	Timber Cut	立方米(cu.m)	299224	185	198
牧业生产	**Production of Animal Husbandry**				
牛存栏	Stocked Cattle	万头(10 000 heads)	15.95		0.07
猪存栏	Stocked Pigs	万头(10 000 heads)	90.62		0.71
羊存栏	Stocked Sheep	万只(10 000 heads)	71.18		4.46
家禽存栏	Stocked Poultry	万只(10 000 heads)	3060.81		22.54
猪出栏数	Slaughtered Pigs	万头(10 000 heads)	203.67		1.60
羊出栏数	Slaughtered Sheep	万只(10 000 heads)	130.04		7.26
猪牛羊肉产量	Meat	吨(ton)	209163		2935
猪肉	Pork	吨(ton)	167302		1289
牛肉	Beef	吨(ton)	23289		497
羊肉	Mutton	吨(ton)	18571		1149
禽肉	Poultry Meat		85826		269
奶类	Milk	吨(ton)	453831		
#牛奶	Cow Milk	吨(ton)	453831		
禽蛋	Poultry & Eggs	吨(ton)	292042		4028
渔业生产	**Aquatic Products**				
水产品产量	Total Aquatic Products	吨(ton)	15380		
捕捞	Fishing	吨(ton)	805		
养殖	Cultured	吨(ton)	14575		
养殖面积	Breeding Area of Aquatic Products	公顷(ha)	4350		
养殖单产	Aquaculture Yield	公斤/公顷(kg/ha)	3351		

槐荫区 Huai yin	天桥区 Tian qiao	历城区 Li cheng	长清区 Chang qing	章丘区 Zhang qiu	济阳区 Ji yang	莱芜区 Lai wu	钢城区 Gang cheng	平阴县 Ping yin	商河县 Shang he
	27	60	80	367	27	160	40		
70	20	250	128	201	176	186	60	89	103
		1034	1533	700	290	129	3	73	125
	647	280094	33129	22903	8378	119979	117368	13756	9173
3538		4664	135173	19512	41107	4297	49974	19350	21227
0.03	0.09	0.52	1.76	1.41	2.24	1.50	0.28	2.12	5.92
0.05	1.34	3.30	11.54	11.08	7.56	22.63	8.84	9.98	13.59
0.23	4.22	1.81	5.86	8.11	5.46	17.23	6.71	5.91	11.18
4.51	75.19	166.15	272.29	686.81	225.93	611.44	191.15	343.41	461.39
0.11	2.43	6.26	23.01	33.66	14.63	42.68	19.04	23.61	36.65
0.52	8.29	3.56	9.18	12.20	13.72	27.39	13.80	11.45	22.67
271	3314	7172	22673	31024	17422	46085	18209	22509	37549
90	1942	5242	18627	26303	12872	38207	14878	18881	28971
106	243	1451	2622	2805	2784	4002	1377	2025	5376
75	1129	479	1424	1917	1765	3876	1954	1603	3202
109	2300	2975	4135	20350	7919	21254	4993	9401	12122
		10804	61296	6389	42973	2505	3082	92297	234485
		10804	61296	6389	42973	2505	3082	92297	234485
1357	8233	23205	40825	63659	19939	35855	16866	30928	47147
1379	401	421	996	1781	3441	3975	240	818	1928
		29	81	63	50	480			102
1379	401	392	915	1718	3391	3495	240	818	1826
124	179	48	346	360	558	1723	270	446	296
11121	2240	8167	2645	4772	6077	2028	889	1834	6169

11-10 主要农副产品产量与上年和历史最高年份比较
Output of Major Agricultural Products in Comparision with Last Year and Maximum Year

单位：万吨 (10 000 tons)

指标	Item	2023年	2022年	历史最高年 Maximum Year		2023年为历史最高年的% 2023 Account for Historic High	2023年为2022年的% 2023 Account for 2022
				年份 Year	产量 Output		
农产品产量	**Total Output of Farm Crops**						
粮食总产量	Output of Grain Crops	302.89	296.19	2023	302.89	100.0	102.3
#小麦	Wheat	141.36	139.69	2023	141.36	100.0	101.2
稻谷	Rice	0.56	0.66	2000	9.89	5.7	84.8
玉米	Corn	148.69	142.11	2023	148.69	100.0	104.6
薯类	Tubers	6.42	7.80	1995	23.10	27.8	82.3
经济作物	**Commercial Crop**						
#棉花	Cotton	0.36	0.35	1999	5.00	7.2	102.8
油料花生	Peanuts	6.39	6.34	2020	6.48	98.6	100.8
蔬菜总产量	Output of Vegetable	726.39	712.61	2023	726.39	100.0	101.9
水果总产量	Output of Fruits	63.99	61.99	2023	63.99	100.0	103.2
水产品总产量	**Total Aquatic Products**	**1.5**	**1.5**	**2015**	**4.80**	**32.0**	**104.1**

主要统计指标解释

农林牧渔业总产值 指以货币表现的农、林、牧、渔业全部产品和对农林牧渔业生产活动进行的各种支持性服务活动的价值总量，它反映一定时期内农林牧渔业生产总规模和总成果。

农林牧渔业总产值采用“产品法”进行计算，通常是按农、林、牧、渔业产品及其副产品的产量分别乘以各自单位产品价格求得；少数生产周期较长，当年没有产品或产品产量不易统计的，则采用间接方法匡算其产值；然后将四业产品产值及农林牧渔专业及辅助性活动产值相加即为农林牧渔业总产值。

粮食产量 指日历年度内生产的全部粮食数量。按收获季节包括夏收粮食、早稻和秋收粮食，按作物品种包括谷物、豆类和薯类。其产量计算方法：谷物按脱粒后的原粮计算，豆类按去豆荚后的干豆计算；薯类(包括甘薯和马铃薯，不包括芋头和木薯)1964年以前按每4公斤鲜薯折1公斤粮食计算，从1964年开始改为按5公斤鲜薯折1公斤粮食计算；城市郊区作为蔬菜的薯类(如马铃薯等)按鲜品计算，并且不作粮食统计。1989年以前全国粮食产量数据主要靠全面报表取得，1989年开始使用抽样调查数据。

棉花产量 指全社会棉花的产量。包括春播棉和夏播棉。产量按皮棉计算。不包括木棉。

油料产量 指全部油料作物的生产量。包括花生、油菜籽、芝麻、向日葵籽、胡麻籽（亚麻籽）和其他油料。不包括大豆、木本油料和野生油料。花生以带壳干花生计算。

水产品产量 指渔业（捕捞和养殖）生产活动的最终有效成果，包括全部海水和淡水鱼类、甲壳类（虾、蟹）、贝类、头足类、藻类和其他类渔业产品的最终产量。水产品产量是通过各级渔业主管部门逐级上报取得数据。1995年及以前，贝类中牡蛎按鲜肉计算；蚶、蛤、蛙按5斤鲜品折1斤计算。1996年以后则统一按鲜品计算。

猪、牛、羊、禽肉产量 指当年出栏并已屠宰、除去头蹄下水后带骨肉(即胴体重)的重量。1996年以前为全面统计并逐级上报数据。1996年第一次农业普查以后，根据普查结果，对畜牧业主要年报数据进行了修正。1999年，国家统计局在部分地区开展了猪、牛、羊、禽等主要畜禽品种的抽样调查，并用抽样数据作为国家定案数据使用。未开展抽样调查的地区，仍使用各级统计部门逐级上报数据。2008年，建立了主要畜禽监测调查制度，猪、牛、羊、禽等主要畜禽数据均以抽样调查数为法定数据。

农作物播种面积 指日历年度内收获农作物在全部土地（耕地或非耕地）上的播种或移植面积。凡是本年内收获的农作物，无论是本年还是上年播种，都算为播种面积，但不包括本年播种，下年收获的农作物面积。

农用化肥施用量 指本年内实际用于农业生产的化肥数量，包括氮肥、磷肥、钾肥和复合肥。化肥施用量要求按折纯量计算数量。折纯量是指把氮肥、磷肥、钾肥分别按含氮、含五氧化二磷、含氧化钾的百分之百成份进行折算后的数量。复合肥按其所含主要成分折算。公式为：

折纯量=实物量×某种化肥有效成份含量的百分比

农业机械总动力 指全部农业机械动力的额定功率之和。农业机械是指用于种植业、畜牧业、渔业、农产品初加工、农用运输和农田基本建设等活动的机械及设备。

Explanatory Notes on Main Statistical Indicators

Gross Output Value of Farming, Forestry, Animal Husbandry and Fishery refers to the total value of products (expressed in monetary terms) of farming, forestry, animal husbandry and fishery, and total value of services in support of farming, forestry, animal husbandry and fishery activities. It reflects the total scale and results of agricultural production during a given period.

Gross output value of farming is calculated by product method, and is obtained by multiplying the output of each product or by-product by its price, resulting in the output value of each single item. For a small number of products, annual output of which is not available or difficult to get due to the long production (growing) process involved, the output value is estimated through an indirect approach. The sum of output values of all products of farming, forestry, animal husbandry and fishery and professional and support activities in farming, forestry, animal husbandry and fishery is then equal to the gross output value of agriculture.

Grain Output refers to the total output of grains produced within a calendar year. It includes summer crops, early rice and autumn crops by harvest seasons; and covers cereals, beans and tubers by type of crops. Output of cereals cover husked grain only. Output of beans refers to dry beans without pods. The output of tubers (sweet potatoes and potatoes, not including taros and cassava) are converted with the ratio of 4:1, i.e. 4 kilograms of fresh tubers were equivalent to 1 kilogram of grain before 1964. Since 1964 the ratio has been changed to 5:1. Tubers consumed as vegetables (such as potatoes) in cities and suburbs are calculated as fresh vegetables and their output is not included in the output of grain. Data on grain production before 1989 were obtained through the comprehensive statistical reporting system. Since 1989, data from sample surveys are used.

Cotton Output refers to cotton production in the whole country including cotton planted in spring and in summer. Output is measured as the weight of ginned cotton. Ceiba is not included.

Output of Oil-bearing Crops refers to the total production of oil-bearing crops of various kinds, including peanuts (dry, in shell), rapeseeds, sesame, sunflower seeds, flax seeds, and other oil-bearing crops. Soybeans, oil-bearing woody plants, and wild oil-bearing crops are not included.

Output of Aquatic Products refers to final output actually yielded from fishing production (fishery and breeding), including all output of marine and freshwater fish, crustaceans (shrimps, crabs), shellfish, cephalopod, seaweed and other fishery products. Data on output of aquatic products are reported by fishery agencies level by level. Before 1995, among the shellfish, oyster was counted as fresh meat; and 5 kilograms of ark shell, clams and frogs were equivalent to 1 kilogram of fresh aquatic products; they have all been counted as fresh aquatic products since 1996.

Output of Pork, Beef, Mutton and Poultry refers to the meat of slaughtered hogs, cattle, sheep and goats with head, feet, and offal taken away. Before 1996, data were obtained through bottom-up comprehensive reporting system. The first agricultural census of China in 1996 revealed some discrepancy between the production of animal products from the annual reports and that from the census. Efforts were made to adjust the output value of animal husbandry to make the figures from the annual reports consistent with the census data. Since 1999, the NBS conducted sample surveys in selected regions for the major animal husbandry products, such as hogs, cattle, sheep and goats and fowls, and the data from sample surveys are used as finalized national data. Production of other regions which are not covered by the sample survey is still reported by statistical agencies level by level. A monitoring and survey program was set up in 2008 on main livestock, and data on the main livestock such as hog, cattle, sheep and poultry from the sample survey became the official data.

Sown Area of Crops refers to area of all land (cultivated or non-cultivated area) sown or transplanted with crops that are harvested within the calendar year. All crops harvested within the year are counted as sown area, regardless of being sown in this year or the previous year. Crops sown this year but will be harvested in the coming year are excluded.

Consumption of Chemical Fertilizers in Agriculture refers to the quantity of chemical fertilizers applied in agriculture in the year, including nitrogenous fertilizer, phosphate fertilizer, potash fertilizer, and compound fertilizer. The consumption of chemical fertilizers is calculated in terms of volume of effective components by means of converting the gross weight of the respective fertilizers into weight containing effective component (e.g. nitrogen content in nitrogenous fertilizer, phosphorous pentoxide contents in phosphate fertilizer, and potassium oxide contents in potash fertilizer). Compound fertilizer is converted in regard to its major components. The formula is:

Volume of effective component= physical quantity× effective component of certain chemical fertilizer (%)

Total Power of Agricultural Machinery refers to the total rated capacity of all agricultural machinery. Agricultural machinery refers to the machines and equipment which are used for activities of farming, animal husbandry, fishery, primary processing of agricultural products, agricultural transport and infrastructure construction of farmland.

12

工 业

INDUSTRY

12-1 各时期全部工业基本情况
Basic Statistics on Total Industry in Each Period

年份 Year	全部工业单位数 (个) Number of Industrial Enterprises (Unit)		工业总产值 (亿元) Gross Industrial Output Value (100 million yuan)		工业增加值 (亿元) Value Added of Industry Enterprises (100 million yuan)		国有独立核算工业 (万元) State-owned Independent Accounting Industrial (10 000 yuan)	
	合计 Total	#国有单位 State-owned	合计 Total	#国有单位 State-owned	合计 Total	#国有单位 State-owned	利润总额 Total Profits	利税总额 Total Profits and Taxes
1949	52	-	1.20	0.52	0.40	0.15	190	541
1952	92	-	2.97	1.65	1.09	0.52	1616	2761
1957	399	-	6.90	6.13	2.18	1.84	5742	10065
1962	847	286	6.67	5.61	2.36	1.80	3293	8242
1965	724	247	11.99	10.09	4.34	3.39	16246	22906
1970	828	285	23.12	17.93	7.56	5.64	19347	31834
1975	1041	326	26.41	18.87	8.46	5.50	11555	27846
1978	1319	398	39.06	25.87	12.89	7.11	28852	53031
1979	1353	359	42.95	28.90	14.10	8.01	31875	57532
1980	1535	356	45.31	30.37	14.24	8.85	32909	59572
"六五" 时期								
1981	1538	350	47.61	31.72	15.11	9.47	35077	62657
1982	1619	357	51.98	33.91	15.79	10.01	32062	64673
1983	1674	369	59.06	36.99	17.96	11.49	35870	60308
1984	1981	325	66.96	39.78	20.10	13.17	45869	83520
1985	2584	477	74.41	44.66	27.54	16.97	61274	112154
"七五" 时期								
1986	3005	369	86.93	48.71	28.69	17.53	54804	115006
1987	3957	361	107.63	56.16	32.88	19.40	58715	125775
1988	5252	372	138.05	68.58	47.49	25.09	80173	156056
1989	7655	380	158.53	76.19	54.66	30.51	76571	170703
1990	11020	394	222.63	116.92	60.43	37.11	25084	125522
"八五" 时期								
1991	12211	376	245.73	131.35	67.73	43.35	36715	151718
1992	15374	373	303.33	162.35	86.85	48.97	55463	193000
1993	19392	376	448.25	230.93	115.36	69.65	57984	223445
1994	22009	366	614.08	236.40	154.49	69.64	60393	240473
1995	24621	495	752.23	279.16	194.16	83.12	65335	316289
"九五" 时期								
1996	32902	425	834.45	260.16	238.31	91.30	79615	337807
1997	33000	325	897.59	263.34	278.87	92.99	95267	343426
1998	32793	227	966.62	234.03	298.41	94.28	42152	292991
1999	29319	211	981.78	212.95	318.80	79.51	-2340	254619
2000	30899	195	994.00	237.14	336.61	81.00	34824	292198
"十五" 时期								
2001	34135	169	1090.70	140.44	356.72	64.69	49222	226242
2002	30064	155	1302.00	144.78	410.98	49.16	28011	234986

12-1 续表 continued

年份 Year	全部工业单位数 (个) Number of Industrial Enterprises (Unit)		工业总产值 (亿元) Gross Industrial Output Value (100 million yuan)		工业增加值 (亿元) Value Added of Industry Enterprises (100 million yuan)		国有独立核算工业 (万元) State-owned Independent Accounting Industrial (10 000 yuan)	
	合计 Total	#国有单位 State-owned	合计 Total	#国有单位 State-owned	合计 Total	#国有单位 State-owned	利润总额 Total Profits	利税总额 Total Profits and Taxes
2003	30258	126	1544.50	167.30	494.55	68.80	53363	302975
2004	31163	115	1981.80	150.70	620.14	37.21	-3943	72684
2005	31370	102	2447.51	177.00	786.11	66.49	268573	354111
“十一五”时期								
2006	35370	86	2806.94	193.10	861.48	73.95	315323	458191
2007	36112	76	3389.09	283.32	985.78	103.65	364790	751182
2008	36416	80	4829.16	338.24	1140.14	136.55	418265	853091
2009	37656	77	5096.98	345.44	1191.36	166.36	422898	885006
2010	37521	66	5800.39	404.38	1352.42	284.75	643216	1162785
“十二五”时期								
2011	36750	54	5544.60	478.10	1507.88		561683	1217350
2012	35917	52	5535.25	491.20	1603.08		646193	1401892
2013	38443	30	5711.48	280.63	1690.63		551967	665206
2014	38753	25	5861.98	246.26	1822.11		507491	611865
2015	38793	24	5877.28	204.79	1844.37		517575	571354
“十三五”时期								
2016	34310	16	6059.16	157.83	1878.83		540739	622714
2017	33725	12	6395.21	147.27	2003.10		583734	589999
2018	31270	13	5641.61	15.50	2145.10		-4140	5014
2019					2167.87			
2020					2360.48			
“十四五”时期								
2021					2746.00			
2022					2869.00			
2023	34092				2886.07			

注：1.工业增加值、工业总产值按当年价格计算。
2.1985、1995年因工业普查对教育局校办工厂统计方法的规定，故国有单位较多。
3.2001年后炼油、浪潮、将军等原国有企业陆续改制，故国有数字较以前年份有所减小。
4.2004年第一次经济普查后，统计年鉴包含济南供电公司年报数据。
5.非经济普查年度，除“工业增加值”外，其它指标空缺。
6.经济普查年度，2023年“工业增加值”为快报数据。
7.根据相关统计调查制度的调整，规模以下工业已无“工业总产值”指标，登记注册类型中已无“#国有单位”和“国有独立核算工业”分类。

Notes: 1. Industrial value added and total industrial output value are calculated according to the current year's prices.
2. There were many state-owned units in 1985 and 1995 due to the provisions regarding statistical approach for school-run factories of Education Bureau from industrial census.
3. Original state-owned enterprises such as Oil Refining, Inspur and General were subject to restructuring in succession after 2001, so the quantity of state-owned enterprises decreased in comparison to that of previous years.
4. After the economic census for the first time in 2004, statistical yearbook includes annual report data of Jinan Power Supply Company.
5.In years other than the year of economic census, indicators are blank, excluding "Value Added of Industrial Enterprises".
6.In the economic census year, "Value Added of Industrial Enterprises" related indicator in 2023 is the express data.
7.According to the adjusted statistics and survey system, the indicator of "gross industrial output value" was removed from the enterprises below the designed size, and the classification of "state-owned sectors" and "state-owned enterprises with independent accountability" were also removed from the registration type.

12–2 各时期规模以上工业基本情况
Basic Statistics of Industrial Enterprises Above Designated Size in Each Period

单位：亿元 (100 million yuan)

年份 Year	单位数 (个) Number of Enterprises (unit)	工业总产值 Gross Industrial Output Value	工业增加值 Value Added of Industry Enterprises	营业收入 Business Revenue	利税总额 Total Profits and Taxes	利润总额 Total Profits	资产总计 Total Assets	所有者权益 Owner's Equities
1949	52	1.06	0.40	0.91	0.07	0.03	0.58	0.17
1952	92	2.83	1.02	2.40	0.32	0.18	1.89	0.55
1957	399	6.04	2.08	5.85	1.04	0.60	2.85	0.83
1962	847	6.65	2.15	6.87	0.92	0.39	5.66	1.65
1965	724	11.89	4.07	9.49	2.47	1.73	5.93	1.73
1970	828	22.94	7.29	19.30	3.66	2.22	10.67	3.10
1975	1041	26.16	7.94	19.70	3.47	1.55	17.21	5.01
1978	1319	37.67	9.94	31.39	6.80	3.88	25.68	7.47
1979	1353	38.79	11.18	35.51	7.21	4.13	27.19	7.91
1980	1535	43.60	12.15	36.90	7.51	4.26	29.22	8.50
“六五”时期								
1981	1538	42.26	12.77	39.84	7.98	4.37	31.49	9.20
1982	1619	45.58	13.63	42.94	8.13	4.18	34.52	10.08
1983	1674	49.64	14.86	46.38	8.84	4.74	38.09	11.12
1984	1981	55.95	17.91	52.16	10.46	5.82	41.66	12.16
1985	1915	66.98	23.10	64.76	13.98	7.62	47.09	13.75
“七五”时期								
1986	2036	75.67	24.54	73.98	14.38	7.07	56.79	16.70
1987	2004	88.17	27.24	86.19	15.88	7.52	64.21	18.88
1988	1984	107.76	35.39	113.84	19.65	10.37	81.67	24.01
1989	1993	118.88	43.20	131.86	20.88	9.73	104.34	30.68
1990	2008	174.89	41.63	136.29	15.57	3.23	125.25	36.82
“八五”时期								
1991	1985	194.29	44.84	160.58	18.46	4.97	138.34	40.81
1992	1941	236.37	60.16	200.54	23.48	7.84	167.44	49.39
1993	2156	319.49	104.43	309.91	31.88	10.26	338.15	99.61
1994	2202	414.81	113.71	346.13	41.69	13.61	462.34	136.14
1995	2648	526.48	130.88	432.17	53.59	16.30	578.55	180.86
“九五”时期								
1996	2301	549.40	175.21	494.99	66.82	27.83	705.50	225.53
1997	1843	603.30	194.42	605.81	70.12	26.99	882.36	286.59
1998	1060	593.83	189.88	539.29	58.56	18.62	882.38	297.81
1999	1064	628.59	201.38	579.64	59.17	15.97	931.22	302.21
2000	1038	680.04	219.19	629.72	64.62	21.69	958.10	363.37

注：1.工业增加值、工业总产值按当年价格计算。
2.1997年及以前统计口径为乡及乡以上工业企业，1998年及以后为全部国有及年销售收入500万元以上工业企业，2011年及以后为年主营业务收入2000万元以上工业企业。
3.1991年及以前“工业增加值”指标为“工业净产值”指标。
4.2019年及以前“营业收入”“营业成本”“税金及附加”指标为“主营业务收入”“主营业务成本”及“主营业务税金及附加”指标。以下相关各表同。
5.自2019年起，不再包含省直单位相关数据。以下相关各表同。
6.自2019年起，数据为济南市、莱芜市区划调整后合并数据，之前年度数据为原济南市数据。以下相关各表同。
7.自2023年起，山东省统计局不再反馈“利税总额”相关数据。
8.表中的合计数和部分计算数据因小数取舍而产生的误差，均未作机械调整。以下相关各表同。

12-2 续表 continued

单位：亿元 (100 million yuan)

年份 Year	单位数(个) Number of Enterprises (unit)	工业总产值 Gross Industrial Output Value	工业增加值 Value Added of Industry Enterprises	营业收入 Business Revenue	利税总额 Total Profits and Taxes	利润总额 Total Profits	资产总计 Total Assets	所有者权益 Owner's Equities
"十五"时期								
2001	1015	786.70	252.61	746.92	77.79	28.45	984.71	369.40
2002	1125	1009.04	325.98	917.31	92.71	32.13	1120.60	407.36
2003	1319	1318.54	426.30	1223.76	132.84	54.71	1312.97	440.85
2004	1512	1781.78	560.15	1677.93	175.98	83.68	1473.90	507.63
2005	1670	2237.51	722.11	2142.84	244.61	131.30	1868.06	630.06
"十一五"时期								
2006	1752	2591.65	797.70	2490.94	289.78	153.74	2000.62	702.78
2007	1820	3189.09	926.58	3086.85	358.87	199.73	2337.09	903.87
2008	2016	3862.64	1052.48	3766.93	425.72	220.79	2899.47	1123.03
2009	2156	3950.77	1154.01	3868.70	500.63	275.85	3478.94	1572.11
2010	2021	4485.61	1313.00	4497.17	584.53	339.76	3904.42	1481.75
"十二五"时期								
2011	1417	4028.49		4165.19	453.47	242.63	3932.90	1407.89
2012	1647	4248.29		4454.97	498.24	253.06	4109.29	1582.77
2013	1901	4777.47		4926.11	539.49	312.95	4249.79	1671.91
2014	1984	5253.05		5406.67	606.60	357.82	4564.86	1846.32
2015	2021	5339.97		5417.16	685.71	396.13	4987.76	2159.78
"十三五"时期								
2016	1962	5486.56		5714.29	729.75	421.11	5501.88	2301.94
2017	2051	5770.91		5810.16	686.80	415.23	6319.64	2268.27
2018	1889	4992.28		5192.15	535.39	307.98	5892.64	2386.75
2019	2153	5839.18		6512.66	545.70	310.86	6663.13	2743.28
2020	2215	6765.08		7575.34	659.87	423.31	7724.85	2967.31
"十四五"时期								
2021	2543	7591.25		8492.55	645.49	408.38	8494.19	3380.30
2022	2665	7246.05		8370.30	593.57	344.86	9637.65	3779.62
2023	2811	8272.05		9613.31		448.14	11412.84	4350.58

Notes: 1. Industrial value added and total industrial output value are calculated according to the current year's prices.

2. Industrial statistical indicators In 1997 and before, the statistical caliber was industrial enterprises at or above the township level. In 1998 and after, they were all state-owned and with an annual sales income of more than 5 million yuan. In 2011 and beyond,the annual main business income was 20 million yuan and above industrial enterprises legal entities.

3.The index of "industrial added value" in 1991 and before is "net industrial output value".

4. "Operating income", "operating cost" and "taxes and surcharges" indicators in year 2019 and before refer to "main operating income", "main operating cost" and "main operating taxes and surcharges" (the same below).

5. Since 2019, statistics does not include data of units directly under provincial jurisdiction (the same below).

6. Since 2019, the data used refer to the combined data after the adjustment of administrative division between Jinan City and Laiwu City, and the data before 2019 are data of original Jinan City (the same below).

7.Since 2023,Shandong Provincial Bureau of Statistics no longer provide relevant data of total profits and taxes.

8.Errors in totals and part of calculations in the table are produced by decimal trade-offs, not mechanically adjusted(the same below).

12-3 各时期主要工业产品产量
Output of Major Industrial Products in Each Period

年份 Year	钢 (万吨) Steel (10 000 tons)	发电量 (亿千瓦小时) Electricity Generation (100 million kWh)	水泥 (万吨) Cement (10 000 tons)	化肥 (万吨) Chemical Fertilizer (10 000 tons)	金切机床 (台) Metal-cutting Machine Tools (unit)	汽车 (辆) Motor Vehicles (unit)	服务器 (万台) Servers (10 000 unit)	布 (万米) Cloth (10 000 m)
1949	-	0.29	0.15	-	40	-	-	2682
1952	-	0.55	1.08	1.62	565	-	-	5104
1957	0.03	1.07	1.29	0.48	2312	-	-	5573
1962	0.57	4.20	4.85	0.81	1140	12	-	2160
1965	0.54	5.65	19.24	3.79	2061	335	-	4853
1970	7.01	11.28	38.06	4.87	4718	1775	-	11665
1975	22.81	11.07	58.48	9.06	3994	3507	-	12547
1978	34.54	12.65	87.55	18.02	3610	4025	-	13806
1979	33.19	11.92	93.77	11.07	3771	4515	-	14300
1980	36.34	11.95	98.86	12.78	4414	5641	-	15236
"六五"时期								
1981	34.23	11.12	96.50	11.62	3336	5099	-	16290
1982	34.96	11.15	104.64	13.23	4262	5993	-	17657
1983	41.24	13.01	112.38	15.37	4816	7249	-	17963
1984	43.80	23.49	117.17	14.53	5533	7947	-	16522
1985	52.64	26.44	135.10	11.44	6686	9400	-	18082
"七五"时期								
1986	57.24	27.01	154.51	12.31	7472	7600	-	12346
1987	64.09	28.83	158.92	13.00	7007	5225	-	20137
1988	75.23	42.97	182.80	13.69	7280	6741	-	19374
1989	81.58	43.98	198.95	14.48	6806	7701	-	21744
1990	87.68	44.71	211.56	14.44	5121	6239	-	20155
"八五"时期								
1991	105.42	56.43	248.33	14.90	5330	7096	-	20119
1992	113.34	61.46	335.61	14.64	7443	8544	-	14896
1993	139.35	69.00	340.35	14.47	6724	10132	-	13205
1994	166.19	66.87	384.00	15.62	3297	9380	-	16062
1995	172.72	68.75	425.02	14.03	4109	5657	-	15046
"九五"时期								
1996	205.49	63.50	379.32	13.73	3855	7125	-	13710
1997	237.70	59.14	392.23	13.89	2526	5656	-	14213
1998	267.33	60.06	379.40	17.29	1508	3615	-	11286

12-3 续表 continued

年份 Year	钢 (万吨) Steel (10 000 tons)	发电量 (亿千瓦小时) Electricity Generation (100 million kWh)	水泥 (万吨) Cement (10 000 tons)	化肥 (万吨) Chemical Fertilizer (10 000 tons)	金切机床 (台) Metal-cutting Machine Tools (unit)	汽车 (辆) Motor Vehicles (unit)	服务器 (万台) Servers (10 000 unit)	布 (万米) Cloth (10 000 m)
1999	265.29	64.24	474.47	22.91	1955	3738	-	14782
2000	277.04	69.29	485.12	28.41	2908	3078	-	16493
"十五"时期								
2001	293.83	69.81	572.28	28.71	3528	7395	-	14107
2002	394.41	69.12	867.71	28.29	4522	12152	-	16027
2003	507.70	77.60	925.20	28.50	6751	19989	-	17040
2004	688.30	74.70	1343.90	40.30	8904	29648	-	16336
2005	1046.60	90.80	1595.70	28.90	7166	42214	-	14018
"十一五"时期								
2006	1131.26	100.14	1960.64	31.44	10057	59242	-	22852
2007	1214.90	130.37	733.98	40.31	9473	100133	-	27469
2008	1123.20	124.25	734.58	48.52	5110	109107	8.3	11786
2009	1051.67	128.76	761.72	57.77	2400	129900	9.7	7500
2010	959.33	131.45	729.79	49.09	2165	212047	9.9	8191
"十二五"时期								
2011	835.80	154.48	824.70	44.20	2024	170717	13.0	11461
2012	694.50	156.60	776.00	55.20	4237	141269	14.7	14908
2013	711.14	162.55	782.20	33.29	4297	165963	17.1	14574
2014	746.20	178.47	832.40	28.60	4902	139751	28.1	14070
2015	699.80	175.87	781.50	23.50	3807	96184	40.6	15539
"十三五"时期								
2016	805.70	177.20	719.80	32.50	4679	124200	46.8	15585
2017	452.03	160.12	604.48	21.00	6013	201883	56.5	16407
2018	160.92	152.90	604.32	20.77	5964	232082	99.6	4032
2019	2144.18	295.10	1287.82	16.91	7237	175488	116.5	4095
2020	2228.91	276.70	1335.88	21.09	8998	394133	143.5	1144
"十四五"时期								
2021	1921.86	315.06	1561.13	16.66	14049	320349	113.7	1099
2022	2021.42	318.16	1361.58	4.23	12518	164370	77.1	808
2023	1944.96	322.95	1229.43	29.47	19387	238834	67.9	1831

注：按经济普查规定汽车产量不含底盘。
Note: The automotive output excludes chassis in line with the provisions of economic census.

12-4 规模以上工业主要经济指标(2023年)
Main Economic Indicators of Industrial Enterprises Above Designated Size(2023)

指标	Item	企业单位数(个) Number of Enterprises (unit)	亏损企业数(个) Loss Enterprises (unit)	工业总产值(现价)(亿元) Gross Industrial Output Value (Current Prices) (100 million yuan)	平均用工人数(万人) Annual Average Employees (10 000 persons)
总计	**Total**	**2811**	**622**	**8272.05**	**43.93**
按登记注册类型分组	**by Status of Registration**				
内资企业	Domestic Invested Enterprises	2651	590	6718.58	36.33
国有独资公司	State-owned Sole-proprietorship Enterprises	12	2	398.91	0.59
私营有限责任公司	Private Limited Liability Corporations	1686	344	1963.72	15.00
其他有限责任公司	Other Limited Liability Corporations	690	195	2690.48	13.84
私营股份有限公司	Private Share-holding Corporations Ltd.	144	33	228.43	2.04
其他股份有限公司	Other Share-holding Corporations Ltd.	69	9	1336.19	4.33
全民所有制企业(国有企业)	State-owned Enterprises	5	2	32.03	0.10
集体所有制企业(集体企业)	Collective-owned Enterprises	7		54.92	0.26
股份合作企业	Cooperative Enterprises	NA		0.41	0.01
联营企业	Joint Ownership Enterprises	NA		0.66	0.02
个人独资企业	Sole-proprietorship Enterprises	34	5	12.13	0.12
合伙企业	Partnership Enterprises	NA		0.70	0.01
其他内资企业	Other Domestic Invested Enterprises				
港澳台投资企业	Enterprises with Investment from Hong Kong, Macao and Taiwan	66	13	1083.51	4.68
港澳台投资有限责任公司	Limited Liability Corporations	64	13	814.93	**4.17**
港澳台投资股份有限公司	Share-holding Corporations Ltd.	NA		268.58	0.50
港澳台投资合伙企业	Partnership Enterprises				
其他港澳台投资企业	Other Enterprises				
外商投资企业	Foreign Invested Enterprises	94	19	469.96	2.92
外商投资有限责任公司	Limited Liability Corporations	85	17	297.77	2.23
外商投资股份有限公司	Share-holding Corporations Ltd.	9	2	172.19	0.69
外商投资合伙企业	Partnership Enterprises				
其他外商投资企业	Other Enterprises				

注：NA表示企业个数小于或等于3(以下相关表同)。
Note:NA refers to less than or equal to three. The same applies to the tables following.

12-4 续表 1 continued 1

指标	Item	企业单位数(个) Number of Enterprises (unit)	亏损企业数(个) Loss Enterprises (unit)	工业总产值(现价)(亿元) Gross Industrial Output Value (Current Prices) (100 million yuan)	平均用工人数(万人) Annual Average Employees (10 000 persons)
按轻重工业分	**by Light & Heavy Industry**				
轻工业	Light Industry	709	172	1334.51	12.61
重工业	Heavy Industry	2102	450	6937.54	31.32
按企业规模分	**by Enterprise Size**				
大型企业	Large-sized Enterprises	60	8	4145.89	16.97
中型企业	Medium-sized Enterprises	162	26	1285.17	8.91
小型企业	Small-sized Enterprises	2147	481	2652.94	17.28
微型企业	Micro-sized Enterprises	442	107	188.06	0.78
按工业行业分	**by Sector**				
煤炭开采和洗选业	Mining and Washing of Coal	NA	1	4.97	0.18
石油和天然气开采业	Extraction of Petroleum and Natural Gas	NA		14.14	0.04
黑色金属矿采选业	Mining and Processing of Ferrous Metal Ores	14	2	109.53	0.79
有色金属矿采选业	Mining and Processing of Non-Ferrous Metal Ores				
非金属矿采选业	Mining and Processing of Non-metal Ores	10	4	10.62	0.06
开采专业及辅助性活动	Professional and Support Activities for Mining				
其他采矿业	Mining of Other Ores				
农副食品加工业	Processing of Food from Agricultural Products	111	33	176.36	0.92
食品制造业	Manufacture of Foods	83	20	154.97	1.74
酒、饮料和精制茶制造业	Manufacture of Liquor, Beverages and Refined Tea	23	7	69.08	0.53
烟草制品业	Manufacture of Tobacco	NA	1	5.51	0.24
纺织业	Manufacture of Textile	68	11	46.47	0.54
纺织服装、服饰业	Manufacture of Textile, Wearing Apparel and Accessories	20	3	13.11	0.42
皮革、毛皮、羽毛及其制品和制鞋业	Manufacture of Leather, Fur, Feather and Related Products and Footwear	NA		1.37	0.02
木材加工和木、竹、藤、棕、草制品业	Processing of Timber, Manufacture of Wood, Bamboo, Rattan,Palm and Straw Products	15	3	8.37	0.08
家具制造业	Manufacture of Furniture	17	8	12.66	0.23
造纸和纸制品业	Manufacture of Paper and Paper Products	42	9	40.27	0.33

12-4 续表 2 continued 2

指标	Item	企业单位数(个) Number of Enterprises (unit)	亏损企业数(个) Loss Enterprises (unit)	工业总产值(现价)(亿元) Gross Industrial Output Value (Current Prices) (100 million yuan)	平均用工人数(万人) Annual Average Employees (10 000 persons)
印刷和记录媒介复制业	Printing and Reproduction of Recording Media	50	14	53.34	0.71
文教、工美、体育和娱乐用品制造业	Manufacture of Articles for Culture, Education, Arts and Crafts, Sport and Entertainment Activities	25	5	12.60	0.20
石油、煤炭及其他燃料加工业	Processing of Petroleum, Coal and Other Fuels	15	5	398.83	0.28
化学原料和化学制品制造业	Manufacture of Raw Chemical Materials and Chemical Products	139	28	362.38	1.56
医药制造业	Manufacture of Medicines	87	19	425.38	3.95
化学纤维制造业	Manufacture of Chemical Fibres	7		28.68	0.09
橡胶和塑料制品业	Manufacture of Rubber and Plastics Products	80	11	41.84	0.47
非金属矿物制品业	Manufacture of Non-metallic Mineral Products	329	91	455.92	3.18
黑色金属冶炼和压延加工业	Smelting and Pressing of Ferrous Metals	48	17	1193.18	3.08
有色金属冶炼和压延加工业	Smelting and Pressing of Non-ferrous Metals	48	13	53.15	0.20
金属制品业	Manufacture of Metal Products	312	57	346.53	3.08
通用设备制造业	Manufacture of General Purpose Machinery	348	63	515.51	4.60
专用设备制造业	Manufacture of Special Purpose Machinery	248	50	276.46	2.37
汽车制造业	Manufacture of Automobiles	131	28	1247.09	5.32
铁路、船舶、航空航天和其他运输设备制造业	Manufacture of Railway, Ship, Aerospace and Other Transport Equipments	24	3	71.15	0.65
电气机械和器材制造业	Manufacture of Electrical Machinery and Apparatus	156	26	480.96	2.65
计算机、通信和其他电子设备制造业	Manufacture of Computers, Communication and Other Electronic Equipment	95	29	845.89	1.86
仪器仪表制造业	Manufacture of Measuring Instruments and Machinery	89	16	75.46	0.87
其他制造业	Other Manufacture	NA		6.80	0.03
废弃资源综合利用业	Utilization of Waste Resources	16	6	31.37	0.22
金属制品、机械和设备修理业	Repair Service of Metal Products, Machinery and Equipment	8	2	20.32	0.24
电力、热力生产和供应业	Production and Supply of Electric Power and Heat Power	77	25	225.68	1.46
燃气生产和供应业	Production and Supply of Gas	34	6	398.63	0.35
水的生产和供应业	Production and Supply of Water	29	6	37.51	0.38

12-5 规模以上国有及国有控股工业主要经济指标(2023年)

Main Economic Indicators of State-Owned and State-Controlled Industrial Enterprises Above Designated Size(2023)

指标	Item	企业单位数(个) Number of Enterprises (unit)	亏损企业数(个) Loss Enterprises (unit)	工业总产值(现价)(亿元) Gross Industrial Output Value (Current Prices) (100 million yuan)	平均用工人数(万人) Annual Average Employees (10 000 persons)
总计	**Total**	**307**	**62**	**3233.86**	**10.65**
按登记注册类型分组	**by Status of Registration**				
内资企业	Domestic Invested Enterprises	288	59	3037.13	9.49
国有独资公司	State-owned Sole-proprietorship Enterprises	12	2	398.91	0.59
其他有限责任公司	Other Limited Liability Corporations	244	52	1509.17	6.39
其他股份有限公司	Other Share-holding Corporations Ltd.	21	2	1086.34	2.36
港澳台投资企业	Enterprises with Investment from Hong Kong,Macao and	10	1	139.90	0.78
港澳台投资有限责任公司	Limited Liability Corporations	10	1	139.90	0.78
外商投资企业	Foreign Invested Enterprises	9	2	56.83	0.39
外商投资有限责任公司	Limited Liability Corporations	8	1	54.95	0.38
外商投资股份有限公司	Share-holding Corporations Ltd.	NA	1	1.88	0.01
按轻重工业分	**by Light & Heavy Industry**				
轻工业	Light Industry	39	9	110.81	1.37
重工业	Heavy Industry	268	53	3123.05	9.28
按企业规模分	**by Enterprise Size**				
大型企业	Large-sized Enterprises	21	5	1795.97	5.56
中型企业	Medium-sized Enterprises	54	11	454.11	3.03
小型企业	Small-sized Enterprises	196	39	949.54	1.98
微型企业	Micro-sized Enterprises	36	7	34.24	0.09

12-5 续表 1 continued 1

指标	Item	企业单位数(个) Number of Enterprises (unit)	亏损企业数(个) Loss Enterprises (unit)	工业总产值(现价)(亿元) Gross Industrial Output Value (Current Prices) (100 million yuan)	平均用工人数(万人) Annual Average Employees (10 000 persons)
按工业行业分	**by Sector**				
煤炭开采和洗选业	Mining and Washing of Coal	NA		4.37	0.13
石油和天然气开采业	Extraction of Petroleum and Natural Gas	NA		8.98	0.02
黑色金属矿采选业	Mining and Processing of Ferrous Metal Ores	4	1	17.42	0.43
有色金属矿采选业	Mining and Processing of Non-Ferrous Metal Ores				
非金属矿采选业	Mining and Processing of Non-metal Ores	NA		2.18	0.01
开采专业及辅助性活动	Professional and Support Activities for Mining				
其他采矿业	Mining of Other Ores				
农副食品加工业	Processing of Food from Agricultural Products	NA		6.76	0.07
食品制造业	Manufacture of Foods	5	1	13.68	0.16
酒、饮料和精制茶制造业	Manufacture of Liquor, Beverages and Refined Tea	NA		21.25	0.16
烟草制品业	Manufacture of Tobacco	NA	1	5.51	0.24
纺织业	Manufacture of Textile	NA	2	2.26	0.04
纺织服装、服饰业	Manufacture of Textile, Wearing Apparel and Accessories	NA	1	2.90	0.14
皮革、毛皮、羽毛及其制品和制鞋业	Manufacture of Leather, Fur, Feather and Related Products and Footwear				
木材加工和木、竹、藤、棕、草制品业	Processing of Timber, Manufacture of Wood, Bamboo, Rattan,Palm and Straw Products	NA		0.26	
家具制造业	Manufacture of Furniture				
造纸和纸制品业	Manufacture of Paper and Paper Products				
印刷和记录媒介复制业	Printing and Reproduction of Recording Media	7	1	9.80	0.21
文教、工美、体育和娱乐用品制造业	Manufacture of Articles for Culture, Education, Arts and Crafts,Sport and Entertainment Activities				
石油、煤炭及其他燃料加工业	Processing of Petroleum, Coal and Other Fuels	NA		355.12	0.15
化学原料和化学制品制造业	Manufacture of Raw Chemical Materials and Chemical Products	12	4	83.06	0.33

12-5 续表 2 continued 2

指标	Item	企业单位数(个) Number of Enterprises (unit)	亏损企业数(个) Loss Enterprises (unit)	工业总产值(现价)(亿元) Gross Industrial Output Value (Current Prices) (100 million yuan)	平均用工人数(万人) Annual Average Employees (10 000 persons)
医药制造业	Manufacture of Medicines	4		20.51	0.20
化学纤维制造业	Manufacture of Chemical Fibres	NA		2.28	0.03
橡胶和塑料制品业	Manufacture of Rubber and Plastics Products	NA	1	2.93	0.06
非金属矿物制品业	Manufacture of Non-metallic Mineral Products	33	7	81.02	0.48
黑色金属冶炼和压延加工业	Smelting and Pressing of Ferrous Metals	8	3	645.67	1.79
有色金属冶炼和压延加工业	Smelting and Pressing of Non-ferrous Metals	NA		21.61	0.03
金属制品业	Manufacture of Metal Products	17	2	54.77	0.34
通用设备制造业	Manufacture of General Purpose Machinery	21	4	150.23	0.97
专用设备制造业	Manufacture of Special Purpose Machinery	15	3	30.37	0.30
汽车制造业	Manufacture of Automobiles	11	1	163.74	0.69
铁路、船舶、航空航天和其他运输设备制造业	Manufacture of Railway, Ship, Aerospace and Other Transport Equipments	10	1	57.86	0.48
电气机械和器材制造业	Manufacture of Electrical Machinery and Apparatus	21	3	156.40	0.47
计算机、通信和其他电子设备制造业	Manufacture of Computers, Communication and Other Electronic Equipment	17	2	707.74	0.78
仪器仪表制造业	Manufacture of Measuring Instruments and Machinery	5		21.69	0.14
其他制造业	Other Manufacture	NA		3.18	0.01
废弃资源综合利用业	Utilization of Waste Resources	NA		17.45	0.01
金属制品、机械和设备修理业	Repair Service of Metal Products, Machinery and Equipn	NA		12.03	0.20
电力、热力生产和供应业	Production and Supply of Electric Power and Heat Power	49	17	202.63	1.05
燃气生产和供应业	Production and Supply of Gas	15	2	320.29	0.22
水的生产和供应业	Production and Supply of Water	21	5	27.92	0.34

12-6 规模以上私营工业企业主要经济指标(2023年)
Main Economic Indicators of Private Industrial Enterprises Above Designated Size(2023)

指标	Item	企业单位数(个) Number of Enterprises (unit)	亏损企业数(个) Loss Enterprises (unit)	工业总产值(现价)(亿元) Gross Industrial Output Value (Current Prices) (100 million yuan)	平均用工人数(万人) Annual Average Employees (10 000 persons)
总计	**Total**	**1866**	**382**	**2204.98**	**17.18**
按登记注册类型分组	**by Status of Registration**				
内资企业	Domestic Invested Enterprises	1866	382	2204.98	17.18
私营有限责任公司	Private Limited Liability Corporations	1686	344	1963.72	15.00
私营股份有限公司	Private Share-holding Corporations Ltd.	144	33	228.43	2.04
个人独资企业	Sole-proprietorship Enterprises	34	5	12.13	0.12
合伙企业	Partnership Enterprises	NA		0.70	0.01
按轻重工业分	**by Light & Heavy Industry**				
轻工业	Light Industry	468	98	607.55	6.01
重工业	Heavy Industry	1398	284	1597.43	11.17
按企业规模分	**by Enterprise Size**				
大型企业	Large-sized Enterprises	15	2	622.57	3.96
中型企业	Medium-sized Enterprises	42	4	352.93	2.11
小型企业	Small-sized Enterprises	1473	297	1109.63	10.55
微型企业	Micro-sized Enterprises	336	79	119.85	0.55
按工业行业分	**by Sector**				
煤炭开采和洗选业	Mining and Washing of Coal	NA	1	0.60	0.05
石油和天然气开采业	Extraction of Petroleum and Natural Gas	NA		12.25	0.04

12-6 续表 1 continued 1

指标	Item	企业单位数(个) Number of Enterprises (unit)	亏损企业数(个) Loss Enterprises (unit)	工业总产值(现价)(亿元) Gross Industrial Output Value (Current Prices) (100 million yuan)	平均用工人数(万人) Annual Average Employees (10 000 persons)
黑色金属矿采选业	Mining and Processing of Ferrous Metal Ores	5	1	62.92	0.06
有色金属矿采选业	Mining and Processing of Non-Ferrous Metal Ores				
非金属矿采选业	Mining and Processing of Non-metal Ores	7	4	6.79	0.04
开采专业及辅助性活动	Professional and Support Activities for Mining				
其他采矿业	Mining of Other Ores				
农副食品加工业	Processing of Food from Agricultural Products	77	18	122.18	0.59
食品制造业	Manufacture of Foods	48	13	75.94	0.89
酒、饮料和精制茶制造业	Manufacture of Liquor, Beverages and Refined Tea	8	4	4.16	0.05
烟草制品业	Manufacture of Tobacco				
纺织业	Manufacture of Textile	56	6	25.32	0.29
纺织服装、服饰业	Manufacture of Textile, Wearing Apparel and Accessories	14	2	6.45	0.16
皮革、毛皮、羽毛及其制品和制鞋业	Manufacture of Leather, Fur, Feather and Related Products and Footwear	NA		0.30	
木材加工和木、竹、藤、棕、草制品业	Processing of Timber, Manufacture of Wood, Bamboo, Rattan,Palm and Straw Products	14	3	8.11	0.07
家具制造业	Manufacture of Furniture	12	5	2.75	0.07
造纸和纸制品业	Manufacture of Paper and Paper Products	36	8	23.98	0.22
印刷和记录媒介复制业	Printing and Reproduction of Recording Media	34	10	29.16	0.41
文教、工美、体育和娱乐用品制造业	Manufacture of Articles for Culture, Education, Arts and Crafts,Sport and Entertainment Activities	21	4	10.51	0.16
石油、煤炭及其他燃料加工业	Processing of Petroleum, Coal and Other Fuels	9	4	10.81	0.05
化学原料和化学制品制造业	Manufacture of Raw Chemical Materials and Chemical Products	86	17	124.41	0.56
医药制造业	Manufacture of Medicines	50	8	236.76	2.36

12-6 续表 2 continued 2

指标	Item	企业单位数(个) Number of Enterprises (unit)	亏损企业数(个) Loss Enterprises (unit)	工业总产值(现价)(亿元) Gross Industrial Output Value (Current Prices) (100 million yuan)	平均用工人数(万人) Annual Average Employees (10 000 persons)
化学纤维制造业	Manufacture of Chemical Fibres	NA		1.64	0.02
橡胶和塑料制品业	Manufacture of Rubber and Plastics Products	67	9	34.47	0.35
非金属矿物制品业	Manufacture of Non-metallic Mineral Products	245	65	282.81	1.95
黑色金属冶炼和压延加工业	Smelting and Pressing of Ferrous Metals	32	12	342.51	0.74
有色金属冶炼和压延加工业	Smelting and Pressing of Non-ferrous Metals	40	11	22.34	0.11
金属制品业	Manufacture of Metal Products	236	40	140.62	1.45
通用设备制造业	Manufacture of General Purpose Machinery	250	41	159.56	1.92
专用设备制造业	Manufacture of Special Purpose Machinery	173	28	97.08	1.35
汽车制造业	Manufacture of Automobiles	81	18	73.02	0.95
铁路、船舶、航空航天和其他运输设备制造业	Manufacture of Railway, Ship, Aerospace and Other Transport Equipments	6	2	3.65	0.05
电气机械和器材制造业	Manufacture of Electrical Machinery and Apparatus	99	13	95.03	0.79
计算机、通信和其他电子设备制造业	Manufacture of Computers, Communication and Other Electronic Equipment	54	14	102.96	0.67
仪器仪表制造业	Manufacture of Measuring Instruments and Machinery	61	8	37.07	0.51
其他制造业	Other Manufacture				
废弃资源综合利用业	Utilization of Waste Resources	8	4	3.98	0.04
金属制品、机械和设备修理业	Repair Service of Metal Products, Machinery and Equipment	4	1	7.76	0.03
电力、热力生产和供应业	Production and Supply of Electric Power and Heat Power	13	5	12.72	0.10
燃气生产和供应业	Production and Supply of Gas	11	2	23.98	0.07
水的生产和供应业	Production and Supply of Water	NA	1	0.37	

12–7 规模以上工业资产实力(2023年)
Capital Power of Industrial Enterprises Above Designated Size(2023)

单位：亿元

指标	Item	流动资产合计 Current Assets	其中of which 应收账款 Accounts Receivable	存货 Inventories
总计	**Total**	**6832.00**	**2229.63**	**1131.07**
按登记注册类型分组	**by Status of Registration**			
内资企业	Domestic Invested Enterprises	5419.58	1861.02	931.90
国有独资公司	State-owned Sole-proprietorship Enterprises	107.98	14.41	15.07
私营有限责任公司	Private Limited Liability Corporations	1860.25	723.61	260.84
其他有限责任公司	Other Limited Liability Corporations	2170.82	742.59	384.41
私营股份有限公司	Private Share-holding Corporations Ltd.	239.99	78.28	49.34
其他股份有限公司	Other Share-holding Corporations Ltd.	972.15	283.27	211.40
全民所有制企业(国有企业)	State-owned Enterprises	23.61	13.36	3.30
集体所有制企业(集体企业)	Collective-owned Enterprises	36.26	0.88	5.64
股份合作企业	Cooperative Enterprises	0.47	0.02	0.11
联营企业	Joint Ownership Enterprises	0.29	0.22	0.02
个人独资企业	Sole-proprietorship Enterprises	7.59	4.30	1.73
合伙企业	Partnership Enterprises	0.17	0.08	0.03
其他内资企业	Other Domestic Invested Enterprises			
港澳台投资企业	Enterprises with Investment from Hong Kong,Macao and Taiwan	1011.13	204.96	122.67
港澳台投资有限责任公司	Limited Liability Corporations	774.57	155.41	85.25
港澳台投资股份有限公司	Share-holding Corporations Ltd.	236.56	49.55	37.42
港澳台投资合伙企业	Partnership Enterprises			
其他港澳台投资企业	Other Enterprises			
外商投资企业	Foreign Invested Enterprises	401.29	163.66	76.51
外商投资有限责任公司	Limited Liability Corporations	208.90	74.38	45.62
外商投资股份有限公司	Share-holding Corporations Ltd.	192.39	89.28	30.89
外商投资合伙企业	Partnership Enterprises			
其他外商投资企业	Other Enterprises			
按轻重工业分	**by Light & Heavy Industry**			
轻工业	Light Industry	1199.95	302.73	205.35
重工业	Heavy Industry	5632.06	1926.90	925.72
按企业规模分	**by Enterprise Size**			
大型企业	Large-sized Enterprises	3109.80	925.97	449.56
中型企业	Medium-sized Enterprises	1260.03	322.57	249.84
小型企业	Small-sized Enterprises	2206.69	832.53	409.14
微型企业	Micro-sized Enterprises	255.49	148.56	22.53
按工业行业分	**by Sector**			
煤炭开采和洗选业	Mining and Washing of Coal	5.88	1.19	0.35
石油和天然气开采业	Extraction of Petroleum and Natural Gas	19.53	4.79	0.08
黑色金属矿采选业	Mining and Processing of Ferrous Metal Ores	74.78	15.08	7.03
有色金属矿采选业	Mining and Processing of Non-Ferrous Metal Ores			

(100 million yuan)

固定资产净额 Net Fixed Assets	固定资产原价 Original Value of Fixed Assets	流动负债合计 Current Liabilities Total	非流动负债合计 Non-Current Liabilities Total	所有者权益合计 Total Owner's Equities	其中of which 实收资本 Paid-up Capital	其中of which 国家资本 State Capital
2362.74	**4274.56**	**5925.22**	**1137.04**	**4350.58**	**1897.51**	**252.36**
2009.75	3616.09	4744.56	1023.58	3250.02	1481.75	233.25
142.18	242.05	126.93	96.02	103.93	38.26	35.51
363.81	799.43	1518.23	137.97	869.29	294.67	1.32
1083.16	1842.23	2200.06	532.83	1253.88	856.02	168.43
66.57	113.86	157.41	41.62	210.02	68.23	0.15
245.11	459.40	609.68	191.54	775.88	207.38	18.41
18.43	48.97	31.18	5.50	8.05	8.96	8.96
87.86	103.89	95.62	17.98	22.81	5.40	
0.29	0.50	0.03		0.74	0.03	
0.29	0.96	0.31	0.08	0.40	0.02	
2.06	4.64	4.95	0.06	4.94	2.78	0.47
	0.16	0.17		0.09		
264.64	448.59	935.07	74.69	733.80	294.36	18.11
231.44	396.12	781.35	72.15	596.48	282.49	15.66
33.20	52.48	153.72	2.54	137.32	11.86	2.45
88.35	209.88	245.58	38.77	366.76	121.41	1.00
76.51	157.46	147.39	19.05	174.66	96.47	1.00
11.85	52.42	98.20	19.73	192.10	24.95	
377.27	684.54	787.31	85.52	1112.43	350.84	27.12
1985.48	3590.03	5137.90	1051.52	3238.15	1546.68	225.25
1188.58	2207.12	2648.33	554.45	2107.09	662.21	73.49
496.49	896.24	1161.47	224.59	962.21	435.89	81.06
571.17	1018.78	1888.64	285.96	1167.62	708.77	84.38
106.51	152.42	226.77	72.04	113.66	90.65	13.43
3.37	11.54	17.60	0.40	-7.79	1.42	0.30
2.26	34.32	-3.23	16.92	21.29	1.68	0.70
29.92	75.62	97.33	13.28	22.50	32.97	2.43

12-7 续表 continued

单位：亿元

指标	Item	流动资产合计 Current Assets	其中of which 应收账款 Accounts Receivable	存货 Inventories
非金属矿采选业	Mining and Processing of Non-metal Ores	9.77	2.82	2.57
开采专业及辅助性活动	Professional and Support Activities for Mining			
其他采矿业	Mining of Other Ores			
农副食品加工业	Processing of Food from Agricultural Products	72.43	17.53	17.14
食品制造业	Manufacture of Foods	82.34	23.37	16.06
酒、饮料和精制茶制造业	Manufacture of Liquor, Beverages and Refined Tea	53.93	5.32	9.85
烟草制品业	Manufacture of Tobacco	11.15	0.97	0.45
纺织业	Manufacture of Textile	36.57	10.79	10.96
纺织服装、服饰业	Manufacture of Textile, Wearing Apparel and Accessories	15.28	4.14	3.70
皮革、毛皮、羽毛及其制品和制鞋业	Manufacture of Leather, Fur, Feather and Related Products and Footwear	1.72	0.27	0.11
木材加工和木、竹、藤、棕、草制品业	Processing of Timber, Manufacture of Wood, Bamboo, Rattan,Palm and Straw Products	5.12	1.74	1.71
家具制造业	Manufacture of Furniture	11.76	2.03	7.59
造纸和纸制品业	Manufacture of Paper and Paper Products	25.68	8.28	9.06
印刷和记录媒介复制业	Printing and Reproduction of Recording Media	42.22	9.22	7.90
文教、工美、体育和娱乐用品制造业	Manufacture of Articles for Culture, Education, Arts and Crafts,Sport and Entertainment Activities	9.15	1.90	4.89
石油、煤炭及其他燃料加工业	Processing of Petroleum, Coal and Other Fuels	115.77	71.91	15.52
化学原料和化学制品制造业	Manufacture of Raw Chemical Materials and Chemical Products	251.07	39.49	44.55
医药制造业	Manufacture of Medicines	505.31	123.28	67.17
化学纤维制造业	Manufacture of Chemical Fibres	23.32	1.35	4.29
橡胶和塑料制品业	Manufacture of Rubber and Plastics Products	34.61	15.33	8.48
非金属矿物制品业	Manufacture of Non-metallic Mineral Products	547.98	265.96	62.07
黑色金属冶炼和压延加工业	Smelting and Pressing of Ferrous Metals	654.68	173.76	89.56
有色金属冶炼和压延加工业	Smelting and Pressing of Non-ferrous Metals	85.42	12.84	7.75
金属制品业	Manufacture of Metal Products	304.04	104.78	56.62
通用设备制造业	Manufacture of General Purpose Machinery	494.42	154.30	119.20
专用设备制造业	Manufacture of Special Purpose Machinery	384.53	152.50	84.24
汽车制造业	Manufacture of Automobiles	925.49	312.88	121.57
铁路、船舶、航空航天和其他运输设备制造业	Manufacture of Railway, Ship, Aerospace and Other Transport Equipments	66.97	17.82	11.11
电气机械和器材制造业	Manufacture of Electrical Machinery and Apparatus	551.92	222.37	82.95
计算机、通信和其他电子设备制造业	Manufacture of Computers, Communication and Other Electronic Equipment	779.67	306.23	191.12
仪器仪表制造业	Manufacture of Measuring Instruments and Machinery	99.87	37.84	21.77
其他制造业	Other Manufacture	15.65	4.86	3.95
废弃资源综合利用业	Utilization of Waste Resources	15.07	5.53	2.32
金属制品、机械和设备修理业	Repair Service of Metal Products, Machinery and Equipment	17.21	5.27	3.58
电力、热力生产和供应业	Production and Supply of Electric Power and Heat Power	324.14	50.15	19.47
燃气生产和供应业	Production and Supply of Gas	92.72	18.42	10.33
水的生产和供应业	Production and Supply of Water	64.84	23.31	4.03

(100 million yuan)

固定资产净额 Net Fixed Assets	固定资产原价 Original Value of Fixed Assets	流动负债合计 Current Liabilities Total	非流动负债合计 Non-Current Liabilities Total	所有者权益合计 Total Owner's Equities	其中of which	
					实收资本 Paid-up Capital	其中of which 国家资本 State Capital
3.94	6.67	12.02	1.27	3.51	3.00	1.25
23.46	33.79	82.40	6.79	24.00	15.65	
51.77	98.86	65.04	4.63	88.98	41.96	0.57
30.26	63.59	42.47	1.53	58.40	45.46	0.06
3.89	11.94	2.89		14.42	10.95	10.95
17.25	31.33	37.92	4.50	20.81	13.42	0.93
10.09	15.30	15.99	2.86	9.75	3.66	
0.23	0.53	1.56		0.51	0.11	
1.28	2.48	5.43	0.50	1.40	0.83	
3.94	6.16	13.05	0.31	7.45	5.56	
10.65	21.55	25.18	2.31	14.69	8.15	
24.75	51.91	31.36	3.45	45.24	25.09	7.17
2.95	4.68	7.84	1.39	6.14	4.80	
34.65	113.13	99.09	16.31	50.32	32.47	27.96
188.90	290.81	297.40	49.34	191.92	68.34	7.24
105.15	198.86	189.99	31.68	566.69	111.78	3.80
5.87	10.58	10.04	0.03	23.20	13.64	
8.75	20.57	23.96	2.01	21.07	17.42	2.61
117.93	229.36	553.25	49.92	322.58	121.69	10.24
397.67	802.90	785.21	100.54	377.27	218.10	4.08
5.04	9.91	88.70	0.78	8.19	5.57	1.18
73.66	168.56	235.43	34.83	232.17	79.55	2.17
98.52	204.64	327.74	28.24	336.81	172.43	9.82
68.08	102.37	277.15	25.93	216.23	76.66	5.93
232.49	397.41	886.35	53.02	452.88	164.62	20.93
11.12	25.86	48.88	3.45	60.07	40.90	0.55
113.25	178.65	492.26	29.37	297.79	140.39	17.33
105.11	149.77	484.10	139.04	410.81	173.91	14.09
15.41	25.82	51.43	3.27	77.48	24.80	4.72
2.05	2.90	10.69	0.11	8.03	1.89	1.00
7.98	11.38	21.37	1.79	4.74	4.90	0.46
12.15	16.57	14.28	7.95	10.68	4.37	
416.80	658.91	392.05	368.98	220.43	151.27	76.37
53.40	80.30	88.03	33.22	77.74	26.56	6.79
68.74	104.99	92.96	97.12	52.19	31.57	10.73

12-8 规模以上国有及国有控股工业资产实力(2023年)

Capital Power of State-Owned and State-Controlled Industrial Enterprises Above Designated Size(2023)

单位：亿元

指标	Item	流动资产合计 Current Assets	其中 of which 应收账款 Accounts Receivable	存货 Inventories
总计	**Total**	**2194.58**	**640.32**	**398.26**
按登记注册类型分组	**by Status of Registration**			
内资企业	Domestic Invested Enterprises	1998.97	607.23	379.37
国有独资公司	State-owned Sole-proprietorship Enterprises	107.98	14.41	15.07
其他有限责任公司	Other Limited Liability Corporations	1217.88	386.59	209.79
其他股份有限公司	Other Share-holding Corporations Ltd.	614.88	191.63	150.97
港澳台投资企业	Enterprises with Investment from Hong Kong,Macao and Taiwan	150.38	20.63	11.17
港澳台投资有限责任公司	Limited Liability Corporations	150.38	20.63	11.17
外商投资企业	Foreign Invested Enterprises	45.23	12.45	7.72
外商投资有限责任公司	Limited Liability Corporations	43.14	12.31	7.64
外商投资股份有限公司	Share-holding Corporations Ltd.	2.09	0.14	0.08
按轻重工业分	**by Light & Heavy Industry**			
轻工业	Light Industry	103.16	15.55	19.87
重工业	Heavy Industry	2091.42	624.77	378.39
按企业规模分	**by Enterprise Size**			
大型企业	Large-sized Enterprises	1008.48	238.00	199.70
中型企业	Medium-sized Enterprises	503.84	123.36	104.03
小型企业	Small-sized Enterprises	634.36	265.87	91.97
微型企业	Micro-sized Enterprises	47.91	13.09	2.56
按工业行业分	**by Sector**			
煤炭开采和洗选业	Mining and Washing of Coal	2.43	0.11	0.09
石油和天然气开采业	Extraction of Petroleum and Natural Gas	16.63	1.91	0.06
黑色金属矿采选业	Mining and Processing of Ferrous Metal Ores	14.48	2.12	0.86
有色金属矿采选业	Mining and Processing of Non-Ferrous Metal Ores			
非金属矿采选业	Mining and Processing of Non-metal Ores	4.79	1.51	0.30
开采专业及辅助性活动	Professional and Support Activities for Mining			
其他采矿业	Mining of Other Ores			
农副食品加工业	Processing of Food from Agricultural Products	2.59	0.14	0.29
食品制造业	Manufacture of Foods	10.11	2.33	1.62
酒、饮料和精制茶制造业	Manufacture of Liquor, Beverages and Refined Tea	10.40	1.03	1.30
烟草制品业	Manufacture of Tobacco	11.15	0.97	0.45

(100 million yuan)

固定资产净额 Net Fixed Assets	固定资产原价 Original Value of Fixed Assets	流动负债合计 Current Liabilities Total	非流动负债合计 Non-Current Liabilities Total	所有者权益合计 Total Owner's Equities	其中 of which 实收资本 Paid-up Capital	其中 of which 国家资本 State Capital
1084.26	**2012.40**	**2064.22**	**721.89**	**1338.85**	**791.58**	**240.01**
1009.81	1886.70	1902.77	685.68	1213.28	733.78	223.63
142.18	242.05	126.93	96.02	103.93	38.26	35.51
667.32	1213.37	1302.44	400.95	657.09	536.87	163.13
169.31	335.64	427.73	164.82	421.75	143.82	15.15
65.01	103.94	124.46	33.62	103.44	46.07	15.61
65.01	103.94	124.46	33.62	103.44	46.07	15.61
9.44	21.76	36.99	2.59	22.13	11.73	0.77
8.15	17.49	35.49	2.30	19.66	10.23	0.77
1.29	4.26	1.50	0.29	2.46	1.50	
43.06	84.12	65.43	8.01	100.33	43.72	24.85
1041.21	1928.28	1998.80	713.88	1238.51	747.86	215.16
604.54	1192.31	937.88	424.06	729.53	381.97	68.43
264.09	464.78	491.52	142.62	335.57	221.36	80.44
163.83	287.15	583.09	118.38	237.83	160.09	77.85
51.80	68.16	51.74	36.83	35.92	28.17	13.30
2.77	10.54	11.74	0.01	-5.76	1.05	0.30
1.90	33.36	2.01	3.54	18.14	0.70	0.70
13.57	41.41	9.09	9.60	29.89	26.88	2.02
0.13	0.38	1.51	0.95	2.74	1.25	1.25
0.35	0.82	2.05	0.02	1.07	0.38	
3.79	8.39	4.72	0.07	12.83	0.59	0.57
6.82	15.05	5.57	0.71	11.90	6.70	
3.89	11.94	2.89		14.42	10.95	10.95

12–8 续表 continued

单位：亿元

指标	Item	流动资产合计 Current Assets	其中 of which 应收账款 Accounts Receivable	存货 Inventories
纺织业	Manufacture of Textile	1.61	0.38	0.96
纺织服装、服饰业	Manufacture of Textile, Wearing Apparel and Accessories	7.29	0.35	1.21
皮革、毛皮、羽毛及其制品和制鞋业	Manufacture of Leather, Fur, Feather and Related Products and Footwear			
木材加工和木、竹、藤、棕、草制品业	Processing of Timber, Manufacture of Wood, Bamboo, Rattan, Palm and Straw Products	0.64	0.25	0.01
家具制造业	Manufacture of Furniture			
造纸和纸制品业	Manufacture of Paper and Paper Products			
印刷和记录媒介复制业	Printing and Reproduction of Recording Media	12.53	1.99	1.80
文教、工美、体育和娱乐用品制造业	Manufacture of Articles for Culture, Education, Arts and Crafts, Sport and Entertainment Activities			
石油、煤炭及其他燃料加工业	Processing of Petroleum, Coal and Other Fuels	29.30	9.89	9.67
化学原料和化学制品制造业	Manufacture of Raw Chemical Materials and Chemical Products	39.75	5.94	8.81
医药制造业	Manufacture of Medicines	22.29	3.64	3.28
化学纤维制造业	Manufacture of Chemical Fibres	3.22	0.03	2.75
橡胶和塑料制品业	Manufacture of Rubber and Plastics Products	6.05	2.49	1.80
非金属矿物制品业	Manufacture of Non-metallic Mineral Products	90.29	51.06	10.69
黑色金属冶炼和压延加工业	Smelting and Pressing of Ferrous Metals	136.68	1.52	33.65
有色金属冶炼和压延加工业	Smelting and Pressing of Non-ferrous Metals	11.98	5.85	0.90
金属制品业	Manufacture of Metal Products	49.40	17.42	10.04
通用设备制造业	Manufacture of General Purpose Machinery	175.87	42.16	41.44
专用设备制造业	Manufacture of Special Purpose Machinery	75.79	23.72	10.82
汽车制造业	Manufacture of Automobiles	136.07	30.80	13.72
铁路、船舶、航空航天和其他运输设备制造业	Manufacture of Railway, Ship, Aerospace and Other Transport Equipments	51.68	12.01	6.58
电气机械和器材制造业	Manufacture of Electrical Machinery and Apparatus	212.65	86.00	36.11
计算机、通信和其他电子设备制造业	Manufacture of Computers, Communication and Other Electronic Equipment	630.31	263.95	162.57
仪器仪表制造业	Manufacture of Measuring Instruments and Machinery	24.19	7.26	6.62
其他制造业	Other Manufacture	4.23	3.60	0.11
废弃资源综合利用业	Utilization of Waste Resources	5.67	3.47	0.69
金属制品、机械和设备修理业	Repair Service of Metal Products, Machinery and Equipment	14.00	3.31	3.24
电力、热力生产和供应业	Production and Supply of Electric Power and Heat Power	264.44	33.49	16.03
燃气生产和供应业	Production and Supply of Gas	63.16	4.63	6.20
水的生产和供应业	Production and Supply of Water	52.90	14.98	3.63

(100 million yuan)

固定资产净额 Net Fixed Assets	固定资产原价 Original Value of Fixed Assets	流动负债合计 Current Liabilities Total	非流动负债合计 Non-Current Liabilities Total	所有者权益合计 Total Owner's Equities	其中 of which: 实收资本 Paid- up Capital	其中 of which: 国家资本 State Capital
1.85	2.88	3.29	0.63	1.18	0.69	0.69
4.91	6.63	9.47	1.56	3.47	0.55	
0.01	0.01	0.44		0.20	0.20	
6.96	17.61	5.65	0.43	16.63	10.11	6.67
29.24	95.37	16.31	9.83	45.76	27.96	27.96
36.79	71.36	85.38	6.84	2.57	10.03	6.52
7.06	11.16	17.22	3.86	17.24	3.28	2.34
2.64	3.30	1.99		5.10	5.00	
2.11	4.74	8.13	0.30	0.27	7.00	2.61
25.10	46.79	91.88	8.04	45.50	20.12	9.82
283.21	547.24	288.30	89.78	223.92	174.86	4.08
1.50	2.11	10.50	0.70	5.13	1.18	1.18
14.34	24.23	60.74	2.48	22.71	13.09	2.04
21.77	70.86	101.90	7.71	120.65	72.87	7.99
19.62	26.61	85.73	5.62	16.98	20.71	5.76
15.78	46.46	112.59	2.21	45.47	25.22	18.48
9.21	21.15	41.24	2.93	49.28	37.20	0.55
26.02	54.01	197.73	4.57	83.44	62.53	17.16
47.08	65.08	402.42	129.41	247.17	85.82	14.01
5.72	9.06	14.44	0.39	18.20	5.93	4.56
0.51	0.86	3.18		1.58	1.00	1.00
1.31	1.48	6.28	0.27	1.02	1.68	0.02
11.57	15.64	11.26	7.88	9.70	3.57	
368.27	587.98	304.51	304.33	181.93	115.88	73.27
45.26	60.09	61.78	30.86	56.38	18.74	6.79
63.20	97.83	82.28	86.37	32.17	17.87	10.73

12–9 规模以上工业损益及分配(2023年)

Profit, Loss and Distribution of Industrial Enterprises Above Designated Size(2023)

单位：亿元

指标	Item	营业收入 Business Revenue	营业成本 Business Cost
总计	**Total**	**9613.31**	**8234.00**
按登记注册类型分组	**by Status of Registration**		
内资企业	Domestic Invested Enterprises	7895.70	6830.35
国有独资公司	State-owned Sole-proprietorship Enterprises	411.80	316.90
私营有限责任公司	Private Limited Liability Corporations	2161.52	1750.67
其他有限责任公司	Other Limited Liability Corporations	3174.40	2856.05
私营股份有限公司	Private Share-holding Corporations Ltd.	229.48	177.90
其他股份有限公司	Other Share-holding Corporations Ltd.	1777.19	1603.88
全民所有制企业(国有企业)	State-owned Enterprises	47.19	44.31
集体所有制企业(集体企业)	Collective-owned Enterprises	81.15	69.25
股份合作企业	Cooperative Enterprises	0.42	0.32
联营企业	Joint Ownership Enterprises	0.66	0.47
个人独资企业	Sole-proprietorship Enterprises	11.12	9.95
合伙企业	Partnership Enterprises	0.76	0.64
其他内资企业	Other Domestic Invested Enterprises		
港澳台投资企业	Enterprises with Investment from Hong Kong,Macao and Taiwan	1221.62	1023.73
港澳台投资有限责任公司	Limited Liability Corporations	879.45	698.04
港澳台投资股份有限公司	Share-holding Corporations Ltd.	342.17	325.69
港澳台投资合伙企业	Partnership Enterprises		
其他港澳台投资企业	Other Enterprises		
外商投资企业	Foreign Invested Enterprises	496.00	379.92
外商投资有限责任公司	Limited Liability Corporations	304.91	239.21
外商投资股份有限公司	Share-holding Corporations Ltd.	191.09	140.71
外商投资合伙企业	Partnership Enterprises		
其他外商投资企业	Other Enterprises		
按轻重工业分	**by Light & Heavy Industry**		
轻工业	Light Industry	1413.86	970.30
重工业	Heavy Industry	8199.45	7263.70
按企业规模分	**by Enterprise Size**		
大型企业	Large-sized Enterprises	5041.48	4320.77
中型企业	Medium-sized Enterprises	1519.91	1277.85
小型企业	Small-sized Enterprises	2834.92	2440.40
微型企业	Micro-sized Enterprises	217.00	194.98
按工业行业分	**by Sector**		
煤炭开采和洗选业	Mining and Washing of Coal	4.94	3.57
石油和天然气开采业	Extraction of Petroleum and Natural Gas	14.28	6.90
黑色金属矿采选业	Mining and Processing of Ferrous Metal Ores	151.67	123.97
有色金属矿采选业	Mining and Processing of Non-Ferrous Metal Ores		

(100 million yuan)

税金及附加 Taxes and Other Charges	销售费用 Selling Expenses	管理费用 Management Expenses	利息费用 Interest Expenses	利润总额 Total Profits	所得税费用 Income Tax Payable	亏损企业 亏损总额 Total Loss of Loss Enterprises	应交增值税 Value-added Tax Payable
117.75	**276.36**	**269.19**	**60.46**	**448.14**	**51.42**	**65.26**	**165.77**
109.22	225.40	214.09	53.40	274.29	30.06	59.08	130.22
73.08	0.86	6.75	1.47	17.01	4.64	1.18	13.51
10.78	108.04	77.75	11.48	106.08	8.61	14.28	41.70
18.10	51.45	86.89	30.46	79.16	13.27	40.43	50.74
1.42	11.79	13.13	2.13	15.27	1.57	2.00	4.95
5.10	52.62	26.99	6.37	49.35	1.58	1.01	17.79
0.43	0.05	0.34	0.39	0.97	0.33	0.18	0.79
0.22	0.15	1.63	1.06	6.14	0.04		0.39
0.01	0.01	0.08		0.02			0.01
0.03		0.09		0.04	0.01		0.06
0.06	0.42	0.40	0.04	0.19	0.01	0.01	0.24
		0.03		0.08			0.03
5.52	26.22	32.14	4.78	121.28	12.49	1.64	25.92
4.84	22.69	29.42	4.68	111.45	11.76	1.64	23.59
0.68	3.53	2.72	0.10	9.83	0.74		2.33
3.01	24.75	22.96	2.27	52.56	8.87	4.54	9.64
2.09	12.85	17.16	1.18	27.15	5.53	3.81	7.03
0.92	11.90	5.80	1.09	25.41	3.33	0.73	2.60
9.95	129.95	63.25	6.87	166.44	18.33	9.47	40.67
107.80	146.41	205.94	53.58	281.69	33.10	55.79	125.10
90.70	131.32	95.49	21.72	268.89	26.88	14.03	82.72
10.47	63.49	55.35	16.18	66.58	9.43	14.00	31.02
15.84	78.41	111.43	19.31	106.01	14.07	33.34	47.97
0.74	3.14	6.92	3.25	6.66	1.04	3.89	4.07
0.26	0.08	0.65	0.36	-0.24		0.26	0.37
2.52		0.09	0.36	4.52	0.34		1.33
1.77	0.23	4.57	1.19	7.58	1.31	0.15	4.17

12-9 续表 continued

单位：亿元

指标	Item	营业收入 Business Revenue	营业成本 Business Cost
非金属矿采选业	Mining and Processing of Non-metal Ores	10.04	6.98
开采专业及辅助性活动	Professional and Support Activities for Mining		
其他采矿业	Mining of Other Ores		
农副食品加工业	Processing of Food from Agricultural Products	196.37	183.68
食品制造业	Manufacture of Foods	166.08	132.43
酒、饮料和精制茶制造业	Manufacture of Liquor, Beverages and Refined Tea	74.86	61.30
烟草制品业	Manufacture of Tobacco	6.94	4.02
纺织业	Manufacture of Textile	51.70	46.70
纺织服装、服饰业	Manufacture of Textile, Wearing Apparel and Accessories	14.32	11.94
皮革、毛皮、羽毛及其制品和制鞋业	Manufacture of Leather, Fur, Feather and Related Products and Footwear	1.30	1.02
木材加工和木、竹、藤、棕、草制品业	Processing of Timber, Manufacture of Wood, Bamboo, Rattan,Palm and Straw Products	8.73	7.80
家具制造业	Manufacture of Furniture	13.06	10.59
造纸和纸制品业	Manufacture of Paper and Paper Products	46.33	39.35
印刷和记录媒介复制业	Printing and Reproduction of Recording Media	53.90	43.31
文教、工美、体育和娱乐用品制造业	Manufacture of Articles for Culture, Education, Arts and Crafts,Sport and Entertainment Activities	13.55	10.96
石油、煤炭及其他燃料加工业	Processing of Petroleum, Coal and Other Fuels	442.42	345.09
化学原料和化学制品制造业	Manufacture of Raw Chemical Materials and Chemical Products	391.82	318.77
医药制造业	Manufacture of Medicines	418.43	163.44
化学纤维制造业	Manufacture of Chemical Fibres	29.59	14.07
橡胶和塑料制品业	Manufacture of Rubber and Plastics Products	44.54	36.86
非金属矿物制品业	Manufacture of Non-metallic Mineral Products	482.51	412.25
黑色金属冶炼和压延加工业	Smelting and Pressing of Ferrous Metals	1751.17	1685.39
有色金属冶炼和压延加工业	Smelting and Pressing of Non-ferrous Metals	60.15	56.07
金属制品业	Manufacture of Metal Products	344.52	286.51
通用设备制造业	Manufacture of General Purpose Machinery	539.02	417.09
专用设备制造业	Manufacture of Special Purpose Machinery	301.81	232.09
汽车制造业	Manufacture of Automobiles	1341.48	1190.86
铁路、船舶、航空航天和其他运输设备制造业	Manufacture of Railway, Ship, Aerospace and Other Transport Equipments	75.10	60.81
电气机械和器材制造业	Manufacture of Electrical Machinery and Apparatus	610.03	515.82
计算机、通信和其他电子设备制造业	Manufacture of Computers, Communication and Other Electronic Equipment	1089.73	1009.58
仪器仪表制造业	Manufacture of Measuring Instruments and Machinery	86.03	55.16
其他制造业	Other Manufacture	7.11	5.07
废弃资源综合利用业	Utilization of Waste Resources	49.37	46.98
金属制品、机械和设备修理业	Repair Service of Metal Products, Machinery and Equipment	23.44	18.23
电力、热力生产和供应业	Production and Supply of Electric Power and Heat Power	246.07	237.75
燃气生产和供应业	Production and Supply of Gas	406.62	393.89
水的生产和供应业	Production and Supply of Water	44.29	37.69

(100 million yuan)

税金及附加 Taxes and Other Charges	销售费用 Selling Expenses	管理费用 Management Expenses	利息费用 Interest Expenses	利润总额 Total Profits	所得税费用 Income Tax Payable	亏损企业亏损总额 Total Loss of Loss Enterprises	应交增值税 Value-added Tax Payable
0.33	0.42	1.44	0.07	0.71	0.23	0.22	0.39
0.40	4.53	4.84	1.12	2.61	0.43	1.41	1.40
1.12	8.39	7.17	0.21	16.29	2.75	0.79	4.46
2.08	3.74	1.88	0.45	5.38	1.30	0.45	2.23
0.19	0.42	2.02		0.33	0.15	0.45	0.57
0.19	0.88	2.01	0.54	-0.25	-0.06	0.80	0.38
0.21	0.68	1.46	0.21	0.37	0.03	0.08	0.33
		0.08		0.11			0.04
0.04	0.22	0.25	0.12	0.17	0.01	0.02	0.09
0.12	0.81	0.67	0.23	0.54	0.20	0.24	0.52
0.23	2.09	1.96	0.36	0.84	0.11	0.22	1.08
0.42	1.79	3.60	0.28	4.22	0.53	0.35	1.46
0.06	1.02	0.76	0.19	-0.06		0.34	0.17
72.96	1.01	4.86	0.86	16.39	4.51	1.40	14.18
2.05	17.44	12.40	5.26	23.88	2.51	3.69	6.52
3.35	81.03	23.87	1.99	90.53	8.25	1.29	15.83
0.21	0.46	0.35	0.05	13.61	1.94		0.05
0.21	1.48	2.31	0.23	1.94	0.22	0.48	0.89
3.54	15.72	24.54	5.48	14.94	2.74	6.35	12.47
3.76	5.20	13.43	10.50	3.49	0.27	7.77	9.23
0.13	0.64	1.31	0.34	1.93	0.17	0.26	0.42
1.84	10.46	13.52	3.37	16.74	1.97	1.74	7.05
3.18	29.34	28.39	2.20	36.98	4.64	3.63	11.65
1.46	15.34	16.26	1.79	22.10	2.74	3.90	5.15
4.99	20.25	27.10	2.57	79.88	5.84	2.68	23.74
0.52	2.08	5.89	0.21	4.11	0.78	0.60	1.65
2.34	16.51	17.40	2.55	42.20	3.20	2.08	14.86
1.82	18.29	16.14	4.69	8.97	-1.28	9.48	11.60
0.54	7.38	7.07	0.32	11.56	1.15	0.33	2.45
0.02	0.06	0.32		1.39	0.10		0.40
0.34	0.43	0.80	0.15	0.99	0.09	0.39	2.04
0.15	0.62	2.28	0.06	2.05	0.30	0.05	0.12
2.12	1.44	11.09	9.78	2.80	2.72	11.05	4.48
0.38	3.92	3.46	0.82	5.82	0.76	1.45	1.22
1.90	1.96	2.95	1.54	2.71	0.50	0.86	0.74

12-10 规模以上国有及国有控股工业损益及分配(2023年)

Profit, Loss and Distribution of State-Owned and State-Controlled Industrial Enterprises Above Designated Size(2023)

单位：亿元

指标	Item	营业收入 Business Revenue	营业成本 Business Cost
总计	**Total**	**3877.81**	**3492.71**
按登记注册类型分组	**by Status of Registration**		
内资企业	Domestic Invested Enterprises	3665.20	3316.42
国有独资公司	State-owned Sole-proprietorship Enterprises	411.80	316.90
其他有限责任公司	Other Limited Liability Corporations	1680.06	1524.79
其他股份有限公司	Other Share-holding Corporations Ltd.	1515.66	1424.12
港澳台投资企业	Enterprises with Investment from Hong Kong,Macao and Taiwan	154.79	126.02
港澳台投资有限责任公司	Limited Liability Corporations	154.79	126.02
外商投资企业	Foreign Invested Enterprises	57.82	50.27
外商投资有限责任公司	Limited Liability Corporations	55.86	48.30
外商投资股份有限公司	Share-holding Corporations Ltd.	1.96	1.97
按轻重工业分	**by Light & Heavy Industry**		
轻工业	Light Industry	125.57	84.44
重工业	Heavy Industry	3752.24	3408.26
按企业规模分	**by Enterprise Size**		
大型企业	Large-sized Enterprises	2244.80	2015.67
中型企业	Medium-sized Enterprises	552.99	468.46
小型企业	Small-sized Enterprises	1044.77	977.84
微型企业	Micro-sized Enterprises	35.25	30.74
按工业行业分	**by Sector**		
煤炭开采和洗选业	Mining and Washing of Coal	4.29	2.87
石油和天然气开采业	Extraction of Petroleum and Natural Gas	9.00	3.96
黑色金属矿采选业	Mining and Processing of Ferrous Metal Ores	19.01	12.42
有色金属矿采选业	Mining and Processing of Non-Ferrous Metal Ores		
非金属矿采选业	Mining and Processing of Non-metal Ores	3.01	2.17
开采专业及辅助性活动	Professional and Support Activities for Mining		
其他采矿业	Mining of Other Ores		
农副食品加工业	Processing of Food from Agricultural Products	8.09	7.50
食品制造业	Manufacture of Foods	14.44	11.69
酒、饮料和精制茶制造业	Manufacture of Liquor, Beverages and Refined Tea	26.65	20.66
烟草制品业	Manufacture of Tobacco	6.94	4.02

(100 million yuan)

税金及附加 Taxes and Other Charges	销售费用 Selling Expenses	管理费用 Management Expenses	利息费用 Interest Expenses	利润总额 Total Profits	所得税费用 Income Tax Payable	亏损企业 亏损总额 Total Loss of Loss Enterprises	应交增值税 Value-added Tax Payable
91.06	**61.61**	**76.21**	**27.21**	**96.88**	**16.24**	**26.25**	**56.86**
89.95	53.10	67.32	26.31	80.72	12.13	23.95	53.03
73.08	0.86	6.75	1.47	17.01	4.64	1.18	13.51
12.07	24.46	46.16	19.93	42.02	8.03	21.93	25.89
2.99	27.71	13.93	4.24	18.31	-0.94	0.19	12.00
0.74	7.18	5.18	0.63	12.44	3.44	1.06	2.54
0.74	7.18	5.18	0.63	12.44	3.44	1.06	2.54
0.37	1.32	3.71	0.26	3.72	0.67	1.25	1.30
0.36	1.31	3.57	0.17	4.37	0.68	0.60	1.28
0.01	0.02	0.14	0.09	-0.65	-0.01	0.65	0.02
1.89	22.39	7.15	0.22	10.55	1.27	1.01	4.61
89.17	39.22	69.05	26.98	86.33	14.96	25.24	52.25
79.99	26.72	36.63	12.82	50.41	10.08	11.51	34.54
5.30	26.02	21.00	7.96	19.63	2.66	4.44	9.07
5.62	8.38	17.26	5.30	24.54	2.87	8.69	12.75
0.15	0.48	1.32	1.12	2.30	0.63	1.60	0.50
0.21	0.07	0.57	0.29	0.02			0.32
1.68		0.09	0.07	3.20			0.92
0.97		1.72	0.15	2.24	0.63	0.14	1.40
0.07	0.02	0.29	0.03	0.47	0.12		0.16
0.02	0.10	0.08	0.02	0.39			0.01
0.11	0.73	0.81	-0.38	0.94		0.07	0.11
0.85	2.44	0.26		2.65	0.67		0.87
0.19	0.42	2.02		0.33	0.15	0.45	0.57

12-10 续表 continued

单位：亿元

指标	Item	营业收入 Business Revenue	营业成本 Business Cost
纺织业	Manufacture of Textile	2.30	2.38
纺织服装、服饰业	Manufacture of Textile, Wearing Apparel and Accessories	3.51	3.13
皮革、毛皮、羽毛及其制品和制鞋业	Manufacture of Leather, Fur, Feather and Related Products and Footwear		
木材加工和木、竹、藤、棕、草制品业	Processing of Timber, Manufacture of Wood, Bamboo, Rattan,Palm and Straw Products	0.50	0.38
家具制造业	Manufacture of Furniture		
造纸和纸制品业	Manufacture of Paper and Paper Products		
印刷和记录媒介复制业	Printing and Reproduction of Recording Media	10.37	7.34
文教、工美、体育和娱乐用品制造业	Manufacture of Articles for Culture, Education, Arts and Crafts, Sport and Entertainment Activities		
石油、煤炭及其他燃料加工业	Processing of Petroleum, Coal and Other Fuels	354.90	260.05
化学原料和化学制品制造业	Manufacture of Raw Chemical Materials and Chemical Products	81.70	63.79
医药制造业	Manufacture of Medicines	21.07	10.34
化学纤维制造业	Manufacture of Chemical Fibres	2.91	2.62
橡胶和塑料制品业	Manufacture of Rubber and Plastics Products	5.02	4.64
非金属矿物制品业	Manufacture of Non-metallic Mineral Products	81.55	67.42
黑色金属冶炼和压延加工业	Smelting and Pressing of Ferrous Metals	874.69	844.44
有色金属冶炼和压延加工业	Smelting and Pressing of Non-ferrous Metals	30.40	28.88
金属制品业	Manufacture of Metal Products	60.22	54.18
通用设备制造业	Manufacture of General Purpose Machinery	171.54	139.75
专用设备制造业	Manufacture of Special Purpose Machinery	40.39	34.46
汽车制造业	Manufacture of Automobiles	166.19	142.68
铁路、船舶、航空航天和其他运输设备制造业	Manufacture of Railway, Ship, Aerospace and Other Transport Equipments	61.78	51.32
电气机械和器材制造业	Manufacture of Electrical Machinery and Apparatus	224.98	200.70
计算机、通信和其他电子设备制造业	Manufacture of Computers, Communication and Other Electronic Equipment	938.78	881.04
仪器仪表制造业	Manufacture of Measuring Instruments and Machinery	23.70	15.99
其他制造业	Other Manufacture	3.46	3.22
废弃资源综合利用业	Utilization of Waste Resources	32.07	30.92
金属制品、机械和设备修理业	Repair Service of Metal Products, Machinery and Equipment	14.82	10.66
电力、热力生产和供应业	Production and Supply of Electric Power and Heat Power	219.54	218.62
燃气生产和供应业	Production and Supply of Gas	325.03	316.50
水的生产和供应业	Production and Supply of Water	34.95	31.96

(100 million yuan)

税金及附加 Taxes and Other Charges	销售费用 Selling Expenses	管理费用 Management Expenses	利息费用 Interest Expenses	利润总额 Total Profits	所得税费用 Income Tax Payable	亏损企业亏损总额 Total Loss of Loss Enterprises	应交增值税 Value-added Tax Payable
0.02	0.01	0.10		-0.20		0.20	-0.04
0.08	0.15	0.78	0.11	0.09	0.02	0.06	0.08
		0.03		0.04			0.01
0.16	0.34	1.34	0.01	0.97	0.13	0.13	0.49
72.75	0.18	3.94	0.35	17.48	4.46		12.61
0.58	10.80	1.72	2.15	0.67	0.21	2.62	2.03
0.23	7.46	0.86	0.39	3.25	0.14		1.11
0.02	0.01	0.06		0.04			
0.04	0.10	0.30	0.03	-0.19		0.24	0.07
1.11	0.85	4.17	1.11	5.13	0.75	1.25	2.60
2.29	3.91	8.85	6.72	-5.92	-0.16	6.71	5.15
0.06	0.12	0.68	0.24	1.86	0.17		0.18
0.37	0.52	1.97	0.40	0.81	0.19	0.58	1.15
1.22	4.13	6.28	0.34	13.36	1.84	0.67	4.73
0.27	1.42	1.83	0.66	-0.31	0.03	0.61	0.56
0.78	1.74	2.58	0.32	16.54	3.38	0.10	3.79
0.39	1.44	4.94	0.14	2.62	0.57	0.60	1.14
1.00	4.92	5.60	0.64	8.98	0.60	0.34	4.63
1.24	11.75	8.03	3.96	12.10	-1.16	0.32	4.67
0.15	1.33	1.13		4.07	0.43		0.40
0.01	0.01	0.02		0.10			0.15
0.22	0.08	0.09	0.09	0.64			1.40
0.12	0.25	2.05	0.04	1.85	0.28		-0.04
1.80	1.16	8.15	7.65	-1.10	2.24	9.08	3.98
0.29	3.19	2.35	0.59	3.52	0.42	1.25	0.94
1.74	1.95	2.50	1.10	0.22	0.14	0.83	0.71

12-11 分地区规模以上工业主要经济指标(2023年)

Main Economic Indicators of Industrial Enterprises Above Designated Size By Region(2023)

单位：亿元

指标	Item	全市 Total	历下区 Li xia	市中区 Shi zhong	槐荫区 Huai yin	天桥区 Tian qiao	历城区 Li cheng
企业单位数(个)	**Number of Industrial Enterprises (unit)**	**2811**	**51**	**83**	**71**	**135**	**194**
工业总产值	**Gross Industrial Output Value**	**8272.05**	**444.09**	**428.57**	**194.14**	**180.59**	**447.07**
资产与负债	**Assets and Liabilities**						
资产总计	Total Assets	11412.84	465.58	774.27	365.01	233.50	754.36
流动资产合计	Current Assets	6832.00	194.35	480.87	242.86	149.50	510.97
存货	Inventories	1131.07	22.11	73.82	39.49	34.75	63.87
应收账款	Accounts Receivable	2229.63	41.75	127.19	59.83	56.99	141.82
固定资产净额	Net Fixed Assets	2362.74	167.01	156.14	31.41	34.20	113.78
流动负债合计	Current Liabilities Total	5925.22	197.77	365.97	137.85	161.62	439.35
非流动负债合计	Non-Current Liabilities Total	1137.04	103.80	148.63	7.76	17.23	60.01
所有者权益合计	Total Owner's Equities	4350.58	164.00	259.67	219.41	54.65	255.00
实收资本	Paid- up Capital	1897.51	65.96	66.60	54.89	43.10	164.07
国家资本	Official Capital	252.36	38.48	23.79	4.09	4.44	16.59
损益及分配	**Profit,Loss and Distribution**						
营业收入	Business Revenue	9613.31	467.48	533.66	232.73	189.71	474.52
营业成本	Business Cost	8234.00	364.68	504.33	191.57	160.54	388.34
税金及附加	Taxes and Other Charges	117.75	73.20	1.97	1.29	0.78	2.26
管理费用	Management Expenses	269.19	10.37	11.44	8.75	8.59	22.50
利润总额	Total Profits	448.14	15.22	12.24	17.42	6.38	31.80
应交所得税	Income Tax Payable	51.42	5.00	1.48	2.70	1.16	4.59
亏损企业亏损总额	Total Loss of Loss Enterprises	65.26	4.98	4.32	0.45	3.34	6.23
本年应交增值税	Value-added Tax Payable	165.77	14.04	4.87	5.22	2.89	8.94

(100 million yuan)

长清区 Chang qing	章丘区 Zhang qiu	济阳区 Ji yang	莱芜区 Lai wu	钢城区 Gang cheng	平阴县 Ping yin	商河县 Shang he	济南高新区 Jinan Gao xin	济南起步区（直管） Jinan Start-up Area (Directly under)	南部山区 Nan shan
217	**594**	**164**	**326**	**153**	**162**	**201**	**398**	**47**	**15**
238.91	**1210.01**	**226.17**	**1042.48**	**819.05**	**351.39**	**228.80**	**1863.77**	**584.46**	**12.56**
655.89	1586.35	311.44	1465.35	891.74	512.97	319.77	2691.36	357.42	27.82
313.72	877.38	186.12	994.39	297.06	310.14	165.52	1891.85	200.87	16.40
67.24	142.08	36.28	133.16	68.69	58.03	35.80	331.13	18.80	5.81
99.99	252.05	42.24	361.67	46.97	77.07	58.29	712.31	146.92	4.54
73.47	370.31	68.59	319.94	371.66	106.24	96.86	351.01	95.17	6.96
389.70	810.79	136.82	971.63	420.30	185.43	123.40	1248.63	315.76	20.20
44.98	100.17	36.63	131.77	104.78	40.76	66.46	270.15	3.30	0.61
221.21	675.38	137.99	361.95	366.67	286.78	129.91	1172.58	38.35	7.01
166.41	287.85	56.88	223.48	226.83	71.94	63.22	380.39	23.64	2.24
7.86	41.29	3.45	32.02	3.93	4.92	3.97	67.04	0.37	0.12
251.15	1251.70	238.40	1496.52	1060.95	368.35	229.06	2224.04	581.75	13.29
206.27	1040.03	175.25	1380.76	997.56	307.55	196.24	1770.30	540.63	9.96
1.76	8.20	3.13	5.85	3.95	2.40	2.18	9.08	1.02	0.65
18.31	41.39	11.08	23.39	15.76	13.48	9.06	68.09	6.21	0.77
8.16	86.37	32.15	24.95	10.22	22.81	9.73	151.50	18.55	0.65
0.80	6.70	4.86	3.74	1.49	3.87	1.23	12.70	1.06	0.05
2.84	5.14	2.06	8.64	7.78	3.61	1.62	13.66	0.57	0.03
6.04	25.98	5.83	17.21	11.02	8.49	4.01	43.76	7.20	0.28

12-12 规模以上大中型工业企业经营情况(2023年)
Main Indicators of Large and Medium-Sized Enterprises(2023)

单位：亿元

指标	Item	企业单位数(个) Number of Enterprises (unit)	亏损企业数(个) Loss Enterprises (unit)
总计	**Total**	**222**	**34**
按登记注册类型分组	**by Status of Registration**		
内资企业	Domestic Invested Enterprises	172	28
国有独资公司	State-owned Sole-proprietorship Enterprises	4	1
私营有限责任公司	Private Limited Liability Corporations	46	5
其他有限责任公司	Other Limited Liability Corporations	76	20
私营股份有限公司	Private Share-holding Corporations Ltd.	11	1
其他股份有限公司	Other Share-holding Corporations Ltd.	32	1
全民所有制企业(国有企业)	State-owned Enterprises	NA	
集体所有制企业(集体企业)	Collective-owned Enterprises	NA	
股份合作企业	Cooperative Enterprises		
联营企业	Joint Ownership Enterprises		
个人独资企业	Sole-proprietorship Enterprises		
合伙企业	Partnership Enterprises		
其他内资企业	Other Domestic Invested Enterprises		
港澳台投资企业	Enterprises with Investment from Hong Kong,Macao and Taiwan	24	1
港澳台投资有限责任公司	Limited Liability Corporations	23	1
港澳台投资股份有限公司	Share-holding Corporations Ltd.	NA	
港澳台投资合伙企业	Partnership Enterprises		
其他港澳台投资企业	Other Enterprises		
外商投资企业	Foreign Invested Enterprises	26	5
外商投资有限责任公司	Limited Liability Corporations	22	4
外商投资股份有限公司	Share-holding Corporations Ltd.	4	1
外商投资合伙企业	Partnership Enterprises		
其他外商投资企业	Other Enterprises		
按轻重工业分	**by Light & Heavy Industry**		
轻工业	Light Industry	67	6
重工业	Heavy Industry	155	28
按企业规模分	**by Enterprise Size**		
大型企业	Large-sized Enterprises	60	8
中型企业	Medium-sized Enterprises	162	26
按工业行业分	**by Sector**		
煤炭开采和洗选业	Mining and Washing of Coal	NA	1
石油和天然气开采业	Extraction of Petroleum and Natural Gas		
黑色金属矿采选业	Mining and Processing of Ferrous Metal Ores	5	
有色金属矿采选业	Mining and Processing of Non-Ferrous Metal Ores		
非金属矿采选业	Mining and Processing of Non-metal Ores		

(100 million yuan)

工业总产值(现价) Gross Industrial Output Value (Current Prices)	资产总计 Total Assets	负债合计 Total Liabilities	营业收入 Business Revenue	利润总额 Total Profits	平均用工人数(万人) Annual Average Employees (10 000 persons)
5431.06	**7658.15**	**4588.85**	**6561.39**	**335.47**	**25.88**
4041.53	5567.52	3416.38	5028.83	188.54	19.38
389.72	304.14	207.35	402.00	16.48	0.52
852.84	1137.75	715.07	1009.08	71.07	5.15
1583.13	2354.84	1585.36	1940.71	44.09	8.68
122.66	193.41	63.73	122.96	9.50	0.93
1021.08	1422.52	716.82	1455.54	40.69	3.86
21.82	22.75	15.67	21.73	0.75	0.06
50.27	132.11	112.39	76.83	5.97	0.20
1013.31	1619.90	957.78	1148.95	102.13	4.38
745.25	1327.21	802.02	807.32	92.36	3.89
268.05	292.69	155.76	341.63	9.77	0.49
376.22	470.73	214.69	383.61	44.80	2.12
214.86	210.36	109.95	219.50	20.93	1.51
161.37	260.37	104.74	164.11	23.87	0.61
850.90	1298.41	507.43	890.51	134.37	7.92
4580.16	6359.75	4081.43	5670.88	201.10	17.95
4145.89	5309.87	3202.79	5041.48	268.89	16.97
1285.17	2348.28	1386.07	1519.91	66.58	8.91
4.91	9.41	17.24	4.79	-0.24	0.18
91.53	116.65	99.86	133.74	5.54	0.70

12-12 续表 continued

单位：亿元

指标	Item	企业单位数（个）Number of Enterprises (unit)	亏损企业数（个）Loss Enterprises (unit)
开采专业及辅助性活动	Professional and Support Activities for Mining		
其他采矿业	Mining of Other Ores		
农副食品加工业	Processing of Food from Agricultural Products	6	1
食品制造业	Manufacture of Foods	12	1
酒、饮料和精制茶制造业	Manufacture of Liquor, Beverages and Refined Tea	6	
烟草制品业	Manufacture of Tobacco	NA	1
纺织业	Manufacture of Textile	5	
纺织服装、服饰业	Manufacture of Textile, Wearing Apparel and Accessories	4	1
皮革、毛皮、羽毛及其制品和制鞋业	Manufacture of Leather, Fur, Feather and Related Products and Footwear		
木材加工和木、竹、藤、棕、草制品业	Processing of Timber, Manufacture of Wood, Bamboo, Rattan,Palm and Straw Products		
家具制造业	Manufacture of Furniture	NA	1
造纸和纸制品业	Manufacture of Paper and Paper Products	NA	
印刷和记录媒介复制业	Printing and Reproduction of Recording Media	NA	
文教、工美、体育和娱乐用品制造业	Manufacture of Articles for Culture, Education, Arts and Crafts, Sport and Entertainment Activities		
石油、煤炭及其他燃料加工业	Processing of Petroleum, Coal and Other Fuels	NA	1
化学原料和化学制品制造业	Manufacture of Raw Chemical Materials and Chemical Products	9	2
医药制造业	Manufacture of Medicines	17	1
化学纤维制造业	Manufacture of Chemical Fibres		
橡胶和塑料制品业	Manufacture of Rubber and Plastics Products	NA	
非金属矿物制品业	Manufacture of Non-metallic Mineral Products	20	4
黑色金属冶炼和压延加工业	Smelting and Pressing of Ferrous Metals	8	2
有色金属冶炼和压延加工业	Smelting and Pressing of Non-ferrous Metals	NA	
金属制品业	Manufacture of Metal Products	14	
通用设备制造业	Manufacture of General Purpose Machinery	21	2
专用设备制造业	Manufacture of Special Purpose Machinery	8	1
汽车制造业	Manufacture of Automobiles	18	3
铁路、船舶、航空航天和其他运输设备制造业	Manufacture of Railway, Ship, Aerospace and Other Transport Equipments	5	1
电气机械和器材制造业	Manufacture of Electrical Machinery and Apparatus	17	1
计算机、通信和其他电子设备制造业	Manufacture of Computers, Communication and Other Electronic Equipment	13	2
仪器仪表制造业	Manufacture of Measuring Instruments and Machinery	NA	
其他制造业	Other Manufacture		
废弃资源综合利用业	Utilization of Waste Resources	NA	
金属制品、机械和设备修理业	Repair Service of Metal Products, Machinery and Equipment	NA	
电力、热力生产和供应业	Production and Supply of Electric Power and Heat Power	8	5
燃气生产和供应业	Production and Supply of Gas	NA	1
水的生产和供应业	Production and Supply of Water	NA	2

(100 million yuan)

工业总产值(现价) Gross Industrial Output Value (Current Prices)	资产总计 Total Assets	负债合计 Total Liabilities	营业收入 Business Revenue	利润总额 Total Profits	平均用工人数(万人) Annual Average Employees (10 000 persons)
50.54	26.62	21.81	64.22	1.12	0.27
109.05	103.54	41.18	117.04	13.59	1.12
50.60	35.74	15.99	55.23	4.33	0.36
3.73	12.30	2.02	4.89	-0.45	0.22
14.67	21.17	15.57	20.35	0.17	0.22
6.80	21.88	15.72	8.10	0.19	0.30
9.74	15.06	10.71	10.12	0.57	0.15
14.49	13.18	7.31	18.27	0.63	0.10
11.75	23.43	9.20	12.77	0.98	0.24
379.32	91.47	46.63	404.05	16.54	0.19
193.22	357.77	238.01	221.71	16.21	0.71
381.29	696.15	169.42	375.87	86.26	3.40
2.24	1.71	5.18	2.21	0.04	0.04
195.41	487.92	274.51	212.62	9.00	1.23
1128.75	1216.55	854.28	1661.21	3.71	2.89
6.99	9.92	6.37	5.46	0.06	0.03
137.03	244.13	106.35	128.95	11.70	1.24
296.73	389.57	172.10	317.97	29.20	2.16
138.80	278.02	176.29	150.16	14.87	0.57
1156.48	1266.54	850.17	1253.25	75.23	4.29
56.80	87.05	41.02	59.55	2.42	0.47
297.12	528.81	347.86	377.72	34.77	1.71
441.12	760.90	424.89	664.66	6.87	1.15
9.29	24.28	12.33	11.07	1.69	0.12
4.89	7.38	6.18	7.32	0.06	0.14
8.51	20.14	13.62	8.33	1.17	0.17
171.46	539.84	401.53	184.03	0.54	1.08
38.38	108.02	56.12	42.89	-0.59	0.22
19.41	143.01	129.37	22.85	-0.69	0.20

12-13 规模以上大中型工业企业一览表(2023年)
Summary of Large and Medium-Sized Enterprises(2023)

企业名称 Name	登记注册类型 Status of Registration	企业规模 Enterprise Size	所属行业 Industry
浪潮电子信息产业股份有限公司	其他股份有限公司	大型	计算机整机制造
山东钢铁股份有限公司	其他股份有限公司	大型	钢压延加工
山东泰山钢铁集团有限公司	其他有限责任公司	大型	钢压延加工
中国石油化工股份有限公司济南分公司	国有独资公司	大型	原油加工及石油制品制造
中国重汽集团济南卡车股份有限公司	港澳台投资股份有限公司	大型	汽柴油车整车制造
济南比亚迪汽车有限公司	其他有限责任公司	大型	汽车零部件及配件制造
中国重汽集团济南商用车有限公司	港澳台投资有限责任公司	大型	汽柴油车整车制造
莱芜钢铁集团银山型钢有限公司	其他有限责任公司	大型	钢压延加工
山东富伦钢铁有限公司	私营有限责任公司	大型	钢压延加工
齐鲁制药有限公司	私营有限责任公司	大型	化学药品制剂制造
济南弗迪电池有限公司	港澳台投资有限责任公司	大型	锂离子电池制造
中国重汽集团济南动力有限公司	港澳台投资有限责任公司	大型	汽车用发动机制造
济南市九羊福利钢铁有限公司	私营有限责任公司	大型	炼铁
临工重机股份有限公司	外商投资股份有限公司	大型	矿山机械制造
山东泰威冶金材料制造有限公司	私营有限责任公司	中型	铁矿采选
济南二机床集团有限公司	其他有限责任公司	大型	金属成形机床制造
重汽(济南)车桥有限公司	港澳台投资有限责任公司	大型	汽车零部件及配件制造
启征新能源汽车(济南)有限公司	其他有限责任公司	大型	汽车零部件及配件制造
山东泰山轧钢有限公司	私营有限责任公司	中型	钢压延加工
山东晋控明水化工集团有限公司	集体所有制企业(集体企业)	大型	氮肥制造
山东泰山焦化有限公司	其他有限责任公司	中型	炼焦
山东电力设备有限公司	其他有限责任公司	中型	变压器、整流器和电感器制造
华能莱芜发电有限公司	其他有限责任公司	中型	火力发电
山东圣泉新材料股份有限公司	私营股份有限公司	大型	初级形态塑料及合成树脂制造
齐鲁安替制药有限公司	港澳台投资有限责任公司	大型	化学药品原料药制造
济南热力集团有限公司	国有独资公司	大型	热力生产和供应
济南万瑞炭素有限责任公司	私营有限责任公司	中型	石墨及碳素制品制造
中车山东风电有限公司	其他有限责任公司	中型	发电机及发电机组制造
费斯托气动有限公司	外商投资有限责任公司	大型	气压动力机械及元件制造
玫德集团有限公司	其他有限责任公司	大型	建筑装饰及水暖管道零件制造
济南圣泉集团股份有限公司	其他股份有限公司	中型	初级形态塑料及合成树脂制造
伊莱特能源装备股份有限公司	外商投资股份有限公司	大型	锻件及粉末冶金制品制造
中国石油集团济柴动力有限公司	其他有限责任公司	大型	内燃机及配件制造
华能济南黄台发电有限公司	其他有限责任公司	大型	热电联产
中国重汽集团济南专用车有限公司	其他有限责任公司	中型	改装汽车制造
济南澳海炭素有限公司	私营有限责任公司	中型	石墨及碳素制品制造
济南伊利乳业有限责任公司	私营有限责任公司	大型	液体乳制造

12-13 续表 1 continued 1

企业名称 Name	登记注册类型 Status of Registration	企业规模 Enterprise Size	所属行业 Industry
山东安信制药有限公司	港澳台投资有限责任公司	大型	化学药品原料药制造
华熙生物科技股份有限公司	外商投资股份有限公司	大型	生物药品制造
济南轻骑铃木摩托车有限公司	外商投资有限责任公司	大型	摩托车整车制造
济南邦德激光股份有限公司	其他股份有限公司	大型	金属切割及焊接设备制造
山东正泰电缆有限公司	其他有限责任公司	中型	电线、电缆制造
山东旺旺食品有限公司	外商投资有限责任公司	大型	液体乳制造
济南热电集团有限公司	其他有限责任公司	大型	热力生产和供应
山东明泉新材料科技有限公司	集体所有制企业(集体企业)	中型	有机化学原料制造
山东港华燃气集团有限公司	港澳台投资有限责任公司	中型	天然气生产和供应业
华电章丘发电有限公司	全民所有制企业(国有企业)	中型	热电联产
山东福瑞达生物股份有限公司	其他股份有限公司	中型	化妆品制造
中国重汽集团济南特种车有限公司	其他有限责任公司	中型	汽柴油车整车制造
山东海鼎农牧有限公司	私营有限责任公司	中型	其他饲料加工
重汽(济南)传动轴有限公司	其他有限责任公司	大型	汽车零部件及配件制造
浪潮计算机科技有限公司	其他有限责任公司	中型	计算机整机制造
中车山东机车车辆有限公司	其他有限责任公司	大型	铁路机车车辆制造
中粮可口可乐饮料(济南)有限公司	港澳台投资有限责任公司	大型	碳酸饮料制造
金雷科技股份公司	其他股份有限公司	大型	发电机及发电机组制造
济南海川投资集团有限公司	其他有限责任公司	中型	石墨及碳素制品制造
中国重汽集团济南橡塑件有限公司	其他有限责任公司	大型	汽车零部件及配件制造
济南裕兴化工有限责任公司	其他有限责任公司	大型	工业颜料制造
济南西门子能源变压器有限公司	外商投资有限责任公司	中型	变压器、整流器和电感器制造
卧龙电气(济南)电机有限公司	私营股份有限公司	中型	电动机制造
山东省章丘鼓风机股份有限公司	其他股份有限公司	大型	风机、风扇制造
积成电子股份有限公司	私营股份有限公司	大型	配电开关控制设备制造
山东鲁碧建材有限公司	其他有限责任公司	大型	水泥制造
济南龙山炭素有限公司	私营有限责任公司	中型	石墨及碳素制品制造
山东宏济堂制药集团股份有限公司	其他股份有限公司	大型	中成药生产
山东济华燃气有限公司	港澳台投资有限责任公司	中型	天然气生产和供应业
山东省万兴食品有限公司	私营有限责任公司	中型	蔬菜加工
山东天岳先进科技股份有限公司	其他股份有限公司	中型	电子专用材料制造
福士汽车零部件(济南)有限公司	外商投资有限责任公司	大型	汽车零部件及配件制造
山东电工电气日立高压开关有限公司	外商投资有限责任公司	中型	配电开关控制设备制造
平阴山水水泥有限公司	港澳台投资有限责任公司	中型	水泥制造
济南水务集团有限公司	其他有限责任公司	大型	自来水生产和供应
齐鲁动物保健品有限公司	私营有限责任公司	大型	兽用药品制造
济南重工股份有限公司	其他股份有限公司	中型	矿山机械制造
山东晋控日月新材料有限公司	其他有限责任公司	中型	氮肥制造

12-13 续表 2 continued 2

企业名称 Name	登记注册类型 Status of Registration	企业规模 Enterprise Size	所属行业 Industry
国网智能科技股份有限公司	其他股份有限公司	中型	工业机器人制造
济南达利食品有限公司	私营有限责任公司	大型	饼干及其他焙烤食品制造
凯傲(济南)叉车有限公司	外商投资有限责任公司	中型	生产专用车辆制造
维达纸业(山东)有限公司	港澳台投资有限责任公司	中型	机制纸及纸板制造
鲁中矿业有限公司	其他有限责任公司	大型	铁矿采选
济南森峰激光科技股份有限公司	其他股份有限公司	中型	金属切削机床制造
华润双鹤利民药业(济南)有限公司	其他有限责任公司	大型	化学药品制剂制造
济南顶津食品有限公司	外商投资有限责任公司	中型	瓶(罐)装饮用水制造
山东国舜建设集团有限公司	私营有限责任公司	中型	环境保护专用设备制造
济南金威刻科技发展有限公司	其他股份有限公司	大型	金属切割及焊接设备制造
山东鲁银新材料科技有限公司	其他有限责任公司	中型	锻件及粉末冶金制品制造
莱芜泰禾生化有限公司	其他有限责任公司	中型	食品及饲料添加剂制造
西电济南变压器股份有限公司	其他股份有限公司	中型	变压器、整流器和电感器制造
山东汉方制药有限公司	私营有限责任公司	中型	中成药生产
济南金麒麟刹车系统有限公司	私营有限责任公司	大型	汽车零部件及配件制造
济南统一企业有限公司	港澳台投资有限责任公司	中型	茶饮料及其他饮料制造
莱芜钢铁集团莱芜矿业有限公司	其他有限责任公司	大型	铁矿采选
大汉科技股份有限公司	私营股份有限公司	大型	生产专用起重机制造
济南迈科管道科技有限公司	港澳台投资有限责任公司	中型	金属结构制造
山东捷晶生物科技有限公司	其他有限责任公司	中型	营养食品制造
山东宏业纺织股份有限公司	其他股份有限公司	中型	棉纺纱加工
山东力诺特种玻璃股份有限公司	私营股份有限公司	大型	玻璃包装容器制造
山东鲁欣冶金科技有限公司	其他有限责任公司	中型	铁矿采选
科兴生物制药股份有限公司	其他股份有限公司	中型	生物药品制造
山东奥太电气有限公司	其他有限责任公司	中型	金属切割及焊接设备制造
莱芜万兴果菜食品加工有限公司	港澳台投资有限责任公司	中型	蔬菜加工
山东华凌电缆有限公司	其他有限责任公司	中型	电线、电缆制造
山东朗进科技股份有限公司	其他股份有限公司	中型	制冷、空调设备制造
山东太古飞机工程有限公司	港澳台投资有限责任公司	大型	航空航天器修理
济南宇飞食品有限公司	私营有限责任公司	中型	禽类屠宰
济南重工集团有限公司	港澳台投资有限责任公司	中型	隧道施工专用机械制造
济南黄河特钢有限责任公司	其他有限责任公司	中型	钢压延加工
山东山水水泥集团有限公司	港澳台投资有限责任公司	中型	水泥制造
山东齐发药业有限公司	私营有限责任公司	中型	化学药品原料药制造
泉意光罩光电科技(济南)有限公司	其他有限责任公司	中型	集成电路制造
济南和盛热力有限公司	其他有限责任公司	中型	热力生产和供应
莱芜新希望六和食品有限公司	其他有限责任公司	中型	禽类屠宰

12-13 续表 3 continued 3

企业名称 Name	登记注册类型 Status of Registration	企业规模 Enterprise Size	所属行业 Industry
山东博士伦福瑞达制药有限公司	外商投资有限责任公司	中型	化学药品制剂制造
济南迈克阀门科技有限公司	港澳台投资有限责任公司	中型	阀门和旋塞制造
济南佳宝乳业有限公司	私营有限责任公司	大型	液体乳制造
中孚安全技术有限公司	私营有限责任公司	大型	信息安全设备制造
山东济钢环保新材料有限公司	其他有限责任公司	中型	建筑用石加工
莱芜钢铁集团泰东实业有限公司	其他有限责任公司	大型	金属废料和碎屑加工处理
山东爱普电气设备有限公司	其他有限责任公司	中型	其他输配电及控制设备制造
山东天鹅棉业机械股份有限公司	其他股份有限公司	中型	棉花加工机械制造
山东晨熙智能科技有限公司	私营有限责任公司	中型	包装装潢及其他印刷
山东泰莱电气股份有限公司	其他股份有限公司	中型	其他输配电及控制设备制造
青岛啤酒(济南)有限公司	其他有限责任公司	中型	啤酒制造
济南新峨嵋实业有限公司	外商投资有限责任公司	中型	耐火陶瓷制品及其他耐火材料制造
济南鲁冠混凝土有限责任公司	私营有限责任公司	中型	水泥制品制造
山东平阴丰源炭素有限责任公司	私营有限责任公司	中型	石墨及碳素制品制造
山东水泥厂有限公司	其他有限责任公司	中型	水泥制造
山东力诺瑞特新能源有限公司	外商投资有限责任公司	中型	太阳能器具制造
济南沃德汽车零部件有限公司	私营有限责任公司	大型	汽车零部件及配件制造
山东福牌阿胶股份有限公司	私营股份有限公司	中型	中成药生产
山东阳光铸业有限公司	其他有限责任公司	中型	炼铁
浪潮商用机器有限公司	港澳台投资有限责任公司	中型	计算机整机制造
章丘重型锻造有限公司	私营有限责任公司	大型	锻件及粉末冶金制品制造
山东银鹭食品有限公司	其他有限责任公司	中型	含乳饮料和植物蛋白饮料制造
山东德源电力科技股份有限公司	其他股份有限公司	中型	配电开关控制设备制造
山东金晔农法食品有限公司	私营有限责任公司	中型	蜜饯制作
济南比亚迪半导体有限公司	其他有限责任公司	中型	集成电路制造
山东山大电力技术股份有限公司	其他股份有限公司	中型	其他专用仪器制造
山东福贞金属包装有限公司	外商投资有限责任公司	中型	金属包装容器及材料制造
济南市冶金科学研究所有限责任公司	其他有限责任公司	中型	有色金属合金制造
济南泉华包装制品有限公司	港澳台投资有限责任公司	中型	纸和纸板容器制造
济南弘正科技有限公司	港澳台投资有限责任公司	中型	摩托车零部件及配件制造
山东赖氏家具股份有限公司	其他股份有限公司	中型	木质家具制造
山东鲁中啤酒原料有限公司	私营有限责任公司	中型	玻璃包装容器制造
齐鲁宏业纺织集团有限公司	私营有限责任公司	中型	棉纺纱加工
神思电子技术股份有限公司	其他股份有限公司	中型	其他计算机制造
山推建友机械股份有限公司	其他股份有限公司	中型	建筑材料生产专用机械制造
济南市莱芜燃气热力有限责任公司	私营有限责任公司	中型	天然气生产和供应业
济南晶恒电子有限责任公司	其他有限责任公司	中型	半导体分立器件制造

12-13 续表 4 continued 4

企业名称 Name	登记注册类型 Status of Registration	企业规模 Enterprise Size	所属行业 Industry
山东烟叶复烤有限公司	其他有限责任公司	中型	烟叶复烤
山东温岭精锻科技有限公司	私营有限责任公司	中型	锻件及粉末冶金制品制造
山东铂源药业股份有限公司	其他股份有限公司	中型	化学药品原料药制造
山东欧锐激光科技有限公司	其他有限责任公司	中型	金属切削机床制造
山东明仁福瑞达制药股份有限公司	其他股份有限公司	中型	中成药生产
山东汇金股份有限公司	其他有限责任公司	中型	汽车零部件及配件制造
山东济南发电设备厂有限公司	其他有限责任公司	中型	发电机及发电机组制造
济南东区供水有限公司	其他有限责任公司	中型	自来水生产和供应
山东华氟化工有限责任公司	其他有限责任公司	中型	初级形态塑料及合成树脂制造
济南二机床铸造有限公司	国有独资公司	中型	黑色金属铸造
山东明化新材料有限公司	其他有限责任公司	中型	有机化学原料制造
山东万祥矿业有限公司	其他有限责任公司	中型	烟煤和无烟煤开采洗选
山东北辰机电设备股份有限公司	私营股份有限公司	中型	金属压力容器制造
安莉芳(山东)服装有限公司	港澳台投资有限责任公司	中型	运动休闲针织服装制造
山东聚鑫集团钢结构有限公司	私营有限责任公司	中型	金属结构制造
莱芜莱新铁矿有限责任公司	其他有限责任公司	中型	铁矿采选
中建八局建筑科技(山东)有限公司	其他有限责任公司	中型	金属门窗制造
济南中船设备有限公司	私营有限责任公司	中型	紧固件制造
山东大旺食品有限公司	外商投资有限责任公司	中型	饼干及其他焙烤食品制造
迈大食品(山东)有限公司	外商投资有限责任公司	中型	饼干及其他焙烤食品制造
赛克赛斯生物科技股份有限公司	其他股份有限公司	中型	化学药品制剂制造
山东华光光电子股份有限公司	其他股份有限公司	中型	光电子器件制造
济南鲁东耐火材料有限公司	外商投资有限责任公司	中型	耐火陶瓷制品及其他耐火材料制造
山东大鲁阁织染工业有限公司	外商投资有限责任公司	中型	棉印染精加工
济南泓泉制水有限公司	其他有限责任公司	中型	自来水生产和供应
济南宜和食品有限公司	外商投资有限责任公司	中型	酱油、食醋及类似制品制造
济南轻骑标致摩托车有限公司	外商投资有限责任公司	中型	摩托车整车制造
济南中燃科技发展有限公司	私营有限责任公司	中型	其他金属加工机械制造
济南锅炉集团有限公司	私营有限责任公司	中型	锅炉及辅助设备制造
山东金钟科技集团股份有限公司	其他股份有限公司	中型	衡器制造
山东科源制药股份有限公司	私营股份有限公司	中型	化学药品原料药制造
山东新升实业发展有限责任公司	其他有限责任公司	中型	热电联产
山东耀华玻璃有限公司	其他有限责任公司	中型	其他玻璃制造
山东上好佳食品工业有限公司	港澳台投资有限责任公司	中型	饼干及其他焙烤食品制造
济南圣都食品有限公司	私营有限责任公司	中型	肉制品及副产品加工
山东新华印务有限公司	其他有限责任公司	中型	书、报刊印刷
山东鲁信天一印务有限公司	其他有限责任公司	中型	包装装潢及其他印刷

12-13 续表 5 continued 5

企业名称 Name	登记注册类型 Status of Registration	企业规模 Enterprise Size	所属行业 Industry
山东中维世纪科技股份有限公司	私营股份有限公司	中型	计算机外围设备制造
山东小鸭精工机械有限公司	外商投资有限责任公司	中型	汽车零部件及配件制造
济南新天科技有限公司	私营有限责任公司	中型	金属切削机床制造
山东巧夺天工家具有限公司	其他有限责任公司	中型	木质家具制造
济南轻骑大韩摩托车有限责任公司	外商投资有限责任公司	中型	摩托车整车制造
平阴鲁西装备科技有限公司	国有独资公司	中型	金属压力容器制造
济南中海炭素有限公司	私营有限责任公司	中型	石墨及碳素制品制造
济南台有玻璃制品有限公司	其他有限责任公司	中型	日用玻璃制品制造
力创科技股份有限公司	私营股份有限公司	中型	供应用仪器仪表制造
中集车辆(山东)有限公司	外商投资有限责任公司	中型	改装汽车制造
济南虫洞智能家居设施有限公司	其他有限责任公司	中型	木质家具制造
章丘华明水泥有限公司	其他有限责任公司	中型	水泥制造
山东九龙新材料有限公司	私营有限责任公司	中型	耐火陶瓷制品及其他耐火材料制造
山东枣矿中兴慧通轮胎有限公司	其他有限责任公司	中型	轮胎制造
济南实达紧固件股份有限公司	其他股份有限公司	中型	紧固件制造
山东泰东新材料有限公司	其他有限责任公司	中型	锻件及粉末冶金制品制造
济南科盛电子有限公司	私营有限责任公司	中型	光电子器件制造
莱芜环球汽车零部件有限公司	外商投资有限责任公司	中型	汽车零部件及配件制造
济南元首针织股份有限公司	其他股份有限公司	中型	运动休闲针织服装制造
济南翼菲智能科技股份有限公司	外商投资股份有限公司	中型	工业机器人制造
山东通发实业有限公司	其他有限责任公司	中型	其他建筑、安全用金属制品制造
济南明鑫制药股份有限公司	私营股份有限公司	中型	化学药品原料药制造
山东高速生物工程有限公司	其他有限责任公司	中型	液体乳制造
济南市白象科技发展有限公司	私营有限责任公司	中型	冶金专用设备制造
山东仁科测控技术有限公司	私营有限责任公司	中型	敏感元件及传感器制造
莱芜钢铁集团金鼎实业有限公司	其他有限责任公司	中型	热力生产和供应
山东裕兴电工器材有限公司	私营有限责任公司	中型	变压器、整流器和电感器制造
山东莱芜煤矿机械有限公司	其他有限责任公司	中型	矿山机械制造
山东百脉泉酒业股份有限公司	其他股份有限公司	中型	白酒制造
山东豪驰智能汽车有限公司	其他有限责任公司	中型	新能源车整车制造
山东新华泰纺织有限公司	私营有限责任公司	中型	棉纺纱加工
济阳元首针织有限责任公司	其他有限责任公司	中型	其他针织或钩针编织服装制造
山东莱威新材料有限公司	其他有限责任公司	中型	其他产业用纺织制成品制造
山东华东风机有限公司	私营有限责任公司	中型	风机、风扇制造
济南思迈迩制衣有限公司	私营有限责任公司	中型	其他针织或钩针编织服装制造
山东省莱芜市辛庄煤矿有限公司	私营有限责任公司	中型	烟煤和无烟煤开采洗选

12-14 主要工业产品生产量(2023年)
Output of Major Industrial Products(2023)

主要工业产品名称	Major Industrial Products above Designated Size	单位 Unit	生产量 Production
铁矿石原矿	Crude Iron ore	万吨 (10 000 tons)	556.1
铁矿石成品矿	Iron ore finished ore	万吨 (10 000 tons)	1900.6
铁精矿	Iron ore concentrate	万吨 (10 000 tons)	1822.6
石灰石	Lime Powder	万吨 (10 000 tons)	448.8
饲料	Feed	万吨 (10 000 tons)	150.8
鲜、冷藏肉	Frozen,Fresh Meat	万吨 (10 000 tons)	18.4
乳制品	Milk Products	万吨 (10 000 tons)	48.4
液体乳	Liquid Milk	万吨 (10 000 tons)	46.6
酱油	Soy Sauce	万吨 (10 000 tons)	6.0
食品添加剂	Food Additives	万吨 (10 000 tons)	17.0
饲料添加剂	Feed Additive	万吨 (10 000 tons)	7.9
饮料酒	Liquor	万千升 (10 000 kiloliter)	25.9
白酒(折65度，商品量)	Liquor (65 degree discount, commercial quantity)	万千升 (10 000 kiloliter)	0.7
啤酒	Beer	万千升 (10 000 kiloliter)	25.2
饮料	Drinks	万吨 (10 000 tons)	295.7
碳酸饮料(汽水)	Carbonated Drinks	万吨 (10 000 tons)	72.7
包装饮用水	Bottled Drinking Water	万吨 (10 000 tons)	54.5
果蔬汁类及其饮料	Juice and Vegetable Juice Beverage	万吨 (10 000 tons)	59.6
布	Cloth	万米(10 000 m)	1831.5
服装	Garments	万件(10 000 pieces)	3658.4
家具	Furniture	万件(10 000 pieces)	72.9
纸制品	Paper Products	万吨 (10 000 tons)	29.2
瓦楞纸箱	Corrugated Box	万吨 (10 000 tons)	16.9
单色印刷品	Monochrome Print	万令(10 000 ream)	92.3
多色印刷品	Ploychrome Print	万对开色令 (10 000 color folio ream)	1984.1
纯苯	Purified Petroleum Benzin(e)	万吨 (10 000 tons)	11.1
精甲醇	Extracted Methanol	万吨 (10 000 tons)	67.8
合成氨(无水氨)	Synthetic Ammonia	万吨 (10 000 tons)	77.7
农用氮、磷、钾化学肥料(折纯)	Chemical Fertilizer	万吨 (10 000 tons)	29.5
尿素(折含氮100%)	Urea	万吨 (10 000 tons)	29.2
化学农药原药(折有效成分100%)	Chemical Pesticide	吨(ton)	1543
涂料	Paint	万吨 (10 000 tons)	18.8
初级形态塑料	Primary Plastic	万吨 (10 000 tons)	92.3
合成橡胶	Chemical Reagent	万吨 (10 000 tons)	0.3
化学试剂	Surface Active Agent	万吨 (10 000 tons)	14.4
表面活性剂	Synthetic Detergents	万吨 (10 000 tons)	3.7
化学药品原药	Chemical Medicine	万吨 (10 000 tons)	1.1

12-14 续表 1 continued 1

主要工业产品名称	Major Industrial Products above Designated Size	单位 Unit	生产量 Production
中成药	Traditional Chemical Medicine	吨(ton)	9305
兽用药品	Veterinary Drugs	吨(ton)	23280
化学纤维	Chemical Fiber	万吨 (10 000 tons)	7.9
橡胶轮胎外胎	Rubber Tyre Cover	万条(10 000 tires)	84.2
塑料制品	Plastic Articles	万吨 (10 000 tons)	15.5
硅酸盐水泥熟料	Portland Cement Clinker	万吨 (10 000 tons)	541.5
水泥	Cement	万吨 (10 000 tons)	1229.4
石灰	Lime	万吨 (10 000 tons)	282.9
商品混凝土	Concrete	万立方米(10 000 cu.m)	3014.6
水泥混凝土排水管	Cement and Concrete Drainage Pipes	千米(km)	297.7
水泥混凝土压力管	Cement and Concrete Pressure Pipes	千米(km)	155.0
砖	Brick	亿块(100 million unit)	1.6
钢化玻璃	Stalinite	万平方米(10 000 sq.m)	198.6
中空玻璃	Hollow Glass	万平方米(10 000 sq.m)	187.8
耐火材料制品	Refractory Product	万吨 (10 000 tons)	49.7
石墨及碳素制品	Graphite and Carbon Products	万吨 (10 000 tons)	208.7
生铁	Cast Iron	万吨 (10 000 tons)	1688.1
粗钢	Crude Steel	万吨 (10 000 tons)	1746.7
钢材	Rolled Steel	万吨 (10 000 tons)	1945.0
钢结构	Steel Structure	万吨 (10 000 tons)	106.5
金属切削工具	Metal Cutting Tool	万件 (10 000 unit)	380.4
锻件	Forge Piece	万吨 (10 000 tons)	135.1
粉末冶金制品	Sintered Metal Products	万吨 (10 000 tons)	2.0
电站锅炉	Utility Boilers	蒸发量吨 (evaporation ton)	970
发动机	Engine	万千瓦(10 000kW)	2826.4
汽车用发动机	Automotive Engine	万千瓦(10 000kW)	2737.6
金属切削机床	Metal-cutting Machine Tools	台(unit)	19387
起重机	Lifting Equipment	万吨 (10 000 tons)	13.6
电梯、自动扶梯及升降机	Elevators, Escalators and Lifts	台(unit)	72922
液压元件	Hydraulic Components	万件(10 000 unit)	51.1
气动元件	Pneumatic Components	万件(10 000 unit)	1915.9
鼓风机	Air Blower	万台(10 000 unit)	3.6
工商用制冷、空调设备	Commercial Refrigeration Equipment	万台(套)(10 000 unit)	3.7
金属紧固件	Metal Fastener	万吨 (10 000 tons)	3.7
弹簧	Spring	万吨 (10 000 tons)	8.3
矿山专用设备	Mining Equipment	万吨 (10 000 tons)	5.7
金属冶炼设备	Metal Smelting Equipment	万吨 (10 000 tons)	1.7
炼油、化工生产专用设备	Special Equipment for Oil Refining and Chemical Protection	吨(ton)	23560

12-14 续表 2 continued 2

主要工业产品名称	Major Industrial Products above Designated Size	单位 Unit	生产量 Production
农产品初加工机械	Agricultural Primary Processing Machinery	万台(10 000 unit)	0.2
电子工业专用设备	Special Equipment for Electronic Industry	万台(10 000 unit)	19.3
棉花加工机械	Cotton Processing Machinery	台(unit)	1489
医疗仪器设备及器械	Medical Instruments	万台(10 000 unit)	35.5
工业机器人	Industrial Robot	套(unit)	3415
汽车	Motor Vehicles	万辆(10 000 unit)	23.9
载货汽车	Trucks	万辆(10 000 unit)	23.9
改装汽车	Modified Cars	万辆(10 000 unit)	2.7
铁路货车	Railway Freight Wagons	辆(unit)	3464
摩托车整车	Motorcycles	万辆(10 000 unit)	46.0
发电机组(发电设备)	Power Generating Equipment	万千瓦(10 000kW)	469.8
电动机	Electromotor	万千瓦(10 000kW)	300.8
变压器	Transformers	万千伏安(10 000 KVA pm)	16509.2
高压开关设备(11万伏以上)	High Voltage Switchgear (over 110,000 volts)	万台(10 000 unit)	0.3
安全、自动化监控设备	Safety and Automatic Monitoring Equipment	台(套、面)(unit)	58885
通信及电子网络用电缆	Cable for Communications and Electronic Network	万对千米(10 000 couples.km)	1.8
电力电缆	Power Cable	万千米(10 000 km)	9.6
太阳能热水器	Solar Water Heater	万平方米(10 000 sq.m)	137.6
灯具及照明装置	Lamps and Lighting Fixtures	万套(台个)(10 000 unit)	189.5
电子计算机整机	Computers	万台(10 000 unit)	74.7
服务器	Servers	万台(10 000 unit)	67.9
半导体分立器件	Discrete Semiconductor Devices	亿只(100 million unit)	65.2
传感器	Transducer	万只(10 000 unit)	1528.2
集成电路	Integrated Circuit	万块(10 000 unit)	8666.2
电子元件	Eletronic Components	亿只(100 million unit)	67.2
电声器件	Electroacoustic Device	万只(10 000 unit)	583.5
印制电路板	Print-circuit Board	万平方米(10 000 sq.m)	103.2
工业自动调节仪表与控制系统	Industrial Automatic Instrument and Control System	台(套)(unit)	182646
电工仪器仪表	Electrical Instrument	万台(10 000 unit)	1076.4
汽车仪器仪表	Automobile Instrument	万台(10 000 unit)	83.2
钟表与计时仪器	Clock	万只(10 000 unit)	46.7
自来水生产量	Tap Water Production	亿立方米(100 million cu.m)	9.6
发电量	Electricity Generation	亿千瓦时(100 million kWh)	323.0
其中：火力发电量	Thermal Power	亿千瓦时(100 million kWh)	294.4
风力发电量	Wind Power	亿千瓦时(100 million kWh)	25.0
垃圾发电量	Garbage Power	亿千瓦时(100 million kWh)	10.3
煤气生产量	Gas Power Generation	亿立方米(100 million cu.m)	197.0

12-15 工业企业能源购进、消费及库存(2023年)
Purchases, Consumption and Inventory of Main Energy Source in Industrial Enterprises(2023)

能源名称	Type of Energy	计量单位 Unit	年初库存量 Beginning Stock	本年购进量 Purchases This Year	本年工业生产消费 Industrial Consumption of This Year	年末库存量 Year-end Stock
能源合计	Total Energy	吨标准煤 (tons of SCE)			49751716	
原煤	Raw Coal	吨(ton)	844590	18401531	18723525	913162
洗精煤	Cleaned Coal	吨(ton)	197029	6748771	6728606	217195
其他洗煤	Other Cleaned Coal	吨(ton)	114177	2720643	2723514	117168
煤制品	Coal Product	吨(ton)	84981	625219	551869	53753
焦炭	Coke	吨(ton)	156978	6603447	7745404	131256
天然气	Natural Gas	万立方米 (10 000 cu.m)		118557	106338	22
液化天然气	Liquefied Natural Gas	吨(ton)	219	96227	14101	158
氢气	Hydrogen	万立方米 (10 000 cu.m)		6009	9677	
汽油	Gasoline	吨(ton)	13	4256	4329	13
煤油	Kerosene	吨(ton)	1.49	23	42	
柴油	Diesel Oil	吨(ton)	1875	51009	47496	1726
液化石油气	Liquefied Petroleum	吨(ton)		9409	1726	
石油焦	Petroleum coke	吨(ton)	54120	2441287	2255129	48656
热力	Heating	百万千焦(mkj)		11601906	12540395	
电力	Electricity	万千瓦时 (10 000 kWh)		1736430	2427851	
城市生活垃圾(用于燃料)	Municipal household waste (for fuels)	吨(ton)	27543	2676228	2325727	27653
生物燃料	Biofuel	吨标准煤 (tons of SCE)	19552	295521	383606	23419
余热余压	Residual heat and residual pressure	百万千焦(mkj)		138558	19650519	
其他燃料	Other Fuel	吨标准煤 (tons of SCE)		9	9	

注:按照经济普查要求，免填能源合计中，年初库存、购进量、年末库存。

Note: According to requirements of economic census, it's unnecessary to fill in inventory and volume of purchase at the beginning of the year and the inventory at the end of the year in the total energy.

12-16 工业分行业主要能源消费量(2023年)
Consumption of Main Energy Source in Industrial Enterprises by Sector (2023)

指标	Item	原煤(吨) Coal(ton)
总计	**Total**	**18723525**
采矿业	**Mining**	
煤炭开采和洗选业	Mining and Washing of Coal	465726
石油和天然气开采业	Extraction of Petroleum and Natural Gas	
黑色金属矿采选业	Mining and Processing of Ferrous Metal Ores	21054
非金属矿采选业	Mining and Processing of Non-Ferrous Metal Ores	
制造业	**Manufacture**	
农副食品加工业	Processing of Food from Agricultural Products	304
食品制造业	Manufacture of Foods	
酒、饮料和精制茶制造业	Manufacture of Wine, Drinks and Refined Tea	
纺织业	Manufacture of Textile	
纺织服装、服饰业	Manufacture of Textile Wearing Apparel and Finery	
皮革、毛皮、羽毛及其制品和制鞋业	Manufacture of Leather, Fur, Feather and Related Products and Footwear	
木材加工及木、竹、藤、棕、草制品业	Processing of Timbers, Manufacture of Wood, Bamboo, Rattan, Palm, and Straw Products	
家具制造业	Manufacture of Furniture	
造纸及纸制品业	Manufacture of Paper and Paper Products	
印刷和记录媒介复制业	Printing and Reproduction of Recording Media	
文教、工美、体育和娱乐用品制造业	Manufacture of Articles for Culture, Education, Arts and Crafts, Sport and Entertainment Activities	
石油、煤炭及其他燃料加工业	Processing of Petroleum, Coal and Other Fuels	278243
化学原料及化学制品制造业	Manufacture of Chemical Raw Material and Chemical Products	2525467
医药制造业	Manufacture of Medicines	34862
化学纤维制造业	Manufacture of Chemical Fiber	
橡胶和塑料制品业	Manufacture of Rubber and Plastic	
非金属矿物制品业	Manufacture of Non-metallic Mineral Products	819616
黑色金属冶炼及压延加工业	Manufacture and Processing of Ferrous Metals	2431445
有色金属冶炼及压延加工业	Manufacture & Processing of Non-ferrous Metals	
金属制品业	Manufacture of Metal Products	
通用设备制造业	Manufacture of General Purpose Machinery	
专用设备制造业	Manufacture of Special Purpose Machinery	
汽车制造业	Manufacture of Automotive	
铁路、船舶、航空航天和其他运输设备制造业	Manufacture of Railroad,Marine,Aerospace and Other Transportation Equipment	
电气机械及器材制造业	Manufacture of Electrical Machinery & Equipment	
计算机、通信和其他电子设备制造业	Manufacture of Computer, Communications and Other Electronic Equipment	
仪器仪表制造业	Manufacture of Measuring Instrument	
其他制造业	Other Manufacture	
废弃资源综合利用业	Utilization of Waste Resources	
金属制品、机械和设备修理业	Metal Products, Machinery and Equipment Repair Industry	
电力、热力、燃气及水生产和供应业	**Production and Supply of Electric Power and Heat Power**	
电力、热力生产和供应业	Production and Supply of Electric Power and Heat Power	12146808
燃气生产和供应业	Production and Supply of Gas	
水的生产和供应业	Production and Supply of Water	

天然气 (万立方米) Natural Gas (10 000 cu.m)	液化天然气 (吨) Liquefied Natural Gas (ton)	汽油 (吨) Gasoline (ton)	柴油 (吨) Diesel Oil (ton)	热力 (百万千焦) Heating (mkj)	电力 (万千瓦时) Electricity (10 000 kWh)
106338	**14101**	**4329**	**47496**	**12540395**	**2427851**
			209		4946
		1	13		6312
		61	3235	312204	70333
			2724		2434
1398	347	73	83	156398	17822
4249	483	58	381	1434491	42904
2006		43	13	158895	20788
1054		2	41	153568	33392
251		7	5		1483
112			3		318
23			190		5164
34		35	96		2136
646	246	81	140	1019440	16846
212	3	150	107	21587	15660
424		44	1		3848
1379	354	90	154	356414	57227
5627	1043	90	895	3165605	275003
4664	17	120	37	2996145	82759
1908		3	28	192602	8296
278		71	182	152964	17018
18892	5127	363	20174	353202	190945
1700	2295	86	6238	181497	676521
77			50		7501
11134	3430	275	574	172	158572
2189	80	616	2303	4959	49445
493	30	533	309	11614	18955
5565		67	4262	359724	127327
165	30	169	95	35868	10986
5923	4	254	143	614699	72345
401		317	17	5677	34276
4		444	22	1647	2706
		5			1064
		7	1432		9063
			14		923
35527	356	42	3264	851023	297804
5	257	127	18		2092
		95	44		82637

主要统计指标解释

工业　指从事自然资源的开采，对采掘品和农产品进行加工和再加工的物质生产部门。具体包括：(1)对自然资源的开采，如采矿、晒盐等(但不包括禽兽捕猎和水产捕捞)；(2)对农副产品的加工、再加工，如粮油加工、食品加工、缫丝、纺织、制革等；(3)对采掘品的加工、再加工，如炼铁、炼钢、化工生产、石油加工、机器制造、木材加工等，以及电力、燃气及水的生产和供应等；(4)对工业品的修理、翻新，如机器设备的修理等。

工业统计调查单位为工业法人单位。

工业法人单位指从事工业生产经营活动的法人单位。工业法人单位应同时具备以下条件：①依法成立，有自己的名称、组织机构和场所，能够独立承担民事责任；②独立拥有（或授权）使用资产，承担负债，有权与其他单位签订合同；③具有包括资产负债表在内的账户，或者能够根据需要编制账户。

国有控股企业　即原来的国有及国有控股企业，根据企业实收资本中国有经济成分的出资人的实际投资情况，或国有经济成分的出资人对企业资产的实际控制、支配程度进行分类。以下情况为国有控股：（1）在企业的全部实收资本中，国有经济成分的出资人拥有的实收资本（股本）所占企业全部实收资本（股本）的比例大于50%的国有绝对控股。(2) 在企业的全部实收资本中，国有经济成分的出资人拥有的实收资本（股本）所占比例虽未大于50%，但相对大于其他任何一方经济成分的出资人所占比例的国有相对控股；或者虽不大于其他经济成分，但根据协议规定拥有企业实际控制权的国有协议控股。（3）投资双方各占50%，且未明确由谁绝对控股的企业，若其中一方为国有经济成分的，一律按国有控股处理。

本篇涉及的企业登记注册类型的解释详见综合篇。

资产总计　指企业过去的交易或者事项形成的、由企业拥有或者控制的、预期会给企业带来经济利益的资源。包括企业拥有的土地、办公楼、厂房、机器、运输工具、存货等实物资产和现金、存款、应收账款和预付账款等金融资产。资产一般按流动性分为流动资产和非流动资产。其中流动资产可分为货币资金、交易性金融资产、应收票据、应收账款、预付款项、其他应收款、存货等；非流动资产可分为长期股权投资、固定资产、无形资产及其他非流动资产等。来源于会计“资产负债表”中“资产总计”项目的期末余额数。

流动资产合计　资产满足以下条件之一应归为流动资产：(1) 预计在一个正常营业周期中变现、出售或耗用，主要包括存货、应收账款等；（2）主要为交易目的而持有；（3）预计在资产负债表日起一年内（含一年）变现；（4）自资产负债日起一年内，交换其他资产或清偿负债的能力不受限制的现金或现金等价物。包括货币资金、应收票据、应收账款、存货等项目。来源于会计“资产负债表”中“流动资产合计”项目的期末余额数。

负债合计　指企业过去的交易或者事项形成的，预期会导致经济利益流出企业的现时义务。包括银行贷款、借款、应付账款、应付职工工资、应付职工福利费、应交税金等企业负有偿还责任的债务。负债一般按偿还期长短分为流动负债和非流动负债。来源于会计“资产负债表”中“负债合计”项目的期末余额数。

应收账款　指资产负债表日以摊余成本计量的、企业因销售商品、提供服务等经营活动应收取的款项。来源于会计“资产负债表”中“应收账款”项目的期末余额数。

存货　指企业在日常活动中持有以备出售的产成品或商品、处在生产过程中的在产品、在生产过程或提供劳务过程中耗用的材料或物料等，通常包括原材料、在产品、半成品、产成品、商品以及周转材料等。来源于会计“资产负债表”中“存货”项目的期末余额数。

营业收入　指企业从事销售商品、提供劳务和让渡资产使用权等生产经营活动形成的经济利益流入。营业收入包括“主营业务收入”和“其他业务收入”。来源于会计“利润表”中“营业收入”项目的本年累计数。

营业成本　指企业从事销售商品、提供劳务和让渡资产使用权等生产经营活动发生的实际成本。包括企业（单位）在报告期内从事销售商品、提供劳务等日常活动发生的各种耗费。包括“主营业务成本”和“其他业务成本”。来源于会计“利润表”中“营业成本”项目的本年累计数。

销售费用　指企业在销售商品和材料、提供劳务的过程中发生的各种费用，包括保险费、包装费、展览费和广告费、商品维修费、预计产品质量保证损失、运输费、装卸费等以及为销售本企业商品而专设的销售机构（含销售网点、售后服务网点等）的职工薪酬、业务费、折旧费等经营费用。

管理费用　指企业为组织和管理企业生产经营所发生的费用，包括企业在筹建期间内发生的开办费、董事会和行政管理部门在企业经营管理中发生的，或者应当由企业统一负担的公司经费等。来源于会计“利润表”中“管理费用”项目的本年累计数。

利润总额　指企业在一定会计期间的经营成果，是生产经营过程中各种收入扣除各种耗费后的盈余，反映企业在报告期内实现的盈亏总额。来源于会计“利润表”中“利润总额”项目的本年累计数。

平均用工人数　指报告期企业平均实际拥有的、参与本企业生产经营活动的人员数。

Explanatory Notes on Main Statistical Indicators

Industry refers to the material production sector which is engaged in the extraction of natural resources and processing and reprocessing of minerals and agricultural products, including (1) extraction of natural resources, such as mining, salt production (but not including hunting and fishing); (2) processing and reprocessing of farm and sideline produces, such as grain and oil processing, food processing, silk reeling, spinning and weaving and leather making; (3) processing and reprocessing of mineral products, such as steel making, iron smelting, chemicals manufacturing, petroleum processing, machine building, timber processing, and production and supply of electricity, gas and water; (4) repairing and renovating of industrial products such as the machinery.

In industrial surveys, the units of enquiry are industrial corporate units.

Industrial corporate units refer to corporate units engaging in industrial production and operation activities, which meet the following requirements: (1) They are established legally, having their own names, organizations, location, and are able to take civil liability independently; (2) They possess (or are authorized to use) assets independently, assume liabilities and are entitled to sign contracts with other units; (3) They have accounts including the balance sheets or can compile the accounts according to the need.

State-holding Enterprises cover the original state-owned enterprises and state-holding enterprises. They are classified according to the actual investment made by the contributors of state-owned part in the paid-in capital of the enterprises, or the degree of control or dominance of the contributor on the assets of the enterprises. The following cases are regarded as state-holding: (1) Absolute state-holding in which the contributors of state-owned parts possess more than 50% of all the paid-in capital (stocks) of the enterprises; (2) Relative state-holding in which the contributors of state-owned parts possess no more than 50% of the paid-in capital (stocks) of the enterprises, but more than that of any other contributors; or agreed state-holding in which the contributors of state-owned parts possess no more than other contributors but have actual control over the enterprises according to agreements; (3) In case both contributors possess 50% and it is not clear which one is in absolute holding position, the enterprise is regarded as state-holding enterprise if one of the contributor has state-owned elements.

For explanation of types of registration covered in this chapter, please refer to Chapter 1 on General Survey.

Total Assets refer to all resources that are owned or controlled by enterprises through previous trades or transactions, with expectation of making economic profits to enterprises. Included are all assets owned by enterprises such as land, office buildings, factories, machines, vehicles, inventories and other physical assets as well as cash, deposits, accounts receivable, prepayments and other financial assets. Classified by the degree of liquidity, total assets include current assets and non-current assets. Current assets can be classified into monetary capital, trading financial assets, notes receivable, accounts receivable, advanced payments, other receivables and inventories. Non-current assets can be divided into long-term equity investment, fixed assets, intangible assets and other non-current assets. Data on this indicator can be obtained from the year-end figures of total assets in the Balance Sheet of accounting records.

Current Assets refer to the assets that meet one of the following requirements: (1) expected to be cashed, sold or used in a normal operation cycle, mainly including inventory and accounts receivable; (2) owned for transaction purpose mainly; (3) expected to be cashed within one year (including one year) from the day of the Balance Sheet; (4) unlimited cash or cash equivalents that can be exchanged with other assets or capable of settling debts during one year since the day of the Balance Sheet. Included are monetary capital, notes receivable, accounts receivable and inventories. Data on this indicator can be obtained from the year-end figures of total current assets in the Balance Sheet of accounting records.

Total Liabilities refer to payable liabilities of enterprises that are accumulated from earlier transactions with expectation of leaking out of economic profits. Included are debts that enterprises are responsible for repaying such as bank loans, borrowings, accounts payable, wages payable, employee benefits payable, taxes payable, etc. In terms of payment, it can be divided into liquid liabilities and long-term liabilities. Data on this indicator can be obtained from the year-end figures of total liabilities in the Balance Sheet of accounting records.

Accounts Receivable refers to creditor's rights through business activities such as selling goods and providing labor. It comes from the ending balance of accounts receivable in balance sheet.

Inventories refers to finished goods or commodities held in preparation for sale in enterprises' daily activities, goods in the production process, material or the physical materials consumed in the production process or in the process of providing labor, usually include raw materials, goods in the production process, semi-finished products, finished products, goods and materials in flow. It comes from the ending balance of inventory in balance sheet.

Business Revenue refers to the inflow of economic benefits

through production and operation activities of enterprises, such as selling commodities, providing labor services and transferring the right to use of assets. Business revenue includes "revenue from principal business" and " revenue from other business". It comes from current year's cumulative report of "business revenue" items from the "income statement".

Business Cost refers to the actual costs incurred by the enterprises in such production and operation activities as selling commodities, providing labor services and transferring the right to use of assets. It includes various expenditures incurred by enterprises (units) in their daily activities of selling goods and providing labour services during the reporting period. It includes "cost of principal business" and "cost of other business". It comes from current year's cumulative report of "operating cost" items from the "income statement".

Selling Expenses refer to the cost during the sale of goods and materials, providing labour services, including insurance, packing, exhibition fees and advertising fees, merchandise maintenance costs, expected product quality guarantee loss, transportation fees, handling fees, and operating expenses for the sales of the company's products, such as employee compensation, business expenses, depreciation costs for dedicated sales offices (including sales outlets, after-sales service outlets, etc.).

Management Expenses refer to the expenses for the organization and management of enterprise operation, including the start-up costs during the construction of enterprises, funds occurred during enterprises operation by board of directors and executive management in the enterprise management, and other costs to be paid by enterprises. It comes from current year's cumulative amount of management cost in income statement.

Total Profits refer to the operational results in a certain accounting period, and it is the balance of various incomes minus various spendings in the course of operation, reflecting the total profits and losses of enterprises in reference period. Data are obtained from current year's cumulative amount of total profits in the profit statement of the accounting record of enterprise.

Annual Average Employees refer to the number of persons engaged in the production and operation activities of enterprises in the reporting period, which are actually employed by the enterprises.

13

建 筑 业

CONSTRUCTION

13-1 建筑业主要指标
Main Indicators of Construction Enterprises

指标	Item	单位 Unit	2019年	2020年	2021年	2022年	2023年
企业单位数	Number of Enterprises	个(unit)	895	1033	1182	1371	1519
建筑业总产值	Gross Output Value	万元(10 000 yuan)	35139777	37481222	41260343	44607549	47770851
按隶属关系分	by Ownership						
中央属	Central	万元(10 000 yuan)	17350365	20148118	21677643	24519759	26861268
地方属	Local	万元(10 000 yuan)	11793174	10596000	10417195	10155041	10385173
其他	Others	万元(10 000 yuan)	5996238	6737105	9165505	9932748	2073363
按工程性质分	by Sector						
建筑工程	Building and Civil Engineering Construction	万元(10 000 yuan)	31199367	33447869	35981015	38174842	42151761
安装工程	Construction Installation	万元(10 000 yuan)	3015885	3288008	3749267	4594480	4913836
其他产值	Others	万元(10 000 yuan)	924525	745346	1530061	1838227	705254
竣工产值	Value of Construction Completed	万元(10 000 yuan)	12943615	12789160	13373476	12501477	12674904
房屋施工面积	Floor Space of Buildings under Construction	万平方米(10 000 sq.cm)	14955	17090	19410	19971	20690
#本年新开工	Started This year	万平方米(10 000 sq.cm)	4705	5349	5621	5223	5610
房屋竣工面积	Floor Space of Buildings Completed	万平方米(10 000 sq.cm)	3418	3323	3730	3128	3735
#住宅	Residential	万平方米(10 000 sq.cm)	2170	1916	2247	1808	1921
所有者权益	Owners' Equity	万元(10 000 yuan)	8130630	7894051	9363017	12683470	15125647
利润总额	Total Profits	万元(10 000 yuan)	1051261	1087848	1360873	1747800	1998849
工资总额	Total wages	万元(10 000 yuan)	3793574	3295738	3454592	4500399	7700968

13-2 建筑企业资产实力(2023年)
Assets of Construction Enterprises (2023)

单位：万元

指标 (总承包与专业承包)	Item	流动资产合计 Total Current Assets	#存货 Inventory
总计	**Total**	**59146032**	**4926329**
其中：国有及国有控股企业	State-owned and State-controlled Enterprises	46470065	2842257
一、按登记注册类型分组	**By Status of Registration**		
内资企业	Domestic Invested Enterprises	59142278	4924944
港澳台投资企业	Enterprises with Investment from Hong Kong,Macao and Taiwan		
外商投资企业	Foreign Invested Enterprises	3755	1385
二、按国民经济行业分组	**By Sector**		
房屋建筑业	Construction of Buildings	16213164	1815960
土木工程建筑业	Civil Engineering	37056680	2418457
建筑安装业	Construction Installation	2614077	271976
建筑装饰装修和其他建筑业	Building Decoration and Other Construction	3262111	419936
三、按隶属关系分组	**By Ownership**		
中央	Central	22933315	1255654
地方	Local	19358157	1354948
其他	Others	4178593	231655
四、按企业资质等级分组	**By Qualification Criteria**		
施工总承包	Construction Contract	53503216	4254858
特级	Special Grade	30371474	1595853
一级	First Grade	15445361	1314408
二级	Second Grade	4558996	932612
三级及以下	Third Grade and below	3127384	411986
专业承包	Professional Contract	5642816	671471
一级	First Grade	3553253	346941
二级	Second Grade	1462451	266589
三级及以下	Third Grade and below	627113	57942

(10 000 yuan)

固定资产原价 Original Value of Fixed Assets	资产合计 Total Assets	流动负债合计 Current Liabilities	非流动负债合计 Non-Current Liabilities	负债合计 Total Liabilities	所有者权益合计 Owners' Equity
3428495	**72668724**	**54051617**	**2972574**	**57543077**	**15125647**
2260842	58501553	44126670	2682085	46926621	11574932
3428354	72664965	54049789	2972574	57541249	15123716
142	3759	1828		1828	1931
780354	18436267	13003774	449989	13744813	4691454
2146234	47313651	36231433	2234730	38613991	8699660
294310	3108845	2185428	144763	2399195	709650
207598	3809961	2630983	143092	2785078	1024883
1420831	30435047	23043598	1465367	24508965	5926082
705211	23551152	17771629	1032119	18904764	4646388
134800	4515354	3311444	184599	3512892	1002461
2909229	66137079	49604896	2807559	52835440	13301639
1425980	39658008	30401831	1444887	31846718	7811291
750732	17641561	13217718	961262	14254706	3386855
425709	5218504	3705914	98341	3976068	1242436
306808	3619006	2279434	303069	2757949	861057
519266	6531645	4446721	165015	4707637	1824008
237524	3932429	2862232	101277	2969411	963019
131544	1867249	1105695	39107	1198427	668822
150198	731967	478794	24631	539800	192167

13-3 建筑业施工产值构成(2023年)
Output Value of Construction Structure(2023)

单位：万元 (10 000 yuan)

指标 (总承包与专业承包)	Item	合计 Total	建筑工程 Construction	安装工程 Installation	其他产值 Other Value	竣工产值 Output Value of Completed
总计	**Total**	**47770851**	**42151761**	**4913836**	**705254**	**12674904**
其中：国有及国有控股企业	State-owned and State-controlled Enterprises	39319804	35568489	3461141	290174	8054782
一、按登记注册类型分组	**By Status of Registration**					
内资企业	Domestic Invested Enterprises	47770362	42151761	4913347	705254	12674904
港澳台投资企业	Enterprises with Investment from Hong Kong,Macao and Taiwan					
外商投资企业	Foreign Invested Enterprises	489		489		
二、按国民经济行业分组	**By Sector**					
房屋建筑业	Construction of Buildings	19962534	18844529	1057064	60942	8645422
土木工程建筑业	Civil Engineering	23498019	21214185	1985317	298517	2719617
建筑安装业	Construction Installation	2304491	420293	1714713	169484	569773
建筑装饰装修和其他建筑业	Building Decoration and Other Construction	2005806	1672754	156743	176310	740093
三、按隶属关系分组	**By Ownership**					
中央	Central	26861268	24728660	2056621	75988	5585984
地方	Local	10385173	9313657	919992	151525	2160523
其他	Others	2073363	1526173	484529	62662	308276
四、按企业资质等级分组	**By Qualification Criteria**					
施工总承包	Construction Contract	44203362	39773002	4032862	397498	11378561
特级	Special Grade	30749638	29151947	1584718	12973	8097440
一级	First Grade	9534469	7439458	1994159	100851	2100702
二级	Second Grade	2099729	1693315	246180	160234	657532
三级及以下	Third Grade and below	1819527	1488282	207805	123440	522887
专业承包	Professional Contract	3567488	2378759	880974	307756	1296344
一级	First Grade	2292872	1567825	527452	197595	828116
二级	Second Grade	942688	551021	288967	102701	372558
三级及以下	Third Grade and below	331928	259913	64555	7461	95669

13-4 建筑企业主要经济指标(2023年)
Main Economic Indicators of Construction Enterprises(2023)

单位：万元 (10 000 yuan)

指标 (总承包与专业承包)	Item	营业收入 Business Revenue	利税总额 Total Pre-tax Profits	营业利润 Profits from Business	利润总额 Total Profits	应付职工薪酬 (本年贷方累计发生额) Total Wages Payable
总计	**Total**	**56960696**	**2827501**	**1978398**	**1998849**	**7700968**
其中：国有及国有控股企业	State-owned and State-controlled Enterprises	46028891	2176343	1664832	1662559	6214012
一、按登记注册类型分组	**By Status of Registration**					
内资企业	Domestic Invested Enterprises	56947134	2827132	1978229	1998680	7700110
港澳台投资企业	Enterprises with Investment from Hong Kong,Macao and Taiwan					
外商投资企业	Foreign Invested Enterprises	13562	369	168	168	858
二、按国民经济行业分组	**By Sector**					
房屋建筑业	Construction of Buildings	21320506	1092038	781401	774868	3462208
土木工程建筑业	Civil Engineering	29950718	1434516	1020576	1046956	3669005
建筑安装业	Construction Installation	3142593	126070	65791	66893	280754
建筑装饰装修和其他建筑业	Building Decoration and Other Construction	2546879	174877	110630	110131	289002
三、按隶属关系分组	**By Ownership**					
中央	Central	31985989	1296880	959254	956524	4138538
地方	Local	11474444	705855	578749	580063	1826267
其他	Others	2568458	173609	126829	125972	249207
四、按企业资质等级分组	**By Qualification Criteria**					
施工总承包	Construction Contract	52063784	2504003	1817753	1801232	7165642
特级	Special Grade	36446753	1573274	1206228	1198852	5385458
一级	First Grade	10324380	562285	396287	389747	1180806
二级	Second Grade	2714171	174144	99250	99481	324020
三级以下	Third Grade and below	2578481	194300	115989	113152	275358
专业承包	Professional Contract	4896912	323499	160645	197617	535326
一级	First Grade	3052378	180746	69525	106441	322879
二级	Second Grade	1385217	114521	81706	81594	134261
三级以下	Third Grade and below	459317	28231	9414	9581	78186

13–5 施工工程施工面积(2023年)
Number of Floor Space Under Construction(2023)

单位：万平方米 (10 000 sq.m)

指标（总承包与专业承包）	Item	房屋建筑施工面积 Floor Space under Construction	# 本年新开工面积 Started This Year	房屋建筑竣工面积 Floor Space Completed	# 住宅房屋 Residential	竣工房屋价值(万元) Output Value of Completed (10 000 yuan)
总计	**Total**	**20690**	**5610**	**3735**	**1921**	**8929075**
其中：国有及国有控股企业	State-owned and State-controlled Enterprises	15685	4600	2295	1153	6053087
一、按登记注册类型分组	**By Status of Registration**					
内资企业	Domestic Invested Enterprises	20690	5610	3735	1921	8929075
港澳台投资企业	Enterprises with Investment from Hong Kong,Macao and Taiwan					
外商投资企业	Foreign Invested Enterprises					
二、按国民经济行业分组	**By Sector**					
房屋建筑业	Construction of Buildings	19137	5149	3397	1757	8166516
土木工程建筑业	Civil Engineering	1462	402	297	147	714341
建筑安装业	Construction Installation	14	7	10	0	22886
建筑装饰装修和其他建筑业	Building Decoration and Other Construction	77	53	31	17	25332
三、按隶属关系分组	**By Ownership**					
中央	Central	12712	3765	1663	812	4684775
地方	Local	2494	722	575	320	1278764
其他	Others	478	114	57	21	89549
四、按企业资质等级分组	**By Qualification Criteria**					
施工总承包	Construction Contract	20151	5476	3447	1780	8837655
特级	Special Grade	16044	4175	2621	1351	7160497
一级	First Grade	2985	793	584	338	1256237
二级	Second Grade	736	356	152	76	287928
三级及以下	Third Grade and below	386	152	89	17	132993
专业承包	Professional Contract	539	134	288	140	91420
一级	First Grade	375	54	218	84	36006
二级	Second Grade	135	64	66	55	36093
三级及以下	Third Grade and below	30	16	4	2	19322

13-6 济南市建筑业特级、一级资质企业一览表(2023年)
List of Special and First Class Qualification in the Construction Enterprises of Jinan City(2023)

企业名称 Name	资质等级 Ownership	经济类型 Economic Type	所属行业 Industry
中建八局第一建设有限公司	特级	其他有限责任公司	住宅房屋建筑
中建八局第二建设有限公司	特级	其他有限责任公司	住宅房屋建筑
中铁十四局集团有限公司	特级	其他有限责任公司	铁路工程建筑
中铁十局集团有限公司	特级	其他有限责任公司	铁路工程建筑
山东省路桥集团有限公司	特级	其他有限责任公司	公路工程建筑
济南城建集团有限公司	特级	其他有限责任公司	市政道路工程建筑
中铁十四局集团第四工程有限公司	特级	其他有限责任公司	铁路工程建筑
中国电建集团山东电力建设第一工程有限公司	特级	其他有限责任公司	火力发电工程施工
中国电建集团核电工程有限公司	特级	其他有限责任公司	火力发电工程施工
济南四建(集团)有限责任公司	特级	其他有限责任公司	其他房屋建筑业
山东高速工程建设集团有限公司	特级	其他有限责任公司	公路工程建筑
中铁十四局集团第三工程有限公司	特级	其他有限责任公司	铁路工程建筑
济南黄河路桥建设集团有限公司	特级	其他有限责任公司	市政道路工程建筑
山东省建设建工(集团)有限责任公司	特级	其他有限责任公司	住宅房屋建筑
中儒科信达建设集团有限公司	特级	其他有限责任公司	住宅房屋建筑
山东三箭建设工程股份有限公司	特级	其他股份有限公司	住宅房屋建筑
中铁铁工城市建设有限公司	特级	其他有限责任公司	住宅房屋建筑
山东平安建设集团有限公司	特级	私营有限责任公司	住宅房屋建筑
中化学交通建设集团有限公司	特级	其他有限责任公司	公路工程建筑
山东长兴建设集团有限公司	特级	私营有限责任公司	住宅房屋建筑
山东港基建设集团有限公司	特级	其他有限责任公司	住宅房屋建筑
中铁十四局集团建筑工程有限公司	特级	其他有限责任公司	住宅房屋建筑
山东铁信建设集团有限公司	特级	其他有限责任公司	住宅房屋建筑
济南二建集团工程有限公司	特级	其他有限责任公司	住宅房屋建筑
中铁十局集团第一工程有限公司	一级	其他有限责任公司	铁路工程建筑
山东省公路桥梁建设集团有限公司	一级	其他有限责任公司	公路工程建筑
济南能源工程集团有限公司	一级	其他有限责任公司	管道和设备安装
中铁十四局集团隧道工程有限公司	一级	其他有限责任公司	铁路工程建筑
济南一建集团有限公司	一级	其他有限责任公司	住宅房屋建筑
山东省高速养护集团有限公司	一级	其他有限责任公司	其他道路、隧道和桥梁工程建筑
山东省邮电工程有限公司	一级	其他有限责任公司	架线及设备工程建筑
嘉林建设集团有限公司	一级	私营有限责任公司	建筑幕墙装饰和装修
中铁十四局集团电气化工程有限公司	一级	其他有限责任公司	架线及设备工程建筑
中铁十局集团电务工程有限公司	一级	其他有限责任公司	铁路工程建筑
山东三箭建设工程管理有限公司	一级	私营有限责任公司	住宅房屋建筑
山东送变电工程有限公司	一级	其他有限责任公司	架线及设备工程建筑
山东汇通建设集团有限公司	一级	其他有限责任公司	市政道路工程建筑
山东黄河工程集团有限公司	一级	其他有限责任公司	港口及航运设施工程建筑
山东济铁工程建设集团有限公司	一级	其他有限责任公司	铁路工程建筑
济南市市政工程建设集团有限公司	一级	国有独资公司	市政道路工程建筑
山东省水利工程局有限公司	一级	其他有限责任公司	河湖治理及防洪设施工程建筑

13-6 续表 1 continued 1

企业名称 Name	资质等级 Ownership	经济类型 Economic Type	所属行业 Industry
山东中恒建设集团有限公司	一级	私营有限责任公司	住宅房屋建筑
山东福源建设集团有限公司	一级	私营有限责任公司	管道和设备安装
山东省工业设备安装集团有限公司	一级	其他有限责任公司	其他建筑安装
济南金曰公路工程有限公司	一级	其他有限责任公司	公路工程建筑
山东正元建设工程有限责任公司	一级	其他有限责任公司	其他房屋建筑业
山东水利建设集团有限公司	一级	其他有限责任公司	河湖治理及防洪设施工程建筑
中国电建集团山东电力建设有限公司	一级	其他有限责任公司	火力发电工程施工
山东长箭建设集团有限公司	一级	私营有限责任公司	住宅房屋建筑
中化学交通建设集团第三工程有限公司	一级	其他有限责任公司	公路工程建筑
山东莱芜建设集团有限公司	一级	其他有限责任公司	住宅房屋建筑
山东正顺建设集团有限公司	一级	私营有限责任公司	住宅房屋建筑
山东建勘集团有限公司	一级	其他有限责任公司	场地准备活动
中建三局集团山东投资建设有限公司	一级	其他有限责任公司	住宅房屋建筑
济南铸诚建筑工程集团有限公司	一级	私营有限责任公司	住宅房屋建筑
济南通达公路工程有限公司	一级	其他有限责任公司	公路工程建筑
莱芜钢铁集团建筑安装工程有限公司	一级	其他有限责任公司	其他建筑安装
山东大禹水务建设集团有限公司	一级	其他有限责任公司	管道工程建筑
普利置业集团股份有限公司	一级	其他股份有限公司	住宅房屋建筑
山东泰山建工发展集团有限公司	一级	其他有限责任公司	住宅房屋建筑
山东奥邦交通设施工程有限公司	一级	其他有限责任公司	其他建筑安装
山东汇友市政园林集团有限公司	一级	其他有限责任公司	其他未列明建筑业
山东福缘来装饰有限公司	一级	私营有限责任公司	住宅装饰和装修
山东高速齐鲁建设集团有限公司	一级	其他有限责任公司	其他房屋建筑业
山东省机械施工有限公司	一级	私营有限责任公司	其他土木工程建筑施工
中建五局(山东)投资建设有限公司	一级	其他有限责任公司	住宅房屋建筑
济南普利供水工程有限公司	一级	其他有限责任公司	管道工程建筑
山东科发建设工程有限公司	一级	其他有限责任公司	建筑幕墙装饰和装修
七彩建设发展有限公司	一级	其他有限责任公司	公共建筑装饰和装修
山东省装饰集团有限公司	一级	其他有限责任公司	公共建筑装饰和装修
济南川丽德市政建设工程有限公司	一级	私营有限责任公司	住宅房屋建筑
山东网源电力工程有限公司	一级	其他有限责任公司	电气安装
山东水总有限公司	一级	其他有限责任公司	河湖治理及防洪设施工程建筑
济南建设设备安装有限责任公司	一级	其他有限责任公司	管道和设备安装
金智成建设集团股份有限公司	一级	私营股份有限公司	电气安装
济南四建集团智能消防工程有限责任公司	一级	其他有限责任公司	住宅房屋建筑
山东历控建设发展有限公司	一级	其他有限责任公司	住宅房屋建筑
瑞森新建筑有限公司	一级	其他有限责任公司	其他房屋建筑业
中铁建黄河投资建设有限公司	一级	其他有限责任公司	城市轨道交通工程建筑
山东金宇信息科技集团有限公司	一级	其他有限责任公司	公路工程建筑
山东顺河路桥工程有限公司	一级	其他有限责任公司	市政道路工程建筑
国舜绿建科技有限公司	一级	其他有限责任公司	其他房屋建筑业
齐鲁建工建设发展集团有限公司	一级	其他有限责任公司	公路工程建筑

13-6 续表 2 continued 2

企业名称 Name	资质等级 Ownership	经济类型 Economic Type	所属行业 Industry
海瑞林建设有限公司	一级	私营有限责任公司	公共建筑装饰和装修
山东长泰建设集团工程有限公司	一级	私营有限责任公司	住宅房屋建筑
山东汇富建设集团有限公司	一级	私营有限责任公司	住宅房屋建筑
章丘市第二建筑安装(集团)有限责任公司	一级	私营有限责任公司	住宅房屋建筑
山东联诚电力工程有限公司	一级	私营有限责任公司	电气安装
山东省建设高压容器有限公司	一级	其他有限责任公司	管道和设备安装
山东泉景建设有限公司	一级	其他有限责任公司	住宅房屋建筑
山东环城城建工程有限公司	一级	其他有限责任公司	其他未列明建筑业
中铁建工集团山东投资建设有限公司	一级	其他有限责任公司	其他房屋建筑业
山东鲁建工程集团有限公司	一级	私营有限责任公司	住宅房屋建筑
山东省大通建设集团有限公司	一级	其他有限责任公司	公路工程建筑
永隆装饰工程有限公司	一级	私营有限责任公司	公共建筑装饰和装修
济南华海建设集团有限公司	一级	私营有限责任公司	住宅房屋建筑
奥斯福集团有限公司	一级	私营有限责任公司	电气安装
山东省建设建工集团第二有限公司	一级	其他有限责任公司	其他房屋建筑业
承峻建设集团有限公司	一级	私营有限责任公司	住宅房屋建筑
山东电建建设集团有限公司	一级	其他有限责任公司	架线及设备工程建筑
起航(山东)投资建设集团有限公司	一级	其他有限责任公司	市政道路工程建筑
山东福思特建筑装饰有限公司	一级	私营有限责任公司	建筑幕墙装饰和装修
山东津单幕墙有限公司	一级	私营有限责任公司	建筑幕墙装饰和装修
山东黄河顺成水利水电工程有限公司	一级	其他有限责任公司	管道工程建筑
山东省建设建工集团消防工程有限公司	一级	私营有限责任公司	其他建筑安装
山东德才建设有限公司	一级	其他有限责任公司	公共建筑装饰和装修
山东博科建筑工程有限公司	一级	其他有限责任公司	住宅房屋建筑
山东高速路桥装备工程有限公司	一级	其他有限责任公司	市政道路工程建筑
济南英雄山建筑安装工程有限公司	一级	私营有限责任公司	住宅房屋建筑
山东黄金集团建设工程有限公司	一级	其他有限责任公司	住宅房屋建筑
山东华尔泰建筑工程有限公司	一级	私营有限责任公司	其他建筑安装
万得福实业集团有限公司	一级	其他有限责任公司	公共建筑装饰和装修
山东清华康利城市照明研究设计院有限公司	一级	其他有限责任公司	电气安装
山东宏雁电子系统工程有限公司	一级	私营有限责任公司	其他建筑安装
山东国宸装饰工程有限公司	一级	私营有限责任公司	公共建筑装饰和装修
水电六局华东建设有限公司	一级	其他有限责任公司	住宅房屋建筑
山东彩旺建设有限公司	一级	私营有限责任公司	电气安装
山东坚瑞建设股份有限公司	一级	私营股份有限公司	其他建筑安装
山东建科特种建筑工程技术中心有限公司	一级	私营有限责任公司	其他房屋建筑业
山东省城建工程集团公司	一级	股份合作企业	住宅房屋建筑
中宝鼎盛建设集团有限公司	一级	私营有限责任公司	住宅房屋建筑
中海(山东)科技股份有限公司	一级	私营股份有限公司	公共建筑装饰和装修
济南万泰建筑装饰工程有限公司	一级	其他有限责任公司	住宅装饰和装修
雪山集团有限公司	一级	私营有限责任公司	管道和设备安装
山东振盛建设工程有限公司	一级	私营有限责任公司	住宅房屋建筑

13-6 续表 3 continued 3

企业名称 Name	资质等级 Ownership	经济类型 Economic Type	所属行业 Industry
山东方原建设集团有限公司	一级	私营有限责任公司	其他房屋建筑业
济南振华岩土工程有限责任公司	一级	私营有限责任公司	提供施工设备服务
山东中大净化工程有限公司	一级	私营有限责任公司	公共建筑装饰和装修
辉瑞(山东)环境科技有限公司	一级	私营有限责任公司	公共建筑装饰和装修
山东众联恒信工程集团有限公司	一级	其他有限责任公司	场地准备活动
济南章丘三建弘信建筑有限公司	一级	私营有限责任公司	住宅房屋建筑
山东省建设建工集团装饰装璜有限公司	一级	私营有限责任公司	公共建筑装饰和装修
山东林垄幕墙装饰有限公司	一级	其他有限责任公司	其他房屋建筑业
山东盛桥实业集团有限公司	一级	其他有限责任公司	其他房屋建筑业
圣雅建设集团股份有限公司	一级	私营股份有限公司	住宅装饰和装修
优士科技发展有限公司	一级	私营有限责任公司	电气安装
山东省建设集团有限公司	一级	其他有限责任公司	其他房屋建筑业
山东宏业发展集团有限公司	一级	私营有限责任公司	架线及设备工程建筑
山东双利电子工程有限公司	一级	其他有限责任公司	电气安装
沃尔德建筑装饰集团股份有限公司	一级	其他股份有限公司	住宅装饰和装修
山东兴发建筑工程有限公司	一级	私营有限责任公司	住宅房屋建筑
山东博安智能科技股份有限公司	一级	其他股份有限公司	电气安装
山东土地集团建设投资有限公司	一级	其他有限责任公司	公共建筑装饰和装修
济南消防工程有限公司	一级	私营有限责任公司	电气安装
山东江森机电工程有限公司	一级	私营有限责任公司	管道和设备安装
山东同信智能科技有限公司	一级	其他有限责任公司	其他土木工程建筑施工
济南佳宸装饰安装有限公司	一级	私营有限责任公司	公共建筑装饰和装修
山东深博建筑工程有限公司	一级	私营有限责任公司	管道和设备安装
山东高速交通建设集团有限公司	一级	其他有限责任公司	公路工程建筑
山东启方科技有限公司	一级	私营有限责任公司	其他建筑安装
山东昌舜岩土工程有限公司	一级	私营有限责任公司	住宅房屋建筑
山东聚福来装饰有限公司	一级	私营有限责任公司	住宅装饰和装修
山东舜联城市建设发展有限公司	一级	其他有限责任公司	园林绿化工程施工
山东亚安建筑工程有限公司	一级	其他有限责任公司	其他房屋建筑业
山东创达建设工程有限公司	一级	私营有限责任公司	住宅装饰和装修
山东志坚建筑工程有限公司	一级	私营有限责任公司	其他房屋建筑业
山东通海建设集团有限公司	一级	私营有限责任公司	公共建筑装饰和装修
山东润豪建设工程有限公司	一级	私营有限责任公司	住宅房屋建筑
豪鑫建设集团有限公司	一级	私营有限责任公司	其他未列明建筑业
济南瑞源智能城市开发有限公司	一级	其他有限责任公司	电气安装
中道华泰建设集团有限公司	一级	私营有限责任公司	其他房屋建筑业
山东润诚机电工程有限公司	一级	私营有限责任公司	电气安装
山东昌利建设集团有限公司	一级	私营有限责任公司	水源及供水设施工程建筑
山东泰东公路工程有限公司	一级	其他有限责任公司	公路工程建筑
山东省亘基工程有限公司	一级	私营有限责任公司	其他房屋建筑业
中炬装饰工程集团有限公司	一级	私营有限责任公司	公共建筑装饰和装修

13-6 续表 continued 4

企业名称 Name	资质等级 Ownership	经济类型 Economic Type	所属行业 Industry
山东金勘岩土工程有限公司	一级	其他有限责任公司	城市轨道交通工程建筑
中国铁路通信信号集团济南工程有限公司	一级	其他有限责任公司	架线及设备工程建筑
山东航空港建设工程集团有限公司	一级	其他有限责任公司	其他土木工程建筑施工
山东力盟电力电子有限公司	一级	私营有限责任公司	其他建筑安装
山东德铭工程建设有限公司	一级	私营有限责任公司	住宅装饰和装修
济南舜联建设集团有限公司	一级	私营有限责任公司	住宅房屋建筑
山东圣恩城市建设工程有限公司	一级	私营有限责任公司	工矿工程建筑
山东剑锋消防工程有限公司	一级	私营有限责任公司	其他建筑安装
山东太平洋环保股份有限公司	一级	私营股份有限公司	其他建筑安装
中交未名环保有限公司	一级	其他有限责任公司	市政道路工程建筑
山东环投环境工程有限公司	一级	私营有限责任公司	其他未列明建筑业
山东信达建设工程有限公司	一级	私营有限责任公司	其他房屋建筑业
山东惠诚建筑有限公司	一级	私营有限责任公司	其他房屋建筑业
山东尚邦建设集团有限公司	一级	其他有限责任公司	住宅房屋建筑
山东合盛建设工程有限公司	一级	私营有限责任公司	其他建筑安装
山东北成环境工程有限公司	一级	私营有限责任公司	环保工程施工
山东洁昕建筑装饰工程设计有限公司	一级	私营有限责任公司	公共建筑装饰和装修
山东高新岩土科技有限公司	一级	其他有限责任公司	公路工程建筑
山东玮瑞建筑装饰工程有限公司	一级	其他有限责任公司	其他土木工程建筑施工
山东省鲁美建材装饰有限公司	一级	私营有限责任公司	建筑幕墙装饰和装修
山东涌泉安全科技有限公司	一级	私营有限责任公司	其他建筑安装
山东雷奥建筑工程有限公司	一级	其他有限责任公司	住宅房屋建筑
济南易通城市建设集团股份有限公司	一级	其他股份有限公司	市政道路工程建筑
济南新中安消防安全工程有限公司	一级	私营有限责任公司	其他建筑安装
山东宇宸建设工程有限公司	一级	私营有限责任公司	其他建筑安装
山东柯联信息科技有限公司	一级	私营有限责任公司	电气安装
济南罡晟建筑工程有限公司	一级	私营有限责任公司	建筑幕墙装饰和装修
秦恒建设科技有限公司	一级	私营有限责任公司	其他土木工程建筑施工
山东万和中盛幕墙有限公司	一级	其他有限责任公司	建筑幕墙装饰和装修
山东盛邦实业集团有限公司	一级	私营有限责任公司	建筑幕墙装饰和装修
和瑞滢晞智能产业发展集团有限公司	一级	私营有限责任公司	其他建筑安装
济南市宏强建设有限公司	一级	私营有限责任公司	其他房屋建筑业
山东水发鲁润水务科技有限公司	一级	其他有限责任公司	环保工程施工
山东飞马消防工程有限责任公司	一级	私营有限责任公司	其他建筑安装
山东中消集团有限公司	一级	私营有限责任公司	其他建筑安装
铭正建设发展有限公司	一级	私营有限责任公司	公共建筑装饰和装修
山东华森建筑消防项目管理有限公司	一级	私营有限责任公司	其他建筑安装
神州瑞宸建设集团有限公司	一级	私营有限责任公司	公共建筑装饰和装修
济南神齐建筑装饰有限公司	一级	私营有限责任公司	其他房屋建筑业
山东展鸿华商装饰工程有限公司	一级	私营有限责任公司	住宅装饰和装修
山东华迪智能技术有限公司	一级	其他有限责任公司	其他建筑安装

13-6 续表 5 continued 5

企业名称 Name	资质等级 Ownership	经济类型 Economic Type	所属行业 Industry
山东衍鑫建筑工程有限公司	一级	私营有限责任公司	住宅房屋建筑
济南七彩贝壳工贸有限公司	一级	私营有限责任公司	公共建筑装饰和装修
济南四建建设发展有限公司	一级	其他有限责任公司	住宅房屋建筑
山东思达特信息科技有限公司	一级	私营有限责任公司	电气安装
山东汉成建设工程有限公司	一级	私营有限责任公司	其他建筑安装
山东鑫联通信科技有限公司	一级	私营有限责任公司	电气安装
山东海灏装饰设计工程有限公司	一级	私营有限责任公司	住宅装饰和装修
山东鹰格信息工程有限公司	一级	其他有限责任公司	其他建筑安装
山东中安消防设施维修有限公司	一级	私营有限责任公司	其他未列明建筑业
森鹏建设集团有限公司	一级	其他有限责任公司	公共建筑装饰和装修
山东洪雨防水工程有限公司	一级	私营有限责任公司	其他未列明建筑业
山东诚大装饰工程有限公司	一级	私营有限责任公司	公共建筑装饰和装修
中直科创股份有限公司	一级	私营股份有限公司	建筑幕墙装饰和装修
山东港原建筑工程有限公司	一级	私营有限责任公司	其他土木工程建筑施工
山东飞洋环境工程有限公司	一级	私营有限责任公司	环保工程施工
济南超卓建筑工程有限公司	一级	私营有限责任公司	住宅装饰和装修
山东泰景楼宇安全技术有限公司	一级	私营有限责任公司	其他未列明建筑业
山东绿工城市开发建设有限公司	一级	其他有限责任公司	住宅房屋建筑
山东融晟水利建设工程有限公司	一级	私营有限责任公司	其他未列明建筑业
山东高速齐鲁建设集团装饰工程有限公司	一级	其他有限责任公司	公共建筑装饰和装修
山东普成建设工程集团有限公司	一级	私营有限责任公司	公共建筑装饰和装修
山东亿威市政工程有限公司	一级	私营有限责任公司	市政道路工程建筑
山东鲁控建设集团有限公司	一级	其他有限责任公司	住宅房屋建筑
山东佰丰德建筑装饰工程有限公司	一级	私营有限责任公司	公共建筑装饰和装修
济南百川建设装饰工程有限公司	一级	私营有限责任公司	公共建筑装饰和装修
山东鼎森集团有限公司	一级	私营有限责任公司	住宅房屋建筑
山东鲁光信息工程有限公司	一级	其他有限责任公司	电气安装
山东众海工程有限公司	一级	私营有限责任公司	其他建筑安装
山东英士力建设工程集团有限公司	一级	私营有限责任公司	公共建筑装饰和装修
山东百安建设工程有限公司	一级	私营有限责任公司	其他建筑安装
山东天启智能工程有限公司	一级	私营有限责任公司	其他未列明建筑业
山东万林建设工程有限公司	一级	私营有限责任公司	住宅装饰和装修
中广核宏达环境科技有限责任公司	一级	其他有限责任公司	环保工程施工
山东亚特尔集团股份有限公司	一级	国有独资公司	管道和设备安装
济南蓝海建设工程有限公司	一级	其他有限责任公司	公路工程建筑
山东金桥保安器材有限公司	一级	私营有限责任公司	电气安装
济南润德医用工程有限公司	一级	私营有限责任公司	其他未列明建筑业
山东智领钢结构有限公司	一级	其他有限责任公司	其他未列明建筑业
山东省深基建设工程有限公司	一级	其他有限责任公司	住宅房屋建筑
山东中道实邦建设集团有限公司	一级	其他有限责任公司	住宅房屋建筑
山东净威净化工程有限公司	一级	私营有限责任公司	其他建筑安装

13-6 续表 6 continued 6

企业名称 Name	资质等级 Ownership	经济类型 Economic Type	所属行业 Industry
山东益德净化工程有限公司	一级	私营有限责任公司	环保工程施工
济南金盾工程有限责任公司	一级	私营有限责任公司	其他建筑安装
龙景建设集团有限公司	一级	私营有限责任公司	其他房屋建筑业
山东泰实建筑工程有限公司	一级	私营有限责任公司	住宅房屋建筑
山东金岛消防安全工程有限公司	一级	私营有限责任公司	其他建筑安装
山东锦润安消防科技有限公司	一级	私营有限责任公司	其他道路、隧道和桥梁工程建筑
清尚科源建设集团有限公司	一级	私营有限责任公司	住宅装饰和装修
济南林海装饰工程有限公司	一级	私营有限责任公司	公共建筑装饰和装修
茂绪建设发展有限责任公司	一级	私营有限责任公司	住宅房屋建筑
山东天宝建设集团有限公司	一级	其他有限责任公司	住宅房屋建筑
山东安泰智能工程有限公司	一级	私营有限责任公司	电气安装
山东睿洲建筑装饰工程有限公司	一级	私营有限责任公司	其他房屋建筑业
山东盛顺装饰有限公司	一级	私营有限责任公司	住宅装饰和装修
山东佑安消防系统有限公司	一级	私营有限责任公司	其他建筑安装
山东正琨建设工程有限公司	一级	私营有限责任公司	公共建筑装饰和装修
山东祥地建筑工程有限公司	一级	私营有限责任公司	其他房屋建筑业
山东富力达建筑科技有限公司	一级	私营有限责任公司	建筑幕墙装饰和装修
山东邦运建筑工程有限公司	一级	私营有限责任公司	电气安装
千庭景观建设有限公司	一级	私营有限责任公司	市政道路工程建筑
山东省齐鲁装饰设计有限公司	一级	私营有限责任公司	公共建筑装饰和装修
山东三盛防水工程有限公司	一级	私营有限责任公司	住宅装饰和装修
山东润霖消防工程有限公司	一级	私营有限责任公司	电气安装
山东高速齐鲁机电工程有限公司	一级	其他有限责任公司	太阳能发电工程施工
济南昌汇建筑工程有限公司	一级	私营有限责任公司	其他未列明建筑业
山东费尔消防技术工程有限公司	一级	私营有限责任公司	其他建筑安装
山东青亦蓝装饰工程有限公司	一级	私营有限责任公司	公共建筑装饰和装修
山东耘威医疗科技有限公司	一级	私营有限责任公司	管道和设备安装
中铁济南工程技术有限公司	一级	其他有限责任公司	铁路工程建筑
山东宇顺建筑工程有限公司	一级	私营有限责任公司	住宅房屋建筑
山东杨帆环保工程股份有限公司	一级	私营股份有限公司	环保工程施工
济南信高工程技术有限公司	一级	私营有限责任公司	其他建筑安装
山东豪庭建设集团有限公司	一级	私营有限责任公司	公共建筑装饰和装修
展鹏嘉业信息产业股份有限公司	一级	私营股份有限公司	电气安装
济南岩土工程公司	一级	全民所有制企业(国有企业)	其他土木工程建筑施工
山东中泉建勘岩土工程有限公司	一级	私营有限责任公司	工矿工程建筑
济南利宸泽建筑工程有限公司	一级	私营有限责任公司	住宅房屋建筑
济南剀诚消防自控设备有限公司	一级	私营有限责任公司	其他建筑安装
济南政和消防工程有限公司	一级	私营有限责任公司	管道和设备安装
山东恒霖建设工程有限公司	一级	其他有限责任公司	住宅房屋建筑
山东康桥交通科技有限公司	一级	私营有限责任公司	公路工程建筑
山东永鹏工程有限公司	一级	私营有限责任公司	其他未列明建筑业

13-6 续表 7 continued 7

企业名称 Name	资质等级 Ownership	经济类型 Economic Type	所属行业 Industry
山东国创装饰工程有限公司	一级	私营有限责任公司	住宅装饰和装修
山东省金海龙建工科技有限公司	一级	私营有限责任公司	架线及设备工程建筑
佳泽睿安集团有限公司	一级	私营有限责任公司	公路工程建筑
山东天石集团有限公司	一级	其他有限责任公司	其他土木工程建筑施工
山东宏岳消防工程有限公司	一级	私营有限责任公司	其他建筑安装
山东奥深智能工程有限公司	一级	私营有限责任公司	其他建筑安装
山东宜佳美建设集团有限公司	一级	私营有限责任公司	其他建筑安装
济南百士岩土工程有限公司	一级	私营有限责任公司	市政道路工程建筑
山东印象照明科技股份有限公司	一级	私营股份有限公司	电气安装
山东昊颐建设工程有限公司	一级	私营有限责任公司	管道工程建筑
山东福源设备安装有限公司	一级	私营有限责任公司	管道和设备安装
山东千业建设工程有限公司	一级	私营有限责任公司	其他建筑安装
山东冠达消防科技有限公司	一级	私营有限责任公司	其他建筑安装
山东民生建工集团有限公司	一级	其他有限责任公司	公共建筑装饰和装修
山东麦高建筑装饰工程有限公司	一级	私营有限责任公司	住宅房屋建筑
济南楚浩装饰工程有限公司	一级	私营有限责任公司	建筑幕墙装饰和装修
山东华盛特克科技有限公司	一级	私营有限责任公司	其他建筑安装
山东今生缘建筑装饰工程有限公司	一级	私营有限责任公司	建筑幕墙装饰和装修
山东世联建设工程有限公司	一级	私营有限责任公司	场地准备活动
山东郓城建设工程有限公司	一级	私营有限责任公司	电气安装
山东鸿图科技有限公司	一级	私营有限责任公司	其他建筑安装
山东昶博建筑工程有限公司	一级	私营有限责任公司	其他房屋建筑业
济南爱华建设有限公司	一级	私营有限责任公司	住宅装饰和装修
山东达美建设集团有限公司	一级	私营有限责任公司	公共建筑装饰和装修
山东济开建设有限公司	一级	私营有限责任公司	住宅房屋建筑
山东宏晨智能工程有限公司	一级	私营有限责任公司	市政道路工程建筑
山东创绩建工集团有限公司	一级	私营有限责任公司	住宅装饰和装修
山东齐鲁建业消防工程有限公司	一级	私营有限责任公司	其他建筑安装
济南东元改建加固工程有限公司	一级	私营有限责任公司	其他房屋建筑业
山东建华土木有限公司	一级	私营有限责任公司	住宅房屋建筑
山东天地盛源消防安全工程有限公司	一级	私营有限责任公司	其他建筑安装
山东世纪装饰工程股份有限公司	一级	私营股份有限公司	住宅装饰和装修
山东欧瑞装饰有限公司	一级	私营有限责任公司	住宅装饰和装修
山东蓝润建筑工程有限公司	一级	私营有限责任公司	电气安装
山东天翼安全技术有限公司	一级	私营有限责任公司	其他建筑安装
山东华埠特克智能机电工程有限公司	一级	其他有限责任公司	其他未列明建筑业
济南万达建筑安装工程有限公司	一级	私营有限责任公司	住宅房屋建筑
山东鑫龙装饰工程有限公司	一级	私营有限责任公司	公共建筑装饰和装修
山东美德隆建设有限公司	一级	私营有限责任公司	住宅房屋建筑
鸿鑫工程有限公司	一级	私营有限责任公司	公共建筑装饰和装修

主要统计指标解释

建筑业统计单位 指从事房屋、构筑物建造和设备安装活动的法人企业。建筑业法人企业应具有建筑业资质并能够独立核算，同时还应具备以下条件：①依法成立，有自己的名称、组织机构和场所，能够承担民事责任；②独立拥有和使用资产，承担负债，有权与其他单位签订合同；③独立核算盈亏，能够编制资产负债表。

建筑业总产值 是以货币形式表现的建筑业企业在一定时期内生产的建筑业产品和提供服务的总和。建筑业总产值包括：

（1）建筑工程产值：指列入建筑工程预算内的各种工程价值。

（2）安装工程产值：指设备安装工程价值以及将预制部品部件安装成建筑工程产品的价值，不包括被安装设备本身的价值。

（3）其他产值：建筑业总产值中除建筑工程、安装工程以外的产值。包括房屋构筑物修理产值、非标准设备制造产值、总包企业向分包企业收取的管理费以及不能明确划分的施工活动所完成的产值。

房屋施工面积 指报告期内施工的全部房屋建筑面积，包括本期新开工的房屋建筑面积、上期跨入本期继续施工的房屋建筑面积、上期停缓建在本期恢复施工的房屋建筑面积、本期竣工的房屋建筑面积及本期施工后又停缓建的房屋建筑面积。

房屋竣工面积 指报告期内房屋建筑按照设计要求已全部完工，达到住人和使用条件，经验收鉴定合格或达到竣工验收标准，可正式移交使用的各栋房屋建筑面积的总和。

Explanatory Notes on Main Statistical Indicators

Statistical Units in the Construction Industry refer to corporate enterprises engaged in the construction of buildings and structures and in the installation of equipment. A corporate construction enterprise should have qualification certificates with independent accounting system, and should meet the following 3 requirements: a) being set up in line with relevant legal basis, having its full name, organization and location, and capable of taking civil liabilities; b) independently possessing and using its assets and assuming its liabilities, and entitled to sign contracts with other institutions; c) making independent accounts of its profits and losses, and capable of compiling its own balance sheet.

Gross Output Value of Construction refers to total of construction products and services, expressed in monetary terms, produced or rendered by construction and installation enterprises during a given period of time. It includes:

(1) Output value of construction projects: the value of projects covered by the project budgets;

(2) Output value of installation projects: the value of the installation of equipment, and the value of installing prefabricated components into construction engineering products (excluding the value of the equipment to be installed);

(3) Other output values: the output value of construction industry apart from that of construction projects and installation projects. It includes: output value of repair of buildings and structures; output value of manufacturing of non-standard equipment; overhead expenses received by contracted enterprises from the sub-contracted enterprises, and the completed output value of construction activities for which there is no clear definition.

Floor Space of Buildings under Construction refers to the total floor space area of buildings under construction in the reference period. It includes buildings new started; buildings started earlier and continued during the reference period; buildings suspended earlier but restarted during the reference period; buildings completed during the reference period; and buildings under construction but suspended during the reference period.

Floor Space of Buildings Completed refers to the total floor space area of buildings that have been completed in the reference period in accordance with the requirements of the design, up to the standard for accommodation or putting into use, and have been checked and accepted by departments concerned as qualified or up to the standard of buildings completed and can be handed over for putting into use.

14

运输与邮电

TRANSPORTATION , POST AND TELECOMMUNICATIONS

14-1 邮电业务量
Business Volume of Postal Services and Telecommunication Services

指标	Item	单位 unit	2019年	2020年	2021年	2022年	2023年
国内分类业务量	**Domestic Classified Business Volume**						
固定电话	Number of Fixed Telephone	万户(10 000 subscribers)	148.82	144.78	145.31	147.66	163.2
年末市内电话	Urban Fixed Telephone at Year-end	万户(10 000 subscribers)	136.30	127.65			
年末农村电话	Rural Fixed Telephone at Year-end	万户(10 000 subscribers)	12.20	2.78			
年末住宅电话	Number of Household Telephone at Year-end	万户(10 000 subscribers)	25.56	14.26			
年末移动电话用户	Number of Mobile Phone Subscribers at Year-end	万户(10 000 subscribers)	1122.86	1154.06	1216.34	1266.04	1315.5
4G电话用户	4G Mobile Phone Subscribers	万户(10 000 subscribers)	888.81	922.67	750.03	570.94	600.1
固定互联网宽带接入用户	Broadband Subscribers of Internet	万户(10 000 subscribers)	392.6	445.5	463.0	501.4	559.3
每百人互联网用户	Number of Internet User per 100 Population	户/百人 (subscriber/100 persons)	49.63	55.56	57.05	61.27	67.99
邮电局所	Post & Telecommunication offices	处(unit)	252	252	253	253	254
国际及港澳分类业务量	**International,Hong kong and Macao Classified Business Volume**						
函件	Letters	万件(10 000 pcs)	45.75	13.02	3.54	1.11	0.98
包件	Packages	万件(10 000 pcs)	0.60	0.60	3.72	0.24	0.54

注：按照山东省通信管理局发布的通信业发展情况，年末市内电话、年末农村电话、年末住宅电话等指标不再进行统计。

Note:According to the development of communication industry released by Shandong Communications Administration, data of local telephone, rural telephone and residential telephone indicators at the end of year are not counted.

14-2 交通运输业基本情况
Basic Conditions of Transport

指标	Item	2019年	2020年	2021年	2022年	2023年
客运量（万人）	**Passenger Traffic (10 000 persons)**					
铁路	Railways	15745.1	9797.4	12163.7	7321.5	18264.7
公路	Highways	3244.0	1209.0	2024.0	1438.0	2137.0
民航	Civil Aviation	936.1	1238.5	1361.6	824.2	1756.1
旅客周转量（亿人公里）	**Passenger-Kilometers (100 million passenger-km)**					
铁路	Railways	795.3	431.9	523.9	313.3	809.2
公路	Highways	54.1	17.1	39.6	29.6	46.2
民航	Civil Aviation	376.5	256.3	268.6	136.2	329.7
货运量（万吨）	**Freight Traffic (10 000 tons)**					
铁路	Railways	20869.8	23188.8	22895.4	24716.7	25349.1
公路	Highways	28064.0	22677.0	24669.0	23843.0	24589.0
民航	Civil Aviation	6.7	14.7	16.8	13.8	14.4
货物周转量（亿吨公里）	**Freight Ton-Kilometers (100 million ton-km)**					
铁路	Railways	1460.5	1566.1	1682.1	1831.5	1796.4
公路	Highways	561.4	516.4	577.4	608.8	615.5
公路通车里程(公里)	**Length of Highways in Operation(km)**					
公路通车里程	Length of Highways in Operation	17770.9	18117.2	18200.1	18294.4	18356.5
#高速公路	Expressway	653.6	737.8	737.8	795.3	828.4
有铺装、简易铺装路面	Paved Roads	17290.0	18117.2	18200.1	18294.4	18356.5
未铺装路面	UnPaved Roads	480.9				
民用航空	**Civil Aviation**					
执行航线(条)	Perform Routes(line)	198	208	185	180	175
通航城市(个)	Navigable Cities(unit)	120	91	100	104	94
起降架次(架次)	Plane Flights(Sorties)	129994	102375	112746	78775	136731
民用汽车拥有量(辆)	**Possession of Civil Motor Vehicles(unit)**					
民用汽车拥有量	Possession of Civil Motor Vehicles	2584278	2794278	3025326	3203381	3386516
私人汽车	Private Vehicles	2332421	2512357	2705622	2857295	3010624
载客汽车	Passenger Vehicles	2370437	2556622	2759683	2925704	3092893
#大型	Large	15767	15535	15330	14900	14426
载货汽车	Trucks	194957	224713	250200	261017	275868
#重型	Heavy	41904	46148	51609	51772	53502
其他汽车	Others	18884				
专项作业车	Special Operation vehicles		12943	15443	16660	17755
摩托车	Motorcycle	258382	329477	405497	473433	494981
挂车	Trailer	12538	14842	15590	15307	16409

注：1.铁路系统统计数据来自中国铁路济南局集团有限公司。
2.2020年起，因公安部“公安交通管理综合应用平台”调整，修改了机动车报表统计口径，增加“专项作业车”等部分车型的统计，不再提供“其它”类汽车拥有量。
3.2020年起，民航客运量、货运量统计口径调整为出港和进港合计数。
4.2021年交通运输部采用新的公路货运统计方法，对2020年公路货运量、公路货物周转量数据进行了修正。

Notes:1. Statistical data of railway system comes from China Railway Jinan Group Co., Ltd.
2.Since 2020, due to the adjustment of the “Public Traffic Management Integrated Application Platform”, the statistical caliber of motor vehicles statement is varied, the statistics on “special motor vehicle” is supplemented, while “Population of Other Vehicles” is not listed longer.
3.Since 2020, the passenger transport volume of civil aviation, and the statistical caliber of freight traffic volume are adjusted as the total number of departures and arrivals
4. In 2021, the Ministry of Transport adopted a new statistic method for road freight, and revised the data of road freight volume and road freight turnover in 2020.

14-3 分地区公路交通(2023年)
Road Transportation by Region(2023)

单位：公里 (km)

指标	Item	济南市 Jinan	其中 of which 市区 Districts	平阴县 Ping yin	商河县 Shang he
公路通车里程	Length of Highways in Operation	18356.5	14621.0	1052.7	2682.8
#高速公路	Expressway	828.4	736.0	59.7	32.7
有铺装、简易铺装路面	Paved Road	18356.5	14621.0	1052.7	2682.8

主要统计指标解释

公路里程 指报告期末公路的实际长度。统计范围：包括城间、城乡间、乡（村）间能行驶汽车的公共道路，公路通过城镇街道的里程，公路桥梁长度、隧道长度、渡口宽度。不包括城市街道里程，断头路里程，农（林）业生产用道路里程，工（矿）企业等内部道路里程。统计原则：按已竣工验收或交付使用的实际里程计算；两条或多条公路共同经由同一路段的重复里程，只计算一次。

货(客)运量 指在一定时期内，各种运输工具实际运送的货物重量(旅客数量）。货运按吨计算，客运按人计算。货物不论运输距离长短、货物类别，均按实际重量统计。旅客不论行程远近或票价多少，均按一人一次客运量统计；半价票、儿童票也按一人统计。

货物(旅客)周转量 指在一定时期内，由各种运输工具运送的货物(旅客)数量与其相应运输距离的乘积之总和。该指标可以反映运输业生产的总成果，也是编制和检查运输生产计划，计算运输效率、劳动生产率以及核算运输单位成本的主要基础资料。计算货物周转量通常按发出站与到达站之间的最短距离，也就是计费距离计算。计算公式为：

货物（旅客）周转量=Σ（货物（旅客）运输量×运输距离）

民用汽车拥有量 指报告期末，在公安交通管理部门按照《机动车注册登记工作规范》，已注册登记领有民用车辆牌照的全部汽车数量。汽车拥有量统计的主要分类：根据汽车结构分为载客汽车、载货汽车及其他汽车；根据汽车所有者不同分为个人(私人)汽车、单位汽车；根据汽车的使用性质分为营运汽车、非营运汽车；根据汽车大小规格不同，载客汽车分为大型、中型、小型和微型，载货汽车分为重型、中型、轻型和微型。

移动电话用户 指在电信运营企业营业网点办理开户登记手续，通过移动电话交换机进入移动电话网，占用移动电话号码的各类电话用户。包括各类签约用户、智能网预付费用户、无线上网卡用户。

固定电话用户 指在电信企业营业网点办理开户登记手续并已接入固定电话网上的全部电话用户。

Explanatory Notes on Main Statistical Indicators

Length of Highways refers to the actual length of highways at the end of reference period. It covers public roads running vehicles between cities, between urban and rural areas, and between townships (villages), as well as highways passing through streets at small cities and towns, length of bridges and tunnels, width of ferry piers. It does not include the length of streets in cities, dead end highways, the length of streets built for agricultural (forest) production and inside factories (mines). Mileage can only be included when the road is completed, checked and accepted or put into operation. If two or more highways use the same section, the length of the section is counted only once.

Freight (Passenger) Traffic refers to the weight of freight (number of passengers) transported with various means within a specific period of time. Freight transport is calculated in tons and passenger traffic is calculated in terms of number of persons. Freight transport is calculated in terms of the actual weight of the goods, irrespective of the type of freight and distance of transport. Passenger traffic is calculated by the principle that one person can be counted only once in one trip, irrespective of travelling distance and ticket price. The passengers who travel with a discounted ticket or a children ticket is also calculated as one person.

Freight Ton-kilometres (Passenger-kilometres) refers to the sum of the product of the volume of transported cargo (passengers) multiplied by the transport distance. AS an indicator to reflect the achievement of the transportation industry, this is an important indicator to show the total results of the transport industry; to prepare and examine the transport plan; and to serve as the main basic data for calculating the efficiency, labour productivity and unit cost of transport. Normally, the shortest distance between the departure station and the destination station (i.e., the payable distance) is the basis in calculating the freight ton-kilometres. The formula is as follows:

Freight Ton-kilometres (Passenger-kilometres) = Σ(freight (passenger) traffic* distance of transportation)

Possession of Civil Motor Vehicles refer to the total numbers of vehicles at the end of the reference period that are registered and received vehicles license according to the Working Regulations for Motor Vehicle Registration formulated by the transport management offices. Motor vehicles are classified into different categories. By the structure of motor vehicles, they are divided into passenger vehicles, trucks and others; by ownership, into private vehicles and vehicles for the unit's use; by usage, into business vehicles and non-business vehicles; and by size of vehicles, into large passenger vehicles, medium-sized passenger vehicles, small passenger vehicles and mini passenger vehicles, heavy trucks, light-heavy trucks, light trucks and mini-trucks.

Mobile Phone Subscribers refer to persons who have gone through registration procedures in the operation outlets of enterprises engaged in telecommunications and are hence connected with the mobile phone communication network through the mobile phone switchboards and occupy mobile phone numbers. Included are various types of contracted subscribers, prepaid users for intelligent network and wireless network card users.

Fixed Telephone Subscribers refer to all subscribers who have gone through registration procedures in the operation outlets of enterprises engaged in telecommunications and are hence connected to the local telecommunications service provider through fixed line network.

15

国内贸易

DOMESTIC TRADE

15-1 各时期分行业社会消费品零售
Total Retail Sales of Consumer Goods by Section in Each Period

单位：万元 (10 000 yuan)

年份 Year	社会消费品零售总额 Total Retail Sales of Consumer Goods						
	总计 Total	批发零售业 Wholesale and Retail Trade	住宿业 Hotels	餐饮业 Catering Services	制造业 Manufacturing	其他 Others	农民对非农业居民 Farmers to Non-agricultural Residents
1949	11426	7312		556	3514		44
1952	22248	16985		1223	3592		448
1957	34568	29279		1935	2381	3	970
1962	41436	35784		1655	2946	266	785
1965	40795	36470		1829	1856	287	353
1970	42993	39397		1537	1468	321	270
1975	60105	53239		2565	2914	1217	170
1978	81335	70661		2907	5120	2222	425
1979	96036	80703		4000	9060	823	1450
1980	119775	95121		4392	16489	1299	2474
"六五时期"							
1981	135236	103303		5388	21353	2157	3035
1982	152094	116241		8165	21398	2778	3512
1983	167948	127884		9225	23569	2953	4317
1984	200301	150233		11342	29563	4506	4657
1985	243080	181867		14823	32342	5535	8513
"七五时期"							
1986	294102	219730		17880	35565	5456	15471
1987	331504	240192		20305	45386	8963	16658
1988	425984	300090		30808	60463	12300	22323
1989	484392	343978		28634	71653	9729	30398
1990	528221	382047		25599	71505	10886	38184
"八五时期"							
1991	597989	424836		27443	78452	14186	53072
1992	711774	535080		37096	77951		61647
1993	985251	723914		56059	80101		125177
1994	1426472	1037687		86141	99621		203023
1995	1837618	1345321		133501	115105		243691
"九五时期"							
1996	2234590	1570947		176100	141201		346342
1997	2568584	1744014		216727	177219		430624
1998	2834024	1893486		255616	207595		477327

15-1 续表 continued

单位：万元 (10 000 yuan)

年份 Year	社会消费品零售总额 Total Retail Sales of Consumer Goods 总计 Total	批发零售业 Wholesale and Retail Trade	住宿业 Hotels	餐饮业 Catering Services	制造业 Manufacturing	其他 Others	农民对非农业居民 Farmers to Non-agricultural Residents
1999	3092091	2043078		305333	225132		518548
2000	3444527	2287545		377550	233128		546304
"十五时期"							
2001	3857141	2574216		485494	237545		559886
2002	4321225	2935804		613178	231947		540296
2003	5115396	4373831		741565			
2004	6689452	5691288	57973	940191			
2005	7726458	6575543	66490	1084425			
"十一五时期"							
2006	8974064	7571831	78098	1324135			
2007	10526639	8791908	86322	1648409			
2008	12922856	10684195	96391	2142271			
2009	15254265	12710608	105378	2438279			
2010	17254574	14022650	150810	3081114			
"十二五时期"							
2011	20231045	16338362	175067	3717616			
2012	23235965	18740304	187466	4308195			
2013	26338714	22006709	177160	4154845			
2014	28640303	24120903	182090	4337310			
2015	31410419	26484428	193710	4732280			
"十三五时期"							
2016	34350723	28971634	210316	5168774			
2017	37525226	31658152	228909	5638165			
2018	40910775	34521369	248418	6140988			
2019	44204092	37604716	275686	6323691			
2020	44691335	38570115	255049	5866171			
"十四五时期"							
2021	51260961	43881612	301524	7077825			
2022	48781082	41921612	271524	6587946			
2023	51990277	44332699	335859	7321719			

注：1992年至2019年社会消费品零售总额及分组数据根据第四次全国经济普查数据进行了修订。
Note: Total retail volume of social consumption and grouping data from 1992 to 2019 are revised according to the fourth national economic census.

15-2 限额以上批发零售业法人企业商品销售情况(2023年)

Sales of Commo-dities by Enterprises above Designated Size of Wholesale and Retail Trade(2023)

单位：万元 (10 000 yuan)

指标	Item	商品销售总额 Total Sales of Commodities 合计 Total	批发 Wholesale	零售 Retail
总计	**Total**	**146434941.7**	**128080534.6**	**18354407.1**
批发业	**Wholesale Trade**	**128791603.4**	**126380317.4**	**2411286.0**
农、林、牧、渔产品批发	Wholesale of Agricultural, Forestry, Livestock and Fishery Products	2441461.7	2429854.4	11607.3
食品、饮料及烟草制品批发	Wholesale of Food, Beverages and Tobaccos	7398800.8	6775930.0	622870.8
纺织、服装及家庭用品批发	Wholesale of Textiles, Wearing Apparel and Household Articles	3617397.3	3287146.7	330250.6
文化、体育用品及器材批发	Wholesale of Culture, Sports Appliances and Equipments	5401852.7	4470935.4	930917.3
医药及医疗器材批发	Wholesale of Medicines and Medical Appliances	11935706.6	11861528.3	74178.3
矿产品、建材及化工产品批发	Wholesale of Mineral Products, Building Materials and Chemical Products	80289720.3	80089697.9	200022.4
机械设备、五金产品及电子产品批发	Wholesale of Machinery, Hardware and Electronic Products	17185075.7	16947339.9	237735.8
贸易经纪与代理	Trade Broker and Agency	24070.7	24070.7	
其他批发业	Other Wholesale not Classified Elsewhere	497517.6	493814.1	3703.5
内资企业	Domestic Invested Enterprises	118701760.2	116292784.2	2408976.0
国有独资公司	State-owned Sole-proprietorship Enterprises	1957474.4	1939601.0	17873.4
私营有限责任公司	Private Limited Liability Corporations	54540692.8	53338377.0	1202315.8
其他有限责任公司	Other Limited Liability Corporations	59856597.3	58701060.0	1155537.3
私营股份有限公司	Private Share-holding Corporations Ltd.	514769.0	499308.2	15460.8
其他股份有限公司	Other Share-holding Corporations Ltd.	1681058.7	1665417.6	15641.1
全民所有制企业(国有企业)	State-owned Enterprises	127766.3	126943.4	822.9
集体所有制企业(集体企业)	Collective-owned Enterprises	5697.1	5697.1	
股份合作企业	Cooperative Enterprises			
联营企业	Joint Ownership Enterprises			
个人独资企业	Sole-proprietorship Enterprises	17704.6	16379.9	1324.7
合伙企业	Partnership Enterprises			
其他内资企业	Other Domestic Invested Enterprises			
港澳台投资企业	Enterprises with Investment from Hong Kong,Macao and Taiwan	8508542.2	8508526.9	15.3
港澳台投资有限责任公司	Limited Liability Corporations	8508542.2	8508526.9	15.3
港澳台投资股份有限公司	Share-holding Corporations Ltd.			
港澳台投资合伙企业	Partnership Enterprises			
其他港澳台投资企业	Other Enterprises			
外商投资企业	Foreign Invested Enterprises	1578996.3	1576701.6	2294.7
外商投资有限责任公司	Limited Liability Corporations	1131482.2	1129187.5	2294.7
外商投资股份有限公司	Share-holding Corporations Ltd.	2011.6	2011.6	
外商投资合伙企业	Partnership Enterprises			
其他外商投资企业	Other Enterprises	445502.5	445502.5	
农民专业合作社(联合社)	Professional Farmers Cooperatives	2304.7	2304.7	

15-2 续表 continued

单位：万元 (10 000 yuan)

指标	Item	商品销售总额 Total Sales of Commodities		
		合计 Total	批发 Wholesale	零售 Retail
零售业	**Retail Trade**	**17643338.3**	**1700217.2**	**15943121.1**
综合零售	General Retail	2262655.1	87339.8	2175315.3
食品、饮料及烟草制品专门零售	Special Retail of Food, Beverages and Tobaccos	783161.1	227185.4	555975.7
纺织、服装及日用品专门零售	Special Retail of Textiles, Garments and Daily Consumer Articles	559436.7	65849.7	493587.0
文化、体育用品及器材专门零售	Special Retail of Culture, Sports Appliances and Equipments	418795.7	45782.1	373013.6
医药及医疗器材专门零售	Special Retail of Medicines and Medical Appliances	884959.2	34246.0	850713.2
汽车、摩托车、零配件和燃料及其他动力销售	Retail of Motor Vehicles, Motorcycles, Parts, and Fuel and Other Powers	8808954.0	917456.3	7891497.7
家用电器及电子产品专门零售	Special Retail of Household Electric Appliances and Electronic Products	708129.5	84233.7	623895.8
五金、家具及室内装饰材料专门零售	Special Retail of Hardware, Furniture and Interior Decoration Materials	103226.5	9979.0	93247.5
货摊、无店铺及其他零售业	Stalls, Non-shop and Other Retails	3114020.5	228145.2	2885875.3
内资企业	Domestic Invested Enterprises	15339109.3	1308959.7	14030149.6
国有独资公司	State-owned Sole-proprietorship Enterprises	58111.2	22895.9	35215.3
私营有限责任公司	Private Limited Liability Corporations	5838735.0	402492.5	5436242.5
其他有限责任公司	Other Limited Liability Corporations	7692350.6	818259.4	6874091.2
私营股份有限公司	Private Share-holding Corporations Ltd.	67404.2		67404.2
其他股份有限公司	Other Share-holding Corporations Ltd.	1070679.8	58074.5	1012605.3
全民所有制企业(国有企业)	State-owned Enterprises	44350.6	233.9	44116.7
集体所有制企业(集体企业)	Collective-owned Enterprises	19099.5	1930.3	17169.2
股份合作企业	Cooperative Enterprises	517512.1	349.0	517163.1
联营企业	Joint Ownership Enterprises			
个人独资企业	Sole-proprietorship Enterprises	30866.3	4724.2	26142.1
合伙企业	Partnership Enterprises			
其他内资企业	Other Domestic Invested Enterprises			
港澳台投资企业	Enterprises with Investment from Hong Kong,Macao and Taiwan	1369449.1	25075.2	1344373.9
港澳台投资有限责任公司	Limited Liability Corporations	1369449.1	25075.2	1344373.9
港澳台投资股份有限公司	Share-holding Corporations Ltd.			
港澳台投资合伙企业	Partnership Enterprises			
其他港澳台投资企业	Other Enterprises			
外商投资企业	Foreign Invested Enterprises	931584.1	366182.3	565401.8
外商投资有限责任公司	Limited Liability Corporations	42452.3	4720.4	37731.9
外商投资股份有限公司	Share-holding Corporations Ltd.	4007.0	2762.7	1244.3
外商投资合伙企业	Partnership Enterprises			
其他外商投资企业	Other Enterprises	885124.8	358699.2	526425.6
农民专业合作社(联合社)	Professional Farmers Cooperatives	3195.8		3195.8

15-3 限额以上批发零售贸易企业资产实力(2023年)

Capital Power of Enterprises above Designated Size of Wholesale and Retail Trade(2023)

单位：万元

指标	Item	法人企业数(个) Number of Corporation Enterprises (unit)
总计	**Total**	**6097**
批发业	**Wholesale Trade**	**4844**
农、林、牧、渔产品批发	Wholesale of Agricultural, Forestry, Livestock and Fishery Products	130
食品、饮料及烟草制品批发	Wholesale of Food, Beverages and Tobaccos	346
纺织、服装及家庭用品批发	Wholesale of Textiles, Wearing Apparel and Household Articles	261
文化、体育用品及器材批发	Wholesale of Culture, Sports Appliances and Equipments	161
医药及医疗器材批发	Wholesale of Medicines and Medical Appliances	497
矿产品、建材及化工产品批发	Wholesale of Mineral Products, Building Materials and Chemical Products	2365
机械设备、五金产品及电子产品批发	Wholesale of Machinery, Hardware and Electronic Products	1030
贸易经纪与代理	Trade Broker and Agency	NA
其他批发业	Other Wholesale not Classified Elsewhere	51
内资企业	Domestic Invested Enterprises	4787
国有独资公司	State-owned Sole-proprietorship Enterprises	14
私营有限责任公司	Private Limited Liability Corporations	4009
其他有限责任公司	Other Limited Liability Corporations	701
私营股份有限公司	Private Share-holding Corporations Ltd.	25
其他股份有限公司	Other Share-holding Corporations Ltd.	24
全民所有制企业(国有企业)	State-owned Enterprises	4
集体所有制企业(集体企业)	Collective-owned Enterprises	NA
股份合作企业	Cooperative Enterprises	
联营企业	Joint Ownership Enterprises	
个人独资企业	Sole-proprietorship Enterprises	9
合伙企业	Partnership Enterprises	
其他内资企业	Other Domestic Invested Enterprises	
港澳台投资企业	Enterprises with Investment from Hong Kong,Macao and Taiwan	34
港澳台投资有限责任公司	Limited Liability Corporations	34
港澳台投资股份有限公司	Share-holding Corporations Ltd.	
港澳台投资合伙企业	Partnership Enterprises	
其他港澳台投资企业	Other Enterprises	
外商投资企业	Foreign Invested Enterprises	22
外商投资有限责任公司	Limited Liability Corporations	19
外商投资股份有限公司	Share-holding Corporations Ltd.	NA
外商投资合伙企业	Partnership Enterprises	
其他外商投资企业	Other Enterprises	NA
农民专业合作社(联合社)	Professional Farmers Cooperatives	NA

注：NA表示企业个数小于或等于3(以下相关表同)。
Note:NA refers to less than or equal to three. The same applies to the tables following.

(10 000 yuan)

流动资产合计 Total Current Assets	其中 of which: 存货 Inventories	固定资产原价 Original Value of Fixed Assets	累计折旧 Accumulated depreciation	其中 of which: 本年折旧 Depreciation in the Year	资产总计 Total Assets	负债合计 Total Liabilities	所有者权益合计 Total Owners' Equities	其中 of which: 实收资本 Paid-up Capital
65630030.4	**7894926.7**	**4156394.9**	**1787866.2**	**283700.6**	**78452492.7**	**62917578.3**	**15896020.8**	**14889436.9**
58391737.1	**6530660.3**	**2551754.6**	**1048833.9**	**163559.8**	**68079212.6**	**53645288.2**	**14432019.6**	**11201970.1**
783433.1	224909.0	84345.4	36165.1	4611.4	942883.6	674036.0	268847.6	212329.9
2270800.6	667002.0	343854.9	160547.7	17005.9	2775200.6	1918502.1	856698.5	400574.9
1681910.5	446851.4	150796.9	53000.8	7901.3	1986824.8	1647596.7	339228.1	180093.6
2498891.1	568247.3	418373.5	150218.2	18455.4	3382146.4	2221144.0	1158980.7	362092.1
7655568.9	917784.4	424756.0	188396.8	35836.4	8668910.6	7103361.3	1565549.3	1022161.8
34511112.6	2496889.6	685319.5	269031.6	44777.2	40370185.2	31666286.6	8703898.6	6818447.5
8659043.0	1169608.3	422719.2	184848.0	33250.0	9582461.0	8129825.6	1452752.3	2175604.2
23131.1	2617.7	50.1	32.3	11.2	23148.9	15854.5	7294.4	2050.0
307846.2	36750.6	21539.1	6593.4	1711.0	347451.5	268681.4	78770.1	28616.1
50191964.1	5825543.8	2459582.9	1004709.6	159152.9	59567081.6	48618463.0	10946713.8	9133000.3
1635362.2	249997.1	107204.7	41437.7	9774.8	1883801.1	1480630.4	403170.7	234363.3
17753628.5	2267629.9	1026414.4	465807.7	79251.9	19755666.1	16990878.0	2762883.3	4389575.2
25803756.2	3188685.6	1198952.3	449464.7	65281.3	31892331.2	25147446.5	6744884.7	3904949.4
371055.0	45109.2	53230.7	21145.6	1924.7	921533.0	423379.0	498154.0	191178.1
4508832.0	66180.6	72694.0	26188.7	2821.5	4967950.5	4493318.6	474631.9	357229.3
108939.0	6604.7	412.6	242.8	22.7	134690.1	73337.7	61352.4	54634.9
787.6	317.8	48.3	29.0		864.4	154.2	710.2	50.0
9603.6	1018.9	625.9	393.4	76.0	10245.2	9318.6	926.6	1020.1
4547117.3	644250.0	60448.6	26194.3	3314.4	4710255.0	3667809.2	1042445.8	981246.8
4547117.3	644250.0	60448.6	26194.3	3314.4	4710255.0	3667809.2	1042445.8	981246.8
3652077.3	60859.9	31723.1	17930.0	1092.5	3801297.6	1359016.0	2442281.6	1087223.0
828191.2	73754.4	10846.9	3700.6	379.3	905978.5	665312.5	240666.0	155754.3
1270.9	877.9	2798.4	896.6	128.8	4579.8	1686.9	2892.9	2736.7
2822615.2	-13772.4	18077.8	13332.8	584.4	2890739.3	692016.6	2198722.7	928732.0
578.4	6.6				578.4		578.4	500.0

15-3 续表 continued

单位：万元

指标	Item	法人企业数(个) Number of Corporation Enterprises (unit)
零售业	**Retail Trade**	**1253**
综合零售	General Retail	92
食品、饮料及烟草制品专门零售	Special Retail of Food, Beverages and Tobaccos	123
纺织、服装及日用品专门零售	Special Retail of Textiles, Garments and Daily Consumer Articles	86
文化、体育用品及器材专门零售	Special Retail of Culture, Sports Appliances and Equipments	61
医药及医疗器材专门零售	Special Retail of Medicines and Medical Appliances	70
汽车、摩托车、零配件和燃料及其他动力销售	Retail of Motor Vehicles, Motorcycles, Parts, and Fuel and Other Powers	456
家用电器及电子产品专门零售	Special Retail of Household Electric Appliances and Electronic Products	170
五金、家具及室内装饰材料专门零售	Special Retail of Hardware, Furniture and Interior Decoration Materials	30
货摊、无店铺及其他零售业	Stalls, Non-shop and Other Retails	165
内资企业	Domestic Invested Enterprises	1232
国有独资公司	State-owned Sole-proprietorship Enterprises	NA
私营有限责任公司	Private Limited Liability Corporations	849
其他有限责任公司	Other Limited Liability Corporations	332
私营股份有限公司	Private Share-holding Corporations Ltd.	4
其他股份有限公司	Other Share-holding Corporations Ltd.	9
全民所有制企业（国有企业)	State-owned Enterprises	NA
集体所有制企业（集体企业）	Collective-owned Enterprises	8
股份合作企业	Cooperative Enterprises	NA
联营企业	Joint Ownership Enterprises	
个人独资企业	Sole-proprietorship Enterprises	23
合伙企业	Partnership Enterprises	
其他内资企业	Other Domestic Invested Enterprises	
港澳台投资企业	Enterprises with Investment from Hong Kong,Macao and Taiwan	14
港澳台投资有限责任公司	Limited Liability Corporations	14
港澳台投资股份有限公司	Share-holding Corporations Ltd.	
港澳台投资合伙企业	Partnership Enterprises	
其他港澳台投资企业	Other Enterprises	
外商投资企业	Foreign Invested Enterprises	4
外商投资有限责任公司	Limited Liability Corporations	NA
外商投资股份有限公司	Share-holding Corporations Ltd.	NA
外商投资合伙企业	Partnership Enterprises	
其他外商投资企业	Other Enterprises	NA
农民专业合作社（联合社）	Professional Farmers Cooperatives	NA

(10 000 yuan)

流动资产合计 Total Current Assets	其中 of which 存货 Inventories	固定资产原价 Original Value of Fixed Assets	累计折旧 Accumulated depreciation	其中 of which 本年折旧 Depreciation in the Year	资产总计 Total Assets	负债合计 Total Liabilities	所有者权益合计 Total Owners' Equities	其中 of which 实收资本 Paid-up Capital
7238293.3	**1364266.4**	**1604640.3**	**739032.3**	**120140.8**	**10373280.1**	**9272290.1**	**1464001.2**	**3687466.8**
3018244.2	147377.5	704208.1	321164.7	46540.8	4409143.9	3659914.6	749229.3	511515.3
293326.4	53280.9	79772.6	35637.6	3979.2	351791.7	202270.3	149521.4	69979.2
269147.9	62527.4	45740.2	16275.3	2300.3	377927.9	357865.1	20062.8	124487.4
218398.3	69155.7	31583.1	17048.3	2338.1	276840.2	192066.6	84773.6	40213.4
575155.5	144904.7	27037.4	17462.5	2700.6	899497.0	704367.6	195129.4	70753.6
2099466.7	691596.1	620027.5	295654.2	56503.0	3127640.8	3421587.9	69064.1	2585389.3
290489.4	84313.2	17783.6	7722.6	1573.5	323688.0	257040.2	66647.8	74331.5
47448.6	11954.0	42767.7	14047.3	1705.9	104230.8	70377.5	33853.3	43532.0
426616.3	99156.9	35720.1	14019.8	2499.4	502519.8	406800.3	95719.5	167265.1
7022222.8	1267311.0	1345626.3	610147.3	105096.4	9789929.2	8367228.1	1785712.3	3597262.9
18213.3		98008.1	43481.5	5929.8	83344.2	37574.4	45769.8	32640.0
2030743.2	630059.0	294544.0	148153.8	25576.3	2390072.5	2169704.7	220367.8	2579977.1
2269759.9	507935.4	558254.2	207094.9	41045.8	3471870.7	2625998.0	845872.7	823719.7
35198.8	3751.5	38014.9	22527.2	1612.2	64056.7	35423.4	28633.3	9440.0
2069286.9	99550.6	240832.5	131077.9	14305.7	2755999.4	2639810.5	479200.1	95460.3
14933.3	5665.2	2228.8	967.3	138.8	19795.8	18700.2	1095.6	1435.9
6030.7	1453.5	1646.0	874.3	153.1	7137.0	3023.6	4113.4	844.4
568597.3	16857.4	110159.0	55019.3	15957.1	985348.3	828003.0	157345.3	52557.5
9459.4	2038.4	1938.8	951.1	377.6	12304.6	8990.3	3314.3	1188.0
137136.0	47995.0	95348.8	57185.4	7064.0	260930.7	195651.9	65278.8	37164.2
137136.0	47995.0	95348.8	57185.4	7064.0	260930.7	195651.9	65278.8	37164.2
77795.0	48869.2	163079.6	71670.3	7957.4	320625.1	708388.8	-387763.7	52919.7
12106.7	3453.9	38071.7	13175.9	1503.3	65978.6	39082.9	26895.7	38142.9
13788.9	80.9	12794.3	3474.6	359.7	33289.5	10581.3	22708.2	14776.8
51899.4	45334.4	112213.6	55019.8	6094.4	221357.0	658724.6	-437367.6	
1139.5	91.2	585.6	29.3	23.0	1795.1	1021.3	773.8	120.0

15-4 限额以上批发零售贸易企业损益及分配(2023年)

Profit Loss and Distribution of Enterprises above Designated Size of Wholesale and Retail Trade(2023)

单位：万元

指标	Item	法人企业数(个) Number of Corporation Enterprises (unit)	主营业务收入 Revenue from Principal Business	营业成本 Business Cost
总计	**Total**	**6097**	**128924835.9**	**124035679.2**
批发业	**Wholesale Trade**	**4844**	**113740112.3**	**110435069.9**
农、林、牧、渔产品批发	Wholesale of Agricultural, Forestry, Livestock and Fishery Products	130	2284229.9	2225053.1
食品、饮料及烟草制品批发	Wholesale of Food, Beverages and Tobaccos	346	6672845.5	6077552.9
纺织、服装及家庭用品批发	Wholesale of Textiles, Wearing Apparel and Household Articles	261	3222559.3	2994293.3
文化、体育用品及器材批发	Wholesale of Culture, Sports Appliances and Equipments	161	4954423.8	4569147.2
医药及医疗器材批发	Wholesale of Medicines and Medical Appliances	497	10691820.9	9835162.6
矿产品、建材及化工产品批发	Wholesale of Mineral Products, Building Materials and Chemical Products	2365	69584980.9	69263782.3
机械设备、五金产品及电子产品批发	Wholesale of Machinery, Hardware and Electronic Products	1030	15846140.0	15006258.2
贸易经纪与代理	Trade Broker and Agency	NA	21432.6	20920.6
其他批发业	Other Wholesale not Classified Elsewhere	51	461679.4	442899.7
内资企业	Domestic Invested Enterprises	4787	104420461.6	101222816.6
国有独资公司	State-owned Sole-proprietorship Enterprises	14	1800107.0	1704986.4
私营有限责任公司	Private Limited Liability Corporations	4009	48783787.1	46670021.3
其他有限责任公司	Other Limited Liability Corporations	701	51685935.6	50813024.0
私营股份有限公司	Private Share-holding Corporations Ltd.	25	477430.1	416405.3
其他股份有限公司	Other Share-holding Corporations Ltd.	24	1536881.0	1488913.8
全民所有制企业（国有企业）	State-owned Enterprises	4	115312.6	109905.5
集体所有制企业（集体企业）	Collective-owned Enterprises	NA	5113.1	4988.9
股份合作企业	Cooperative Enterprises			
联营企业	Joint Ownership Enterprises			
个人独资企业	Sole-proprietorship Enterprises	9	15895.1	14571.4
合伙企业	Partnership Enterprises			
其他内资企业	Other Domestic Invested Enterprises			
港澳台投资企业	Enterprises with Investment from Hong Kong,Macao and Taiwan	34	7905770.6	7688707.8
港澳台投资有限责任公司	Limited Liability Corporations	34	7905770.6	7688707.8
港澳台投资股份有限公司	Share-holding Corporations Ltd.			
港澳台投资合伙企业	Partnership Enterprises			
其他港澳台投资企业	Other Enterprises			
外商投资企业	Foreign Invested Enterprises	22	1411575.4	1521273.8
外商投资有限责任公司	Limited Liability Corporations	19	1008266.7	976455.0
外商投资股份有限公司	Share-holding Corporations Ltd.	NA	2844.7	2258.5
外商投资合伙企业	Partnership Enterprises			
其他外商投资企业	Other Enterprises	NA	400464.0	542560.3
农民专业合作社（联合社）	Professional Farmers Cooperatives	NA	2304.7	2271.7

(10 000 yuan)

税金及附加 Taxes and Other Charges	销售费用 Sales Expenses	管理费用 Management Expenses	财务费用 Financial Expenses	营业利润 Profits from Business	利润总额 Total Profits	所得税费用 Income Tax Expense	应付职工薪酬(本年贷方累计发生额) Total Wages Payable	应交增值税 Value-added Tax Payable
284883.8	**3239949.8**	**1775684.1**	**347402.9**	**832869.9**	**1001556.8**	**263211.2**	**1978420.4**	**809252.2**
234709.1	**1829946.9**	**1358479.1**	**267274.3**	**735236.6**	**902224.9**	**218839.2**	**1300017.6**	**632634.6**
836.9	28054.6	22523.8	5086.4	11551.3	13138.8	217.4	20548.2	4525.8
139185.1	180327.7	193518.0	3135.6	154738.2	152332.4	37452.9	159937.7	59813.2
3629.9	153431.8	67247.3	-701.4	23849.1	24768.4	6820.5	77385.7	24679.6
7737.2	150765.1	139164.5	-3950.4	156290.2	155242.7	5236.4	175188.6	10524.8
19923.0	489022.8	248683.7	36122.2	146298.2	141321.4	30477.0	265285.4	131203.2
48720.6	440810.4	393945.7	239164.2	39201.5	212520.9	88109.1	291948.6	217800.4
14180.2	376144.4	281012.0	-10208.9	193762.6	195227.5	49625.2	300290.7	179141.6
20.7	82.1	102.3	-47.3	354.1	366.8	124.6	67.9	69.6
475.5	11308.0	12281.8	-1326.1	9191.4	7306.0	776.1	9364.8	4876.4
226236.3	1660992.1	1259644.2	295894.8	844470.8	834982.9	186910.9	1220083.0	600849.0
2252.2	16405.5	10951.0	18035.5	60671.4	61327.8	15610.1	21108.8	15656.7
148902.7	1011917.9	726529.4	77507.6	242596.8	217435.9	50016.2	575393.4	264947.3
72252.8	581687.8	476478.5	182101.2	502688.1	517239.1	120198.8	576106.5	309761.7
758.0	25973.5	22451.6	9576.1	40638.4	40062.7	887.5	23833.3	2951.0
1823.4	24237.6	20372.4	7913.2	-3862.3	-2857.1	-249.2	21144.3	6647.3
212.6	640.1	1830.7	713.1	1533.5	1538.5	392.0	2017.3	634.1
1.4		19.2	-0.9	104.5	104.5	5.2	6.8	22.1
33.2	129.7	1011.4	49.0	100.4	131.5	50.3	472.6	228.8
6849.2	140853.1	62481.1	-34712.3	59405.3	58501.9	21205.2	60851.3	17578.2
6849.2	140853.1	62481.1	-34712.3	59405.3	58501.9	21205.2	60851.3	17578.2
1623.6	28088.3	36342.7	6091.8	-168648.0	8731.6	10723.1	19042.1	14207.4
893.9	10026.3	12415.7	5561.9	10130.7	7598.2	473.3	12710.3	13478.5
38.4	67.8	294.8	65.5	119.7	135.2	10.4	156.3	42.4
691.3	17994.2	23632.2	464.4	-178898.4	998.2	10239.4	6175.5	686.5
	13.4	11.1		8.5	8.5		41.2	

15-4 续表 continued

单位：万元

指标	Item	法人企业数（个）Number of Corporation Enterprises (unit)	主营业务收入 Revenue from Principal Business	营业成本 Business Cost
零售业	**Retail Trade**	**1253**	**15184723.6**	**13600609.3**
综合零售	General Retail	92	1435248.8	1185697.4
食品、饮料及烟草制品专门零售	Special Retail of Food, Beverages and Tobaccos	123	705778.5	596873.1
纺织、服装及日用品专门零售	Special Retail of Textiles, Garments and Daily Consumer Articles	86	469871.6	347437.6
文化、体育用品及器材专门零售	Special Retail of Culture, Sports Appliances and Equipments	61	384711.3	323292.4
医药及医疗器材专门零售	Special Retail of Medicines and Medical Appliances	70	786990.7	603889.7
汽车、摩托车、零配件和燃料及其他动力销售	Retail of Motor Vehicles, Motorcycles, Parts, and Fuel and Other Powers	456	7859973.6	7510884.6
家用电器及电子产品专门零售	Special Retail of Household Electric Appliances and Electronic Products	170	639216.1	590771.8
五金、家具及室内装饰材料专门零售	Special Retail of Hardware, Furniture and Interior Decoration Materials	30	91949.9	65923.7
货摊、无店铺及其他零售业	Stalls, Non-shop and Other Retails	165	2810983.1	2375839.0
内资企业	Domestic Invested Enterprises	1232	13113689.6	11643268.3
国有独资公司	State-owned Sole-proprietorship Enterprises	NA	76393.9	64345.3
私营有限责任公司	Private Limited Liability Corporations	849	5280617.0	4726260.3
其他有限责任公司	Other Limited Liability Corporations	332	6723328.3	6028789.2
私营股份有限公司	Private Share-holding Corporations Ltd.	4	60041.1	49939.3
其他股份有限公司	Other Share-holding Corporations Ltd.	9	701620.3	541717.8
全民所有制企业（国有企业)	State-owned Enterprises	NA	39055.8	40384.3
集体所有制企业（集体企业）	Collective-owned Enterprises	8	17032.0	15057.6
股份合作企业	Cooperative Enterprises	NA	188315.9	152465.3
联营企业	Joint Ownership Enterprises			
个人独资企业	Sole-proprietorship Enterprises	23	27285.3	24309.2
合伙企业	Partnership Enterprises			
其他内资企业	Other Domestic Invested Enterprises			
港澳台投资企业	Enterprises with Investment from Hong Kong,Macao and Taiwan	14	1236546.9	1157632.2
港澳台投资有限责任公司	Limited Liability Corporations	14	1236546.9	1157632.2
港澳台投资股份有限公司	Share-holding Corporations Ltd.			
港澳台投资合伙企业	Partnership Enterprises			
其他港澳台投资企业	Other Enterprises			
外商投资企业	Foreign Invested Enterprises	4	831291.3	796678.9
外商投资有限责任公司	Limited Liability Corporations	NA	37595.0	24643.4
外商投资股份有限公司	Share-holding Corporations Ltd.	NA	3317.4	1890.2
外商投资合伙企业	Partnership Enterprises			
其他外商投资企业	Other Enterprises	NA	790378.9	770145.3
农民专业合作社（联合社）	Professional Farmers Cooperatives	NA	3195.8	3029.9

(10 000 yuan)

税金及附加 Taxes and Other Charges	销售费用 Sales Expenses	管理费用 Management Expenses	财务费用 Financial Expenses	营业利润 Profits from Business	利润总额 Total Profits	所得税费用 Income Tax Expense	应付职工薪酬(本年贷方累计发生额) Total Wages Payable	应交增值税 Value-added Tax Payable
50174.7	**1410002.9**	**417205.0**	**80128.6**	**97633.3**	**99331.9**	**44372.0**	**678402.8**	**176617.6**
16138.7	303566.6	79935.2	13966.9	46624.7	46930.0	8617.8	161773.9	29477.7
1965.0	36334.2	17769.2	1458.5	55567.0	54596.5	14032.3	34082.5	11784.9
2611.9	90853.5	19005.1	8136.0	4763.7	3512.9	3514.7	39706.4	10435.3
4988.3	36445.4	15110.5	489.4	11113.3	9604.3	2004.1	27349.7	5192.6
1879.2	156468.7	42073.6	9764.1	-3336.4	-4623.5	1189.7	96814.0	16179.4
18056.8	359166.8	162226.2	40426.2	-39228.4	-33529.2	5767.3	230363.1	67540.3
336.0	27230.8	25622.6	2945.5	-1773.1	-2272.9	219.8	23520.2	4684.6
800.9	12977.7	12566.4	1994.0	-2331.9	-2380.4	19.1	8611.4	2075.2
3397.9	386959.2	42896.2	948.0	26234.4	27494.2	9007.2	56181.6	29247.6
42729.5	1304422.5	387353.2	72696.2	78602.8	80898.9	39439.4	618767.0	161215.8
143.2	1142.2	2898.4	200.5	6620.3	6621.1	1764.8	2765.4	1643.8
13893.1	447061.6	201436.2	23980.7	-28502.4	-28598.9	10580.0	241781.7	55442.8
19536.5	636016.0	126657.5	41113.4	47649.5	50363.7	24555.0	250647.8	82455.1
1059.7	5082.5	5214.3	15.0	5004.8	5189.8	771.9	3299.7	999.7
5043.2	157341.2	35426.8	-11575.4	49229.0	47087.6	304.7	82554.0	13190.8
14.1	1538.2	1284.3	95.1	-919.4	-914.8	5.2	1641.2	-70.3
29.3	660.5	1770.1	-20.0	-389.8	-373.8	12.2	709.9	197.5
2946.5	54706.6	10791.8	18859.1	-389.0	1315.3	1391.2	34129.6	6930.9
63.9	873.7	1873.8	27.8	299.8	208.9	54.4	1237.7	425.5
5094.0	68337.8	16646.9	3230.4	12994.0	12652.8	5176.4	39937.0	8884.6
5094.0	68337.8	16646.9	3230.4	12994.0	12652.8	5176.4	39937.0	8884.6
2344.9	37194.6	13129.2	4201.7	6000.9	5744.3	-244.3	19411.9	6511.8
737.7	3767.1	8990.2	1497.6	-2383.0	-2433.3	111.9	3064.8	933.4
182.0	3038.9	-1047.3	-484.9	5169.3	5287.0	0.7	3154.3	53.9
1425.2	30388.6	5186.3	3189.0	3214.6	2890.6	-356.9	13192.8	5524.5
6.3	48.0	75.7	0.3	35.6	35.9	0.5	286.9	5.4

15-5 限额以上餐饮业主要经济指标(2023年)

Main Economic Indicators of Enterprises above Designated Size of Catering Services (2023)

单位：万元

指标	Item	法人企业数(个) Number of Corporation Enterprises (unit)	资产总计 Total Assets	负债合计 Total Liabilities	所有者权益 Owners' Equities
总计	**Total**	**869**	**832747.0**	**609003.4**	**223743.8**
正餐服务	Restaurant	431	515766.3	386932.2	128834.3
快餐服务	Fast Food	386	236502.9	151382.2	85120.7
饮料及冷饮服务	Beverages and Cold Drinks	7	13084.1	17215.9	-4131.8
餐饮配送及外卖送餐服务	Catering Distribution and Delivery Service	38	63789.3	49279.1	14510.2
其他餐饮业	Others	7	3604.4	4194.0	-589.6
内资企业	Domestic Invested Enterprises	865	780434.0	553441.8	226992.4
国有独资公司	State-owned Sole-proprietorship Enterprises	NA	15762.4	1894.6	
私营有限责任公司	Private Limited Liability Corporations	383	344766.6	335420.2	9346.5
其他有限责任公司	Other Limited Liability Corporations	131	390663.9	191544.0	199119.9
私营股份有限公司	Private Share-holding Corporations Ltd.	NA	280.0	139.7	140.3
其他股份有限公司	Other Share-holding Corporations Ltd.				
全民所有制企业(国有企业)	State-owned Enterprises	5	3530.9	7097.9	-3567.0
集体所有制企业(集体企业)	Collective-owned Enterprises				
股份合作企业	Cooperative Enterprises				
联营企业	Joint Ownership Enterprises				
个人独资企业	Sole-proprietorship Enterprises	16	3674.1	4560.8	-886.6
合伙企业	Partnership Enterprises	328	37518.5	14679.2	22839.3
其他内资企业	Other Domestic Invested Enterprises				
港澳台投资企业	Enterprises with Investment from Hong Kong,Macao and Taiwan	NA	48256.8	53762.6	-5505.8
港澳台投资有限责任公司	Limited Liability Corporations	NA	48256.8	53762.6	-5505.8
外商投资企业	Foreign Invested Enterprises	NA	4056.2	1799.0	2257.2
外商投资有限责任公司	Limited Liability Corporations	NA	4056.2	1799.0	2257.2

(10 000 yuan)

其中 of which 实收资本 Paid-up Capital	主营业务收入 Revenue from Principal Business	营业成本 Business Cost	销售费用 Sales Expenses	管理费用 Management Expenses	财务费用 Financial Expenses	营业利润 Profits from Business	利润总额 Total Profits	应付职工薪酬(本年贷方累计发生额) Total Wages Payable
145904.1	**944101.5**	**537655.4**	**270870.1**	**128304.8**	**7683.5**	**33686.5**	**40748.4**	**232331.4**
88417.6	490787.0	254059.0	149928.8	93063.5	5241.9	4386.6	6375.8	127552.1
45047.4	338585.9	193624.7	111549.2	20755.3	1848.9	27622.8	28431.9	80229.6
1300.0	33148.0	22285.4	4814.3	3952.2	126.1	2022.1	2034.2	6030.1
11044.1	73403.9	60692.1	4230.3	9790.8	455.3	-417.6	3834.1	15411.4
95.0	8176.7	6994.2	347.5	743.0	11.3	72.6	72.4	3108.2
140106.0	874659.1	511891.1	237850.0	124662.9	6126.0	27517.7	34496.4	210786.5
	1216.3	714.9	6.2	204.5	-13.3	304.2	304.4	
77167.7	427753.3	243890.9	108864.7	78925.3	3471.8	-3124.2	-843.2	103169.2
53548.2	299924.8	201333.6	63836.6	41028.2	2632.6	20170.2	24018.7	71058.9
300.0	382.2	256.2	90.6	38.2	3.3	-6.1	-6.1	53.0
521.7	2333.7	977.2	1298.9	803.6	3.9	-767.0	-685.1	1298.8
113.0	7248.6	3567.8	1837.3	1816.7	7.0	-10.7	13.6	3072.9
8455.4	137016.5	61865.4	61921.9	2050.9	7.4	11255.5	11998.5	32133.7
4598.1	63906.3	23931.2	30929.1	3438.7	1553.1	4726.9	4799.4	20644.5
4598.1	63906.3	23931.2	30929.1	3438.7	1553.1	4726.9	4799.4	20644.5
1200.0	5536.1	1833.1	2091.0	203.2	4.4	1441.9	1452.6	900.4
1200.0	5536.1	1833.1	2091.0	203.2	4.4	1441.9	1452.6	900.4

15-6 限额以上住宿业主要经济指标(2023年)

Main Economic Indicators of Enterprises above Designated Size of Hotels Services(2023)

单位：万元

指标	Item	法人企业数(个) Number of Corporation Enterprises (unit)	资产总计 Total Assets	负债合计 Total Liabilities	所有者权益 Owners' Equities
总计	**Total**	**337**	**1153651.7**	**1151346.3**	**2305.4**
旅游饭店	Tourist Hotel	68	725951.0	595611.7	130339.3
一般旅馆	General Hotels	250	297632.2	352962.0	-55329.8
民宿服务	Home Lodging Services	NA	5806.8	3513.2	2293.6
露营地服务	Campground Services				
其他住宿业	Others	18	124261.7	199259.4	-74997.7
内资企业	Domestic Invested Enterprises	333	1139113.2	1143225.9	-4112.7
国有独资公司	State-owned Sole-proprietorship Enterprises	NA	2636.9	412.6	2224.3
私营有限责任公司	Private Limited Liability Corporations	244	245089.8	242477.9	2611.9
其他有限责任公司	Other Limited Liability Corporations	77	675860.9	796790.7	-120929.8
私营股份有限公司	Private Share-holding Corporations Ltd.				
其他股份有限公司	Other Share-holding Corporations Ltd.				
全民所有制企业(国有企业)	State-owned Enterprises	8	205797.9	83019.3	122778.6
集体所有制企业(集体企业)	Collective-owned Enterprises	NA	8162.2	18558.5	-10396.3
股份合作企业	Cooperative Enterprises				
联营企业	Joint Ownership Enterprises				
个人独资企业	Sole-proprietorship Enterprises	NA	1565.5	1966.9	-401.4
合伙企业	Partnership Enterprises				
其他内资企业	Other Domestic Invested Enterprises				
港澳台投资企业	Enterprises with Investment from Hong Kong,Macao and Taiwan	NA	12233.1	6599.8	5633.3
港澳台投资有限责任公司	Limited Liability Corporations	NA	12233.1	6599.8	5633.3
外商投资企业	Foreign Invested Enterprises	NA	2301.2	1520.5	780.7
外商投资有限责任公司	Limited Liability Corporations	NA	2301.2	1520.5	780.7
农民专业合作社(联合社)	Professional Farmers Cooperatives	NA	4.2	0.1	4.1

(10 000 yuan)

其中 of which 实收资本 Paid-up Capital	主营业务收入 Revenue from Principal Business	营业成本 Business Cost	销售费用 Sales Expenses	管理费用 Management Expenses	财务费用 Financial Expenses	营业利润 Profits from Business	利润总额 Total Profits	应付职工薪酬(本年贷方累计发生额) Total Wages Payable
168059.4	**465388.2**	**225926.8**	**132268.4**	**145338.9**	**10533.3**	**-23730.7**	**-20914.7**	**148366.8**
95488.7	247844.7	127672.2	66425.2	69347.4	3544.0	-8292.3	-7270.2	92546.9
66651.3	194259.3	71174.0	58472.9	67227.5	3198.6	-2817.2	-1350.7	42370.6
2073.2	269.5	204.6	0.2	248.3	9.0	-147.3	-149.0	72.0
3846.2	23014.7	26876.0	7370.1	8515.7	3781.7	-12473.9	-12144.8	13377.3
163689.4	457938.5	225224.5	128416.1	142930.6	10526.8	-24408.5	-21613.1	145986.2
1100.0	2544.5	314.2	1442.4	744.7	3.7	35.7	49.0	846.8
47293.7	145416.3	64317.0	37462.8	48500.3	1836.7	-5060.7	-3375.7	29530.8
87609.6	226099.2	108690.0	74606.9	69660.4	10634.8	-17883.3	-17509.4	80649.6
27098.3	80958.9	50981.3	10696.4	23118.1	-1938.7	1586.5	1646.7	34358.2
587.8	2719.3	773.4	4103.6	901.8	-11.7	-3049.2	-2392.0	492.3
	200.3	148.6	104.0	5.3	2.0	-37.5	-31.7	108.5
4320.0	4632.7	306.8	1468.7	1925.9	-1.3	607.7	607.5	1899.0
4320.0	4632.7	306.8	1468.7	1925.9	-1.3	607.7	607.5	1899.0
50.0	2676.0	347.0	2383.6	390.9	7.8	69.2	89.6	422.2
50.0	2676.0	347.0	2383.6	390.9	7.8	69.2	89.6	422.2
	141.0	48.5		91.5		0.9	1.3	59.4

15–7 限额以上住宿业和餐饮业法人企业经营情况(2023年)

Main Indicators of Enterprises above Designated Size of Hotels and Catering Services(2023)

指标	Item	法人企业数(个) Number of Corporation Enterprises (unit)	从业人员期末人数(人) Engaged Persons at Year-end (person)
总计	**Total**	**1206**	**57331**
住宿业	**Hotels**	**337**	**18193**
旅游饭店	Tourist Hotel	68	9822
一般旅馆	General Hotels	250	6619
民宿服务	Home Lodging Services	NA	11
露营地服务	Campground Services		
其他住宿业	Others	18	1741
内资企业	Domestic Invested Enterprises	333	17963
国有独资公司	State-owned Sole-proprietorship Enterprises	NA	106
私营有限责任公司	Private Limited Liability Corporations	244	5013
其他有限责任公司	Other Limited Liability Corporations	77	9945
私营股份有限公司	Private Share-holding Corporations Ltd.		
其他股份有限公司	Other Share-holding Corporations Ltd.		
全民所有制企业(国有企业)	State-owned Enterprises	8	2772
集体所有制企业(集体企业)	Collective-owned Enterprises	NA	107
股份合作企业	Cooperative Enterprises		
联营企业	Joint Ownership Enterprises		
个人独资企业	Sole-proprietorship Enterprises	NA	20
合伙企业	Partnership Enterprises		
其他内资企业	Other Domestic Invested Enterprises		
港澳台投资企业	Enterprises with Investment from Hong Kong,Macao and Taiwan	NA	149
港澳台投资有限责任公司	Limited Liability Corporations	NA	149
外商投资企业	Foreign Invested Enterprises	NA	69
外商投资有限责任公司	Limited Liability Corporations	NA	69
农民专业合作社(联合社)	Professional Farmers Cooperatives	NA	12
餐饮业	**Catering Services**	**869**	**39138**
正餐服务	Restaurant	431	20164
快餐服务	Fast Food	386	14148
饮料及冷饮服务	Beverages and Cold Drinks	7	731
餐饮配送及外卖送餐服务	Catering Distribution and Delivery Service	38	3490
其他餐饮业	Others	7	605
内资企业	Domestic Invested Enterprises	865	34937
国有独资公司	State-owned Sole-proprietorship Enterprises	NA	
私营有限责任公司	Private Limited Liability Corporations	383	17927
其他有限责任公司	Other Limited Liability Corporations	131	10764
私营股份有限公司	Private Share-holding Corporations Ltd.	NA	15
其他股份有限公司	Other Share-holding Corporations Ltd.		
全民所有制企业(国有企业)	State-owned Enterprises	5	177
集体所有制企业(集体企业)	Collective-owned Enterprises		
股份合作企业	Cooperative Enterprises		
联营企业	Joint Ownership Enterprises		
个人独资企业	Sole-proprietorship Enterprises	16	550
合伙企业	Partnership Enterprises	328	5504
其他内资企业	Other Domestic Invested Enterprises		
港澳台投资企业	Enterprises with Investment from Hong Kong,Macao and Taiwan	NA	3803
港澳台投资有限责任公司	Limited Liability Corporations	NA	3803
外商投资企业	Foreign Invested Enterprises	NA	398
外商投资有限责任公司	Limited Liability Corporations	NA	398

营业额 (万元) Business Revenue (10 000 yuan)	其中 of which 客房收入 From Hotel Rooms	餐费收入 From Meals	商品销售收入 Revenue from Commodities	其他收入 Other Revenue	客房数 (间) Number of Room (room)	床位数 (张) Number of Beds (bed)	餐位数 (位) Number of Dining-seats (seat)	年末餐饮营业面积(平方米) Operating Area of Catering Enterprises at Year-end (sq.m)
1512755.9	**342808.1**	**1030470.5**	**35091.6**	**104385.7**	**56284**	**88074**	**406125**	**2418574**
510817.0	**295353.6**	**138667.7**	**18388.9**	**58406.8**	**45997**	**69616**	**49484**	**1160935**
266049.5	108932.2	102241.2	16060.9	38815.2	13017	20212	29911	571381
209706.9	167793.8	23418.8	1875.5	16618.8	29573	43958	12382	516420
247.1	132.7	7.2	5.1	102.1	40	100		5000
34813.5	18494.9	13000.5	447.4	2870.7	3367	5346	7191	68134
502954.9	290313.2	137288.0	18369.0	56984.7	45157	68416	48335	1134394
2687.6	2045.0	595.7		46.9	162	282	532	2400
155827.3	133204.4	15808.8	1727.0	5087.1	24859	36688	11303	457087
257741.5	128090.1	82013.1	9224.1	38414.2	17354	27185	26464	571082
83596.4	25342.9	37429.0	7417.9	13406.6	2332	3603	8036	86827
2859.8	1418.4	1441.4			365	523	2000	16998
242.3	212.4			29.9	85	135		
4882.7	2261.0	1219.8		1401.9	330	490	1000	16000
4882.7	2261.0	1219.8		1401.9	330	490	1000	16000
2837.3	2637.7	159.9	19.8	19.9	431	582	149	10431
2837.3	2637.7	159.9	19.8	19.9	431	582	149	10431
142.1	141.7		0.1	0.3	79	128		110
1001938.9	**47454.5**	**891802.8**	**16702.7**	**45978.9**	**10287**	**18458**	**356641**	**1257639**
521830.8	47226.6	436998.0	6428.4	31177.8	10047	18004	223166	903392
358050.6	48.2	344585.8	3916.2	9500.4	172	333	106615	265322
35128.7		34232.1	386.8	509.8			2756	10355
78331.5	179.7	69360.8	5971.3	2819.7	68	121	11110	59600
8597.3		6626.1		1971.2			12994	18970
928299.5	47454.5	822423.8	14597.1	43824.1	10287	18458	344248	1206973
1276.6	363.9	554.6	5.6	352.5				
447225.1	22607.2	391772.2	7197.5	25648.2	5662	10062	230972	736908
323810.5	23512.8	275134.2	7345.8	17817.7	4341	7820	85825	362904
382.2		382.2					180	800
2459.7	631.7	1828.0			230	476	1156	20200
8481.3	338.9	8088.5	48.2	5.7	54	100	3944	20379
144664.1		144664.1					22171	65782
67808.3		63547.9	2105.6	2154.8			11987	48945
67808.3		63547.9	2105.6	2154.8			11987	48945
5831.1		5831.1					406	1721
5831.1		5831.1					406	1721

15-8 销售过亿元的商品交易市场一览表(2023年)
Large Commodity Markets with Transaction Value over 100 Million Yuan (2023)

市场类别 Category	市场数量 (个) Market Quantity (unit)	市场总摊位 (个) Number of booths (unit)	年末出租摊位数 (个) Number of rent booths at Year-End (unit)	年末营业面积 (平方米) Operating Area at Year-End (sq.m)	年成交额 (万元) Annual Turnover (10 000 yuan)
总计	**26**	**18920**	**17583**	**1662745**	**7057221**
工业消费品综合市场	2	3116	2676	93450	176214
农产品综合市场	2	2571	2511	177800	313187
金属材料市场	2	192	189	45000	530336
水产品市场	2	1822	1798	121200	3880000
蔬菜市场	3	1269	1204	95810	343221
干鲜果品市场	1	258	258	61000	242400
茶叶市场	2	800	601	90000	135900
服装市场	1	2430	2430	199000	130692
鞋帽市场	1	889	798	19925	132000
小商品市场	1	1508	1503	45500	103515
通讯器材市场	1	1055	1055	65000	372504
家具市场	5	2005	1804	422122	243671
汽车市场	1	70	70	130000	325000
机动车零配件市场	2	935	686	96938	128581

主要统计指标解释

社会消费品零售总额 指企业（单位、个体户）通过交易直接售给个人、社会集团非生产、非经营用的实物商品金额，以及提供餐饮服务所取得的收入金额。个人包括城乡居民和入境人员，社会集团包括机关、社会团体、部队、学校、企事业单位、居委会或村委会等。

商品销售额 指对本单位以外的单位和个人出售的商品金额（含增值税），以及出售给本单位且开具增值税发票的商品金额。在批发和零售业中，本指标反映国内销售的商品以及出口商品的总价。商品销售包括：（1）售给个人和社会集团消费用的商品；（2）售给农业、工业、建筑业、服务业等国民经济各行业用于生产、经营用的商品，包括售予批发和零售业作为转卖或加工后转卖的商品；（3）对国（境）外直接出口的商品。不包括：（1）未通过买卖行为付出的商品，如因机构变动移交给其他企业单位的商品、借出的商品、归还受其他单位委托代保管的商品、付出的加工原料和赠送给其他单位的样品等；（2）促销返券所销售的、不计入营业收入的商品；（3）经本单位介绍，由买卖双方直接结算，本单位只收取手续费的业务；（4）未发生所有权转移的商品预付卡销售，如加油卡；（5）汽车维修、电话卡销售等服务性经济活动；（6）购货退回的商品；（7）商品损耗和损失；（8）出售本单位自用的废旧物资；（9）期货交易商品；（10）自来水供应企业、电力企业、天然气供应企业提供的水、电、气。

批发业 指向其他批发或零售单位（含个体经营者）及其他企事业单位、机关团体等批量销售生活用品、生产资料的活动，以及从事进出口贸易和贸易经纪与代理的活动，包括拥有货物所有权，并以本单位（公司）的名义进行交易活动，也包括不拥有货物的所有权，收取佣金的商品代理、商品代售活动；还包括各类商品批发市场中固定摊位的批发活动，以及以销售为目的的收购活动。

零售业 指百货商店、超级市场、专门零售商店、品牌专卖店、售货摊等主要面向最终消费者（如居民等）的销售活动，以互联网、邮政、电话、售货机等方式的销售活动，还包括在同一地点，后面加工生产，前面销售的店铺（如面包房）；谷物、种子、饲料、牲畜、矿产品、生产用原料、化工原料、农用化工产品、机械设备（乘用车、计算机及通信设备除外）等生产资料的销售不作为零售活动；多数零售商对其销售的货物拥有所有权，但有些则是充当委托人的代理人，进行委托销售或以收取佣金的方式进行销售。

住宿业 指为旅行者提供短期留宿场所的活动，有些单位只提供住宿，也有些单位提供住宿、饮食、商务、娱乐一体的服务，不包括主要按月或按年长期出租房屋住所的活动。

餐饮业 指通过即时制作加工、商业销售和服务性劳动等，向消费者提供食品和消费场所及设施的服务。

住宿餐饮业营业额 指住宿和餐饮业单位在经营活动中，因提供服务或销售商品等取得的全部收入（含增值税），收入主要来源于提供客房、餐费服务、商品销售和其他服务，如商务服务。不包括多产业法人企业附营的其他行业产业活动单位的餐费收入、商品销售收入等各项收入。其中，客房收入指住宿和餐饮业单位在经营活动中因提供住宿服务取得的收入（含增值税）。不包括多产业法人企业附营的其他行业产业活动单位的客房收入。餐费收入指本单位为顾客提供就餐服务取得的收入（含增值税）。包括：经烹饪、调制加工后出售的各种食品，如主食、炒菜、凉拌菜等的收入。不包括多产业法人企业附营的其他行业产业活动单位的餐费收入。

亿元以上商品交易市场 指年成交额在亿元及以上的商品交易市场。商品交易市场是指经有关部门和组织批准设立，有固定场所、设施，有经营管理部门和监管人员，若干市场经营者入内，常年或实际开业三个月以上，集中、公开、独立地进行生活消费品、生产资料等现货商品交易以及提供相关服务的交易场所，包括各类消费品市场、生产资料市场等。

Explanatory Notes on Main Statistical Indicators

Total Retail Sales of Consumer Goods refer to the revenue received by enterprises (units, self-employed individuals) through direct sales of non-production and non-business physical commodities to individuals and social institutions, and revenue from providing catering services. Individuals include rural and urban households, population from abroad, social institutions include government agencies, social organizations, military units, schools, institutions, neighbourhood (village) committees, etc.

Total Sales of Commodities refers to the amount of goods sold to institutions and individuals outside the institution (including value-added tax), as well as the amount of goods sold to the institution and with VAT invoices provided by the institution. The total sales revenue of wholesale and retail industries is calculated based on the total goods amount of goods sold domestically and abroad. The commodities include: (1) commodities sold to individuals and social groups for their consumption; (2) commodities sold to establishments in all industries for their production and operation, including agriculture, industry, construction, and catering services, including commodities sold to wholesale and retail establishments for re-selling, with or without further processing; (3) commodities for direct export to abroad. Excluded are (1) extended commodities without trading, such as goods handed over to other enterprises and institutions because of the change of organizations, lent goods, return of goods kept for others, extended processing materials and samples donated to others, (2) goods sold by coupon rebates that are not included in business income, (3) goods of direct settlement between buyer and seller with handling fees introduced by others, (4) prepaid cards for goods without transfer of ownership, such as gas cards, (5) Service-oriented economic activities such as automobile maintenance and telephone card sales, (6) goods returned after purchase, (7) damaged and spoiled goods, (8) waste and used goods of self-use, (9) futures trading commodities, (10) water, electricity and gas supplied by water supply enterprises, electric power enterprises and natural gas supply enterprises.

Wholesale Trade refers to the activities of selling wholesale commodities for daily use and capital goods to other enterprises of wholesale and retail trades (including self-employed individuals) and other enterprises, institutions and government agencies and organizations, and the activities of engaging in import and export and acting as a trade agent. The wholesaler may have the ownership of the commodities for wholesale and trade in the name of its own (a company), and the wholesaler can act as commission agent or commodity broker without the ownership of commodities. Also included are the wholesale activities at the fixed stalls in wholesale market and the acquisition for sales purpose.

Retail Trade refers to the activities of department stores, supermarkets, franchised stores, brand stores, retail stalls and on-the-spot-making-selling stores selling commodities to the final consumers (residents) by any means, including internet, post, telephone, sales machine. It also includes shops with sales and production located in the same places (such as bakeries). Retail trade excludes the activities of sales of capital goods such as grain, seed, feed, livestock, mineral products, raw material for production, industrial chemicals, chemical products for agricultural use, machine and equipment (excluding vehicles, computers and communication equipment). Most retailers have the ownership of commodities to sell, but some are acting as agents or brokers to make transactions for a commission.

Hotel Services refer to short-term accommodation services provided to visitors. Some units may provide only accommodation while others provide a combination of accommodation, meals, business services and recreational facilities. It excludes activities related to the provision of long-term primary residences, typically leased on a monthly or annual basis.

Catering Services refer to the activities of providing foods, serving locations and facilities to customers through instant processing, commercial sales and service-type labor.

Hotels and Catering Services Business Revenue refers to total revenue (including VAT) of hotels and catering services received from providing services or selling commodities through business activities. Revenue comes mainly from providing hotels, catering services, selling of commodities and other services, such as commodity services. It does not include revenue from providing meals or selling of commodities by establishments affiliated to other multi-industrial corporate enterprises. Income from hotel rooms refers to income (including VAT) of hotels and catering services by providing lodging services through business activities. Income from meals refers to income (including VAT) from providing catering services, including selling of cooked or prepared foods, such as staple food, cooked dishes, or cold dishes. It does not include income from meals provided by establishments affiliated to other multi-industrial corporate enterprises.

Large Commodity Markets with Transaction Value over 100 Million Yuan refers to the commodity markets with an annual transaction at and above 100 million. The commodity markets refer to markets approved and managed by related departments, where there are fixed sites, facilities, managers and administrative offices, where there are a certain number of traders to operate for at least three months or all the year, where the commodities, including articles for daily consumption and capital goods and services, are traded in a centralized, independent and open way. Such markets include markets for daily goods, markets of capital goods, etc.

16

对外贸易与国际旅游

FOREIGN TRADE AND INTERNATIONAL TOURISM

16-1 海关进出口商品总额
International Trade in Goods of Customs

单位：万美元 (10 000 USD)

指标	Item	2023年进出口总额 Total Value of Imports and Exports in 2023	其中 of which		2022年进出口总额 Total Value of Imports and Exports in 2022	其中 of which	
			出口 Export	进口 Import		出口 Export	进口 Import
总　额	**Total**	**3074109**	**1951475**	**1122634**	**3270583**	**2112951**	**1157632**
按贸易方式分	**By Trade**						
一般贸易	General Trade	2740585	1809304	931281	2850676	1907650	943025
援助物资	Aid Material	175	175		563	563	
捐赠物资	Donation Material				38	38	
补偿贸易	Compensation Trade						
来料加工装配贸易	Processing and Assembling Trade with Sent Materials	27142	13292	13851	37853	20451	17401
进料加工贸易	Processing Trade with Imported Materials	98466	71817	26649	93405	65819	27586
对外承包工程出口货物	Export of Contracted projects	12700	12700		28588	28588	
投资设备	Investment Goods	581		581	576		576
出料加工贸易	Export Processing Trade	166	50	116	189	40	149
海关特殊监管区域进口设备	**Import of Equipment in Special Customs Supervision Area**	**2734**		**2734**	**1523**		**1523**
海关特殊监管区域物流货物	**Logistics Freight of Equipment in Special Customs Supervision Area**	**88101**	**33191**	**54910**	**161415**	**76549**	**84866**
易货贸易	Barter Trade						
保税监管场所进出境货物	**Bonded Supervision Entry and Exit Goods**	**93416**	**2125**	**91291**	**90154**	**9643**	**80511**
来料加工装配进口设备	Imported Equipment for Processing Incoming Materials						
租赁贸易	Leasing Trade						
其他贸易	Other Trade	6815	5594	1220	5602	3608	1994
按运输方式分	**By Ways of Transport**						
水路运输	Waterway Transport	2155283	1535200	620038	2207442	1542729	664714
铁路运输	Railway Transport	55785	42090	13696	43620	32514	11106
公路运输	Road Transport	480224	151084	329140	383667	112339	271328
航空运输	Air Transport	316944	157751	159193	448944	239107	209837
邮件运输	Mail Transport	3335	2792	543	2731	2162	569
其他运输	Others	62582	62558	24	184179	184101	78
按企业性质分	**By Natural of Enterprises**						
国有企业	State-owned Enterprises	487997	68115	419882	602175	83282	518894
集体企业	Collective-owned Enterprises	77533	32941	44592	108507	55582	52925
外商投资企业	Foreign Funded Enterprises	615149	513845	101303	586799	478062	108738
中外合资	Joint-venture Enterprises	117313	98309	19004	146890	123243	23647
中外合作	Cooperation Enterprises	932	932		996	996	
外商独资	Enterprises with Sole Fund	496903	414603	82299	438913	353823	85090
其他	Others	3315	2788	527	2695	2158	537

16-2 主要国别(地区)海关进出口商品总额
International Trade in Goods of Customs by Country (Region)

单位：万美元 (10 000 USD)

国别(地区)	Country (region)	2023年进出口总额 Total Value of Imports and Exports in 2023	其中 of which		2022年进出口总额 Total Value of Imports and Exports in 2022	其中 of which	
			出口 Export	进口 Import		出口 Export	进口 Import
总额	**Total**	**3074109**	**1951475**	**1122634**	**3270583**	**2112951**	**1157632**
亚洲	**Asia**	**1456417**	**879898**	**576520**	**1648022**	**1046603**	**601420**
中国香港	Hong Kong, China	61830	61731	100	61502	61382	120
印度	India	95007	72585	22422	79340	62359	16980
印度尼西亚	Indonesia	87541	57263	30279	70375	60235	10140
日本	Japan	92368	49534	42834	97666	62500	35166
马来西亚	Malaysia	238423	100969	137454	275168	131332	143837
巴基斯坦	Pakistan	10362	10168	194	16517	16243	274
菲律宾	Philippines	74027	59609	14418	80111	61982	18128
卡塔尔	Qatar	3357	2985	372	3974	3667	306
沙特阿拉伯	Saudi Arabia	58279	53029	5250	34240	26093	8148
新加坡	Singapore	43452	34342	9110	132400	115528	16872
韩国	Republic of Korea	86697	64484	22213	146160	107184	38976
泰国	Thailand	84663	30965	53698	100017	45470	54547
土耳其	Türkiye	35165	33765	1401	19382	19077	305
阿拉伯联合酋长国	The United Arab Emirates	52225	46943	5282	69271	65336	3934
越南	Vietnam	74087	58479	15608	110899	76735	34164
中国台湾	Taiwan, China	155284	14759	140525	96461	18982	77478
非洲	**Africa**	**272397**	**258540**	**13857**	**256896**	**233868**	**23028**
埃及	Egypt	9110	8527	583	11724	11522	202
南非	South Africa	17808	13009	4799	22792	14429	8363
尼日利亚	Nigeria	31138	31121	17	32866	32660	206
欧洲	**Europe**	**532943**	**386084**	**146859**	**481058**	**356325**	**124733**

16-2 续表 continued

单位：万美元 (10 000 USD)

国别(地区)	Country (region)	2023年进出口总额 Total Value of Imports and Exports in 2023	其中 of which 出口 Export	进口 Import	2022年进出口总额 Total Value of Imports and Exports in 2022	其中 of which 出口 Export	进口 Import
比利时	Belgium	16756	15587	1169	9998	9043	955
英国	United Kingdom	34105	30355	3750	35402	30351	5052
德国	Germany	92168	45074	47094	94358	49407	44951
法国	France	25054	16843	8210	24474	20501	3973
意大利	Italy	28752	24049	4703	26050	21805	4245
荷兰	Netherlands	29439	24993	4446	32801	29101	3700
西班牙	Spain	22888	21465	1423	18891	16576	2315
芬兰	Finland	2497	1770	727	4014	2308	1706
瑞典	Sweden	8858	2413	6445	8315	3036	5279
瑞士	Switzerland	14527	1348	13179	10125	1679	8446
俄罗斯	Russia	142958	109857	33102	92228	76742	15487
拉丁美洲	**Latin America**	**309924**	**176620**	**133304**	**329536**	**154963**	**174574**
阿根廷	Argentina	14987	5704	9283	21820	8064	13756
巴西	Brazil	119416	47427	71989	142368	38455	103913
智利	Chile	27048	13517	13531	34206	12725	21481
墨西哥	Mexico	46327	44523	1804	39659	38919	741
北美洲	**North America**	**298311**	**204464**	**93846**	**331678**	**240222**	**91456**
加拿大	Canada	62201	45278	16923	73413	56067	17346
美国	United States	228834	159178	69656	253150	184135	69015
大洋洲	**Oceanic**	**203565**	**45868**	**157697**	**222844**	**80970**	**141873**
澳大利亚	Australia	185362	37677	147685	200519	72969	127550
新西兰	New Zealand	14469	4457	10012	18514	4191	14323

16-3 海关进出口商品分类金额
International Trade in Goods by HS Section and Division of Customs

单位：万美元 (10 000 USD)

商品分类	Commodity (by HS Section and Division)	2023年		2022年	
		出口 Export	进口 Import	出口 Export	进口 Import
总　额	**Total**	**1951475**	**1122634**	**2112951**	**1157632**
活动物；动物产品	**Live Animals; Animal Products**	**1416**	**76430**	**1146**	**118455**
活动物	Live Animals				
肉及食用杂碎	Meat and Edible Met Offal	19	46804		87568
鱼、甲壳动物、软体动物及其他水生无脊椎动物	Fish and Crustacean,Mollusc and Other Aquatic Invertebrates	66	25515	10	24856
乳品；蛋品；天然蜂蜜；其他食用动物产品	Dairy Produce; Birds' Eggs; Natural Honey; Edible Products of Animal Origin, not Elsewhere Specified or Included	59	3993	104	5626
其他动物产品	Products of Animal Origin, not Elsewhere Specified or Included	1272	118	1032	404
植物产品	**Vegetables Products**	**78096**	**31863**	**58457**	**23865**
活树及其他活植物；鳞茎、根及类似品；插花及装饰用簇叶	Live Tree and Other Plants; Bulbs, Roots and the Like; Cut Flowers and Ornamental Foliage	17	61	50	49
食用蔬菜、根及块茎	Edible Vegetables and Certain Roots and Tubers	44471	898	31568	97
食用水果及坚果；柑桔属水果或甜瓜的果皮	Edible Fruit and Nuts; Peel of Citrus Fruit or Melons	18788	857	18313	166
咖啡、茶、马黛茶及调味香料	Coffee, Tea, Mate and Spices	14377	2034	8159	2659
谷　物	Cereals		8739		2928
制粉工业产品；麦芽；淀粉、菊粉；面筋	Products of The Milling Industry; Malt; Starches; Inulin; Wheat Gluten	26	8855		3374
含油子仁及果实；杂项子仁及果实；工业用或药用植物；稻草、秸秆及饲料	Oil Seeds and Oleaginous Fruits; Miscellaneous Grains, Seeds and Fruit; Industrial or Medicinal Plants; Straw and Fodder	333	10385	234	14551
虫胶；树胶、树脂及其他植物液、汁	Lac; Gums, Resins And Other Vegetables Saps and Extracts	54	15	90	27
编结用植物材料；其他植物产品	Vegetables Plaiting Materials; Vegetables Products Not Elsewhere Specified or Included	31	21	42	15
动、植物油、脂及其分解产品；精制的食用油脂；动、植物蜡	**Animal or Vegetables Fats and Oils and their Cleavage Products; Prepared Edible Fats; Animal or Vegetables Waxes**	**3003**	**2270**	**3424**	**1196**
动、植物油、脂及其分解产品；精制的食用油脂；动、植物蜡	Animal or Vegetables Fats and Oils and their Cleavage Products; Prepared Edible Fats; Animal or Vegetables Waxes	3003	2270	3424	1196
食品；饮料、酒及醋；烟草、烟草及烟草用品的制品	**Prepared Foodstuffs; Beverages, Spirits And Vinegar; Tobacco and Manufactured Tobacco Substitutes**	**28763**	**4268**	**33317**	**5221**
肉、鱼、甲壳动物、软体动物及其他水生无脊椎动物的制品	Preparations of Meat,of Fish or of Crustaceans,Molluscs or other Aquatic Invertebrates	167	81	285	173
糖及糖食	Sugars and Sugar Confectionery	749	755	602	2865
可可及可可制品	Cocoa and Cocoa Preparations	43	90	70	100

16-3 续表 1 continued 1

单位：万美元 (10 000 USD)

商品分类	Commodity (by HS Section and Division)	2023年 出口 Export	2023年 进口 Import	2022年 出口 Export	2022年 进口 Import
谷物、粮食粉、淀粉或乳的制品；糕饼点心	Preparations of Cereals, Flour, Starch or Milk; Pastry-Cooks' Products	4782	7	4252	9
蔬菜、水果、坚果或植物其他部分的制品	Preparations of Vegetables, Fruit, Nuts or Other Parts of Plants	17720	15	18868	81
杂项食品	Miscellaneous Edible Preparations	1842	318	3580	388
饮料、酒及醋	Beverages, Spirits and Vinegar	850	998	1234	774
食品工业的残渣及废料；配制的动物饲料	Residues and Waste from The Food Industries; Prepared Animal Fodder	1428	2003	733	833
烟草、烟草及烟草代用品的制品	Tobacco and Manufactured Tobacco Substitutes	1180		3694	
矿产品	**Mineral Products**	**469**	**364063**	**2951**	**292428**
盐；硫磺；泥土及石料；石膏料、石灰及水泥	Salt; Sulphur; Earths and Stone; Plastering Materials, Lime and Cement	326	2276	223	1398
矿砂、矿渣及矿灰	Ores, Slag and Ash		192091	1	197692
矿物燃料、矿物油及其蒸馏产品；沥青物质；矿物蜡	Mineral Fuels, Mineral Oils and Products of Their Distillation; Bituminous Substances; Mineral Waxes	143	169696	2727	93338
化学工业及其相关工业的产品	**Products of The Chemical or Industries Allied**	**162833**	**16392**	**186921**	**18281**
无机化学品；贵金属、稀土金属、放射性元素及其同位素的有机及无机化合物	Inorganic Chemicals; Organic or Inorganic Compounds of Precious Metals, of Rare-Earth	4491	394	9987	802
有机化学品	Organic Chemicals	65380	1264	89405	6775
药品	Pharmaceutical Products	36610	1581	35886	1382
肥料	Fertilizers	4796		7083	
鞣料浸膏及染料浸膏；鞣酸及其衍生物；染料、颜料及其他着色料;油漆及清漆;油灰及其他类似胶粘剂；墨水、油墨	Tanning or Dyeing Extracts; Tannins and Their Derivatives; Dyes, Pigments and Other Colouring Matter; Paints and Varnishes; Putty and Other Mastics; Inks	15357	605	14865	548
精油及香膏；芳香料制品及化妆盥洗品	Essential Oils and Retinoid; Perfumery, Cosmetic or Toilet Preparations	960	4142	930	2076
肥皂、有机表面活性剂、洗涤剂、润滑剂、人造蜡、调制蜡、光洁剂、蜡烛及类似品、塑型用膏、“牙科 用蜡”及牙科用熟石膏制剂	Soap,Organic Surface-Active Agents,Washing Preparations, Lubricating Preparations, Artificial Waxes, Prepared Waxes, Polishing or Scouring Preparations, Candles and Similar Articles, Modelling Pastes, "Dental Waxes" And Dental Preparations With a Basis of Plast	1709	597	1853	622
蛋白类物质；改性淀粉；胶；酶	Albuminoidal Substances; Modified Starches; Glues; Enzymes	2163	746	1962	1097
炸药；烟火制品；火柴；引火合金；易燃材料制品	Explosives; Pyrotechnic Products; Matches; Pyrophoric Alloys; Certain Combustible Preparations				
照相及电影用品	Photographic or Cinematographic Goods	70	3464	159	1695
杂项化学产品	Miscellaneous Chemical Products	31297	3598	24790	3282
塑料及其制品；橡胶及其制品	**Plastics and Articles Thereof Rubber and Articles Thereof**	**81360**	**31744**	**91503**	**27957**
塑料及其制品	Plastics and Articles Thereof	72783	29810	82164	23007
橡胶及其制品	Rubber and Articles Thereof	8576	1934	9339	4950

16-3 续表 2 continued 2

单位：万美元 (10 000 USD)

商品分类	Commodity (by HS Section and Division)	2023年		2022年	
		出口 Export	进口 Import	出口 Export	进口 Import
生皮、皮革、毛皮及其制品；鞍具及挽具；旅行用品、手提包及类似容器、动物肠线(蚕胶丝除外)制品	**Raw Hides and Skins, Leather, Fur Skins and Articles Thereof; Saddlery and Harness; Travel Goods, Handbags and Similar Containers; Articles of Animal Gut (Other Than Silk-Worm Gut)**	**12896**	**403**	**21345**	**407**
生皮(毛皮除外)及皮革	Raw Hides and Skins(Other Than Fur Skins) and Leather		366	79	371
皮革制品；鞍具及挽具；旅行用品、手提包及类似容器；动物肠线(蚕胶丝除外)制品	Articles of Leather; Saddlery and Harness; Travel Goods, Handbags and Similar Containers; Articles of Animal Gut (Other Than Silk-Worm Gut)	12830	37	21193	36
毛皮、人造毛皮及其制品	Fur Skins and Artificial Fur; Manufactures Thereof	66		73	
木及木制品；木炭；软木及软木制品；稻草、秸秆、针茅或其他编结材料制品；篮筐及柳条编结品	**Wood and Articles of Wood; Wood Charcoal;Cork and Articles of Cork; Manufactures of Straw, of Esparto or of Other Plaiting Materials; Basket Ware and Wickerwork**	**8802**	**7181**	**9306**	**4853**
木及木制品；木炭	Wood and Articles of Wood; Wood Charcoal	7108	7181	6914	4853
软木及软木制品	Cork and Articles of Cork	7		14	
稻草、秸秆、针茅或其他编结材料制品；篮筐及柳条编结品	Manufactures of Straw, of Esparto or of Other Plaiting Materials; Basket Ware and Wickerwork	1687		2378	
木浆及其他纤维状纤维素浆；回收(废碎)纸或纸板；纸、纸板及其制品	**Pulp of Wood or of Other Fibrous Cellulosic Material; Waste and Scrap of Paper or Paperboard; Paper and Paperboard and Articles Thereof**	**11150**	**53607**	**16353**	**42659**
木浆及其他纤维状纤维素浆；回收(废碎)纸或纸板	Pulp of Wood or of Other Fibrous Cellulosic Material; Waste and Scrap of Paper or Paperboard	55	52409	129	39187
纸及纸板；纸浆、纸或纸板制品	Paper and Paperboard; Articles of Paper Pulp, of Paper or Paperboard	10433	617	14759	3167
书籍、报纸、印刷图画及其他印刷品；手稿、打字稿及设计图纸	Printed Books, Newspapers, Pictures and Other Products of The Printing Industry; Manuscripts, Typescripts and Plans	662	582	1464	305
纺织原料及纺织制品	**Textiles and Textile Articles**	**109786**	**4535**	**118376**	**6225**
蚕丝	Silk	17		18	
羊毛、动物细毛或粗毛；马毛纱线及其机织物	Wool, Fine or Coarse Animal Hair;Horsehair Yarn and Woven Fabric		56	3	126
棉花	Cotton	1518	3239	2537	4544
其他植物纺织纤维；纸纱线及其机织物	Other Vegetables Textile Fibres; Paper Yarn and Woven Fabrics of Paper Yarn	12	3	25	
化学纤维长丝	Man-Made Filaments	3272	256	4369	364
化学纤维短纤	Man-Made Short Fibres	27619	522	10894	509
絮胎、毡呢及无纺织物；特种纱线；线、绳、索、缆及其制品	Wadding, Felt and Nonwoven; Special Yarns; Twine, Cordage, Ropes and Cables and Articles Thereof	5812	71	8201	205
地毯及纺织材料的其他铺地制品	Carpets and Other Textile Floor Coverings	5005	24	4206	32
特种机织物；簇绒织物；花边；装饰毯；装饰带；刺绣品	Special Woven Fabrics; Tufted Textile Fabrics; Lace; Tapestries; Trimmings; Embroidery	1158	51	2187	45
浸渍、涂布、包覆或层压的纺织物；工业用纺织制品	Impregnated, Coated, Covered or Laminated Textile Fabrics; Textile Articles of a Kind Suitable for Industrial Use	1249	42	1342	68

16-3 续表 3 continued 3

单位：万美元 (10 000 USD)

商品分类	Commodity (by HS Section and Division)	2023年		2022年	
		出口 Export	进口 Import	出口 Export	进口 Import
针织物或钩编织物	Knitted or Crocheted Fabrics	886	79	956	109
针织或钩编的服装及衣着附件	Articles of Apparel and Clothing Accessories, Knitted or Crocheted	22472	9	33056	21
非针织或非钩编的服装及衣着附件	Articles of Apparel and Clothing Accessories, not Knitted or Crocheted	26156	42	32686	105
其他纺织制成品；成套物品；旧衣着及旧纺织品；碎织物	Other Made Up Textile Articles; Sets; Worn Clothing And Worn Textile Articles; Rags Articles; Rags	14609	141	17896	98
鞋、帽、伞、杖、鞭及其零件；已加工的羽毛及其制品；人造花；人发制品	**Footwear, Headgear, Umbrellas, Sun Umbrellas, Walking-Sticks, Seat-Sticks, Whips, Riding-Crops and Parts Thereof; Prepared Feathers and Articles Made Therewith; Artificial Flowers; Articles of Human Hair**	**14406**	**91**	**19379**	**52**
鞋靴、护腿和类似品及其零件	Footwear, Gaiters and The Like; Parts of Such Articles	7382	90	10104	42
帽类及其零件	Headgear and Parts Thereof	1296		1575	9
雨伞、阳伞、手杖、鞭子、马鞭及其零件	Umbrellas, Sun Umbrellas, Walking-Sticks, Seat-Sticks, Whips, Riding-Crops And Parts Thereof	282		523	
已加工羽毛、羽绒及其制品；人造花；人发制品	Prepared Feathers and Down and Articles Made of Feathers or of Down; Artificial Flowers; Articles of Human Hair	5445		7177	
石料、石膏、水泥、石棉、云母及类似材料的制品；陶瓷产品；玻璃及其制品	**Articles of Stone, Plaster, Cement, Asbestos, Mica or Similar Materials; Ceramic Products; Glass and Glassware**	**41227**	**966**	**52598**	**1629**
石料、石膏、水泥、石棉、云母及类似材料的制品	Articles of Stone, Plaster, Cement, Asbestos, Mica or Similar Materials	8644	159	14654	124
陶瓷产品	Ceramic Products	11204	145	15246	411
玻璃及其制品	Glass and Glassware	21379	662	22698	1094
天然或养殖珍珠、宝石或半宝石、贵金属、包贵金属及其制品；仿首饰；硬币	**Natural or Cultured Pearls, Precious or Semi-Precious Stones, Precious Metals, Metals Clad With Precious Metal and Stones, Precious Metals, Metals Clad With Precious Metal and Articles Thereof; Imitation Jewellery; Coin**	**2904**	**61**	**7786**	**35**
天然或养殖珍珠、宝石或半宝石、贵金属、包贵金属及其制品；仿首饰；硬币	Natural or Cultured Pearls, Precious or Semi-Precious Stones, Precious Metals, Metals Clad With Precious Metal and Stones, Precious Metals, Metals Clad With Precious Metal and Articles Thereof; Imitation Jewellery; Coin	2904	61	7786	35
贱金属及其制品	**Base Metals and Articles of Base Metal**	**190633**	**12040**	**245747**	**28446**
钢　铁	Iron and Steel	62372	3355	81691	1284
钢铁制品	Articles of Iron or Steel	96832	2785	123651	2843
铜及其制品	Copper and Articles Thereof	2819	2983	3658	21010
镍及其制品	Nickel and Articles Thereof	10	41	43	49
铝及其制品	Aluminium and Articles Thereof	13357	2215	15832	2559
铅及其制品	Lead and Articles Thereof	2			4
锌及其制品	Zinc and Articles Thereof	53	6	72	27
锡及其制品	Tin and Articles Thereof	1	1	1	

16–3 续表 4 continued 4

单位：万美元 (10 000 USD)

商品分类	Commodity (by HS Section and Division)	2023年 出口 Export	2023年 进口 Import	2022年 出口 Export	2022年 进口 Import
其他贱金属、金属陶瓷及其制品	Other Base Metals; Cermets; Articles Thereof	51	235	150	214
贱金属工具、器具、利口器、餐匙、餐叉及其零件	Tools, Implements, Cutlery, Spoons and Forks, of Base Metal; Parts Thereof of Base Metal	6992	212	10164	208
贱金属杂项制品	Miscellaneous Articles of Base Metal	8145	208	10485	249
机器、机械器具、电气设备及其零件；录音机及放声机、电视图像、 声音的录制和重放设备及其零件、附件	**Machinery and Mechanical Appliances; Electrical Equipment; Parts Thereof; Sound Recorders and Reproducers, Television Image and Sound Recorders and Reproducers; and Parts and Accessories of Recorders and Reproducers; and Parts and Accessories of Such Artic**	**607372**	**438067**	**702529**	**515878**
核反应堆、锅炉、机器、机械器具及其零件	Nuclear Reactors, Boilers, Machinery and Mechanical Appliances; Parts Thereof	413801	320004	379772	320965
电机、电气设备及其零件；录音机及放声机、电视图像、声音的录制和重放设备及其零件、附件	Electrical Machinery and Equipment and Parts Thereof; Sound Recorders and Reproducers, Television Image and Sound Recorders and Reproducers, and Parts and Accessories of Such Articles	193571	118063	322756	194913
车辆、航空器、船舶及有关运输设备	**Vehicles, Aircraft, Vessels And Associated Transport Equipment**	**428329**	**6140**	**377455**	**7369**
铁道及电车道机车、车辆及其零件；铁道及电车道轨道固定装置及其零件、附件；各种机械(包括电动机械)交通信号设备	Railway or Tramway Locomotives, Rolling-Stock and Parts Thereof; Railway or Tramway Track Fixtures And Fittings and Parts Thereof; Mechanical(Including Electro-Mechanical) Traffic Signalling Equipment of All Kinds	8642	665	5267	509
车辆及其零件、附件，但铁道及电车道车辆除外	Vehicles Other Than Railway or Tramway Rolling-Stock, and Parts and Accessories Thereof	428202	1299	368757	1071
航空器、航空器及其零件	Aircraft, Spacecraft, and Parts Thereof	135	4089	2017	5691
船舶及浮动结构体	Ships, Boats and Floating Structures	1350	87	1414	98
光学、照相、电影、计量、检验、医疗或外科用仪器及设备、精密仪器及设备；钟表；乐器；上述物品的零件、附件	**Optical, Photographic, Cinematographic, Measuring, Checking, Precision, Medical or Surgical Instruments and Apparatus; Clocks And Watches; Musical Instruments; Parts and Accessories Thereof**	**34507**	**71090**	**37057**	**61385**
光学、照相、计量、检验、医疗或外科用仪器及设备、精密仪器及设备；上述物品的零件、附件	Optical, Photographic, Cinematographic, Measuring, Checking, Precision Medical or Surgical Instruments and Apparatus; Parts and Accessories Thereof	31899	71070	32496	61374
钟表及其零件	Clocks and Watches and Parts Thereof	1279	5	2959	12
乐器及其零件、附件	Musical Instruments; Parts and Accessories of Such Articles	1330	15	1601	
武器、弹药及其零件、附件	**Arms and Ammunition; Parts and Accessories Thereof**			**1**	
武器、弹药及其零件、附件	Arms and Ammunition; Parts and Accessories Thereof			1	
杂项制品	**Miscellaneous Manufactured Articles**	**76362**	**829**	**92672**	**618**
家具；寝具、褥垫、弹簧床垫、软坐垫及类似的填充制品；	Furniture; Bedding, Mattresses, Mattress Supports, Cushions and Similar Stuffed Furnishings	39096	696	40837	570
玩具、游戏品、运动用品及其零件、附件	Toys, Games and Sports Requisites; Parts and Accessories Thereof	30959	17	40609	17
杂项制品	Miscellaneous Manufactured Articles	6307	116	11227	31
艺术品、收藏品及古物	**Works of Art, Collectors' Pieces and Antiques**	**21**	**1**	**37**	**73**
特殊交易品及未分类商品	**Commodities and Transactions not Classified According to Kind**	**46778**	**592**	**30991**	**598**

16-4 按企业性质分海关进出口商品总额(2023年)
International Trade in Goods of Customs by Type of trade(2023)

单位：万美元

指标	Item	合计 Total	国有企业 State-owned Enterprises
进口商品总额	**Total Value of Imports**	**1122634**	**419882**
一般贸易	General Trade	931281	340467
来料加工装配贸易	Processing and Assembling Trade with Sent Materials	13851	
进料加工贸易	Processing Trade with Imported Materials	26649	769
租赁贸易	Leasing Trade	1	
海关特殊监管区域进口设备	Import of Equipment in Special Customs Supervision Area	2734	
海关特殊监管区域物流货物	Logistics Freight of Equipment in Special Customs Supervision Area	91291	76912
投资设备	Investment Goods	581	
保税监管场所进出境货物	Bonded Supervision Entry and Exit Goods	54910	1646
国际无偿援助和捐赠物资	International Aid and Material Donations		
其他贸易	Others	1220	89
出口商品总值	**Total Value of Exports**	**1951475**	**68115**
一般贸易	General Trade	1809304	53842
国际无偿援助和捐赠物资	International Aid and Material Donations	175	151
来料加工装配贸易	Processing and Assembling Trade with Sent Materials	13292	
进料加工贸易	Processing Trade with Imported Materials	71817	11928
对外承包工程出口货物	Export of Contracted projects	12700	2123
保税监管场所进出境货物	Bonded Supervision Entry and Exit Goods	2125	
海关特殊监管区域物流货物	Logistics Freight of Equipment in Special Customs Supervision Area	33191	5
其他贸易	Others	5594	67

(10 000 USD)

外商投资企业 Foreign Funded Enterprises				集体企业 Collective-owned Enterprises	其他 Others
小计 Total	中外合作 Cooperation Enterprises	中外合资 Joint-venture Enterprises	外商独资 Enterprises with Sole Fund		
101303	**19004**		**82299**	**44592**	**226**
51305	9267		42038	44592	
13428			13428		
18632		1468	17165		
1			1		
37		37			
9534			9534		
581		581			
7452		7452			
334		237	97		
513845	**932**	**98309**	**414603**	**32941**	**2788**
436125	932	87367	347825	32800	
12585		17	12568		
39075		10358	28717		
				141	
760		481	279		
23354			23354		
1946		87	1859		

16–5 历年海关进出口总额
Total Imports and Exports of Customs in Major Years

单位：万美元 (10 000 USD)

年份 Year	进出口总额 Total Value of Imports and Exports	进口总额 Total Value of Imports	出口总额 Total Value of Exports
1993	27446	21371	6075
1994	41746	23579	18167
1995	66587	29812	36775
1996	91347	48193	43154
1997	104230	52862	51368
1998	79943	45096	34847
1999	96125	60199	35926
2000	143935	86827	57108
2001	150143	90746	59397
2002	149264	79755	69509
2003	201554	117980	83545
2004	304678	167373	137305
2005	376213	198370	177843
2006	438930	194981	243949
2007	621804	278277	343527
2008	802699	342979	459720
2009	565704	260998	304706
2010	743776	338888	404888
2011	1041422	436966	604456
2012	913286	341844	571442
2013	957442	409126	548316
2014	1048867	442950	605917
2015	911424	311763	599661
2016	1086259	352229	734030
2017	1130449	379887	750562
2018	1318209	463119	855090
2019	1630123	695064	935059
2020	1998749	909323	1089426
2021	3003034	1184182	1818852
2022	3270583	1157632	2112951
2023	3074109	1122634	1951475

16–6 利用外资情况
Utilization of Foreign Capital

单位：万美元 (10 000 USD)

指标	Item	2019年	2020年	2021年	2022年	2023年
新批外商投资企业个数(个)	**Newly Established Foreign Investment Enterprises(unit)**	**228**	**203**	**330**	**251**	**267**
外商直接投资企业个数	Foreign Direct Investments Enterprises	228	203	330	251	267
合同外资金额	**Total Amount of Contracted Foreign Capita**	**683441**	**585244**	**968530**	**784185**	**587039**
外商直接投资	Foreign Direct Investments	683441	585244	968530	784185	587039
实际使用外资	**Total Amount of Foreign Investment Actually Utilized**	**224249**	**192456**	**265840**	**313738**	**247773**
外商直接投资	Foreign Direct Investments	224249	192456	265840	313738	247773

16–7 对外经济技术合作
Economic Cooperation with Foreign Countries or Regions

单位：万美元 (10 000 USD)

指标	Item	2019年	2020年	2021年	2022年	2023年
对外承包和劳务合作合同金额	**Contracted Value of Contracted Projects and Labour Services**	**573114**	**439945**	**660562**	**488850**	**380222**
对外承包	Contracted Projects	573114	439945	660562	488850	380222
对外承包和劳务合作营业额	**Value of Turnover of Contracted Projects and Labour Services**	**408820**	**427206**	**410022**	**409203**	**428553**
对外承包	Contracted Projects	408820	427206	410022	409203	428553
外派劳务人数(人)	**Dispatched Workers(person)**	**8047**	**11996**	**8608**	**4489**	**7302**
境外投资企业数(个)	**Number of Overseas Investment Enterprises(unit)**	**79**	**77**	**60**	**45**	**78**
中方实际投资额	**China Actual Investment**	**110798**	**191321**	**174208**	**174978**	**223226**

16-8 旅游住宿单位接待入境游客
Received Inbound Tourists by Hotels

指标	Item	2019年	2020年	2021年	2022年	2023年
入境游客人数(人次)	**Number of Inbound Tourists(person-time)**	**456585**	**108524**			
外国人	Foreigners	285071	90926			
#日本	Japan	28653	2674			
菲律宾	Philippines	3500	1446			
新加坡	Singapore	18092	2729			
韩国	Republic of Korea	41390	5536			
美国	United States	29556	20623			
加拿大	Canada	7859	1836			
英国	United Kingdom	12910	7623			
德国	Germany	19384	2557			
法国	France	8893	1555			
意大利	Italy	6069	583			
瑞士	Switzerland	1348	156			
澳大利亚	Australia	12422	3783			
新西兰	New Zealand	2113	815			
港澳和台湾同胞	Chinese Compatriots from Hong Kong Macao and Taiwan Province	171514	17700			
#台湾同胞	Chinese Compatriots from Taiwan Province	87086	4355			
入境游客人天数(人天)	**Number of Days on Inbound Tourists(person-day)**	**1276852**	**265436**			
外国人	Foreigners	806837	187665			
港澳和台湾同胞	Chinese Compatriots from Hong Kong Macao and Taiwan Province	959122	77773			
#台湾同胞	Chinese Compatriots from Taiwan Province	317730	45873			
旅游外汇收入(亿美元)	**Foreign Exchange Income of Tourism(100 million USD)**	**2.75**	**0.33**			
#商品性收入	Commercial Income	0.7	0.08			
附:平均每天来济国际旅游人数(人次)	Number of Tourists Per Day(person-time)	1251	296.51			
星级宾馆客房出租率(%)	Star Hotel Room Rate(%)	62.0	47.51	50.57	42.69	58.44

注：1.2018年起接待入境游客包含了过夜游客和一日游游客。
2.根据省文化和旅游厅统一安排，2021年起暂停测算、公布和使用入境旅游数据。

Notes:1.Starting in 2018, Inbound Tourists Include Overnight Visitors and Day-trippers.
2.According to the unified arrangement of the Provincial Department of Culture and Tourism, the measurement, publication and use of inbound tourism data have been suspended since 2021.

16-9 济南与国外结成友好城市一览表(2023年末)
Friendship Cities of Jinan(End of 2023)

国别	Country	城市	City	缔结日期 Day
日本	Japan	和歌山市(和歌山县首府)	Wakayama	1983.01.14
英国	United Kingdom	考文垂市(英国汽车工业故乡，制造业中心之一)	Coventry	1983.10.03
美国	United States	萨克拉门托市(加利福尼亚州首府)	Sacramento	1985.05.29
日本	Japan	山口市(山口县首府)	Yamaguchi	1985.09.20
加拿大	Canada	里贾纳市(萨斯喀彻温省省会)	Regina	1987.08.10
巴布亚新几内亚	Papua New Guinea	莫尔斯比港(巴布亚新几内亚首都)	Port Moresby	1988.09.28
韩国	Republic of Korea	水原市(京畿道首府)	Suwon Special	1993.10.27
俄罗斯	Russia	下诺夫哥罗德市(下诺夫哥罗德州首府)	Nizhny novgorod	1994.09.25
芬兰	Finland	万达市(欧洲机场城市、芬兰第四大城市)	Vantaa	2001.08.27
法国	France	雷恩市(布列塔尼大区首府)	Rennes	2002.07.17
澳大利亚	Australia	郡德勒普市(西澳洲新兴教育科技中心)	Joondalup	2004.09.04
德国	Germany	奥格斯堡市(施瓦本地区首府)	Augsburg	2004.10.10
乌克兰	Ukraine	哈尔科夫市(哈尔科夫州首府)	Kharkiv	2007.05.23
以色列	Israel	卡法萨巴市(沙龙地区中心城市)	Kfar Saba	2009.05.11
白俄罗斯	Belarus	维捷布斯克市(维捷布斯克州首府)	Vitebsk	2009.04.10
佛得角	Cape Verde	普拉亚市(佛得角首都)	Praia	2009.10.22
巴西	Brazil	波多韦柳市(朗多尼亚州首府)	Porto Velho	2011.10.13
土耳其	Türkiye	马尔马里斯市(地中海沿岸港口城市和旅游胜地)	Marmaris	2011.10.21
印度尼西亚	Indonesia	徐图利祖市(东爪哇省泗水市机场城市、新兴经济城市)	Sidoarjo	2012.09.21
保加利亚	Bulgaria	卡赞勒格市(保加利亚玫瑰精油生产中心)	Kazanlak	2013.08.29
墨西哥	Mexico	萨博潘市(哈利斯科州经济首府)	Zapopan	2014.04.18
意大利	Italy	奇维塔韦基亚市(欧洲第三大客运港)	Civitavecchia	2016.06.20
印度	India	那格浦尔市(印度地理中心城市、马哈拉施特拉邦第二首府)	Nagpur	2017.12.08
埃塞俄比亚	Ethiopia	阿尔巴门奇市(格穆戈法省首府、泉水之城)	Arba Minch	2018.09.29
斯洛文尼亚	Slovenia	马里博尔(斯洛文尼亚第二大城市、欧洲足球强市)	Maribor	2019.09.26
		区县级 District and County		
日本	Japan	柳井市(日本山口县东南部城市)	Yanai	2004.05.14
白俄罗斯	Belarus	明斯克市苏维埃区(白俄罗斯首都明斯克市历史最悠久的区之一)	Soviet region of Minsk	2012.08.03
罗马尼亚	Romania	布加勒斯特市第四区(罗马尼亚重要的政治、经济和文化中心)	Sector 4 of Bucharest	2013.04.16
格鲁吉亚	Georgia	库塔伊西市(格鲁吉亚西部历史名城和第二大工业城市)	Kutaisi	2016.05.20

海关进出口商品总额 指实际进出我国关境的货物总金额。包括对外贸易实际进出口货物，来料加工装配进出口货物，国家间、联合国及国际组织无偿援助物资和赠送品，华侨、港澳台同胞和外籍华人捐赠品，租赁期满归承租人所有的租赁货物，进料加工进出口货物，边境地方贸易及边境地区小额贸易进出口货物，中外合资企业、中外合作经营企业、外商独资经营企业进出口货物和公用物品，到、离岸价格在规定限额以上的进出口货样和广告品(无商业价值、无使用价值和免费提供出口的除外)，从保税仓库提取在中国境内销售的进口货物，以及其他进出口货物。该指标可以观察一个国家在货物贸易方面的总规模。我国规定出口货物按离岸价格统计，进口货物按到岸价格统计。

外商投资 是指国外及港澳台地区的法人和自然人在中国大陆地区以现金、实物、无形资产、股权等方式进行投资。其中，外商直接投资是指国外及港澳台地区投资者在非上市公司中的全部投资及在单个外国投资者所占股权比例不低于10%的上市公司中的投资。

对外承包工程 根据《对外承包工程管理条例》，对外承包工程是指中国的企业或者其他单位承包境外建设工程项目的活动。

对外劳务合作 指组织劳务人员赴其他国家或地区为国外的企业或机构工作的经营性活动。

入境游客 指报告期内来中国（大陆）观光、度假、探亲访友、就医疗养、购物、参加会议或从事经济、文化、体育、宗教活动的外国人、港澳台同胞等游客（即入境旅游人数）。统计时，入境游客按每入境一次统计1人次。入境游客包括入境过夜游客和入境一日游游客。

国际旅游收入 指入境游客在中国（大陆）境内旅行、游览过程中用于交通、参观游览、住宿、餐饮、购物、娱乐等全部花费。

Explanatory Notes on Main Statistical Indicators

Import and Export of Goods refer to the value of commodities actually imported or exported across the border of China. They include the actual imports and exports through foreign trade, imported and exported goods under the processing and assembling trades and materials, supplies and gifts as aid given gratis between governments and by the United Nations and other international organizations, and contributions donated by overseas Chinese, compatriots in Hong Kong and Macao and Chinese with foreign citizenship, leasing commodities owned by tenant at the expiration of leasing period, the imported and exported commodities processed with imported materials, commodities trading in border areas, the imported and exported commodities and articles for public use of the Sino-foreign joint ventures, cooperative enterprises and ventures with sole foreign investment. Also included are import or export of samples and advertising goods for which CIF or FOB value are beyond the permitted ceiling (excluding goods of no trading or use value and free commodities for export), imported goods sold in China from bonded warehouses and other imported or exported goods. The indicator of the total imports and exports at customs can be used to observe the total size of external trade in a country. In accordance with the stipulation of the Chinese government, exports are calculated at FOB, while imports are calculated at CIF.

Foreign Investment refers to investment in China by legal or natural persons of foreign countries and of Hong Kong, Macao and Taiwan, in the form of cash、physical assets、intangible assets and equity and others. Foreign direct investment refers to investment by investors from foreign countries and from Hong Kong, Macao and Taiwan in a non-listed company, or the investment of over 10 percent or more in a listed company.

Overseas Contracted Projects refer to activities of contracting overseas construction projects by Chinese enterprises or any other units, which are stipulated in the Regulations on Administration of Foreign Contracted Project.

Overseas Labour Services refer to operational activities of organizing labour force to go abroad providing services to foreign enterprises or agencies.

Overseas Visitor Arrivals refer to the number of tourists of foreigners, Chinese compatriots from Hong Kong, Macao and Taiwan who come to China (mainland) within the reference period for sight-seeing, vacation, visiting relatives, medical treatment, shopping, attending conference, or to engage in economic, cultural, sports and religious activities (namely the number of overseas visitor arrivals). In compiling statistics, each arrival is counted as one person-time. Overseas visitor arrivals includes inbound overnight tourists and one-day tourists.

Foreign Exchange Earnings from International Tourism refer to the total expenditure of overseas visitors during their stay in the mainland of China on transportation, sighting, accommodation, food, shopping and entertainment.

17

科技

SCIENCE AND TECHNOLOGY

17-1 科技综合情况
Basic Statistics on Scientific and Technological Activities

指标	Item	单位 Unit	2018年	2019年	2020年	2021年	2022年
R&D活动单位	R&D Activity Units	个(Unit)	821	1089	1209	1455	1828
R&D人员全时当量	Full-time Equivalent of R&D Personnel	人年(man-years)	59995	52153	53677.5	61894.1	80397.4
R&D经费支出	Expenditure on R&D	万元(10 000 yuan)	2085980.1	2255264.6	2654629.1	3067048.7	3468393.7
#基础研究	Basic Research	万元(10 000 yuan)	144105.1	173425.2	184501.6	267574.4	299283.0
#应用研究	Applied Research	万元(10 000 yuan)	246533.3	304343.7	414305.5	386592.1	444041.3
#试验发展	Experimental Development	万元(10 000 yuan)	1695281.7	1777495.7	2055822.1	2412882.4	2725069.3
#日常性支出	Daily Expenditure	万元(10 000 yuan)	1843653.3	2010202.7	2373932.1	2788617.4	3194505.9
人员劳务费	Staff Service Fee	万元(10 000 yuan)	763134.5	695510.6	864042.4	975737.2	1354717.2
#资产性支出	Capital Expenditure	万元(10 000 yuan)	242326.8	233015.5	277874.7	278431.3	273887.7
仪器设备	Instrument and Equipment	万元(10 000 yuan)	236760.3	218192.1	263337.9	229617.0	230700.4
R&D经费外部支出	External Expenditure on R&D	万元(10 000 yuan)	79731.3	107132.1	218149.6	269409.6	279935.5

注：2018年数据为行政区划调整前口径，以下各表同。
Note: Data used in 2018 is the statistical scale before the adjustment of administrative division (the same below).

17-2 科技投入情况(2022年)
Basic Statistics on Science and Technology Investment(2022)

指标	Item	单位 Unit	合计 Total	科研机构 Research Institutions	高等院校 Higher Education Institutions	规模以上工业 Industrial Enterprises Above Designated Size	其他 Others
有R&D活动单位数	**Number of Enterprises with R&D Activities**	**个(unit)**	**1828**	**85**	**74**	**1224**	**445**
R&D人员	**R&D Personnel**	**人(person)**	**123802**	**8283**	**32723**	**51599**	**31197**
#研究人员	Research Personnel	人(person)	65667	5509	27510	17850	14798
R&D人员折合全时当量	**Full-time Equivalent of R&D Personnel**	**人年(man-years)**	**80397**	**7258**	**16802**	**35658**	**20679**
基础研究	Basic Research	人年(man-years)	11817	1568	9708.9	184	357
应用研究	Applied Research	人年(man-years)	12463	2543	6417.5	1367	2135
试验发展	Experimental Development	人年(man-years)	56117	3147	676	34107	18187
R&D经费支出	**Expenditure on R&D**	**万元(10 000 yuan)**	**3468394**	**342496**	**479656.6**	**1858188**	**788053**
基础研究	Basic Research	万元(10 000 yuan)	299283	59018	201857.6	4852	33556
应用研究	Applied Research	万元(10 000 yuan)	444041	85048	251585.5	56756	50652
试验发展	Experimental Development	万元(10 000 yuan)	2725069	198431	26213.4	1796580	703845
日常性支出	**Routine Expenses**	**万元(10 000 yuan)**	**3194506**	**270846**	**391260**	**1770484**	**761916**
#人员劳务费	Labor Cost	万元(10 000 yuan)	1354717	146506	101958.1	679291	426962
资产性支出	**Assets Expenditure**	**万元(10 000 yuan)**	**273888**	**71650**	**88396.6**	**87704**	**26137**
#仪器和设备	Instrument and Equipment	万元(10 000 yuan)	230700	65808	58605.1	84892	21396

17–3 规模以上工业企业科技活动情况(2022年)

Basic Statistics on Science and Technology Activities of Industrial Enterprises Above Designated Size(2022)

单位:个 (unit)

指标	Item	企业数 Number of Enterprises	#有R&D活动单位数 Number of Enterprises with R&D Activities	有研发机构单位数 Number of R&D Institutions
总计	**Total**	**2667**	**1224**	**597**
按登记注册类型分	**By Status of Registration**			
内资企业	Domestic Invested Enterprises	2510	1149	560
国有企业	State-owned Enterprises	34	9	4
集体企业	Collective-owned Enterprises	7	2	2
股份合作企业	Cooperative Enterprises	4	1	1
联营企业	Joint Ownership Enterprises	2	1	
有限责任公司	Limited Liability Corporations	691	348	183
国有独资公司	State Sole-proprietorship Corporations	43	23	14
其他有限责任公司	Other Limited Liability Corporations	648	325	169
股份有限公司	Share-holding Corporations Ltd.	93	79	41
私营企业	Private Enterprises	1679	709	329
私营独资企业	Private Sole-proprietorship Enterprises	53	4	1
私营合伙企业	Private Partnership Enterprises	7	2	1
私营有限责任公司	Private Limited Liability Corporations	1533	642	286
私营股份有限公司	Private Share-holding Corporations Ltd.	86	61	41
其他企业	Other Enterprises			
港、澳、台商投资企业	Enterprises with Funds from Hong Kong,Macao and Taiwan	66	28	15
合资经营企业	Joint-venture Enterprises	35	14	8
合作经营企业	Cooperative Enterprises			
独资经营企业	Sole-proprietorship Enterprises	27	11	7
投资股份有限公司	Share-holding Corporations Ltd.	2	1	
其他港澳台投资企业	Other Enterprises with Funds from Hong Kong, Macao and Taiwan	2	2	
外商投资企业	Foreign Funded Enterprises	91	47	22
中外合资经营企业	Joint-venture Enterprises	40	22	10
中外合作经营企业	Cooperative Enterprises	2		
外资企业	Sole-proprietorship Enterprises	46	22	10
外商投资股份有限公司	Share-holding Corporations Ltd. with Foreign Investment	3	3	2
其他外商投资企业	Other Foreign Funded Enterprises			
按工业行业大类分	**By Sector**			
煤炭开采和洗选业	Mining and Washing of Coal	3	1	1
石油和天然气开采业	Extraction of Petroleum and Natural Gas	3		
黑色金属矿采选业	Mining and Processing of Ferrous Metal Ores	13	2	2
有色金属矿采选业	Mining and Processing of Non-Ferrous Metal Ores			
非金属矿采选业	Mining and Processing of Nonmetal Ores	7		1
开采专业及辅助性活动	Professional and Support Activities for Mining			

17-3 续表 continued

单位:个 (unit)

指标	Item	企业数 Number of Enterprises	#有R&D活动单位数 Number of Enterprises with R&D Activities	有研发机构单位数 Number of R&D Institutions
其他采矿业	Mining of Other Ores			
农副食品加工业	Processing of Food from Agricultural Products	100	23	10
食品制造业	Manufacture of Foods	79	34	24
酒、饮料和精制茶制造业	Manufacture of Wine, Drinks and Refined Tea	20	7	3
烟草制品业	Manufacture of Tobacco	2	2	1
纺织业	Manufacture of Textile	56	18	6
纺织服装、服饰业	Manufacture of Textile Wearing Apparel and Finery	20	5	3
皮革、毛皮、羽毛及其制品和制鞋业	Manufacture of Leather, Fur, Feather & Its Products and Footwear	3	1	
木材加工和木、竹、藤、棕、草制品业	Processing of Timbers, Manufacture of Wood,Bamboo, Rattan, Palm, and Straw Products	11	2	
家具制造业	Manufacture of Furniture	16	5	
造纸和纸制品业	Manufacture of Paper and Paper Products	45	12	6
印刷和记录媒介复制业	Printing, Reproduction of Recording Media	42	17	5
文教、工美、体育和娱乐用品制造业	Manufacture of Culture, Education,Arts and crafts, Sport and Entertainment Goods	28	12	5
石油、煤炭及其他燃料加工业	Processing of Petroleum, Coal and Other Fuels	15	7	4
化学原料和化学制品制造业	Manufacture of Chemical Raw Material and Chemical Products	128	62	32
医药制造业	Manufacture of Medicines	77	55	35
化学纤维制造业	Manufacture of Chemical Fiber	9	3	3
橡胶和塑料制品业	Manufacture of Rubber and Plastic	71	38	17
非金属矿物制品业	Manufacture of Non-metallic Mineral Products	335	84	34
黑色金属冶炼和压延加工业	Manufacture and Processing of Ferrous Metals	47	17	12
有色金属冶炼和压延加工业	Manufacture & Processing of Non-ferrous Metals	40	14	8
金属制品业	Manufacture of Metal Products	303	111	61
通用设备制造业	Manufacture of General Purpose Machinery	323	201	95
专用设备制造业	Manufacture of Special Purpose Machinery	253	170	82
汽车制造业	Manufacture of Automotive	127	56	29
铁路、船舶、航空航天和其他运输设备制造业	Manufacture of Railroad,Marine,Aerospace and Other Transportation Equipment	24	16	6
电气机械和器材制造业	Manufacture of Electrical Machinery & Equipment	150	92	34
计算机、通信和其他电子设备制造业	Manufacture of Computer, Communications and Other Electronic Equipment	91	67	34
仪器仪表制造业	Manufacture of Measuring Instrument	81	68	35
其他制造业	Other Manufacture	5	2	1
废弃资源综合利用业	Comprehensive Utilization of Waste	12	2	1
金属制品、机械和设备修理业	Metal Products, Machinery and Equipment Repair Industry	9	5	4
电力、热力生产和供应业	Production and Supply of Electric Power and Heat Power	64	8	2
燃气生产和供应业	Production and Supply of Gas	31	3	1
水的生产和供应业	Production and Supply of Water	24	2	

17–4 规模以上工业企业技术改造及引进吸收(2022年)
Innovation and Resorb of Industrial Enterprises Above Designated Size(2022)

单位：万元 (10 000 yuan)

指标	Item	技术改造经费支出 Expenditure for Technical Renovation	引进国外技术经费支出 Expenditure for Acquisition of Foreign Technology	引进技术的消化吸收经费支出 Expenditure for Assimilation of Technology	购买国内技术经费支出 Expenditure for Purchase of Domestic Technology
总计	**Total**	**618075**	**33868**	**6**	**104481**
按登记注册类型分	**By Status of Registration**				
内资企业	Domestic Invested Enterprises	432049	11285	6	35118
国有企业	State-owned Enterprises	2453			
集体企业	Collective-owned Enterprises	165			
股份合作企业	Cooperative Enterprises				
联营企业	Joint Ownership Enterprises				
有限责任公司	Limited Liability Corporations	223520	10135		2869
国有独资公司	State Sole-proprietorship Corporations	119193			560
其他有限责任公司	Other Limited Liability Corporations	104328	10135		2309
股份有限公司	Share-holding Corporations Ltd.	132465	222	6	248
私营企业	Private Enterprises	73445	928		32002
私营独资企业	Private Sole-proprietorship Enterprises				
私营合伙企业	Private Partnership Enterprises				
私营有限责任公司	Private Limited Liability Corporations	46128	928		31968
私营股份有限公司	Private Share-holding Corporations Ltd.	27318			34
其他企业	Other Enterprises				
港、澳、台商投资企业	Enterprises with Funds from Hong Kong, Macao and Taiwan	72412	13053		67838
合资经营企业	Joint-venture Enterprises	71680	12112		53324
合作经营企业	Cooperative Enterprises				
独资经营企业	Sole-proprietorship Enterprises	732	940		14514
投资股份有限公司	Share-holding Corporations Ltd.				
其他港澳台投资企业	Other Enterprises with Funds from Hong Kong,Macao and Taiwan				
外商投资企业	Foreign Funded Enterprises	113615	9530		1525
中外合资经营企业	Joint-venture Enterprises	111572	9012		
中外合作经营企业	Cooperative Enterprises				
外资企业	Sole-proprietorship Enterprises	2043	518		1525
外商投资股份有限公司	Share-holding Corporations Ltd. with Foreign Investment				
其他外商投资企业	Other Foreign Funded Enterprises				
按工业行业大类分	**By Sector**				
煤炭开采和洗选业	Mining and Washing of Coal				
石油和天然气开采业	Extraction of Petroleum and Natural Gas				
黑色金属矿采选业	Mining and Processing of Ferrous Metal Ores				
有色金属矿采选业	Mining and Processing of Non-Ferrous Metal Ores				
非金属矿采选业	Mining and Processing of Nonmetal Ores				
开采专业及辅助性活动	Professional and Support Activities for Mining				

17-4 续表 continued

单位：万元 (10 000 yuan)

指标	Item	技术改造经费支出 Expenditure for Technical Renovation	引进国外技术经费支出 Expenditure for Acquisition of Foreign Technology	引进技术的消化吸收经费支出 Expenditure for Assimilation of Technology	购买国内技术经费支出 Expenditure for Purchase of Domestic Technology
其他采矿业	Mining of Other Ores				
农副食品加工业	Processing of Food from Agricultural Products	633			560
食品制造业	Manufacture of Foods	5952			
酒、饮料和精制茶制造业	Manufacture of Wine, Drinks and Refined Tea	210			210
烟草制品业	Manufacture of Tobacco	118299			
纺织业	Manufacture of Textile	1573			
纺织服装、服饰业	Manufacture of Textile Wearing Apparel and Finery				
皮革、毛皮、羽毛及其制品和制鞋业	Manufacture of Leather, Fur, Feather & Its Products and Footwear				
木材加工和木、竹、藤、棕、草制品业	Processing of Timbers, Manufacture of Wood,Bamboo, Rattan, Palm, and Straw Products				
家具制造业	Manufacture of Furniture				
造纸和纸制品业	Manufacture of Paper and Paper Products	1830	915		662
印刷和记录媒介复制业	Printing, Reproduction of Recording Media	2716			
文教、工美、体育和娱乐用品制造业	Manufacture of Culture, Education,Arts and crafts, Sport and Entertainment Goods				
石油、煤炭及其他燃料加工业	Processing of Petroleum, Coal and Other Fuels	37681			
化学原料和化学制品制造业	Manufacture of Chemical Raw Material and Chemical Products	35576			
医药制造业	Manufacture of Medicines	39506	12125		34559
化学纤维制造业	Manufacture of Chemical Fiber				
橡胶和塑料制品业	Manufacture of Rubber and Plastic	1719			
非金属矿物制品业	Manufacture of Non-metallic Mineral Products	19069			560
黑色金属冶炼和压延加工业	Manufacture and Processing of Ferrous Metals	112094			
有色金属冶炼和压延加工业	Manufacture & Processing of Non-ferrous Metals	1370			
金属制品业	Manufacture of Metal Products	122970			422
通用设备制造业	Manufacture of General Purpose Machinery	24654	740	6	1580
专用设备制造业	Manufacture of Special Purpose Machinery	2037			240
汽车制造业	Manufacture of Automotive	16737	940		14589
铁路、船舶、航空航天和其他运输设备制造业	Manufacture of Railroad,Marine,Aerospace and Other Transportation Equipment	5219	9012		1
电气机械和器材制造业	Manufacture of Electrical Machinery & Equipment	8288			3208
计算机、通信和其他电子设备制造业	Manufacture of Computer, Communications and Other Electronic Equipment	2149	10135		1205
仪器仪表制造业	Manufacture of Measuring Instrument	4806			285
其他制造业	Other Manufacture	25			
废弃资源综合利用业	Comprehensive Utilization of Waste				
金属制品、机械和设备修理业	Metal Products, Machinery and Equipment Repair Industry	46831			46401
电力、热力生产和供应业	Production and Supply of Electric Power and Heat Power	6133			
燃气生产和供应业	Production and Supply of Gas				
水的生产和供应业	Production and Supply of Water				

17–5 规模以上工业企业技术资源(2022年)
Technical Resources of Industrial Enterprises Above Designated Size(2022)

指标	Item	R&D经费支出(万元) Expenditure on R&D (10 000 yuan)	新产品销售收入(万元) Sales Revenue of New Products (10 000 yuan)	研究与试验发展(R&D)人员(人) R&D Personnel (person)	R&D人员折合全时当量(人年) Full-time Equivalent of R&D Personnel (man-years)
总计	**Total**	**1858188**	**29815888**	**51599**	**35658**
按登记注册类型分	**By Status of Registration**				
内资企业	Domestic Invested Enterprises	1653366	23805820	44661	31032
国有企业	State-owned Enterprises	61040	160252	1271	553
集体企业	Collective-owned Enterprises	1923	12516	39	28
股份合作企业	Cooperative Enterprises	33759	942553	467	370
联营企业	Joint Ownership Enterprises	4732	80896	86	77
有限责任公司	Limited Liability Corporations	590463	8668718	18299	12156
国有独资公司	State Sole-proprietorship Corporations	85712	1532953	1993	1042
其他有限责任公司	Other Limited Liability Corporations	504751	7135766	16306	11113
股份有限公司	Share-holding Corporations Ltd.	373071	8256647	8781	6769
私营企业	Private Enterprises	588379	5684238	15718	11078
私营独资企业	Private Sole-proprietorship Enterprises	3273	16012	32	24
私营合伙企业	Private Partnership Enterprises	785	6200	22	6
私营有限责任公司	Private Limited Liability Corporations	540104	4934660	14088	10056
私营股份有限公司	Private Share-holding Corporations Ltd.	44217	727366	1576	993
其他企业	Other Enterprises				
港、澳、台商投资企业	Enterprises with Funds from Hong Kong, Macao and Taiwan	133436	4880282	4089	2842
合资经营企业	Joint-venture Enterprises	68629	848805	1525	1223
合作经营企业	Cooperative Enterprises				
独资经营企业	Sole-proprietorship Enterprises	63612	1825776	2086	1284
投资股份有限公司	Share-holding Corporations Ltd.	573	2192004	463	324
其他港澳台投资企业	Other Enterprises with Funds from Hong Kong, Macao and Taiwan	622	13697	15	11
外商投资企业	Foreign Funded Enterprises	71387	1129787	2849	1784
中外合资经营企业	Joint-venture Enterprises	39571	670588	1166	854
中外合作经营企业	Cooperative Enterprises				
外资企业	Sole-proprietorship Enterprises	27148	176651	1569	858
外商投资股份有限公司	Share-holding Corporations Ltd. with Foreign Investment	4668	282548	114	73
其他外商投资企业	Other Foreign Funded Enterprises				
按工业行业大类分	**By Sector**				
煤炭开采和洗选业	Mining and Washing of Coal	4149		13	8
石油和天然气开采业	Extraction of Petroleum and Natural Gas				
黑色金属矿采选业	Mining and Processing of Ferrous Metal Ores	28909	205745	75	58
有色金属矿采选业	Mining and Processing of Non-Ferrous Metal Ores				
非金属矿采选业	Mining and Processing of Nonmetal Ores		20784		
开采专业及辅助性活动	Professional and Support Activities for Mining				

17-5 续表 continued

指标	Item	R&D经费支出(万元) Expenditure on R&D (10 000 yuan)	新产品销售收入(万元) Sales Revenue of New Products (10 000 yuan)	研究与试验发展(R&D)人员(人) R&D Personnel (person)	R&D人员折合全时当量(人年) Full-time Equivalent of R&D Personnel (man-years)
其他采矿业	Mining of Other Ores				
农副食品加工业	Processing of Food from Agricultural Products	6317	98407	288	189
食品制造业	Manufacture of Foods	14201	338530	1231	708
酒、饮料和精制茶制造业	Manufacture of Wine, Drinks and Refined Tea	3597	41539	170	65
烟草制品业	Manufacture of Tobacco	22576	873175	706	310
纺织业	Manufacture of Textile	6552	193352	422	329
纺织服装、服饰业	Manufacture of Textile Wearing Apparel and Finery	2575	53645	241	131
皮革、毛皮、羽毛及其制品和制鞋业	Manufacture of Leather, Fur, Feather & Its Products and Footwear	824	8939	24	15
木材加工和木、竹、藤、棕、草制品业	Processing of Timbers, Manufacture of Wood,Bamboo, Rattan, Palm, and Straw Products	1910	24888	37	26
家具制造业	Manufacture of Furniture	1238	4372	31	21
造纸和纸制品业	Manufacture of Paper and Paper Products	4151	135310	288	172
印刷和记录媒介复制业	Printing, Reproduction of Recording Media	12573	160304	639	399
文教、工美、体育和娱乐用品制造业	Manufacture of Culture, Education,Arts and crafts, Sport and Entertainment Goods	2131	45773	175	128
石油、煤炭及其他燃料加工业	Processing of Petroleum, Coal and Other Fuels	8932	567283	238	183
化学原料和化学制品制造业	Manufacture of Chemical Raw Material and Chemical Products	69907	1410325	1929	1331
医药制造业	Manufacture of Medicines	346372	2473479	5075	3567
化学纤维制造业	Manufacture of Chemical Fiber	9939	27035	105	64
橡胶和塑料制品业	Manufacture of Rubber and Plastic	17871	124493	497	314
非金属矿物制品业	Manufacture of Non-metallic Mineral Products	34809	1035471	1548	1041
黑色金属冶炼和压延加工业	Manufacture and Processing of Ferrous Metals	38600	3126491	4724	3396
有色金属冶炼和压延加工业	Manufacture & Processing of Non-ferrous Metals	5007	71640	347	251
金属制品业	Manufacture of Metal Products	86297	1603794	3193	2319
通用设备制造业	Manufacture of General Purpose Machinery	206606	1625376	6656	4782
专用设备制造业	Manufacture of Special Purpose Machinery	136249	1781075	3910	2775
汽车制造业	Manufacture of Automotive	117496	4331378	4202	2734
铁路、船舶、航空航天和其他运输设备制造业	Manufacture of Railroad,Marine,Aerospace and Other Transportation Equipment	25668	328983	771	602
电气机械和器材制造业	Manufacture of Electrical Machinery & Equipment	148953	2309288	3215	2111
计算机、通信和其他电子设备制造业	Manufacture of Computer, Communications and Other Electronic Equipment	362696	6153136	6463	4843
仪器仪表制造业	Manufacture of Measuring Instrument	55920	417044	2352	1715
其他制造业	Other Manufacture	3548	58638	66	51
废弃资源综合利用业	Comprehensive Utilization of Waste	2715	73282	80	40
金属制品、机械和设备修理业	Metal Products, Machinery and Equipment Repair Industry	8316	75286	412	341
电力、热力生产和供应业	Production and Supply of Electric Power and Heat Power	59563	11486	1397	609
燃气生产和供应业	Production and Supply of Gas	253		42	14
水的生产和供应业	Production and Supply of Water	770	6144	37	20

17-6 规模以上工业企业科技活动项目(2022年)

Technology Project Activities of Industrial Enterprises Above Designated Size (2022)

指标	Item	新产品开发项目数(项) Projects for New Products Development (unit)	新产品开发经费支出(万元) Expenditure on new products Development (10 000 yuan)
总计	**Total**	**12464**	**2224546**
按登记注册类型分	**By Status of Registration**		
内资企业	Domestic Invested Enterprises	11240	1882142
国有企业	State-owned Enterprises	354	43538
集体企业	Collective-owned Enterprises	8	1162
股份合作企业	Cooperative Enterprises	20	34063
联营企业	Joint Ownership Enterprises	11	4732
有限责任公司	Limited Liability Corporations	3566	720066
国有独资公司	State Sole-proprietorship Corporations	315	57216
其他有限责任公司	Other Limited Liability Corporations	3251	662850
股份有限公司	Share-holding Corporations Ltd.	1172	394615
私营企业	Private Enterprises	6109	683967
私营独资企业	Private Sole-proprietorship Enterprises	29	1582
私营合伙企业	Private Partnership Enterprises	16	500
私营有限责任公司	Private Limited Liability Corporations	5505	628451
私营股份有限公司	Private Share-holding Corporations Ltd.	559	53434
其他企业	Other Enterprises		
港、澳、台商投资企业	Enterprises with Funds from Hong Kong, Macao and Taiwan	685	273007
合资经营企业	Joint-venture Enterprises	197	57302
合作经营企业	Cooperative Enterprises		
独资经营企业	Sole-proprietorship Enterprises	462	213644
投资股份有限公司	Share-holding Corporations Ltd.	5	1276
其他港澳台投资企业	Other Enterprises with Funds from Hong Kong, Macao and Taiwan	21	786
外商投资企业	Foreign Funded Enterprises	539	69396
中外合资经营企业	Joint-venture Enterprises	343	39774
中外合作经营企业	Cooperative Enterprises		
外资企业	Sole-proprietorship Enterprises	187	24953
外商投资股份有限公司	Share-holding Corporations Ltd. with Foreign Investment	9	4669
其他外商投资企业	Other Foreign Funded Enterprises		
按工业行业大类分	**By Sector**		
煤炭开采和洗选业	Mining and Washing of Coal	3	826
石油和天然气开采业	Extraction of Petroleum and Natural Gas		
黑色金属矿采选业	Mining and Processing of Ferrous Metal Ores	15	15162
有色金属矿采选业	Mining and Processing of Non-Ferrous Metal Ores		
非金属矿采选业	Mining and Processing of Nonmetal Ores	8	620
开采专业及辅助性活动	Professional and Support Activities for Mining		

17-6 续表 continued

指标	Item	新产品开发项目数(项) Projects for New Products Development (unit)	新产品开发经费支出(万元) Expenditure on new products Development (10 000 yuan)
其他采矿业	Mining of Other Ores		
农副食品加工业	Processing of Food from Agricultural Products	106	11233
食品制造业	Manufacture of Foods	246	19546
酒、饮料和精制茶制造业	Manufacture of Wine, Drinks and Refined Tea	37	2930
烟草制品业	Manufacture of Tobacco	25	1957
纺织业	Manufacture of Textile	125	9255
纺织服装、服饰业	Manufacture of Textile Wearing Apparel and Finery	38	2217
皮革、毛皮、羽毛及其制品和制鞋业	Manufacture of Leather, Fur, Feather & Its Products and Footwear	3	413
木材加工和木、竹、藤、棕、草制品业	Processing of Timbers, Manufacture of Wood,Bamboo, Rattan, Palm, and Straw Products	13	1910
家具制造业	Manufacture of Furniture	47	930
造纸和纸制品业	Manufacture of Paper and Paper Products	120	10522
印刷和记录媒介复制业	Printing, Reproduction of Recording Media	97	10635
文教、工美、体育和娱乐用品制造业	Manufacture of Culture, Education,Arts and crafts, Sport and Entertainment Goods	80	4484
石油、煤炭及其他燃料加工业	Processing of Petroleum, Coal and Other Fuels	38	10578
化学原料和化学制品制造业	Manufacture of Chemical Raw Material and Chemical Products	605	93092
医药制造业	Manufacture of Medicines	1453	329459
化学纤维制造业	Manufacture of Chemical Fiber	57	9258
橡胶和塑料制品业	Manufacture of Rubber and Plastic	183	13802
非金属矿物制品业	Manufacture of Non-metallic Mineral Products	530	79959
黑色金属冶炼和压延加工业	Manufacture and Processing of Ferrous Metals	314	219626
有色金属冶炼和压延加工业	Manufacture & Processing of Non-ferrous Metals	84	7440
金属制品业	Manufacture of Metal Products	856	102459
通用设备制造业	Manufacture of General Purpose Machinery	1929	206006
专用设备制造业	Manufacture of Special Purpose Machinery	1791	152530
汽车制造业	Manufacture of Automotive	821	259027
铁路、船舶、航空航天和其他运输设备制造业	Manufacture of Railroad,Marine,Aerospace and Other Transportation Equipment	179	23312
电气机械和器材制造业	Manufacture of Electrical Machinery & Equipment	957	158705
计算机、通信和其他电子设备制造业	Manufacture of Computer, Communications and Other Electronic Equipment	694	356111
仪器仪表制造业	Manufacture of Measuring Instrument	618	61091
其他制造业	Other Manufacture	54	3512
废弃资源综合利用业	Comprehensive Utilization of Waste	12	3201
金属制品、机械和设备修理业	Metal Products, Machinery and Equipment Repair Industry	35	7099
电力、热力生产和供应业	Production and Supply of Electric Power and Heat Power	286	35325
燃气生产和供应业	Production and Supply of Gas	5	315
水的生产和供应业	Production and Supply of Water		

17-7 规模以上工业企业R&D经费情况(2022年)
R&D Funds of Industrial Enterprises Above Designated Size(2022)

单位：万元

指标	Item	合计 Total	按支出用途分组 By Object of Expenditure 经常费支出 Daily Expenditure	资产性支出 Capital Expenditure
总计	**Total**	**1858188**	**1770484**	**87704**
按登记注册类型分	**By Status of Registration**			
内资企业	Domestic Invested Enterprises	1653366	1572091	81275
国有企业	State-owned Enterprises	61040	59396	1644
集体企业	Collective-owned Enterprises	1923	1921	2
股份合作企业	Cooperative Enterprises	33759	33479	280
联营企业	Joint Ownership Enterprises	4732	4732	
有限责任公司	Limited Liability Corporations	590463	558146	32317
国有独资公司	State Sole-proprietorship Corporations	85712	81443	4269
其他有限责任公司	Other Limited Liability Corporations	504751	476702	28048
股份有限公司	Share-holding Corporations Ltd.	373071	357528	15543
私营企业	Private Enterprises	588379	556889	31490
私营独资企业	Private Sole-proprietorship Enterprises	3273	3248	25
私营合伙企业	Private Partnership Enterprises	785	785	
私营有限责任公司	Private Limited Liability Corporations	540104	510184	29921
私营股份有限公司	Private Share-holding Corporations Ltd.	44217	42673	1544
其他企业	Other Enterprises			
港、澳、台商投资企业	Enterprises with Funds from Hong Kong, Macao and Taiwan	133436	131067	2368
合资经营企业	Joint-venture Enterprises	68629	67827	802
合作经营企业	Cooperative Enterprises			
独资经营企业	Sole-proprietorship Enterprises	63612	62067	1545
投资股份有限公司	Share-holding Corporations Ltd.	573	573	
其他港澳台投资企业	Other Enterprises with Funds from Hong Kong, Macao and Taiwan	622	600	22
外商投资企业	Foreign Funded Enterprises	71387	67326	4061
中外合资经营企业	Joint-venture Enterprises	39571	38110	1461
中外合作经营企业	Cooperative Enterprises			
外资企业	Sole-proprietorship Enterprises	27148	24588	2560
外商投资股份有限公司	Share-holding Corporations Ltd. with Foreign Investment	4668	4628	40
其他外商投资企业	Other Foreign Funded Enterprises			
按工业行业大类分	**By Sector**			
煤炭开采和洗选业	Mining and Washing of Coal	4149	4149	
石油和天然气开采业	Extraction of Petroleum and Natural Gas			
黑色金属矿采选业	Mining and Processing of Ferrous Metal Ores	28909	28909	
有色金属矿采选业	Mining and Processing of Non-Ferrous Metal Ores			
非金属矿采选业	Mining and Processing of Nonmetal Ores			
开采专业及辅助性活动	Professional and Support Activities for Mining			

(10 000 yuan)

R&D经费支出 Expenditure on R&D				R&D经费外部支出 External expenditure on R&D
按资金来源分组 By Capital Source				
政府资金 Government Appropriation Funds	企业资金 Self-raised Funds by Enterprises	境外资金 Foreign funds	其他资金 Other Funds	
45011	**1804343**	**7299**	**1535**	**180176**
40887	1603745	7200	1535	155096
157	60883			22786
	1923			
	33759			
	4732			
23540	565487		1435	20038
316	84940		456	444
23224	480547		980	19595
11812	361231		29	64686
5378	575730	7200	71	47586
	3273			
	785			
4976	527858	7200	71	46863
403	43814			723
626	132810			23670
478	68151			13258
148	63464			9310
	573			1063
	622			39
3499	67788	100		1410
872	38699			589
	27048	100		821
2627	2041			
	4149			
	28909			

17-7 续表 continued

单位：万元

指标	Item	合计 Total	按支出用途分组 By Object of Expenditure 经常费支出 Daily Expenditure	资产性支出 Capital Expenditure
其他采矿业	Mining of Other Ores			
农副食品加工业	Processing of Food from Agricultural Products	6317	6208	109
食品制造业	Manufacture of Foods	14201	13635	566
酒、饮料和精制茶制造业	Manufacture of Wine, Drinks and Refined Tea	3597	3549	48
烟草制品业	Manufacture of Tobacco	22576	19131	3445
纺织业	Manufacture of Textile	6552	6493	58
纺织服装、服饰业	Manufacture of Textile Wearing Apparel and Finery	2575	2571	4
皮革、毛皮、羽毛及其制品和制鞋业	Manufacture of Leather, Fur, Feather & Its Products and Footwear	824	824	
木材加工和木、竹、藤、棕、草制品业	Processing of Timbers, Manufacture of Wood,Bamboo, Rattan, Palm, and Straw Products	1910	1910	
家具制造业	Manufacture of Furniture	1238	1238	
造纸和纸制品业	Manufacture of Paper and Paper Products	4151	4151	
印刷和记录媒介复制业	Printing, Reproduction of Recording Media	12573	12063	510
文教、工美、体育和娱乐用品制造业	Manufacture of Culture, Education,Arts and crafts , Sport and Entertainment Goods	2131	1953	178
石油、煤炭及其他燃料加工业	Processing of Petroleum, Coal and Other Fuels	8932	8487	445
化学原料和化学制品制造业	Manufacture of Chemical Raw Material and Chemical Products	69907	61418	8489
医药制造业	Manufacture of Medicines	346372	318320	28052
化学纤维制造业	Manufacture of Chemical Fiber	9939	9919	19
橡胶和塑料制品业	Manufacture of Rubber and Plastic	17871	17642	229
非金属矿物制品业	Manufacture of Non-metallic Mineral Products	34809	33252	1557
黑色金属冶炼和压延加工业	Manufacture and Processing of Ferrous Metals	38600	38321	279
有色金属冶炼和压延加工业	Manufacture & Processing of Non-ferrous Metals	5007	4995	12
金属制品业	Manufacture of Metal Products	86297	81431	4867
通用设备制造业	Manufacture of General Purpose Machinery	206606	201997	4610
专用设备制造业	Manufacture of Special Purpose Machinery	136249	133062	3187
汽车制造业	Manufacture of Automotive	117496	113310	4186
铁路、船舶、航空航天和其他运输设备制造业	Manufacture of Railroad,Marine,Aerospace and Other Transportation Equipment	25668	25545	122
电气机械和器材制造业	Manufacture of Electrical Machinery & Equipment	148953	147541	1412
计算机、通信和其他电子设备制造业	Manufacture of Computer, Communications and Other Electronic Equipment	362696	340833	21863
仪器仪表制造业	Manufacture of Measuring Instrument	55920	54718	1201
其他制造业	Other Manufacture	3548	3431	117
废弃资源综合利用业	Comprehensive Utilization of Waste	2715	2715	
金属制品、机械和设备修理业	Metal Products, Machinery and Equipment Repair Industry	8316	7896	421
电力、热力生产和供应业	Production and Supply of Electric Power and Heat Power	59563	57856	1708
燃气生产和供应业	Production and Supply of Gas	253	253	
水的生产和供应业	Production and Supply of Water	770	760	10

(10 000 yuan)

R&D经费支出 Expenditure on R&D				R&D经费外部支出 External expenditure on R&D
按资金来源分组 By Capital Source				
政府资金 Government Appropriation Funds	企业资金 Self-raised Funds by Enterprises	境外资金 Foreign funds	其他资金 Other Funds	
108	6208			42
22	14179			408
38	3559			38
	22121		456	264
2	6549			
	2575			85
	824			
	1910			
	1238			
	4151			3
20	12553			
	2131			148
	8932			246
163	69744			1892
3251	335921	7200		32876
	9939			
155	17715			21
157	34652			211
328	38272			472
11	4996			123
437	85860			171
12821	193777		8	3471
4060	132189			958
1601	114956	100	840	43191
10587	15081			209
814	148093		46	603
6636	356005		55	67926
3616	52304			2972
	3519		29	
	2715			
	8316			10
174	59288		102	23829
8	245			
	770			8

17-8 规模以上工业企业办科技机构情况(2022年)

Science and Technology Institutions of Industrial Enterprises Above Designated Size (2022)

指标	Item	机构数 (个) Number (unit)
总计	**Total**	**841**
按登记注册类型分	**By Status of Registration**	
内资企业	Domestic Invested Enterprises	793
国有企业	State-owned Enterprises	6
集体企业	Collective-owned Enterprises	2
股份合作企业	Cooperative Enterprises	1
联营企业	Joint Ownership Enterprises	
有限责任公司	Limited Liability Corporations	294
国有独资公司	State Sole-proprietorship Corporations	22
其他有限责任公司	Other Limited Liability Corporations	272
股份有限公司	Share-holding Corporations Ltd.	94
私营企业	Private Enterprises	396
私营独资企业	Private Sole-proprietorship Enterprises	1
私营合伙企业	Private Partnership Enterprises	1
私营有限责任公司	Private Limited Liability Corporations	329
私营股份有限公司	Private Share-holding Corporations Ltd.	65
其他企业	Other Enterprises	
港、澳、台商投资企业	Enterprises with Funds from Hong Kong,Macao and Taiwan	20
合资经营企业	Joint-venture Enterprises	12
合作经营企业	Cooperative Enterprises	
独资经营企业	Sole-proprietorship Enterprises	8
投资股份有限公司	Share-holding Corporations Ltd.	
其他港澳台投资企业	Other Enterprises with Funds from Hong Kong,Macao and Taiwan	
外商投资企业	Foreign Funded Enterprises	28
中外合资经营企业	Joint-venture Enterprises	16
中外合作经营企业	Cooperative Enterprises	
外资企业	Sole-proprietorship Enterprises	10
外商投资股份有限公司	Share-holding Corporations Ltd. with Foreign Investment	2
其他外商投资企业	Other Foreign Funded Enterprises	
按工业行业大类分	**By Sector**	
煤炭开采和洗选业	Mining and Washing of Coal	1
石油和天然气开采业	Extraction of Petroleum and Natural Gas	
黑色金属矿采选业	Mining and Processing of Ferrous Metal Ores	2
有色金属矿采选业	Mining and Processing of Non-Ferrous Metal Ores	
非金属矿采选业	Mining and Processing of Nonmetal Ores	1
开采专业及辅助性活动	Professional and Support Activities for Mining	

机构人员(人) Research Personnel(person)			机构经费支出(万元) Agency Expenditure (10 000 yuan)	仪器和设备原价(万元) Original price of Equipment (10 000 yuan)
合计 Total	博士毕业 Doctor	硕士毕业 Master		
34763	**489**	**5881**	**1691818**	**1905440**
29649	420	4713	1403532	1685700
106		8	7755	14473
133			1871	1945
291		79	34789	2092
12338	191	1863	620283	415064
1123	46	303	68063	143930
11215	145	1560	552221	271134
6470	89	1353	405313	212900
10311	140	1410	333520	1039227
11			252	25
8		1	216	18
8860	121	1296	284906	1011622
1432	19	113	48148	27561
3448	54	1028	245029	85336
1039	1	46	38462	17120
2409	53	982	206567	68216
1666	15	140	43258	134404
711	5	56	26676	48071
925	9	80	14663	86078
30	1	4	1920	256
4		1	87	25
115	3	5	34627	1830
15			650	187

17-8 续表 continued

指标	Item	机构数 (个) Number (unit)
其他采矿业	Mining of Other Ores	
农副食品加工业	Processing of Food from Agricultural Products	11
食品制造业	Manufacture of Foods	24
酒、饮料和精制茶制造业	Manufacture of Wine, Drinks and Refined Tea	6
烟草制品业	Manufacture of Tobacco	3
纺织业	Manufacture of Textile	6
纺织服装、服饰业	Manufacture of Textile Wearing Apparel and Finery	3
皮革、毛皮、羽毛及其制品和制鞋业	Manufacture of Leather, Fur, Feather & Its Products and Footwear	
木材加工和木、竹、藤、棕、草制品业	Processing of Timbers, Manufacture of Wood,Bamboo, Rattan, Palm, and Straw Products	
家具制造业	Manufacture of Furniture	
造纸和纸制品业	Manufacture of Paper and Paper Products	6
印刷和记录媒介复制业	Printing, Reproduction of Recording Media	5
文教、工美、体育和娱乐用品制造业	Manufacture of Culture, Education,Arts and crafts, Sport and Entertainment Goods	5
石油、煤炭及其他燃料加工业	Processing of Petroleum, Coal and Other Fuels	5
化学原料和化学制品制造业	Manufacture of Chemical Raw Material and Chemical Products	53
医药制造业	Manufacture of Medicines	52
化学纤维制造业	Manufacture of Chemical Fiber	5
橡胶和塑料制品业	Manufacture of Rubber and Plastic	24
非金属矿物制品业	Manufacture of Non-metallic Mineral Products	37
黑色金属冶炼和压延加工业	Manufacture and Processing of Ferrous Metals	12
有色金属冶炼和压延加工业	Manufacture & Processing of Non-ferrous Metals	8
金属制品业	Manufacture of Metal Products	85
通用设备制造业	Manufacture of General Purpose Machinery	132
专用设备制造业	Manufacture of Special Purpose Machinery	109
汽车制造业	Manufacture of Automotive	31
铁路、船舶、航空航天和其他运输设备制造业	Manufacture of Railroad,Marine,Aerospace and Other Transportation Equipment	7
电气机械和器材制造业	Manufacture of Electrical Machinery & Equipment	48
计算机、通信和其他电子设备制造业	Manufacture of Computer, Communications and Other Electronic Equipment	77
仪器仪表制造业	Manufacture of Measuring Instrument	68
其他制造业	Other Manufacture	1
废弃资源综合利用业	Comprehensive Utilization of Waste	1
金属制品、机械和设备修理业	Metal Products, Machinery and Equipment Repair Industry	8
电力、热力生产和供应业	Production and Supply of Electric Power and Heat Power	4
燃气生产和供应业	Production and Supply of Gas	1
水的生产和供应业	Production and Supply of Water	

机构人员(人) Research Personnel(person)			机构经费支出(万元) Agency Expenditure (10 000 yuan)	仪器和设备原价(万元) Original price of Equipment (10 000 yuan)
合计 Total	博士毕业 Doctor	硕士毕业 Master		
120	4	8	3909	4070
1162	3	61	21849	837894
135	2	5	1703	1912
232	14	64	19897	24027
77		6	2280	6519
191		6	2346	18619
95			2814	908
281		3	6572	16503
64		5	1266	534
154	2	4	19408	1574
1462	40	209	79480	45185
4476	112	1418	99476	209302
95	1	9	8154	5564
347	10	14	8114	7489
816	8	54	30217	21660
2245	27	118	255942	76386
236	4	9	6712	5936
2244	36	63	72443	92021
4457	44	652	142357	103837
2993	23	401	104970	56484
2974	62	1094	216659	88531
508	2	70	15989	7468
1746	17	340	110044	100403
5095	47	1075	369745	106267
1835	9	163	43367	21719
23		1	1179	580
52		1	193	258
404		18	7183	5775
101	19	4	1848	35956
9			339	17

17-9 规模以上工业企业自主知识产权及相关情况(2022年)

Independent Intellectual Property Rights of Industrial Enterprises Above Designated Size(2022)

单位：件

指标	Item	专利申请数 Number of Patent Applications
总计	**Total**	**17532**
按登记注册类型分	**By Status of Registration**	
内资企业	Domestic Invested Enterprises	14122
国有企业	State-owned Enterprises	2940
集体企业	Collective-owned Enterprises	12
股份合作企业	Cooperative Enterprises	79
联营企业	Joint Ownership Enterprises	25
有限责任公司	Limited Liability Corporations	4023
国有独资公司	State Sole-proprietorship Corporations	520
其他有限责任公司	Other Limited Liability Corporations	3503
股份有限公司	Share-holding Corporations Ltd.	1883
私营企业	Private Enterprises	5160
私营独资企业	Private Sole-proprietorship Enterprises	23
私营合伙企业	Private Partnership Enterprises	20
私营有限责任公司	Private Limited Liability Corporations	4586
私营股份有限公司	Private Share-holding Corporations Ltd.	531
其他企业	Other Enterprises	
港、澳、台商投资企业	Enterprises with Funds from Hong Kong,Macao and Taiwan	1359
合资经营企业	Joint-venture Enterprises	218
合作经营企业	Cooperative Enterprises	
独资经营企业	Sole-proprietorship Enterprises	1126
投资股份有限公司	Share-holding Corporations Ltd.	7
其他港澳台投资企业	Other Enterprises with Funds from Hong Kong,Macao and Taiwan	8
外商投资企业	Foreign Funded Enterprises	2051
中外合资经营企业	Joint-venture Enterprises	166
中外合作经营企业	Cooperative Enterprises	
外资企业	Sole-proprietorship Enterprises	64
外商投资股份有限公司	Share-holding Corporations Ltd. with Foreign Investment	1821
其他外商投资企业	Other Foreign Funded Enterprises	
按工业行业大类分	**By Sector**	
煤炭开采和洗选业	Mining and Washing of Coal	3
石油和天然气开采业	Extraction of Petroleum and Natural Gas	
黑色金属矿采选业	Mining and Processing of Ferrous Metal Ores	22
有色金属矿采选业	Mining and Processing of Non-Ferrous Metal Ores	
非金属矿采选业	Mining and Processing of Nonmetal Ores	8
开采专业及辅助性活动	Professional and Support Activities for Mining	

(piece)

#发明专利 Inventions	有效发明专利数 Number of Effective Inventions	拥有注册商标数 Registered Trademarks	形成国家或行业标准数(项) Industry or National Standards(unit)
6692	**24956**	**18880**	**561**
5805	23164	18259	529
2454	7459	31	14
4	48	2	
27	12	37	
4	8	2	
1291	4495	9046	176
215	541	1956	16
1076	3954	7090	160
843	4312	2905	162
1182	6830	6236	177
4	39	177	
10	10	24	
1048	5919	5108	170
120	862	927	7
599	861	61	12
154	388	46	
437	376	11	12
3	78		
5	19	4	
288	931	560	20
46	303	489	20
16	192	66	
226	436	5	
1	1		
5	6		
2	4		

17-9 续表 continued

单位：件

指标	Item	专利申请数 Number of Patent Applications
其他采矿业	Mining of Other Ores	
农副食品加工业	Processing of Food from Agricultural Products	143
食品制造业	Manufacture of Foods	188
酒、饮料和精制茶制造业	Manufacture of Wine, Drinks and Refined Tea	52
烟草制品业	Manufacture of Tobacco	254
纺织业	Manufacture of Textile	78
纺织服装、服饰业	Manufacture of Textile Wearing Apparel and Finery	38
皮革、毛皮、羽毛及其制品和制鞋业	Manufacture of Leather, Fur, Feather & Its Products and Footwear	10
木材加工和木、竹、藤、棕、草制品业	Processing of Timbers, Manufacture of Wood,Bamboo, Rattan, Palm, and Straw Products	13
家具制造业	Manufacture of Furniture	33
造纸和纸制品业	Manufacture of Paper and Paper Products	100
印刷和记录媒介复制业	Printing, Reproduction of Recording Media	87
文教、工美、体育和娱乐用品制造业	Manufacture of Culture, Education,Arts and crafts， Sport and Entertainment Goods	81
石油、煤炭及其他燃料加工业	Processing of Petroleum, Coal and Other Fuels	47
化学原料和化学制品制造业	Manufacture of Chemical Raw Material and Chemical Products	462
医药制造业	Manufacture of Medicines	534
化学纤维制造业	Manufacture of Chemical Fiber	24
橡胶和塑料制品业	Manufacture of Rubber and Plastic	183
非金属矿物制品业	Manufacture of Non-metallic Mineral Products	600
黑色金属冶炼和压延加工业	Manufacture and Processing of Ferrous Metals	562
有色金属冶炼和压延加工业	Manufacture & Processing of Non-ferrous Metals	79
金属制品业	Manufacture of Metal Products	948
通用设备制造业	Manufacture of General Purpose Machinery	2152
专用设备制造业	Manufacture of Special Purpose Machinery	1682
汽车制造业	Manufacture of Automotive	1520
铁路、船舶、航空航天和其他运输设备制造业	Manufacture of Railroad,Marine,Aerospace and Other Transportation Equipment	148
电气机械和器材制造业	Manufacture of Electrical Machinery & Equipment	2714
计算机、通信和其他电子设备制造业	Manufacture of Computer, Communications and Other Electronic Equipment	1015
仪器仪表制造业	Manufacture of Measuring Instrument	673
其他制造业	Other Manufacture	29
废弃资源综合利用业	Comprehensive Utilization of Waste	32
金属制品、机械和设备修理业	Metal Products, Machinery and Equipment Repair Industry	46
电力、热力生产和供应业	Production and Supply of Electric Power and Heat Power	2961
燃气生产和供应业	Production and Supply of Gas	9
水的生产和供应业	Production and Supply of Water	2

(piece)

#发明专利 Inventions	有效发明专利数 Number of Effective Inventions	拥有注册商标数 Registered Trademarks	形成国家或行业标准数(项) Industry or National Standards(unit)
28	219	226	3
38	303	1075	2
11	24	483	5
87	302	1850	
16	183	19	14
15	10	48	
	2	7	3
7	7	26	
1	76	2	
25	113	102	
5	128	59	21
8	82	34	3
5	103	21	
142	958	4419	38
323	1338	6502	94
11	49	4	
35	291	95	10
107	740	160	26
202	1179	44	15
9	56	10	
239	1366	277	24
592	2280	846	65
392	1755	849	58
515	820	334	18
53	229	37	1
465	1764	393	40
653	2266	566	54
190	716	349	50
13	56	30	
9	42		
5	64	2	
2483	7423	8	17
	1	3	

主要统计指标解释

研究与试验发展(R&D)　指为增加知识存量（也包括有关人类、文化和社会的知识）以及设计已有知识的新应用而进行的创造性、系统性工作，包括基础研究、应用研究和试验发展三种类型。国际上通常采用R&D活动的规模和强度指标反映一国的科技实力和核心竞争力。

基础研究　指一种不预设任何特定应用或使用目的的实验性或理论性工作，其主要目的是为获得（已发生）现象和可观察事实的基本原理、规律和新知识。其成果通常表现为提出一般原理、理论或规律，并以论文、著作、研究报告等形式为主。

应用研究　指为获取新知识，达到某一特定的实际目的或目标而开展的初始性研究。应用研究是为了确定基础研究成果的可能用途，或确定实现特定和预定目标的新方法。其研究成果以论文、著作、研究报告、原理性模型或发明专利等形式为主。

试验发展　指利用从科学研究、实际经验中获取的知识和研究过程中产生的其他知识，开发新的产品、工艺或改进现有产品、工艺而进行的系统性研究。其研究成果以专利、专有技术，以及具有新颖性的产品原型、原始样机及装置等形式为主。

R&D人员　指报告期R&D活动单位中从事基础研究、应用研究和试验发展活动的人员。包括直接参加上述三类R&D活动的人员，以及与上述三类R&D活动相关的管理人员和直接服务人员，即直接为R&D活动提供资料文献、材料供应、设备维护等服务的人员。不包括为R&D活动提供间接服务的人员，如餐饮服务、安保人员等。

R&D人员全时当量　指报告期R&D人员按实际从事R&D活动时间计算的工作量，以“人年”为计量单位。为国际上比较科技人力投入而制定的可比指标。

R&D经费支出　指报告期调查单位内部为实施R&D活动而实际发生的全部经费，按支出性质分为日常性支出和资产性支出。不包括调查单位委托其他单位或与其他单位合作开展R&D活动而转拨给其他单位的全部经费。

新产品销售收入　指报告期企业销售新产品实现的销售收入。新产品是指采用新技术原理、新设计构思研制、生产的全新产品，或在结构、材质、工艺等某一方面比原有产品有明显改进，从而显著提高了产品性能或扩大了使用功能的产品。既包括经政府有关部门认定并在有效期内的新产品，也包括企业自行研制开发，未经政府有关部门认定，从投产之日起一年之内的新产品。

专利　是专利权的简称，是对发明人的发明创造经审查合格后，由国家知识产权局依据专利法授予发明人和设计人对该项发明创造享有的专有权。包括发明、实用新型和外观设计。反映拥有自主知识产权的科技和设计成果情况。

发明（专利）　指对产品、方法或者其改进所提出的新的技术方案。是国际通行的反映拥有自主知识产权技术的核心指标。

Explanatory Notes on Main Statistical Indicators

Research and Experimental Development (R&D) refers to creative and systematic work undertaken in order to increase the stock of knowledge (including knowledge of humankind, culture and society) and to devise new applications of available knowledge. R&D includes 3 categories of activities: basic research, applied research and experimental development. The scale and intensity of R&D are widely used internationally to reflect the strength of S&T and the core competitiveness of a country in the world.

Basic Research refers to experimental or theoretical work undertaken primarily to acquire new knowledge of the underlying foundations of phenomena and observable facts, without any particular application or use in view. Basic research usually formulates hypotheses, theories or laws, and its results are mainly released or disseminated in the form of scientific papers or monographs or research reports.

Applied Research refers to original investigation undertaken in order to acquire new knowledge. It is directed primarily towards a specific, practical aim or objective. Purpose of the applied research is to identify the possible uses of results from basic research, or to explore new (fundamental) methods or new approaches. Results of applied research are expressed in the form of scientific papers, monographs, fundamental models or invention patents.

Experimental Development refers to systematic work, drawing on knowledge gained from research and practical experience and producing additional knowledge, which is directed to producing new products or processes or to improving existing products or processes. Results of experimental development activities are embodied in patents, exclusive technology, and monotype of new products or equipment.

R&D Personnel refer to persons of R&D activities units engaged in basic research, applied research, and experimental development at the reference period, including persons of directly participating in the three activities above, as well as management and direct service staff related to R&D activities, such as literature provision, material supply, equipment maintenance staff, it excludes persons providing indirect support and ancillary services, such as canteen and security staff.

Full-time Equivalent of R&D Personnel refers to the ratio of working hours actually spent on R&D during a specific reference period (usually a calendar year) divided by the total number of hours conventionally worked in the same period by an individual or by a group. The measurement unit of the ratio is "man-years". This is an internationally comparable indicator of S&T manpower input.

Expenditure on R&D refers to the real expenditure of surveyed units on their own R&D activities in reporting period. It is divided into current expenditures and gross fixed capital expenditures for R&D according to the nature of expenditure. It doesn't include the fees transferred to cooperated or entrusted agencies on R&D activities.

Sales Income of New Products refers to the sales income of new products of the enterprises at the reference period. New products refer to products developed and produced with new technologies and designs or improved in structure, material, process or other aspects so that their performance are improved or their functions expanded. New products include those affirmed by government authorities in their validity period and also those developed by enterprises without the affirmation of government authorities within one year after they are put into production.

Patent is an abbreviation for the patent right and refers to the exclusive right of ownership by the inventors or designers for the creation or inventions, given from the China National Intellectual Property Administration after due process of assessment and approval in accordance with the Patent Law. Patents are granted for inventions, utility models and designs. This indicator reflects the achievements of S&T and design with independent intellectual property.

Patented Inventions refer to new technical proposals to the products or methods or their modifications. This is universal core indicator reflecting the technologies with independent intellectual property.

18

教育与文化

EDUCATION AND CULTURE

18-1 教育事业基本情况
Basic Statistics on Education

指标	Item	1952年	1957年	1962年	1965年	1970年	1975年
学校数(所)	**Number of Schools(unit)**	**2679**	**3106**	**3731**	**4318**	**5359**	**5412**
#驻济高等学校	Colleges and Universities in Jinan	5	4	12	8	2	4
中等教育	Secondary Education	37	67	112	410	1204	922
#中等职业学校	Vocational Secondary Education	16	16	15	15	17	21
普通中学	Ordinary middle school	21	51	93	159	1024	783
小　学	Elementary school	2636	3034	3606	3899	4152	4485
专任教师(人)	**Full-time Teachers(person)**	**8555**	**13452**	**19606**	**26760**	**32508**	**42432**
#驻济高等学校	Colleges and Universities in Jinan	671	1325	2598	2451	922	2468
中等教育	Secondary Education	1108	2569	3418	5321	9607	15274
#中等职业学校	Vocational Secondary Education	311	787	765	685	914	985
普通中学	Ordinary middle school	797	1782	2629	3502	8445	13571
小　学	Elementary school	6773	9550	13571	18971	21954	24654
在校学生(万人)	**Total Enrollment(10 000 persons)**	**26.87**	**31.95**	**49.82**	**68.27**	**80.20**	**90.28**
#驻济高等学校	Colleges and Universities in Jinan	0.43	0.82	1.65	1.40	0.30	0.61
中等教育	Secondary Education	2.73	5.14	5.80	10.43	18.97	25.43
#中等职业学校	Vocational Secondary Education	0.69	0.93	0.51	0.65	0.12	0.58
普通中学	Ordinary middle school	2.04	4.21	5.22	7.50	17.81	23.86
小　学	Elementary school	23.70	25.98	42.35	56.42	60.91	64.22
各类学校毕业生数(万人)	**Graduates(10 000 persons)**	**4.38**	**8.58**	**10.60**	**10.45**	**12.09**	**22.66**
#驻济高等学校	Colleges and Universities in Jinan	0.14	0.11	0.31	0.43		0.20
中等教育	Secondary Education	0.60	1.14	1.72	1.90	1.02	11.83
#中等职业学校	Vocational Secondary Education	0.13	0.14	0.32	0.03		0.20
普通中学	Ordinary middle school	0.46	1.00	1.40	1.80	0.38	11.58
每一教师负担学生数(人)	**Each Teacher Burden Number of Students(person)**	**31.41**	**23.75**	**25.41**	**23.27**	**24.67**	**21.28**
#驻济高等学校	Colleges and Universities in Jinan	6.41	6.19	6.35	5.71	3.25	2.47
中等教育	Secondary Education	24.64	20.01	16.97	19.60	19.75	16.65
#中等职业学校	Vocational Secondary Education	22.33	11.84	6.64	9.51	1.36	5.95
普通中学	Ordinary middle school	25.63	23.64	19.84	21.41	21.09	17.58
小　学	Elementary school	34.99	27.20	31.21	29.74	27.74	26.05
平均每万人口在校学生(人)	**Number of Enrollment Per 10000 Population(person)**	**843**	**922**	**1418**	**1829**	**1968**	**2062**
#大学生	Undergraduate	14	24	47	38	7	14
中专生	Secondary Students	22	27	14	17	3	13
中学生	Middle School Students	64	122	150	256	463	566
小学生	Elementary School Students	743	750	1206	1513	1494	1466

注：1.驻济高等学校在校生含普通专本科、成人本专科、研究生在校生。
2.驻济高等学校毕业生为普通本专科毕业生。
3.“中等职业学校”中相关教师、学生数据不含技工学校。

1980年	1985年	1990年	1995年	2000年	2005年	2010年	2015年	2020年	2021年	2022年	2023年
5066	**4511**	**3924**	**3360**	**1725**	**1251**	**1025**	**946**	**1108**	**1066**	**1031**	**990**
11	16	16	16	16	59	66	72	52	52	52	52
759	593	529	440	423	348	302	280	390	373	371	364
30	40	39	41	40	91	73	41	41	66	65	32
710	491	417	312	297	247	209	214	320	332	334	332
4295	3899	3368	2890	1273	832	645	582	666	641	608	574
49608	**46806**	**55978**	**58779**	**62869**	**77334**	**83106**	**88487**	**121438**	**123004**	**122248**	**122226**
3744	4614	7245	7500	8269	24341	29526	31693	42202	41894	41936	40098
19062	17530	21618	23946	26817	27435	28370	30589	42017	42643	40438	40755
1338	2367	2890	2941	2916	4738	4511	4068	3642	4040	4273	4315
17294	13572	16065	17621	20585	21915	21943	23643	34796	35587	36165	36440
26775	24579	26922	27417	27417	25201	24801	25795	37219	38467	39874	41373
83.56	**78.38**	**79.48**	**91.69**	**95.79**	**129.28**	**144.60**	**153.71**	**201.27**	**183.14**	**180.08**	**189.53**
1.58	3.02	3.73	5.66	9.30	48.71	64.25	71.40	89.85	69.40	67.07	69.11
20.24	25.34	28.08	36.64	44.99	42.50	41.76	40.77	54.41	52.74	48.59	49.78
0.31	1.92	2.51	4.79	5.75	9.88	8.10	5.93	6.28	6.40	6.49	6.05
19.63	21.49	22.45	27.15	33.82	30.91	30.18	30.16	39.84	40.70	42.10	43.73
61.47	49.98	47.57	49.23	41.40	37.88	38.40	41.44	57.01	61.00	64.42	70.64
18.07	**17.31**	**17.12**	**20.88**	**23.65**	**33.58**	**38.10**	**39.83**	**43.89**	**41.35**	**41.99**	**33.07**
0.03	0.45	1.03	1.68	1.55	13.49	17.57	19.48	18.37	17.86	18.09	17.48
8.41	7.36	8.24	10.39	10.80	14.03	13.55	14.22	17.12	15.27	14.79	15.59
0.46	0.52	0.62	1.16	1.84	3.29	3.13	2.75	1.73	1.72	1.91	2.21
7.89	6.39	6.66	7.78	8.16	10.40	9.20	10.23	12.97	12.28	12.87	13.38
16.84	**16.75**	**14.20**	**15.60**	**15.24**	**16.72**	**17.40**	**17.37**	**16.58**	**14.89**	**14.73**	**15.51**
4.22	6.55	5.15	7.54	11.25	20.01	21.76	22.53	21.29	16.57	15.99	17.24
10.62	14.46	12.99	15.30	16.78	15.49	14.72	13.33	11.00	12.37	12.02	12.21
2.29	8.12	8.69	16.30	18.84	20.86	17.96	14.58	17.24	15.80	15.19	14.03
11.35	15.83	13.98	15.41	16.43	14.10	13.75	12.76	11.45	11.43	11.64	12.00
22.96	20.33	17.67	18.20	15.10	15.03	15.48	16.07	15.32	15.87	16.16	17.07
1822	**1605**	**1518**	**1691**	**1702**	**2177**	**2395**	**2465**	**2510**	**1962**	**2201**	**2304**
34	62	71	104	165	820	1064	1145	1121	855	820	840
7	39	48	88	102	195	192	170	182	184	183	184
429	473	473	553	601	521	500	484	497	501	514	532
1339	1024	908	908	736	638	636	664	711	752	787	859

Notes: 1.Students under high education in Jinan include regular college students, regular junior college students, adult college students, adult junior students and postgraduate students.

2.Graduates under high education in Jinan are Undergraduates and Short-cycle Courses in Regular HEIs.

3.Data related to teachers and students in the "Secondary Vocational Schools" do not include Skilled Workers Schools.

18-2 普通高等院校一览(2023年)
Basic Statistics on Institutions of Higher Education(2023)

单位：人 (person)

名称 Name	普通本专科在校学生数 Total Enrollment	普通本专科毕业生数 Graduates	普通本专科招生数 New Enrollment	教职工人数 Teachers and Staff	#专任教师 Full-time Teachers 合计 Total	#正高级 Senior	#副高级 Sub-Senior
总计(Total)	**653002**	**179413**	**200185**	**54075**	**39532**	**5477**	**12433**
综合性大学(Comprehensive Universities)	**91209**	**24209**	**25708**	**10950**	**7332**	**1852**	**2611**
山东大学	21052	5266	5742	5973	3378	1350	1283
济南大学	32180	8456	7781	2911	2304	356	829
山东青年政治学院	20546	5951	6832	1141	888	65	231
山东女子学院	17431	4536	5353	925	762	81	268
理工院校(Universities of Science and Engineering)	**76082**	**18907**	**20037**	**8340**	**5780**	**841**	**2078**
山东建筑大学	23691	5601	5981	2235	1719	288	664
山东科技大学	2047	702	545	190	90	35	50
齐鲁工业大学	28369	6775	7156	3512	2200	380	752
山东交通学院	18167	5829	6355	1834	1502	114	489
山东电力高等专科学校	3808			569	269	24	123
医药院校(Medical Colleges and Universities)	**62616**	**12087**	**14976**	**6829**	**4420**	**675**	**1432**
山东第一医科大学	22428	2223	2625	3798	2160	303	705
山东中医药大学	17902	4440	4273	1604	1387	266	386
山东医学高等专科学校	13558	3214	4550	926	463	66	244
济南护理职业学院	8728	2210	3528	501	410	40	97
师范院校(Normal Colleges and Schools)	**49893**	**14588**	**14576**	**4344**	**3405**	**491**	**1094**
山东师范大学	24112	7219	5956	2768	2107	369	700
齐鲁师范学院	18495	4898	5889	1037	889	94	279
济南幼儿师范专科学校	7286	2471	2731	539	409	28	115
财经院校(Colleges and Universities of Finance and Economics)	**31667**	**8878**	**8156**	**2808**	**2067**	**403**	**842**
山东财经大学	26184	6701	6529	2381	1690	340	678
山东财经大学燕山学院	5483	2177	1627	427	377	63	164
政法院校(Colleges and Universities of Politics and Law)	**26101**	**6998**	**7280**	**1831**	**1317**	**110**	**340**
山东警察学院	5746	1295	1266	567	341	34	134
山东司法警官职业学院	8613	2818	2886	321	260	3	42
山东政法学院	11742	2885	3128	943	716	73	164
体育院校(Sports Colleges and Universities)	**4010**	**2298**	**2277**	**493**	**391**	**42**	**166**
山东体育学院	4010	2298	2277	493	391	42	166
艺术院校(Art Schools)	**16857**	**3983**	**4273**	**1822**	**1497**	**157**	**527**
山东艺术学院	8959	2144	2147	1045	895	100	324
山东工艺美术学院	7898	1839	2126	777	602	57	203
职业技术学院(Vocational Technical Institutes)	**294567**	**87465**	**102902**	**16658**	**13323**	**906**	**3343**
山东协和学院	35203	9160	11801	1640	1535	119	461
山东商业职业技术学院	16964	5416	5250	1059	986	46	250
山东劳动职业技术学院	14027	4223	4872	700	584	29	135
山东职业学院	11311	4880	3880	630	562	24	130
山东圣翰财贸职业学院	13420	3037	5939	806	562	10	165
山东艺术设计职业学院	6854	1350	2848	458	382	3	33
山东英才学院	24498	6289	9817	1380	994	17	160
山东旅游职业学院	9904	2729	3510	495	406	18	65
济南工程职业技术学院	14387	4757	5383	771	656	47	157
山东电子职业技术学院	11385	3409	4228	655	526	9	120
济南职业学院	15543	5371	5867	1052	830	84	305
山东现代学院	17291	6867	2828	1194	746	19	90
山东工程职业技术大学	24334	7034	8665	949	781	60	176
山东城市建设职业学院	13842	4637	4965	714	601	63	151
山东管理学院	12741	2568	4018	817	600	56	150
齐鲁理工学院	25241	6339	8993	1620	1269	193	383
山东农业工程学院	2829	1156	837	304	202	18	75
山东特殊教育职业学院	1700	510	800	215	135	11	30
山东传媒职业学院	10361	3573	3591	421	383	18	74
莱芜职业技术学院	12732	4160	4810	778	583	62	233

18-3 中等专业学校一览(2023年)
Basic Statistics on Specialized Secondary Schools(2023)

单位：人 (person)

名称 Name	在校学生数 Total Enrollment	毕业生数 Graduates	招生数 New Enrollment	教职工人数 Teachers and Staff	#专任教师 Full-time Teachers 合计 Total	#正高级 Senior	#副高级 Sub-Senior
总计(Total)	**14189**	**4486**	**4685**	**1404**	**1084**	**20**	**337**
工科学校(Engineering Schools)							
济南信息工程学校	3205	1156	1044	213	190	3	72
济南电子机械工程学校	2674	1013	1002	209	174	7	60
济南铁路学校	318	73	139	85	83	1	18
山东冶金中等专业学校	867	328	349	130	77	2	42
财经学校(Finance and Economics Schools)							
山东省济南商贸学校	2502	704	777	213	177	3	59
体育学校(Sports Schools)							
济南市体育运动学校	784	412	264	114	60	1	13
济南市第二体育运动学校	183	61	80		29	1	6
山东体育学院附属中学	1763	345	562				
艺术学校(Art Schools)							
山东省文化艺术学校	916	175	163	233	123		22
山东工艺美术学院附属中等美术学校	139	48	45	21	19	1	4
济南艺术学校	838	171	260	186	152	1	41

18-4 分县区学前教育基本情况(2023年)
Statistics in Pre-school Education Institutions by Region(2023)

单位：人 (person)

县区	Region	幼儿园数(所) Number of Kindergartens (unit)	在园人数 Enrolment	入园人数 Entrants	教职工数 Teachers and Staff	#专任教师 Full-time Teachers
全市	**Total**	**2117**	**309342**	**84059**	**45202**	**25648**
历下区	Li xia	134	28336	7747	4901	2701
市中区	Shi zhong	187	31851	8655	5604	2961
槐荫区	Huai yin	165	32485	8996	4785	2503
天桥区	Tian qiao	156	25341	7058	4193	2064
历城区	Li cheng	231	52653	15127	7567	4266
长清区	Chang qing	91	14555	4010	1696	1089
章丘区	Zhang qiu	184	25048	6944	3444	1985
济阳区	Ji yang	122	13506	3619	1603	1005
莱芜区	Lai wu	323	25616	7049	3372	2341
钢城区	Gang cheng	74	6872	1606	1011	719
济南高新区	Jinan Gao xin	105	19883	5254	2969	1469
南部山区	Nan shan	66	5249	1207	773	391
济南起步区	Jinan Start-up Area	40	3742	885	518	255
平阴县	Ping yin	54	8512	1983	951	708
商河县	Shang he	185	15693	3919	1815	1191

18-5 文化事业机构和人员
Number of Cultural Institutions and Persons in Culture

指标	Item	2019年	2020年	2021年	2022年	2023年
机构数(个)	**Institutions (unit)**					
电影业	Movies	65	64	65	72	73
艺术业	Arts	25	27	26	26	23
文物业	Cultural Relics	67	64	80	91	103
图书馆业	Libraries	14	14	14	14	14
群众文化业	Mass Culture	175	174	174	174	174
艺术教育业	Art Education	1	1	1	1	1
文艺科研业	Culture Research	1	1	1	1	1
从业人员数(人)	**Employed Persons(person)**					
电影业	Movies	1075	641	588	528	534
艺术业	Arts	1475	1512	1492	1480	1373
文物业	Cultural Relics	1365		1637	1604	1823
图书馆业	Libraries	507	567	756	730	639
群众文化业	Mass Culture	745	801	723	775	761
艺术教育业	Art Education	175	181	180	238	238
文艺科研业	Culture Research	47	50	49	54	55

注：电影业机构、从业人员数据为城市电影院线数据，不含农村。
Note: The data of the film industry institutions and employees are urban cinema line data, excluding rural areas.

主要统计指标解释

普通高等学校 指通过国家普通高等教育招生考试，招收高中毕业生为主要培养对象，实施高等学历教育的全日制大学、独立设置的学院、独立学院和高等专科学校、高等职业学校及其他普通高教机构。

大学、独立设置的学院主要实施本科及本科层次以上的教育。独立学院主要实施本科层次的教育。高等专科学校、高等职业学校实施专科层次的教育。其他普通高教机构是指承担国家普通招生计划任务不计校数的机构，包括普通高等学校分校、大专班等。

文化事业机构 指从事专业文化工作和为专业文化工作服务的独立建制的单位。不包括这些单位另外举办独立核算的其他机构和各部门的业余文化组织。

Explanatory Notes on Main Statistical Indicators

Regular Higher Education Institutions refer to educational establishments recruiting graduates from senior secondary schools as the main target through National Matriculation TEST. They include full-time universities, independently established schools, independent colleges, higher professional colleges, higher vocational colleges and other regular higher education institutions.

Universities and independently established schools primarily provide normal courses at undergraduate and higher levels. Independent colleges mainly provide normal undergraduate courses. Higher professional colleges and higher vocational colleges primarily provide undergraduate of short-cycle courses. Other regular higher education institutions refer to educational establishments, which are responsible for enrolling higher education students under the State Plan but not enumerated in the total number of schools, including: branch schools of regular higher education institutions and junior colleges.

Cultural Institutions refer to units which have their own organizational system, work on professional culture work and serve the professional culture work, excluding other institutions for independent accounting established by such units separately and amateur cultural organizations of all departments.

19

体育与卫生

SPORTS AND PUBLIC HEALTH

19-1 体育事业
Statistics of Sports Institutions

指标	Item	2019年	2020年	2021年	2022年	2023年
体育部门职工人数(人)	**Number of Persons of Physical System(person)**	**672**	**677**	**550**	**548**	**536**
#业余体育学校	Spare-time Sports School	402	410	375	375	372
总计中:教练员	Referees	183	181	251	232	222
等级裁判员(人)	**Number of Referees in Grades(person)**					
一级裁判员	First Grade Referees					
二级裁判员	Second Grade Referees	344	155	169	90	420
三级裁判员	Third Grade Referees					
二级运动员发展人数(人)	**Number of Second Grade Sportsmen(person)**	**534**	**564**	**637**	**293**	**1488**
少年儿童业余体校在校学生(人)	Enrollment Spare-time Sports School(person)	1286	1010	1961	1666	1564
业余体校(所)	Spare-time Sports School(unit)	10	10	10	7	8
运动员获奖牌数(枚)	**Number of Medals Won by Athletes(unit)**	**1353**	**715.5**	**784**	**717**	**695**
#世界级 金牌	World Gold Medals	13		3	2	14
银牌	Silver Medals	7				4
铜牌	Copper Medal	8		2		3
#洲 际 金牌	Intercontinental Gold Medals	10		1	1	16
银牌	Silver Medals	11			2	6
铜牌	Copper Medal	7		1		1
#全 国 金牌	Country Gold Medals	100	15	39	26	56
银牌	Silver Medals	91	7	28	30	55
铜牌	Copper Medal	132	10	27	26	52
#全 省 金牌	Province Gold Medals	442	285.5	298	258	200
银牌	Silver Medals	248	182	162	181	126
铜牌	Copper Medal	284	216	223	191	162
体育设施(个)	**Sports Facility(unit)**					
体育场	Stadium	14	14	124	119	64
体育馆	Gymnasium	10	11	28	32	34
游泳馆	Natatorium	9	10	79	122	144
室内外游泳池	Indoor Swimming Pool	10	10	90	13	28
有固定看台的灯光球场	Light Count With Fixed Stand	5	5	8	8	334

注：等级裁判员为当年新评定的人数。
Note: The number of referees is the number of new assessments in the current year.

19-2 各时期卫生事业情况
Statistics of Health Institutions in Major Years

年份 Year	卫生机构(个) Number of Health Institutions (unit)		卫生工作人员(人) Medical Technical Personnel (person)		卫生机构床位(张) Number of Health Institutions Beds (bed)	
	小计 Total	#医院及卫生院 Hospitals and Township Hospitals	小计 Total	#卫生技术人员 Medical Technical Personnel	小计 Total	#医院及卫生院 Hospitals and Township Hospitals
1952	208	22	6277	4778	3160	1906
1957	708	45	10740	7991	5972	3401
1962	1191	98	13705	9648	7917	5662
1965	1144	114	18885	14881	9035	6438
1970	682	130	13273	10341	7878	6462
1975	934	137	20021	14956	9066	8050
1978	1017	148	24949	19198	11496	9856
1979	1078	152	26385	20110	11902	10781
1980	1091	151	27843	21295	12301	11052
"六五"时期						
1981	1188	152	29597	22559	12428	11436
1982	1159	151	30636	22814	12379	11383
1983	1177	156	31924	23948	12966	11674
1984	1160	157	32967	24502	13728	12960
1985	1175	165	34232	26185	14356	13791
"七五"时期						
1986	1184	167	35803	27360	14757	14165
1987	1137	166	37129	28159	15457	14721
1988	1103	171	38384	29167	16165	15580
1989	1137	180	39926	29878	16698	16176
1990	1300	178	41444	31130	18214	17216
"八五"时期						
1991	1233	177	40957	30815	18439	17538
1992	1331	180	41996	31541	18818	18178
1993	1285	193	43274	32871	20243	19320
1994	1228	213	43630	33007	20001	19064
1995	1185	216	43648	32848	20747	19534
"九五"时期						
1996	1674	214	45765	35219	20428	19716
1997	1567	220	44664	34188	21422	20706
1998	1574	227	45110	34596	21965	21130

19-2 续表 continued

年份 Year	卫生机构(个) Number of Health Institutions (unit)		卫生工作人员(人) Medical Technical Personnel (person)		卫生机构床位(张) Number of Health Institutions Beds (bed)	
	小计 Total	#医院及卫生院 Hospitals and Township Hospitals	小计 Total	#卫生技术人员 Medical Technical Personnel	小计 Total	#医院及卫生院 Hospitals and Township Hospitals
1999	1570	226	45121	34000	21735	21086
2000	1414	231	45166	35669	21698	20830
“十五”时期						
2001	1414	231	45296	35790	21906	21033
2002	1708	243	39386	31945	21576	21042
2003	1868	246	41925	33803	22674	22262
2004	1917	243	41625	33998	24044	22588
2005	2138	246	41499	34129	24695	23524
“十一五”时期						
2006	2285	240	43023	35124	27695	26101
2007	2265	243	42513	34579	26055	25328
2008	5092	286	44416	36143	28939	27555
2009	5163	281	46311	37648	30920	28749
2010	5086	277	54711	39366	31947	29844
“十二五”时期						
2011	5159	262	58590	42116	34920	31545
2012	5239	243	60426	44331	38834	35194
2013	5368	255	76955	57700	45465	41287
2014	5784	265	84515	63604	48280	44058
2015	5947	269	89117	71778	49311	45195
“十三五”时期						
2016	6188	270	92060	76447	52191	47524
2017	5770	289	97663	76273	54855	50142
2018	6030	293	104347	82834	57460	51207
2019	7487	351	122370	97532	66623	59697
2020	7514	343	126681	102172	68831	62072
“十四五”时期						
2021	7515	336	131269	108401	72832	66258
2022	7665	329	137111	113536	76367	69642
2023	8136	368	147040	122229	82473	74310

注：2015年及2016年的卫生技术人员为注册卫生技术人员，其他年份为在岗卫生技术人员。
Note: Health technicians in 2015 and 2016 are registered health technicians, and other years are on-the-job health technicians.

19-3 卫生事业机构及床位
Number of Health Institutions and Beds

指标	Item	2019年	2020年	2021年	2022年	2023年
各类卫生机构数(个)	**Number of Health Institutions (unit)**	**7487**	**7514**	**7515**	**7665**	**8136**
医院	Hospital	289	284	279	280	320
社区卫生服务中心(站)	Health Service Center for Community	352	379	385	399	423
卫生院	Health Centers	62	59	57	49	48
门诊部	Outpatient Department	156	163	177	184	214
急救中心(站)	First-Aid Center	1	1	1	1	1
采血供应机构	Pick and Supply Blood Institution	3	2	2	2	2
妇幼保健院(所、站)	Women and Children Care Agencies	15	15	15	15	15
专科疾病防治院(所、站)	Specialized Disease Prevention & Treatment Institution	13	9	8	7	8
疾病预防控制中心(防疫站)	Center for Disease Control and Prevention	15	14	14	14	16
医学科学研究机构	Medical Science Research Institutes	2	2	2	2	2
其他卫生机构	Other Medical Institutions	39	32	30	40	55
各类卫生机构病床数(张)	**Number of Health Institutions Beds(bed)**	**66623**	**68831**	**72832**	**76367**	**82473**
医院	Hospital	56315	58790	62887	66157	70599
社区卫生服务中心(站)	Health Service Center for Community	3791	3899	3873	4371	5176
卫生院	Health Centers	3382	3282	3371	3485	3711
门诊部	Outpatient Department	33	43	138	73	75
妇幼保健院(所、站)	Women and Children Care Agencies	1444	1533	1592	1591	1848
专科疾病防治院(所、站)	Specialized Disease Prevention & Treatment Institution	1658	1284	932	595	963
千人拥有量(张、人)	**Number Per 1000 Population(bed.person)**					
平均每千人拥有病床	Number Of Beds Per 1000 Population	7.48	7.48	7.80	8.11	8.74
每千人拥有卫生技术人员	Number Of Medical Technical Personnel Per 1000 Population	13.43	12.74	13.36	13.88	14.86
每千人拥有医生	Number Of Doctors Per 1000 Population	4.30	4.37	4.55	4.67	4.99
每千人拥有护士	Number Of Nurses Per 1000 Population	4.91	4.97	5.30	5.51	5.96

19–4 分地区卫生事业机构及床位(2023年)
Number of Health Institutions and Beds by District(2023)

指标	Item	全市 Total	市区 Districts	平阴县 Ping yin	商河县 Shang he
各类卫生机构数(个)	**Number of Institutions(unit)**	**8136**	**7413**	**264**	**459**
医院	Hospital	320	309	5	6
疗养院	Sanatorium				
社区卫生服务中心(站)	Health Service Center for Community	423	406	8	9
卫生院	Health Centers	48	31	6	11
门诊部	Outpatient Department	214	207		7
诊所、卫生所、医务室	Infirmaries and Clinics	3528	3348	80	100
急救中心(站)	First-Aid Center	1	1		
采血供应机构	Pick and Supply Blood Institution	2	2		
妇幼保健院(所、站)	Women and Children Care Agencies	15	13	1	1
专科疾病防治院(所、站)	Specialized Disease Prevention & Treatment Institution	8	7	1	
疾病预防控制中心(防疫站)	Center for Disease Control and Prevention	16	14	1	1
卫生监督所	Health Supervision Institute	12	10	1	1
医学科学研究机构	Medical Science Research Institutes	2	2		
其他卫生机构	Other Medical Institutions	55	55		
各类卫生机构病床数(张)	**Number of Institutions Beds(bed)**	**82473**	**76810**	**2847**	**2816**
医院	Hospital	70599	66683	1786	2130
疗养院	Sanatorium				
社区卫生服务中心(站)	Health Service Center for Community	5176	5081	34	61
卫生院	Health Centers	3711	2343	753	615
门诊部	Outpatient Department	75	74		1
妇幼保健院(所、站)	Women and Children Care Agencies	1848	1805	34	9
专科疾病防治院(所、站)	Specialized Disease Prevention & Treatment Institution	963	723	240	
千人拥有量(张、人)	**Number Per 1000 Population(bed.person)**				
平均每千人拥有病床	Number Of Beds Per 1000 Population	8.74	8.95	8.64	5.32
每千人拥有卫生技术人员	Number Of Medical Technical Personnel Per 1000 Population	14.86	13.53	8.34	6.40
每千人拥有医生	Number Of Doctors Per 1000 Population	4.99	5.22	3.07	2.41
每千人拥有护士	Number Of Nurses Per 1000 Population	5.96	6.22	4.00	2.87

19–5 医疗机构年收入与支出 (2023年)
Revenue and Expenditure in Health Institutions(2023)

单位：万元 (10 000 yuan)

机构分类	Institutions	总收入 Total Income 合计 Total	财政补助收入 Financial Subsidy Income	上级补助收入 Grant From Higher Authority	业务收入/事业收入 Business Income
合计	**Total**	**8389605.4**	**909499.7**	**17214.6**	**7177226.5**
医院	Hospital	6939068.2	545877.8	1689.1	6110641.0
社区卫生服务中心(站)	Health Service Center for Community	442335.2	84944.8	3757.0	335180.8
卫生院	Health Centers	133034.8	53045.1	444.3	76501.3
门诊部	Outpatient Department	67495.2			56912.5
诊所.卫生所.医务室	Infirmaries and Clinics	109925.1			97392.6
急救中心(站)	First-Aid Center	3479.0	3081.0	182.5	215.5
妇幼保健院(所、站)	Women and Children Care Agencies	222129.9	39668.7	4.3	172564.8
专科疾病防治院(所、站)	Specialized Disease Prevention & Treatment Institution	18171.7	8143.3		9922.0

19–5 续表 continued

单位：万元 (10 000 yuan)

机构分类	Institutions	总支出 Total Expenditure 合计 Total	单位管理费 Unit Management Fee	业务活动费 Business Activity Fee	总费用中：人员费用 Staff Expenditure
合计	**Total**	**7930677.6**	**1012818.5**	**6541253.6**	**2810003.7**
医院	Hospital	6616408.0	910642.8	5571109.2	2307940.7
社区卫生服务中心(站)	Health Service Center for Community	434104.9	13045.8	401238.3	143053.9
卫生院	Health Centers	128161.9	4241.3	121080.5	58368.9
门诊部	Outpatient Department	43944.2			23280.5
诊所.卫生所.医务室	Infirmaries and Clinics	82424.1	118.8	80.8	45122.3
急救中心(站)	First-Aid Center	3844.6	857.7	2985.4	2096.0
妇幼保健院(所、站)	Women and Children Care Agencies	213654.2	30790.5	180900.6	105956.6
专科疾病防治院(所、站)	Specialized Disease Prevention & Treatment Institution	20159.3	4332.5	11744.2	8834.1

注:门诊部及诊所.卫生所.医务室不填报财政补助收入、上级补助收入、单位管理费、业务活动费四项指标。

Note:Outpatient department and clinic. Health clinic. The medical office does not report four indicators: financial subsidy income, superior subsidy income, Unit Managemen Fee, Business Activity Fee.

19-6 医院卫生院工作情况
Basic Statistics on Hospitals and Health Centers

指标	Item	2019年	2020年	2021年	2022年	2023年
医院	**Hospital**					
单位数(个)	Number(unit)	289	284	279	280	320
诊疗人次数(万人次)	Visits (10 000 person-times)	3922	3397	3993	3584	4105
#门诊人次数	Outpatient Visits	3449	3018	3504	3148	3638
急诊人次数	Emergency Visits	300	235	327	314	355
健康检查人数(万人次)	check-up(10 000 person-times)	260	235	271	253	262
入院人数(万人)	Inpatients(10 000 persons)	182.2	172.3	204.3	203.1	259.7
出院人数(万人)	Patients Discharged(10 000 persons)	181.5	171.8	203.6	202.7	258.8
平均开放病床数(张)	Average Bed Opened(bed)	52359	54692	58399	62570	67958
病床使用率(%)	Utilization Rate of Beds(%)	87.27	77.71	82.71	71.42	79.99
病床周转次数(次)	Number of Medals Won by Athletes(unit)	34.70	31.40	34.90	32.40	38.10
出院者平均住院日(日)	Average Stay Days in Hospital(day)	9.20	9.10	8.50	8.00	7.70
卫生院	**Health Centers**					
单位数(个)	Number(unit)	62	59	57	49	48
诊疗人次数(万人次)	Visits (10 000 person-times)	301.9	304.1	349.4	310.4	356.9
#门诊人次数	Outpatient Visits	292.1	292.7	334.2	302.7	347.2
急诊人次数	Emergency Visits	3.6	5.0	4.5	3.9	2.6
健康检查人数(万人次)	check-up(10 000 person-times)	35.8	25.5	28.3	24.5	16.6
入院人数(万人)	Inpatients(10 000 persons)	7.2	5.8	6.5	6.6	10.2
出院人数(万人)	Patients Discharged(10 000 persons)	7.2	5.7	6.5	6.5	10.2
平均开放病床数(张)	Average Bed Opened(bed)	3187	3203	3240	3153	3611
病床使用率(%)	Occupancy Rate of Hospital Beds(%)	58.03	47.37	51.77	51.27	71.46
病床周转次数(次)	Turnover of Hospital Beds(time)	22.70	17.90	20.00	20.60	28.10
出院者平均住院日(日)	Average Length of Stay in Hospital(day)	7.80	8.50	8.80	8.80	8.70

19-7 分地区卫生技术人员分类情况(2023年)
Medical Technical Personnel by Region(2023)

单位：人 (person)

指标	Item	全市 Total	市区 Districts	平阴县 Ping yin	商河县 Shang he
各类卫生机构工作人员合计	**Total of Personnel in Health Institutions**	**147040**	**139217**	**3466**	**4357**
#卫生技术人员小计	Health Technical Personnel	122229	116096	2746	3387
医生	Licensed Physicians	47103	44817	1012	1274
注册护士	Registered Nurses	56210	53371	1318	1521
其他	Others	4630	4305	112	213

主要统计指标解释

医疗卫生机构　指从卫生健康行政部门取得《医疗机构执业许可证》，或从民政、工商行政、机构编制管理部门取得法人单位登记证书，为社会提供医疗保健、疾病控制、卫生监督服务或从事医学科研和医学在职培训等工作的单位。医疗卫生机构包括医院、基层医疗卫生机构、专业公共卫生机构、其他医疗卫生机构。

医院　包括综合医院、中医医院、中西医结合医院、民族医院、各类专科医院和护理院，不包括专科疾病防治院、妇幼保健院和疗养院。

卫生技术人员　包括执业医师、执业助理医师、注册护士、药师（士）、检验技师（士）、影像技师、卫生监督员和见习医（药、护、技）师（士）等卫生专业人员。不包括从事管理工作的卫生技术人员(如院长、副院长、党委书记等)。

执业医师　指《医师执业证》“级别”为“执业医师”且实际从事医疗、预防保健工作的人员，不包括实际从事管理工作的执业医师。执业医师类别分为临床、中医、口腔和公共卫生四类。

床位数　指年末医疗卫生机构实有床位，又称实有床位数、病床数。实有床位包括正规床、简易床、监护床、超过半年的加床、正在消毒和修理的床位、因扩建或大修而停用的床位。不包括产科新生儿床、接产室待产床、库存床、观察床、临时加床和病人家属陪待床。

Explanatory Notes on Main Statistical Indicators

Health Care Institutions refer to the units which have been qualified with the Certification of Health Care Institution,, or qualified with the Certification of Corporate Unit by the civil affairs, administration for industry and commerce, and engaging in medical care services, disease control services, health supervision services, or medicine research and on-job training, etc., including: hospitals, health care institutions at grass-root level, specialized public health institutions, and other health care institutions.

Hospitals include general hospitals, traditional Chinese medicine hospitals, hospitals of integrated traditional Chinese and western medicine, nationalities hospitals, specialized hospitals and nursing hospitals, as well as affiliated hospitals of medical colleges, excluding specialized disease prevention and treatment institutes, maternal and child health centers and convalescent hospitals.

Health Technical Personnel refer to the professional staff engaged in health care, including licensed physicians and physician assistants, registered nurses, pharmacists, laboratory and imaging technicians, health care supervisors and intern doctors, pharmacists, nurses, and technical personnel, excluding health technical personnel engaged in management (e.g. president, vice president and secretary of the party committee etc).

Licensed Physicians refer to the medical workers with licenses of qualified doctors and are employed in medical treatment, disease prevention or healthcare institutions, excluding the licensed doctors engaged in management. The physicians are divided into 4 categories: clinician, Chinese medicine, stomatology and public health.

Number of Beds refer to the actual number of beds in health care institutions at year-end, also known as the actual number of beds or hospital beds, including regular beds, simple beds, monitoring beds, extra bed over 6 months, beds under disinfection or repairing, beds deactivated due to expansion or overhaul, not including neonatal beds, pre-delivery beds, inventory beds, observation beds, temporary beds and family accompany beds.

20

民政、司法和其他

SOCIAL WELFARE CIVIL ADMINISTRATION AND JUSTICE

20–1 社会治安主要指标
Main Indicators of Public Order

指标	Item	2019年	2020年	2021年	2022年	2023年
刑事案件(件)	**Criminal Cases(case)**					
当年全部立案数	Put on Record	25382	32965	40583	36275	37583
破获当年刑事案件数	Cracked the Number of Criminal Cases	9259	18983	17316	16099	21289
治安案件(件)	**Public Security Cases(case)**					
受理数	Cases Accepted	79355	68614	64550	63708	59836
查处数	Cases Investigated and Treated	72593	60633	58043	62628	59023
城市交通事故	**Traffic Accidents**					
交通事故(起)	Number of Traffic Accidents(case)	3334	3313	3317	3257	2937
伤亡人数(人)	Number of Injuries and Deaths(person)	3925	3747	3631	3771	3207
#死亡人数(人)	Number of Deaths(person)	472	465	447	439	380
损失折款(万元)	Direct Losses(10 000 yuan)	905	1006	1207	857	704.12
火灾事故	**Fires**					
火灾起数(起)	Number of Fire Accidents(case)	4577	4319	5907	5892	6535
伤亡人数(人)	Number of Injuries and Deaths(person)	12	16	35	13	14
#死亡人数(人)	Number of Deaths(person)	10	13	24	9	7
损失折款(万元)	Direct Losses(10 000 yuan)	1529	2153	6231.8	3817	5494

20-2 分地区社会治安主要指标(2023年)
Main Indicators of Public Order by District(2023)

指标	Item	全市 Total	其中 of which 市区 Districts	平阴县 Ping yin	商河县 Shang he
刑事案件(件)	**Criminal Cases(case)**				
当年全部立案数	Put on Record	37583	35641	811	1131
破获当年刑事案件数	Cracked the Number of Criminal Cases	21289	20038	506	745
治安案件(件)	**Public Security Cases(case)**				
受理数	Cases Accepted	59836	56261	1386	2189
查处数	Cases Punished	59023	55573	1379	2071
城市交通事故	**Traffic Accidents**				
交通事故(起)	Number of Traffic Accidents(case)	2937	2833	65	39
伤亡人数(人)	Number of Injuries and Deaths(person)	3207	3086	77	44
#死亡人数(人)	Number of Deaths(person)	380	353	18	9
损失折款(万元)	Direct Losses(10 000 yuan)	704.12	694.77	4.36	4.99
火灾事故	**Fires**				
火灾起数(起)	Number of Fire Accidents(case)	6535	5703	279	553
伤亡人数(人)	Number of Injuries and Deaths(person)	14	13	1	
#死亡人数(人)	Number of Deaths(person)	7	7		
损失折款(万元)	Direct Losses(10 000 yuan)	5494	4891	160	443.0

20-3 社会保障和救济

Basic Statistics on Social Security and Receiving Relief Flinds

指标	Item	2019年	2020年	2021年	2022年	2023年
优抚情况(人)	**Veteran Benefit and Placement(person)**					
享受定期抚恤金人数	Number of Receiving Periodic Pensions	587	623	651	663	683
在乡复员军人	Demobilized Soldiers in Countryside	1327	1256	1179	1106	834
参战退役人员	Veterans	5104	5125	5154	5150	5159
社会救济情况(人)	**Social Relief(person)**					
城镇居民最低生活保障人数	Number of Urban Residents for Minimum Livelihood Guarantee	15491	14159	13063	10932	10548
农村居民最低生活保障人数	Number of Rural residents for Minimum Livelihood Guarantee	73305	84209	84367	83049	85340
民政经费(万元)	**Civil Affairs Expenditures(10 000 yuan)**					
城市居民最低生活保障费	Urban Residents for Minimum Livelihood Guarantee	9657	11030	11774	12952	11907
农村最低生活保障费	Rural residents for Minimum Livelihood Guarantee	26039	39218	51177	66311	66397
其它社会救助费	Other Social Assistance Expenses	1158	1175	1367	1214	573
社会福利费	Social Welfare Funds	60731	69771	92454	96830	95320
退役安置费(万元)	**Decommissioning Costs(10 000 yuan)**	**13538**	**11504**	**10582**	**4955**	**7096**
自然灾害生活救助费(万元)	**Natural Disaster Assistance Expenses(10 000 yuan)**	**2450**				
医疗救助费(万元)	**Medical Assistance Expenses(10 000 yuan)**	**3680**	**9280**	**10409**	**9656**	**11127**
社会保障及扶贫(个、元)	**Social Security and Poverty Alleviation(unit.yuan)**					
建立社会保障服务网络的乡镇数	Number of Towns With Social Security Service Network	40	29	29	192	
城市市区居民最低生活保障金标准	Minimum Living Standards for Urban Residents	685	821	904	995	1045

注：1.“优抚情况”根据部门数据进行修订。
2. 2022年，“建立社会保障服务网络的乡镇数”的口径为全市可以经办居民养老保险业务的乡镇。

Note:1.The statistical data of preferential treatment were revised based on data provided by related department.
2.The unified standard for the "number of towns and villages establishing social security service networks" in 2022 refers to the towns and villages that can handle residents' endowment insurance business in the whole city.

20–4 分地区社会保障和救济(2023年)

Basic Statistics on Social Security and Receiving Relief Flinds by Region (2023)

指标	Item	济南市(汇总) Total	济南市(市本级) Cities	历下区 Li xia	市中区 Shi zhong
社会救济情况(人)	**Social Relief(person)**				
城镇居民最低生活保障人数	Number of Urban Residents for Minimum Livelihood Guarantee	10548		1486	1639
农村居民最低生活保障人数	Number of Rural residents for Minimum Livelihood Guarantee	85340			1331
民政经费(万元)	**Civil Affairs Expenditures(10 000 yuan)**				
城市居民最低生活保障费	Urban Residents for Minimum Livelihood Guarantee	11907.4		1925.7	1807.6
农村最低生活保障费	Rural residents for Minimum Livelihood Guarantee	66396.5			1368.8
其它社会救助费	Other Social Assistance Expenses	573.3		73.3	245.3
社会福利费	Social Welfare Funds	95319.8	26696.7	6937.1	3229.7
社会保障(元)	**Social Security(yuan)**				
城市市区居民最低生活保障金标准	Minimum Living Standards for Urban Residents	1045	1045	1045	1045

槐荫区 Huai yin	天桥区 Tian qiao	历城区 Li cheng	长清区 Chang qing	章丘区 Zhang qiu	济阳区 Ji yang	莱芜区 Lai wu	钢城区 Gang cheng	济南高新区 Jinan Gao xin	济南起步区 (直管) Jinan Start-up Area (Directly under)	南部山区 Nan shan	平阴县 Ping yin	商河县 Shang he
1233	2529	423.0	568	543	62	853	544	23	111	44	177	313
548	479	1933.0	10422	17892	5177	17759	3725	749	2223	4731	4131	14240
1341.6	2927.5	533.2	512.8	574.2	54.0	909.7	624.2	29.0	128.8	56.8	187.2	295.1
573.9	370.0	2282.8	7142.3	13343.8	3571.2	14007.9	3107.4	860.2	2037.8	4387.7	2961.3	10381.4
		208.4			21.0		0.4					24.9
2441.2	2225.2	3870.9	5672.9	12553.3	4040.2	9134.4	3603.8	1912.1	1792.9	2743.8	3749.7	4715.9
1045	1045	1045	1045	1045	1045	1045	1045	1045	1045	1045	1045	1045

20-5 律师、公证、司法基本情况(2023年)
Basic Statistics on Law, Notarizations and Mediation (2023)

指标	Item	单位 Unit	全市 Total	市区 Districts	平阴县 Ping yin	商河县 Shang he
律师工作	**Lawyers**					
律师事务所	Number of Law Offices	个(unit)	518	507	8	3
执业律师	Number of Lawyers	人(person)	8899	8845	37	17
担任常年法律顾问	Permanent Legal Advisor	家(unit)	12169	11990	144	35
民事诉讼代理	Civil Agent	件(case)	127444	126170	848	426
刑事诉讼辩护及代理	Criminal Defense and Agent	件(case)	12855	12509	109	237
行政诉讼代理	Administrative Agent	件(case)	5696	5632	57	7
非诉讼法律事务	Non-litigation Legal Matters	件(case)	25520	25488	3	29
公证工作	**Notarization**					
公证处	Number of Notary Offices	个(unit)	15	13	1	1
公证处人员	Personnel of Notary Offices	人(person)	475	456	8	11
#公证员	Notaries	人(person)	166	158	4	4
办理公证总数	Number of Notarized Affair	件(case)	198948	196590	1191	1167
#国内民事公证	Domestic Civil Notarization	件(case)	92856	91042	976	838
国内经济公证	Domestic Commerce Notarization	件(case)	69779	69251	215	313
涉外公证	Foreign-related Notarization	件(case)	80434	80421		13
办理经济公证涉及金额	Money of Commerce Notarization	亿元(100 million yuan)	652.68	644.41	4.62	3.65
基层司法行政工作	**Basic Mediation Administration**					
人民调解委员会	People's Mediation Committee	个(unit)	6123	5201	361	561
人民调解员	People's Mediators	人(person)	24430	20516	1445	2469
调解纠纷总数	Number of Mediation Disputes	件(case)	35579	31401	2067	2111
#调解成功	Success Mediation	件(case)	35318	31142	2067	2109
法律服务所	Legal Service Office	个(unit)	147	136	8	3
基层法律工作者	Grassroots Legal Workers	人(person)	841	795	32	14
担任法律顾问	Legal Advisor	家(unit)	692	605	79	8
民事诉讼代理	Civil Agent	件(case)	7663	6544	566	553
非诉讼代理	Non-litigation Agent	件(case)	3172	3050	110	12
法律援助工作	**Legal Aid**					
法律援助机构	Legal Aid Institution	个(unit)	13	11	1	1
执业人员	Practitioners	人(person)	19	19		
办理法律援助案件	Legal Aid Cases	件(case)	21578	19247	1111	1220

主要统计指标解释

律师 是指依法取得律师执业证书，接受委托或指定，为当事人提供法律服务的执业人员。

公证员 是指符合法定条件，在公证机构从事公证业务的执业人员。

调解人员 指在人民调解委员会担负调解民间一般民事纠纷和轻微违法行为引起纠纷的工作人员，包括调解委员会的委员和调解小组的调解员。

Explanatory Notes on Main Statistical Indicators

Lawyers refer to practitioners who have obtained a lawyer's practice certificate in accordance with the law, accept commissions or appointments, and provide legal services to clients.

Notary refers to a practitioner who meets the legal requirements and engages in notarization business at a notary institution.

Mediation Personnel refers to staff taking charge of mediating ordinary civil disputes among the people and disputes arising from minor infraction at the people's mediation committee, including the member of the mediation committee and the mediator of the mediation team.

附 录

APPENDIX

附录一 山东省十六城市主要经济指标(2023年)
Main Statistical Indicators of 16 Cities in Shandong(2023)

单位：亿元

城市名称	Region	地区生产总值 Gross Domestic Product	第一产业 Primary Industry	第二产业 Secondary Industry	第三产业 Tertiary Industry	固定资产投资比上年增长(%) Growth Rate Investment in Fixed Assets (%)	房地产开发投资额 Estate Development Investment	一般公共预算收入 General Public Budget Revenue	一般公共预算支出 General Public Budget Expenditure	金融机构本外币存款余额 The Balance of RMB and Foreign Currencies Deposits in Financial Institutions
全　省	**Total**	**92068.7**	**6506.2**	**35987.9**	**49574.6**	**5.2**	**8168.9**	**7464.7**	**12582.7**	**159927.0**
济南市	**Jinan**	**12757.4**	**429.5**	**4312.0**	**8015.9**	**2.1**	**1399.7**	**1060.8**	**1365.3**	**27952.8**
青岛市	Qingdao	15760.3	492.8	5268.4	9999.2	5.0	1441.3	1337.8	1719.0	27114.0
淄博市	Zibo	4561.8	194.2	2221.0	2146.6	5.9	373.2	395.3	551.9	7542.3
枣庄市	Zaozhuang	2156.7	200.8	822.9	1133.1	7.2	334.7	181.0	352.1	3315.4
东营市	Dongying	3899.1	195.2	2222.9	1480.9	8.0	193.6	284.6	381.9	6017.6
烟台市	Yantai	10162.5	696.2	4278.3	5188.0	5.8	593.0	673.9	952.7	13345.2
潍坊市	Weifang	7606.0	674.3	3088.2	3843.6	0.8	606.1	608.3	889.4	13552.8
济宁市	Jining	5516.5	627.9	2073.6	2815.0	7.1	513.8	475.0	782.8	8749.9
泰安市	Taian	3323.9	361.8	1349.8	1612.2	7.8	268.2	239.2	463.4	6273.6
威海市	Weihai	3513.5	368.7	1331.6	1813.3	4.3	205.6	237.4	430.4	6594.9
日照市	Rizhao	2390.9	218.5	934.3	1238.1	1.4	200.5	195.3	320.1	4114.2
临沂市	Linyi	6105.2	529.5	2374.2	3201.4	6.5	674.2	445.8	920.1	10849.8
德州市	Dezhou	3805.3	378.0	1527.4	1900.0	7.1	395.9	250.6	622.8	6056.7
聊城市	Liaocheng	2926.4	413.9	1083.5	1429.0	7.3	386.0	244.6	535.5	6186.4
滨州市	Binzhou	3118.9	303.2	1300.5	1515.2	7.4	209.5	292.1	526.9	4756.1
菏泽市	Heze	4464.5	422.1	1799.5	2242.8	7.9	373.4	316.5	734.7	7109.4
济南位次	Position	2	6	2	2	14	2	2	2	1

注：本表内其他城市数据根据内部资料整理，不做正式发布，仅供参考。各项指标最终数据，敬请关注各城市官方发布机构。

(100 million yuan)

#住户存款 Household Deposits	金融机构本外币贷款余额 The Balance of RMB and Foreign Currencies Loans in Financial Institutions	社会消费品零售总额比上年增长(%) Growth Rate Total Retail Sales of Consumer Goods (%)	货物进出口总额 Total Import & Export	#出口总额 Total Export	实际使用外资(亿美元) Actual Use of Foreign Capital (100 million USD)	城镇居民人均可支配收入(元) Per Capita Disposable Income of Urban Households (yuan)	城镇居民人均消费支出(元) Per Capita Consumption Expenditure of Urban Households (yuan)	农村居民人均可支配收入(元) Per Capita Disposable Income of Rural Households (yuan)	农村居民人均消费支出(元) Per Capita Consumption Expenditure of Rural Households (yuan)	居民消费价格指数 Consumer Price Indices
97230.0	**138667.3**	**8.7**	**32642.6**	**19430.2**	**175.3**	**51571**	**30251**	**23776**	**16075**	**100.1**
11870.7	**28756.6**	**6.6**	**2161.0**	**1373.4**	**24.8**	**62506**	**37831**	**25587**	**16267**	**100.6**
12894.4	30146.9	7.3	8759.7	4713.6	37.5	65751	39663	29736	19070	100.5
5334.1	5270.7	9.6	1035.1	625.0	6.2	55181	32988	26338	18962	100.3
2444.9	2690.5	11.3	513.1	479.5	5.9	42084	22862	22410	14313	100.1
3338.9	4176.1	9.2	2494.3	657.0	8.0	62175	34677	25474	18745	99.6
8585.4	9121.3	9.2	4568.5	2653.1	23.2	59126	35605	28349	19836	100.5
9078.1	10936.0	7.0	3403.1	2302.3	8.9	51155	29396	27460	17332	100.4
6390.6	7318.9	11.0	971.5	788.6	10.7	45505	24992	23851	14895	99.5
4596.4	4519.8	10.8	457.6	393.5	5.7	45955	25629	24965	15801	99.9
4370.0	5345.8	6.0	2006.8	1501.7	7.9	58799	34719	29013	17294	100.1
2643.0	4156.0	9.1	1373.0	506.3	4.6	42674	24453	22835	12006	99.7
7724.2	10028.1	10.6	1682.7	1534.9	7.4	47005	21168	20509	12854	99.3
4608.5	3779.6	10.0	698.5	576.4	5.8	35303	19859	21922	16807	100.0
4540.8	3787.3	10.5	591.9	360.8	5.6	35574	19670	20071	13999	99.8
3019.8	3892.4	10.9	1191.8	602.5	7.5	45288	27340	23423	15781	99.7
5790.0	4553.3	11.2	733.9	361.4	5.5	35454	20926	19493	15422	99.7
2	2	15	5	6	2	2	2	6	8	1

Note: The data regarding other cities in this table is sorted out according to internal data which is for reference only instead of being released officially. As for final data regar various indicators, refer to official release mechanism in each city.

附录二 十五副省级城市主要经济指标(2023年)
Main Statistical Indicators of 15 Vice-provincial Cities(2023)

单位：亿元

城市名称	Region	地区生产总值 Gross Domestic Product	第一产业 Primary Industry	第二产业 Secondary Industry	第三产业 Tertiary Industry	固定资产投资比上年增长(%) Growth Rate Investment in Fixed Assets (%)	房地产开发投资上年增长(%) Growth rate Estate Development Investment (%)	一般公共预算收入 General Public Budget Revenue	一般公共预算支出 General Public Budget Expenditure
济南	**Jinan**	**12757.4**	**429.5**	**4312.0**	**8015.9**	**2.1**	**-19.7**	**1060.8**	**1365.3**
沈阳	Shenyang	8122.1	334.4	2953.1	4834.5	1.5	-34.8	800.9	1082.1
大连	Dalian	8752.9	595.9	3715.3	4441.7	0.6	-24.8	750.2	1013.5
长春	Changchun	7002.1	531.0	2616.5	3854.6	4.2	-16.7	576.5	1075.0
哈尔滨	Harbin	5576.3	630.1	1293.6	3652.5	-24.7	-33.3	313.1	1080.7
南京	Nanjing	17421.4	317.8	5929.0	11174.7	-1.9	-0.2	1620.0	1838.7
杭州	Hangzhou	20059.0	347.1	5666.9	14045.0	2.8	11.6	2616.8	2636.2
宁波	Ningbo	16452.8	383.8	7540.5	8528.5	7.5	3.8	1785.9	2235.1
厦门	Xiamen	8066.5	27.7	2867.9	5170.8	0.5	33.8	932.1	1084.7
青岛	Qingdao	15760.3	492.8	5268.4	9999.2	5.0	-19.4	1337.8	1719.0
武汉	Wuhan	20011.7	474.4	6800.9	12736.4	0.3	2.5	1601.2	2204.1
广州	Guangzhou	30355.7	317.8	7775.7	22262.2	3.6	-8.7	1944.2	2971.7
深圳	Shenzhen	34606.4	24.7	13015.3	21566.4	11.0	10.6	4112.8	5012.1
成都	Chengdu	22074.7	594.9	6370.9	15109.0	2.0	-23.6	1929.3	2586.8
西安	Xi'an	12010.8	325.2	4146.9	7538.6	0.1	-11.3	951.6	1728.8
济南位次	Position	9	7	9	9	7	11	9	10

注：1.为便于排序，广州实际使用外资数据为人民币口径根据平均汇率推算；厦门、成都、西安实际使用外资为FDI口径。
2.本表内其他城市数据根据内部资料整理，不做正式发布，仅供参考。各项指标最终数据，敬请关注各城市官方发布机构。

(100 million yuan)

金融机构本外币存款余额 The Balance of RMB and Foreign Currencies Deposits in Financial Institutions	金融机构本外币贷款余额 The Balance of RMB and Foreign Currencies Loans in Financial Institutions	社会消费品零售总额 Total Retail Sales of Consumer Goods	货物进出口总额 Total Import & Export	#出口总额 Total Export	实际使用外资(亿美元) Actual Use of Foreign Capital (100 million USD)	城镇居民人均可支配收入(元) Per Capita Disposable Income of Urban Households (yuan)	农村居民人均可支配收入(元) Per Capita Disposable Income of Rural Households (yuan)	居民消费价格指数 Consumer Price Indices
27952.7	**28756.6**	**5199.0**	**2161.0**	**1373.4**	**24.8**	**62506**	**25587**	**100.6**
21842.7	20333.3	4210.4	1469.4	524.5	12.1	53650	24197	100.3
19886.0	14404.9	2008.6	4552.8	2080.8	9.7	53689	26430	100.4
18839.9	17953.7	2109.8	1225.9	331.3	3.3	45480	20443	99.8
18559.2	15129.8	2384.0	495.3	212.8	1.6	45784	23647	100.7
54279.9	54337.9	8201.1	5659.9	3333.1	49.4	79858	36789	100.6
77589.0	68642.0	7670.6	8029.7	5338.7	88.3	80587	48180	100.2
34071.6	38133.0	5212.6	12779.3	8287.8	46.9	80144	48350	100.4
16724.7	18575.3	2743.3	9470.4	4474.5	19.3	72880	34206	100.2
27114.0	30146.9	6319.0	8759.7	4713.6	37.5	65751	29736	100.5
38483.9	47517.1	7531.9	3606.2	2167.3		61693	31560	100.4
86638.3	76674.2	11012.6	10914.3	6502.6	69.3	80501	38607	101.0
133350.5	92140.9	10486.2	38710.7	24552.1	90.2	76910	-	100.8
58074.0	60498.0	10001.6	7489.8	4538.6	22.9	54489	30089	100.2
34129.3	35528.5	4811.6	3597.6	2334.0	12.5	51178	19826	100.0
9	10	9	12	12	7	8	10	4

Notes: 1. To facilitate ranking, the data regarding actual use of foreign capital actually used by Guangzhou is calculated as per RMB caliber and average annual rate;The actual Use of foreign capital in Xiamen Chengdu and Xi'an is Based on FDI Criteria

2.The data regarding other cities in this table is sorted out according to internal data which is for reference only instead of being released officially. As for final data regarding various indicators, refer to official release mechanism in each city.

附录三 二十六省会城市主要经济指标(2023年)
Main Statistical Indicators of 26 Provincial Capitals (2023)

单位：亿元

城市名称	Region	地区生产总值 Gross Domestic Product	第一产业 Primary Industry	第二产业 Secondary Industry	第三产业 Tertiary Industry	固定资产投资比上年增长(%) Growth Rate Investment in Fixed Assets (%)	房地产开发投资上年增长(%) Growth rate Estate Development Investment (%)
济南	**Jinan**	**12757.4**	**429.5**	**4312.0**	**8015.9**	**2.1**	**-19.7**
石家庄	Shijiazhuang	7534.2	576.9	2309.2	4648.1	7.6	-23.5
太原	Taiyuan	5573.7	46.0	2341.7	3186.1	-18.3	-5.6
呼和浩特	Hohhot	3802.0	167.5	1337.7	2296.3	25.5	-1.3
沈阳	Shenyang	8122.1	334.4	2953.1	4834.5	1.5	-34.8
长春	Changchun	7002.1	531.0	2616.5	3854.6	4.2	-16.7
哈尔滨	Harbin	5576.3	630.1	1293.6	3652.5	-24.7	-33.3
南京	Nanjing	17421.4	317.8	5929.0	11174.7	-1.9	-0.2
杭州	Hangzhou	20059.0	347.1	5666.9	14045.0	2.8	11.6
合肥	Hefei	12673.8	377.2	4642.2	7654.4	3.0	4.6
福州	Fuzhou	12928.5	721.6	4675.1	7531.8	3.2	-35.3
南昌	Nanchang	7324.5					
郑州	Zhengzhou	13617.8	172.2	5373.4	8072.2	6.8	-0.1
武汉	Wuhan	20011.7	474.4	6800.9	12736.4	0.3	2.5
长沙	Changsha	14332.0	451.9	5365.5	8514.6	-6.8	
广州	Guangzhou	30355.7	317.8	7775.7	22262.2	3.6	-8.7
南宁	Nanning	5469.1	636.4	1194.6	3638.1	-23.7	-32.6
海口	Haikou	2358.4	103.5	432.9	1822.0	4.7	10.1
成都	Chengdu	22074.7	594.9	6370.9	15109.0	2.0	-23.6
贵阳	Guiyang	5154.8	207.5	1805.3	3142.0	-10.3	
昆明	Kunming	7864.8	353.4	2281.9	5229.5	-24.9	-40.2
西安	Xi'an	12010.8	325.2	4146.9	7538.6	0.1	-11.3
兰州	Lanzhou	3487.3	73.1	1120.6	2293.6	-7.4	-17.3
西宁	Xining	1801.1	65.1	692.6	1043.5	-6.6	-33.4
银川	Yinchuan	2685.6	99.5	1302.9	1283.3	8.5	-2.7
乌鲁木齐	Urumqi	4168.5	33.1	1146.7	2988.6	12.6	1.3
济南位次	Position	9	9	10	8	12	15

注：本表内其他城市数据根据内部资料整理，不做正式发布，仅供参考。各项指标最终数据，敬请关注各城市官方发布机构。

(100 million yuan)

一般公共预算收入 General Public Budget Revenue	一般公共预算支出 General Public Budget Expenditure	金融机构本外币存款余额 The Balance of RMB and Foreign Currencies Deposits in Financial Institutions	金融机构本外币贷款余额 The Balance of RMB and Foreign Currencies Loans in Financial Institutions	社会消费品零售总额 Total Retail Sales of Consumer Goods	货物进出口总额 Total Import & Export	#出口总额 Total Export	城镇居民人均可支配收入(元) Per Capita Disposable Income of Urban Households (yuan)	农村居民人均可支配收入(元) Per Capita Disposable Income of Rural Households (yuan)	居民消费价格指数 Consumer Price Indices
1060.8	**1365.3**	**27952.7**	**28756.6**	**5199.0**	**2161.0**	**1373.4**	**62506**	**25587**	**100.6**
737.9	1274.8	23236.6	18135.0	2751.2	1237.1	774.3	47564	21242	100.7
449.2	777.3	19265.2	19570.3	1912.9	1349.7	826.9	45835	24488	99.7
238.1	593.0			1202.6	194.4	118.1	57085	25518	100.5
800.9	1082.1	21842.7	20333.3	4210.4	1469.4	524.5	53650	24197	100.3
576.5	1075.0	18839.9	17953.7	2109.8	1225.9	331.3	45480	20443	99.8
313.1	1080.7	18559.2	15129.8	2384.0	495.3	212.8	45784	23647	100.7
1620.0	1838.7	54279.9	54337.9	8201.1	5659.9	3333.1	79858	36789	100.6
2616.8	2636.2	77589.0	68642.0	7670.6	8029.7	5338.7	80587	48180	100.2
929.6	1411.3	25452.8	27748.0	5270.8	3588.1	2327.1	59609	31140	100.0
754.1	1007.8	23547.2	24490.7	4963.8	3435.3	2558.5	58009	28636	100.2
500.2	925.6	17266.1	19894.4		1112.9	787.6	54911	25803	100.6
1165.8	1519.6			5623.1	5522.3	3569.1	48740	30383	99.4
1601.2	2204.1	38483.9	47517.1	7531.9	3606.2	2167.3	61693	31560	100.4
1227.1	1626.8	30715.6	32970.6	5561.7	2813.5	1896.9	67276	43200	100.4
1944.2	2971.7	86638.3	76674.2	11012.6	10914.3	6502.6	80501	38607	101.0
400.9	816.5	14361.0	21753.2	2424.8	1259.1	623.0	44469	20369	99.7
266.9	378.0	7115.2		1088.8	790.1	291.8	46321	22203	100.3
1929.3	2586.8	58074.0	60498.0	10001.6	7489.8	4538.6	54489	30089	100.2
446.2	778.6	15422.7	15350.3	2526.8	471.7	305.4	48364	23640	100.1
558.0	837.8	19358.4	25261.5	3574.3	1346.8	439.6	55501	22144	100.8
951.6	1728.8	34129.3	35528.5	4811.6	3597.6	2334.0	51178	19826	100.0
255.3	501.9	10446.1	15861.7	1796.3	117.4	47.3	48039	18604	100.6
144.1	418.8			624.8	38.8	20.0	41917	17076	100.3
197.8	438.2	6604.9	6989.5	806.5	130.2	88.2	46983	20859	100.6
369.8	504.1	13089.0	11667.2	1175.7	700.1	545.6	49033	28290	100.2
8	10	8	8	9	11	11	5	12	5

Note: The data regarding other cities in this table is sorted out according to internal data which is for reference only instead of being released officially. As for final data regarding various indicators, refer to official release mechanism in each city.

附录四

中华人民共和国统计法

Statistical Law of The People's Republic of China

（1983 年 12 月 8 日第六届全国人民代表大会常务委员会第三次会议通过　根据 1996 年 5 月 15 日第八届全国人民代表大会常务委员会第十九次会议《关于修改〈中华人民共和国统计法〉的决定》第一次修正　2009 年 6 月 27 日第十一届全国人民代表大会常务委员会第九次会议修订　根据 2024 年 9 月 13 日第十四届全国人民代表大会常务委员会第十一次会议《关于修改〈中华人民共和国统计法〉的决定》第二次修正）

目　录

第一章　总　则

第一条　为了科学、有效地组织统计工作，保障统计资料的真实性、准确性、完整性和及时性，加强统计监督，发挥统计在了解国情国力、服务经济社会高质量发展中的重要作用，推动全面建设社会主义现代化国家，制定本法。

第二条　本法适用于各级人民政府、县级以上人民政府统计机构和有关部门组织实施的统计活动。

统计的基本任务是对经济社会发展情况进行统计调查、统计分析，提供统计资料和统计咨询意见，实行统计监督。

第三条　统计工作坚持中国共产党的领导。

国家建立集中统一的统计系统，实行统一领导、分级负责的统计管理体制。

第四条　国务院和地方各级人民政府、各有关部门应当加强对统计工作的组织领导，为统计工作提供必要的保障。

第五条　国家加强统计科学研究，根据经济社会发展的新情况，健全科学合理的统计标准和统计指标体系，将新经济新领域纳入统计调查范围，并不断改进统计调查方法，提高统计的科学性。

国家有计划地加强统计信息化建设，推动现代信息技术与统计工作深度融合，促进统计信息搜集、处理、传输、共享、存储技术和统计数据库体系的现代化。

第六条　国家构建系统完整、协同高效、约束有力、权威可靠的统计监督体系。

统计机构根据统计调查制度和经批准的计划安排，对各地区、各部门贯彻落实国家重大经济社会政策措施情况、履行统计法定职责情况等进行统计监督。

第七条　统计机构和统计人员依照本法规定独立行使统计调查、统计报告、统计监督的职权，不受侵犯。

地方各级人民政府、县级以上人民政府统计机构和有关部门以及各单位的负责人，不得自行修改统计机构和统计人员依法搜集、整理的统计资料，不得以任何方式要求统计机构、统计人员及其他机构、人员伪造、篡改统计资料，不得明示、暗示下级单位及其人员或者统计调查对象填报虚假统计数据，不得对依法履行职责或者拒绝、抵制统计违法行为的单位和个人打击报复。

第八条　国家机关、企业事业单位和其他组织以及个体工商户和个人等统计调查对象，必须依照本法和国家有关规定，真实、准确、完整、及时地提供统计调查所需的资料，不得提供不真实或者不完整的统计资料，不得迟报、拒报统计资料。

第九条　地方各级人民政府、县级以上人民政府统计机构和有关部门应当根据国家有关规定，将防范和惩治统计造假、弄虚作假纳入依法行政、依法履职责任范围，建立健全相关责任制，加强对领导干部统计工作的考核管理，依法对统计造假、弄虚作假行为追究法律责任。

第十条　统计工作应当接受社会公众的监督。任何单位和个人有权检举统计中弄虚作假等违法行为。对检举有功的单位和个人应当给予表彰和奖励。

第十一条　统计机构和统计人员对在统计工作中知悉的国家秘密、工作秘密、商业秘密、个人隐私和个人信息，应当予以保密，不得泄露或者向他人非法提供。

第十二条　任何单位和个人不得利用虚假统计资料骗取荣誉称号、物质利益或者职务职级等晋升。

第二章　统计调查管理

第十三条　统计调查项目包括国家统计调查项目、部门统计调查项目和地方统计调查项目。

国家统计调查项目是指全国性基本情况的统计调查项目。部门统计调查项目是指国务院有关部门的专业性统计调查项目。

地方统计调查项目是指县级以上地方人民政府及其部门的地方性统计调查项目。

国家统计调查项目、部门统计调查项目、地方统计调查项目应当明确分工，互相衔接，不得重复。

第十四条 国家统计调查项目由国家统计局制定，或者由国家统计局和国务院有关部门共同制定，报国务院备案；重大的国家统计调查项目报国务院审批。

部门统计调查项目由国务院有关部门制定。统计调查对象属于本部门管辖系统的，报国家统计局备案；统计调查对象超出本部门管辖系统的，报国家统计局审批。

地方统计调查项目由县级以上地方人民政府统计机构和有关部门分别制定或者共同制定。其中，由省级人民政府统计机构单独制定或者和有关部门共同制定的，报国家统计局审批；由省级以下人民政府统计机构单独制定或者和有关部门共同制定的，报省级人民政府统计机构审批；由县级以上地方人民政府有关部门制定的，报本级人民政府统计机构审批。

第十五条 统计调查项目的审批机关应当对调查项目的必要性、可行性、科学性进行审查，对符合法定条件的，作出予以批准的书面决定，并公布；对不符合法定条件的，作出不予批准的书面决定，并说明理由。

第十六条 制定统计调查项目，应当同时制定该项目的统计调查制度，并依照本法第十四条的规定一并报经审批或者备案。

统计调查制度应当对调查目的、调查内容、调查方法、调查对象、调查组织方式、调查表式、统计资料的报送和公布等作出规定。

统计调查应当按照统计调查制度组织实施。变更统计调查制度的内容，应当报经原审批机关批准或者原备案机关备案。

第十七条 统计调查表应当标明表号、制定机关、批准或者备案文号、有效期限等标志。

对未标明前款规定的标志或者超过有效期限的统计调查表，统计调查对象有权拒绝填报；县级以上人民政府统计机构应当依法责令停止有关统计调查活动。

第十八条 搜集、整理统计资料，应当以周期性普查为基础，以经常性抽样调查为主体，综合运用全面调查、重点调查等方法，并充分利用行政记录、社会大数据等资料。

重大国情国力普查由国务院统一领导，国务院和地方人民政府组织统计机构和有关部门共同实施。

第十九条 国家制定统一的统计标准，保障统计调查采用的指标涵义、计算方法、分类目录、调查表式和统计编码等的标准化。

国家统计标准由国家统计局制定，或者由国家统计局和国务院标准化主管部门共同制定。

国务院有关部门可以制定补充性的部门统计标准，报国家统计局审批。部门统计标准不得与国家统计标准相抵触。

第二十条 国家实施统一的国民经济核算制度。

国家统计局统一组织和实施地区生产总值核算工作。

第二十一条 县级以上人民政府统计机构根据统计任务的需要，可以在统计调查对象中推广使用计算机网络报送统计资料。

第二十二条 县级以上人民政府应当将统计工作所需经费列入财政预算。

重大国情国力普查所需经费，由国务院和地方人民政府共同负担，列入相应年度的财政预算，按时拨付，确保到位。

第三章 统计资料的管理和公布

第二十三条 县级以上人民政府统计机构和有关部门以及乡、镇人民政府，应当按照国家有关规定建立统计资料的保存、管理制度。

县级以上人民政府统计机构和有关部门建立健全统计信息共享机制，明确统计信息的共享范围、标准和程序。

第二十四条 国家机关、企业事业单位和其他组织等统计调查对象，应当按照国家有关规定设置原始记录、统计台账，推动统计台账电子化、数字化、标准化，建立健全统计资料的审核、签署、报送、归档等管理制度。

统计资料的审核、签署人员应当对其审核、签署的统计资料的真实性、准确性和完整性负责。

第二十五条 县级以上人民政府有关部门应当及时向本级人民政府统计机构提供统计所需的行政记录资料和国民经济核算所需的财务资料、财政资料及其他资料，并按照统计调查制度的规定及时向本级人民政府统计机构报送其组织实施统计调查取得的有关资料。

县级以上人民政府统计机构应当及时向本级人民政府有关部门提供有关统计资料。

第二十六条 县级以上人民政府统计机构按照国家有关规定，定期公布统计资料。

国家统计数据以国家统计局公布的数据为准。

第二十七条 县级以上人民政府有关部门统计调查取得的统计资料，由本部门按照国家有关规定公布。

第二十八条 统计调查中获得的能够识别或者推断单个统计调查对象身份的资料，任何单位和个人不得对外提供、泄露，不得用于统计以外的目的。

第二十九条 县级以上人民政府统计机构和有关部门统计调查取得的统计资料，除依法应当保密的外，应当及时公开，供社会公众查询。

第四章 统计机构和统计人员

第三十条 国务院设立国家统计局，依法组织领导和协调全国的统计工作。

国家统计局根据工作需要设立的派出调查机构，承担国家统计局布置的统计调查等任务。

县级以上地方人民政府设立独立的统计机构，乡、镇人民政府设置统计工作岗位，配备专职或者兼职统计人员，依法管理、开展统计工作，实施统计调查。

第三十一条 县级以上人民政府有关部门根据统计任务的需要设立统计机构，或者在有关机构中设置统计人员，并指定统计负责人，依法组织、管理本部门职责范围内的统计工作，实施统计调查，在统计业务上受本级人民政府统计机构的指导。

第三十二条 统计机构、统计人员应当依法履行职责，如实搜集、报送统计资料，不得伪造、篡改统计资料，不得以任何方式要求任何单位和个人提供不真实的统计资料，不得有其他违反本法规定的行为。

统计人员应当坚持实事求是，恪守职业道德，对其负责搜集、审核、录入的统计资料与统计调查对象报送的统计资料的一致性负责。

第三十三条 统计人员进行统计调查时，有权就与统计有关的问题询问有关人员，要求其如实提供有关情况、资料并改正不真实、不准确的资料。

统计人员进行统计调查时，应当出示县级以上人民政府统计机构或者有关部门颁发的工作证件；未出示的，统计调查对象有权拒绝调查。

第三十四条 国家实行统计专业技术职务资格考试、评聘制度，提高统计人员的专业素质，保障统计队伍的稳定性。

统计人员应当具备与其从事的统计工作相适应的专业知识和业务能力。

县级以上人民政府统计机构和有关部门应当加强对统计人员的专业培训和职业道德教育。

第五章 监督检查

第三十五条 县级以上人民政府对下级人民政府、本级人民政府统计机构和有关部门执行本法的情况，实施监督。

第三十六条 国家统计局组织管理全国统计工作的监督检查，查处重大统计违法行为。

县级以上地方人民政府统计机构依法查处本行政区域内发生的统计违法行为。但是，国家统计局派出的调查机构组织实施的统计调查活动中发生的统计违法行为，由组织实施该项统计调查的调查机构负责查处。

法律、行政法规对有关部门查处统计违法行为另有规定的，从其规定。

第三十七条 县级以上人民政府有关部门应当积极协助本级人民政府统计机构查处统计违法行为，及时向本级人民政府统计机构移送有关统计违法案件材料。

第三十八条 县级以上人民政府统计机构在调查统计违法行为或者核查统计数据时，有权采取下列措施：

（一）发出统计检查查询书，向检查对象查询有关事项；

（二）要求检查对象提供有关原始记录和凭证、统计台账、统计调查表、会计资料及其他相关证明和资料；

（三）就与检查有关的事项询问有关人员；

（四）进入检查对象的业务场所和统计数据处理信息系统进行检查、核对；

（五）经本机构负责人批准，登记保存检查对象的有关原始记录和凭证、统计台账、统计调查表、会计资料及其他相关证明和资料；

（六）对与检查事项有关的情况和资料进行记录、录音、录像、照相和复制。

县级以上人民政府统计机构进行监督检查时，监督检查人员不得少于二人，并应当出示执法证件；未出示的，有关单位和个人有权拒绝检查。

第三十九条 县级以上人民政府统计机构履行监督检查职责时，有关单位和个人应当如实反映情况，提供相关证明和资料，不得拒绝、阻碍检查，不得转移、隐匿、篡改、毁弃原始记录和凭证、统计台账、统计调查表、会计资料及其他相关证明和资料。

第六章 法律责任

第四十条 地方各级人民政府、县级以上人民政府统计机构或者有关部门、单位的负责人有下列行为之一的，由任免机关、单位或者监察机关依法给予处分，并由县级以上人民政府统计机构予以通报：

（一）自行修改统计资料、编造虚假统计数据的；

（二）要求统计机构、统计人员或者其他机构、人员伪造、篡改统计资料的；

（三）明示、暗示下级单位及其人员或者统计调查对象填报虚假统计数据的；

（四）对本地方、本部门、本单位发生的统计数据严重失实情况和严重统计违法行为失察的；

（五）有其他统计造假、弄虚造假行为的。

对依法履行职责或者拒绝、抵制统计违法行为的单位和个人打击报复的，依照前款规定给予处分和予以通报。

第四十一条 县级以上人民政府统计机构或者有关部门有下列行为之一的，由本级人民政府、上级人民政府统计机构或者本级人民政府统计机构责令改正，予以通报；对负有责任的领导人员和直接责任人员，由任免机关或者监察机关依法给予处分：

（一）未经批准或者备案擅自组织实施统计调查的；

（二）未经批准或者备案擅自变更统计调查制度的内容的；

（三）伪造、篡改统计资料的；

（四）要求统计调查对象或者其他机构、人员提供不真实的统计资料的；

（五）未按照统计调查制度的规定报送有关资料的。

统计人员有前款第三项至第五项所列行为之一的，责令改正，依法给予处分。

第四十二条 县级以上人民政府统计机构或者有关部门有下列行为之一的，对负有责任的领导人员和直接责任人员由任免机关或者监察机关依法给予处分：

（一）违法公布统计资料的；

（二）泄露或者向他人非法提供统计调查对象的商业秘密、个人隐私、个人信息的；

（三）对外提供、泄露在统计调查中获得的能够识别或者推断单个统计调查对象身份的资料的；

（四）违反国家有关规定，造成统计资料毁损、灭失的。

统计人员有前款所列行为之一的，依法给予处分。

第四十三条 统计机构、统计人员泄露国家秘密、工作秘密的，依法追究法律责任。

第四十四条 作为统计调查对象的国家机关、企业事业单位或者其他组织有下列行为之一的，由县级以上人民政府统计机构责令改正，给予警告，可以予以通报；其负有责任的领导人员和直接责任人员属于公职人员的，由任免机关、单位或者监察机关依法给予处分：

（一）拒绝提供统计资料或者经催报后仍未按时提供统计资料的；

（二）提供不真实或者不完整的统计资料的；

（三）拒绝答复或者不如实答复统计检查查询书的；

（四）拒绝、阻碍统计调查、统计检查的；

（五）转移、隐匿、篡改、毁弃或者拒绝提供原始记录和凭证、统计台账、统计调查表及其他相关证明和资料的。

企业事业单位或者其他组织有前款所列行为之一的，可以并处十万元以下的罚款；情节严重的，并处十万元以上五十万元以下的罚款。

个体工商户有本条第一款所列行为之一的，由县级以上人民政府统计机构责令改正，给予警告，可以并处一万元以下的罚款。

第四十五条 作为统计调查对象的国家机关、企业事业单位或者其他组织迟报统计资料，或者未按照国家有关规定设置原始记录、统计台账的，由县级以上人民政府统计机构责令改正，给予警告，可以予以通报；其负有责任的领导人员和直接责任人员属于公职人员的，由任免机关、单位或者监察机关依法给予处分。

企业事业单位或者其他组织有前款所列行为之一的，可以并处五万元以下的罚款。

个体工商户迟报统计资料的，由县级以上人民政府统计机构责令改正，给予警告，可以并处一千元以下的罚款。

第四十六条 县级以上人民政府统计机构查处统计违法行为时，认为对有关公职人员依法应当给予处分的，应当向该公职人员的任免机关、单位提出给予处分的建议，该公职人员的任免机关、单位应当依法及时作出决定，并将结果书面通知县级以上人民政府统计机构；向监察机关移送的，由监察机关按照有关规定办理。

第四十七条 作为统计调查对象的个人在重大国情国力普查活动中拒绝、阻碍统计调查，或者提供不真实或者不完整的普查资料的，由县级以上人民政府统计机构责令改正，予以批评教育。

第四十八条 违反本法规定，利用虚假统计资料骗取荣誉称号、物质利益或者职务职级等晋升的，除对其编造虚假统计资料或者要求他人编造虚假统计资料的行为依法追究法律责任外，由作出有关决定的单位或者其上级单位、监察机关取消其荣誉称号，追缴获得的物质利益，撤销晋升的职务职级等。

第四十九条 当事人对县级以上人民政府统计机构作出的行政处罚决定不服的，可以依法申请行政复议或者提起行政诉讼。对国家统计局派出的调查机构作出的行政处罚决定不服的，向国家统计局申请行政复议。

第五十条 违反本法规定，造成人身损害、财产损失的，依法承担民事责任；构成犯罪的，依法追究刑事责任。

第七章 附 则

第五十一条 本法所称县级以上人民政府统计机构，是指国家统计局及其派出的调查机构、县级以上地方人民政府统计机构。

第五十二条 民间统计调查活动的管理办法，由国务院制定。

中华人民共和国境外的组织、个人需要在中华人民共和国境内进行统计调查活动的，应当按照国务院的规定报请审批。

利用统计调查危害国家安全、损害社会公共利益或者进行欺诈活动的，依法追究法律责任。

第五十三条 本法自 2010 年 1 月 1 日起施行。

附录五

济南市统计局2023年统计大事要事

Chronicle of Events of Jinan Statistical Undertaking

1月5日，济南市统计局组织开展市属副局级及以下事业单位服务高质量发展绩效考核服务对象评价电话调查。

1月8日，省委常委、市委书记刘强对济南市统计局报送的《关于驻济央企情况的分析报告》作出批示。

1月16日，济南市统计局党组召开全面从严治党暨党风廉政建设专题会议。

1月17日，济南市统计局党组书记、局长程伟主持召开建立经济运行监测分析旬报机制工作专题会。

1月18日，济南市统计局到派驻“第一书记”帮包村、驻村工作队、“双报到”社区及基层联系点开展“走基层·送温暖”春节走访慰问系列活动。

1月30日，济南市统计局组织召开2022年年报和首月经济运行工作调度会。局党组书记、局长程伟主持会议并讲话。

1月30日，济南市统计局组织中层干部集体观看典型案例警示教育纪录片。

1月31日，济南市统计局党组书记、局长程伟到济南魏家庄万达广场进行城市商业综合体专题调研。

2月1日至8日，济南市统计局统筹开展“四上”专业年报集中轮训，全面部署年报统计调查工作，夯实基层基础，提高年报工作质量。

2月2日，济南市统计局2021年度文书档案和照片档案专项实体验收通过入馆。

2月3日，济南市统计局组织召开区县（功能区）统计局长（主任）视频会议，落实经济网格体系建设部署会议要求，调度第五次全国经济普查准备工作。局党组书记、局长程伟主持会议。

2月6日，山东省统计局党组成员、副局长、一级总监周尊考来济围绕落实全省工业经济高质量发展大会、省委农村工作会议精神情况、做好第五次全国经济普查、经济运行监测、统计数据质量等方面工作进行调研座谈。济南市委常委、副市长王宏志，济南市统计局党组书记、局长程伟参加座谈并交流有关情况。

2月9日，济南市统计局召开全市分类培育高质量纳统工作专班会议。

2月17日，济南市统计局参加济南市经济网格培训会议，对全市经济网格员开展系统业务培训。

2月24日，济南市统计局召开机关党委党建工作专题会议，研究部署机关党建和机关党支部评星定级等工作。

3月1日，省委常委、市委书记刘强听取济南市统计局关于第五次全国经济普查筹备工作开展情况专题汇报。

3月9日，济南市统计局到“双报到”社区开展“践行雷锋精神 争做志愿先锋”主题党日暨志愿服务系列活动。

3月14日，济南市统计局召开党组扩大会议，安排部署全市统计造假专项治理行动阶段性工作。

3月16日至17日，济南市统计局组织举办全市统一核算制度培训，集体学习地区生产总值统一核算方法，安排部署第五次全国经济普查和投入产出调查工作。

3月22日，济南市统计局召开局党组理论中心组（扩大）学习会议，专题学习《济南市优化营商环境条例》有关内容。

3月24日，国家统计局贸易外经统计司副司长俞炳彬来济调研商业综合体与电商企业统计情况。山东省统计局党组成员、副局长陆万明，济南市统计局党组书记、局长程伟陪同调研。

3月31日，济南市委、济南市政府印发《关于做好第五次全国经济普查的通知》，开展全市第五次全国经济普查工作。

4月6日，济南市统计局召开专项治理行动推进会。局党组成员、副局长李士营主持会议。

4月14日，济南市统计局举办第五次全国经济普查单位清查试点工作业务培训班。

4月20日，济南市统计局召开学习贯彻习近平新时代中国特色社会主义思想主题教育工作会议。市委学习贯彻习近平新时代中国特色社会主义思想主题教育第十二巡回指导组到会指导。

4月21日，济南市统计局与济南市地方金融监管局联合召开金融行业运行分析座谈会。

4月24日至25日，济南市统计局邀请济南市纪委监委参加全市统计“双随机”执法检查工作，开展嵌入式监督执法。

4月25日，济南市统计局举办学习贯彻习近平新时代中国特色社会主义思想主题教育第一专题读书班暨第四次理论中心组集体学习。

4月27日至29日，济南市统计局组织开展局领导分区县包挂督导检查统计造假专项治理工作。

5月5日，济南市统计局召开市直部门统计工作培训会，安排部署统计造假专项治理和清理纠正违反统计法律法规的文件和做法等工作，提高部门统计工作水平。

5月5日，山东省统计局党组成员、副局长陈汉臻到济南开展投入产出电子台账督导及数据质量座谈会。局党组书记、局长程伟，局党组成员、副局长谈友军参加座谈。

5月10日，国家统计局党组书记、局长康义到济南二机床集团有限公司调研第五次全国经济普查、统计数据报送等工作。山东省委常委、副省长曾赞荣，济南市委副书记、市长于海田参加调研活动。

5月22日，国家统计局固定资产投资统计司司长翟善清到济南开展投资工作专题调研。山东省统计局党组书记、局长马金栋，济南市委常委、副市长王宏志，济南市统计局党组书记、局长程伟参加调研活动。

5月23日，济南市统计局召开学习贯彻习近平新时代中国特色社会主义思想主题教育推进会议。

5月25日至26日，济南市统计局组织经普业务骨干到杭州市交流学习第五次全国经济普查工作。

5月26日，济南市统计局到槐荫区五里沟街道办事处开展群众工作教育实践工作，现场召开“三联系三调研”和“双报到”工作对接会。

6月2日，第五次全国经济普查省级综合试点（天桥）启动活动在济南市天桥区举行。山东省统计局党组成员、副局长李涛，济南市人民政府副秘书长吴剑，济南市天桥区委书记孙战宇，济南市统计局党组书记、局长程伟参加启动活动。

6月14日，济南市统计局举办学习贯彻习近平新时代中国特色社会主义思想主题教育第四专题读书班暨第七次理论学习中心组集体学习。

6月16日，济南市第五次全国经济普查领导小组印发《市第五次全国经济普查领导小组办公室成员名单的通知》。

6月21日至30日，济南市统计局围绕扎实推进主题教育、统筹做好第五次全国经济普查等重点工作，组织开展局领导班子到支部、到区县讲党课。

6月25日，济南市统计局召开全市统计系统网络和数据安全视频培训会，传达全省统计系统网络和数据安全会议精神，部署全市网络和数据安全重点工作。

6月28日，济南市统计局在市委党校组织统计干部政治与业务素质双提升培训班。

7月3日，济南市统计局第7批次投入产出调查专题业务培训班结课，实现全市500余家投入产出调查单位业务培训全覆盖。

7月6日，山东省统计局党组成员、副局长，一级总监周尊考带队到济南市历城区和平阴县开展能源领域专题调研。

7月11日，济南市第五次全国经济普查领导小组办公室安排部署特殊类型普查对象摸排工作。

7月12日，济南市第五次全国经济普查领导小组办公室组织开展经普工作线上实机演示培训。

7月14日，济南市统计局主题教育领导小组办公室召开第十次工作推进会暨阶段工作总结会议，局党组书记、局长，局主题教育领导小组组长程伟主持会议，局领导班子成员，局主题教育领导小组副组长、成员及局主题教育领导小组办公室主任、副主任参加会议。

7月27日，济南市统计局召开主题教育调研成果交流暨典型案例剖析会议。局党组书记、局长程伟主持会议并讲话，市委主题教育第十二巡回指导组组长秦贵昌出席会议。

8月2日，济南市政府官方网站公开发布《济南市第五次全国经济普查单位清查告知书》。

8月8日，济南市统计局高标准通过市委主题教育专项整治工作专班关于统计造假专项整治工作质量抽检。

8月14日，济南市第五次全国经济普查领导小组办公室组织召开济南市第五次全国经济普查培训动员大会。省委常委、市委书记、市五经普领导小组组长刘强讲话，市委副书记、市长、市五经普领导小组组长于海田主持。济南市统计局党组书记、局长程伟作专题业务培训。

8月16日，济南市统计局召开主题教育第十四次工作推进会。局党组书记、局长程伟主持会议，局领导班子成员参会。

8月22日，济南市统计局党组理论学习中心组专题学习习近平总书记关于推动高质量发展的重要论述，邀请市委市直机关工委列席旁听第二工作组到会指导。

8月29日，济南市统计局开展统计系统网络安全自查排查，确保网络系统安全。

9月1日，济南市统计局组织开展习近平法治思想专题培训，邀请市习近平法治思想济南律师宣讲团成员、山东政法学院教授隋洪明作专题辅导报告。

9月1日，济南市第五次全国经济普查领导小组办公室召开全市第五次全国经济普查宣传工作专题会议。

9月2日至3日，济南市统计局组织开展第五次全国经济普查主题灯光秀，为第五次全国经济普查助力。

9月4日，济南市统计局组织开展“五经普”单位清查入户登记情况电话调查。

9月13日，山东省统计局党组书记、局长马金栋到济南调研座谈第五次全国经济普查工作开展情况。济南市委常委、副市长王宏志陪同调研。济南市统计局党组书记、局长程伟汇报济南市第五次全国经济普查工作开展情况。

9月18日，济南市统计局组织开展局领导包挂区县服务“五经普”专题实地督导调研。

9月20日，济南市统计局、国家统计局济南调查队联合举办第十四届“中国统计开放日”暨第五次全国经济普查宣传活动。

9月25日起，济南市统计局、济南广播电视台联合开展经济普查宣传活动，济南电视台新闻综合频道《今晚20分》节目播放经济普查宣传，高频次播出第五次全国经济普查单位清查滚动字幕。

10月2日，济南市第五次全国经济普查领导小组召开全市第五次全国经济普查工作调度会。

10月9日，济南市统计局组织召开升规纳统工作推进会议，安排部署年度升规纳统工作。

10月9日，济南市第五次全国经济普查领导小组组织召开全市第五次全国经济普查工作专题调度会。

10月13日，济南市统计局组织召开全市统计系统网络和数据安全视频培训会。

10月16日，济南市统计局组织开展“经济大普查 数说新时代”五经普主题展走进市直机关系列活动。

10月18日，济南市十八届人大常委会第十一次会议听取审议市政府关于全市第五次全国经济普查工作开展情况的报告。受市政府委托，济南市统计局局长程伟作工作报告。

10月19日，济南市统计局组织召开前三季度“四下”经济运行分析会。

10月26日至31日，济南市统计局在山东大学苏州研究院举办全市统计干部政治与业务素质双提升培训班。

11月2日，济南市统计局、济南市农业农村局联合开展蔬菜、瓜果生产情况调研。

11月6日，济南市统计局组织开展2023年“慈心一日捐”活动。

11月7日至9日，济南市统计局组织开展上规入库工作专项督导，对接帮助达规达限企业开展申报，确保应纳尽纳、应统尽统。

11月9日，济南市统计局2022年度文书档案和照片档案顺利通过档案验收。

11月28日至30日，济南市统计局组织召开全市统计系统政务服务培训会议。

12月4日，济南市统计局举办第五次全国经济普查登记工作培训班。

12月19日，济南市统计局组织举办“依法普查 服务发展”第五次全国经济普查宣传月暨统计法颁布40周年主题宣传活动。

12月21日，济南市委、市政府主要领导同志分别对济南市统计局撰写的《关于第五次全国经济普查暨上规入库工作情况的报告》作出肯定性批示。

12月27日，济南市统计局走进“12345”市民服务热线中心，参加热线接听活动，并对群众关心的统计问题进行答疑解惑。